⍟ tripadvisor®

The Best of Sri
by travellers li

Visit TripAdvisor for millions o
Find the best places to eat, sta

Top-Rated Hotels

1 Asian Jewel Boutique Hotel ⊚⊚⊚⊚⊚
Hikkaduwa
"Wonderful, fantastic, understated luxury"

2 Ceylon Tea Trails ⊚⊚⊚⊚⊚
Hatton
"Magical and so relaxing"

3 Galle Fort Hotel ⊚⊚⊚⊚⊚
Galle
"Oozing with colonial charm and character"

Popular Restaurants

1 Restaurant Diya Sisila ⊚⊚⊚⊚⊚
Bentota
"Fresh seafood in a spectacular setting"

2 Malli's Seafood Restaurant ⊚⊚⊚⊚⊚
Bentota
"Intimate, charming and elegant"

3 SANKAREST Garden Restaurant ⊚⊚⊚⊚⊚
Kosgoda
"Delicious food prepared by a lovely woman"

Amazing Things to Do

1 Citadel of Sigiriya - Lion Rock ⊚⊚⊚⊚⊚
Sigiriya
"Enthralling experience for adventure seekers"

2 The Millennium Elephant Foundation ⊚⊚⊚⊚⊚
Kegalle
"You can go and actually ride the elephants"

3 Golden Cave Temple ⊚⊚⊚⊚⊚
Dambulla
"Well worth the climb"

tripadvisor.co.uk | tripadvisor.it | tripadvisor.es | tripadvisor.de | tripadvisor.fr | tripadvisor.se | nl.tripadvisor.com
tripadvisor.dk | tripadvisor.ie | tripadvisor.no | pl.tripadvisor.com | tripadvisor.ru

Ratings were accurate as of April 2011 and may change over time. Visit tripadvisor.co.uk online for current ratings.

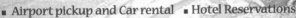

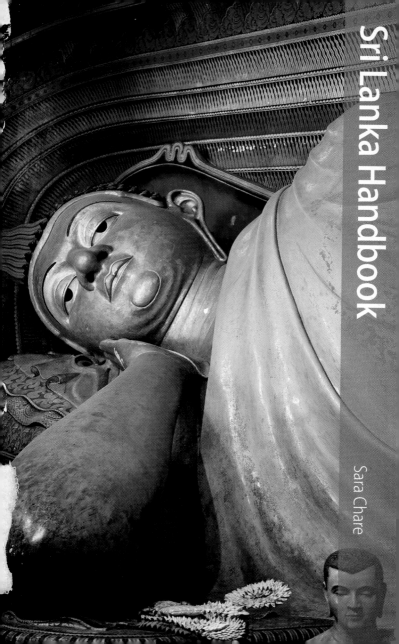

Sri Lanka Handbook

Sara Chare

Part of Sri Lanka's irresistible charm lies in the way it interweaves past and present. Whilst being forward-looking and progressive, this remains an island deeply imbued with a sense of pride in its traditions. Commuters and taxi drivers will stop on busy highways and queue at roadside temples to pay respects to their ancestors; businessmen will swap the comfort of their air-conditioned offices for an exhausting pilgrimage to the island's most sacred sites; and at special occasions the timing of even the simplest events is governed by ritual and auspicious moments determined by astrology.

That Sri Lanka's diverse ethnic groups have clung fiercely on to their traditions is perhaps not surprising in the wake of centuries of invasion by foreign powers. The island's early settlers migrated from India, to which, recent evidence suggests, Sri Lanka was once linked by an ancient causeway. They established a 2500-year-old Buddhist tradition that survives here as a potent symbol of the national identity, despite having long since faded in its native land. Hinduism, too, made its mark, proudly protected by Tamils across the nation. Arab traders brought Islam, while in later years the colonial powers of Europe fought over the island's riches. Their legacy survives in the island's tumble-down forts and creaking railways, tea plantations and passion for cricket.

What gives Sri Lanka its edge, though, is that this intoxicating mix of cultures is so accessible. Marco Polo declared this the 'finest island of its size in the world.' Centuries later, it would be hard to disagree.

This page Tea pickers dot the hillsides of the Highland plantations.
Previous page The reclining Buddha at Wewurukannala Vihara Temple is eight storeys high.

Jaffna ⑫

Paranthan

Talaimannar

Mankulam

Mannar

Bay of Bengal

Vavuniya

Nilaveli
Uppeveli
⑩ Trincomalee

⑦ Mihintale

Anuradhapura

Habarana

Puttalam

Aukana

Sigiriya
⑧ Polonnaruwa
Dambulla ⑨

Batticaloa

Maha Oya

Chilaw

Kurunegala

Matale

Indian Ocean

④ Kandy
Peradeniya

Mahiyangana

Negombo

Bibile

Komariya

COLOMBO
①

Kitulgala

Nuwera Eliya

Badulla

Pottuvil
⑪

Mount Lavinia

⑤

Bandarawela ⑥

Ella

Adam's Peak

Wellawaya

Ratnapura

Kalutara

Madampe

Beruwela
Bentota

Kataragama

③ ♦ Yala West (Ruhuna) National Park

Hikkaduwa ②

Hambantota

Galle

Mirissa   Matara   Tangalla

4

Highlights

See colour maps at the end of book

1 Colombo Buzzing capital and a foodie's paradise. ▶▶page 55.

2 Galle UNESCO-protected Dutch old town. ▶▶page 143.

3 Yala West (Ruhuna) National Park The best chance of spotting the elusive leopard. ▶▶page 179.

4 Kandy Home to the worshipped Tooth and the island's grandest festival. ▶▶page 192.

5 Adam's Peak Perfectly conical, a holy mountain worth climbing. ▶▶page 228.

6 Ella Mountain walks, waterfalls and vistas. ▶▶page 238.

7 Anuradhapura and Mihintale Mighty *dagobas*, the holiest tree and the birthplace of Sri Lankan Buddhism. ▶▶page 259.

8 Sigiriya Spectacular 'Lion Rock', bare-breasted damsels and a fifth-century playboy's penthouse. ▶▶page 274.

9 Polonnaruwa Well-preserved and compact ancient city in a peaceful shaded park. ▶▶page 285.

10 Uppuveli and Nilaveli Beautiful beaches with hardly a soul around. ▶▶page 306.

11 Arugam Bay The island's best surf and its latest beach hotspot. ▶▶page 311.

12 Jaffna Peninsula Eerie islands, half-submerged churches and a proud Tamil culture, open for the first time in two decades. ▶▶page 335.

Delhi

Kolkata

Mumbai

Chennai

Colombo

N

20 km
20 miles

Stilt fishermen of Weligama still practise this centuries-old tradition.

The 'king' of coconuts, and the best thirst quencher on the island.

Contents

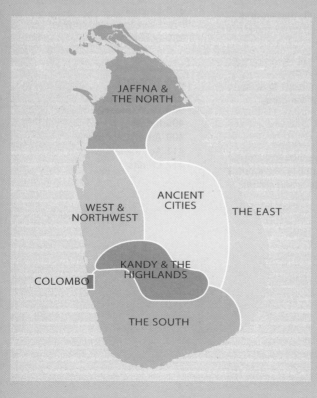

JAFFNA &
THE NORTH

ANCIENT
CITIES

WEST &
NORTHWEST

THE EAST

KANDY & THE
HIGHLANDS

COLOMBO

THE SOUTH

Contents

Footprint features

Essentials

Planning your trip

Where to go

Sri Lanka's superb beaches lie all along its coastline, with sandy coves and estuaries and long palm-fringed stretches. They vary greatly in character. Beaches on the west coast of the island, conveniently close to Colombo and the airport, tend to be the most crowded, but offer opportunities for watersports and buzz with busy bars and restaurants. Here, also, away from the package hotels, are some of the most exquisite places to stay, notably in **Bentota**. For many travellers however, the picturesque beaches of the south coast, often with magnificent sweeps of white sand, are the biggest draw. Quieter than the west coast, **Unawatuna** and **Tangalla** are the best established here, offering opportunities for diving and packed with reasonably priced accommodation. Picture-perfect, laid-back **Mirissa** is increasingly popular with budget travellers, and there are plenty of other options in this area that you might just get to yourself. Further off the beaten track, but at last accessible once more, the beautiful and deserted beaches of the east coast are worth seeking out during the off-season in the west coast. **Arugam Bay**, Sri Lanka's surf capital, is the latest hotspot, while north of Trincomalee, **Nilaveli** and **Uppuveli**, with gentle clear waters perfect for swimming, are beginning to come alive again.

However, most of Sri Lanka's most beautiful and interesting sights are away from the coast. By venturing a few hours inland you can explore the island's abundant cultural heritage. In lush verdant hills, the last Buddhist capital of **Kandy** is found. To the north are the other two points of the Cultural Triangle – the ancient capitals of **Anuradhapura** and **Polonnaruwa** – and the extraordinary royal citadel atop the giant rocky outcrop of **Sigiriya**, decorated with its world famous frescoes. Close to Anuradhapura is **Mihintale** where the first royal conversion to Buddhism was inspired, while **Dambulla** has impressive paintings in its rock cave. While visiting Kandy you can also see baby elephants at bath time at the **Pinnawela Elephant Orphanage**. Nearby, are interesting spice plantations and several temples.

The central mountains provide a refreshing break, with spectacular waterfalls and some great walking trails around **Nuwara Eliya**, surrounded by tea gardens. To the east, the 'gaps' at **Ella** and **Haputale** provide spectacular views, while some travellers are lured by the attractive gem capital of **Ratnapura**.

Sri Lanka's varied wildlife can be explored in its impressive network of national parks, such as **Ruhuna-Yala** to the southeast where the fortunate may even spot a leopard, and **Uda Walawe**, famous for its herds of elephants. There is plenty of birdwatching along the shallow coastal lagoons, while **Sinharaja Biosphere Reserve** is the last significant stretch of pristine rainforest.

Choosing a route obviously depends on your interests, the time of year and to a certain extent your mode of travel. Hiring a car allows you greater flexibility. A good option can be to take the train to Kandy and then to take buses or hire a car for visiting the rest of the Cultural Triangle and the hill country. Even if you are staying at a beach hotel on the southwest or south coast it is easy to get up to Kandy and make that a base for further exploration. ▸▸ *See Safety, page 47, and the box on page 329 for areas that are out of bounds.*

🌙 *Sri Lanka's population at just over 20 million is comparable to that of Australia and exceeds that of the city of Mumbai (Bombay) in India.*

The #1 Essential Travel Download*

Get TripAdvisor Mobile - **FREE**

- Browse millions of traveller reviews, photos & maps
- Find hotels, restaurants & things to do
- See what's nearby
- Apps available for iPhone, Android, Nokia, Palm Pre, & Windows Mobile

Packing for Sri Lanka

Travel light. Most essentials are available in the cities; items are cheap and laundry services generally speedy. Take light cotton clothes – it is a good idea to have some very lightweight long sleeve cotton tops and trousers in pale colours for evenings, as they also give some protection against mosquitoes. It can be cool at night in the Central Highlands and some warm clothing is essential. Dress is usually informal, though one or two clubs and hotels expect guests to be formally dressed at evening meals. In Colombo short-sleeved shirts and ties are often worn for business. For travelling, loose clothes are most comfortable. Trainers or canvas shoes are good options for protecting feet against cuts and so on. Women should dress modestly. Even on the beach, very revealing swimwear attracts unnecessary attention. Remember the adage, take twice as much money and half the clothes that you think you will need.

Items you might find particularly useful include: toiletries, including barrier contraceptives and tampons (available in the larger towns but you may prefer to take your own supply); personal medicines and inhalers and a copy of a prescription; international driving licence; photocopies of essential documents (flight information, passport identification and visa pages) or email yourself this information; spare passport photographs (in case you want to extend your visa); student (ISIC) card which can be used for discounts on some site entrance fees; hat and sunglasses; insect repellent; high factor sun protection cream; Swiss army knife; torch; wet wipes; zip-lock bags; contact lens cleaning solutions (available in the larger towns and cities but it is best to bring your own).

Budget travellers may also want to take the following: sheet sleeping bag (for when the sheets are less than clean); earplugs; eyeshades; padlock (for room and baggage); soap; string (or washing line); towel; washbasin plug; a spork (useful for eating lunch packets with when you don't feel like plunging your filthy fingers into the rice). Mosquito mats/coils are readily available in Sri Lanka but take your own mosquito net (these are standard in all but the very cheapest hotels but many have holes or are filthy).

One week

If you only have a week, you'd better get your skates on. A typical itinerary would head straight to **Kandy**, either on the scenic railway or by car (stopping at **Pinnawela**). On day two, after exploring the city and surrounds, travel north to **Dambulla** and spend the night at **Sigiriya**. Climb the rock first thing the next morning, and then head east to explore **Polonnaruwa** in the afternoon. Those interested in Sri Lanka's ancient ruins could then head northwest to **Anuradhapura** and **Mihintale**, returning to **Colombo** on the Puttalam road; or for those who prefer relaxation on the beach return to Colombo and spend a couple of days on the west coast. This trip can also be done in reverse, starting in **Negombo** and then heading north. An alternative one-week trip by car might head straight along the coast, via **Galle**, for a day on one of the south's beautiful beaches, then to Tissamaharama for a safari at **Yala National Park**, perhaps with a side trip to the temple town of **Kataragama**. From there it is a picturesque drive into the highlands, where you could explore the tea estates, walking trails and fading colonial grandeur of **Nuwara Eliya**, and return to Colombo via Kandy.

Two weeks

Two weeks gives you time for a 'classic' tour of Sri Lanka. You might start in **Anuradhapura** and spend a few days covering the ancient cities, perhaps with a side trip to the east coast for the beaches north of **Trincomalee**, looping south to **Kandy** via **Dambulla** or **Mahiyangana**. From Kandy tour the **Central Highlands**, perhaps climbing Adam's Peak and continue east to **Ella** or **Haputale** and then south to the national parks at **Yala** or **Uda Walawe** for wildlife spotting. You could finish by flopping on a south coast beach for a couple of days, or return to Colombo via **Sinharaja Reserve** and **Ratnapura**.

Three weeks and more

Three weeks or longer gives you a chance to explore the above sites in greater depth and to get off the beaten track. You could easily spend a week exploring the villages of the south coast, or a few days trekking in the hill country, visiting some of lesser visited ancient sites of **Northwest** and **North Central Provinces**, or exploring the island's wildlife and birdlife in greater depth. Accessible once more, the unspoilt beaches and wild country of the east are an increasingly draw for travellers, with laid back **Arugam Bay** the island's latest 'cool' beach destination. Or you could see a very different side of Sri Lanka by visiting the Tamil heartland of **Jaffna** for a few days.

When to go

Climate → *The best times to visit Sri Lanka are between the two main rainy seasons.*

Because the island lies just north of the equator temperatures remain almost constant throughout the year. However, rainfall varies widely. Sri Lanka is affected by two main monsoon seasons, sweeping over the country at different times of year. The **southwest monsoon** (June-October) brings heavy rain to the south; the best time to visit this area is from late October to early March, after the monsoon has finished. The **northeast monsoon** (October-January) can be a good time to visit despite the rain as the countryside becomes lush with tropical vegetation. The north and east are dry but hot from June to October. The Central Highlands are much cooler throughout the year, but are very wet both during the southwest monsoon and the northeast monsoon. ▶▶ *See also Background, page 380.*

What to do

Ayurveda → *See box, page 16.*

With the renewed interest in alternative forms of therapy in the West, Ayurvedic healing in Sri Lanka has become a serious subject for research and scientists have begun exploring the island's wealth of wild plants. There has been a regeneration of special Ayurvedic herbal cure centres, which are increasingly attracting foreign visitors. Day treatment centres can be found around Kandy and most large hotels now have Ayurveda massage centres attached. A number of authentic specialist Ayurvedic 'resorts' are opening up, especially along the west coast;

some of these are exquisite (such as the **Ayurveda Pavilions** in Negombo).

Birdwatching

Sri Lanka is an ornithologist's paradise with 233 resident species, of which 26 (mainly in the Wet Zone) are endemic. Together with almost 200 migrant species recorded, birdwatching is highly rewarding.

Sinharaja Forest Reserve, the **Peak Wilderness Sanctuary** and the **Ruhuna-Yala National Park** are particularly rewarding since they offer diverse habitats, while the reservoirs and coastal lagoons to

Ayurvedic healing

Ayurveda (the science of life/health) is the ancient Hindu system of medicine – a naturalistic system depending on diagnosis of the body's 'humours' (wind, mucus, gall and sometimes blood) to achieve a balance. In the early form, gods and demons were associated with cures and ailments; treatment was carried out by using herbs, minerals, formic acid (from ant hills) and water, and hence was limited in scope. Ayurveda classified substances and chemicals compounds in the theory of *panchabhutas* (five 'elements'). It also noted the action of food and drugs on the human body. Ayurvedic massage using aromatic and medicinal oils to tone up the nervous system has been practised for centuries.

This ancient system, which developed in India over centuries before the Buddha's birth, was written down as a *samhita* by Charaka. It probably flourished in Sri Lanka up to the 19th century when it was overshadowed by the Western system of allopathic medicine.

In addition to the use of herbs as cures, many are used daily in the Sri Lankan kitchen (chilli, coriander, cumin, fennel, garlic, ginger), some of which will be familiar in the West, and have for centuries been used as beauty preparations.

the southeast (especially **Bundala**) attract a large variety of water birds. Local specialist tour operators are listed on page 84.

Buddhism → *See page 360.*
The ancient Buddhist centres hold great attraction for visitors and certainly for those interested in the living religion. Sri Lanka provides rewarding opportunities to discover more about the practice of Theravada (Hinanaya) Buddhism and meditation. Several centres offer courses on Buddhism in English (and occasionally in French and German). Visit the **Buddhist Cultural Centre** (see page 82) and www.buddhanet.net, for a list of addresses and websites of retreats which accept foreigners for teaching and meditation.

Cricket
Many visitors come to Sri Lanka to support their touring cricket teams. Sri Lanka is the home of some of the most magnificently sited cricket grounds in the world, and the vibrant buzz at a Test or One-Day International is unforgettable. In early 2011 Sri Lanka co-hosted the Cricket World Cup with Bangladesh and India, and made it to the final (India won by 6 wickets). Games were played in Colombo, Kandy and the new stadium at Hambantota.

In the UK, **Gulliver Sports Travel**, T01684-878371, www.gulliversports.co.uk, is the official tour operator to the England Cricket Board; in Australia contact **Australian Sports Tours**, T1-800-026 668, www.astsports.com.au.

Cycling → *See also page 24.*
An increasing number of tour operators, both within Sri Lanka and abroad, run mountain-bike tours of the island. A waymarked **National Cycling Trail** has been developed, which runs for 240 km along the length of the southwest coast from Wadduwa (near Kalutara) to Koggala, and into the interior. The trail covers varied terrain and is divided into sections of 20-30 km (approximately 2 hrs of cycling), taking in hill country, Ancient Cities and parts of Sabaragamuwa Province.

Diving and watersports
The warm waters along Sri Lanka's palm-fringed coast are dotted with beach resorts ideal for **swimming**. Dec-Mar is the only suitable time to swim on the west coast, while Nov and Apr are usually also fine on

One-day wonders

In a football-fixated world, the universal Sri Lankan passion for the gentler charms of cricket can seem both strange and refreshing. When the national team plays, everyone watches. The economy suffers as attendance at work drops dramatically with fans clustering around their radios and TVs without a care for anything else. Cricket is played on any spare patch of grass going. The fact that they may not have a bat or ball doesn't stop them: a plank and piece of fruit will do.

The Test team is one of the main focuses of national identity, and its players national icons – they become stars, politicians and sure-fire revenue-earners in the advertising world. Adoring schoolboys who speak no other word of English can reel off the names and batting averages of every international cricketer around the world.

Cricket's origins in Sri Lanka are of course colonial, but it wasn't until 1981 that the national team achieved Test status. Though they proved themselves far from minnows it was almost 20 years until 'senior' nations such as England finally agreed to play them in a full series. In the meantime, they transformed themselves with flair into kings of the one-day international, the game's shorter form, surprising everyone but themselves when they blasted their way to victory in the 1996 World Cup. The key to their success lay in the attacking batting of the openers, particularly Sanath Jayasuriya, who abandoned traditional caution at the start of an innings and smashed the opposition bowlers from the off, setting unassailable targets. Their success revolutionized the game as all teams adopted these tactics, transforming the one-day game forever. More recently Sri Lank co-hosted the 2011 World Cup with Bangladesh and India, and reached the final before being beaten by six wickets by India. Kumar Sangakkara – one of the most consistent players in world cricket and one of the stars of the recent World Cup, scoring the third most runs (465), including 48 in Mumbai – has since resigned as captain.

Serious cricket starts at school in Sri Lanka, and though the game can be a great national unifier, there is an undeniable bias towards privilege. Public school cricket garners enormous media coverage, and its young players are idolized like their senior counterparts – perhaps at its most bizarre in the *Sunday Observer*'s 'Most Popular Schoolboy Cricketer of the Year' competition. Until recently progress to the Test team was virtually impossible without money, but the national team's variable showing prompted the game's administrators to spread cricket to the regions, setting up clinics, seminars and tournaments in the outstations to encourage talented youngsters from less wealthy backgrounds. A role model for many, as well as a political bridge, has been the extraordinarily gifted Muttiah 'Murali' Muralitharan (retired in 2010), one of the few Indian Tamils to play for Sri Lanka. He won Test matches almost single-handed with his sometimes unplayable off-spin bowling.

See www.srilankacricket.lk for further information.

---

the south. Avoid swimming outside these months, when the southwest monsoon batters the coast – there are a number of drownings each year. Particular care should be taken of rip currents; check the situation locally. Many large hotels have excellent swimming pools and will usually accept non-residents for a small fee, or even for free.

Dive centres on the west and south coasts have equipment for rent and some

Clear waters

Corals, invertebrates and dazzling fish – blue surgeon, comical parrot, butterfly, lion, large and small angels, snappers, groupers, barracudas and jackfish – enjoy Sri Lanka's warm coastal waters, yet the island has yet to become renowned as a diving destination. Much of the coastline, particularly in the southwest, was adversely affected by 'bleaching' in 1998 but was not seriously damaged by the tsunami in 2004. The reefs are slowly beginning to recover, but to avoid disappointment seek out clearer waters by taking a boat further out to sea. It is worth noting that there is only one decompression chamber in Sri Lanka, at the Trincomalee naval base.

There remain nonetheless some superb sites to explore. As long as you travel away from the coast, visibility up to 25 m is possible, especially in the morning, and a wealth of marine life can be seen at popular sites such as Negombo and Hikkaduwa. The south coast is even better and many rate the wrecks in the bays at Galle and Weligama. From April to June, Dondra to Tangalla are fine in calm seas, while the more adventurous should enquire about the Great and Little Basses off Kirinda, made famous by Arthur C Clarke, before setting sail. Some of Sri Lanka's most spectacular sites are on the east coast, where the wreck of *HMS Hermes*, a Second World War aircraft carrier, lies in good condition buried deep off Passekudah Bay, near Batticaloa (for trips to the wreck, see page 324).

offer a full range of PADI courses. Diving is best avoided during the monsoons. The best time in the southwest is the winter (Nov-Mar) when the sea is relatively calm and clear. The far south and the east coast are better Apr-Sep (but avoid Jul). Specialist companies will advise you on good reefs and the website **www.divesrilanka.com** if a useful resource.

Several popular beach areas offer good **snorkelling** at reefs within walking distance of shore, notably **Hikkaduwa**, **Unawatuna**, **Mirissa** and **Polhena** (near Matara), while the clear waters of **Pigeon Island**, a short boat ride from Nilaveli near Trincomalee, are also once again accessible.

The **surf** at **Arugam Bay** on the east coast is regarded as some of the best in Asia, though only Apr-Oct. **Hikkaduwa** is the main centre during the winter (Nov-Mar), sometimes attracting international tournaments, while **Midigama** and **Mirissa** are smaller and quieter. Surfing equipment can be bought or hired and cheap accommodation aimed at long-stay surfers is available.

Larger hotels on the west coast offer **windsurfing**, **parasailing** and **waterskiing**. **Bentota** is said to be the best spot.

Golf

A legacy from the British period, there are some excellently maintained courses in **Colombo**, **Nuwara Eliya** and on the banks of the **Victoria Reservoir** east of Kandy.

Hiking

There is little organized trekking in Sri Lanka, but some richly rewarding countryside to explore, especially in the hill country. Existing paths include ancient pilgrim routes and colonial-era bridal pathways. Moderately fit walkers should not miss climbing the sacred mountain of **Adam's Peak**, especially during pilgrimage season (Dec-May), while **Horton Plains** offers crisp mountain air and stunning views at World's End with the option of camping. The **Knuckles Range** (Dumbara Hills) has some hard treks, while **Nuwara Eliya**, **Ella** and **Haputale** are particularly good bases for walkers.

Whitewater rafting and canoeing

Kelani River, which falls through a rocky gorge just above Kitulgala, is the most popular area for rafting and canoeing, offering grade IV-V rapids. There are several operators in Colombo and Kitulgala. Gentle rafting is possible on the **Walawe River** in Uda Walawe, while the **Mahaweli Ganga**, Sri Lanka's longest river, offers more challenging opportunities.

Wildlife → www.dwlc.lk; see also page 381.

Sri Lanka's wildlife reserves are home to a wide range of native species, and wildlife 'safaris' offer the chance to see elephant, spotted deer, buffalo, wild pig, jackal, sambar and, with time and luck, the leopard and sloth bear. Around 24% of Sri Lanka's land area is covered by forest, most large tracts of which are protected by the government. The Forestry Department runs the island's forest reserves (such as the **Knuckles Range**) and biosphere reserves (notably **Sinharaja**), while the national parks, sanctuaries and nature reserves, which offer the best chance of wildlife spotting, belong the Department of Wildlife Conservation. Most of Sri Lanka's national parks are in the Dry Zone areas of the north and east, the most frequently visited by tourists being **Yala National Park**, where a remarkable array of bird and animal life is easily visible; **Uda Walawe**, famous for its elephants; and **Minneriya** to the north. Closed for many years owing to the civil war, the island's largest reserve, **Wilpattu** reopened in 2010.

All national parks are open 0630-1830. Entrance fees for most are US$15 for foreigners and US$7 for children under 12, plus fees for a compulsory tracker, taxes and service charge. These hidden charges can add up and make a visit quite expensive, however, the money is ploughed back into wildlife conservation (theoretically at least). Most people choose to visit the parks on a day trip. Bungalows and campsites are available but these are difficult to arrange and often booked up well in advance.

Getting there

Air

All international flights arrive at Katunayake, 30 km north of Colombo. International airlines flying to Sri Lanka include: **Aeroflot, Cathay Pacific, El Al, Emirates, Gulf Air, Indian Airlines, Korean Airlines, Kuwait Airways, Lufthansa, Malaysia Airlines, Oman Air, Pakistan International Airways, Qatar Airways, Royal Jordanian, Saudi Arabian, Singapore Airlines** and **Thai International. Sri Lankan Airlines**, www.srilankan.lk, the national carrier, flies to over 20 countries, and has offices all over the world. A source of great national pride, it compares favourably with the best of the Southeast Asia airlines for comfort and service.

November to March is high season with Christmas, New Year and Easter the most expensive times to visit. Shop around, book early and if using a 'bucket shop' confirm with the airline that your name appears on their list. It is possible to get a significant discount from a reputable travel agent especially outside European holiday times, most notably from London. The airlines invariably quote a higher price as they are not able to discount tickets but off-load surplus tickets on agents who choose to pass on part of their commission to passengers. It is possible to get Christmas bargains, but the lowest prices are often during May-June when it's monsoon season in the south.

A number of charter companies offer package tours, operating mainly from Central Europe (Germany, Italy, etc). These can work out cheaper than scheduled flight fares, but may have limitations. They are not available to Sri Lankan nationals and usually must include accommodation. You can also arrange a stop-over in Sri Lanka on a 'Round the World' and other long-distance tickets.

From the UK and Ireland

Sri Lankan Airlines flies eight to nine times a week direct from London to Colombo. Jet Airways offers some good deals, transiting through India. It is usually cheaper to fly via the Middle East; Gulf Air, Emirates, Oman Air and Qatar Airways tend to offer similar fares.

There are various discount flight booking agencies which offer significantly better deals than the airlines oneself. The national press carry their advertisements as well as magazines such as *TNT*. Many now have branches across the UK as well as in London.

Discount travel agents
Bridge the World, T0800-988 6884, www.bridgetheworld.com.
Flightbookers, www.ebookers.com.
North South Travel, T01245-608291, www.northsouthtravel.co.uk. Donates its profits to charity
Sri Lanka Tours, T020-743 43921, www.srilankatours.co.uk. Offers deals on flights with Sri Lankan, Emirates, Kuwait Airways, Qatar Airways, Ethihad Airways, Oman Airways and Jet Airways.
STA, T0871-230 0040, www.statravel.co.uk. With over 65 branches in the UK, offers special deals for under-26s.
Trailfinders, T0845-054 6060, www.trail finders.com. Has branches in 20 British cities with a good range of tailor-made and round-the-world deals.
Travelbag, T0871-703 4701, www.travelbag.co.uk. Quotes competitive fares.

From the USA and Canada

From the east coast, it is best to fly from New York via London or pick up a direct flight from the UK but this will usually involve a stopover in London. From the west coast, it is best to fly via Hong Kong, Singapore or Bangkok using one of those countries' national carriers.

Discount travel agents
Other online agents worth checking out include **www.expedia.com**, **www.travelocity.com** and **www.orbitz.com**.
Discount Airfares Worldwide On-Line, www.etn.nl. A hub of consolidator and discount agent links.
STA Travel, T1800-781 4040, www.statravel.com. Discount student/ youth travel company with over 100 stores across North America.
Travel Cuts, T1-800 667 2887, www.travel cuts.com. Specialist in student discount fares, IDs and other travel services. Branches in other Canadian cities and in the USA.

From Australasia via the Far East

There are no direct flights to Colombo from Australia or New Zealand, but **Cathay Pacific**, **Malaysian Airlines**, **Singapore Airlines** and **Thai International** are the main linking airlines and offer the best deals. **Sri Lankan** also flies to the major Southeast Asian regional capitals.

Discount travel agents
Flight Centre, T133133, www.flight centre.com.au, and New Zealand, T0800-243544, www.flightcentre.co.nz, with branches in major towns and cities.
STA Travel, T134782, www.statravel.com.au; New Zealand, T0800-474400, www.statravel.co.nz, branches in major towns and campuses around both countries.
Travel.com.au, Sydney, T1300-130 483, www.travel.com.au.

From South Asia

Sri Lankan Airlines flies to a growing number of Indian destinations, including Bangalore, Chennai, Delhi, Kochi, Mumbai, Thiruvananthapuram and Tiruchirappalli, as well as Male in the Maldives. **Jet Airways** flies to Colombo from Chennai and Delhi.

Airport information → *www.airport.lk.*

Disembarkation Cards are handed out to passengers during the inward flight. Complete parts 1 and 2 and hand them in at the immigration counter on arrival along with your passport. Keep your baggage identification tag safe as this must be handed in when leaving the Arrivals hall.

Bandaranaike International Airport, at present Sri Lanka's only international airport (although a new one will be opening in 2012 in the south of the island), is at Katunayake, 30 km north of Colombo. It has modern facilities including duty free shops (with a large selection of electrical goods). Major banks are represented by branches in the Arrivals hall, offering a good rate of exchange, and there is an ATM which accepts most cards. The tourist information counter has limited information although it is worth picking up copies of *Travel Lanka* and the *Sri Lanka Tourist Board Accommodation Guide*.

There is a pre-paid taxi stand and several hotel and tour company booths just after the Arrivals hall (see page 58). Outside, porters will offer to transport your luggage; alternatively, the trolleys are free. There are several hotels and guesthouses within a few kilometres of the airport (see page 73), and a wider choice of accommodation at Negombo, 6 km away (see page 97). Stringent baggage and personal security checks are often carried out, especially on departure, so be prepared to repack your bags.

Visitors to Departures or Arrivals must buy an entrance permit for Rs 200 at the special booths before entering the terminal, but access is limited due to security controls.

A few flights each night arrive in Sri Lanka in the small hours. If you are going to arrive late, it is best to book a hotel or guesthouse in Negombo for the first night (and arrange in advance to be picked up from the airport) and move to Colombo or another beach resort the following day. Avoid accommodation touts. At the airport bank exchange counters and taxis operate 24 hours, though public transport does not.

On departure, give yourself enough time to pass through security. Travellers are not allowed into the terminal building before their luggage has been x-rayed and their documents have been scrutinized.

Sea → *For further details, see page 86.*

At the time of writing passenger services between Colombo Harbour and **Tuticorin**, India, had just started running after a long hiatus. Two voyages a week are planned and the journey takes 10-13 hours. Prices range between Rs5500-Rs75,000 depending on the level of comfort. Contact **Unicorn** ① *12 Galle Face Court 2, Colombo 3, T230 2100*. Other routes may also open. Once established, Indian visas will be obtainable at Colombo port.

Cruise ships occasionally stop at Colombo and you may be able to get a berth on a cargo or container ship from ports in the Gulf region or Southeast Asia but it is impossible to book trips in advance. Sailors in their own vessels may be able to berth in Galle, although immigration formalities should be carried out in Colombo. Check with your nearest Sri Lankan representative in advance.

Getting around

Public transport in Sri Lanka is very cheap and, in the case of buses, island-wide. Due to overcrowding on buses, train is a (marginally) more comfortable alternative, although the network is limited and there are often delays. The majority of travellers hire a car – whether self-drive or with a chauffeur – for at least part of their stay, especially if only here for a short time. Note that some areas of the north and east remain out of bounds (see page 47).

Air

There are still few internal flights in Sri Lanka, but there are flights between Colombo's domestic airport at Ratmalana and Jaffna (see page 85). Those visitors with money to burn can charter planes or helicopters to take them to their destination.

Sri Lankan Airlines (T19733 5500, www.srilankan.aero) has re-launched their air taxi service, which was suspended in 2007, and flights currently operate from Colombo to Kandy, Bentota, Dickwella, Nuwara Eliya, Ampara, Koggala, Hambantota and Tangalle. There are plans by expand this to encompass Negombo, Tissamaharama, Arugam Bay, Trincomalee, Dambulla and Jaffna. Most are charter flights at the moment, but there are scheduled departures to Bentota, Koggala and Dickwella.

Road

The main roads in Sri Lanka are generally well maintained but traffic often moves very slowly, especially in Colombo and its surrounds. There has been some investment in recent years and there are now 'carpet' roads from Colombo to Kandy, Puttalam and Galle. Work began on the Colombo–Matara Expressway in March 2003 and is ongoing.

Bus

Government-run CTB buses are the cheapest, slowest and most uncomfortable of the options as they are always very crowded. Private buses follow the same routes, offer a higher degree of comfort (if you can get a seat) and cost a little more.

Private intercity buses are often air-conditioned minibuses (sometimes coaches on popular routes). They cost about double the fare of ordinary buses but they are quicker and you are guaranteed a seat since they operate on a 'leave when full' basis. They can be quite cramped, especially if you have a lot of luggage (if it takes up a whole seat you will probably have to pay for it) but on the whole they are the best option for travelling quickly between the main towns. They are generally non-stop but will let you off on request en route (ask the conductor in advance) although you will still have to pay the full fare to the end destination. If you do want to get off en route it is best to sit near the door since the aisle is used by passengers on fold-away seats. The fare is usually displayed on the front or side window.

In general it is best to board buses at the main bus stand in order to get a seat. Once out on the road it is normally standing room only.

Car hire

Many people choose to travel by car for at least part of their trip. This gives you greater flexibility if you want to tour, giving you the chance to see some places which are almost inaccessible any other way. Sharing a vehicle can make this possible for even those travelling on a small budget. On the downside however it cuts out some of the interaction with local people which can be one of the most rewarding aspects of travel by public transport, and may give you a lesser sense of 'achievement'.

There are several **self-drive** car hire firms based in Colombo including some linked to international firms. You have to be 25-65 years old and have an International Driving Permit (contact your local Automobile Association) in order to get a Sri Lankan driving permit through their AA. To get this 'recognition permit', which is issued up to the expiry date of your International Driving Permit, is a simple process and costs Rs 500. Just call at the **Automobile Association of Sri Lanka** ① *3rd floor, 40 Sir MM Markar Mawatha, Galle Face, Colombo 3, T242 1528, Mon-Fri 0830-1630.* Some hire firms (eg **Avis**) will arrange this. If you do not have an International Driving Permit but do have your national licence, you must apply for a temporary Sri Lankan Driving Licence from the **Register of Motor Vehicles** ① *Department of Motor Traffic, 341 Elvitigala Mawatha, Colombo 5, T269 4331.* Temporary Driving Licences are issued on payment of Rs 600 plus GST per month up to a maximum of three months.

The rule of 'might is right' applies in Sri Lanka, and the standard of driving can be appalling. Many foreign visitors find the road conditions difficult, unfamiliar and sometimes dangerous. If you drive yourself it is essential to take great care and you should attempt to anticipate the mistakes that Sri Lankan road users might make. Most Sri Lankan drivers appear to take unbelievable risks, notably overtaking at inopportune times, such as when approaching a blind bend. Pedestrians often walk along, or in the middle of, a narrow road in the absence of pavements and cattle and dogs roam at will. Never overtake a vehicle in front of you which indicates to the right. It usually means that it is unsafe for you to overtake and rarely means that they are about to turn right. Flashing headlights mean 'get out of the way, I'm not stopping'. In these circumstances it is best to give the oncoming vehicle space, since they usually approach at great speed. Roundabouts are generally a free-for-all, so take your chance cautiously. Horns are used as a matter of course, but most importantly when overtaking, to warn the driver being overtaken.

It may actually be safer (and more relaxing) to hire a **car with a driver**. These are available through travel agents and tour operators, or you can book with a freelance driver direct (the latter usually works out considerably cheaper). A driver may be helpful in being able to communicate with local people and also make a journey more interesting by telling you more about the places and local customs. Before setting off, however, you should agree some ground rules, as there are a number of potential pitfalls: first, check that the driver is content for you to pick the route and accommodation, as some can be inflexible. It is best not to depend on the driver for suggestions of hotels, restaurants and gift shops since you may not get an unbiased opinion. Most large hotels have free driver accommodation and will provide a meal for them, but guesthouses and hotels off the beaten track often do not – in these instances you should agree in advance who will pay for drivers' accommodation. It is also worth checking that the driver will stop for photographs; that his allowance will cover parking fees at sites; and, if you plan a long trip that he is prepared to spend the time away from home. Hire charges vary according to make and mileage and can be very high for luxury models.

The following rates quoted by **Quickshaw's** (see Colombo, page 86) for air-conditioned cars were valid in 2011. 20% tax is additional:

Self-drive Nissan Sunny: €18 per day (up to 100 km), €130 per week (up to 700 km), plus €0.12 per excess kilometre. Nissan Blue Bird: €22 per day, €155 per week, plus

€0.12 per kilometre. A refundable deposit of Rs 25,000 is required, which covers insurance for accidental damage and loss (with a police report) up to this value. It is prohibited to drive in wildlife sanctuaries. Petrol costs, which are extra, are rising fast.

Car with driver Nissan Sunny: €35 per day (up to 100 km) or €240 per week (up to 700 km), plus €0.30 per excess kilometre. Mercedes Benz: €90 per day, €630 per week, plus €0.80 per kilometre. Chauffeur's subsistence is an extra Rs 750 per day. Alternatively, some companies charge a flat rate. Much cheaper rates are possible with freelance drivers.

Cycling

Cycling is very worthwhile in Sri Lanka as it gives you the opportunity to see authentic village life well off the beaten track. Foreign cyclists are usually greeted with cheers, waves and smiles. It is worth taking your own bike (contact your airline well in advance) or mountain bikes can be hired from **Adventure Sports Lanka** in Colombo (see page 84) and other adventure tour companies, though they may not be up to international standards. Bicycles can be transported on trains, though you will need to arrive two hours ahead at Colombo Fort station. While cycling is fun on country byways, hazardous driving means that you should avoid the major highways (especially the Colombo–Galle road) as far as possible. Cycling after dark can be dangerous because of the lack of street lighting and poor road surfaces. Take bungee cords (to strap down a backpack), spare parts and good lights from home, and take care not to leave your bike parked anywhere unattended. Repair shops are widespread and charges are nominal. Always carry plenty of water.

Local bikes tend to be heavy and often without gears but on the flat they offer a good way of exploring short distances outside towns. Many people choose to hire one to explore ancient city areas such as Polonnaruwa and Anuradhapura. Expect to pay Rs 200-300 per day for cycle hire from hotels and guesthouses, depending on the standard of hotel and condition of the bike. ▶ See also Cycling, page 16.

Hitchhiking

This is rare in Sri Lanka, partly because public transport is so cheap.

Motorcycling

Motorcycles are popular locally and are convenient for visiting different beaches and also for longer distance sightseeing. Repairs are usually easy to arrange and quite cheap. Motorcycle hire is possible for around €14 per day (unlimited mileage) in some beach resorts (eg Hikkaduwa, Mirissa) or in towns nearby. You will generally need to leave a deposit or your passport. Check all bikes thoroughly for safety. If you have an accident you will usually be expected to pay for the damage. Potholes and speed-breakers add to the problems of a fast rider.

Taxi

Taxis have yellow tops with red numbers on white plates, and are available in most towns. Negotiate price for long journeys beforehand. **Radio cabs** (eg Ace, Quick, GNTC) are more expensive and have a higher minimum charge, but are fixed price, very reliable, convenient and some accept credit cards. They are air-conditioned, have digital meters and are available 24 hours at the airport, Colombo and Kandy. The car usually arrives within 10-15 minutes of phoning (give exact location).

In tourist resorts, taxis are often Toyota **vans** which can carry up to 10 people. Ask at your hotel/guesthouse for an estimate of the fare to a particular destination. There is usually a 'going-rate', but you will probably have to bargain to reach this. Agree on the fare before getting in.

Three-wheeler

These three-wheeled motorized tricycles, the Indian auto-rickshaws made by Bajaj, move quickly through traffic but compare poorly against taxis for price. Sri Lanka's three-wheeler drivers are always keen to procure business, and you will be beeped constantly by any without a passenger. An alarming 40% lack licences, and the driving is frequently of the kamikaze variety but they are often the only option available. Three-wheeler fares are negotiable as they are unmetered but fix a price before starting – the going rate is around Rs 25-50 per km. You can offer about 60% of the asking price though it is unlikely that you will get to pay the same rate as locals.

Train

Although the network is limited there are train services to a number of major destinations. Journeys are comparatively short, and very cheap by Western standards. Train journeys are leisurely (bar the intercity sevice between Colombo and Kandy) and an ideal way to see the countryside and meet the people without experiencing the downside of a congested bus journey through dusty crowded roads. You should be aware of touts on major train routes (especially Colombo to Kandy and Galle).

There are three principal 'lines':
1 **Northern Line** This runs from Colombo up to Anuradhapura and continues north to Vavuniya, though no longer to Jaffna or Mannar. A line branches east at Maho (67 km south of Anuradhapura) towards Habarana, then splitting at Gal Oya junction, the northern section terminating at Trincomalee, the southern section continuing via Polonnaruwa to Batticaloa.

2 **Main Line** East from Colombo Fort to Kandy (with a branch line to Matale) with the ascent starting at Rambukkana. From Peradeniya the Main Line continues to Badulla through the hills, including stops at Nanu Oya (for Nuwara Eliya), Hatton (for Adam's Peak), Ohiya (for the Horton Plains) and Ella. This line is very scenic and a recommended way of travelling to the hill country, though book well in advance (up to 10 days).

3 **Colombo–Matara Line** South, originating at Maradana/Fort, and following the coast to Galle and as far as Matara, connecting all the popular coastal resorts. Running initially through the commuter belt south of the city, it can be crowded in the rush hour.

There are also the following lines: on the **Puttalam Line**, there are slow trains north from Fort to Puttalam via Katunayake (for the airport), Negombo and Chilaw. The **Kelani Valley Line** goes from Maradana to Avissawella.

Third class has hard seats; second has some thin cushioning; first class is fairly comfortable. Many slow trains may have second- and third-class coaches only, with first-class only available on some express trains. The time of the next train in each direction is usually chalked onto a blackboard.

Intercity trains

There are air-conditioned intercity trains running to Kandy and Vavuniya (via Anuradhapura), which should be booked in advance. Kandy train also has a first-class observation car, which must be booked well in advance as it is very popular (for information on reserving these whilst in Colombo, see page 215). You will need to specify your return date at the time of booking the outward journey as tickets are not open-ended.

There are also some special through trains such as a weekly service from Matara all the way to Anuradhapura, and another from Matara to Kandy, both via Colombo. Extra services are put on during festivals and holidays, eg from January for four months to Hatton (for the Adam's Peak pilgrimage season); April holiday season to the hills; in May and June for full moon days to Buddhist sites such as Kandy, Anuradhapura, Mihintale; and July/August for **Kandy Perahera**.

Maps

The Survey Department's *Road Map of Sri Lanka* (scale 1:500,000), available at Survey Department branches in large towns, as well as some shops, including Odel in Colombo, is useful and up-to-date. It has some street maps for larger towns. For more detail the department's four large sheet maps covering the island (scale 1:250,000) are the best available. These may not be available to buy for security reasons but you can ask to consult these at the Survey Department's Map Sales Branch in Colombo. *Arjuna's Atlas of Sri Lanka*, Arjuna, 1997 (see www.lankadotcom.com) is a comprehensive demographic survey of Sri Lanka. Sri Lanka Tourist Board branches both in Sri Lanka and abroad gives out a 1:800,000 Sri Lanka itinerary map plus several city and site guides with sketch maps free, but these are not particularly clear.

There are a number of user-friendly fold-out sheet maps produced abroad. These are mainly 1:500,000 scale and show tourist sights. Some have town street maps and some tourist information. Insight and Berndtson & Berndtson maps are both nicely laminated; Periplus's has some tourist information and clear street maps of Colombo, Kandy, Anuradhapura, Galle, Negombo, Nuwara Eliya and Polonnaruwa; Nelles Verlag also has some city insets; the Reise *Know How* map is probably the most detailed.

Sleeping

Sri Lanka has a surprisingly uneven range of accommodation. At the top end, there are international five-star hotels in Colombo and a handful of very exclusive 'boutique' hotels in some other areas. Below this level, you can stay safely and relatively cheaply in most major tourist areas, where there is a choice of quality hotels offering a full range of facilities (though their food can be bland and uninspired). At the lower end of the scale, there is an increasing range of family-run guesthouses in tourist areas offering bed and breakfast (and sometimes other meals). In smaller centres even the best hotels are far more variable and it may be necessary to accept much more modest accommodation. In the high season (December to March for much of the island) bookings can be extremely heavy. It is therefore best to reserve rooms well in advance if you are making your own arrangements, and to arrive reasonably early in the day.

Prices are highly inflated in Kandy during the **Esala Perahera** festival and in Nuwara Eliya during the April holiday season. 'Long weekends' (weekends when a public holiday

Sleeping price codes

LL	US$450 and over	B	US$71-114	F	Rs 1500-2499
L	US$250-449	C	US$40-70	G	Rs 1499
AL	US$165-249	D	Rs 3500-4500		and under
A	US$115-164	E	Rs 2500-3499		

Prices are for a double room excluding taxes during the high (not 'peak') season. Rates for hotels in categories C or above tend to be quoted in US dollars, or, in west coast package resorts, in euros. Prices are 'spot-rates' for individual travellers. Tour operators can get large discounts for 'package' clients in the top categories. Prices are exclusive of service charge and tax, both 10%. Single rooms are rare and single occupancy of a double room rarely attracts a significant discount.

or *poya* day falls on a Thursday, Friday, Monday or Tuesday) also attract a substantial increase in room rates in Nuwara Eliya. Many hotels charge the highest room rate over Christmas and New Year (between mid-December to mid-January). Large reductions are made by hotels in all categories out-of-season in most resorts. Always ask if any is available. During the monsoon rooms may feel damp and have a musty smell.

International class hotels
Mainly in the capital and around Kandy, these have a full range of facilities where prices and standards are sometimes comparable with the West. In Colombo, these are often genuinely luxurious.

Boutique hotels and villas
One of the fastest growing sectors of the market, these can be quite special offering a high degree of luxury, superb and very personal service, and a sense of privacy and exclusiveness lacking in resort-style hotels. Often they are innovatively designed with environmental sensitivity. Some sumptuous villas can also be rented by the day or week – see www.villasinsrilanka.com.

Colonial-era hotels
The colonial period has left a legacy of atmospheric colonial-era hotels, notably in Colombo, Kandy and Nuwara Eliya. Some were purpose built, others converted from former governors' residences, etc. A number have been carefully modernized without losing their period charm. Some very good deals are available.

Resort hotels
Catering mainly to tourists on package holidays, most larger tourist hotels on beaches and near important sites come into this category. Some are luxurious with a good range of facilities, others, notably in some west coast resorts, are rather tired and dated. Food served here tends to be of the 'all-you-can-eat' buffet variety. It pays to make bookings through tour operators, which offer large discounts on most resort-style hotels.

Best colonial hotels

Galle Face Hotel, Colombo, see page 74.
Mount Lavinia Hotel, Mount Lavinia, see page 76.
Hill Club, Nuwara Eliya, see page 230.

Bandarawela Hotel, Bandarawela, see page 245.
Closenburg Hotel, Galle, see page 159.

Guesthouses

Guesthouses are the staple of budget travellers, and are in plentiful supply in tourist haunts such as the west and south coasts, in Kandy, Nuwara Eliya, Anuradhapura and a few other towns. Some are effectively small hotels, usually at the upper end of the price bracket (D and E); others are simpler and more basic affairs. At their best, usually when family owned, they can be friendly, homely, and rich sources of local information. Those offering quality home cooking are well worth searching out. In addition, some private homes in Colombo, Kandy and some beach areas offer rooms, which can be very good value. Homestays are currently being championed by the Sri Lankan government, so these will be more readily available in the near future.

Ayurvedic resorts

Mainly on the west coast, very popular with tourists from mainland Europe, these offer a degree of luxury combined with ready or tailor-made programmes of Ayurvedic treatment. The authenticity of the treatments on offer tends to vary. **Ayurveda Pavilions** in Negombo (see page 98), and **Siddhalepa Ayurveda Health Resort** in Kalutara (see page 134), are two of the most highly regarded resorts, while more basic accommodation is offered with treatment at the Ayurvedic hospitals in Mount Lavinia (see page 89).

Government rest houses

These are sometimes in converted colonial houses, often in superb locations, though compared to privately run enterprises are now often run down, overpriced with poor service. In some cases however they are the best (or only) option in town. **Ceylon Hotels Corporation (CHC)** ① *Central Reservations: 2 Galle Rd, Colombo 3, T558 5858, www.ceylon hotels.lk*, is responsible for management of several of the old government rest houses across the island. It's best to book through Central Reservations as occasionally an individual rest house may not honour a direct booking. Prices charged by some on arrival may vary from what is quoted on the phone or the CHC's 'official' typed list showing the tariff which only a few managers acknowledge exists. Rice and curry lunches at rest houses are often good, though more expensive than similar fare elsewhere.

National park accommodation

National park bungalows are expensive, with accommodation costs, national park fees, service charges and linen charges. If the bungalow is within the park boundaries then you will have to pay park entrance fees for two days for an overnight stay. Camping is also possible in many national parks. Accommodation must be booked at the Department of Wildlife Conservation in Colombo (see page 90) but at the time of writing, excessive demand, the complex lottery system and the difficulty in getting to the office was making this difficult to arrange. The bungalows and campsites also have to be booked up to a month in advance.

Plantation bungalows

Some attractive rubber and tea plantation bungalows in the hill country can be rented out by small or large groups and provide an interesting alternative place to stay. A caretaker/cook is often provided. There is no centralized booking agency, but see individual entries in the text, speak to the tourist board or contact **Red Dot Tours**, www.reddottours.com.

Circuit bungalows

Designed mainly for government workers, these may be the only option in areas well off the beaten track. They should be booked through the government offices in Colombo. Contact details are given under individual entries.

Railway Retiring Rooms

Railway Retiring Rooms may be hired for up to 24 hours. However, there are only a few stations with rooms and they are generally rather poor value. Some are open to people without rail tickets and can be useful in an emergency. Stations with rooms include: Anuradhapura, Galle, Kandy, Mihintale, Polgahawela, Maho and Trincomalee.

Eating and drinking

Although it shares some similarities with Indian cooking, Sri Lankan cuisine is distinct from its neighbour. While at its heart lies the island's enviable variety and bountiful supply of native vegetables, fruits and spices, Sri Lanka's history of trade and colonization has contributed to the remarkable range of dishes available today. Even before the arrival of the Europeans, Indians, Arabs, Malays and Moors had all left their mark. The Portuguese brought chilli from South America, perhaps the most significant change to food across the East, while the Dutch and even the British have also bequeathed a number of popular dishes. Sampling authentic Sri Lankan fare is a highlight of any trip.

Cuisine

Rice and curry is Sri Lanka's main 'dish', but the term 'curry' conceals an enormous variety of subtle flavours. Coriander, mustard seeds, cumin, fenugreek, peppercorns, cinnamon, cloves and cardamoms are just some of the spices that, roasted and blended, give a Sri Lankan curry its richness, while most cooks also add Maldive fish, or dried sprats. *Rampe* (screw-pine leaf) and tamarind pulp are also distinctive ingredients. The whole is then usually cooked in coconut milk.

Sri Lankan food is renowned for its fieriness, and **chilli** is the most noticeable ingredient in some curries. While most tourist restaurants, aware of the sensitivity of some Western palates, normally tone down its use, real home cooking will usually involve liberal quantities. If a dish is still too hot, a spoonful of rice or curd, or a sip of beer or milk (not water) will usually tone down its effects.

A typical Sri Lankan meal would comprise a large portion of rice, with a 'main curry' – for Buddhists usually fish, although chicken, beef and mutton are also often available – and several pulse and vegetable and (sometimes) salad dishes. *Dhal* is invariably one of these, and vegetable curries may be made from jackfruit, okra, breadfruit, beans, bananas, banana flowers or pumpkin, amongst others. Deliciously salty poppadums are also usually served, and the offering is completed by numerous side dishes: spicy pickles, sweet and sour chutneys and 'sambols', made of ground coconut (*pol sambol*) or onion

Eating price codes

℟℟℟ over Rs 1000   ℟℟ Rs 500-1000   ℟ below Rs 500

Prices are for the cost of a main meal, excluding drinks and taxes.

mixed with Maldive fish, red chilli and lime juice (*seeni sambol*). *Mallung*, a milder dish prepared with grated coconut, shredded leaves, red onions and lime, is an alternative to try. *Kiri hodhi* is a mild 'white' curry prepared with coconut milk.

Rice-based alternatives to rice and curry include the Dutch-inspired *lamprais*, rice boiled in meat stock with curry, accompanied by dry meat and vegetable curries, fried meat and fish or meat balls (*frikkadels*), then parcelled in banana leaf and baked; and the ubiquitous *buriyani*, a Moorish dish of rice cooked in stock with pieces of chopped spiced meat and garnished with sliced egg.

The **rice** generally served is usually plain white boiled rice but it is worth searching out the healthier red rice. There are some tasty alternatives. '**String hoppers**', a steamed nest of thin rice flour noodles, are often eaten with thin curries at breakfast but are often available at any time. '**Hoppers**' (*appam*), a breakfast speciality, are small cupped pancakes made from fermented rice flour, coconut milk and yeast. Crispy on the edges (like French crêpes), thick at the centre, they are often prepared with an egg broken into the middle of the pan ('egg hoppers'). *Pittu* is a crumbly mixture of flour and grated coconut steamed in a bamboo mould, usually served with coconut milk and sambol.

As befits a tropical island, Sri Lanka's **fish** and **seafood** is excellent. The succulent white seerfish, tuna and mullet, usually grilled and served with chips and salad, are widely available along the coast, while crab, lobster and prawns (often jumbo prawns) are magnificent and reasonably priced. Cuttlefish is very versatile and prepared a number of ways. Meat varies in quality; though it is cheap and usually better than you get in India.

Unsurprisingly, **Indian** food is also popular, particularly from the south. Cheap filling traditional 'plate' meals (*thali*) are often available in Colombo, the north and east, as are *dosai*, crispy pancakes made from rice and lentil-flour batter, often served with a spiced potato filling.

Sri Lanka has a spectacular variety of superb tropical **fruit**, and this is reflected in the variety of juices on offer. Available throughout the year are pineapple, papaya (excellent with lime) and banana, of which there are dozens of varieties (red bananas are said to be the best). The extraordinarily rich jack (*jak*) fruit is also available all year. Seasonal fruit include the lusciously sweet mango (for which Jaffna is especially famous), the purplish mangosteen (July to September), wood-apple, avocado, the spiky foul-smelling durian and hairy red rambutan from July to October. In addition to ordinary green coconuts, Sri Lanka has its own variety – the golden king coconut (*thambili*); the milk is particularly sweet and nutritious.

Breakfast

The tendency amongst most smaller hotels and guesthouses is to serve a 'Western breakfast' comprising fruit and white bread with some jam. It is well worth ordering a Sri Lankan alternative in advance – ie the night before. This could comprise hoppers, string hoppers, *kiribath* (see below) or, best of all, the delicious **rotty** (roti), a flat circular unleavened bread cooked on a griddle.

Lunch

Lunch is the main meal of the day for many Sri Lankans. Rice and curry is the standard, often served in larger hotels as a buffet. The better rest houses are a good option for sampling a variety of authentic curries (usually Rs 400-500). A cheaper and quicker alternative is to pick up a **'lunch packet'**, available from local restaurants and street vendors. This takeaway option usually comprises a portion of rice, a meat, fish or vegetable curry, plus *dhal*, all wrapped up in a paper parcel. Usually costing Rs 100-150, this is a cheap and filling meal. A lighter alternative still is a plate of **short eats**, a selection of meat and vegetable rolls, 'cutlets' (deep-fried in bread crumbs), *rotis* and *wadais*, a Tamil speciality of deep-fried savoury lentil doughnut rings, sometimes served in yoghurt (*thair vadai*). You will normally be given a full plate and charged for however many you eat.

Dinner

In larger hotels, dinner is usually the main meal of the day, often with enormous all-you-can-eat buffets. Sri Lankans tend to eat late but light, and be aware that outside Colombo and the major tourist centres, the offering in guesthouses and restaurants may be limited unless you order in advance. It may not be possible to get rice and curry but Chinese food, such as fried rice, and devilled dishes are nearly always available.

Desserts

Sri Lankans tend to have a sweet tooth. Rice forms the basis of many Sri Lankan sweet dishes, palm treacle (*kitul*) being used as the main traditional sweetener. This is also served on curd as a delicious dessert (*kiri peni*) and boiled and set into *jaggery*. *Kavun* is an oil cake, made with rice flour and treacle and deep-fried until golden brown. Malay influence is evident in the popular *watalappam*, a steamed pudding made with coconut milk, eggs and jaggery, rather reminiscent of crème caramel. *Kiribath*, rice boiled in milk, is something of a national dish, often served at weddings and birthdays. It can be eaten with jaggery or as a breakfast dish with *seeni sambol*. Sri Lankan ice cream varies in quality; the best is made by soft drinks company Elephant House. Jaffna is also famous for its 'cream houses'.

Eating out → *Sri Lankans usually eat with their hands, mixing rice and curry together with the right thumb and forefingers. As a foreigner, however, you will always be supplied with a fork.*

Eating out in Sri Lanka is remarkably cheap. Most restaurants serve a choice of Indian, Chinese and continental dishes. Sadly, it is not easy to get good Sri Lankan food in most resort hotels which tend to concentrate on Western dishes. The upmarket hotels in Colombo, however, serve first-class buffets at lunch and dinnertime, and there are an increasing number of excellent Sri Lankan restaurants in the city. Upcountry, home cooking in family-owned guesthouses is often unbeatable. It is essential to order well in advance as Sri Lankan curries take a long time to prepare. This is one of the reasons for the universal popularity of Chinese and 'devilled' dishes available throughout the island, which can be knocked together in a few minutes. **Vegetarian** food is much less common in Sri Lanka than in India, and in places can be difficult to get. Check out www.lankarestaurants.com, for interesting and helpful reviews of restaurants, including food and ambience.

Drinks → *Do not add ice to drinks as the water from which it is made may not be pure.*

As they are year-round fruits, fresh papaya, pineapple and lime **juice** are always excellent. Sour-sop and wood-apple juice are two more unusual alternatives worth trying. One of the most popular and widespread drinks is King Coconut (the golden *thambili*). Always pure, straight from the nut, it is very refreshing. Mineral **water** is available everywhere, though is relatively expensive. There is a huge variety of bottled **soft drinks**, including international brands. Local favourites include ginger beer, cream soda, lemonade and Necto. These are perfectly safe but always check the seal. Elephant House is the main soft drinks manufacturer, and all their products are palatable. One potent soft drink is **Peyawa**, a ginger beer made with pepper and coriander for added kick.

The island's **coffee** harvest failed in 1869, and it would seem that Sri Lankans have never quite forgiven it, such are the crimes committed in the name of the drink. Colombo's upmarket hotels do however serve decent coffee, and there are a couple of new Western-style coffee bars opening up. As befits one of the world's great producers, **tea** is of course a much better option, although the highest quality varieties are generally exported.

Drinking **alcohol** in Sri Lanka is a no-nonsense male preserve. Bars, except in Colombo and tourist areas, tend to be spit-and-sawdust affairs. **Beer** is strong (5%+), popular and served in large 660 ml bottles. **Lion**, **Carlsberg** and **Three Coins** are the three main brands, each producing a Pilsner style lager slightly thin to Western tastes but quite palatable. **Three Coins** make some good specialist beers: their 8% **Sando stout** is smooth and chocolatey, and **Riva** is a more than passable wheat beer. The locally brewed **arrack**, distilled from palm toddy, is the most popular spirit and a cheaper option than beer. Superior brands include **Old Arrack**, **Double distilled**, the matured **VSOA** and **seven-year- old** arrack. The frothy, cloudy cider-like **toddy** is the other national drink, produced from the fermented sap of coconut, kitul (palm treacle) or palmyra palms. It is available from very basic toddy 'taverns', usually makeshift shacks that spring up in toddy-producing areas. Alcohol is not sold on *poya* days (see Festivals and events, below). Orders for alcoholic drinks in hotels are usually taken on the previous day. Note that hotels and restaurants will serve foreign tourists expensive, imported spirits and beers unless told otherwise.

Festivals and events

Since the significant days of all four of its religions are respected, Sri Lanka has an remarkable number of festivals, and probably more public holidays (29) than anywhere else in the world – a matter of increasing consternation to the island's business leaders. In mid-April, the **Sinhala** and **Tamil New Year** celebrations are colourful and feature traditional games. In May and June the **Wesak** and **Poson Poya** (full moon) days are marked with religious pageants. **Esala Perahera** (around July-August full moon) is the most striking of all, particularly in Kandy though major festivals are also held in Colombo, Kataragama and other major temples. Drummers, dancers, decorated elephants, torch-bearers and whip-crackers all add colour and drama to the 10 days of celebrations. All full moon (*poya*) days are holidays, as are Saturday and Sunday. There are also several secular holidays. Most religious festivals (Buddhist, Muslim and Hindu) are determined by the lunar calendar and therefore change from year to year. Check at the tourist office (www.srilankatourism.org) for exact dates.

Full moon festivities

Full Moon *poya* days of each month are holidays. Buddhists visit temples with offerings of flowers, to worship and remind themselves of the precepts. Certain temples hold special celebrations in connection with a particular full moon, eg Esala at Kandy. Accommodation may be difficult to find and public transport is crowded during these festivals. No alcohol is sold (you can however order your drinks at your hotel the day before) and all places of entertainment are closed.

Dates for 2011 *poya* days include: 11 October, 10 November and 10 December. Dates for 2012 include: 8 January, 7 February, 7 March, 6 April, 8 May, 4 June. Check http://www.qpp studio.net/publicholidays2012/sri_lanka.htm for the latest dates.

Holidays and festivals

Jan Duruthu Poya Sri Lankan Buddhists believe that the Buddha visited the island. There is a large annual festival at the **Kelaniya Temple** near Colombo.

Tamil Thai Pongal On 14th, observed by Hindus, celebrating the first grains of the rice harvest.

Jan/Feb Navam Poya In late-Jan/early Feb, this is celebrated at Colombo's grandest *perahera* at Gangaramaya Temple, with caparisoned elephants, dancing, drummers and processions.

Feb National (Independence) Day Celebrated on the 4th and involves processions, dances, parades.

Feb/Mar Maha Sivarathri Marks the night when Siva danced his celestial dance of destruction (*Tandava*), celebrated with feasting and fairs at Siva temples, preceded by a night of devotional readings and hymn singing.

Mar/Apr Easter Good Friday with Passion plays in Negombo and other coastal areas, in particular on Duwa Island.

Mar Medin Poya Day.

Apr Bak Poya Day.

Sinhala and Tamil New Year Day The 13-14th is marked with celebrations (originally harvest thanksgiving), by closure of many shops/restaurants. Many Colombo residents decamp to the highlands, see box, page 233.

May Day 1 May.

Wesak Poya Day The day following is the most important *poya* in the calendar, celebrating the key events in the Buddha's life: his birth, Enlightenment and death. Clay oil-lamps are lit across the island and there are also folk theatre performances. Wayside stalls offer food and drink free to passers-by. These are special celebrations at Kandy, Anuradhapura and Kelaniya (Colombo).

National Heroes' Day On the 22nd of the month but not a public holiday.

Jun Poson Poya Day Marks Mahinda's arrival in Sri Lanka as the first Buddhist missionary; Mihintale and Anuradhapura hold special celebrations.

Bank Holiday On the 30th.

Jul/Aug Esala Poya The most important Sri Lankan festival. It takes place in Jul/early Aug with grand processions of elephants, dancers, etc, honouring the Sacred Tooth of the Buddha in Kandy lasting 10 days, and elsewhere including Dewi Nuwara (Dondra) and Bellanwila Raja Maha Vihare, South Colombo.

Culmination of the **Pada Yatra** pilgrimage to Kataragama, where purification rituals including firewalking are held.

Munneswaram (Chilaw) Vel Festival and in Colombo from Sea St Hindu temple, procession to Bambalapitiya and Welawatta.

Nikini Poya Day Celebrations at Bellanwila, Colombo.

Sep Binara Poya Day A Perahera is held in Badulla.

Oct/Nov Wap Poya Day.

Deepavali Festival of Lights, celebrated by Hindus with fireworks, commemorating Rama's return after his 14 years exile in the forest when citizens lit his way with earthen oil lamps.

Nov Il Poya Day.

Dec Unduwap Poya Day Marks the arrival of Emperor Asoka's daughter, Sanghamitta, with a sapling of the Bodhi Tree from India. Special celebrations at Anuradhapura, Bentota and Colombo.

Christmas Day Bank holiday on 25th.

Special Bank Holiday 31st.

Muslim holy days

These are fixed according to the lunar calendar, see page 370. According to the Gregorian calendar, they tend to fall 11 days earlier each year, dependent on the sighting of the new moon.

Ramadan Start of the month of fasting when all Muslims (except young children, the very elderly, the sick, pregnant women and travellers) must abstain from food and drink from sunrise to sunset.

Id ul Fitr The 3-day festival marks the end of Ramadan.

Id-ul-Zuha/Bakr-Id Muslims commemorate Ibrahim's sacrifice of his son according to God's commandment; the main time of pilgrimage to Mecca (the Hajj). It is marked by the sacrifice of a goat, feasting and alms giving.

Muharram When the killing of the Prophet's grandson, Hussain, is commemorated by Shi'a Muslims. Decorated *tazias* (replicas of the martyr's tomb) are carried in procession by devout wailing followers who beat their chests to express their grief. Shi'as fast for the 10 days.

Shopping

Local craft skills are still practised widely across the country. Pottery, coir fibre, carpentry, handloom weaving and metalwork all receive government assistance. Some of the crafts are concentrated in just a few villages.

What to buy

Of Indonesian origin but Sri Lankan design, good-quality **batiks**, from wall hangings to *lungis* (sarongs), are widely available. **Handloom** has seen a major revival in recent years, and there is also a wide range of handwoven cotton and silk textiles in vibrant colours and textures.

The 'city of arts', Kalapura, has over 70 families of craftsmen making superb **brass**, wood, silver and gold items. Some specialize in fine carvings, inlays and damascene. Oil lamps are popular.

Ratnapura is Sri Lanka's **gem** capital, but they are sold throughout the country. Sapphires, rubies, cats eye, amethyst, topaz, moonstone and zircon are a few of the stones mined in the country.

A popular craft in the southwest of the island, especially around Ambalangoda, based on traditional **masks** used in dance dramas. Good-quality masks in a range sizes can also be picked up in the craft outlets in Colombo. See box, page 129.

Another Kandyan specialism is **silverware**, with jewellery, tea sets, trays, candle stands and ornaments available. Inlay work is a further specialization. Fine gold and silver chain work is done in the Pettah area of Colombo.

Mlesna is a government-run chain of **tea** shops, where good-quality tea can be bought. Tea is sometimes presented in attractive wooden or woven packages, and accessories such as teapots can make good gifts. Some tea and spice gardens welcome visitors and have retail outlets for their produce. Matale is noted for its spices.

Introduced by the Portuguese, Galle is famous for its **pillow lace** and crochet. Musical instruments, especially **drums** are a popular gift. Matara is a good place to pick them up. **Coir and palm leaf** are made into mats, rugs, baskets and bags (see box, page 358), while **reed, cane** and **rattan** are fashioned into attractive household goods, including mats, chairs, lampshades, bags and purses. **Lacquerware** is another craft centred on the Kandy region. The quality of **leather** goods especially bags, is often fairly high.

Where to buy

Craft department stores in the larger cities offer a range under one roof – **Lakpahana, Lanka Hands, Craft Link, Viskam Nivasa** are some you will come across. There are government **Laksala** shops in many towns, where prices are fixed. Private upmarket shops and top hotel arcades offer better quality, choice and service but at a price. Vibrant and colourful local bazaars (markets) are often a great experience but you must be prepared to bargain.

Bargaining

In some private shops and markets bargaining is normal and expected. It is best to get an idea of prices being asked by different stalls for items you are interested in before taking the plunge. Some shopkeepers will happily quote twice the actual price to a foreigner showing interest, so you might well start by halving the asking price. On the other hand it would be inappropriate to do the same in an established shop with price-tags, though a plea for the 'best price' or a 'special discount' might reap results even here. Remain good humoured throughout.

Tips and trends

Gem stones, gold jewellery and silver items are best bought in reputable shops. Taxi (and three-wheeler) drivers often receive commission when they take you to shops. If you arrive at a shop with a tout you may well end up paying absurdly high prices to cover the commission he earns. The quality of goods in a shop that needs to encourage touts may be questionable too. Try to select and enter a shop on your own and be aware that a tout may follow you in and pretend to the shopkeeper that he has brought you.

Batik 'factories', mask and handicrafts 'workshops', spice 'gardens', gem 'museums' across the island attract a traveller's attention by suggesting that a visit will be particularly interesting, but the main purpose of most is to get you into their shop where you may feel obliged to buy something in exchange for the free 'demonstration' or visit.

Export of certain items such as antiquities, ivory, furs and skins is controlled or banned, so it is essential to get a certificate of legitimate sale and permission for export.

Responsible tourism

The benefits of international travel are evident for both hosts and travellers – employment, increased understanding of different cultures, business and leisure opportunities. At the same time there is clearly a downside to the industry. Where visitor pressure is high and/or poorly regulated, adverse impacts to society and the natural environment may be apparent. Paradoxically, this is as true in undeveloped and pristine areas – where culture and the natural environment are less 'prepared' for even small numbers of visitors – as in major resort destinations.

How big is your footprint?

The point of a holiday is, of course, to have a good time, but if it's relatively guilt-free as well, that's even better. Perfect eco tourism would ensure a good living for local inhabitants while not detracting from their traditional lifestyles, encroaching on their customs or spoiling their environment. Perfect eco tourism probably doesn't exist, but everyone can play their part. Here are a few points worth bearing in mind:

1 Think about where your money goes. Try and put money into local people's hands; drinking local beer or fruit juice rather than imported brands.
2 Haggle with humour and not aggressively. Remember that you are likely to be much wealthier than the person you're buying from.
3 Think about what happens to your rubbish. Take biodegradable products and a water bottle filter. Be sensitive to limited resources like water, fuel and electricity.
4 Help preserve local wildlife and habitats by respecting rules and regulations, such as sticking to footpaths, not standing on coral and not buying products made from endangered plants or animals.
5 Don't treat people as part of the landscape. Ask if you want a photo.
6 Learn the local language and be mindful of local customs and norms. It can enhance your experience and you'll earn respect of local people.

The travel industry is growing rapidly and increasingly the impacts of this supposedly 'smokeless' industry are becoming apparent. These impacts can seem remote and unrelated to an individual trip or holiday (eg air travel is clearly implicated in global warming and damage to the ozone layer, resort location and construction can destroy natural habitats and restrict traditional rights and activities) but, individual choice and awareness can make a difference in many instances (see below), and collectively, travellers are having a significant effect in shaping a more responsible and sustainable industry.

Of course travel can have beneficial impacts and this is something to which every traveller can contribute. Sri Lanka's national parks for example are part funded by receipts from visitors. Similarly, travellers can promote patronage and protection of important archaeological sites and heritage through their interest and contributions via entrance and performance fees. They can also support small-scale enterprises by staying in locally run hotels and hostels, eating in local restaurants and by purchasing local goods, supplies and arts and crafts.

There has been a phenomenal growth in tourism that promotes and supports the conservation of natural environments and is also fair and equitable to local communities. This eco-tourism segment is probably the fastest growing sector of the travel industry and provides a vast and growing range of destinations and activities.

While the authenticity of some ecotourism operators claims need to be interpreted with care, there is clearly both a huge demand for this type of activity and also significant opportunities to support worthwhile conservation and social development initiatives.

International organizations such as **Tourism Concern** ① *T020-7133 3800, www.tourism concern.org.uk*, and **Conservation International** ① *T1-703-341 2400, www.conservation. org*, develop and/or promote ecotourism projects and destinations and their web sites are an excellent source of information. **Ethical Consumer Research Assocation** ① *www.ethicalconsumer.org*, publish a guide on ethical shopping. It is also worth picking up a copy of Mark Mann's *Good Alternative Tourism Guide* (London: Earthscan, 2002), published in association with Tourism Concern.

In Sri Lanka, the **Sri Lanka Ecotourism Foundation** ⓘ *www.ecotourismsrilanka.net*, is a non-profit making NGO dedicated to building sustainable community-based ecotourism.

Local customs and laws

Greeting

'Ayubowan' (may you have long life) is the traditional welcome greeting among the Sinhalese, said with the hands folded upwards in front of the chest. You should respond with the same gesture. The same gesture accompanies the word 'vanakkam' among Tamils.

Conduct

Cleanliness and modesty are appreciated even in informal situations. Nudity and topless bathing are prohibited and heavy fines can be imposed. Displays of intimacy are not considered suitable in public and will probably draw unwanted attention. Women in rural areas do not normally shake hands with men as this form of contact is not traditionally acceptable between acquaintances. Use your right hand for giving, taking, eating or shaking hands as the left is considered to be unclean.

Visiting religious sites

Visitors to Buddhist and Hindu temples are welcome though the shrines of Hindu temples are sometimes closed to non-Hindus. Visitors should be dressed decently – skirts or long trousers – shorts and swimwear are not suitable. Shoes should be left at the entrance and heads should be uncovered. In some Hindu temples, especially in the north, men will be expected to remove their shirts.

Do not attempt to shake hands with Buddhist *bhikkus* (monks). See also Photography, below. Monks are not permitted to touch money so donations should be put in temple offering boxes. Monks renounce all material possessions and so live on offerings. Visitors may offer flowers at the feet of the Buddha.

Mosques may be closed to non-Muslims shortly before prayers. In mosques women should be covered from head to ankle.

Photography

Do not attempt to be photographed with Buddhist *bhikkus* (monks) or to pose for photos with statues of the Buddha or other deities and paintings. Photography is prohibited in certain sections of the sacred sites as well as in sensitive areas such as airports, dams and military areas.

Begging

The sight of beggars especially near religious sites can be very disturbing. A coin to one child or a destitute woman on the street will make you the focus of demanding attention from a large number before long. Many Sri Lankans give alms to street beggars as a means of gaining spiritual merit or out of a sense of duty but the sum is often very small – Rs 10 or so. Some people find it appropriate to give food to beggars rather than money. Children sometimes offer to do 'jobs' such as call a taxi, show you the way or pose for a photo. You may want to give to a registered charity rather than individual handouts.

Essentials A-Z

Accident and emergency

Emergencies T119/118. **Police** T243 3333;
Tourist Police T243 3342; **Fire and
ambulance** T242 2222; **Hospital**
(Colombo) T269 1111.

Children

Children of all ages are widely welcomed and
greeted with warmth which is often extended
to those accompanying them. Sri Lanka's
beaches and wildlife are especially likely to
appeal, and of course a visit to Pinnawela
Elephant Orphanage. Keep children away from
stray animals which may carry parasites or
rabies, monkeys too can be aggressive.

Care should be taken when travelling
to remote areas where health services are
primitive since children can become ill more
rapidly than adults. Extra care must be taken
to protect children from the strong sun by
using high factor sun cream, hats, umbrellas,
etc, and by avoiding being out in the hottest
part of the day. Cool showers or baths help
if children get too hot. Dehydration may be
counteracted with plenty of drinking water -
bottled, boiled (furiously for 5 mins) or
purified with tablets. Preparations such as
'Dioralyte' may be given if the child suffers
from diarrhoea. Moisturizer, zinc and castor
oil (for sore bottoms due to change of diet)
are worth taking. Mosquito nets or electric
insect repellents at night may be provided
in hotel rooms which are not a/c. To help
young children to take anti-malarial tablets,
one suggestion is to crush them between
spoons and mix with a teaspoon of dessert
chocolate (for cake-making) bought in a
tube. Wet wipes and disposable nappies
are not readily available in many areas.

In the big hotels there is no difficulty
with obtaining safe baby foods. For older
children, tourist restaurants will usually have
a non-spicy alternative to Sri Lankan
curries. Grilled or fried fish or chicken is a
good standby, often served with boiled
vegetables, as are eggs. Fruit is magnificent
but should be peeled first. Toast and jam
are usually served for breakfast, or hoppers
(with bananas). Fizzy drinks are widely
available, although king coconut is a
healthier and cheaper alternative.
Bottled water is available everywhere.

Many hotels and guesthouses have triple
rooms, at little or no extra cost to the price of
a double, or you can ask for an extra bed. The
biggest hotels provide babysitting facilities.

Buses are often overcrowded and are
probably worth avoiding with children.
Train travel is generally better (under 12s
travel half-price, under 3s free) but hiring
a car hire is by far the most comfortable
and flexible option; see page 22.

Customs and duty free

On arrival visitors to Sri Lanka are officially
required to declare all currency, valuable
equipment, jewellery and gems even
though this is rarely checked. All personal
effects should be taken back on departure.
Visitors are not allowed to bring in goods
in commercial quantities, or prohibited/
restricted goods such as dangerous drugs,
weapons, explosive devices or gold. Drug
trafficking or possession carries the death
penalty, although this is very rarely carried
out on foreigners. In addition to completing
Part II of the Immigration Landing Card, a
tourist may be asked by the Customs Officer
to complete a Baggage Declaration Form.

Duty free

You are allowed 1.5 litres of spirits, 2 bottles
of wine, 200 cigarettes, 50 cigars or 250 g
rolling tobacco, a small quantity of perfume
and 250 ml of eau de toilette. You can also

import a small quantity of travel souvenirs not exceeding US$250 in value. For more information visit Sri Lanka Customs, www.customs.gov.lk.

Export restrictions

Up to 10 kg of tea is allowed to be exported duty free. Note that the 'Ceylon Tea' counter at the airport *outer* lobby accepts rupees. The following are not permitted to be exported from Sri Lanka: all currencies in excess of that declared on arrival; any gems, jewellery or valuable items not declared on arrival or not purchased in Sri Lanka out of declared funds; gold (crude, bullion or coins); Sri Lankan currency in excess of Rs 250; firearms, explosives or dangerous weapons; antiques, statues, treasures, old books, etc (antiques are considered to be any article over 50 years old); animals, birds, reptiles or their parts (dead or alive); tea, rubber or coconut plants; dangerous drugs.

Import of all the items listed above and in addition, Indian and Pakistani currency, obscene and seditious literature or pictures is prohibited.

If transiting through another country after leaving Sri Lanka, check beforehand that any duty free alcohol you purchase will be accepted, if you not you may find yourself in India or the Middle East pouring it down a sink in front of customs officials.

Disabled travellers

The country isn't geared up specially for making provisions for the physically handicapped or wheelchair-bound traveller. Access to buildings, toilets, pavements and kerbs and public transport can prove frustrating but it is easy to find people to give a hand with lifting and carrying. Provided there is an able-bodied companion to scout around and arrange help, and so long as you are prepared to spend on at least mid-price hotels or guesthouses, private car hire and taxis, Sri Lanka should prove to be rewarding.

Some travel companies now specialize in exciting holidays, tailor-made for individuals depending on their level of disability. **Global Access – Disabled Travel Network Site**, www.globalaccessnews.com, is dedicated to providing information for 'disabled adventurers' and includes a number of reviews and tips from members of the public. You might want to read *Nothing Ventured* edited by Alison Walsh (Harper Collins), which gives personal accounts of world-wide journeys by disabled travellers, plus advice and listings.

Organizations in Sri Lanka include **Sri Lanka Federation of the Visually Handicapped (SLFVH)**, 74 Church St, Col 2, Colombo, T011-243 7758, www.slfvh.org.

Drugs

Penalties for possession of, use of, or trafficking in illegal drugs in Sri Lanka are strict, and convicted offenders may expect jail sentences and heavy fines.

Embassies and consulates

Foreign diplomatic representations in Sri Lanka are listed on page 88.
Australia, 35 Empire Circuit, Forrest, Canberra, ACT 2603, T6239 7041, www.slh caust.org; Level 11, 48 Hunter St, Sydney NSW 2000, T9223 8729, www.slcgsyd.com.
Austria, Rainergasse 1/2/5, 1040, Vienna, T503 7988, www.srilankaembassy.at.
Belgium, rue Jules Lejeune, 27, 1050 Brussels, T2344 5394, www.srilankaembassy.be.
Canada, Suite 1204, 333 Laurier Av West, Ottawa, Ontario K1P 1Cl, T233 8449, www.srilankahcottawa.org.
France, 16 rue Spontini, 75016 Paris, T5573 3131, www.srilankaembassy.fr.
Germany, Niklasstr 19, 14163 Berlin, T8090 9749, www.srilanka-botschaft.de.

India, 27 Kautilya Marg, Chanakyapuri, New Delhi 110021, T2301 0201, www.slhcindia.org; 196, TTK Rd, Alwarpet, Chennai 600018, T2498 7896, T2498 7894, www.srilankain chennai.org; 34 Homi Modi St, Mumbai 400 001, T204 5861, slcon@mtnl.net.in.
Indonesia, 70 Jalan Diponegoro, No 70, Central Jakarta 10320, T314 1018, lankaemb@vision.net.id
Italy, Via Adige No 2, 00198, Rome, T855 4560, www.srilankaembassyrome.org.
Japan, 2-1-54, Takanawa, Minato-ku, Tokyo 108-0074, T03 3440 6911, www.lankaembassy.jp.
Maldives, 1st and 4th floor, H Haifa Building, Bodufungadu Magu, Male, T322 845, www.slhcmaldives.com.
The Netherlands, Jacob de Graefflaan, 2517 JM, The Hague, T365 5910, www.infolanka.nl.
Pakistan, House No 2C, Street No 55 F-6/4, Islamabad, T282 8723, www.slhcpakistan.org.
Singapore, 13-07/12 Goldhill Plaza, 51 Newton Rd, Singapore 308900, T6254 4595, www.lanka.com.sg.
South Africa, 410 Alexander St, Brooklyn, Pretoria 0181, T460 7679, www.srilanka.co.za.
Sweden, Strandvagen 39, Box 24055, S-104 50, Stockholm, T663 6523, www.slembassy.se.
Thailand, Ocean Tower 11, 13th floor, No 75/6-7 Sukhumvit Soi 19, Bangkok 10110, T261 1934, slemb@ksc.th.com.
UK, 13 Hyde Park Gardens, London W2 2LU, T020-7262 1841, www.slhclondon.org.
USA, 2148 Wyoming Av, NW, Washington DC 20008, T483 4025, www.slembassy usa.org; 3250 Wilshire Blvd, Suite 1405, Los Angeles, CA 90010, T387 0210, www.srilankaconsulatela.com.

Gay and lesbian travellers

Homosexuality between men remains technically illegal in Sri Lanka, even in private, and may lead to a prison sentence of up to 12 years. The situation does seem to be relaxing but it's wise to be discreet to avoid the attentions of over zealous and homophobic police officers.

Campaigning gay group **Companions on a Journey**, 46/50 Robert E Gunawardena Maw, Col 6, T485 1535, has a drop-in centre and arranges events.

The internet is a good source of information: www.utopia-asia.com/tipssri.htm, it lists some gay- and lesbian-friendly accommodation and tour operators.

Another resource is **Equal Ground**, T11-567 9766, www.equal-ground.org, which regularly holds activities for lesbian and bisexual women. Travellers are welcome to call for information about activities in the gay community.

Health

Local populations in Sri Lanka are exposed to a range of health risks not encountered in the Western world. Many of the diseases are major problems for the local poor and destitute and, although the risk to travellers is more remote, they cannot be ignored. Obviously 5-star travel is going to carry less risk than backpacking on a budget.

Healthcare in the region is varied, with the best being facilities being available in Colombo where there are some excellent private clinics/hospitals. As with all medical care, first impressions count. It's worth contacting your embassy or consulate on arrival and asking where the recommended (ie those used by diplomats) clinics are. You can also ask about locally recommended medical do's and don'ts. If you do get ill, and you have the opportunity, you should also ask your medical insurer whether they are satisfied that the medical centre/hospital you have been referred to is of a suitable standard.

Before you go
Ideally, you should see your GP or travel clinic at least 6 weeks before your departure

Cash Sale

Date:

Sold To. _____

QTY	DESCRIPTION	RATE	AMOUNT
1	S. O/M		350.
1	p-CHrg		475-
			~~1125~~ -
			325
			82 -
	S/C		
			907-
		TOTAL	
		DISCOUNT	
		GRAND TOTAL	

NO: 739 907/

Leeches

When trekking in the monsoon be aware of leeches. They usually wait on the ground for a passerby and get into your boots when you are walking. Then, when they are gorged with blood, they drop off.

Don't try pulling one off as the head will be left behind and cause infection. Salt or a lighted cigarette have always been heralded as ways to remove leeches, but if neither are to hand a Dettol solution works wonders and even a hand sanitizer will encourage them to fall off. It helps to spray socks and bootlaces with an insect repellent before starting in the morning and tucking trousers into socks. If planning to do a lot of trekking it may be worth purchasing the leech socks sold in some camping stores.

for general advice on travel risks, malaria and vaccinations. Make sure you have travel insurance, get a dental check (especially if you are going to be away for more than a month), know your blood group and if you suffer a long-term condition such as diabetes or epilepsy make sure someone knows or that you have a Medic Alert bracelet/necklace with this information on it. Remember that it is risky to buy medicinal tablets abroad because the doses may differ there is the risk of being given fake drugs.

A-Z of health risks

If you are unlucky (or careless) enough to receive a venomous **bite or sting** by a snake, spider, scorpion or sea creature, try to identify the creature, without putting yourself in further danger (do not try to catch a live snake). Snake bites in particular are very frightening, but in fact rarely poisonous – even venomous snakes bite without injecting venom. Victims should be taken to a hospital or a doctor without delay. Commercial snake bite and scorpion kits are available, but are usually only useful for the specific types of snake or scorpion. Most serum has to be given intravenously so it is not much good equipping yourself with it unless you are used to making injections into veins. It is best to rely on local practice in these cases, because the particular creatures will be known about locally and appropriate treatment can be given. To prevent bites, do not walk in snake territory in bare feet or sandals -

wear proper shoes or boots and walk heavily to warn the snake you are coming. For scorpions and spiders, keep beds away from the walls and look inside your shoes and under the toilet seat every morning. Certain tropical sea fish when trodden upon inject venom into bathers' feet. This can be very painful. Wear plastic shoes if such creatures are reported. The pain can be relieved by immersing the foot in hot water (as hot as you can bear) for as long as the pain persists. Citric acid juices in fruits such as lemon are reported as being useful.

Chikungunya is a relatively rare mosquito-borne disease that has had outbreaks in Sri Lanka, particularly during the monsoon when flooded areas encourage the carrier mosquitoes to breed. The disease manifests within 12 days of infection and symptoms resemble a severe fever, with headaches, joint pain, arthritis and exhaustion lasting from several days to several weeks; in vulnerable sections of the population it can be fatal. Neither vaccine nor treatment are available, so rest is the best cure.

Unfortunately there is no vaccine against **dengue fever** and the mosquitoes that carry it bite during the day. You will be ill for 2-3 days, then get better for a few days and then feel ill again. It should all be over in 7-10 days. Heed all the anti-mosquito measures that you can.

The standard advice for **diarrhoea** prevention is to be careful with water and ice for drinking. If you have any doubts about where the water came from then boil it or filter and treat it. There are many filter/treatment devices now available on the market. Food can also transmit disease. Be wary of salads (what were they washed in, who handled them), re-heated foods or food that has been left out in the sun having been cooked earlier in the day. There is a simple adage that says wash it, peel it, boil it or forget it. Also be wary of unpasteurized dairy products, these can transmit a range of diseases from brucellosis (fevers and constipation), to listeria (meningitis) and tuberculosis of the gut (constipation, fevers and weight loss).

The key treatment with all diarrhoea is rehydration. Try to keep hydrated by taking the right mixture of salt and water. This is available as Oral Rehydration Salts (ORS) in ready-made sachets or can be made up by adding a teaspoon of sugar and a half teaspoon of salt to a litre of clean water. You can also use flat carbonated drinks. Drink at least 1 large cup of this drink for each loose stool. Alternatively, Immodium (or Pepto-Bismol, used a lot by Americans) is useful if you have a long coach/train journey or on a trek, although is not a cure. Antibiotics like Ciproxin (Ciprofloxacin) – obtained by private prescription in the UK – can be a useful antibiotic for some forms of travellers' diarrhoea. If it persists beyond 2 weeks, with blood or pain, seek medical attention. One good preventative is taking probiotics like Vibact or Bifilac which are available over the counter.

If you go **diving** make sure that you are fit to do so. The **British Sub-Aqua Club (BSAC)**, Telford's Quay, South Pier Rd, Ellesmere Port, Cheshire CH65 4FL, UK, T01513-506200, www.bsac.com, can put you in touch with doctors who do medical examinations. Protect your feet from cuts, beach dog parasites (larva migrans) and sea urchins. The latter are almost impossible to remove but can be dissolved with lime or vinegar. Keep an eye out for secondary infection. Check that the dive company

know what they are doing, have appropriate certification from BSAC or **PADI**, Unit 7, St Philips Central, Albert Rd, St Philips, Bristol, BS2 OTD, T0117-300 7234, www.padi.com, and that the equipment is well maintained.

Hepatitis means inflammation of the liver. The most obvious symptom is a yellowing of your skin or the whites of your eyes. However, prior to this all that you may notice is itching and tiredness. Early on, depending on the type of hepatitis, a vaccine or immunoglobulin may reduce the duration of the illness. There are vaccines for hepatitis A and B; the latter spread through blood and unprotected sexual intercourse, both of these can be avoided. Unfortunately there is no vaccine for hepatitis C or the increasing alphabetical list of other hepatitis viruses.

If infected with **leishmaniasis**, you may notice a raised lump, which leads to a purplish discolouration on white skin and a possible ulcer. The parasite is transmitted by the bite of a sandfly. Sandflies do not fly very far and the greatest risk is at ground levels, so if you can avoid sleeping on the jungle floor do so, under a permethrin-treated net and use insect repellent. Seek advice for any persistent skin lesion or nasal symptom. Several weeks of treatment is required under specialist supervision.

Various forms of **leptospirosis** occur throughout the world, transmitted by a bacterium which is excreted in rodent urine. Fresh water and moist soil harbour the organisms, which enter the body through cuts and scratches. If you suffer from any form of prolonged fever consult a doctor.

A **malaria** risk exists throughout the year in Sri Lanka, predominantly in the area north of Vavuniya and the northeastern coastal districts. There is a low to no risk in the rest of the country. In the UK we still believe that Chloroquine and Paludrine are sufficient for Sri Lanka. Other countries may recommend either Malarone, Mefloquine or Doxycycline.

For **mosquito repellents**, remember that DEET (Di-ethyltoluamide) is the gold standard. Apply the repellent 4-6 hrs but more often if you are sweating heavily. If a non-DEET product is used check who tested it. Validated products (tested at the London School of Hygiene and Tropical Medicine) include Mosiguard, Non-DEET Jungle formula and non-DEET Autan. If you want to use citronella remember that it must be applied very frequently (hourly) to be effective. If you are a target for insect bites or develop lumps quite soon after being bitten, carry an Aspivenin kit.

Prickly heat is a common intensely itchy rash, avoided by frequent washing and by wearing loose clothing. It is cured by allowing skin to dry off through use of powder – and spending a few nights in an a/c hotel.

Rabies is endemic in most districts in Sri Lanka, so avoid dogs that are behaving strangely. If you are bitten by a domestic or wild animal, do not leave things to chance: scrub the wound with soap and water and/or disinfectant, try to at least determine the animal's ownership, where possible, and seek medical assistance at once. The course of treatment depends on whether you have already been satisfactorily vaccinated against rabies. If you have (and this is worthwhile if you are spending lengths of time in developing countries) then some further doses of vaccine are all that is required. If you are not already vaccinated then anti-rabies serum (immunoglobulin) may be required in addition. It is important to finish the course of treatment. Note that Sri Lanka suffers from shortages of immunoglobulin, so if planning to spend time in rural areas it may be worth investing in the pre-travel vaccine.

The range of visible and invisible **sexually transmitted diseases** is mind-boggling. Unprotected sex can spread HIV, hepatitis B and C, gonorrhea (green discharge), chlamydia (nothing to see but may cause painful urination and later female infertility), painful recurrent herpes, syphilis and warts, just to name a few. You can cut down the risk by using condoms, a femidom or avoiding sex altogether.

Make sure you protect yourself from the **sun** with high-factor sun screen and don't forget to wear a hat.

Ticks usually attach themselves to the lower parts of the body often after walking in areas where cattle have grazed. They swell up as they start to suck blood. The important thing is to remove them gently, so that they do not leave their head parts in your skin, because this can cause a nasty allergic reaction later. Do not use petrol, Vaseline, lighted cigarettes, etc, to remove the tick, but, with a pair of tweezers remove the gently by gripping it at the attached (head) end and rock it out in very much the same way that a tooth is extracted.

Certain **tropical flies** which lay their eggs under the skin of sheep and cattle also occasionally do the same thing to humans with the unpleasant result that a maggot grows under the skin and pops up as a boil or pimple. The best way to remove these is to cover the boil with oil, Vaseline or nail varnish to stop the maggot breathing, then to squeeze it out gently the next day.

Vaccinations

If you need vaccinations, see your doctor well in advance of your travel. Most courses must be completed by a minimum of 4 weeks. Travel clinics may provide rapid courses of vaccination, but are likely to be more expensive. The following vaccinations are recommended: typhoid, polio, tetanus, infectious hepatitis and diptheria. For details of malaria prevention, see page 42.

The following vaccinations may also be considered: rabies, possibly BCG (since TB is still common in the region) and in some cases meningitis and diphtheria (if you're staying in the country for a long time). Yellow fever is not required in Sri Lanka but you may be asked to show a certificate if you have travelled from Africa or South America. Japanese encephalitis may be required for rural travel at certain times of the year (mainly rainy seasons). An effective oral cholera vaccine (Dukoral) is now available as 2 doses providing 3 months' protection.

Further information
Websites
Blood Care Foundation (UK), www.bloodcare.org.uk A Kent-based charity "dedicated to the provision of screened blood and resuscitation fluids in countries where these are not readily available". They will dispatch certified non-infected blood of the right type to your hospital/clinic. The blood is flown in from various centres around the world.
British Travel Health Association (UK), www.btha.org This is the official website of an organization of travel health professionals.
Fit for Travel, www.fitfortravel.scot.nhs.uk This site from Scotland provides a quick A-Z of vaccine and travel health advice requirements for each country.
Foreign and Commonwealth Office (FCO) (UK), www.fco.gov.uk This is a key travel advice site, with useful information on the country, people, climate and lists the UK embassies/consulates. The site also promotes the concept of 'know before you go' and encourages travel insurance and appropriate travel health advice. It has links to Department of Health travel advice site, see above.
The Health Protection Agency, www.hpa.org.uk Up-to-date malaria advice guidelines for travel around the world. It gives specific advice about the right drugs for each location. It also has useful information for those who are pregnant, suffering from epilepsy or planning to travel with children.
Medic Alert (UK), www.medicalalert.co.uk This is the website of the foundation that produces bracelets and necklaces for those with existing medical problems. Once you have ordered your bracelet/necklace you write your key medical details on paper inside it, so that if you collapse, a medic can identify you as having epilepsy or a nut allergy, etc.

Travel Screening Services (UK), www.travelscreening.co.uk A private clinic dedicated to integrated travel health. The clinic gives vaccine, travel health advice, email and SMS text vaccine reminders and screens returned travellers for tropical diseases.
World Health Organisation, www.who.int The WHO site has links to the *WHO Blue Book* on travel advice. This lists the diseases in different regions of the world. It describes vaccination schedules and makes clear which countries have yellow fever vaccination certificate requirements and malarial risk.

Books
International Travel and Health World Health Organisation, Geneva ISBN 92 4 158026 7.
Lankester, T, *The Travellers Good Health Guide*, ISBN 0-85969-827-0.
Warrell, D and Anderson, A (eds), *Expedition Medicine* (The Royal Geographic Society), ISBN 1 86197 040 4.
Young Pelton, R, Aral, C and Dulles, W, *The World's Most Dangerous Places*, ISBN 1 566952 140 9.

Insurance

Although Sri Lanka does not suffer from being a crime-ridden society, accidents and delays can still occur. Full travel insurance is advised but at the very least get medical insurance and coverage for personal effects. There are a wide variety of policies to choose from, so it's best to shop around. Your local travel agent can also advise on the best and most reliable deals available. Always read the small print carefully. Check that the policy covers the activities you intend or may end up doing. Also check exactly what your medical cover includes, eg ambulance, helicopter rescue or emergency flights back home. Also check the payment protocol. You may have to pay first before the insurance company reimburses you.
STA Travel, www.statravel.co.uk, offers a range of good-value policies.

Internet

Internet access is now widespread across Sri Lanka but prices can vary considerably. Hotels and guesthouses are beginning to offer Wi-Fi, and in the main tourist areas cafés are also getting in on the act. Most major towns will usually have communication centres where terminals are available. Connections are usually much slower and less reliable and charges rise. Sometimes post offices offer the cheapest internet connection in town, so it is worth dropping in to ask. Skype is increasingly available.

Language

Sinhala and Tamil are the official languages, but English is widely spoken and understood in the main tourist areas though not by many in rural parts. Some German is spoken by a growing number of Sri Lankans in the southwestern beach resorts. See page 394 for Sinhala and Tamil phrases.

Media

Newspapers and magazines
It is well worth reading the newspapers, which give a good insight into Sri Lankan attitudes. The *Daily News* and *The Island* are national daily newspapers published in English; there are several Sunday papers including the *Sunday Observer* and *Sunday Times*. Each has a website with archive section which is worth investigating. In Colombo and some other hotels a wide range of international daily and periodical newspapers and magazines is available. The *Lanka Guardian* is a respected fortnightly offering news and comment. *Lanka Monthly Digest* is aimed primarily at the business world but has some interesting articles.

Travel Lanka is a free monthly tourist guide available at larger tourist offices and in major hotels. It has some useful information and listings for Colombo and the main tourist areas, though much is out of date. If the copy on display in the tourist office is months out of date ask for the more recent edition, it's usually tucked away in a cupboard. For a more contemporary view, pick up a copy of *Leisure Times*. Also monthly, it has the latest restaurant, bar and nightclub openings, and a rundown of the month's events in Colombo. Free copies are available at the airport, big hotels, shopping complexes, and some bars and clubs.

Radio and television

Sri Lanka's national radio and television network, broadcasts in Sinhalese and English. **SLBC** operates between 0540 and 2300 on 95.6 FM in Colombo and 100.2 FM and 89.3 FM in Kandy. **BBC World Service** (1512khz/19m and 9720khz/31m from 2000 to 2130 GMT) has a large audience in both English and regional languages. Liberalization has opened the door to several private channels and an ever-growing number of private radio stations. **Yes FM** (89.5 FM), **TNL** (101.7 FM) and **Sun FM** (99.9 or 95.3 FM) broadcast Western music in English 24 hrs a day.

The 2 state TV channels are **Rupavahini** which broadcasts 24 hrs a day, and **ITN**. Many Sri Lankans now watch satellite TV with a choice of channels, which offer good coverage of world news and also foreign feature films and 'soaps'.

Money → *£1 = Rs 175, US$1= Rs 110, €1 = Rs 154 (Jul 2011)*

The Sri Lankan rupee is made up of 100 cents. Notes in denominations of Rs 1000, 500, 200, 100, 50, 20, 10 and coins in general use are Rs 10, 5, 2 and 1. Visitors bringing in excess of US$10,000 into Sri Lanka should declare the amount on arrival. All Sri Lankan rupees should be re-converted upon leaving

Sri Lanka. It is also illegal to bring Indian or Pakistani rupees into Sri Lanka, although this is rarely, if ever, enforced. See Customs, page 38. It is now possible to bring Sri Lankan rupees into the country but at the time of writing the limit was set at Rs 5000 and it was only available at some foreign exchange desks in the UK and had to be ordered in advance.

It is best to carry TCs and credit cards in a money belt worn under clothing. Only carry enough cash for your daily needs, keeping the rest in your money belt or in a hotel safe. Keep plenty of small change and lower denomination notes as it can be difficult to change large notes, this is especially helpful if taking 3-wheelers or bargaining for goods.

Banks

Banks are generally open Mon-Fri 0900-1500, although some banks in Colombo have extended opening hours. Private banks (eg **Commercial Bank**, **Hatton National Bank**, **Sampath Bank**) are generally more efficient and offer a faster service than government-owned banks like **Bank of Ceylon** and **People's Bank**.

Automated Telling Machines (ATMs) are now common in Sri Lanka, especially in Colombo and larger towns. A small fee (less than the commission charged for changing TCs) will be charged on your bill at home and will vary depending of your bank. The majority of Sri Lankan banks now accept Visa, MasterCard and Cirrus, but check the sign for assurance. Queues at ATMs can be very long on public holidays.

Changing money

There is an ATM and several 24-hr exchange counters at the airport which give good rates of exchange. Larger hotels often have a money exchange counter (sometimes open 24 hrs), but offer substantially lower rates than banks. In the larger cities and resorts you will often find private dealers who will exchange cash notes or travellers' cheques. Rates are comparable to banks and are

entirely above board. There is no black market money-changing in Sri Lanka, although it may be useful to carry some small denomination foreign currency notes (eg £10, US$10) for emergencies.

Keep the **encashment receipts** you are given when exchanging money, as you may need at least 1 to re-exchange any rupees upon leaving Sri Lanka. Unspent rupees may be reconverted at a commercial bank when you leave. Changing money through unauthorized dealers is illegal.

Cost of travelling

The Sri Lankan cost of living remains well below that in the industrialized world, although is rising quite sharply. Food and public transport, especially rail and bus, remain exceptionally cheap, and accommodation, though not as cheap as in India, costs much less than in the West. The expensive hotels and restaurants are also less expensive than their counterparts in Europe, Japan or the US. Budget travellers (sharing a room) could expect to spend about Rs 2000 (about £11, €12 or US$18) each per day to cover cost of accommodation, food and travel. Those planning to stay in fairly comfortable hotels and use taxis or hired cars for travelling to sights should expect to spend at least Rs 8000 (about £45, €50 or US$70) a day. Single rooms are rarely charged less than about 80% of the double room price.

Many travellers are irritated by the Sri Lankan policy of '**dual pricing**' for foreigners – one price for locals, another for tourists. Sites that see a lot of tourists, particularly in Kandy and the Cultural Triangle, carry entrance charges comparable to those in the West, while national park fees have increased exponentially in recent years and carry a catalogue of hidden extra taxes. Hotels have one price for Sri Lankans and expats and another for foreign tourists. In common with many other Asian countries, some shops and 3-wheeler drivers will try to overcharge foreigners – experience is the only way to combat this.

Credit cards

Major credit cards are increasingly accepted in the main centres of Sri Lanka both for shopping and for purchasing Sri Lankan rupees, but do not let the card out of your sight. Ensure that transactions are carried out in front of you and check the amounts before confirming payment. Larger hotels also accept payment by credit card. Cash can also be drawn from ATMs using credit cards but charges will be applied. Notify your bank in advance that you will be using your credit card and/or debit card whilst in Sri Lanka to avoid the card being stopped. It is also recommended that you check your statements on returning home.

Travellers' cheques (TCs)

Travellers' cheques issued by reputable companies (eg **American Express**, **Thomas Cook**) are accepted without difficulty and give a slightly better exchange rate than currency notes in Sri Lanka. They also offer the security of replacement if lost or stolen assuming the case is straightforward. TCs in pounds sterling, US dollars and euro are usually accepted without any problem and the process normally takes less than 15 mins in private banks and moneychangers (longer in government-owned banks). Larger hotels will normally only exchange TCs for resident guests but will offer a substantially lower rate than banks or private dealers. A 1% stamp duty is payable on all TCs transactions plus a small commission which varies from bank to bank.

Take care to keep the proof of purchase slip and a note of TCs numbers separately from the cheques. In the case of loss, you will need to get a police report and inform the travellers' cheques company.

Service charge

A service charge of 10% is applied to some accommodation, and a further 15% government tax, which is added to food and drink as well, can also apply. The upmarket the establishment the more chance these will be added to the total. Enquire beforehand

about additional taxes, otherwise it can give you a nasty shock when you come to pay.

Opening hours

Banks Mon-Fri 0900-1500 (some 1300), some open Sat morning
Government offices Mon-Fri 0930-1700, some open Sat 0930-1300 (often alternate Sat only).
Post offices Mon-Fri 1000-1700, and Sat mornings.
Shops Mon-Fri 1000-1900 and Sat mornings with most closed on Sun. Sun street bazaars in some areas.

Poya days (full moon) are holidays and government offices, etc, will be closed. In tourist areas more is open that elsewhere.

Post

Postcards to most countries beyond the Middle East cost Rs 20. Try to use a franking service in a post office when sending mail, or hand in your mail at a counter. Many towns often have private agencies which offer most postal services.

For valuable items, it is best to use a **courier**, eg **DHL Parcel Service** in Colombo. It takes 2-3 working days to the UK or USA; 3-4 working days to mainland Europe.

Poste restante at the GPO in larger towns will keep your mail (letters and packages) for up to 3 months.

Safety

Restricted and protected areas

Since 2009, many roads have reopened in the north and east, and major towns and tourists areas are once again accessible. Some places, however, remain no-go or have limited access due to high security and/or land mines. Check www.fco.gov.uk for the latest information. Travel off road should not be undertaken.

Other areas with restricted access include certain archaeological sites, national parks and reserves which require permits before visiting. Refer to the relevant sections of the travelling text for details.

Confidence tricksters

Confidence tricksters and touts who aim to part you from your money are found in most major towns and tourist sites. It is best to ignore them and carry on your own business while politely, but firmly, declining their offers of help.

Accommodation touts are common at rail and bus stations often boarding trains some distance before the destination. After engaging you in casual conversation to find out your plan one will often find you a taxi or a 3-wheeler and try to persuade you that the hotel of your choice is closed, full or not good value. They will suggest an alternative where they will, no doubt, earn a commission (which you will end up having to pay). It is better to go to your preferred choice alone. Phone in advance to check if a place is full and make a reservation if necessary. If it is full then the hotelier/ guesthouse owner will usually advise you of a suitable alternative. Occasionally, touts operate in groups to confuse you or one may pose as the owner of the guesthouse you have in mind and tell you that it is sadly full but he able to 'help' you by taking you to a friend's place.

Another trick is to befriend you on a train (especially on the Colombo to Galle or Kandy routes), find out your ultimate destination and 'helpfully' use their mobile to phone for a 3-wheeler in advance, telling you that none will be available at the station. Once at the other end, the 3-wheeler driver may take you on an indirect route and charge up to 10 times the correct fee. In fact, 3-wheeler drivers are nearly always waiting at major stations. It's worth checking the distance to your destination (usually given in the guidebook) and remember that the going rate for 3-wheeler hire is around Rs 25-50 per km.

Another breed of tout is on the increase especially in towns attracting tourists (Kandy, Galle). Someone may approach on the street, saying they recognize you and work at your hotel. Caught off-guard, you feel obliged to accept them as your guide for exploring the sights (and shops), and so are ripe for exploitation. Some may offer to take you to a local watering hole, where at the end of your drinking session the bill will be heavily inflated. Be polite, but firm, when refusing their offer of help.

A gem shop may try to persuade you to buy gems as a sample for a client in your home country – usually your home town (having found out which this is in casual conversation). A typical initial approach is to request that you help with translating something for the trader. The deal is that you buy the gems (maybe to the value of US$500 or US$1000) and then sell them to the client for double the price, and keep the difference. Of course, there is no client at home and you are likely to have been sold poor-quality gems or fakes. Only buy gems for yourself and be sure of what you are buying. This is a common trick in Galle and Ratnapura where various methods are employed. It is worth getting any purchase checked by the State Gem Corporation in Colombo. It is also essential to take care that credit cards are not 'run off' more than once when making a purchase.

Travel arrangements, especially for sightseeing, should only be made through reputable companies; bogus agents operate in popular seaside resorts.

Personal security

In general the threats to personal security for travellers in Sri Lanka are small. In most areas it is possible to travel without any risk of personal violence, though violent attacks, still very low by Western standards, are on the increase. Care should be taken in certain lesser visited areas of popular beach resorts such as Hikkaduwa, Negombo and Mirissa, and don't walk along the beach at night after the restaurants and bars have closed.

Basic common sense needs to be used with respect to looking after valuables. Theft is not uncommon especially when travelling by train or crowded bus. It is essential to take good care of personal possessions both when you are carrying them, and when you have to leave them anywhere. You cannot regard hotel rooms as automatically safe. It is wise to use hotel safes for valuable items, though even they cannot guarantee security. It is best to keep TCs and passports with you at all times. Money belts worn under clothing are one of the safest options, although you should keep some cash easily accessible in a purse.

Police

Even after taking all reasonable precautions people do have valuables stolen. This can cause great inconvenience. You can minimize this by keeping a record of vital documents, including your passport number and TCs in a separate place from the documents themselves, with relatives or friends at home, or even email them to yourself before setting off. If you have items stolen, they should be reported to the police as soon as possible. Larger hotels will be able to help in contacting and dealing with the police.

Many tourist resorts now have an English-speaking tourist police branch. The paper work involved in reporting losses can be time consuming and irritating, and your own documentation (eg passport and visas) will normally be demanded. Tourists should not assume that if procedures move slowly they are automatically being expected to offer a bribe. If you face really serious problems, for example in connection with a driving accident, you should contact your consular office as quickly as possible.

Student travellers

Full-time students qualify for an **ISIC** (International Student Identity Card) which is issued by student travel and specialist agencies at home (eg **STA Travel**). A card allows some few travel benefits (eg reduced prices) and acts as proof of student status. Only a few sites in Sri Lanka will offer concessions, however.

Telephone

Dialling Sri Lanka from abroad: T+94. National operator: T1200. International operator: T101 to change to T1201. Directory enquiries: T1234 International directory enquiries T1236.

Calls within Sri Lanka STD codes are listed for each town in the text. Dial the local number within the town but use the STD area code first (eg Kandy 081) when dialling from outside the town. Mobile prefixes are 071, 072, 077 and 078.

IDD (International Direct Dialling) is now straightforward in Sri Lanka with many private call offices throughout the country. Calls made from hotels usually cost a lot more (sometimes three times as much). They can be made cheaply from post offices though you may need to book. There are also IDD card-operated pay phones, phone cards can be bought from post offices, kiosks near the pay phones and some shops. Pay phones can of course be used for local calls as well.

The cheapest way to phone abroad is to use **Skype**, and this is becoming increasingly available in Sri Lanka at internet cafés and some guesthouses.

Mobile phones

Mobile phones or 'hand phones' are very popular in Sri Lanka and networks extend across much of the island. Most foreign networks are able to roam within Sri Lanka; enquire at home before leaving. If staying in Sri Lanka for several weeks, consider getting a pay-and-go SIM card. You will need to provide a copy of your passport for their records, but topping up is straightforward once everything is set up. When topping up in shops the process is completed by the shopkeeper and you are not handed a voucher, wait until the confirmation text comes through before leaving the premises. The main mobile phone providers are **Etisalat**, **Mobitel** and **Dialog**. Dialog currently has the best island coverage.

Time

GMT + 5½ hrs. Perception of time is sometimes rather vague in Sri Lanka (as in the rest of South Asia). Unpunctuality is common so you will need to be patient.

Tipping

A 10% service charge is added to room rates and meals in virtually all but the cheapest hotels and restaurants. Therefore it is not necessary to give a further tip in most instances. In many smaller guesthouses staff are not always paid a realistic wage and have to rely on a share of the service charge for their basic income.

Tour companies sometimes make recommendations for 'suitable tips' for coach drivers and guides. Some of the figures may seem modest by European standards but are very inflated if compared with normal earnings. A tip of Rs 100 per day from each member of the group can safely be regarded as generous.

Taxi drivers do not expect to be tipped but a small extra amount over the fare is welcomed.

Tour operators

If you don't wish to travel independently, you may choose to try an inclusive package holiday or let a specialist operator quote for a tailor-made tour. The lowest prices quoted by package tour companies in 2011 vary from about £900 for a fortnight (flights, hotel and breakfast) in the low season, to £1500+ during the peak season at Christmas and the New Year. For the cheaper hotels, you pay very little extra for an additional week. Package operators include: **Monarch**, T0871-940 5040, www.monarch.co.uk, **Thomas Cook**, T0870-010 9386, www.thomascook.com, and **Virgin**, T0844-557 3865, www.virgin holidays.co.uk. All allow you to book a return flight with the 1st night's accommodation, leaving you free to arrange the rest yourself.

UK and Ireland
Abercrombie & Kent, T0845-618 2204, www.abercrombiekent.co.uk.
Adventures Abroad, T1800-665 3998, www.adventures-abroad.com. Outward bound adventures.
Andrew Brock (Coromandel), T01572-821 330, abrock3650@aol.com. Special interest including crafts, textiles, botany, etc.
Audley Travel, T01993-838 335, www.audleytravel.com. Fairs, festivals, culture, religion.
Barefoot Traveller, T020-8741 4319, www.barefoot-traveller.com. Diving specialist (with Maldives).
Cox & Kings, T020-7873 5000, www.coxandkings.co.uk. Ancient sites and tourist high spots.
Exodus Travels, T020-8772 3936, www.exodus.co.uk. Includes cycling holidays.
Experience Sri Lanka, T020-7924 7133, www.experiencesrilanka.com. Can arrange homestays and takes in lesser-publicized sights such as Mannar.
Explore, T0845-013 1537, www.explore.co.uk.

Indus Tours, T020-8901 7320, www.industours.co.uk.

Kuoni, T0130-674 7002, www.kuoni.co.uk. Upmarket package tours and tailor-made trips.

Pettits, T01892-515 966, www.pettits.co.uk. Upmarket, individual service.

Red Dot Tours, Orchard House, Folly Lane, Bramham, Leeds LS23 6RZ, T0870-231 7892, www.reddottours.com. Tailor-made tours but also an excellent accommodation booking service (good range of villas and bungalows). Professional service, knowledgeable advice.

Sri Lanka Holidays, 4 Kingly St, London, T020-7439 0944, www.srilanka-holidays.co.uk. Country specialists.

Sri Lanka Insider Tours, T01233-811771, www.insider-tours.com. Cooperative tour organization using local transport, homestays or locally owned hotels.

Steppes Travel, 51 Castle St, Cirencester, Gloucestershire, T01285-880980, www.steppestravel.co.uk. Specializes in tailor-made tours.

Trans Indus, T020-85663739, www.transindus.co.uk. Tailor-made tours in Southeast Asia, Japan, China, India and Sri Lanka.

North America

Absolute Asia, 15 Watts St, 5th floor, New York, NY 10013, T800-736 8187, www.absoluteasia.com. Upmarket, offering including Ayurveda and adventure travel.

Adventures Abroad, T1-800-665-3998, www.adventures-abroad.com. Range of tours, small groups guaranteed.

Australia and New Zealand

Exotic Lanka Holidays, T1300 374734, www.exoticlankaholidays.com.au. Specializes in Sri Lanka, tours include birding and cricket.

Passport Travel, T+61 3 9500 0444, www.travelcentre.com.au. For cycling holidays.

Visiting archaeological sites

If you intend to visit most of the major archaeological sites of the Ancient Cities, it is worth buying a **Cultural Triangle Round Ticket**. This covers a single entry, valid for 21 days from the date of first use to Sigiriya, Polonnaruwa, Dambulla, most of Anuradhapura, Ritigala, Nalanda, Medirigiriya, the National Museum at Kandy, Katharagama Museum and the Maritime Archaeology Museum in Galle, and includes the cost of a camera, though not normally a video camera. The tickets are available from Anuradhapura, Polonnaruwa and Sigiriya or less conveniently from Colombo, Central Cultural Fund, 212/1 Bauddhaloka Mawatha, Col 7, T250 0732, www.ccf.lk. The ticket price is US$50 (or equivalent in Rupees), US$25 for five to 12 year olds; there is not normally a student reduction.

However, not all parts of these sites are included: there is a separate fee to visit Kandy's Dalada Maligawa (Temple of the Tooth), Aukana, and Issurumuniya Museum (and occasionally Sri Maha Bodhi) at Anuradhapura.

Alternatively, individual tickets to Sigiriya, Anuradhapura and Polonnaruwa cost US$25, children under 12 US$12.50. Other sights are cheaper. Entry fees are much lower for Sri Lankans.

The sites are usually open 0600-1800; the ticket office often only opens at 0700. If you are keen to miss the crowds and visit a site early in the day, buying the triangle permit in advance enables you to avoid having to wait for the ticket office to open. If you visit a site during the heat of the day, it is best to take thick socks for protection against the hot stone.

Sri Lanka

See also Colombo, page 84.
Boutique Sri Lanka, T11-269 9213, www.boutiquesrilanka.com. Also offers yoga and Ayurvedic holidays.
Lion Royal Tourisme, 45 Braybrook St, Col 2, Colombo, T11-471 5996, www.lion royaltourisme.com. Tailor-made tours with an excellent network of hotels. Also extends services to the Maldives.

Tourist information

The **Sri Lanka Tourist Board**, 3rd floor, Devonshire Sq, London EC2M 4WD, T0845-8806 3333, www.srilanka.travel, has some information for planning your trip. The website has details of sights, accommodation and transport. There are Sri Lanka Tourist Board offices in Colombo and a few major tourist centres, such as Kandy. They are listed in the relevant sections throughout the book.

Useful websites

www.divesrilanka.com Information on dive sites, and when and where to dive.
www.infolanka.com Has an extensive list of travel links, some useful articles, recipes and downloadable Sri Lankan music files.
www.lakdasun.org A site for Sri Lankans rather than foreign tourists, but useful tips about accommodation and transport can be found on the forum
www.srilanka.travel The official website of the Sri Lanka Tourist Board, with useful general tourist information.
www.tamilnet.com Has a fairly balanced Tamil perspective.

Blogs

There are a number of blogs written by people living in Sri Lanka and travellers passing through.

www.lankareviewed.blogspot.com
Hotel reviews, places to eat and sites.
www.riceandcurry.wordpress.com
A food site with Sri Lankan recipes and
some restaurant reviews.

Visas and permits

There are plans to introduce an online visa
service, whereby visitors would have to
obtain visas before setting off, but at the time
of writing this had not come into effect.

At present nationals of the following
countries are issued with a free 30-day visa
upon arrival: Albania, Armenia, Australia,
Austria, Bahrain, Bangladesh, Belarus,
Belgium, Bhutan, Bosnia-Herzegovina,
Bulgaria, Canada, China, Croatia, Cyprus,
Czech Republic, Denmark, Estonia, Finland,
France, Germany, Greece, Hong Kong,
Hungary, India, Indonesia, Iran, Ireland,
Israel, Italy, Japan, Kuwait, Latvia, Lithuania,
Luxembourg, Malaysia, Maldives, Nepal,
Netherlands, New Zealand, Norway, Oman,
Pakistan, Philippines, Poland, Portugal,
Romania, Russia (plus most former
republics), Saudi Arabia, Serbia, Singapore,
Slovakia, Slovenia, South Africa, South Korea,
Spain, Sweden, Switzerland, Thailand,
Turkey, UAE, UK, USA. Nationals of all other
countries need a visa prior to arrival. All
tourists should have a valid passport (valid
for 6 months upon entry) and also have a
valid visa for the country that is their next
destination (if a visa is necessary); check
with your nearest Sri Lankan representative
before travelling. It may sometimes be
necessary to show proof of sufficient funds
(US$30 per day) and a return or onward
ticket, although this is rarely checked on
arrival. Transit passengers are issued with
a **Transit Visa**.

A 60-day **extension** is available to
nationals of all countries upon paying a fee,
which varies according to the charge to Sri
Lankans of entering your country. This can
be arranged before leaving for Sri Lanka,

or apply in person during office hours,
to the **Department of Immigration
and Emigration**, 41 Ananda Rajakaruna
Mawatha, Col 10, Colombo, T94-11-532
9000, www.immigration.gov.lk. Bring
passport, flight information and passport
photo. It is not necessary to wait until
shortly before the expiry of your original
visa. Extensions will be granted at any
time within the original 30-day period.
In 2011, the following fees applied:
Australia Rs 3300 (US$30); Canada Rs 5500
(US$50); France Rs 2860 (US$26); Germany
Rs 2948 (US$26.80); India Rs 330 (US$3);
Ireland Rs 1760 (US$16); Netherlands
Rs 5390 (US$49); New Zealand Rs 3795
(US$34.50); UK Rs 5940 (US$53), USA
Rs 11,000 (US$100).

Voltage

230-240 volts, 50 cycles AC. There may be
pronounced variations in the voltage, and
power cuts are common. 3-pin (round)
sockets are the norm. Universal adaptors
are widely available.

Women travellers

Compared with many other countries it is
relatively easy and safe for women to travel
around Sri Lanka, even on their own,
although they may experience a lot of
unwanted attention and have unsavoury
remarks directed at them. Travelling with
a male companion does not guarantee a
quiet life, although those travelling solo may
want to invent an imaginary husband and
consider wearing a fake wedding ring.

Modest dress for women is always
advisable: loose-fitting, non-see through
clothes. Cover the shoulders, and wear
skirts, dresses or shorts that are at least
knee-length. Don't walk through towns in
bikinis and take the time to cover up. Make
a note of how the local women are dressing

and act accordingly, you'll soon notice a difference between say Colombo and Trincomalee town.

It is always best to be accompanied when travelling by 3-wheeler or taxi at night. Do not get into a taxi or 3-wheeler if there are men accompanying the driver. Travelling on buses can be uncomfortable because of the number of people packed into a small space, and wandering hands occur. If someone is pressing themselves against you a little too enthusiastically, jam your bag in between. If travelling alone, try and sit next to another woman, on the East coast this is expected of you and they will pat the seat to invite you to join them. Do the same on trains, or sit with a family.

Remember that what may be considered to be normal, innocent friendliness in a Western context may be misinterpreted by some Sri Lankan men. It's not recommended for women to frequent the local bars, instead drink in hotel bars or restaurants.

Avoid visiting remote areas of archaeological sites such as Polonnaruwa late in the day (ie after the tour groups have left) and care should be taken in certain lesser visited areas of popular beach resorts such as Hikkaduwa, Negombo and Mirissa.

As at home, do not walk around alone at night, or on deserted stretches of beach, and use your common sense. Sri Lanka is on the whole is a safe destination, and solo women travellers will have the added bonus of meeting and speaking to Sri Lankan women.

Working in Sri Lanka

All foreigners intending to work need **work permits**. No one is allowed to stay longer than 6 months in a calendar year, or to change their visa status. The employing organization should make formal arrangements. Apply to the Sri Lankan representative in your country of origin.

UK and Ireland
The **World Service Enquiry directory**, www.wse.org.uk, lists voluntary placements overseas.
International Voluntary Service, Thorn House, 5 Rose St, Edinburgh EH2 2PR, www.ivsgb.org.
i-to-i International projects, Woodside House, 261 Low Lane, Leeds LS18 5NY, T0113-205 4620, www.i-to-i.com. Arranges for students and young people to spend part of a gap year teaching English, looking after the disabled or helping with conservation work.
Link Overseas Exchange, The Hayloft, Wards of Keithock, Near Brechin, Angus DD9 7PZ, T01356-629134, www.linkoverseas.org.uk.
Project Trust, The Hebridean Centre, Isle of Coll, Argyll PA78 6TE, T01879-230444, www.projecttrust.org.uk.
Teaching and Projects Abroad, Aldsworth Parade, Goring, Sussex BN12 4TX, T01903-708300, www.projects-abroad.co.uk.
VSO, Carlton House, 27A Carlton Dr, Putney, London SW15 2BS, www.vso.org.uk.

USA and Canada
Council for International Programs, 3500 Lorain Av, Suite 504, Cleveland, OH 44113, T216-566 1088, www.cipusa.org.
i-to-i, T800 985 4864 (see above). English-teaching placements.
Projects Abroad, 347 West 36th St, Suite 903, New York NY 10018, T1-888-839 3535, www.projects-abroad.org. Also has an office in Canada.
United Nations Volunteers, www.unv.org. Usually mature, experienced people with specific qualifications.
World University Service of Canada, T1-800-267 8699, www.wusc.ca. Runs a development project on a tea plantation.

Australia
Australian Volunteers International, 71 Argyle St, Fitzroy Victoria 3065, T3-9279 1788, www.australianvolunteers.com.

Contents

Footprint features

Colombo

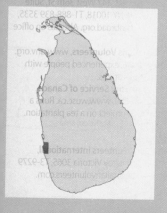

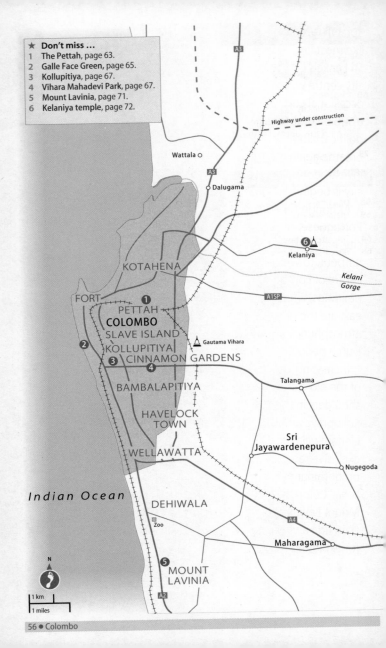

★ Don't miss ...
1 The Pettah, page 63.
2 Galle Face Green, page 65.
3 Kollupitiya, page 67.
4 Vihara Mahadevi Park, page 67.
5 Mount Lavinia, page 71.
6 Kelaniya temple, page 72.

Highway under construction

Wattala ○

A3

○ Dalugama

6 ⛩
Kelaniya

Kelani
Gorge

KOTAHENA

FORT
1 PETTAH
COLOMBO
SLAVE ISLAND
2
KOLLUPITIYA
3 CINNAMON GARDENS
4
⛩ Gautama Vihara

A1SP

BAMBALAPITIYA

HAVELOCK
TOWN

WELLAWATTA

Talangama ○

Sri
Jayawardenepura

○ Nugegoda

Indian Ocean

DEHIWALA

□ Zoo

A4

Maharagama ○

N

5 MOUNT
LAVINIA

A2

1 km
1 miles

Sprawling, choked with traffic and invariably chaotic, Colombo, like most large Asian cities, may not be to everyone's taste. As Sri Lanka's commercial capital and its only conurbation, the city centre was an obvious target for Tamil separatists and saw occasional curfews and a high military presence during recent troubled times. Today, however, buoyed by the most positive political climate, the barriers are down and Colombo is able to breathe again. With both eyes firmly fixed on the future, investment is flowing in and this characterful and diverse city is beginning to buzz with a new found energy.

Although Colombo's origins pre-date the arrival of the Portuguese, culturally and architecturally it appears a modern city, with few established tourist sights. Close to the enormous harbour, to which Colombo owes its pre-eminence, the banking centre of Fort houses some impressive red brick and whitewashed buildings, which give an impression of its colonial origins. To the east are the narrow lanes of the bustling Pettah district with its atmospheric and colourful bazaars and some reminders of the Dutch period.

Increasingly the heart of modern Colombo lies to the south of the old centre, where the city's wealthy young elite rub shoulders in the fashionable boutiques and restaurants of Kollupitiya and Bambalapitiya, while the broad avenues and elegant villas of Cinnamon Gardens nearby reveal the city's most exclusive residential district. Inland from here, or south to the predominantly Tamil suburb of Wellawatta, brings you to a more 'local' Colombo. Alternatively, the pleasant colonial resort of Mount Lavinia with its narrow strip of beach is only a 30-minute train ride away from the centre, and a laid-back alternative base for exploring the city.

Getting there

Air Almost all international visitors to Colombo arrive by air at **Bandaranaike International Airport** at Katunayake, about 30 km north of the city and 6 km from Negombo, www.airport.lk. Available at the airport are regular buses to Colombo's Bastian Mawatha Stand in the Pettah; catch the free shuttle from outside Arrivals to where the buses leave from. There are also pre-paid taxis (Rs 1900 depending on which part of town you're heading to) and more expensive air-conditioned taxis (from Rs 2100), which can be arranged from the taxi service counter. A breakdown of fares is available at www.airport.lk/getting-around/taxi-rates.php and includes prices to reach other destinations such as Kandy and Hikkaduwa. Taxis are also available from the travel agent counters.

Trains leave from **Katunayake train station**, which is about 1 km from the airport. From here suburban commuter trains run north to Negombo (15 minutes) and south to Colombo (1¼ hours). Trains run infrequently but there are plans for 15-minute shuttles.

It is also possible to rent a car at the airport, though rates tend to be steep and it usually pays to shop around in Colombo. Moreover, if you wish to self-drive a Sri Lankan Recognition Permit is needed to accompany International Driving Permits, so it may not be possible to drive immediately. These are available from the AA or the Department of Motor Traffic in Colombo (see page 23). Domestic air passengers arrive at Ratmalana Airport to the south of the city. ►► *See Transport, page 85.*

Bus Government and private buses run to Colombo from virtually every significant town in Sri Lanka. There are three bus stands, all close to each other, 1 km east of Fort station in the Pettah. There are regular bus services along Galle Road to Colombo's southern suburbs, where many visitors choose to stay.

Train Nearly all of Sri Lanka's railway lines originate in Fort Railway Station at the south-western corner of the Pettah (Colombo 11), which is within walking distance of the major hotels in Fort. There are regular services from Kandy, main tourist areas in the highlands, Anuradhapura, west and south coast beach resorts and Trincomalee on the east coast.

Getting around

Although the city is quite spread out, it is fairly simple to get your bearings. If you venture beyond Fort you will need transport to explore. Short hops by three-wheeler should cost no more than Rs 150 – you will need to bargain. Radio cabs are a reliable alternative and quite affordable if you can share one. Some streets in Fort, around the president's house and major banks, are blocked or have strict security checks so it is often impossible for transport to take the most obvious route. The **Colombo City Tour** ⓘ *www.colombocitytour.com, US$30, children US$22 for 7 hrs,* is easily recognisable by its red double decker buses, but currently this isn't a hop-on hop-off service so isn't ideal unless you want to tour the sights for between 2½ and seven hours, and it only runs at weekends.

Orientation

If you are going to spend any time here, it pays to become familiar with the city's postcodes, by which areas are often referred (see box, opposite). The main coastal road,

I'm in heaven ... Colombo Seven

Even more than London, Colombo's citizens define their city by its postcodes. Aside from recognizing the snob value of having an office in Colombo 1 or a residence in Colombo 7 (and being suitably impressed), having a grasp of the most important postcodes will help you find your way around the city.

Colombo 1	Fort
Colombo 2	Slave Island
Colombo 3	Kollupitiya
Colombo 4	Bambalapitiya
Colombo 5	Havelock Town
Colombo 6	Wellawatta
Colombo 7	Cinnamon Gardens
Colombo 8	Borella
Colombo 9	Dermatagoda
Colombo 10	Maradana
Colombo 11	Pettah
Colombo 12	Hultsdorf
Colombo 13	Kotahena
Colombo 14	Grandpass
Colombo 15	Mutwal

Galle Road, which leads to Galle and beyond, is the spine of the city, and many of the areas of interest lie on it or within a few kilometres inland. Officially the city's centre, and the area from which all suburbs radiate, is **Fort**, containing the harbour, the president's house and banks, and to the south some of the most exclusive hotels. East is the busy bazaar of the **Pettah**, which contains the main train and bus stations, and which turns into **Kotahena**. South of Fort is **Galle Face Green**, a popular place for a stroll, which soon becomes **Kollupitiya**, a wealthy shopping area with many excellent restaurants. Inland, and separated from Fort and the Pettah by Beira Lake, is **Slave Island** and the busy thoroughfare of Union Place. South of here (and inland from Kollupitiya) is leafy **Cinnamon Gardens**, the most exclusive area of Colombo, with the city's biggest park, main museums and some attractive guesthouses, so many visitors choose to stay here. To the east is **Borella**. Back on the coast, Galle Road continues south to **Bambalapitiya**, another shopping area but progressively less exclusive, which is parallel to **Havelock Town**. Further south is **Wellawatta**, a large Tamil area, then **Dehiwala** (not strictly speaking part of Colombo), which houses Colombo's zoo. Then you reach **Mount Lavinia**, a traditional bolt-hole from the city for both locals and tourists, see page 71. Yet none of these areas constitute Sri Lanka's administrative capital, which was moved to **Sri Jayawardenepura Kotte**, 11 km southeast of Fort, in 1982.

Tourist information

Sri Lanka Tourist Board ① *80 Galle Rd, Col 3, T243 7059, www.srilankatourism.org, Mon-Fri 0830-1615, Sat 0830-1230,* has free literature in English (and some in German, French, Italian, Swedish and Japanese) and will arrange guides, though not much information on transport (Cultural Triangle tickets are not sold here; best bought at sites). There is also an information counter at Bandaranaike Airport, T245 2411. **Railway Tourist Office** ① *Fort Station, Col 11, T244 0048,* offers friendly advice to anyone planning a rail journey. They will suggest an itinerary, book train tickets and hotels, and arrange a car with driver. Some may find their sales techniques a little pushy. Special steam train excursions are offered on the *Viceroy Special* (usually groups of 30 are required for a two-day one-night trip to Kandy).

Travel Lanka is a free monthly tourist guide available at larger tourist offices and in major hotels. It has some useful information and listings for Colombo and the main tourist areas, though much is out of date. If the copy on display in the tourist office is months out of date ask for the more recent edition, it's usually tucked away in a cupboard. For a more contemporary view, pick up a copy of *Leisure Times*. Also monthly, it has the latest restaurant, bar and nightclub openings, and a rundown of the month's events in Colombo. Free copies are available at the airport, big hotels, shopping complexes, and some bars and clubs.

Background

Sheltered from the southwest monsoon by a barely perceptible promontory jutting out into the sea, Colombo's bay was an important site for Muslim traders long before the colonial period. Its name derives from 'Kotomtota', or port to the kingdom of Kotte founded in 1369, close to present-day Sri Jayawardenepura Kotte, see page 72.

However, Colombo is essentially a colonial city. Soon after arrival in Sri Lanka, the Portuguese set up a fortified trading post in modern-day Fort, captured in 1656 by the Dutch. The canals constructed to link up the coastal lagoons are a lasting legacy, as well as the churches and mansions of the Pettah, Kotahena and Hultsdorf. Colombo's rise to pre-eminence however did not start until the 19th century and the establishment of British power. When the British took control of Kandy and encouraged the development of commercial estates, the island's economic centre of gravity moved north, thereby lessening the importance of Galle as the major port. The town became the banking and commercial hub and benefited from its focal position on the rapidly expanding transport system within the island. From 1832 the British encouraged the rapid development of a road network which radiated from Colombo. In the late 19th century this was augmented by an expanding rail network. Since independence Colombo has retained its dominant position.

Sights

Colombo is a modern city with plenty of buzz but few 'must-see' sights. Its historical centre is the colonial Fort, which combined with a visit to the hectic bazaar and Dutch period legacy of the Pettah area to its east, can make for an interesting walking tour. Most of the rest of the city's sights are spread out in the southern suburbs, where the attractive wide boulevards of Cinnamon Gardens, the city's most exclusive district, are a highlight. Here you can visit the city's principal park and museums, and perhaps even more enticingly, sample some of the fare that is fast making Colombo one of the culinary capitals of Asia. ▸▸ *For listings, see pages 73-90.*

The city

Fort area
Lying immediately south of the harbour, the compact fort area, historically Colombo's commercial centre, is a curious blend of old and new, modern tower blocks rubbing shoulders with reminders of its colonial past. It can be an eerily quiet place outside office hours. Because it houses the president's residence and the principal banking area, it was a separatist target during the war and remains the only road-blocked area of the city with continued high security. The harbour and much of the northwest section remain off-limits. Though it houses many fine British colonial buildings (many of which are

Colombo

To Kelaniya Raja Maha Vihara (A1)
To Negombo (A3)

Santa Lucia Cathedral
Stadium

KOTAHENA

St Anthony's
Wolfendahl
M Zain Mawatha
New Moor St
Dam St

Abdul Cader Rd
Sirimavo Bandaranaike Mawatha
Dr Danister Silva Maw

Harbour

Jayatilleke Maw
FORT
PETTAH
Fort
Olcott Maw
Secretariat Halt
Wijewardana Maw

SLAVE
ISLAND
Beira Lake

Kompanna Vidiya

Union Place

Kollupitiya

Duplication Rd
B Jetti Maw
Dharmapala Maw

Galle Rd
R A De Mel Maw
A Coomaraswamy Maw

Indian Ocean

KOLLUPITIYA
Independence Av

CINNAMON GARDENS

C Mundasa Maw
Bauddhaloka Maw

Kollupitiya

Bambalapitiya
BAMBALAPITIYA

Vajira Rd
Havelock Rd
Fife Rd

Dickman's Rd
Dharmarama Maw

Galle Rd
HAVELOCK TOWN
Lumbini Theatre

Wellawatta
Methodist
W A Silva Maw

Survey Dept
ITI Net

WELLAWATTA

Roxy Cinema
Buddha Statue

St Mary's

Maradana Rd
Panchikawatta Rd

Maradana

MARADANA

TB Jayah Rd
Deans Rd
Kularatnam
Rajkaruna M

Baseline

Ward Place
Rosemead Pl
Barnes Place
Horton Place
Gregory's Rd

Rajkaruna M
Kynsey Rd

BORELLA
Gautama Vihara
Cotta Rd

Otter's Club

Ridgeway Golf Links

D de S Senanayaka Maw

To Sri Jayawardenapura Kotte

Jawatte Rd

Asiri
Kirula Rd
Narahenpita

Elvitigala Maw

Kirillapona

KIRILLAPONA

Avissawella Rd

PAMANKADA

Dutugemunu St

(High Level Rd)

Kotagama Sri Vachisara Maw

DEHIWALA

Zoo

To ① & Mount Lavinia

Colombo maps

1 Colombo, page 61
2 Fort & Pettah, page 62
3 Galle Face & Union Place, page 65
4 Kollupitiya & Cinnamon Gardens, page 66
5 Bambalapitiya & Havelock Town, page 70

N

800 metres
800 yards

Sleeping
Chamenka Guest House 1
Mrs Jayawardhana's 3
Omega Inn 2
Cinnamon Lakeside 7

Eating
Shanmugas 1

boarded up), little remains from either the Portuguese or Dutch periods, and the last traces of the fort itself were destroyed in the 19th century. Many offices have moved out of Fort, leaving it a rather empty shell, though it is still interesting to explore the accessible areas by foot.

The **Grand Oriental Hotel** is a good place to start a tour. Formerly the first port of call for all travellers arriving by steamship, it was once the finest hotel in Colombo. It used to be said that if you waited long enough in its hall, you would meet everyone worth meeting in the world. It is rather faded now, but you can get fascinating views of the harbour area from the hotel's third-floor restaurant. From here, **York Street**, Fort's main shopping area, runs due south, passing the brick-built colonial-era department stores of **Cargill's** and **Miller's**, and the government emporium **Laksala**.

To the east on Bristol Street is the central YMCA, next to the Moors Islamic Cultural Home. Across Duke Street is the Young Men's Buddhist Association. The shrine houses a noted modern image of the Buddha.

2 Fort & Pettah

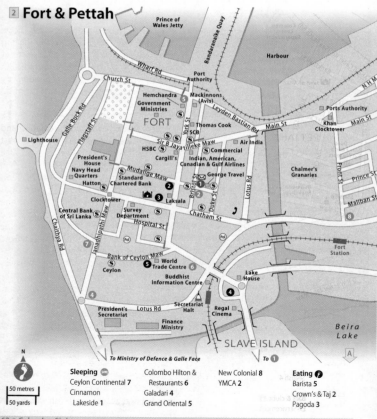

Sleeping 🛏	Colombo Hilton &	New Colonial 8	Eating 🍴
Ceylon Continental 7	Restaurants 6	YMCA 2	Barista 5
Cinnamon	Galadari 4		Crown's & Taj 2
Lakeside 1	Grand Oriental 5		Pagoda 3

Sir Baron Jayatilleke Mawatha, once the main banking street, stretches west of York Street. Nearly all the buildings are in red brick. At the western end of Chatham Street to the south, past the Dutch period Fort Mosque, is the **Lighthouse Clocktower**, now replaced as a lighthouse by the new tower on Chaithya Road. A modern clocktower (with Big Ben chimes) takes its place. The northern end of Janadhipathi Mawatha, which includes the **president's house** (*Janadhipathi Mandiraya*), is normally closed to the public.

Heading south along Janadhipathi Mawatha, a quite different, more vibrant Fort comes into view. The 1960s **Ceylon Continental Hotel** has magnificent views along the coast to Mount Lavinia, while on Bank of Ceylon Mawatha is Fort's modern day commercial hub, the twin steel and glass towers of the 39-floor **World Trade Centre** (1991), Sri Lanka's tallest building, along with some other high-rise offices. To the south, opposite the Galadari Hotel, the colonial **Old Parliament House** is now used as the president's secretariat.

Seafish **4**

Bars & clubs
Ex-Servicemen's Institute **1**   Barrier —

The Pettah and Kotahena

To the north and east of Fort Station is a busy market area with stalls lining Olcott Mawatha and Bodhiraja Mawatha, making pedestrian movement slow and tedious at times. The central area of the Pettah, with many wholesale outlets, bounded by these two roads as well as Main Street and Front Street, is frantic, dirty and noisy, the cries of the traders mingling with the endless traffic horns. It is fascinating and enervating in equal measure. Specialist streets house craftsmen and traders such as goldsmiths (Sea Street), fruit and vegetable dealers (the end of Main Street) and Ayurvedic herbs and medicines (Gabo's Lane). In the market area to the north, Arabs, Portuguese, Dutch and British once traded. Today, most of the traders are Tamil or Muslim, as evidenced by the many *kovils* and mosques.

About 100 m northeast of Fort Railway Station at the south western edge of the Pettah, the **Dutch Period Museum**, ① *Prince St, T244 8466, Tue-Sat 0900-1700, Rs 500, children Rs 300, camera Rs 250,* was originally the residence of the Dutch governor, Thomas van Rhae (1692-1697); it was sold to the VOC (Vereenigde Oostindische Compagnie or Dutch East India Company) before becoming the Colombo seminary in 1696. Then in 1796 it was handed over to the British who turned it into a military hospital and later a post

Colombo harbour

Given Sri Lanka's historical reliance on trade, its harbours, of which Colombo is the most important, are a nerve centre of the economy. Colombo's success lay in its strategic position on the Indian Ocean sea route between Europe, the Far East and Australasia, almost equidistant between the Red Sea and the Straits of Malacca. Development did not begin until the late 19th century – the small promontory offered little protection for larger ships, so in 1875 the British started work on a series of breakwaters which were to provide an effective harbour all year round. By 1912, when the dockyard and fourth breakwater were completed, Colombo was considered one of the top seven harbours in the world.

Currently handling almost 4000 ships a year, today Colombo is at the forefront of plans to make Sri Lanka the shipping hub of South Asia. Having developed its container terminals in recent years and refurbished its passenger terminal in anticipation of establishing ferry links with India and the Maldives, the Sri Lankan Ports Authority is planning a new container terminal, the South Port, with 12 new berths and a new breakwater. The intention is to attract mega container vessels and double capacity within 20 years.

The best views of the harbour are offered at the **Harbour Restaurant** at the Grand Oriental Hotel.

office. It has now been restored and offers a fascinating insight to the Dutch period. The museum surrounds a garden courtyard and has various rooms dedicated to different aspects of Dutch life including some interesting old tombstones. Upstairs, several rooms display Dutch period furniture.

To the north, halfway along Main Street on the left-hand side after 2nd Cross Street is the **Jami-ul-Alfar Mosque** with its interesting white and red brick facade but little of architectural interest inside. At the eastern end of Main Street, Mohamed Zain Mawatha (once Central Road) goes east from a large roundabout, just north of the market, and you enter **Kotahena**. A left turn off Mohamed Zain Mawatha immediately after the roundabout leads to a right fork, Ratnajothi Saravana Mawatha (formerly Wolfendahl Street). At the end (about 500 m) is the **Wolfendahl Church**. Built in 1749 on the site of an earlier Portuguese church, it is prominently placed on a hill, commanding a view over the harbour. Its Doric facade is solid and heavy, and inside it has many tombstones and memorial tablets to Dutch officials. It is the most interesting surviving Dutch monument in Sri Lanka. Some 200 m to the south in New Moor Street is the **Grand Mosque**, a modern building in the style, as one critic puts it, of a "modern international airport covered in metallic paint".

About 1 km to its northeast is **Santa Lucia**, the Roman Catholic cathedral, in some people's eyes the most remarkable church building in Sri Lanka. It is a huge grey structure with a classical facade and a large forecourt, begun in 1876, and completed in 1910. Inside are the tombs of three French bishops but little else of interest. The Pope conducted a service here during his visit in 1994. **Christ Church**, the Anglican cathedral back towards the harbour, is a kilometre northwest of here and is the main church in a diocese that dates from 1845.

Also in the Pettah are three modest Hindu temples, of little architectural interest, but giving an insight into Hindu building style and worship. Perhaps the most striking is that of **Sri Ponnambula Vanesvara** at 38 Sri Ramanathan Road. The *gopuram* (gateway) has typical sculptures of gods from the Hindu pantheon. A Siva lingam is in the innermost shrine, with a Nandi bull in front and a dancing Siva (*Nataraja*) to one side.

Galle Face, Union Place and Beira Lake

Heading south from Fort past the **Ceylon Continental Hotel** and Old Parliament, you reach **Galle Face Green**, to the south of the mouth of the canal feeding Beira Lake. Originally laid out in 1859, the area has been redeveloped and, green once more, is a pleasant place to wander and relax and very popular with Sri Lankans. There are lots of food stalls and hawkers selling knick-knacks, kites and children's toys. **Speaker's Corner** is at its southwestern corner opposite the historic **Galle Face Hotel**. Be on guard for pickpockets and touts, especially at night when the whole area comes alive.

Cross Galle Road, and then the canal, and head into **Slave Island** (see box, page 68). On Kew Street, near the **Nippon Hotel**, city tours often visit the **Sri Siva Subharamaniya Kovil**,

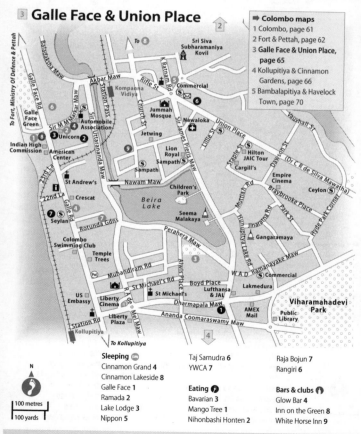

3 Galle Face & Union Place

➡ Colombo maps
1 Colombo, page 61
2 Fort & Pettah, page 62
3 Galle Face & Union Place, page 65
4 Kollupitiya & Cinnamon Gardens, page 66
5 Bambalapitiya & Havelock Town, page 70

Sleeping
Cinnamon Grand 4
Cinnamon Lakeside 8
Galle Face 1
Ramada 2
Lake Lodge 3
Nippon 5

Taj Samudra 6
YWCA 7

Eating
Bavarian 3
Mango Tree 1
Nihonbashi Honten 2

Raja Bojun 7
Rangiri 6

Bars & clubs
Glow Bar 4
Inn on the Green 8
White Horse Inn 9

Kollupitiya & Cinnamon Gardens

4

To Maradana

Beira Lake

To Slave Island

Union Place

City Dispensary

de Soysa Circus

Odel

Commercial ⑤

⑦

Town Hall

Thai Embassy

Perahera Maw

Sir P Peris Maw

ViP Tours

Lakmedura

Dharmapala Maw

Entrance

Viharamahadevi Park

Alliance Francaise

St Michael's Rd

Citibank ⑤

Capri Club

AMEX Mail

Public Library

Museum of Natural History

Horton Pl

Liberty Cinema ⑧

③

Ananda Coomaraswamy Maw

New Town Hall

Art Gallery ⑪

St Bridget's Convent

Premasiri Supermarket

Italian Embassy

National Museum

CINNAMON GARDENS

Liberty Plaza

Clifford Av

Palm Grove

Ernest de Silva Maw

Sir M Fernando Rd

Albert Cres

Sea View Av

Milepost Ln

Abdul Gafoor Maw

KOLLUPITIYA

④

Seylan

Maitland Cres

Commercial ⑤

St Anthony's Maw

Russian Embassy

Cambridge Place

Colombo Cricket Club

Independence Av

Hatton ⑤

②

Guildford Crescent

Standard Chartered

Deal Place

Walukarama Temple

Lionel Wendt Centre

Deanstone Place

Walukarama Rd

⑤

Rajakeeya Maw

5th Lane

Navarangashela

Craft Lanka

Charles Circus

Kumaratunga Munidasa Maw

Colombo University

Stanley Wijesundera Maw

Reid Av

Sampath ⑤

Union Place

⑩

University Library

Rheinland Pl ⑨

Alfred Place

①

Planetarium

Premadasa

Bagatale Rd

⑫

⑰

British Council

Queen's Rd

Viskam Niwasa

Jawatta Rd

Nations Trust ⑤

⑮

④ ⑭

German Embassy

Laksala

Bauddhaloka Maw

Stanmore Cres

People's ⑤

Standard Chartered Lanka Hands

UN Office

Central Culture Fund Office

Parsee Tower of Silence

Barefoot

Temple Lane

⑥

Irish Consulate

Havelock Rd

⑤

To Bambalapitiya

➡ Colombo maps
1 Colombo, page 61
2 Fort & Pettah, page 62
3 Galle Face & Union Place, page 65
4 Kollupitiya & Cinnamon Gardens, page 66
5 Bambalapitiya & Havelock Town, page 70

N

200 metres
200 yards

Sleeping
Colombo House 1
Mrs Jayawardhana's 7
Parisare 5
Ranjit's Ambalama 6
Renuka, Renuka City & Palmyrah Restaurant 3
Tintagel 2

Wayfarer's Inn 4

Eating
Barefoot Garden Café 21
Bars Café 1
Chesa Swiss 2
Chinese Garden 3
Commons 4

Cricket Club Café 4
Flower Drum 5
Flower Lounge 17
Gallery Café & Shop 15
Great Wall 6
Green Cabin 20
Lemon Bar 8
Paradise Road Café 7

66 ● Colombo Sights

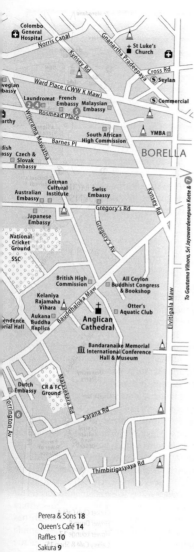

Perera & Sons **18**
Queen's Café **14**
Raffles **10**
Sakura **9**
Summer Garden **11**
Tea Cup **12**

with its enormous colourful *gopuram*. Along Sir James Pieris Mawatha to the south is the pea-green **Beira Lake**, where the endangered spot-billed pelican can be seen. At its northern end along Navam Mawatha is an important commercial zone, with some restaurants and bars, and a pavement leads some of the way around the lake. It is possible to hire out a **swan pedalo** ① *Rs 100, children Rs 50 for 30 mins*, for a trip around a section of the lake. There are jetties to two tiny islands, one a park, the other the tranquil **Seema Malakaya**, designed for meditation by Geoffrey Bawa with various Buddha statues. It belongs to the **Gangaramaya Temple** to the east, which has an interesting selection of rare curios, including an impressive set of gold Buddhas and some intricate carved ivory on show. You might also see the temple elephant shackled up in the grounds. The temple comes alive during the **Navam Perahera** in January.

Kollupitiya, Cinnamon Gardens and Borella

Inland and parallel with Galle Road runs RA de Mel Mawatha (formerly Duplication Road), built up all the way south. Kollupitiya and, further south, Bambalapitiya have some of Colombo's best shopping areas, with some upmarket boutiques, notably **Barefoot**, see page 83. Wealthy locals also flock to the numerous excellent restaurants.

East of Kollupitiya station, Ananda Coomaraswamy Mawatha leads to the most prestigious residential area of Colombo, **Cinnamon Gardens** – widely referred to by its postal code, Colombo 7 – where cinnamon trees used to grow during colonial times. Broad roads and shaded avenues make it a very attractive area, more reminiscent of Singapore than South Asia, though an increasing number of offices and government buildings have moved here in recent years from Fort. Its centrepiece is the attractive **Vihara Mahadevi Park** ① *0600-1800, approach*

Slave Island

The high rise hotels and offices that occupy the northward jutting peninsula in Beira Lake facing the fort show no trace of the earlier uses of what was known as Slave Island. 'Island' was a misnomer, but slaves played a very real part in the colonial history of Colombo.

During the Dutch period this tongue of open land was known as Kaffir Veldt. The Kaffirs – Africans from the East Coast around Mozambique – were brought to Sri Lanka for the first time by the Portuguese from Goa in 1630. When the Dutch ousted the Portuguese they made use of the slave labour force to build the fort in Colombo, when there may have been 4000 of them. Their numbers grew, but after an unsuccessful insurrection in the 18th century the Dutch authorities decided to insist that all slave labour must be identifiably accommodated. The Kaffir Veldt was the nearest open space on which special shanty houses could be built, and a nightly roll call would be held to ensure that every slave was there.

By 1807, the number of slaves had fallen to 700, though the British did not abolish slavery in Sri Lanka until 1845. Nonetheless, the name Slave Island has persisted.

from the northeast, opposite the Town Hall, with the museums and art gallery to its south. The park was re-named after the mother of the King Dutthagamenu. Early morning is an excellent time to visit. In the southwest is a **botanical garden** with a range of tropical trees including a Bo tree, ebony, mahogany, *sal* and lemon eucalyptus which attract a wide variety of birds. There is also an enormous profusion of climbing and parasitic plants as well as rare orchids. The park is particularly colourful in the spring. You may catch sight of elephants which are bathed in the water tank to the southwest. A series of rectangular lakes to the east of the park leads to a golden statue of the seated Buddha. The white cupola of the impressive **Town Hall** stands out on Kannangara Mawatha to the northeast corner of the park. It was completed in 1927. At the De Soysa Circus roundabout is an equally interesting red-brick building, the **Victoria Memorial Rooms**, built in 1903.

In **Borella**, the suburb east of Cinnamon Gardens, the modest shrine room of the **Gautama (Gotami) Vihara** contains impressive modern murals depicting the life of the Buddha by the Sri Lankan artist George Keyt, painted in 1939-1940.

The **National Museum** ⓘ *8 Marcus Fernando Mawatha (Albert Crescent), T269 4768, Sat-Thu 0900-1830 (last entry 1730), closed public holidays, Rs 500, children Rs 300, cameras Rs 250, video cameras Rs 2000*, has a statue of Sir William Gregory, governor 1872-1877, in front of the imposing facade. Opened in 1877, it has a good collection of paintings, sculptures, furniture, porcelain and Kandyan regalia. The library houses a unique collection of over 4000 *ola* (palm manuscripts) – an extremely rich archaeological and artistic collection. Very well labelled and organized, a visit is an excellent introduction for a tour of Sri Lanka. Exhibits include an outstanding collection of 10th- to 12th-century bronzes from Polonnaruwa, and the lion throne of King Nissankamalla, which has become the symbol of Sri Lanka. There are interesting details and curiosities: for example the origin of *kolam* dancing is traced back to the pregnancy craving of the Queen of the legendary King Maha Samnatha. The ground floor displays Buddhist and Hindu sculptures, including a striking 1500-year-old stone statue of the Buddha from Toluvila. 'Demon-dance' masks line the stairs to the first floor. One visitor noted, "These are more 'satire' than 'demon' in nature, with lots of characters of court officials, soldiers and 'outsiders' such as Muslims. Some were very elaborate and capable of moving their eyes, etc. It is interesting to see how these evolved as different fashions swept the court." The first floor has superb scale reproductions of the wall paintings at Sigiriya and Polonnaruwa. Other exhibits include ancient jewellery and carvings in ivory and wood.

The **Natural History Museum** ⓘ *entered via the National Museum or from A Coomeraswamy Mawatha, T269 4767, daily 0900-1700 (last entry 1630), closed public holidays, Rs 300, children Rs 150, cameras Rs 250, video cameras Rs 2000*, is a Victorian-style array of ageing stuffed animals and lizards in formaldehyde, although the scope is quite impressive. The 'applied botany' section introduces you to how various industries work, such as rubber, timber, tea and coconut (note the 13 different types), while there is also a collection of fossils found in Sri Lanka dating back to the Pleistocene Age. The **National Art Gallery**, next door, a one-room collection by Sri Lankan artists, is somewhat disappointing.

A little further south, the **Lionel Wendt Centre** ⓘ *19 Guildford Cres, Mon-Fri 0900-1245 and 1400-1700, Sat-Sun 1000-1200 and 1400-1700*, is a registered charity fostering the arts in Sri Lanka. Local artists are supported with temporary exhibitions, while there is a permanent exhibition of Wendt's pictures. Plays and dance recitals are also performed here.

The well-presented **Bandaranaike Museum** ⓘ *Bauddhaloka Mawatha, 0900-1600, closed Mon and poya holidays*, is housed inside the massive and imposing Bandaranaike Memorial International Conference Hall (BMICH), built by the Chinese government. As well as commemorating the life and times of the assassinated prime minister, with some interesting letters, diaries and personal effects on display, it offers a useful insight into Sri Lanka's steps into post-colonial nationhood. Opposite the BMICH is a replica statue of the Aukana Buddha.

South of the centre

Bambalapitiya and Havelock Town

South of Kollupitiya, Bambalapitiya extends south along Galle Road. This is a busy shopping area with two popular indoor malls at Majestic City and Liberty Plaza and some enticing eateries, but few interesting sights although the **Vajirarama Temple**, whose missionary monks have taken Buddhism to the west, is worth a look. To the east, south of Bauddhaloka Mawatha, **Havelock Road**, lined with some more excellent restaurants, is another traffic-filled thoroughfare, stretching south to Havelock Town. The **Isipathanaramaya Temple**, just north of Havelock Park, is famous for its beautiful frescoes.

Wellawatta and Dehiwala

South of Bambalapitiya, Wellawatta is the last busy suburb within the city limits. Home to many of Colombo's Tamils (and sometimes called 'Little Jaffna' as a result), it has a bustling charm away from the pretensions of wealthier suburbs further north.

Near the busy bazaar of Dehiwala, the **Subbodaramaya Temple** is a Buddhist complex with a shrine room dating from 1795. There is the usual *dagoba*, a Bo-tree and also a 'Seven-Week House' which illustrates the weeks following the Buddha's Enlightenment. There are several Buddha statues, some well-preserved wall paintings and woodcarvings but the most arresting figure is the supremely serene 4.5 m-reclining Buddha with eyes set in blue sapphires.

Dehiwala Zoo ① *A Dharmapala Mawatha (Allan Av), 10 km southeast of the centre, T271 2751, 0830-1800, Rs 2000, children Rs 1000, Rs 250, video camera Rs 2000*, is often very crowded during holidays and weekends. The 22 ha of undulating grounds is beautifully laid out with shrubs, flowering trees and plants, orchids, lakes and fountains. There are more than 3000 animals from all around the world, including big cats, crocodiles, bears and so on. The aquarium has over 500 species of fish. The zoo is particularly noted for its collection of

5 Bambalapitiya & Havelock Road

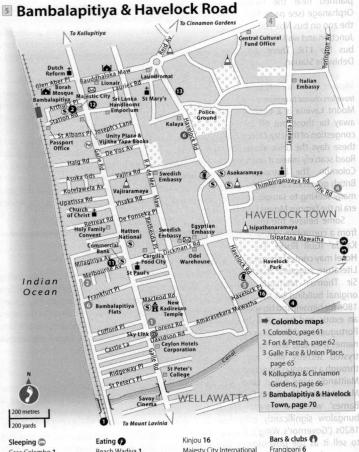

Sleeping ⊜
Casa Colombo 1
Havelock Place Bungalow 5
Janaki 4
Ottery Tourist Inn 2
Westeern 6

Eating ⊙
Beach Wadiya 1
Chinese Dragon 11
Curry Bowl & Perera 13
Jack Tree 3
Hotel de Majestic 12

Kinjou 16
Majesty City International
  Food Hall 2
Mathura Madras
  Woodlands 4
Regina Margherita 5

Bars & clubs ⊙
Frangipani 6

➡ **Colombo maps**
1 Colombo, page 61
2 Fort & Pettah, page 62
3 Galle Face & Union Place,
  page 65
4 Kollupitiya & Cinnamon
  Gardens, page 66
5 Bambalapitiya & Havelock
  Town, page 70

birds – there is a large walk-in aviary for Sri Lankan species. Sea-lions perform at 1600 and a troupe of trained elephants, around 1715. By Asian standards, the animals are well housed, though some, such as the big cats, have insufficient space. Partly to help ease this crowding, a new 15-ha site is planned near the Pinnawela Elephant Orphanage (see page 194). You can reach the zoo on bus Nos 100 or 155 to Dehiwala Junction and walk the last kilometre or take bus No 118. There are also trains to Dehiwala Station.

Mount Lavinia → 12 km south of Fort. Many travellers choose to explore the city from here.

Mount Lavinia is a pleasant place to stay away for those put off by the noise and congestion of the city. Once a fishing place, these days the drive along the busy Galle Road scarcely marks it apart from the rest of Colombo. The historic connection with British governors in the 19th century brings many seeking to sample something of that era in the famous Mount Lavinia Hotel here.

Some believe the town takes its name from a corruption of the Sinhalese 'Lihinia Kanda' ('Gull Rock'). The Mount Lavinia Hotel may contest the origins of the name. Literature suggests that British Governor Sir Thomas Maitland established the original building on the headland here in 1806 for himself and his secret lover Lovina, an exotic and beautiful dancer of mixed Portuguese and Sinhalese race – hence the name. It is said that for seven years she trysted secretly with him by creeping through a tunnel connecting her garden to Maitland's wine cellar! Later, the original Mount Lavinia Hotel was Governor Edward Barnes' weekend retreat. He had the bungalow significantly extended in the 1820s ('Governor's Wing'), but was forced to sell it as the government in England approved neither of the expenditure nor his luxurious lifestyle.

Mount Lavinia is famous for its 'golden mile' of beach, from which the high-rise

Mount Lavinia

200 metres
200 yards

Sleeping
Berjaya 6 C1
Beverley Hills &
  Hollywood Karaoke 1 C2
Blue Seas Guest House 2 B2
Haus Chandra &
  Carrington Villa 3 A1
Ivory Inn 9 B2
Lotus Inn 7 B2
Mount Lavinia 14 D1
Mount Lavinia House 5 B1
Rivi Ras 18 C1
Tropic Inn 23 C2
Windsurf 24 C1
YMCA 4 D2

Eating
Angler 1 D1
Boat Haus 10 B1
Golden Mile 4 C1
La Langousterie 7 C1
La Rambla 2 D1
Lavinia Breeze 3 B1
La Voile Blanche 5 B1
Loon Tao 6 C1

Bars & clubs
Lion Pub 11 B2

buildings of central Colombo are easily visible. The attractive colonial villas and lovely scent of frangipani and bougainvillea, however, mask a slightly seedier side. Theft is more common than elsewhere and if visiting the beach do not take anything valuable with you; beware of walking around at night after the restaurants have closed.

The beach itself is cleanest south of **Mount Lavinia Hotel**, where it is 'private' for the use of the hotel residents only, although non-residents can pay for access as well as use of the pool. North of the hotel, it gets rather narrow and has a noticeable amount of litter especially at weekends and holidays. There are a number of bars/restaurants here, mostly run by the hotels immediately behind them.

Hotels close to the beach are also close to the railway line, with trains passing at regular intervals from early morning to late at night, invariably using their horns to alert pedestrians on the track. Take care when crossing the railway en route to the beach.

North and east of the city

Kelaniya

Some 13 km northeast from Fort, across the Kelaniya River, is the **Raja Maha Vihara**, the most visited Buddhist temple in Sri Lanka after the Temple of the Tooth in Kandy. In the 13th century Kelaniya was an impressive city but for Buddhists its chief attraction today is the legendary visit of the Buddha to the site. The *Mahavansa* recorded that the original stupa enshrined a gem-studded throne on which the Buddha sat when he visited Sri Lanka. Ultimately destroyed by the Portuguese, the present *dagoba* is in the shape of a 'heap of paddy'. The first city on the site was believed to have been built by King Yatala Tissa. According to legend this was destroyed by a flood from the sea which was a punishment given to the king for mistreating the Buddhist *sangha*. He tried to placate the sea by setting his daughter afloat on a golden boat. Having drifted ashore in the south of the island she married King Kavan Tissa, and became the mother of one of Sri Lanka's great heroes, King Dutthagamenu. The city is subsequently believed to have been destroyed by Tamil invasions, and was only re-built in the 13th century by King Vijayabahu.

The present temple, which dates to the late 19th century, is set amongst attractive frangipani trees and has an impressive bell-tower. There is a famous image of the reclining Buddha, but there are also many images of Hindu deities. **Duruthu Perahera** each January draws thousands of pilgrims from all over the island. Take a Biyagama bus from Bastion Mawatha. They leave every half an hour and the trip takes 20-30 minutes.

Sri Jayawardenepura Kotte

Built in the shadow of the modern city of Colombo, most government offices have relocated in this new artificially planned capital 11 km southeast, but Colombo still retains its importance as the commercial capital. The decision to put the new 'Parliament' here was based partly on the fact that the site was formerly the almost sacred territory of Kotte, the ancient capital of Sri Lanka under Alakeswara who built a large fortress and defeated the Tamil leader Chakravarthi. Parakramabahu VI (ruled 1412-1467) transformed the fortress into a prosperous modern city, building a magnificent three-storey temple to hold the Tooth relic which he had placed within several bejewelled gold caskets. However, subsequent weak rulers left the city relatively defenceless and it fell easy prey to the Portuguese. They destroyed the city so that there are no traces of its former glory left. Some panels from the old temple can be seen in the National Museum.

The impressive **Parliament Building** itself was designed by the renowned modern Sri Lankan architect Geoffrey Bawa, see box, page 374. It stands in the middle of a lake surrounded by parkland but is not open to the public.

The **Gramodaya Folk Arts Centre** has craftsmen working with brass, silver, leather, coir and producing jewellery, pottery, natural silk, lace and reed baskets. There is a craft shop and a restaurant serving Sri Lankan specialities. Ask the tourist office for details.

The drive from Colombo's Fort area through the suburbs takes about 30 minutes. Buses run from the city or you can take a three-wheeler.

● Sleeping

Hotel prices
LL over US$450   L US$250-449   AL US$165-249
A US$115-164   B US$71-114   C US$40-70
D Rs 3500-4500   E Rs 2500-3499   F Rs 1500-2499
G under Rs 1499
Restaurant prices
₩₩₩ over Rs 1000   ₩₩ Rs 500-1000   ₩ under Rs 500

There are some very high-quality hotels, mainly in Fort, Galle Face and Union Place, with luxurious rooms, 1st-class service, several restaurants, pool(s), bars, nightclub, etc. Good-quality mid-range accommodation is rather thin on the ground and decent budget options are almost non-existent. Booking in advance is recommended. Many hotels and guesthouses offer airport transfers.

Close to the airport p58
Those arriving late or departing early may prefer to find a hotel close to the international airport at Katunayake (30 km north of Colombo). Another alternative is to stay at Negombo, some 6 km north of the airport, where the accommodation choice is much wider, see page 97.

AL-B Taj Airport Garden, 234 Negombo Rd, Seeduwa, 3.5 km from airport, T225 3771, www.tajhotels.com. Very attractive setting on the lagoon (watersports possible), 120 rooms and suites, all with views, pool. Plush and convenient.

A-B Ramada, 842 Negombo Rd, Katunayake, T225 3646, www.ramada.com. Standard, deluxe rooms and suites, pool and gym. Reasonable food and airport shuttle available if arranged in advance.

A-B Tamarind Tree, 1 Andiambalama Estate, Yatiyana, Minuwangoda (4 km from airport), T225 3802, www.thetamarindtreehotels.com. 20 a/c rooms, 30 self-catering apartments, all a bit tired, and attractive gardens and good pool. Luxurious and well designed though service can be iffy.

C-E Full Moon Garden Hotel, 754 Colombo Rd, Katunayake, T535 3534, www.avenra gardenhotel.com. 30 a/c rooms that aren't up to much but close to the airport. Wi-Fi, restaurant, pool, friendly staff.

Fort area and the Pettah p60, map p62
There are several F and G hotels around Fort Railway Station though they are very basic.
LL-AL Colombo Hilton, 2 Sir Chittampalam A Gardiner Mawatha, Col 2, T249 2492, www.hilton.com. 387 rooms, best views in the city, all facilities including 6 restaurants, 4 bars, pool, Wi-Fi, leisure centre. There is another Hilton hotel, the **Colombo Residence**, 200 Union Pl, T534 4644, www.hilton.com, which is smaller and popular with families.
LL-B Ceylon Continental, 48 Janadhipathi Mawatha, Col 1, T242 1221, www.ceylon continental.com. 250 fully equipped rooms with good views, nice pool, 3 restaurants.
AL-A Galadari, 64 Lotus Rd, Col 1, T254 4544, www.galadarihotel.lk. 446 rooms with good views, all facilities including a Mlesna shop in the lobby. Staff are helpful and efficient.
A-B Grand Oriental, 2 York St, Col 1, T232 0391, www.grandoriental.com. Colonial-era hotel built to accommodate travellers arriving by sea and a Colombo

legend (once advertised as "the largest and best equipped hotel in the East"), though faded now and rooms in need of renovation. Fascinating view of the docks from **Harbour Room** restaurant (no photos), good food, nightclub, friendly staff, good location.

G New Colonial, opposite Fort Station, T232 3074. 7 singles, 5 doubles, fine for a night if catching an early train.

G YMCA (Central), 39 Bristol St, Col 1, T232 5252. Cheap, basic rooms, opt for private bathroom if possible as shared is 'filthy'. Dorm (Rs 150), membership (obligatory) is returnable, cafeteria serves simple local food. Really only for the brave or desperate.

Galle Face, Union Place and Beira Lake
p65, map p65

LL-A Cinnamon Grand, 77 Galle Rd, Col 3, T243 7437, www.cinnamonhotels.com. Popular hotel with over 500 rooms and suites in 2 wings, 8 restaurants, and direct access to Crescat Mall. Beautiful open spaces, all facilities, good pool.

LL-A Cinnamon Lakeside, 115 Sir CA Gardiner Mawatha, Col 2, T249 1000, www.cinnamonhotels.com. Slightly north of Galle Face in Slave Island, 340 rooms and suites, good restaurants, beautiful pool, nightclub. Currently being refurbished. Service can leave something to be desired.

L-A Galle Face Hotel, 2 Galle Rd, Col 3, T558 5858, www.gallefacehotel.com. Originally built in 1864 and re-designed by Geoffrey Bawa (see box, page 374), probably the most atmospheric place to stay in Colombo. Room price varies and there are 2 wings, Regency and Classic. Avoid rooms overlooking Galle Rd, as these can be very noisy. Carefully maintained colonial atmosphere, with beautiful furniture. Friendly staff, 'superb' service, 30-m saltwater pool over-looking the Indian Ocean; the **Verandah** bar is the best in Colombo for a sunset drink. Very competent travel desk.

L-A Taj Samudra, 25 Galle Face Centre Rd, Col 3, T244 6622, www.tajhotels.com. Well situated overlooking Galle Face Green and

the ocean, pleasant seating areas in the lobby, attractive gardens behind. Comfortable rooms; some with good views but opt for those that have been refurbished. Excellent food, nightclub, pool.

AL-A Ramada, 30 Sir MM Markar Mawatha, Col 3, T242 2001, www.ramadacolombo.com. Modern hotel built in Moghul style. 94 reasonable rooms, very good Mughlai food, large pool.

B-C Lake Lodge, 20 Alwis Terrace, Col 3, T232 6443, www.taruhotels.com. Boutique hotel offering 12 a/c rooms with attached bath. Quiet, good food, rooftop terrace with lake views, Wi-Fi. Recommended.

C Nippon, Manning Mansions, 123 Kumaran Ratnam Rd, Col 2, T236 3306. Colonial style in attractive plant-lined colonnade. Spacious rooms, most with a/c. Bar and good oriental restaurant.

E YWCA, 7 Rotunda Garden, T232 8589, natywca@sltnet.lk. The best are the large double rooms with balcony, but cheaper accommodation with shared bathroom also available (Rs550). Clean, very central, breakfast included in the price. Has an old-fashioned, institutional feel but good value. Currently undergoing repairs to the roof so can be noisy. Couples accepted but not single men.

Kollupitiya, Cinnamon Gardens and Borella *p67, map p66*

L-AL Tintagel, 65 Rosemead Pl, Col 7, T460 2122, www.tintagelcolombo.com. This 10-room boutique hotel from the owners of the **Paradise Road** franchise (see Shopping, page 82), used to be the home of the Bandaranaike family, a political dynasty in Sri Lanka. SWRD Bandaranaike was shot here in 1959. The suites are as stylishly decorated as one would expect, and each are individual. There is a restaurant and bar, although the government has not yet granted an alcohol licence (guests can BYO), pool and free 3-wheeler to other Paradise Road properties. Staff are excellent.

B Renuka & Renuka City, 328 Galle Rd, T257 3598, www.renukahotel.com. Twin hotels with 81 comfortable a/c rooms aimed mainly at business travellers, with TV, fridge and IDD phone. Small pool a short walk away, basement **Palmyrah** restaurant recommended for Sri Lankan curries (see Eating, page 78). Good location.

D Parisare, 97/1 Rosmead Pl, Col 7 (no sign, next to UNHCR, ring on arrival), T269 4749, sunsep@visualnet.lk. Exceptionally well-designed and beautiful house, 3 extremely good-value fan rooms, all with attached bath; best room has 4-poster bed, bathtub, separate dressing room, desk, sofa and its own (small) garden. The 2 upstairs rooms are also excellent. Pleasant seating area with TV and roof-top sun terrace, all meals offered. Often booked up weeks in advance.

D Wayfarer's Inn, 77 Rosmead Pl, Col 7, T269 3936, wayfarer@slt.lk. Fan and a/c rooms with TV, tea-making facilities and fridge, and studio with kitchen facilities. Restaurant, garden, table tennis, not as homely as other guesthouses though.

D-E Colombo House, 26 Charles Pl, off Bagatelle Rd, Col 3, T257 4900, www.colombohouse.com. Impressive 1939 mansion, but the 4 rooms are past their best and as such are overpriced. Still, the location is excellent and it's very quiet.

D-E Ranjit's Ambalama, 53/19 Torrington Av, T250 2403, www.ranjitsambalama.com. 7 rooms, some with shared bathroom and 6 with the option of a/c (Rs 1500), in house with attractive terrace for breakfasts. Ask about 4-room bungalow on edge of the city.

F Mrs Jayawardhana's, 42 Kuruppu Rd (off Cotta Rd), Col 8, T269 3820. 3 rooms, 1 with private bathrooms, in charming family guesthouse, library, garden, meals on request, clean, good value.

Bambalapitiya and Havelock Town
p69, map p70

LL-L Casa Colombo, 231 Galle Rd, Col 4, T452 0130, www.casacolombo.com. 12 spacious suites in a boutique hotel,
ranging in size and layout, and each individually decorated. Stylish mix of old and new, 200-year-old mansion with colonial touches, designer furniture, flatscreen TVs, free Wi-Fi, etc. Attentive service, pool, spa, dining areas and bar.

A-B Havelock Place Bungalow, 6/8 Havelock Pl, Col 5, T258 5191, www.havelockbungalow.com. Stylishly designed modern guesthouse. 3 suites and 4 standard rooms, simple, beautiful individual furnishings, restaurant, gardens, pool and jacuzzi. Homely and quiet.

B-C Janaki, 43 Fife Rd, Col 5, T250 2169, www.hoteljanakicolombo.com. 50 reasonable a/c rooms with TV and balcony, pool and restaurant.

D-F Westeern, 35 Frankfurt Pl, Col 4, T250 7161, www.hotelwesteern.com. 55 comfortable a/c rooms in hotel by the sea (and railway line).

E-F Ottery Tourist Inn, 29 Melbourne Av (off Galle Rd), Col 4, T258 3727, www.ottery touristinn.com. 8 large rooms, some with balcony, in a colonial building. Run down but quiet location.

Wellawatta and Dehiwala *p69, map p61*

B Sapphire, 371 Galle Rd, Col 6, T236 3306, www.hotelsapphirelk.com. Ugly building but 40 comfortable a/c rooms, attached bath, good rooftop Chinese restaurant, pool.

C Omega Inn, 324 Galle Rd, Col 6, T258 2277, www.hotelomegainn.com. Comfortable a/c rooms with TV, some with tea-making facilities and minibar. **Regency Pub** next door. Can be noisy.

G Chamenka Guest House, 44 Pallidora Rd, Dehiwala, T077-905 5635, www.chamenka. hostel.com. Family-run guesthouse offering 4 rooms with shared bathroom.

Mount Lavinia *p71, map p71*

Note that some of the accommodation in Mount Lavinia is very close to the railway line, and although trains do not run all night the early commuter services make disturb light sleepers.

AL-A Mount Lavinia, 100 Hotel Rd, T271 1711, www.mountlaviniahotel.com. Renovated and extended former governors' weekend retreat located on a small but prominent headland retaining a rich colonial atmosphere. 275 rooms and suites, many with sea views and retaining old world ambience, a 'must-stay'. Huge public areas and labyrinthine corridors, all facilities, range of restaurants, terrace bar (good for sunset drinks), nightclub (see Bars and clubs), shopping arcade, sports including tennis, gym, elephant rides (Sun 1000-1400), impressive terrace pool, peaceful private beach (cleaner than public beach to the north).

A-B Mount Lavinia House, 9 Samudra Mawatha, T273 9554, www.laviniahouse.com. 6 rooms, most with sea views, in small but chic guesthouse. All are a/c with attached bath except the circular Fantasy Suite on the top floor with its jungle bathroom. Restaurant, pool that starts inside and extends into the garden. Self-catering apartments are available at the sister hotel, **Lavinia House Residence**, T777-267 872, next door.

B Berjaya, 36 College Av, T273 9610, www.berjayahotel.com. 95 large a/c rooms in comfortable resort hotel, private balconies, restaurants, pool.

C Haus Chandra & Carrington Villa, 37 Beach Rd, T228 7575, www.plantationgrouphotels.com. 27 small a/c and fan rooms, plus 4 suites and 1 excellent **AL** villa for 6 people, restaurants (on rooftop plus cheaper food at **Boat Haus Café** on the beach), small but deep pool, chauffeur-driven Rolls Royce available for hire. Ask about excellent hotels in Kitulgala.

C Rivi Ras, 50/2 De Saram Rd, T271 7731, rivirasph@eureka.lk. Rooms and suites, fan slightly cheaper, in 2-storey villas with verandas set in attractive garden, excellent **La Langousterie** seafood restaurant on beach.

D Beverley Hills, 27 De Saram Rd, T273 3555, bhills@eureka.lk. Large, well laid out rooms, some a/c, very clean, Korean and Sri Lankan food, bar, karaoke, Wi-Fi. Extension in progress.

D-E Tropic Inn, 30 College Av, T273 8653, www.tropicinn.com. 16 a/c rooms with hot water, sizes vary so check first, breakfast included, helpful management. Internet available.

E-F Blue Seas Guest House, 9/6 De Saram Rd, T271 6298. Good clean rooms with a/c or fan (including breakfast), some with balconies, in family-run guesthouse. Quiet location, very friendly and helpful.

E-F Ivory Inn, 21 De Saram Rd, T271 5006. Reasonable fan and a/c rooms with balcony, attractive garden.

F Lotus Inn, 5 Beach Rd. 3 clean a/c rooms in quiet villa. Breakfast available on request.

F Windsurf, 15a De Soysa Av, T273 2299. 15 large, simple rooms with basic bathrooms, sea views. Restaurant, rooftop beer garden, friendly.

G YMCA, 55 Hotel Rd, T271 3786. 7 rooms with attached bath. Good value. Home of the Mt Lavinia tennis club.

🍴 Eating

There are many excellent places to eat in Colombo. As well as Sri Lankan and Indian fare, most other types of Asian cuisine are very popular with Thai, Japanese, Korean and even Mongolian restaurants in particular popping up all over the place to add to ubiquitous Chinese offering.

Some of the best speciality restaurants are to be found in the upper category hotels, which also serve good Western food. Their eat-all-you-want buffets are particularly recommended at lunchtime, where you have the added benefit of sitting in cool comfort during the hottest part of the day. American/European-style venues are also becoming increasingly popular, particularly the 'Irish' pub.

For those on a tighter budget, lunch packets (available from street stalls all over the city) are a good idea. These normally comprise rice plus a meat, fish or vegetable curry, and cost Rs 100-150.

Fort area and the Pettah p60, map p62
There are lots of cheap 'rice and curry' places in Fort, the Pettah and along Galle Rd, (🍴).

🍴🍴🍴 **Harbour Room**, **Grand Oriental**, see Sleeping, page 73. Serves unexceptional food but the views over the harbour are spectacular.

🍴🍴🍴 **Il Ponte**, **Ginza Hohsen** and **Curry Leaf** restaurants, **Colombo Hilton**, see Sleeping, page 73. For 1st-class Italian, Japanese and Sri Lankan cuisine.

🍴🍴🍴-🍴🍴 **Stix Chinese Corner**, **Galadari Hotel**, see Sleeping, page 73. Good Chinese food.

🍴🍴 **Seafish**, 15 Sir CA Gardiner Mawatha, just behind Regal Cinema, Col 2, T232 6915. Excellent fish at reasonable prices, hoppers with curry (evenings).

🍴 **Crown's**, next to **Laksala**, 54 York St (basement). Open 0630-1830. South Indian style vegetarian, simple but good, friendly, cheap.

🍴 **Pagoda**, Chatham St, Col 1. Offers good-value Chinese plus Sri Lankan and Western.

🍴 **Shakthi**, YMCA, see Sleeping, page 74. Very cheap authentic Sri Lankan food, self-service.

🍴 **Taj**, 54 York St, T242 2812. Popular with local office workers at lunchtime, cheap rice and curry, kotthu rotty, short eats, a/c upstairs.

Cafés
The luxury hotels in Fort and Galle Face have 24-hr coffee shops.
Barista, 3rd floor, World Trade Centre, Col 1. Mon-Fri 0800-2000, Sat 1100-1600. Western-style coffee shop, with cappuccinos, lattes, etc, pastries and snacks for local office workers.

Galle Face, Union Place and Beira Lake p65, map p65
City dwellers take in the sea air on Galle Face Green while eating out off the street vendors.

🍴🍴🍴 **The Bavarian German Restaurant**, 11 Galle Face Court 2 (opposite **Galle Face Hotel**), Col 3, T242 1577. Open 1800-2400. German specialities in big portions, slow service.

🍴🍴🍴 **Golden Dragon**, **Taj Samudra**, see Sleeping, page 74. Open 1900-2330. Excellent Chinese.

🍴🍴🍴 **Nihonbashi Honten**, 11 Galle Face Terrace, Col 3, T232 3847. Open 1200-1430, 1800-2230. The best Japanese food in Colombo, There are set menus and fusion dishes, as well as sushi and sashimi. The menu is provided on an iPad.

🍴🍴🍴 **Raja Bojun**, Seylan Towers, Galle Rd, Col 3, T471 6171. Open 1200-2300. Excellent Sri Lankan buffet overlooking the ocean. Huge variety, reasonably priced.

🍴🍴🍴 **Sea Spray**, **Galle Face Hotel**, see Sleeping, page 74. Good seafood and Western dishes in one of the city's most atmospheric locations.

🍴🍴🍴-🍴🍴 **The Mango Tree**, 83 Dharmapala Mawatha, Col 3, T587 9790, www.the mangotree.net. Open 1200-1500, 1900-2300. Offers a wide range of Indian fare, including vegetarian options, seafood, meat and Indian breads. Has an outlet at **Crescat Food Court**. Standard of service varies.

🍴🍴 **7 Degrees North**, **Cinnamon Lakeside**, see Sleeping, page 74. Tapas and cocktails overlooking the lake, or Mediterranean cuisine by the pool. Live music at weekends, good atmosphere.

🍴🍴 **Chutneys**, **Cinnamon Grand**, see Sleeping, page 74. Excellent South Indian food, with the dishes on the menu separated into regions. Helpful and friendly staff.

🍴 **Crescat Food Court**, (next to **Cinnamon Grand**). Not the most authentic surroundings (self-service in Western-style shopping mall basement) but a good way to sample a wide range of Asian cuisines. Wi-Fi available.

🍴 **Rangiri**, 67 Union Place, Col 2. Eye-watering but tasty Sri Lankan curry plus full range of sambols. Friendly and popular with locals.

Kollupitiya, Cinnamon Gardens and Borella p67, map p66
🍴🍴🍴 **Chesa Swiss**, 3 Deal Pl, off RA de Mel Mawatha, Col 3, T257 3433. Open 1900-2300, closed poya days. Excellent Swiss food, though at a price.

🍴🍴🍴 **Gallery Café**, 2 Alfred House Rd, Col 3, T258 2162, gallerycafe@paradiseroadsl.com. Open 1000-2400. Once the office of famed

Sri Lankan architect Geoffrey Bawa, see box, page 374 (his old work table is still there), exclusive setting with unbeatable ambience, minimalist chic decor, good fusion food, fabulous desserts and cakes, excellent wine list. Book in advance.

††† Lemon Bar, 41 Maitland Cres, Col 7, T077-155 4149. Open 1700-2400. A rooftop restaurant with great atmosphere, serving interesting and tasty international cuisine. **Silk** nightclub is downstairs, see page 81.

†††-†† Cricket Club Café, 34 Queen's Rd (near British Council), Col 3, T150 1384. Open 1100-2300. International range of dishes, many named after famous cricketers (such as Murali's Mulligatawny or Gatting's Garlic Prawns), in a cricket-lover's heaven, though shows other sports on TV too. Local and touring teams usually visit. Good bar popular with expats. Food is pub fare at restaurant prices.

†††-†† Palmyrah, Hotel Renuka, see Sleeping, page 75. Open 0700-1430, 1900-2200. Widely praised for its Sri Lankan food and Jaffna specialties, it also serves Western and South Indian dishes. Attentive service, popular, try the hoppers. Recommended.

†††-†† Raffles, 35 Bagatalle Rd, Col 03, T576 7814, www.rafflescolombo.com. Good range of Western and Sri Lankan food in tasteful surroundings. Staff are attentive and professional. Lunch buffet available.

†† Bars Café, 24 Deal Pl, opposite Chesa Swiss, Col 3, T257 5157. Modern restaurant with a coffee bar feel, serving good Eastern and Western cuisine. The hoppers and the rice and curry are good choices. Beautiful cakes. A/c.

†† Chinese Garden, 32 Dharmapala Mawatha, Col 3. Wide range of Chinese dishes, unimpressive exterior and a bit grubby but popular with locals (may have to wait for table).

†† Flower Drum, 26 Thurstan Rd, Col 3, T257 4811, www.flowerdrum.net. Excellent Chinese, extensive choice, quiet atmosphere, reasonable prices.

†† Flower Lounge, 18 Bagatelle Rd, Col 3, T259 3032, www.flowerdrum.net. Good

range of Chinese in salubrious surroundings, same owners as **Flower Drum** (see above).

†† Great Wall, 491 Galle Rd, Col 3. Chinese, offers reasonable lunchtime set menus.

†† Green Cabin, 453 Galle Rd, Col 3, T258 8811. Open 1000-2300. Good-value authentic Sri Lankan food (curry and string hoppers) in pleasant surroundings. Lunchtime buffet, cakes and snacks for sale in the front area. Devilled dishes are particularly good.

†† Queen's Café, 417 RA de Mel Mawatha, Col 3, T250 8345. Open 1100-2400, closed Fri lunchtime. Indian and Chinese, curries, tandooris, snacks, plus milkshakes and juices, not much atmosphere but a/c and good value, pool lounge upstairs.

†† Sakura, 14 Rheinland Place, Col 3, T257 3877. Open 1130-1400, 1730-2400. Good food in what was Colombo's 1st Japanese restaurant, reasonably priced.

† Summer Garden, 110 Green Path, off A Coomaraswamy Mawatha, Col 7, T494 0540. Has a selection of cheap Sri Lankan and Chinese dishes in an open-air setting, handy for museums.

Cafés

Barefoot Garden Café, 706 Galle Rd, Col 3, T255 3075. Daily 1000-1900. Wonderfully chic terrace café serving light meals, sandwiches and cakes in frangipani gardens next to bookshop and art gallery.

The Commons, 39A Ernest de Silva Mawatha, T269 4435. Sun-Thu 1000-2200, Fri-Sat 1100-2400. Flavoured coffees (excellent frappuccinos), juices and snacks (bagels, burgers, wraps, etc).

Paradise Road Café, 213 Dharmapala Mawatha, Col 7, T268 6043. Open 1000-1900. Beautiful old colonial mansion open daytime for light meals and drinks.

Perera & Sons, 17 Galle Rd, Col 3, T232 3295. Cakes, snacks, breads, mainly takeaway but some tables. Other branches around the city, 24 Deal Pl, Col 3; 2 Dharmapala Mawatha; off Pieris Maw, Col 2, and on Havelock Rd.

The Tea Cup, 399 RA De Mel Mawatha, Col 3. Free Wi-Fi. Range of hot and cold teas, as well as cakes and snacks served at tables set out on a grassy lawn. Friendly and relaxing.

Bambalapitiya and Havelock Town
p69, map p70

🍴🍴 **Regina Margherita**, 151 Park Rd, Col 5, T739 4440. Open 1800-2300. Popular restaurant serving authentic Italian food, try the pizza.

🍴🍴 **Chinese Dragon**, 11 Milagiriya Av, Col 4, T250 3637. Open 1100-1500, 1800-2300. Long-established local favourite, outside barbecues as well.

🍴🍴 **International Food Hall**, **Majestic City** (basement), Bambalapitiya, Col 4. Great place to try out a range of different cuisines.

🍴🍴 **Jack Tree**, 200 Park Rd, Col 5, T574 7788, www.jacktree.com. Thai cuisine, run by the same people as **The Mango Tree** (see Eating, page 77).

🍴🍴 **Kinjou**, 33 Amarasekera Mawatha (off Havelock Rd), Col 5, T258 9477. Open 1145-1430, 1830-2300. Good Szechuan cooking in plush Japanese surroundings.

🍴 **Curry Bowl**, Havelock Rd, T257 5157. Open 1000-2200. Dosai and string hoppers, **Perera** bakers attached, takeaway available.

🍴 **Hotel de Majestic**, 17 Galle Rd, Col 4 (opposite Majestic City), T537 7760. String hoppers and superb Pakistani and Singaporean curries.

🍴 **Mathura Madras Woodlands**, 185 Havelock Rd, Col 5, T258 2909. Open 1100-2300. A/c, choice of good North and South Indian cuisine, good value lunch-time buffets.

Wellawatta and Dehiwala
p69, maps p61 and p70

🍴🍴 **Beach Wadiya**, 2 Station Av, Col 6, T258 8568 (see map, page 70). Open 1200-2300. Very popular beachside seafood restaurant, well-stocked bar, rustic surroundings, good food but small portions and service can be slow. Book in advance.

🍴🍴 **Shanmugas**, 53/3 Ramakrishna Rd, Col 6, near Roxy Cinema, T236 1384.

Open 1100-2200. Excellent South Indian vegetarian restaurant boasting 15 varieties of dosai, plus some North Indian specialities, civilized atmosphere, close to beach. Recommended, considered by many as the best veggie spot in town.

Mount Lavinia *p71, map p71*

Most hotels and guesthouses in Mt Lavinia have a restaurant, though many serve fairly bland food (family guesthouses and private houses tend to be the exception, although lunch and dinner should be ordered in advance). Breakfast is often included. Most hotel restaurants are only open for breakfast, lunch and dinner. For other times head for the beach shacks which are open all day. Seafood is, naturally enough, the speciality. Restaurants on the beach tend to be quite expensive, but the views at sunset are magnificent. Live music at weekends.

🍴🍴🍴 **Golden Mile**, 43/14 Mount Beach (off College Av), T273 3997. Attractive timber constructed beachside restaurant, wide menu from around the world (lobster thermidor Rs 2450, Tasmanian T-bone Rs 4490), expensive but atmospheric. Veggie dishes are significantly cheaper.

🍴🍴🍴 **Governor's Restaurant**, **Mount Lavinia**, see Sleeping, page 71. Atmospheric colonial surroundings.

🍴🍴🍴 **La Langousterie**, part of **Rivi Ras** hotel, see Sleeping, page 76. One of the best for seafood.

🍴🍴🍴 **La Rambla**, 69 Hotel Rd, T272 5403. Tastefully decorated restaurant serving good-quality seafood and Mediterranean cuisine, desserts are a bit disappointing.

🍴🍴🍴 **Lavinia Breeze**, 43/7, De Alwis Av, off De Saram Rd, T077-321 5951, www.laviniabreeze.lk. Seafood. Raised covered eating area and candlelit tables in the sand in the evening, with live music at weekends. Seafood and international dishes, platters are especially good.

🍴🍴🍴 **Seafood Cove**, also at **Mount Lavina Hotel**, see Sleeping, page 76. Excellent seafood in great beachside position.

♥♥♥-♥♥ **La Voile Blanche**, 43/10 Beach Rd, T456 1111. Unsurprisingly specializes in seafood, but has extensive menu with Asian and Western choices. Beachfront, with chilled atmosphere. Good cocktail list and range of spirits.

♥♥♥-♥♥ **Loon Tao**, 43/12 College Av, T272 2723, www.loontao.com. Chinese restaurant serving predominantly seafood, but meat and tofu dishes also available. Extensive menu, upmarket beach hut feel.

♥♥ **The Angler**, 71 Hotel Rd. Family-run, also 4 **E** rooms and apartment to let. Good Sri Lankan, Chinese and Western dishes.

♥♥ **Boat Haus**, Haus Chandra, see Sleeping, page 76. Seafood, pizzas and snacks.

⊙ Bars and clubs

→ *Some bars open until 0300, or even later.*
Once the preserve of the big hotels, new bars are opening up around the city all the time. Since drinking alcohol in Sri Lanka remains a predominantly male preserve, some of the older affairs may feel a little uncomfortable for women, but the newer plusher bars have a broader appeal. Almost all **AL**, **A** and **B** hotels have pleasant, if expensive, bars. On *poya* days alcohol is not generally available until midnight. The nightclub scene is largely restricted to top category hotels, most impose a hefty cover charge on non-residents at weekends (ladies often free) and expensive drinks. Some have early evening 'Happy Hours', though few get going much before midnight.

Fort area and the Pettah *p60, map p62*
Bars
Echelon Pub, Colombo Hilton,
see Sleeping, page 73. Open 1100-0230. Smarter than most and popular with expats at the weekends.
Sri Lanka Ex-Serviceman's Institute, 29 Bristol St, Col 1, T242 2650. Serves very cheap beer, but a male-only venue.

Clubs
The majority of the following are hotel nightclubs. Music varies depending on the night and with it, the clientele.
Blue Elephant, Colombo Hilton,
see Sleeping, page 73.
Blue Leopard, Grand Oriental,
see Sleeping, page 73.
Zouk, Galadari Hotel, see Sleeping, page 73. Open Tue-Sun. Highly rated.

Galle Face, Union Place and Beira Lake *p65, map p65*
Bars
A sunset drink overlooking the sea at the Galle Face is a must.
Glow Bar, 3rd floor, AA Building, 42 Sir MM Markar Mawatha, Col 3. Cocktails, fusion food and eclectic mix of music. Popular with the under 30s, happy hour is 1800-1900.
Inn on the Green, Galle Rd, Col 3, T223 9440. Open 1600-2400. Styled as an English pub, serves draught bitter and a variety of imported lagers as well as expensive English crisps.
White Horse Inn, 2 Navam Mawatha, Col 2, T230 4922. Fairly inexpensive drinks, busy at weekends, otherwise quiet.

Clubs
Amuseum, Galle Face Hotel,
see Sleeping, page 74. Currently the place to be seen and to flash your cash.
Club Nouvo, Taj Samudra,
see Sleeping, page 74.
Mojo, Taj Samudra, see Sleeping, page 74.

Kollupitiya, Cinnamon Gardens and Borella *p67, map p67*
Bars
Cricket Club Café, see Eating, page 78. Serves draught Carlsberg by the pint or Guinness, with a good selection of wines. Good atmosphere.
Frangipani, 126 Havelock Rd, Col 5. Where colonial meets retro. Psychedelic bar in colonial house, high ceilings and fuschia lights, good cocktail range.

Gallery Café Bar, see Eating, page 77.
An open-air (stone) bar in courtyard,
very chic, good cocktails.

Clubs
Silk, in the same building as **Lemon**,
see Eating, page 78. Popular.

Mount Lavinia *p71, map p71*
The more expensive hotels often provide
live music over dinner, especially at
weekends. Almost all restaurants serve
alcohol. A couple of hotels host karaoke
nights, including **Beverley Hills Hotel**.

Bars
Mount Lavinia Hotel, see Sleeping, page 76.
The terrace bar offers probably the best
setting for an end of day drink (although the
beach bars will provide a cheaper option to
enjoy the sunset).
Lion Pub, corner of Galle and Beach Rds,
T276 1961. You enter through a big lion's
mouth, food nothing special but reasonably
priced. The sunken beer garden is popular with
tourists and locals and has a good atmosphere.

Clubs
The Hut, Mount Lavinia Hotel, see Sleeping,
page 76. Open Wed-Sun. A local, friendly
crowd. Ideal for those who want a retro
night out.

⊙ Entertainment

Casinos
Casinos are open through the night and
some are 24-hr, those mentioned below
are just a small selection.
Bally's, 14 Dharmapala Maw, Col 3.
Upmarket casino open 24 hrs.
MGM Grand Club, 772 Galle Rd,
Bambalapitiya, Col 4, T250 2268.
Offers banco, blackjack, roulette,
baccarat, has VIP 'foreigners only' lounge.

Ritz Club, 5 Galle Face Terr, Col 3
(behind Ramada).

Cinemas
There are a number of cinemas in Colombo,
the following are your best bet for
English-language recent releases.
Liberty, 35 Dharmapala Mawatha, Col 3.
Majestic, Level 4, Majestic City, Col 4.
  Alternatively, films are also shown at
Alliance Française, **British Council** and
American Center. See Directory, page 88,
for addresses.

Cultural shows
Some top hotels put on regular folk dance
performances (also Western floor shows/live
music for dancing); open to non-residents.

Theatres
Lionel Wendt Centre, see page 69.
Stages both Western and local productions,
and occasional classical music concerts.
Box office 1000-1200, 1400-1700.
Lumbini Hall, Havelock Town. Specializes
in Sinhalese theatre.

⊛ Festivals and events

Jan **Duruthu Perahera**, Kelaniya Temple,
a 2-day festival with caparisoned elephants,
acrobats and floats.
Feb **Navam Maha Perahera**, Gangaramaya
Temple, celebrates the full-moon with
processions around Beira Lake-Viharam
ahadevi Park area. A large number of
elephants, torch-bearers, drummers, dancers,
acrobats, stilt walkers and pilgrims take part.

⊙ Shopping

Most shops are open 1000-1900 on weekdays
and 0845-1500 on Sat, though tourist shops
will be open for longer and sometimes on
Sun. You can shop with confidence at
government-run shops, although it is

interesting to wander in the bazaars and look for good bargains. Shops in Fort tend to be good but more expensive than equally good quality items in Kollupitiya. Boutiques in the Pettah are worth a visit too. The top hotels have shopping arcades selling quality goods but prices are often higher than elsewhere.

Bazaars

Sunday Bazaar, Main St, the Pettah; and Olcott St, Fort.

Bookshops

Colombo has plenty of good bookshops, especially along Galle Rd in Kollupitiya.
Barefoot, 704 Galle Rd, Col 3, T258 9305 www.barefootceylon.com. Has an excellent selection, with good coverage of Sri Lanka and books on design, photography, architecture and modern fiction, as well as cards and postcards.
Bookland, 430-432 Galle Rd, Col 3, T471 4444.
Buddhist Book Centre with branches at Buddhist Information Centre, 380 Sarana Rd (off Bauddhaloka Maw), Col 7, T268 9786.
Buddhist Cultural Centre, 125 Anderson Rd, Nedimala, Dehiwala, T272 6234, bcc@sri.lanka.net. Daily 0830-1730 including *poya* and public holidays.
Cultural Bookshop, Ananda Cooraswam Mawatha, Col 7 (next to Art Gallery). Has a wide selection.
Lakehouse, 100 Sir CA Gardiner Mawatha, Col 2, booklhb@sltnet.lk. Branch upstairs at Liberty Plaza. Very good range.
MD Gunasena, 217 Olcott Mawatha, Col 11, T232 3981, www.mdgunasena.com. The largest bookshop in Sri Lanka, with branches around Colombo and the island.
Odel, 5 Alexandra Pl, Lipton Circus, Col 7, T268 2712. Good selection of books in English, especially lifestyle and cookery.
Sarasavi, 30 Stanley Thilakaratne Mawatha, Nugegoda, T285 2519, sarasavi@slt.lk. Branches at YMBA Buildings in Fort and Borella.
Serendib, 36 Rosmead Place, Col 7. Antiquarian books and maps.

Survey Department, York St, Col 1, T243 5328. Maps of Colombo and Sri Lanka.
Vijitha Yapa, Unity Plaza, Col 3, T259 6960, www.vijithayapa.com. Recommended for range. Branches at **Crescat**, T551 0100 and 32 Thurstan Rd, Col 3.

Boutique shops

'Lifestyle' shops are becoming increasingly popular with Colombo's wealthy elite, and some high-quality gifts can be picked up amongst them.
Barefoot, 704 Galle Rd, Col 3, T258 9305 www.barefootceylon.com. Funky homewares in the signature bright colours.
Elephant Walk, 61 Ward Pl, Col 7, T077-773 3791. Well-crafted, homeware and chic gifts.
Kalaya, 116 Havelock Rd. Modern designer homestore, with some goods imported from India.
Paradise Road, 213 Dharmapala Mawatha, Col 7, also **Gallery Shop** at **Gallery Café** (1000-2230). Kitchen accessories, candles, beautiful leather diaries, address books, etc, well-made sarongs. For larger pieces, including furniture visit Paradise Road Design Ware House, 61/3 Ward Pl, Col 7, T269 1056.

Clothes

Textiles represent Sri Lanka's biggest industry, and clothes made here are exported to major brand names around the world. Very cheap clothes can be found in the Pettah, though don't buy off street stalls.
Barefoot, 704 Galle Rd, Col 3, T258 9305 www.barefootceylon.com. Beautiful handmade cotton and silk sarongs, dresses, skirts, bags, etc, in bright primary colours.
Cotton Collection, 40 Ernest de Silva Mawatha, Col 7, www.cottoncollection.lk. Similar to **Odel** (see below), clothes for men, women and children.
French Corner, 24 Hyde Park Corner, Col 2.
House of Fashions, 28 RA de Mel Mawatha, Col 3. Cheaper and popular with locals.
Odel, 5 Alexandra Pl, Lipton Circus, Col 7, T268 2712. The place for shirts, t-shirts, sportswear and even jumpers, lots of choice

and the quality is good. The warehouse branch at Dickman's Rd, Col 5 is worth a visit, as it stocks different things.

Department stores and complexes

Crescat, Galle Rd, Col 3 (next to **Cinnamon Grand**). A small but upmarket shopping mall, brighter than the others. Internet café, Dilmah Tea, Mlesna, and branch of Vijitha Yapa bookshop. Foodcourt (see Eating, page 77) and supermarket in the basement.
Liberty Plaza, Dharmapala Mawatha, Col 3. Ageing mall.
Majestic City, Galle Rd, Col 4. The largest mall, it has a branch of Odel, as well as a cinema (see page 81) and a foodcourt (see Eating, page 79).
Odel, 5 Alexandra Pl, Lipton Circus, Col 7, T268 2712. A classy department store that sells clothes, shoes, soaps, cosmetics, jewellery, music and homewares, and has cafés, including Delifrance and a sushi bar.
Unity Plaza, opposite **Majestic City**. Branch of Vijitha Yapa bookshop and there is a Perera & Sons in the basement (see Eating, page 78).

Gemstones, silver and gold

These should only be bought at reputable shops; it is probably best to avoid the private jewellers in Sea St, the Pettah.
Sri Lanka Gem & Jewellery Exchange, World Trade Centre, East Tower, is a government institution with 34 wholesalers and retailers. The Gem Testing Laboratory, 5th floor, will test gems for foreigners (Rs 150 per stone).

Handloom and handicrafts

The government outlets offer good quality and reasonable prices, and the added bonus of not having to haggle. Here you can pick up masks, batiks, brasswork, silverwork, etc. Government outlets include: **Laksala**, 60 York St, Col 1, www.laksala.lk, which carries a wide range; **Lakmedura**, 113 Dharmapala Mawatha, Col 7, open until 1900;

Lanka Hands, 135 Bauddhaloka Mawatha, Col 4, 0930-1830; **Lakpahana**, 21 Rajakeeya Mawatha, Col 7, www.lakpahana.com.
Barefoot, 704 Galle Rd, Col 3, T258 9305 www.barefootceylon.com. Very popular shop with tourists and wealthy locals. Started by Barbara Sansoni, the artist, excellent handloom fabrics, home furnishings, batiks, clothes; also toys, bookshop (see above).
Prasanna Batiks, 35 Main St, Col 11. Batiks.

Supermarkets

Cargill's, 40 York St, Col 1; 407 Galle Rd, Col 3 (24-hr branch with pharmacy); 21 Staples St, Col 2; and at Majestic City.
Keells, at Crescat and Liberty Plaza.

Tea

The supermarkets listed above all stock a wide selection of tea.
Dilmah, www.dilmahtea.com. At Crescat and Odel shopping malls and the airport.
Mlesna Tea Centre, 44 Ward Place, Col 7, T269 6348, www.mlesnateas.com. Excellent range of teas, pots, etc. Several branches over town at Hilton, Crescat, Liberty Plaza, Majestic City and at the airport.
Sri Lanka Tea Board, 574 Galle Rd, Col 3.

▲ Activities and tours

Cricket

Colombo has several cricket stadiums.
Colombo Cricket Club, Maitland Place, Col 7, which has a very attractive colonial style pavilion, and **Nondescript's Cricket Club** (NCC), are next door to each other.
R Premadasa Stadium, Khettarama, Col 10. This large stadium hosts Tests and One-Days (sometimes day/night), and is where the 2011 World Cup matches were played.
Sinhalese Sports Club Ground (SSC), Maitland Pl, Col 7, T269 5362. Headquarters where Test matches and One-Day Internationals are played. Contact the Cricket Board here for tickets.

Diving

Though diving is possible off Colombo, most of the dive schools operate from coastal resorts, notably Hikkaduwa.

Colombo Divers, Mount Lavinia, on beach, near **Golden Mile**, T077-366 8679 (Olivenzo), www.colombodivers.com. Dives for US$55 plus US$10 for equipment; 2 reef, 1 wreck and 1 reef, or 2 wreck. The wrecks nearby are a tug and a cargo ship, 30 mins by boat to site. SSI and PADI courses available. Also operates from Negombo (see page 100).

Lanka Sportreizen, 29-b BS de S Jayasinghe Mawatha, Dehiwala, T276 7500, www.lsr-srilanka.com. Organizes diving, as well as nature and wildlife holidays.

Underwater Safaris, 25c Barnes Place, Col 7, T269 4012, www.underwatersafaris.org. Offers diving trips and PADI courses from Colombo and Hikkaduwa.

Football

Sugathadasa Stadium, A de Silva Mawatha, Col 13. For international matches.

Golf

Royal Colombo Golf Club, Ridgeway Golf Links, Col 8, T269 5431, www.rcgcsl.com. Offers temporary membership and has a dress code.

Rowing

Colombo Rowing Club, 51 Sir CA Gardiner Mawatha, Col 2 (opposite Lake House Bookshop), T243 3758. Offers temporary membership.

Swimming

Many hotels allow non-residents to use their pool on a daily basis for a fee.

Colombo Swimming Club, 148 Galle Rd, Col 3 (opposite Temple Trees, the President's Residence), T242 1645, www.colombo swimmingclub.org. Popular expats' hangout with pool, tennis, gym, bar, restaurant, initial membership Rs 100,000 (of which Rs 60,000 is refundable), temporary membership is available for Rs 1750 per week; you must be recommended by an existing member.

Tennis and squash

At the **Cinnamon Grand, Ceylon Continental, Taj Samudra** and **Cinnamon Lakeside** hotels. Also at: **Gymkhana Club**, 31 Maitland Cres, Col 7, T269 1025, and **Sri Lanka Ladies Squash Association**, T269 6256.

Tours and tour operators

Most tour operators offer half- or full-day city tours by car, typically visiting Kelaniya, Fort and the Pettah, the National Museum and usually Buddhist and Hindu temples. All tour operators will offer car hire and island tours. Some (eg **Aitken Spence, Jetwing, Keells**) run a number of luxury hotels on the southwest coast and elsewhere. Prices include their hotel and breakfast (if you choose your own hotel, a large reservation fee may be added). It is also possible to arrange trips to then national parks from Colombo.

Adventure Sports Lanka, Koswatte, T279 1584, www.actionlanka.com. Recommended for adventure activities such as whitewater rafting, mountain biking, canoeing and diving.

Aitken Spence, 305 Vauxhall St, Col 2, T230 8308, www.aitkenspencetravels.com. One of Sri Lanka's largest operators, with some of Sri Lanka's finest hotels, full range of services, excellent if expensive tours.

A Baur, 5 Upper Chatham St, Col 1, T244 8087, www.travel.baurs.com. Tours, including birdwatching.

Cox & Kings, 315 Vauxhall St, Col 2, T243 4295, www.coxandkings.co.uk.

George Travel, 2nd floor, 29 Ex-Serviceman's Building, Bristol St, Col 1, T242 2345. Recommended for international flight tickets, very popular with budget travellers.

Hemtours, 75 Braybrooke Pl, Col 2, T230 0001, www.hemas.com. Includes wildlife tours.

Jetwing, 46/26 Navam Mawatha, Col 2, T234 5700, www.jetwingtravels.com. Highly recommended for personalized service, good car and driver/guide, excellent network of hotels.

Jetwing Eco Tours, (as above),
www.jetwingeco.com. Excellent nature
and wildlife tours, personal service.
Keells, 130 Glennie St, Col 2, T232 0862,
www.johnkeellshotels.com. Wide range of
hotels, see also **Walkers Tours**, below.
Leopard Safaris, 45 Ambagahawatta,
Colombo Rd, Katunayake, T077-731 4004,
www.leopardsafaris.com. Excellent tented
safaris in Yala, Uda Walawe, Wilpattu and
the Knuckles.
Lion Royal Tourisme, 45 Braybrook St, Col 2,
T471 5996, www.lionroyaltourisme.com.
Personal service, reliable fleet of drivers and
generous discounts on a wide range of hotels.
Shanti Travel, 138/2-3 Kynsey Rd, Col 8, T465
4500, www.shantitravel.com. Predominantly
for the French market but staff speak
excellent English. Personal service, reliable.
Walkers Tours, 130 Glennie St, Col 2, T230
6727, www.walkerstours.com. Expensive
but recommended for excellent service.

Trekking, nature and weddings
Quickshaw's, 3 Kalinga Pl, Col 5, T258 3133,
www.quickshaws.com. Includes special tours
for birders, divers, cricketers, authors and
honeymooners.

Yachting
Royal Colombo Yacht Club, Colombo
Harbour. Welcomes experienced sailors.

◉ Transport

→ *Beware of pickpockets and avoid hotel touts
at bus and railway stations. See page 48 for
more information.*

Air
Domestic airport at Ratmalana, just south
of Mount Lavinia (500 m off Galle Rd), is used
for domestic flights. It remains primarily a
military airport, security is high and there are
few facilities. Domestic airlines include: **Expo
Aviation**, 466 Galle Rd, Col 3, T257 6941,
www.expoavi.com. Also check out the

Sri Lankan Airlines air taxi service. Airlines
provide a free bus to and from the city.
Bandaranaike International Airport,
T245 2911, www.airport.lk, (or Colombo),
is at Katunayake, about 6 km south of
Negombo and 30 km north of Colombo.
Aviation Services, T225 2861. The tourist
information counter will give advice,
brochures, maps, and the useful monthly
Travel Lanka magazine. See page 21
if arriving at night.

International airlines include: **Aeroflot**,
Taj Samudra Hotel, Col 2, www.aeroflot.org;
Air Canada, East Tower, World Trade Centre,
Col 1, T254 2875, www.aircanada.com;
Air France, Galle Face Hotel, Galle Rd,
Col 3, T232 7605, www.airfrance.com;
Air India, 4 Bristol St, Col 1, T232 6844,
www.airindia.in; **American Airlines**, Mack
Air (PVT) Ltd, 11A York St, Col 1, T234 8100,
www.aa.com; **British Airways**, 400 Deans
Rd, Col 10, T476 7767, www.ba.com; **Cathay
Pacific**, 186 Vauxhall St, Col 2, T233 4145,
www.cathaypacific.com; **Czech Airlines**,
Jetwing Air, 'Jetwing House', 140A Vauxhall
St, Col 2, T473 2481, www.csa.cz; **Delta**,
45 Jandhipathi Mawatha, Col 1, T233 8734,
www.delta.com; **Emirates**, Hemas House,
9th floor, 75 Braybrooke Place, Col 2,
T470 4070, www.emirates.com; **Gulf Air**,
1 Justice Akbar Mawatha, Col 2, T235 9888,
www.gulfair.com; **Kuwait Airways**, Ceylinco
House, 69 Janadhipathi Mawatha, Col 1,
T244 5531, www.kuwait-airways.com;
Oman Air, 400 Deans Rd, Col 10, T446
2222, www.omanair.com; **Pakistan
International Airlines**, 45 Ananda
Coomaraswamy Mawatha, Col 7, T257 6781,
www.piac.com.pk ; **Royal Jordanian**, 40 A
Kumaratunge Munidasa, Col 3, T230 1626,
www.rj.com; **Saudi Airlines**, 466 Galle Rd,
Col 6, T257 7242, www.saudiairlines.com;
Singapore Airlines, 315 Vauxhall St,
Col 2, T249 9699, www.singaporeair.com;
Sri Lankan Airlines, 3rd floor, East Tower,
World Trade Centre, Echelon Sq, Col 1,
T019-733 5500, www.srilankan.lk;
STA, 3rd floor, East Tower, World Trade

Centre, Echelon Sq, Col 1, T522 0027, www.statravel.com; **Thai Airways**, Hilton Residence, Union Place, Col 2, T230 7100, www.thaiairways.com; **United Airlines**, 06-02 East Tower, World Trade Centre, Echelon Sq, Col 1, T234 6026, www.united.com.

Boat

At the time of writing passenger services between Colombo Harbour and **Tuticorin**, India, had just started running after a long hiatus. 2 voyages a week are planned and the journey takes 10-13 hrs. Prices range from Rs 5500-75,000 depending on the level of comfort. Contact **Unicorn**, 12 Galle Face Court 2, Col 3, T230 2100.

Bus

Local Colombo has an extensive network of public and private buses competing on popular routes. Although the system can get very crowded, it is not difficult to use since the destinations are usually displayed in English. Useful services are those that run from Fort Railway Station down the Galle Rd (including Nos 100, 101, 102, 106, 133). No 138 goes from Fort past the Town Hall and the National Museum (Glass House stop, across the road); No 187 between Fort and the International airport. Numerous buses run up and down Galle Rd to **Mount Lavinia**. Nos 100, 101, 102, 105, 106, 133 and 134 go to **Fort**. Local buses have white signs, while long distance have yellow. Details of the 3 bus stations near Fort Railway Station are given below. **Ceylon Transport Board** (CTB), T258 1120. **Long distance** There is a good island-wide network and travel is cheap. Most major towns have an express service at least every 30 mins to 1 hr. There are 3 main bus stations in Colombo, all close to Fort Railway Station. All 3 are quite chaotic, choking with fumes, with services usually operating on a 'depart when full' basis.

CTB/Central, Olcott Mawatha, southeast corner of the Pettah (right from Fort station, and across the road), T232 8081. CTB buses, which are the cheapest, oldest

and slowest, and offer services to almost all island-wide destinations. Left luggage here is sometimes full.

Bastion Mawatha, to the east of Manning Market. Transport Authority, T242 1731. The buses are privately run, with the cost and journey time depending on whether you get an ancient bone-shaker ('normal' bus), 'semi-luxury', 'luxury' (with a/c), or the wanton sensuousness of a 'super-luxury' coaster. It serves most destinations to the east, southeast and south, including **Kandy** (luxury bus 3½ hrs), **Nuwara Eliya** (6 hrs), **Hikkaduwa** (2½ hrs), **Galle** (3 hrs), **Matara** (5 hrs), **Tangalla** (6 hrs), **Hambantota** (6½ hrs) and **Kataragama** (7½-8 hrs).

Saunders Place, just to the north of the CTB bus station, which also offers private a/c coasters and bone-shakers to destinations to the north and northeast, including **Ampara** (9 hrs), **Anuradhapura** (5-6 hrs), **Badulla** (7½ hrs), **Bandarawela** (7½ hrs), **Batticaloa** (7½ hrs), **Chilaw** (2 hrs), **Dambulla** (4 hrs), **Kurunegala** (2½ hrs), **Negombo** (1½ hrs), **Polonnaruwa** (5-6 hrs), **Puttalam** (3 hrs), **Trincomalee** (7 hrs), and **Vavuniya** (6 hrs). Private and public buses to **Jaffna** leave from Wellawatta (12-14 hrs).

Car hire

For general information on car hire, charges and self-drive versus being driven, see page 22. Most hotels and travel agents can arrange car hire (with or without driver). Agents include: **Avis**, Walkers Tours (see Activities and tours, above), www.avis.com, recommended; **Hertz**, Level 1, 130 Nawala Rd, T236 9333, www.hertz.com; **Lion Royal** (see Activities and tours, above), www.lionroyaltourisme.com; **Mal-Key**, 58 Pamankada Rd, Kirulapana, Col 6, T250 2008, www.malkey.lk; **Quickshaw's** (see Activities and tours, above), www.quick shaws.com, with chauffeur rates from Rs 5300 per day (Rs 37,000 per week) for 100 km per day, plus Rs 750 for driver's subsistence; self-drive from Rs 2900, the website has a good breakdown of costs and types of car.

Motorbike hire
Gold Wing Motors, 346 Deans Rd, Col 10, T268 5750. Rental on daily, weekly or monthly terms.

Taxi
Metered taxis have yellow tops and red-on-white number plates. Make certain that the driver has understood where you wish to go and fix a rate for long-distance travel. **Radio cabs** are very convenient and reliable (see page 24); **GNTC**, T268 8688, gntc@isplanka.lk, also has a branch at the airport, T225 1688, recommended but pricey; **Kangaroo Cabs**, T258 8588; **Unique Cabs**, T273 3733; **Yellow Cabs**, T294 2942.

Three-wheeler
3-wheelers are quick but you need to bargain hard (minimum usually Rs 50 per km), however there are now some metered 3-wheelers. Trips around Fort will cost Rs 150; Fort to Cinnamon Gardens, Rs 300. Fort to Mount Lavinia will cost upwards of Rs 500, the exact fee depending upon your negotiating skills (see page 24).

Train
Local Suburban train halts are Fort, Secretariat, Kompanna, Kollupitiya, Bambalapitiya, Wellawatta, Dehiwala, Mount Lavinia.

To Mount Lavinia from Fort, buy ticket from counter No 13. Suburban services run regularly between Fort and Mount Lavinia (and beyond), approximately every 30 mins (less frequently at weekends and holidays) between 0436 and 2135, though they can get packed at rush hour. They take 30 mins. Timings of the next train are chalked up on a blackboard. If heading south after Mount Lavinia, it is quicker to change at Moratuwa than retrace your steps to Fort.

Long distance The main station is Fort, actually located at the southwestern corner of the Pettah, though many trains originate in Maradana. There are trains to most places of interest on 4 separate lines.

Enquiries (express and commuter trains), T243 4215. Berths reservations, T243 2908. For foreign travellers, the **Railway Tourist Office**, Fort Station, T243 5838, can be useful (see page 59). Left luggage ('Cloak Room') is just past the **Intercity Reservation Office**, Rs 56 per locker per day but is often full. The Intercity Reservation Office is open 0630-1430, and this is where the tickets to Kandy can be arranged. The white board in the office outlines which trains and classes are full.

There are special a/c **Hitachi** trains for day tours to Kandy and Hikkaduwa. Occasional tours are arranged on vintage steam trains – details from the Railway Tourist Office.

Intercity trains to **Kandy** leave Fort at 0700 and 1535 (1st class, including observation car, Rs 360; 2nd class, reservation also required, Rs 220; 3rd class Rs 150; 2½ hrs). Return tickets are valid for 10 days, but the return date must be booked in advance. Normal trains to **Kandy** (2nd class Rs 190, 3rd class Rs 105, 3¼ hrs), via **Gampaha** (for **Heneratogoda**) and **Rambukkana** (for **Pinnawela**) leave at 1035, 1240 (to **Hatton**), 1635, 1745.

Trains to **Badulla** leave at 0555, 0930, 2000 (mail train). The 0930 (Udarata Menike) is express (9 hrs) with observation car (1st class Rs 750); the 2000 has 1st-class sleeping berths (Rs 750), and 2nd- (Rs 450) and 3rd- (Rs 270) class sleeperettes. Normal trains take 10-11 hrs (2nd class Rs 370, 3rd class Rs 205). All trains call at **Hatton** (for **Adam's Peak**, 4½-5½ hrs), **Nanu Oya** (for **Nuwara Eliya**, Rs 290/160, 6-7 hrs), **Ohiya** (for **Horton Plains**, 7-8 hrs), **Haputale** (8½-9½ hrs), **Bandarawela** (Rs 340/185, 9-10 hrs) and **Ella** (9½-10½ hrs).

On the Northern line to **Anuradhapura** (4 hrs) and **Vavuniya** (for **Jaffna**), an intercity train leaves Fort daily at 0545, 1620 (1st class a/c, 1620 train, with reservation Rs 750, 2nd class Rs 450). Normal trains to **Vavuniya** at 1345 and 2200 (mail train) (4½-5 hrs to **Anuradhapura**), via **Kurunegala** (2 hrs).

Vavuniya night train 1st-class sleeperette Rs 700, 2nd-class sleeper Rs 400, and 3rd-class sleeper Rs 250. For **Polonnaruwa**, 0600, 1030 (intercity), 1915 (intercity), (1st class Rs 750, 2nd class Rs 500, 3rd class Rs 320, 7½ hrs). To **Trincomalee**, take the 0600, 1030 (intercity), 2100 (1st-class sleeperette Rs 750, 2nd-class sleeper Rs 450, 3rd-class sleeper Rs 270), alternatively take the Batticaloa train, 0600, 1030 (intercity), 1915 (intercity, Rs 900, Rs 500, Rs 400), and change at Gal Oya.

Trains run every 1-2 hrs from 0520 to 2020 on the Puttalam line to **Negombo** (1½ hrs), via **Katunayake** (for the **airport**), a few continuing to **Chilaw** and **Puttalam** (4 hrs).

Trains south to **Galle** (2½-3 hrs) leave Fort at 0710 (1st class available), 0900, 1030, 1405, 1640, 1700, 1725, 1750 and 1930. Most call at **Kalutara**, **Aluthgama**, **Ambalangoda** and **Hikkaduwa**, and continue to **Matara** (3½-4 hrs), with stops at **Talpe** and **Weligama** and in some cases other south coast beach resorts.

● Directory

Banks
Banks with 24-hr ATMs are widespread throughout Colombo. York St has a large concentration. Banks usually open at 0900 and close at 1300 or 1500, though are keeping increasingly flexible hours. Some branches open for Sat morning and have an evening service; most are closed on Sun, *poya* days and national holidays.

Bank of Ceylon, Bureau de Change, York St, Fort, is now open 24 hrs a day, including holidays for encashment of TCs and foreign currency. Cirrus ATMs are found mainly at private banks such as **Commercial Bank** and **Sampath Bank** and foreign banks in Fort. Most give cash advances on Visa and MasterCard. There are numerous licensed moneychangers in Fort area, notably on Mudalige Mawatha, offering marginally better rates for cash. Hotels generally offer

a poor rate of exchange for cash and TCs, though they may be convenient for residents.

Couriers
DHL, Keells (Pvt) Ltd, 130 Glennie St, Col 2, T254 1285, www.dhl.com. See page 47 for details of rates.

Cultural centres
Most have a library and a reading room and have regular music and film programmes. **Alliance Française**, 11 Bomes Place, Col 7, T269 4162, www.alliancefr.lk. Tue-Fri 0900-1800, Sat 0900-1530. Shows films on Fri. **American Center**, 44 Galle Rd, Col 3, T233 2725. Tue-Sat 1000-1800. Shows film on Tue from 1800. **British Council**, 49 Alfred House Gardens, Col 3, T258 1171, www.britishcouncil.org/srilanka. Tue-Sat, 0900-1800, Sun 0900-1630. **German (Goethe) Cultural Institute**, 39 Gregory's Rd, Col 7, T269 4562, www.goethe.de/srilanka. Mon-Fri 0900-1300, 1500-1700. **Indian Cultural Centre**, 16/2 Gregory's Rd, Col 7, T268 4698. **Russian Cultural Centre**, 10 Independence Av, Col 10, T268 5440. Mon-Fri 0900-1700.

Embassies and consulates
Australia, 21 Gregory's Rd, Col 7, T246 3200, www.srilanka.embassy.gov.au. **Canada**, 33A, 5th Lane, Colpetty, Col 3, T522 6232. **France**, 89 Rosmead Place, Col 5, T263 9400, www.ambafrance-lk.org. **Germany**, 40 Alfred House Av, Col 3, T258 0431, www.colombo.diplo.de. **India**, 36-38 Galle Rd (next to Galle Face Hotel), Col 3, T232 7587, www.hcicolombo.org. Mon-Fri 0900-1730, visas 0930-1200. Can take up to 5 working days to process visas, take 2 passport photos, expect a long wait; or go to Kandy where it is usually quicker. **Italy**, 55 Jawathe Rd, Col 5, T258 8388, www.ambcolombo.esteri.it. **Japan**, 20 Gregory's Rd, Col 7, T269 3831, www.lk.emb-japan.go.jp. **New Zealand**, 329 Park Rd, Col 5, T250 1139. **South Africa**, 114 Rosmead Pl, Col 7, T268 9926. **UK**, 389 Bauddhaloka Mawatha, Col 7, T539 0639,

www.ukinsrilanka.fco.gov.uk. Mon-Thu 0800-1630, Fri 0800-1300. **USA**, 210 Galle Rd, Col 3, T249 8500, www.srilanka.usembassy. gov. Mon-Fri 0800-1700.

Emergency services
Fire and ambulance, T242 2222. **Police**, T243 3333. Police stations, south of Maradana Railway Station, Kollupitiya, Bambalapitiya and Wellawatta.

Internet
Internet is widely available, though varies wildly in price. A number of hotels and guesthouses now offer internet, although some charge an additional fee which can be high. American chain restaurants and coffee houses often have free internet available for patrons, for example McDonald's and Baskin-Robbins. Internet cafés abound.

Libraries
Colombo Public Library, 15 Sir Marcus Fernando Mawatha, Col 7, T469 1968, www.colombopubliclibrary.org. Mon-Fri 0830-2000, Sat-Sun 0830-1900. Small fee.

Medical services
Chemists There are a number on Galle Rd, Union Place and in the Pettah and Fort. **State Pharmaceutical** outlets at Hospital Junction, Col 7 and Main St, Fort. Pharmacies in **Keells Supermarket**, Liberty Plaza, Dharmapala Mawatha, Col 3 and **Cargill's**, Galle Rd, Col 3 (24 hrs). **City Dispensary**, 505 Union Pl, Col 2. **Ward Place Pharmacy**, 24a Ward Pl, Col 7.
   Herbal and Ayurvedic centres
Mount Clinic of Oriental Medicine, 41 Hotel Rd, Mount Lavinia, T272 3464, offers acupuncture, Ayurvedic and Chinese medical massage, including 'milk rice massage'. **Siddhalepa Ayurveda Hospital**, 106 Templer's Rd, Mount Lavinia, T272 2524. Authentic herbal and Ayurvedic health programmes include herbal/steam baths and massage but fairly 'stark and institutional'; rooms available for longer stays.

Hospitals If you need an English-speaking doctor, ask at your hotel or guesthouse. There is also a list of suggested practitioners and dentists on the British Embassy website www.ukinsrilanka.fco. gov.uk. **General Hospital,** 10 Regent St, T269 2222, T269 1111 (24-hr A&E), is the main public hospital. **Government Ayurvedic Hospital**, 325 Cotta Rd, Borella, T269 5855, or see Mount Lavinia, below. Homeopathy and herbal medicine. Foreigners often prefer to use the more expensive private hospitals: **Asha Central**, 33 Horton Pl, Col 7, T269 6411. **Asiri**, 181 Kirula Rd, Col 5, T250 0608; **Durdan's**, 3 Alfred Pl, Col 3, T541 0000; **McCarthy's**, 22 Wijerama Mawatha, Col 7, T697 760; **Nawaloka**, 23 Sri Saugathodaya Mawatha, Col 2, T244 6258, T254 4444 (24-hr).

Post
GPO, Bristol St, next to the Ex-Serviceman's Institute, Fort, T232 6203, open 0700-1800, Mon-Sat (Poste Restante 0845-1645). Post office in Mount Lavinia is on Station Rd.

Telephone
Skype is increasingly available. Numerous private telephone offices offer more or less standard rates for IDD (International Direct Dialling) calls. Card pay phones offer 24-hr service and much lower rates than hotels. Phone cards of various denominations are sold in shops and kiosks near pay phones. Alternatively, if staying in Sri Lanka for longer than a couple of weeks invest in a SIM card, Dialog provides good coverage.

Useful addresses
Automobile Association of Ceylon, 40 Sir MM Markar Mawatha, Galle Face, Col 3, T242 1528, www.aaceylon.lk. Mon-Fri 0800-1630, for issue of temporary Sri Lankan driving permit (bring 2 photos, photocopy of your national licence and international driving permit) and go to the 3rd floor. At the time of writing the endorsement cost Rs 500 per month.

Central Cultural Fund (Cultural Triangle Office), 212/1 Bauddhaloka Mawatha, Col 7 (to the right and halfway to the back of building), T250 0732, www.ccf.lk. The 21-day Visitors' Permit is on sale (US$50) for entry to the sites and photography; information booklets are also available. The permits are easier and quicker to get at the sites (Anuradhapura, Kandy, Polonnaruwa or Sigiriya).

Department of Wildlife Conservation Department, 382 New Kandy Rd, Malabe, on the outskirts of Colombo, T288 8585.

Ministry of Defence, Galle Face Rd, opposite Galle Face Green and on the right if coming from Galle Face Hotel. Look for a checkpoint with a wealth of military personnel and vehicles and you're in the right place. Visit the permit office and submit a letter requesting permission to travel to the North. Include your name, address, passport number, intended dates of travel, and specify if you require a land or air permit. You also need to provide a copy of your passport and an address where you will be staying. It can take up to 4 days to process, so try to leave yourself enough time to travel up there as you can only undertake the journey on the dates on your permit (and the trains are often booked up). Carry this and your passport with you at all times when in the North.

Contents

West & Northwest

★ Don't miss ...
1 Negombo, page 94.
2 Kalpitiya Peninsula, page 103.
3 Yapahuwa, page 109.

Portugal Bay

Wilpattu National Park

Anuradhapura

A20

Nuwara Wewa

A13

Kalpitiya

Karaitivu

Nochchiyagama

Talawa

Kala Oya

Kala Oya

Tambuttegama

A28

Eppawala

Puttalam Lagoon

Talawila

A12

Mahagalkadawala

Kalpitiya Peninsula

Puttalam

Sasseruwa

Palavi

A10

Yapahuwa

Daladagama

Medagalla

Maho

Polpitigama

Mundel Lake

Andigama

Udappuwa

Kiriyankalli

Nikaweratiya

Battulu-Oya

A28

Padeniya

Ganewatta

A10

Arankele

A6

Panduwasnuwara

Wariyapola

Hettipola

Chilaw

Ridigama

Munneswaram

Madampe

Kuliyapitiya

Kurunegala

Dandagamuwa

Dambokka

Naramala

Mawatagama

A10

Marawila

Galketigedara

A3

Dambadeniya

Polgahawela

Pannala

Giriulla

Pinnawela

Waikkal

Alawwa

Kegalla

Maha Oya

Dankotuwa

N

Diwulapitiya

Mirigama

A1

Negombo

Warakapola

10 km

10 miles

Other than a day or two spent on the beach at Negombo, one of the most developed and least prepossessing resorts on the west coast, most travellers tend to pass through the West and Northwest regions, heading straight for the more spectacular sights of the Ancient Triangle or the cooler climes of Kandy. Yet this region possesses its own proud history, with a reasonable claim to be the cradle of Sri Lankan civilization. It was here that Prince Vijaya, the founder of the Sinhalese race, first landed in AD 543. It also boasts no fewer than four ancient capitals, founded in a game of medieval cat-and-mouse to hide the sacred Tooth Relic from foreign invaders.

The area is also where the Wet Zone meets the Dry Zone. Around the densely populated northern suburbs of Colombo, closely packed coconut groves, occasional strands of forest and intensive cultivation contribute to the lush, evergreen landscape. A few kilometres north of Chilaw, however, the Deduru Oya marks the ancient boundary between the wet western hill country and the dry irrigated lands of the north. The landscape becomes increasingly barren and beyond the recently reopened Wilpattu National Park, Sri Lanka's largest protected area, in the northern boundary of the region, lie the arid wastes of the Wanni.

From west to east the landscape also undergoes a transformation. The wide shallow lagoons of the sand-fringed coast give way to the forest-clad hills and mountains of the highlands.

Negombo

→ *Phone code: T031. Colour map 2, C1. Population: 140,000.*

Owing to its proximity to the international airport, 6 km away, Negombo is the principal resort north of Colombo. It has a wide range of accommodation, and is a convenient place to end a holiday (or begin it if the flight schedules are unkind), although the beach can be dirty – if you are looking for an unspoilt strip of white sand head down south where the beaches are far superior. Moreover, some find Negombo seedy – Sri Lankans regard it as their vice capital, with visible evidence of prostitution and worse, though on an international scale its problems are fairly minor. Negombo town, although a little scruffy, does have a picturesque lagoon and a few interesting reminders of the Portuguese and Dutch periods. → For listings, see pages 97-101.

Ins and outs

Getting there Negombo town is easily accessible from the airport by taxi, three-wheeler or bus. It takes about 20 minutes. Hotels can often arrange a transfer on request. From Colombo, take the No 240 bus (every 15-20 minutes) from Saunders Place bus stand in the Pettah which takes about an hour. The train from Fort Station also takes about an hour.

Getting around The main tourist area is 2-4 km north of the town itself. You can walk most of the way along the beach (which gets progressively more inviting), or take a three-wheeler (Rs 150), or the Kochchikade bus (No 905) from the bus station. Frequent buses run along the main beach road from the bus and railway stations in Negombo Town. Bicycles can be hired to explore area. Three-wheelers offer Negombo town tours.

Best time to visit Swimming and watersports are only safe from November to April, outside the southwestern monsoon period. Easter is celebrated with Passion plays, particularly on Easter Saturday on Duwa island. In July the **Fishermen's festival** at St Mary's Church is a major regional celebration.

Sights

The Portuguese originally built a **fort** on the headland guarding the lagoon in about 1600. Since the area was rich in spices, particularly the much prized cinnamon, it changed hands several times before the Portuguese were finally ousted by the Dutch in 1644. In attempting to make Negombo an important centre, the Dutch built a much stronger structure but this was largely destroyed by the British who pulled much of it down to build a jail. Today, only the gatehouse to the east (dated 1678) with its rather crooked clocktower survives. The place is still used as a prison and the District Court is tucked away in a corner of the grounds.

A more enduring monument to the Dutch is the **canal system**. Originally explored in the 15th century, they were improved and expanded by the Dutch who recognised their advantage in transporting spices – cinnamon, cloves, pepper, cardamoms – and precious gems from the interior and along the coast to the port of Negombo for loading on ships sailing for distant shores. Today you can see this if you follow St Joseph Road into Custom House Road and around the headland. It skirts the lagoon where mainly fishing boats are moored (witness to its thriving fishing industry). The junction of the canal is just past the bridge crossing the lagoon. Unfortunately at its mouth it is dirty and not that appealing.

St Mary's Church dominates the town. It is one of many churches that bears witness to the extent of Portuguese conversions to Roman Catholicism, especially among the fishermen in Negombo District. Work began in 1874 and was only completed in 1922. There are a number of alabaster statues of saints and of the Easter story as well as a colourfully painted ceiling.

There are three **Hindu temples** on Sea Street. The largest, Sri Muthu Mari Amman, has a colourful *gopuram* in the inner courtyard.

The area is very rich in marine life and although there is much evidence of a motorized fleet in the harbour, you can still see fishermen using catamarans and

Negombo Beach

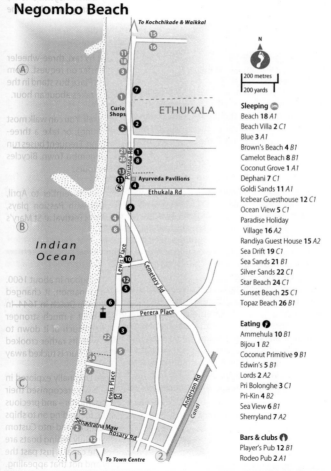

To Kochchikade & Waikkal

ETHUKALA

Curio Shops

Indian Ocean

Lewis Place

Cemetery Rd

Potutala Rd

Ayurveda Pavilions

Ethukala Rd

Perera Place

Anderson Rd

Canal

Senaviratna Maw

Rosary Rd

To Town Centre

N

200 metres
200 yards

Sleeping
Beach 18 *A1*
Beach Villa 2 *C1*
Blue 3 *A1*
Brown's Beach 4 *B1*
Camelot Beach 8 *B1*
Coconut Grove 1 *A1*
Dephani 7 *C1*
Goldi Sands 11 *A1*
Icebear Guesthouse 12 *C1*
Ocean View 5 *C1*
Paradise Holiday
 Village 16 *A2*
Randiya Guest House 15 *A2*
Sea Drift 19 *C1*
Sea Sands 21 *B1*
Silver Sands 22 *C1*
Star Beach 24 *C1*
Sunset Beach 25 *C1*
Topaz Beach 26 *B1*

Eating
Ammehula 10 *B1*
Bijou 1 *B2*
Coconut Primitive 9 *B1*
Edwin's 5 *B1*
Lords 2 *A2*
Pri Bolonghe 3 *C1*
Pri-Kin 4 *B2*
Sea View 6 *B1*
Sherryland 7 *A2*

Bars & clubs
Player's Pub 12 *B1*
Rodeo Pub 2 *A1*

Catholicism and canals

The coastal road runs through the region most affected by Portuguese colonialism. Their imprint is clearly visible in the high proportion of Roman Catholics, and the number of Catholic churches in the numerous villages through which the road passes. Nearly a quarter of the population immediately inland from Negombo is Christian, increasing in the north to almost 40%. The common nature of names like Fernando and Perera gives one clue as to why their resolve to convert was so successful!

Dutch influence is also evident in the now unused canal which was built between Colombo and Negombo. Once it was busy with the flat-bottomed 'padda' boats which travelled the 120 km between Colombo and Puttalam. As the Rev James Cordimer wrote in 1807 "the top of the canal (near Colombo) is constantly crowded with large flat-bottomed boats, which come down from Negombo with dried fish and roes, shrimps, firewood, and other articles. These boats are covered with thatched roofs in the form of huts". The Dutch built canals extensively not just around Colombo but also around Galle in the south, but they were relatively minor works compared to the 1000 km of irrigation canals already dug by the Sinhalese by the 12th century. The boats on these canals were often pulled by two men in harness. Now though the canal banks are largely the preserve of people strolling along the waterway. You can hire bikes at several points, including Negombo, and ride along a section of the banks.

ancient outrigger canoes to bring up their catch onto the beach every day. The outrigger canoes known as *oruva* here are not made from hollowed-out tree trunks but rather the planks are sewn together and caulked to produce a fairly wide canoe with an exceptionally flat bottom. Look out for them as some are often beached in front of the hotels. You can usually see the fleet early in the morning returning to harbour, each canoe under a three-piece sail. Their catch includes seer, skipjack, herring, mullet, pomfret, amberjack, and sometimes sharks. Prawns and lobster are caught in the lagoon. There are a number of fish markets – one is near the bridge on Duwa Island across the lagoon and there is another beyond the fort.

The nearest **reef** is 3 km off the beach hotel area with corals within 10-20 m, though the quality of this inner reef is poor. There are much better reefs further out, teeming with marine life including barracuda (even rare giant barracuda), blue-ringed angels and unusual starfish. Make sure you go with a registered (eg PADI) dive school.

Muthurajawela marsh in the lagoon is an estuarine wetland which harbours the saltwater crocodile, which can grow up to 9 m in length, as well as many species of birds such as the pied kingfisher. More information and boat tours (with wildlife guide) can be obtained from the **Visitor Centre** ① *T074-830150, Tue-Sun 0700-1800*. Tours are also arranged by hotels and guesthouses in Negombo, and tour operators, see page 100.

For Sleeping and Eating price codes and other relevant information, see pages 26-32.

⊕ Sleeping

Most people choose to stay in the beach area north of Negombo town. Hotels are spread out for almost 2 km, mostly on Lewis Place and further north on Porutota Rd in Ethukala. The junction of Lewis Place, Porutota and Cemetery roads forms a convenient mid-point. To its south are most of the cheaper guesthouses while to the north are the more expensive package hotels. Some hotels don't allow Sri Lankans accompanying tourists to stay, partly because the area has been a suspect destination for shady practices. Most larger hotels offer watersports. There is currently a lot of building work going on in Negombo, so new hotels and restaurants will be open by the time you read this.

Negombo Town *p94*

F New Rest House, 14 Circular Rd, T222 2299. Slightly tired rooms, some in the 300-year-old villa, others in the new building at the back. All with fan, some with a veranda, spacious open areas with pleasant furnishings, bar, restaurant. Attractive position though a little too close to the fish market.

Negombo Beach *p94, map p95*

LL-L Beach (Jetwing), Porutota Rd, T227 3500, www.jetwinghotels.com. 75 rooms with balcony, and 3 suites with rain shower and jacuzzi. Pool (open to non-residents when occupancy is low), sports (non-residents tennis Rs 1000, gym. **LL-L Blue** (Jetwing), Porutota Rd, T229 9003, www.jetwinghotels.com. Recently renovated, with 103 large rooms, 6 suites and 3 family rooms, not all with good views. Typical resort hotel, with all amenities and excellent service, good pool, entertainment, and watersports such as kitesurfing organized.

AL Brown's Beach (Aitken Spence), 175 Lewis Pl, T555 5000, www.aitkenspence hotels.com. 140 a/c rooms, including 25 beachside rooms in busy resort hotel popular with families. Full facilities, good reasonable restaurants, large pool (non-residents Rs 400), nightclub (2130, Rs 1000, ladies free), sports. Book in advance.
A-B Paradise Holiday Village, 154/9 Porutota Rd, T227 4588, www.paradise holidayvillage.com. 32 rooms and 17 apartments with kitchenette and living area built around central courtyard. Restaurant, pool, pleasant gardens.
B Goldi Sands, Poutota Rd, T227 9021, www.goldisands.com. At the time of writing construction work on this hotel was just coming to an end. 75 a/c rooms with balcony, some with sea views. Bar, restaurant and tours. Helpful and professional staff.
B-D Topaz Beach, 21 Porutota Rd, T227 9265, www.topazbeachhotel.com. 30 good-sized rooms, fan and a/c. Views better from 2nd and 3rd floors, restaurant.
C Camelot Beach, 345 Lewis Pl, T223 5881, camelothotel@sltnet.lk. 86 mainly a/c rooms, ugly modern exterior but attractive wood panelling inside, very friendly and helpful. Focus is around the swimming pools (non-residents, Rs 500), 2 bars, restaurant. Popular with package tourists.
C Sunset Beach, 5 Carron Pl, T222 2350, www.hotelsunsetbeach.com. 42 small a/c rooms in 3-storey block on the beach, upper floors more spacious, clean, light and airy, pool, useful local information. Can organize fishing trips.
C-D Icebear Guesthouse, 103-2 Lewis Pl, T223 3862, www.icebearhotel.com (English), www.icebearhotel.net (German). Attractively furnished rooms in bungalows and 'villas', in well-kept Swiss-owned guesthouse. Pleasant garden with wonderful secluded feel, personal attention, good home cooking (book in advance for evening meal), free Wi-Fi and bicycles.

D-E Randiya Guest House, 154/7 Porutota Rd, T227 9568, www.randiya.com. 15 rooms with verandas in peaceful bird-filled setting, 10 fan only, 5 with a/c, breakfast included.

E Coconut Grove, Porutota Rd, T487 2375. 15 decent fan rooms set back from the road, good view upstairs, restaurant, also Ayurveda health centre.

E-F Ocean View, 104 Lewis Pl, T223 8689, www.oceanview-negombo.com. Upstairs rooms cleaner and more spacious, lower ones small and grubby but with nice seating areas outside. As it's on the road, downstairs rooms can be noisy. Friendly, organizes tours.

F Dephani, 189/15 Lewis Pl, T223 4359, dephanie@slt.lk. 11 clean, comfortable rooms with nets (some with sea views), in very friendly family-run guesthouse, small balconies (better upstairs), restaurant.

E-G Silver Sands, 229 Lewis Pl, T222 2880, www.silversands.go2lk.com. 15 large, well-kept, clean fan and a/c rooms, cheaper downstairs, best with large sea-facing balconies, good restaurant, helpful owner, reliable taxi service, best value in this class, popular so book ahead.

E-G Star Beach, 83/3 Lewis Pl, T222 2606. Clean rooms, downstairs are cheap but gloomy, upstairs most have balcony, private or shared, and some rooms have sea view. Restaurant looks out onto the beach. Friendly.

F Sea Sands, 7 Porutota Rd, T227 9154. 11 simple fan rooms with attached bath and shared balcony, friendly, reasonable. **Dolce Vita** at back, see Eating, page 99.

F-G Beach Villa, 3/2 Senaviratne Mawatha, T222 2833, www.beachvillanegombo.com. 15 a/c and fan rooms, restaurant next to the beach, travel desk. Internet and Ayurvedic treatments. The budget option so don't expect too much.

F-G Sea Drift, 2A Carron Pl, T223 5534, himanthajayaweera@yahoo.com. Fan rooms in family guesthouse (one of the originals in Negombo), kitchen facilities available, friendly.

Ayurvedic resort

Ayurveda Pavilions (Jetwing), Porutota Rd, T487 0764, www.jetwinghotels.com. 12 exquisitely, though deceptively simply furnished villas (King's villa US$260, Queen's villa US$220, prices vary depending on the season so check the website for up-to-date tariffs). Each villa has beautiful front garden with frangipani tree, open-air bath, own massage table, and DVD player. Very ecologically sound, attention to detail and personal service is breathtaking. Treatment packages from 3 days (US$300) to 30 days (US$1800). The ultimate treat.

Towards the airport

F Srilal Fernando, 67 Parakrama Rd, Kurana, T222 2481. 5 rooms set around a courtyard, with very clean bath and fan in spacious family home, excellent food, good value, German spoken.

● Eating

Negombo Town *p94*

¶¶ **Icebear Century Café**, 25 Main St, T223 8097. Owned by the same people as the **Icebear Guesthouse** (see Sleeping, page 97), this café offers coffee, tea, cake and sandwiches in an airy space in the town centre.
¶ **Choys**, 31 Custom House Rd, T222 2807. In a pleasant location on the lagoon.
¶ **Sapuna** and **Wonshis**, St Joseph's Rd. Serves reasonable Chinese.

Negombo Beach *p94, map p95*

Most of the upmarket hotels in Porutota Rd serve all-you-can-eat buffets. The tendency is towards Western food or mild and rather insipid curries but seafood is the speciality: lobster, crab and prawns are all excellent, and the fish, particularly tuna and seer, are also excellent. The restaurants and bars along Lewis Pl tend to be cheaper.
¶¶¶ **Lords**, 80B Portutota Rd, T077-723 4721, www.lordsrestaurant.net. Chic eatery with catfish in small pools in the courtyard.

Expensive but tasty food, beautifully presented. British meals such as shepherd's pie if you're feeling homesick but also Asian fusion. If you can't afford a meal, just go for one of the fresh juices. Extensive mocktail menu for non-drinkers. Art gallery.

¶¶¶-¶¶ Edwin's, 204 Lewis Pl, T223 9164. Excellent Sri Lankan meals, devilled prawns, Rs 700. Generous portions, attentive host, try the rice and curry.

¶¶¶-¶ Ammehula, 286 Lewis Pl, opposite **Camelot Beach Resort**, T077-962 0349. Small but good restaurant, seafood speciality (fish is presented to you for inspection), good pancakes, rice and curry (Rs 600); huge portions.

¶¶¶-¶ Sea View, 319 Lewis Pl, T223 3762. Popular seafood restaurant, serving Sri Lankan and Western food. Small and busy.

¶¶ Bijou, opposite **Sea Sands**. Swiss-owned and moderately expensive (although much cheaper than the tourist hotels), fondue Rs 2200-2900 (order in advance), excellent for seafood and noodles.

¶¶ Coconut Primitive, 108 Lewis Pl, on Browns Beach Junction, T487 4766. Have just moved to new premises next door to their old spot and will soon be offering rooms. Food is Sri Lankan and Western, quality is good and price is reasonable.

¶¶-¶ Dolce Vita, 27 Porutota Rd, T077-743 6318, www.freewebs.com/dolcevitasrilanka. Coffee shop selling cake and more filling meals. A good place to watch the kitesurfers.

¶¶-¶ Pri-Kin, 10 Porutota Rd, T227 8646. Don't be put off by the outside. Friendly and offers excellent northern Chinese dishes, as well as Western and Sri Lankan; try the soups and prawn dishes.

¶¶-¶ Sherryland, set back from Porutota Rd in a garden. Attentive service, lively bar and good range of cocktails, good value. Set menu and Lion lager Rs 430-900.

¶ Pri Bolonghe 146 Lewis Pl, T223 3733. Authentic Sri Lankan breakfast if order the night before; evening meals of rice and curry, etc. Seating in a large leafy garden so bring mosquito repellent.

◐ Bars and clubs

Negombo *p94, map p95*
Most hotels have at least one bar, or serve alcohol in their restaurant. Some of the larger hotels have nightclubs (open 2130, dress 'smart but casual'). There are also an increasing number of Western-style bars.
Players Pub, has 2 billiard tables, is popular with Brits and boasts that it stays open longer than anywhere else in Negombo (0130 or when the last person left standing leaves!).
Rodeo Pub is very popular.

✷ Festivals and events

Negombo *p94, map p95*
Mar/Apr Easter, holds a special place in this strongly Catholic area. There are numerous passion plays usually held on Easter Sat, the most famous of which is on Duwa Island which involves the whole community. Station yourself between the 2 churches on Sea St (1 km south of Lewis Place) if short of time. Young girls in spotless white dresses are carried shoulder high by 4 men between the churches. This takes place in the afternoon but preparations take most of the day.

◎ Shopping

Negombo *p94, map p95*
The curio stalls near the large hotels are handy for getting last-minute presents. Quality varies considerably and they are not nearly as good as when you buy direct upcountry. Visit them all before deciding and then bargain hard. There are tailors all along Porutota Rd.

▲ Activities and tours

Negombo *p94, map p95*
Ayurvedic massage
Many hotels now offer Ayurvedic massage.

Boat trips

Fishermen take tourists out to see the lagoon and canal. These can be arranged directly with the fishermen on the beach; alternatively hotels and guesthouses can organize trips. Prices vary depending on who you go with, how long the trip is and what is involved.

Diving and snorkelling

Fishermen offer boat trips for snorkelling. Only dive with a PADI-qualified operation and be careful of other dive operations.
Colombo Divers, **Jetwing Beach Hotel**, T077-366 8679, www.colombodivers.com. PADI and SSI dive centre, 2 standard dives with equipment €53/US$70, €61/US$80 for the outer reef. €188/US$250 for 10 dives. Open Water €315-338/US$420-450, also offers advanced and specialty courses.
Sri Lanka Diving Tours, T77-764 8459, www.srilanka-divingtours.com. PADI dive centre offering 2 dives for US$70 and Open Water for US$410, German and English spoken. Also arranges diving in Trincomalee and trips to the wreck of *HMS Hermes* (see page 321).

Fishing

Major hotels offer deep-sea fishing and 'leisure fishing'

Swimming

It is dangerous to swim in the sea, particularly during the southwest monsoon May-Oct. Most of the larger hotels allow non-residents to use their pools (Rs 400-500).

Tennis

Brown's Beach (see Sleeping) allows non-residents to use their tennis facilities (Rs 500 includes racquets and balls). **Beach** (see Sleeping) allows non-residents to use their tennis courts for Rs 1000.

Tour operators

In addition to hotel travel desks, independent travel agents include:

Airwing Tours, 68 Colombo Rd, T223 8116, www.airwingtours.com. Offers several 'eco' tours for birdwatchers, photographers, trekkers, etc.). Also has an office at the airport.
Mr Lakshman Bolonghe, 146 Lewis Pl, T077-497 6919. Good English-speaking guide, who can arrange half-day birdwatching tours.

Watersports

Windsurfing can be arranged through **Blue** (see Sleeping). Hire is US$20 per hr but if combined with a lesson is US$25 per hr.

⊝ Transport

Negombo *p94, map p95*
To the airport

Frequent buses (No 240 to Colombo) stop close to the airport from early morning to late evening but can be crowded. Taxis cost Rs 1000 from Ethukala hotels. Expect to pay a little more at night. Most hotels/guesthouses can arrange taxis for you. 3-wheelers charge Rs 800 but the journey is not for the faint-hearted, there is a lot of traffic.

Bicycle hire

Available from many hotels/guesthouses; about Rs 250 per day. The flat roads make a short trip out of Negombo attractive.

Bus

Long-distance services depart from the bus stand. There are regular services to **Colombo** (No 240), both intercity express (1-1½ hrs) and the cheaper, slower CTB buses. There are frequent buses to **Kandy** (No 1), which leave mainly early morning or mid-late afternoon. Also to **Kurunegala** (No 34), and **Chilaw** (No 907).

Car/motorbike hire/taxi

Car hire/taxi is mostly through hotels; inspect vehicles carefully and expect to pay about US$200-270 per week with driver. For motorbike hire costs from Rs 2000 per day.

Alma Tours, 217 Lewis Pl, T487 3624, almatours65@yahoo.com. Hires out cars, motorbikes and mopeds.

Three-wheeler
Drivers cruise the main beach road from Lewis Pl to Ethukala. From Lewis Pl to the bus or railway stations expect to pay around Rs 150, and up to Rs 200 from the hotels in Ethukala. Beware of touts.

Train
The regular commuter train goes to **Colombo** via **Katunayake** (for the airport). Avoid this train during rushhour, and especially Mon morning, when it gets very crowded. Also 6 trains a day to **Chilaw** and **Puttalam**.

❶ Directory

Negombo *p94, map p95*
Banks Bank of Ceylon, Main St nearly opposite St Mary's. **Sampath Bank** and **Seylan Bank**, Rajapasksha Broadway.
Laundry There are many places where visitors can get their laundry done, or it can be organized through the hotel or guesthouse. Some charge by the garment, others by weight. **Medical services** Most hotels and guesthouses have doctors on call. **General Hospital**, Colombo Rd, T222 2261.
Post office Main St towards the fort. The **H20 Centre**, Lewis Pl, currently offers the cheapest rates and is open until 2230. It is also where you'll find the Agency post office. In Negombo town **Jezi Cyber Spot**, 84 St Joseph's St (near the bus station), T222 1821. **Useful numbers** Tourist **police**, Ethukala, T222 4287.

Northwest coast

North of Negombo, you cross from the West to Northwest Province, traditionally known as Wayamba Province. It is an area of fishing hamlets and seemingly endless groves of coconut palms, while inland is a rich agricultural patchwork of paddy fields and plantations. The 'carpeting' of the coastal road to Puttalam in 2002 made this the quickest route from Colombo to Anuradhapura, and many pass through without stopping. However, there are some worthwhile attractions: secluded beaches, ancient Hindu temples, a 'forgotten' peninsula and Sri Lanka's recently reopened largest national park. ⟶ For listings, see pages 104-106.

Beaches north of Negombo → Phone code: Waikkal 031 and Marawila 032. Colour map 2, C1.

There are two main beach areas which lack the bustle (and hassle) of Negombo but are still within easy reach of the airport. **Waikkal**, 12 km north of Negombo, is attractively sited on a meandering river but is quite remote so you are dependent on transport to get anywhere. It is, however, the site of one of the island's most impressive eco-resorts, which organizes a wide array of nature-based activities.

A further 11 km north is **Marawila**, which has a large Roman Catholic church, curious Italianate houses and a reputation for producing good-quality batiks. There are a growing number of resort-style hotels here, though the area has never really taken off on the scale of resorts further south. The beach is good in places but sometimes gives way to breakwaters constructed of large rocks.

Along the west coast to Puttalam → Phone code: 032. Colour map 2, B1/C1.

Beyond Marawila and after crossing the estuary, the road passes between the lagoon and the railway through **Madampe**, which is known for its Coconut Research Institute and **Taniwella Devale**, a colourful harvest festival held in August in which the whole farming community participates.

Chilaw, 75 km north of Colombo, is a small town with a large fish market and a big Roman Catholic church. Its shady claim to fame is as a smuggling centre though there is little in town to warrant a stop. However, 2 km east is **Munneswaram**, which is worth a detour, especially on Fridays, the busiest day for this Hindu temple complex of three shrines. The 1500-year-old inner sanctum of the main Siva temple has Tamil inscriptions and is an important pilgrimage centre. In August there is a month-long festival, which includes firewalking.

A left turn at Battulu Oya leads to the prawn-fishing Tamil village of **Udappuwa** on the Kalpitiya Peninsula, 26 km north of Chilaw. As at Munneswaram, there is a festival with firewalking in July/August at its seaside three-temple shrine complex. Experiments in 1935-1936 showed that the coals were heated to about 500°C.

Marshes and lagoons lie between the road and the sea for much of the route north, which crosses a series of minor rivers and a few major ones such as the Battulu Oya. The largely Muslim and Catholic town of **Puttalam**, 131 km north of Colombo, is a centre for prawn farming, dried fish and coconut plantations. It used to be famous for its ancient pearl fishery but is now better known for its donkeys, and is thus a target of many Sinhalese jokes. The A12 continues northeast through to Anuradhapura.

Kalpitiya Peninsula → *Phone code: 032. Colour map 2, A1/B1.*

Though easily accessible by causeway from the main road, few travellers choose to explore this narrow, sandy spit of land – partly due to local skirmishes during the war, particularly at sea, it is also well off the beaten track. It has a quite distinctive, almost otherworldly landscape, and there are some important monuments to its history. Kalpitiya's position at the head of Puttalam's lagoon made it an important port for Arab traders from the seventh century and the peninsula remains predominantly Muslim to this day. Later, the Portuguese and the Dutch recognized its strategic use and the Dutch built a fort here in order to strangle King Rajasingha's trade with India. Today it is famous for its dried fish and prawn farming. Its sandy soil has also made its farmers some of Sri Lanka's richest. Despite its proximity to the sea, the land overlies an abundant supply of fresh, rather than brackish, water. Simple wells have been constructed for irrigation and crops including tobacco, shallots, chilli and even potatoes grow abundantly.

In recent years Kalpitiya Peninsula has also been recognized as an excellent place to see dolphins, and even whales between December and mid-April. Tours are run from a number of hotels (see Sleeping, page 105). Twitchers will also enjoy the abundance of birdlife here. Things may not remain so peaceful for long, as a large resort is currently being constructed in Dutch Bay.

Talawila → *Colour map 2, B1. 22 km from Puttalam, 5 km off the main road.*

Here, there is an important shrine at **St Anne's Church**. There are two accounts of its history. In one, a shipwrecked Portuguese sailor brought the image of St Anne to shore, placed it under a banyan tree and vowed to build a church here if his business prospered. In the other, a vision of St Anne appeared and left gold coins for the construction of a chapel. The present day church, set in extensive tree-lined grounds, was built in 1843 and has fine satinwood pillars. Remove shoes before you enter, and photography is not allowed. There is also a wide beach behind. There are two major festivals in March and June featuring huge processions, healing and a rural fair. These draw up to 50,000 people, with some pilgrims arriving by boat.

Kalpitiya → *Colour map 2, A1. 19 km beyond Talawila.*

The bustling, predominantly Muslim village of Kalpitiya, marks the end of the road. The small **Dutch fort**, built in 1676 on the site of a Portuguese stockade and Jesuit chapel, is one of the best preserved in Sri Lanka. It has a VOC gate (1760), an original wooden door, and inside the remains of the barracks, commander's house, chapel and prison. The navy has been *in situ* throughout the war and you will need to ask permission from the sentry to enter. In the modern base, you may be shown a number of rusting Indian trawlers, impounded for fishing in Sri Lankan waters. Two tunnels lead from the fort to St Peter's Kirk and a school, though these were blocked up during the war. Photography is prohibited and you may need to leave ID before entering. A naval officer will accompany you around the ramparts.

In contrast, the impressively gabled **St Peter's Kirk** nearby has lost many of its original features although inside a heavy stone font remains. There are some well-preserved 17th- and 18th-century Dutch gravestones inside. The church's columns and semi-circular porch date from a 19th-century renovation. Outside, there is a small, weathered cemetery.

Wilpattu National Park → *Colour map 2, A1/2.*

ⓘ *The park office, information centre and entrance are at Hunuwilagama, 7 km from the Wilpattu Junction turn-off at Maragahawewa on the A12. US$16.*

In March 2010 a clamour of excitement greeted the reopening of Wilpattu National Park, Sri Lanka's largest, oldest and – before the war – most popular wildlife sanctuary. The 131,693 ha park had been an important historical and archaeological site, as well as home to some of Sri Lanka's most visible populations of large mammals.

The park was closed in 1985, immediately after an attack on its wardens and officers by a group of LTTE cadres, it was reopened in 2003 before being closed again in 2006 when six Sri Lankan tourists and their guide were killed by a landmine. There has been some dispute over the past year, as roads are being laid in the park causing damage to the ecology and distress to the animals, visitors may see construction vehicles rumbling around.

Wilpattu has a unique topographical landscape of gently undulating terrain dominated by *villus*, natural sand-rimmed water basins, which fill up with rain and to which animals come to drink. These used to be the best places to see leopards. Certain sections have a distinctive rich, red, loamy soil and there are also areas of dense forest. The western part of the park is reminiscent of Yala (see page 179), while out to sea Dutch and Portugal bays may still support populations of dugong. A further protected area, the Wilpattu Sanctuary, lies to the north within Northern Province.

These days few animals are visible, many deer and water buffalo having been poached. A small population of leopard remains but is hard to see, while elephants are more likely to be glimpsed in the farming areas to the south. The bird population of resident and migratory waterfowl and scrub and forest species is said to be fairly healthy, as is the reptile population.

 The Mahavansa records that Prince Vijaya landed at Kudrimalai, to the southwest of the park, married Kuveni, the local jungle princess, and founded the Sinhalese race.

◉ Northwest coast listings

For Sleeping and Eating price codes and other relevant information, see pages 26-32.

● Sleeping

Beaches north of Negombo *p102*
AL Club Palm Bay, Thalawila Wella, Thoduwawa, near Marawila, T225 4954, www.club-palm-bay-hotel-marawila-sri-lanka. lakpura.ca. 104 well-furnished a/c chalets, plus 2 suites, in an attractive setting surrounded on 3 sides by a lagoon. Sports including fishing and boating, 9-hole golf course, health centre, huge pool. Good beach close by.
A Clubhotel Dolphin, Kammala South, Waikkal, sandwiched between the sea and the old Dutch canal, T227 7788, www.serendibleisure.com. Older deluxe

rooms and newer, more private villas. Popular with European packages, swimming pools, spa, activities organized and plenty of sports and entertainment laid on, good restaurant. Can also arrange tours.
A-B Ranweli Holiday Village, Waikkal, T227 7359, www.ranweli.com. Sea and river view bungalows in award-winning eco-friendly resort. Located in a 9-ha mangrove peninsula between the river and the sea, activities on offer include boat trips, birdwatching, guided nature walks, yoga and fishing. Well-designed and furnished rooms, plants in bathrooms, whole concept well thought out. Peaceful atmosphere, 'a naturalist's paradise'. Plans to renovate and update rooms shortly.

B Olenka Sunside Beach, Moderawella, near Marawila, T225 2170, www.olenkahotel.lk. 38 comfortable a/c rooms and 4 suites with balcony/terrace around small pool.

C Sanmali Beach, Beach Rd, Marawila, T225 4766, www.sanmali.com. 20 a/c rooms with balcony, close to beach. Small pool, restaurant, lower end package resort.

E-F Palm Haven, Beach Rd, Marawila, T225 1469. 18 clean comfortable chalets with hot water, beach restaurant and small pool.

Along the west coast to Puttalam p102

AL The Mudhouse, Pahaladuwelweva, Anamaduwa, T77-301 6191, www.the mudhouse.lk. For those who want to get back to nature, look no further. Huts made from natural, local materials, scattered around jungle and some even in the trees. No electric lights, lanterns and candles in the evenings, and outdoor showers (no hot water). Prices are all-inclusive, a lot of the fruit and veg comes from **The Mudhouse's** organic garden, Due to its remote location a member of staff can meet visitors in the nearest town, pick-ups can be arranged from anywhere in Sri Lanka, or your driver can ring for detailed directions.

D-E Senatilaka Guest Inn, 81/a Kurunegala Rd, Puttalam, T226 5403. 10 a/c and fan rooms with attached hot bath, some with balcony, a/c and TV, open-air terrace, restaurant, good value.

D-F Rest House, across the lagoon in Chilaw, close to the beach, T222 2299. 16 a/c and fan rooms, some with balcony overlooking sea. Kitchens lack hygiene – avoid the food.

Kalpitiya Peninsula p103

There are a number of all-inclusive resorts here, with more being built. Below are just a few suggestions.

AL-B Alankuda Beach Resort, Alankuda, T077-772 5200, www.alankudabeachresort. com. 4 large cabanas, 2 family villas, and a house where meals can be prepared by the chef. Saltwater pool, trips arranged, restaurant.

AL-B Palagama Beach, 12 Palmyra Rd, Alankuda, T077-350 7088, www.palagama beach.com. 4 cabanas, the 3 not on the beach have hot water, modelled on fishing shacks. There is a more luxurious villa option, or a house with kitchen and living area. Restaurant, infinity pool, dolphin-watching trips, watersports and trips to Wilpattu.

B-C Dolphin View Eco Lodge, off Km 40 post Kalpitiya Rd, 2 km towards the sea, Sethawadiya, T11-281 9457, www.dolphin viewecolodge.com. 4 cabanas with great views, 2 are larger than the others. Note that accommodation is rustic and simple, there's no hot water and no a/c (nets provided), but it's a great place to get away from it all. Restaurant serves good seafood as well as other options. Dolphin-watching trips.

G Taniya, Kalpitiya, T329 3031, www.taniya hotel.com. 14 a/c and fan rooms, as well as 2 cabanas. Restaurant, fishing trips and dolphin-watching.

Wilpattu National Park p104

At the time of writing a number of travellers were basing themselves in Anuradhapura (see page 260) and journeying to Wilpattu. The park bungalows were reopened in Dec 2010 and can be booked by contacting the Department of Wildlife Conservation, T11-288 8585, well in advance.

B-C Anawila Bungalow, 1 km from the park, T077-771 8045. The bungalow has 2 rooms, as well as sleeping arrangements in the upstairs lounge where it's much cooler. Note that at the time of writing electricity was still generator-dependent and this was switched off at 2200. Food and linens not supplied but this may have changed, so check before arrival. Rented on a bungalow only basis.

F Preshamal Safari Hotel, Wilpattu Junction, Pahala Maragahawewa, T011-252 1866. 4 basic, spartan rooms with fan and attached bath. Sri Lankan breakfast, rice and curry and breakfast packets for the park available.

⦿ Eating

Many of the hotels have restaurants serving reasonable food.

▲ Activities and tours

Kalpitiya Peninsula p103
Dolphin and whale watching
Most resorts organize dolphin- and whale-watching trips. See Sleeping, above.

Kitesurfing
Kalpitiya Peninsula is popular with windsurfers and some resorts hire out gear. **KiteKuda**, www.srilankakiteschool.com. Lessons for beginners, a discover session is €45 for 2 hrs (€50 for a private lesson), and more advanced kiters (€135 for 4 hrs). Accommodation also available in 4 new bungalows.

Wilpattu National Park p104
Hotels in Anuradhapura (see page 271) and the Kalpitiya Peninsula organize tours to Wilpattu and this is probably the easiest way to visit at the moment.
Leopard Safaris (see page 85), based near Colombo. Offers excellent tented safaris.

⊖ Transport

Along the west coast to Puttalam p102
Bus
Frequent buses go along the coast between **Puttalam** and **Colombo** (3 hrs), some stopping at **Chilaw** (1 hr) and **Negombo** (2 hrs), and inland to **Anuradhapura** and **Kurunegala** (both 2 hrs).

Train
The line can flood after heavy rain. Regular trains run from Colombo Fort station to **Chilaw**, via **Negombo** and **Madampe**, 3 of which continue to **Puttalam**, the end of the line.

Kalpitiya Peninsula p103
Bus
Buses run along the main road from **Puttalam**.

Wilpattu National Park p104
Bus
Buses ply the **Puttalam–Anuradhapura** road. Ask to be let out at Wilpattu Junction.

Kurunegala and around

As the chosen capital of four medieval kingdoms, the inland heart of Northwestern Province contains some important archaeological ruins, the highlight of which, Yapahuwa, rivals the rock fortress at Sigiriya. They can be visited either as a detour en route to Anuradhapura or Dambulla, or they can make a rewarding day trip from the provincial capital of Kurunegala. ▶▶ *For listings, see page 110.*

Kurunegala → *Phone code: 037. Colour map 2, C3. Population: 28,500. 93 km from Colombo.*

Kurunegala is an important crossroads town astride the route from Colombo to Anuradhapura and Kandy to Puttalam. It enjoys a pleasant location overlooked by huge rocky outcrops, some of which have been given names of the animals they resemble: Elephant Rock, Tortoise Rock, etc. According to a legend, these 'animals' were magically turned into stone when they threatened the city's water supply during a drought. Situated at the foot of the 325-m black rock, **Etagala**, there are excellent views across the lake from the temple, where there is an enormous **Buddha statue**.

Kurunegala was the royal capital for only half a century, starting with the reign of Bhuvanekabahu II (1293-1302) who was followed by Parakramabahu IV (ruled

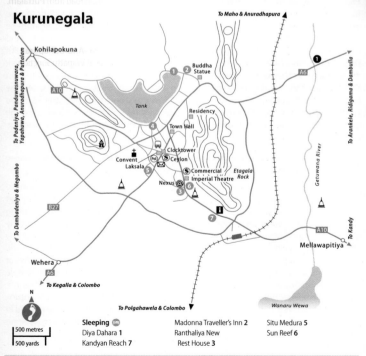

Kurunegala

Sleeping 😴
Diya Dahara **1**
Kandyan Reach **7**
Madonna Traveller's Inn **2**
Ranthaliya New
Rest House **3**
Situ Medura **5**
Sun Reef **6**

1302-1326). There is little left of the Tooth Relic (see page 199) temple save a few stone steps and part of a doorway. Elsewhere in the town, you can drive up to **Elephant Rock** for wonderful views, or take a trip around the attractive lake. The town is best used though as a base to visit the deserted ruins in the surrounding countryside.

Arankele → *Colour map 2, B3. 24 km north of Kurunegala.*

Up a forested hillside is this sixth-century **cave** hermitage. Ancient Brahmi inscriptions have been found in some caves. Excavations have revealed meditation halls, stone-faced double platform structures and ambulatories for the *Tapovana* (forest-dwelling) sect of austere Buddhist hermits here. Typically, the platforms aligned east–west, with the entrance porch to the east, would be bridged by a large monolith. The smaller of the double-platform structure here was probably divided into nine 'cells' or monks' dwellings – the roof being supported on columns.

After travelling 14 km along the Kurunegala–Dambulla road, turn left on to the Ibbagamuwa–Moragollagama Road for 10 km. It is hard to reach by public transport.

Ridigama → *Colour map 2, C4. 18 km northeast of Kurunegala.*

The 'Silver Temple' marks the place where silver ore was discovered in the second century BC, during the reign of Dutthagamenu (Dutugemunu). It is an ancient Buddhist temple site with rock cave hermitages and an image house with Kandyan paintings. Among the finds, which mostly date from the 18th century, are Buddha statues (seated and reclining), a door frame beautifully carved and inlaid with ivory, and a curious altar with Dutch (Delft) tiles with Biblical figures gifted by a Dutch consul. There is an attractive artificial lake at the foot of the hills. The journey there is tricky. Head north from Kurunegala on the A6 (Dambulla road). Having passed Ibbagamuwa (11.5 km), take the first right onto the B409. At 7 km, turn right at the junction onto the B264; after 9 km you reach Ridigama. Turn left at the main junction, then right at the clocktower and follow the dirt track for 200 m. Turn left onto the sealed road, then turn right at the T-junction. Follow the road past the lake and go uphill for 1.5 km to the *vihara*.

Dambadeniya → *Colour map 2, C2. 30 km southwest of Kurunegala.*

Dambadeniya became prominent in the mid-13th century when the capital was moved there by Parakramabahu II (ruled 1236-1270) together with the Tooth Relic. Legend states that it was the site of a monumental battle with the Indian King Kalinga, during which 24,000 men were successfully repelled and the Tooth kept safe, though shortly afterwards it was moved to the more secure site of Yapahuwa. Little remains of the ancient rock palace buildings though six ponds, where the courts used to bathe, are still there. The 272-step climb to the top is nevertheless worth it for the panoramic views of the surrounding rocks, and across to the ocean on a clear day. The two-storey temple (originally three) about 400 m south, which has Buddha images, is identified as the Vijayasundaramaya. It has some interesting wall paintings dating from the 18th century, when it was restored. It was used to exhibit the Tooth Relic which was normally housed in another temple near the palace. The site is just off the Kurunegala–Negombo road, along which buses ply. If coming from Colombo turn off at Ambepussa.

Panduwasnuwara → *Colour map 2, C2. 27 km northwest of Kurunegala.*

The oldest of the royal capitals in the district, Panduwasnuwara was used by King Parakramabahu I as a stepping stone to his great citadel at Polonnaruwa. Legend states that Panduwasdeva, Sri Lanka's second king, had his capital here in the fifth century BC. A forested mound has been identified as his predecessor King Vijaya's tomb.

The archaeological remains, in a sprawling, only part excavated, 20-ha site date to the 12th century AD. There is an impressive 1.25-km-long ancient wall around the citadel with a moat in which crocodiles may have acted as an extra deterrent. Inside are the remains of a palace (once three-storey), audience hall and storehouses as well as a monastic complex and several bathing pools. A guide may show you around, though you can clamber at will around the ruins.

Nearby, a small **Tooth temple** ① *0900-1700*, reminiscent of the Tooth temple at Kandy has been restored, while back on the main road at the turn-off to the site is a small museum containing finds from local excavations, such as coins, images and jewellery. To get there, follow the Kurunegala–Puttalam road for around 17 km, and turn left at Wariyapola towards Chilaw. The site is a kilometre from the main road. Buses run between Chilaw and Kurunegala.

Yapahuwa → *Colour map 2, B3. 47 km north of Kurunegala, 69 km south of Anuradhapura.*

① *Rs 1000 and guide will expect a tip.*

Yapahuwa, arguably Wayamba's most impressive ruins, lies off the route north from Kurunegala to Anuradhapura. To reach the site follow the A10 past the turn-off to Panduwasnuwara to **Padeniya**. Here there is a *vihara* with 28 carved pillars, an elaborately carved door, and an ancient clay image house and library. At Padeniya, the A28 forks right to Anuradhapura. Yapahuwa lies 6 km east of the main road, close to the pleasant town of Maho.

Yapahuwa is a huge **rock fortress**, suggestive of Sigiriya, which stands on a very pleasant, shaded site. Bhuvanekabahu I (ruled 1272-1284) moved his capital from Dambadeniya to Yapahuwa, seeing the need for stronger fortification against Tamil invaders, and built a palace and a temple where the Tooth and the Alms Bowl relics were housed for 11 years.

A vast granite rock, rising 100 m from the surrounding plain, is encircled by a 1-km-long path rising to the top. The fort palace, built of stone, is surrounded by two moats and ramparts and there are signs of other ancient means of defence. The impressive ornamental stairway, with some fine lions and guardstones, is still well preserved and somewhat reminiscent of Far Eastern art. The steps are fairly steep so can be tiring to climb. The ruins at the head of the remarkable flight of granite steps are unique and the views over the palms towards the highlands are not to be missed. The temple (restored in 1886) illustrates South Indian artistic influence in its fine carvings on the pillars, doorway and windows which show dancers, musicians and animals. One of the window frames is now exhibited in the Colombo National Museum (see page 68). The remains of a temple to the northeast, outside the fortification (which was thought at one time to have housed the Tooth Relic), has some sculptures visible. There is a small, fairly modern museum on site.

This fortress capital of the Sinhalese kings when abandoned was inhabited by Buddhist monks and religious ascetics. The relics were carried away from the temple here to South India by the Pandyas, and then recovered in 1288 by Parakramabahu III (ruled 1287-1293), who temporarily placed them in safety at Polonnaruwa.

Yapahuwa is 5 km east of Maho, which is easily accessible by bus or train. Take a three-wheeler from here. Buses leave every two hours from Kurunegala and hourly from Anuradhapura. Since Maho lies on the Colombo–Vavuniya line, there are several trains a day from Kurunegala taking an hour. From Anuradhapura it takes two hours.

◉ Kurunegala and around listings

For Sleeping and Eating price codes and other relevant information, see pages 26-32.

● Sleeping

Kurunegala *p107, map p107*
C Kandyan Reach, 344-350 Kandy Rd (1 km southeast of the centre), T222 4218, www.kandyanreach.com. Large a/c rooms with hot water, balcony and TV. Restaurant and good (if rather shallow) pool.
D Diya Dahara, 7 North Lake Rd, T222 3452, diyadahara@sltnet.lk. 7 a/c rooms (some larger than others), No 3 has large balcony, best located restaurant in town overlooking the lake, good buffet lunch.
D Madonna Traveller's Inn, 44 North Lake Rd, T222 3276. 9 good-sized rooms, a/c and fan, clean and well-furnished. Restaurant, quiet location close to the lake.
D Situ Medura, 21 Mihindu Mawatha, T222 2335. 2 a/c if slightly gloomy rooms in large traditional mansion once belonging to local aristocrat, restaurant.
D-F Ranthaliya New Rest House, South Lake Rd (1 km from centre), T222 2298. 11 comfortable a/c and fan rooms, some with view overlooking the tank (with a bit of a stretch!), restaurant.
F Sun Reef, 51/1 Kandy Rd (by the Lion lager sign), T222 2433. 8 clean rooms with attached bath including 1 larger a/c room, simple but comfortable, friendly, good English spoken, reasonably priced restaurant, towards the railway station.

Yapahuwa *p109*
C Yapahuwa Paradise Resort, T397 5055, www.hotelyapahuwaparadise.com. Bright rooms with private balconies and a/c, pleasant gardens, restaurant and pool.

❼ Eating

Kurunegala *p107, map p107*
Many of the hotels have restaurants serving reasonable food.

◉ Transport

Kurunegala *p107, map p107*
Bus
Frequent buses to **Colombo** (2-2½ hrs depending on route); to **Negombo** (2 hrs); **Dambulla** (2 hrs); **Anuradhapura** (3 hrs); **Kandy** (1½ hrs).

Train
The station is 1.5 km southeast of the town centre. Kurunegala is on the Northern line to **Anuradhapura** and **Vavuniya**. 5 trains to **Colombo Fort**, 0559, 1147, 1338, 1436 and 1714 (2 hrs). To **Anuradhapura** (Vavuniya train), takes 3 hrs. 0745, 1545, 1820, 2400. To **Trincomalee**, 0800.

❶ Directory

Kurunegala *p107, map p107*
Banks Plenty of banks in town including **Commercial Bank** and **Sampath Bank** with ATM facilities. **Internet** Several places on Kandy Rd.

Contents

Footprint features

The South

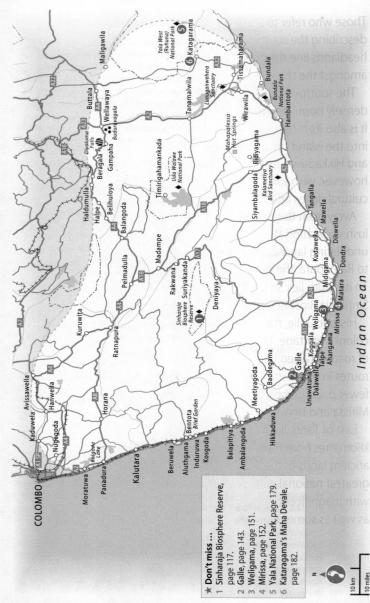

Indian Ocean

★ Don't miss ...
1 Sinharaja Biosphere Reserve,
   page 117.
2 Galle, page 143.
3 Weligama, page 151.
4 Mirissa, page 152.
5 Yala National Park, page 179.
6 Kataragama's Maha Devale,
   page 182.

N

10 km
10 miles

COLOMBO

Maligawila
Katagarama
Yala West
(Ruhuna)
National Park
Tissamaharama
Buttala
Wellawaya
Bundala
Bundala
National Park
Budurwagala
Wirawila
Lunuganwehera
Sanctuary
Tanamalwila
Hambantota
Diyaluma
Falls
Beragala
Gampaha
Haldumulla
Halpe
Belihuloya
Belihuloya
Mahapalessa
Hot Springs
Ridiyagama
Balangoda
Timirigahamankada
Uda Walawe
National Park
Kalametiya
Bird Sanctuary
Madampe
Rakwana
Siyambalagoda
Tangalla
Pelmadulla
Suriyakanda
Mawella
Kudawella
Ratnapura
Kuruwita
Sinharaja
Biosphere
Reserve
Deniyaya
Dikwella
Dondra
Midigama
Matara
Hanwella
Avissawella
Baddegama
Meetiyagoda
Ahangama
Mirissa
Weligama
Galle
Koggala
Talpe
Dalawella
Unawatuna
Kaduwela
Nugegoda
Bolgoda
Lake
Horana
Bentota
Brief Garden
Hikkaduwa
Morauwa
Panadura
Kalutara
Beruwela
Aluthgama
Induruwa
Kosgoda
Balapitiya
Ambalangoda

Those who refer to Sri Lanka as a tropical paradise are usually describing the south. Here magnificent bays, beaches and rocky headlands line the coast while small-scale farms are scattered amongst the thick cover of trees in the interior.

The southwest region, from Colombo to Galle, is the most densely populated part of the island and its centre of industry. It is also its most developed with Western sun-seekers packing into the island's major resorts, such as Beruwela, Bentota and Hikkaduwa. It requires little effort to escape the hordes however, with some short trips inland to explore the region's cultural riches and its tranquil rivers and lagoons.

Away from the palm-fringed coastal belt, dense forests and lush vegetation stretch inland. The heart of the Wet Zone is an undulating landscape of tea and rubber plantations, leading to Ratnapura, the centre of the island's gem-producing region. To its south lies Sri Lanka's largest remaining tract of rainforest, Sinharaja Biosphere Reserve, a World Heritage Site.

Historic Galle, the province's unrivalled capital, is rich with colonial heritage. The outstandingly beautiful 80-km stretch of road between here and Tangalla is one of the most scenic routes in the country. Though no longer a secret, there are fewer package hotels, and amongst the popular and laid-back Mirissa and Unawatuna, a few idyllic beach hideaways remain.

East of Tangalla the landscape changes over just a few kilometres from lush to the comparatively barren. Here, in the ancient lands of the Ruhuna kingdom, are some of Sri Lanka's greatest national parks, in particular Yala and Uda Walawe, with magnificent opportunities for spotting wildlife and birdlife, as well as some of the island's most sacred pilgrimage sites.

Interior of the Wet Zone

Stretching inland away from Colombo and the west coast beaches towards the Central Highland ridge, Sabaragamuwa Province, with its luxuriantly verdant, gently hilly landscape, is one of Sri Lanka's most beautiful regions. Beyond the gem capital of Ratnapura, lies the wonderful UNESCO-protected Sinharaja rainforest, while scattered around the region are some remarkable, if rarely visited, prehistoric cave sites. ▶▶ *For listings, see pages 121-123.*

Inland to Ratnapura

The most frequently used route inland to Ratnapura heads east from Colombo along the congested A4 through Nugegoda, though a more attractive route follows the B1 along the south bank of the Kelaniya River. This passes through the picturesque **Kaduwela**, 16 km from Colombo, where there is a large Buddhist temple and the irrigation tank of Mulleriyawa, where you can watch a constant succession of varied river traffic from the beautifully positioned Rest House. The two routes converge near Hanwella (33 km), where the A4 traffic begins to clear. **Hanwella** is built on the site of a Portuguese fort, and is noted as the place where the last king of Kandy, Sri Vikrama Rajasinha, was defeated.

Avissawella (57 km), the ancient capital of the Sitawaka kings and now the centre of the rubber industry, is in beautiful wooded surroundings. The ruins of the royal palace of Rajasinha, a Buddhist king who converted to Hinduism, can still be seen. He was responsible for starting work on the unfinished **Berendi Kovil**, which still has some fine stonework despite the Portuguese attack. It is just off the Ginigathena road on the opposite bank of the river.

At Avissawella, the A4 turns south towards Ratnapura, while the A7 leads off east through Kitulgala (see page 229), Hatton and ultimately to Nuwara Eliya. The road to Ratnapura periodically crosses rivers that come tumbling down from the southwest highlands. It passes through Pusella and crosses the Kuruwita River, running through a landscape that was the site of some of Sri Lanka's earliest settlements and is also a gem-bearing area. At **Batadombalena Cave**, near Kuruwita, fragmentary human skeletal remains have been found, as well as those of several large mammal skeletons including elephants and cattle, dating back at least as far as 28,000 years ago, or possibly very much earlier. To reach the caves take the road towards Eratne, turn right after 2 km and follow it to the end (2 km). A path reaches the cave in 5 km.

An alternative route from Colombo to Ratnapura follows the coastal road south to **Panadura** (see page 124), turning inland along the A8 through **Horana**, where there is a Rest House built in the remains of an ancient Buddhist monastery. On the opposite side of the road is a large Buddhist temple with a particularly noteworthy bronze candlestick, over 2 m tall. Heading east from here there are some good views of Adam's Peak.

Ratnapura → *Phone code: 045. Colour map 3, B3. Population: 109,000. 100 km from Colombo.*

The climate of Ratnapura has been likened to a Turkish bath. One of Sri Lanka's wettest towns, even February, the driest month, normally has nearly 100 mm of rain, while May, the wettest, has nearly 500 mm. The vegetation is correspondingly luxuriant, and the city has a beautiful setting on the banks of the Kalu Ganga, with views of rubber plantations and paddies. When fine, its views of Adam's Peak are also unmatched. This town is aptly

A gem of a place

Sri Lanka's gems place it among the top five gem-bearing nations of the world. Washed out from the ancient rocks of the highlands themselves, the gems are found in pockets of alluvial gravel known as *illama*, usually a metre or two below the surface. Ratnapura (the 'City of Gems') is still the heart of the industry, though new pits are being explored in other parts of the island.

The quality of Ratnapura's gems is legendary. In the seventh century Hiuen Tsang claimed that there was a ruby on the spire of the temple at Anuradhapura whose magnificence illuminated the sky. Marco Polo (1293) described the flawless ruby as 'a span long and quite as thick as a man's arm'! Today, sapphires are much more important and since the latest royal engagement featured a Sri Lankan sapphire ring, the industry is seeing a sharp increase in demand.

Traditional gem mining makes use of only the simplest technology. Pits are dug in the gravel. Divided in two, one half is used for extracting water while the gravel is dug out from the other half. When after two or three days a large enough pile of gravel has been excavated it is systematically washed in a stream, sifting the gems and heavy minerals from the lighter material. The work is done in teams, everyone getting a share of the value of any gems found. The cutting and polishing is carried out largely in Ratnapura itself. Dressed, cut and then polished, the methods and materials used are still largely local. Hand-operated lathes, and polishing paste made from the ash of burnt paddy straw have been used for generations.

A number of precious stones are found nearby including sapphire, ruby, topaz, amethyst, cat's eye, alexandrite, aquamarine, tourmaline, garnet and zircon. Genuine stones are common. Valuable stones by definition are more rare. Advice given to travellers at the beginning of the century still holds: 'As regards buying stones, it is a risky business unless the passenger has expert knowledge or advice. It is absolute folly to buy stones from itinerant vendors. It is far better to go to one of the large Colombo jewellers and take the chance of paying more and obtaining a genuine stone.'

named the 'City of Gems' as Ratnapura is best known for its gemstones that are washed down the riverbed. The gravel beds that contain the gemstones are also the source of evidence of some of Sri Lanka's earliest cultures and of the wildlife that is now extinct. Discoveries of animal bones as well as of a variety of stone tools have made it clear that the area is probably one of the first sites to have been occupied by humans in Sri Lanka.

Sights

Although people seem to trade gems all over town, there are certain areas that specialize in uncut and unpolished stones, polished stones, cut stones, while other streets will only deal in star sapphires or cat's eyes. From 0700-1000 the area around the clocktower is a fascinating place to visit, where you can watch hundreds of people buying and selling gems. If you do buy a gem, it is worth checking its authenticity at the **State Gem Corporation** ① *in the fort, 0800-1630*. If the gem merchant is genuine, he should not mind if you check its authenticity before the transaction.

There are around 200 working **gem mines**, in the Ratnapura area. The mines are around 30 m deep, each with a series of interconnecting tunnels. Travel agents can organize visits (a tip is expected), or you can take a three-wheeler to Warallupa Road, where there are several working mines. At each mine there is a shack housing a generator, where you will be shown the mining process. Miners will demonstrate washing and sifting the stones, and it may also be possible to walk inside some mines – ask locally.

Ratnapura is surrounded by rubber and tea estates in a lush and beautiful setting, and gives better views of Adam's Peak than almost anywhere else on the island. The old **Fort** above the clocktower offers good views. Further afield, it is well worth going to the big **Buddha statue**, built by a wealthy young gem merchant, on a hill behind the Rest House, for the views. Driving up to **Gilimale** from the bridge gives you a chance to see the massive curtain wall of the Central Highlands to the north. The surrounding forests are rich in flowers, one of the most notable being the **Vesak Orchid**, which takes its name from the month of Vesak in which it flowers.

Maha Saman Dewale, some 4 km west of town, is the richest Buddhist temple in Sri Lanka. Dedicated to the guardian god of Adam's Peak, it is thought to date from the 13th century, but was rebuilt by Parakramabahu IV in the 15th century before being damaged by the Portuguese soldiers. The temple, which has been restored, has an ornamental doorway

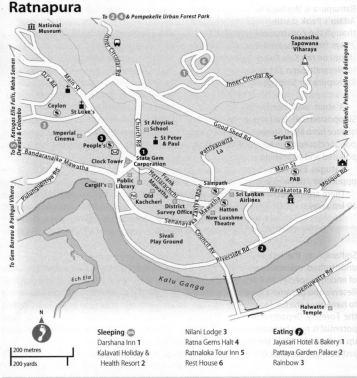

Ratnapura

Sleeping
Darshana Inn **1**
Kalavati Holiday &
 Health Resort **2**

Nilani Lodge **3**
Ratna Gems Halt **4**
Ratnaloka Tour Inn **5**
Rest House **6**

Eating
Jayasari Hotel & Bakery **1**
Pattaya Garden Palace **2**
Rainbow **3**

and fine wall paintings inside. Interesting features include the remains of a Portuguese fort. On the temple wall is a Portuguese soldier sculpted in stone while a slab bearing their coat of arms was also found here. There is a major **Perahera** procession during the July-August full moon, when decorated boats sail along the Kalu Ganga.

There are a few museums in Ratnapura. Private museums tend to be primarily retail outlets for gems but at the same time demonstrate the craft of gem polishing. The **Gem Bureau and Museum** ① *Pothgul Vihara Rd, Getangama (2 km south), 0900-1700*, has gems from different parts of Sri Lanka, and an art gallery. The **Gem Bank Gemmological Museum** ① *6 Ehelepola Mawatha, Batugedera, 2 km along A4 towards Pelmadulla, T222 2724, 0900-1700*, has an interesting private collection of gems and precious minerals and mining-related exhibits including a model of a pit. Don't miss the museum's rare elephant pearl. **Ratnapura National Museum** ① *Ehelapola Walauwa, Colombo Rd, T222 2451, Sat-Wed 0900-1700, Rs 45, children Rs 25*, has a small dated exhibition of prehistoric fossil skeletons of elephants, hippos and rhinoceros found in gem pits, plus stuffed animals and snakes in jars. There is also a section on the arts and culture of the province with musical instruments, masks, jewellery, textiles and flags.

Excursions

Ratnapura is the base for the much steeper and more strenuous route which leads to **Adam's Peak** starting at Siripagama, 15 km away. The climb takes about seven hours, though the construction of new steps may shorten the time. Some pilgrims walk the 25 km from Ratnapura to Adam's Peak during the winter months. It begins at **Malwala** (8 km) on the Kalu Ganga to **Palabadelle** (11 km, 375 m), then follows a very steep path to **Heramitipana** (13 km, 1100 m), and to the summit (5 km, 2260 m). Buses leave Ratnapura for Siripagama regularly until 1900. ▸▸ *See page 228 for the shorter and more frequently used route.*

A short walk northeast of town is **Pompakelle Urban Forest Park** ① *0800-1700*. Signposted trails lead you through the surprisingly large 15 ha forest – a welcome change of pace from Main Street. Close to the entrance is a large, now defunct, natural swimming pool. Enclosed originally by the British as a reservoir for the town, the water is muddy and polluted and swimming is prohibited, though a clean-up is planned.

Katugas Ella Falls, 2 km north from the centre, are attractive waterfalls with the opportunity to swim in the river. Avoid visiting on Sundays when it can get busy.

There are impressive **caves** at Kosgalla, 8 km from Ratnapura and at Eratna/Baṭatota, 19 km away.

Sinharaja Biosphere Reserve → *Phone code: 045; Colour map 3, B3/4.*

Sinharaja, as the last significant stretch of rainforest on the island to be left largely undisturbed, maintains enormous national importance. It is home to a remarkable array of endemic species. In 1989 it was recognized by UNESCO as an international Biosphere Reserve and became a World Heritage Site. 'Sinharaja' means 'Lion King' and is believed to have been the final refuge of the now extinct lion on the island. While it is managed by the Forestry Department with less than maximum efficiency, Sinharaja's ecotourism potential is now beginning to be recognized, with some good accommodation opening up in the area. While the wildlife is harder to see than at some of the big national parks, just being in the thick of the rainforest can be an exhilarating experience.

Ins and outs → *For tour operators, see page 123.*
Getting there and around There are two entrances to the reserve, from Colombo, the west coast or Ratnapura, most people enter at the main gate at Kudawa at the northwestern edge of the reserve. East of Ratnapura, turn off the A4 at Tiruwanaketiya, head for Kalawana, and then turn right at Weddagala, 6 km from the park entrance. Alternatively, you can approach from Rakwana through Pothupitiya, though the road may be impassable in the wet season. From the south coast it is best to enter at Mederipitiya, 12 km from Deniyaya, on the Galle–Ratnapura road, which is also accessible by car from Embilipitiya to the southeast.

There are several walking trails for exploring the forest on foot with a guide. Bring water, food, binoculars, rainwear and a lighter or salt to get rid of leeches (see box, page 41).

Best time to visit December to early April and August and September, when rainfall tends to be lighter. The shaded forest, with an average temperature of 23.6°C, is fairly cool throughout the day, though afternoons are usually wet – come prepared.

Park information An entry ticket (Rs 575, children Rs 290), plus (compulsory) guide ticket must be purchased before entry. The guide fee varies according to the length of the trail and they will probably expect an additional tip. There are about 30 guides, all local villagers, and although very knowledgeable they don't always speak English. Video cameras costs Rs 500. The reserve is open 0600-1800 though guides rarely arrive before 0700-0730. If you wish to make an early start, make arrangements the previous day. Facilities and information at the park offices (Kudawa and Mederipitiya) are limited, and leaflets may not be available, so it is worth calling in at the **Forestry Department** ① *82 Rajamalwatta Rd, Battaramulla (Colombo outskirts), T011-286 6626*, for further information.

Background

The first records on Sinharaja date back to Portuguese time when detailed lists on not only names but also agricultural produce were collected for taxation purposes. Having been mapped first by the Dutch, the British made the forest Crown Property in 1840. Naturalist George Henry Thwaites undertook the first surveys in the 1850s, recording many plants found in Sinharaja, and in May 1875, 2430 ha of the 'Sinharaja Mukalana' were recognized as reserved forest. Through the 20th century, numerous studies assessed the area's suitability as a source of wood, but owing to its inaccessibility the reserve remained untouched until 1968, when the government sanctioned selective logging. From 1971 to 1977, about 1400 ha of forest was selectively logged, but pressure from conservation groups brought about a complete ban in 1978 when the area was designated a Man and Biosphere Reserve. In 1988 it was declared a National Heritage Area, and a World Heritage Site in 1989. Despite this, the forest remains an important source of income for inhabitants of the 22 villages surrounding the reserve. The sap from the kitul palm produces a fermented toddy and a treacle produced by heating it which in turn makes the dry brown sugar, jaggery. Rattan is collected to make baskets and mats, and also leaves and wood for construction and fuel. There is also some illicit gem-mining in some eastern areas of the reserve.

The reserve

Sinharaja's importance lies not just in its pristine nature, but also in the high degree of endemism of its species. For example, 95% of the endemic birds of Sri Lanka, and more than half of its mammals and butterflies, have been recorded here. This said, in the dense forest animals can be hard to see, so don't expect game spotting on the level of Yala. The purple-faced leaf monkey is the most commonly seen mammal, and others include giant squirrel, dusky squirrel and sambar. The leopard population is estimated to be around 15 (very seldom seen) and there are no elephants. Birdlife, as ever, is the most rewarding to observe. Rare endemics include red-faced malkoha, Sri Lanka blue magpie, the white-headed starling and even the green-billed coucal, with plenty of others including orange minivets, orioles and babblers. An interesting and colourful spectacle is the presence of mixed flocks, sometimes comprising up to 80 species. The most commonly seen reptile is the green garden lizard, while snakes include the endemic green pit viper and the hump-nosed viper. There are several endemic amphibian species, including the torrent toad, wrinkled frog and Sri Lankan reed frog.

Lying in the southwest lowland Wet Zone, the reserve's rolling hills with ridges and valleys between 200-1300 m stretch 21 km from east to west, though north to south it only measures 3.7 km, bounded by the Kalu Ganga in the north and the Gin Ganga in the south. It spans the districts of Ratnapura, Kalutara, Galle and Matara. Vegetation consists of tropical wet evergreen forest and tropical lowland forest, with lofty, very straight dominant trees a distinctive feature. As with its fauna, the forest's trees, ferns and epiphytes are also largely endemic.

There are three main **nature trails** from Kudawa. Guide leaflets are sometimes available. **Waturawa Trail** is 4.7 km long; about three hours of gentle walking. The path starts 250 m from the camp and leads through the forest up to the visitors centre. From here, most guides will take you to the giant newada tree, some 43 m high. There are 14 observation posts which are marked on the guide leaflet and there are two good places for spotting birds and watching monkeys. This trail is a good introduction to the rainforest. **Moulawella Trail** is 7.5 km long. Taking about seven hours, this is a fairly strenuous trek. It takes you through primary forest up to Moulawella Peak (760 m) and from there you can see Adam's Peak and look over the forest canopy. The walk gives you a chance to see fascinating leaf-shaped frogs, lizards, tropical fish, snakes, crabs and a 300-year-old vine. **Sinhagala Trail** is 14 km long. This trek takes a full day. It leads through the heart of the rainforest to the 742-m 'Lion Rock' from where you can look out over the unbroken tree canopy of an undisturbed forest and see the various hill ranges – 'twice as good as Moulawella'.

Ratnapura to the highlands

The A4 between Ratnapura and Pelmadulla (18 km) continues across the fertile and undulating low country, while the hills on either side come closer and closer to the road. It is a major gem-bearing area. **Pelmadulla** is a main junction, the road from Colombo running east and then northeast, curving round the southern flank of the Central Highland massif towards Haputale, while the A18 goes southeast to Madampe. From Pelmadulla the A4 continues to Balangoda and the caves beyond, through superb lush scenery all the way. This is the heart of the rubber-producing area, and there are many rubber estates. Adam's Peak and the Maskeliya Range rise magnificently to the north, although during the southwest monsoon they are almost permanently covered in cloud.

Balangoda and around → Phone code: 045. Colour map 3, B4.
Balangoda is one of an increasing number of towns overlooked by an enormous cement Buddha. The town itself has little of interest; most visitors use it as a base for excursions

into the Peak Wilderness Sanctuary and to visit the nearby prehistoric cave sites. **Kuragala Cave**, with the Jailani Muslim shrine nearby, can be reached by following a path uphill from Taniantenna on the Kaltota Road. It is 25 km along the Kaltota Road. In August Muslims congregate here for a large festival. **Budugala Cave Temple**, 25 km away, is across a deep gully from the shrine. Take the road to Uggalkaltota, to the east, which follows the downward sloping ridge (buses go most of the way).

From Balangoda, after passing Rajawaka on the Kaltota Road, a track leads 4 km down to the south to **Diyainna Cave**, near the village of the same name, which was also inhabited between 8000 and 2500 BC. If you continue along the track southeast towards Uda Walawe Reservoir, you will reach **Handagiriya** on the river bank. It is claimed that the old Buddhist stupa once held the Tooth Relic (see page 199). This is close to **Bellan Bendi Pelessa**, the plain where large finds of prehistoric skeletons has confirmed it as an open-air site once used by *Homo sapiens belangodensis*.

Belihuloya → *Phone code: 045. Colour map 3, B5.*

A small settlement on the Ratnapura–Badulla road, Belihuloya is best known as a picturesque rest point set among tea estates on the banks of a gushing river. There is a track from here leading up to World's End on the Horton Plains (see page 224), though from this side it is a four-hour uphill walk.

Belihuloya to Haputale

Heading northeast for 16 km, you reach the **Non Pareil Tea Estate**, where a dirt track winds 24 km up to World's End. Passing through **Halpe** (6 km), the road continues for a further 7 km to a turn off for the **Bambarakanda Falls**, which at 237 m – in three stages – is Sri Lanka's highest waterfall. The falls, which are impressive after the rains, are reached by a sealed road, 5 km off the A4. Just beyond the turn off for the falls is the settlement of Kalupahana. **Haldumulla**, nearby, has excellent views across to the sea. It is possible to visit an organic tea garden here, the **Bio Tea Project**, run by Stassen Exports Ltd. Their centre is signposted 3 km off the road. Further east from Kalpahana is **Beragala**, and then a further steep climb of 10 km is Haputale. *For details of Haputale, Ella and Badulla, see Uva Province, page 236.*

To the south coast

After Pelmadulla the A18 runs southeast through Kahawatta Ford. After 10 km, at **Madampe**, the A17 branches off to the right towards Galle and Matara. On the way you pass through various towns and villages, of which **Rakwana** is the largest. The chief village of a tea-growing district, it has a large Tamil and Muslim population and a beautiful setting. There are many beautiful flowering trees in season and wild orchids, notably the large flowered *Dendrobium maccarthaie*. The Sinharaja Biosphere Reserve is accessible from Rakwana. The road west out of town leads eventually close to the main entrance at **Kudawa**, via Pothupitiya and Weddagala. Alternatively, you can continue south to Deniyaya for the Mederipitiya entrance.

The road south of Rakwana is very scenic, with fabulous views across to the mountains and valleys of the Peak Wilderness Sanctuary, numerous fine waterfalls and some grand, if rickety, old iron bridges. Tea and rubber plantations cover the landscape with *pinus* trees often lining the road. Crossing the Bulutota Pass there are ten hair-pin bends, marked by white markers, after which you pass just to the east of **Gongala Peak** (1358 m). This is the easternmost edge of the Wet Zone. From **Panilkande**, the road continues west to **Deniyaya**, one of the centres of low-altitude tea production and a main gateway to Sinharaja (see page 117). Just south of **Akuressa** the road forks, the A24 turning left to Matara down the valley of the Nilwala Ganga, and passing from one of the wettest areas of Sri Lanka to one of the driest in under 20 km. The right fork continues as the A17 to Galle, remaining in typically Wet Zone vegetation and cultivation throughout.

◉ Interior of the Wet Zone listings

For Sleeping and Eating price codes and other relevant information, see pages 26-32.

● Sleeping

Inland to Ratnapura *p114*
C-D Rest House (CHC), on the Kelaniya River, Hanwella, T011-250 3497, www.ceylonhotels.lk. 8 fan and a/c rooms with beautiful view along the river. Edward VII (then Prince of Wales) planted a jack tree in the garden here in 1875.
C-E Rest House, Avissawella, T036-222 2299. Clean rooms with balcony, a/c rooms well furnished but expensive, non a/c are simpler. Popular lunch-time spot with fiery rice and curry, but overpriced.

Ratnapura *p114, map p116*
C Ratnaloka Tour Inn, Kosgala, Kahangama (6 km from town), T222 2455, www.ratna loka.com. 53 a/c rooms, deluxe are carpeted with TV, bathtub and private balcony (views across to lotus pond and tea estates). All comfortable, good restaurant, long pool.
D-E Kalavati Holiday and Health Resort, Polhengoda Village, Outer Circular Rd, 1.6 km from bus stand, T222 2465. 18 rooms, some with a/c, no hot water, restaurant, house decorated with collector's pieces (antiques cabinets, palm leaf manuscripts, statues, betel cutters, etc), beautiful tropical garden, some interesting tours (Dec to May only), natural therapy 'healing arts' practised here including oil baths and massage, herbal treatments.
D-E Rest House, Rest House (Inner Circle) Rd, on a hill 1 km from centre, T222 2299, udarest@sltnet.lk. 11 large, simple rooms (best upstairs) though no hot water, food good

value, peaceful, delightful site and outstanding views from atmospheric veranda.
E Nilani Lodge, 21 Dharmapala Mawatha, T222 2170, hashani@sltnet.lk. 9 a/c and fan rooms with balcony and hot water, in large modern white apartment-style building. Restaurant, tours and gem museum and shop on site, tours to mines and cutters. Basically a gem shop with beds.
E-F Darshana Inn, 68/5 Rest House (Inner Circle) Rd, just below **Rest House**, T222 2674. 4 basic rooms, fan, rather damp attached bath, restaurant, popular bar, pleasant owner.
F-G Ratna Gems Halt, 153/5 Outer Circular Rd (short climb), T222 3745, rathnagems@ yahoo.com. Spotless, excellent value rooms, all with bath, in family house. Upstairs rooms with shared veranda overlooking paddy fields and mines, smaller, darker box-like rooms downstairs. Good meals available. Small gem centre (no pressure to buy) where you can watch stones being dressed, cut and polished. Also runs a 5-day gem polishing and cutting courses; contact in advance.

Sinharaja Biosphere Reserve *p117*
There is accommodation at the Kudawa entrance, in Kudawa itself and at Kalawana, 17 km away. If entering from the Mederipitiya entrance, the nearest accommodation is at Deniyaya, 12 km away.
LL-L Boulder Garden, Sinharaja Rd, Kalawana, Kudawa nearest entrance, T225 5812, www.bouldergarden.com. Genuinely creative 'eco' concept, a sort of prehistoric luxury resort or upmarket hermitage, with 8 smart but simple rooms (plus 2 cave 'suites') built into a complex of

28 caves. Fully inclusive, though expensive, rates include a trip to Sinharaja, and also a 3-hr walk along cave route within grounds.
C Blue Magpie Lodge, very close to Kudawa entrance, T011-243 1872, bluemagpielodge@gmail.com. 12 simple rooms with hot water. Restaurant, walking trails, perfect for birdwatchers.
C-D Rainforest Lodge, Temple Rd, Deniyaya, for Mederipitiya entrance, T041-492 0444, rainforestlodge@ymail.com. Family-run lodge set amidst tea plantations, offering 5 clean rooms and good food.
D-E Singraj Rest, Koswatta, 1 km from Kalawana, for Kudawa entrance, T225 5201. 7 modern rooms. Pleasant position between tea plantations and paddy fields, friendly, good food.
E-F Martin Wijeysinghe's Lodge, 200 m from park entrance, 3.5 km by jeep from Kudawa village, 2 km shortcut on foot, T490 0863. Knowledgeable and highly respected former park ranger. Magnificent forest views, 7 clean and simple rooms.
F Rest House, Deniyaya, for Mederipitiya entrance, T041-227 3600. Fine position and very large, simple but clean rooms. Popular lunch spot.
F Sathmala Ella Rest, Deniyaya, 4 km towards Mederipitiya, 7 km from entrance, T041-227 3481. 10 fan rooms with balcony or terrace, restaurant, bar, pleasant position close to Ging Ganga, though little English spoken and rather disorganized.
F Sinharaja Rest, Temple Rd, Deniyaya, for Mederipitiya entrance, T041-227 3368. 7 tired fan rooms, run by Bandula and Palitha Ratnayake, very knowledgeable and enthusiastic guides. Recommended trips to Sinharaja, good food.
F-G Rainforest Edge, Balawatukanda, Weddagala, T045-225 5912, www.rainforest edge.com. 7 fan rooms, with hot water, in an eco-lodge on top of a hill with great views. Pool and restaurant serving Sri Lankan food.

Ratnapura to the highlands *p119*
C Rest House (CHC), near the bridge, Belihuloya, T228 0156, www.ceylonhotels.lk. 14 a/c and fan rooms (best in a newer extension) in over 100-year-old building by an attractive though very noisy stream. Rooms a little shabby and could be cleaner. Restaurant on pleasant covered terrace.
D-E River Garden Resort, Badulla Rd, Ratnapura side of the bridge, Belihuloya, T228 0222, www.srilankaecotourism.com. Great position, with attractive thatched huts on the hillside, fan, attached hot bath, in extensive gardens. Camping also available. Wide variety of sports offered include canoeing and mountain-biking, a 'natural pool' for bathing in the river (though take care). Good food.
E Landa Holiday Houses, Badulla Rd, Belihuloya, T228 0288, www.landa holidays.com. 4 cottages and 1 treehouse, Dutch designed and built by the stream in a jungle setting. Meals on request.

🍴 Eating

Ratnapura *p114, map p116*
There are plenty of good bakeries near the bus station and in town.
🍴 **Jayasiri Hotel & Bakery**, 198 Main St. Open 1030-2130. Sri Lankan rice and curry downstairs, Chinese on 1st floor, bustling with activity, friendly staff, full of local colour.
🍴 **Pattaya Garden Palace**, 14 Senanayake Mawatha, T222 3029. Modern a/c restaurant with a wide choice of Chinese and Thai dishes.
🍴 **Rainbow**, 163 Main St. Good for rice and curry meals, large airy room looking onto part of gem traders street market.
🍴 **Rest House**, see Sleeping, above. A good spot for lunch (good rice and curry, reasonably priced drinks) and dinner.

▲ Activities and tours

Sinharaja Biosphere Reserve *p117*
Bandula and Palitha Ratnayaka, who run **Sinharaja Rest** in Deniyaya (see Sleeping, page 122) are long-established, experienced guides with excellent English. Tours range from 4 hrs to all day. The full-day walk takes you to Lion Rock where you can look out over the forest canopy. Walks can vary according to fitness.

⊖ Transport

Ratnapura *p114, map p116*
Bus
There are regular services to **Colombo** (2½-3 hrs), **Kalawana** for **Sinharaja** (2 hrs), and **Balangoda** (1 hr). 2 CTB buses a day to **Haputale** (4 hrs) via **Belihuloya** (2 hrs), 1 going on to **Badulla**; several buses to **Kandy** (4 hrs), via **Avissawella** and **Kegalla**; and 3 buses a day via **Embilipitiya** to **Hambantota** and **Matara** (1 hr). For **Galle**, take an a/c bus along the A8 to Panadura and change to a Colombo–Galle bus there.

Sinharaja Biosphere Reserve *p117*
Bus
To **Kudawa**: buses from **Colombo**, 1 direct a day to Kalawana (4 hrs), otherwise change

in Ratnapura (2 hrs). 4 buses from **Kalawana** to Kudawa (45 mins). Walkers can ask locally for the short cut from Weddagala or use the 4-km track.

At **Deniyaya** the bus stand fields buses to **Colombo** (6½ hrs), **Ratnapura** (4½ hrs), and **Embilipitiya** (3½ hrs). For **Galle**, change at **Akuressa** (2½ hrs).

Occasional buses also run to the **Mederipitiya** entrance (45 mins), though it is easier to take your own transport.

Ratnapura to the highlands *p119*
Bus
Buses run from Ratnapura east to **Balangoda** (1 hr) and **Belihuloya** (2 hrs), with 3 services running on to **Haputale** (4 hrs). From Pelmadulla and Balangoda hourly services to **Colombo** (3-4 hrs). For the south coast, buses run from Pelmadulla to **Tangalla** via **Embilitipiya** (2 hrs).

❶ Directory

Ratnapura *p114, map p116*
Post office Main post office, clocktower square, Mon-Fri 0830-1900. **Useful address** Tourist police, main police station, opposite clocktower, corner with Bandaranaike Mawatha.

Beaches along the southwest coast

Beyond Colombo's urban sprawl lie the golden beaches that serve Sri Lanka's package tourism industry. To some, the coast's wealth of quality accommodation, beach restaurants and bars makes for a perfect indulgent holiday; to others it has been spoilt by over-development. Yet away from the resorts traditional life continues. Many people still depend on fishing with fishermen bringing in their catch at numerous points along the coast. The coconut palms that line the shore also provide a livelihood for many. The road and railway line hug the ocean as they go south – an enjoyable journey.
➤➤ *For listings, see pages 133-142.*

South to Kalutara

Moratuwa, 23 km south of Colombo, has a large Catholic population, and some fine churches. The town is also noted for its furniture making and its college, and you will see by the side of the road furniture workshops carving wood into a wide variety of intricate designs. There is plenty of accommodation in Moratuwa, mainly by **Bolgoda Lake**, popular for local weddings and as a weekend escape from Colombo. Here you can fish for barramundi, or take boat trips out to the lake's islands.

Panadura, to the south of a wide estuary, has many fine colonial mansions. From here, the A8 road leads east to Ratnapura and beyond, hugging the southern edge of the highlands. The town is known for producing some of the highest quality **batik** in Sri Lanka. It is well worth the small diversion to the workshop and showroom of **Bandula Fernando** ① *289/5 Noel Mendis Rd, just off the A2, T034-223 3369.* One of the foremost batik designers in Sri Lanka, Bandula Fernando combines traditional and modern styles to produce some exceptionally vibrant and original batik designs. He is also credited with evolving mosaic art in batik, acknowledged as a uniquely individual style of batik. The designs on offer are quite different from those seen elsewhere on the island and are sold at fair prices considering the detail and excellence.

Kalutara → *Phone code: 034. Colour map 3, B2. 42 km from Colombo. Population 38,000.*

Kalutara is a busy district capital renowned for its basket-making. Leaves of the wild date are dyed red, orange, green and black, and woven into hats, mats and baskets. To guard the spice trade the Portuguese built a fort on the site of a Buddhist temple here. The Dutch took it over and a British agent converted it into his residence. The site, by the bridge across the Kalu Ganga, now again has a modern Buddhist shrine, the **Gangatilaka Vihara**, with a sacred Bo tree outside. It is worth stopping to visit the hollow *dagoba* (actually a *dagoba* within a *dagoba*), as others on the island contain relics and are not accessible. Most remarkable are the extraordinary acoustics, which can be quite disorienting. There are 75 paintings inside, illustrating events from the Buddha's life.

Kalutara has a huge stretch of fine sand with **Wadduwa**, to the north, home to the area's top resorts. Kalutara itself divides into **Mahawaskaduwa** (Kalutara North) where the beach is more scenic, right down to **Katukurunda** (Kalutara South).

At **Palatota**, a little inland, is **Richmond Castle** ① *0900-1600, Rs 100.* A fine country house in a 17-ha fruit garden estate, it is now used as an education centre for underprivileged local children. Built in 1896, it originally belonged to landowner-turned-philanthropist NDA Silva Wijayasinghe, the local Padikara Mudah (village leader), and was

Sap tappers

Palm toddy is a universal favourite for Sri Lankans, as is the stronger distilled arrack, both of which are found throughout the island. They (as well as sweet palm juice, treacle or jaggery) are produced from the sap which is collected in earthen pots that you'll notice hanging at the base of the long green fronds at the crown of the palms which have been set aside for 'tapping'.

The sap flows when the apex of an unopened flower bunch is 'tapped' by slicing it off and tapping it with a stick to make the cells burst and the juice to flow. This usually starts in about three weeks of the first cut. From then on successive flower buds are tapped so that sap collecting can continue for half a year. Fruit production, of course, stops during this period, but tapping seems to result in an improved crop of nuts where the yield had previously been poor.

The sap is extracted from the crown of the palms by the *duravas* (toddy tappers). The skilful tapper usually ties a circle of rope around his ankles and shins up the tall smooth trunk two or three times a day to empty the sap pot into one he has tied around his waist. An agile man collecting from a group of palms will often get from tree to tree by using pairs of coconut fibre ropes tied from one tree top to the next, which saves the tapper time and energy wasted in climbing down and up again.

used during the British period as a circuit bungalow for officials. Note the audience hall, with intricately carved pillars and beams (two shiploads of teak were brought from Burma for its construction) and a spiral staircase leading to a gallery. Another room shows some fascinating photographs from the time. Turn left immediately after the *vihara* along the Kalutara–Palatota road. After 2 km, a track leads left to the house.

The large number of coconut palms along the coast road marks this as the centre of the arrack industry. The island's best quality mangosteen (introduced from Malaya in the early 19th century) and rubber are economically important. Graphite is also mined. Wild hog deer, introduced by the Dutch from the Ganga Delta, are reputedly still found nearby.

Beruwela, Aluthgama and Bentota

The coast at this point becomes more developed, with half a dozen villages indistinguishably joined together. Beruwela and its adjoining villages, with several large hotel resorts popular primarily with Germans, is at the north end, while Aluthgama, a little further south, is protected from the sea by a spit of land. Some characterful smaller guesthouses and restaurants can be found here, with a more peaceful riverside setting. The Bentota Bridge spans one of Sri Lanka's largest rivers, south of which Bentota, and particularly Walauwa, contain some sumptuous, and very expensive, places to stay.

Beruwela → *Phone code: 034. Colour map 3, B2. Population 34,000. 58 km from Colombo. The beach is notorious for its 'beach boys', who crowd around the beach entrances to the hotels.*
The name Beruwela is derived from the Sinhalese word *Baeruala* ('the place where the sail is lowered'). It marks the spot where the first Arab Muslim settlers are believed to have landed in around the eighth century. **Kitchimalai Mosque**, on a headland 3 km north along the beach from the main hotel area, is worth seeing. It is a major pilgrimage centre at the end of **Ramadan** since there is also a shrine of a 10th-century Muslim saint; guides

guides may tell you that it is the oldest mosque in Sri Lanka but this is unlikely to be true. Looking east from the mosque, **Beruwela harbour** is an interesting place to watch the fishermen unload their catch. The harbour has over 600 boats, many of which are quite sizeable since the fishermen spend up to two months at sea. The fish market is busy in the early morning – you may well see fresh shark or tuna change hands even before the sun is up. You can also hire a boat to the lighthouse raised on a small island offshore which offers an excellent view of the coastline from the top.

All the hotels listed in this section are actually in **Moragalla**, an adjoining settlement to the south of Beruwela, with some of the more upmarket hotels further south at **Kaluwamodara**. Fishermen offer to ferry holidaymakers across the narrow estuary to Bentota, the next resort.

Beruwela

Sleeping
Bavarian Guest House 1
Belfry Guest House 3
Club Palm Garden 4
Eden Resort & Spa 5
Panorama 7
Riverina 8
Ypsylon Guest House
& Dive Centre 12
The Palms 2

Aluthgama → *Phone code: 034. Colour map 3, B2. 60 km from Colombo.*

Aluthgama, the principal town here, has a busy fish market and is famous for its oysters. The sand spit which separates the river from the sea where most of the hotels are built provides excellent waters for windsurfing and sailing. Many of the hotels referred to as being in Bentota are to the north of the Bentota Bridge and so are actually in Aluthgama.

Bentota → *Phone code: 034. Colour map 3, B2. 63 km from Colombo. The sea is rough during the monsoons – best between Nov and Apr.*

Bentota Bridge marks the border between the Western and Southern Provinces. The 40-ha **National Resort Complex** is built entirely for foreign tourists with shops, a bank and a post office. A full range of sports is available and the area is also gaining a reputation for providing first-class Ayurvedic healing centres, with many more under construction. South of Bentota, along Galle Road towards Induruwa, the area feels less of a tourist ghetto, and the natural beauty of the coastline returns. Here are some of the most sumptuous places to stay in the entire island. Unofficial 'guides' offer nearby river and lagoon trips and visits to temples, coir factories and woodcarvers. They are very overpriced.

The splendid **Brief Garden** ① *T227 0462, daily 0800-1700, Rs 800*, at Kalawila was created between 1929 and 1989 by the late Bevis Bawa, the landscape architect, writer,

Aluthgama & Bentota

Sleeping 🛏️
Ayubowan **4**
Bentota Beach **2**
Club Bentota **12**
Club Villa **5**
Ganga Garden **3**
Hemadan **7**
Nilwala **10**

Saman Villas **9**
Sun and Moon **8**
Susantha & Palm
Restaurant **15**
Terrena **1**
The Villa **18**
Vivanta by Taj **17**
Wunderbar Beach Club **6**

Eating 🍴
Anushka River Inn **3**
Diya Sisila **1**
Singharaja **4**

sculptor, bon vivant and brother to Geoffrey (see box, page 374) – the name refers to a court brief! It is an enchanting garden in an undulating landscape of paddies and scattered villages on a hillside. The 2-ha garden with cool, shady paths and many mature specimen trees, was really created as a series of wonderfully composed views, designed in different moods. There are many references to European- and Japanese-style gardens, with shade-loving anthurium and alocasia plants common throughout. Bawa's house though is the highlight, with its eclectic private collection of paintings, sculptures, photographs (note Edward VIII and Lord Olivier, both of whom stayed here) and furniture (many colonial antiques), providing an added incentive to visit. Some of the paintings were composed by Australian artist Donald Friend, who came for a week and stayed for six years. Bawa himself appears in a number of forms, both in the house and garden, at one point representing Bacchus, holding a birdbath shaped as a giant clam-shell. In his outside bathroom, he appears again as a water-spouting gargoyle with wild hair and blue marble eyes. From Aluthgama, take the road inland to Matugama, and then Dhargatown (8 km). From here, a 2-km rough track (right at the first fork and left at the second) takes you to the gardens.

Induruwa to Ambalangoda

Induruwa → *Phone code: 034. Colour map 3, B2. 68 km from Colombo.*

Induruwa, with its pleasant stretch of beach, is being developed and some new hotels and guesthouses are opening up. Attractions in the area include several turtle hatcheries.

Visitors are welcome at the **turtle hatchery** ⓘ *Galle Rd, Bentota South, T227 5850, Rs 200; donations appreciated.* Formerly part of the Victor Hasselblad Project, the hatchery has been running for about 20 years, buying eggs from local fishermen at a higher price than they would normally get if sold for food. The eggs are buried as soon as possible in batches of 50. After hatching, the baby turtles are placed in holding tanks for two to three days before being released into the sea in the evening under supervision. Depending on the time of year (best November to April), you can see the hatchlings of up to five species – green, olive ridley, hawksbill, leatherback and loggerhead – at any one time. An example of each species is also held in separate tanks for research purposes.

Kosgoda → *Phone code: 091. Colour map 3, B2. 73 km from Colombo.*

Kosgoda's 4-km stretch of beach has the highest density of turtle nesting in the country. In August 2003, the **Turtle Conservation Project (TCP)** launched a programme with the financial assistance of the UNDP to protect 1 km of the beach with the assistance of former nest poachers, retrained as 'nest-protectors' and tour guides. The **Kosgoda Sea Turtle Conservation Project** ① *Galle Rd, T226 4567, www.kosgodaseaturtle.org, 0900-1700, Rs 200*, is open nearly every day and welcomes visitors and volunteers. Learn more about turtles and visit the hatchery. Contact them in advance if you want to take part in an evening turtle watch.

Balapitiya → *Phone code: 091. Colour map 3, C2. 81 km from Colombo.*

A few kilometres north of Ambalangoda near the small town of Balapitiya, a bridge fords the Madu Ganga. The estuary is a major **wetlands** area, famous for its 64 islands. Tours are offered which usually include a visit to the 150-year-old **Koth Duwa temple**, and an island where you can watch cinnamon being cut and prepared, though bear in mind that the finished oil, bark and powder for sale is overpriced. You will also see some wildlife as the estuary is home to more than 300 varieties of plant, including 95 families of mangrove, marshes and scrub supporting 17 species of birds, and a wide variety of amphibians and reptiles; water monitors are common. River safari operators leave from either side of the bridge. A 1½-hour trip, visiting two islands, costs around Rs 12,000 for a six-person boat.

Ambalangoda → *Phone code: 091. Colour map 3, C2. Population 20,100. 85 km from Colombo.*

The busy town of Ambalangoda is an important commercial and fish trading centre. With some local colour, and a fine sweep of sandy beach to its north, some visitors opt to stay here over its more touristy resort neighbours along the coast. The town is chiefly famous as the home of **devil dancing** and **mask making**, which many families have carried out for generations. It may be possible to watch a performance of *kolama* (folk theatre); ask at the museum or School of Dancing (see below). Ambalangoda is also famous as a major centre for cinnamon cultivation and production. Ask your hotel or guesthouse about visiting a plantation and factory. The colourful fish market is worth visiting early in the morning.

Sights

There are actually two **Ariyapala Mask museums** ① *426 Patabendimulla, 0830-1730*, run by the two sons of the late mask-carver, who set up in competition. The museums are opposite one another: the smaller one houses the museum proper, while the other 'mask museum' is primarily a workshop and showroom. Some of the exhibits tracing the tradition of mask dancing are interesting and informative. The masks can be very elaborate. The *naga raksha* mask from the **Raksha Kolama** (Devil Dance), for example, has a fearsome face with bulging eyes that roll around, a bloodthirsty tongue hanging from a

Dance of the sorcerers

The **Devil Dance** evolved from the rural people's need to appease malevolent forces in nature and seek blessing from good spirits when there was an evil spirit to be exorcised, such as a sickness to be cured. It takes the form of a ritual dance, full of high drama, with a sorcerer 'priest' and an altar. As evening approaches, the circular arena in the open air is lit by torches, and masked dancers appear to the beating of drums and chanting. During the exorcism ritual, which lasts all night, the 'priest' casts the evil spirit out of the sick. There are 18 demons associated with afflictions for which different fearsome *sanni* masks are worn. There is an element of awe and grotesqueness about the whole performance and these dances have a serious purpose and are, therefore, not on offer as 'performances'.

The **Kolam Dance** has its origins in folk theatre. The story tells of a queen, who, while expecting a child, had a deep craving to see a masked dance. This was satisfied by the Carpenter of the Gods, Visvakarma, who invented the dances.

The *kolam* dances tell stories and again make full use of a wonderful variety of masks (often giant in size) representing imaginary characters from folk tales, Buddhist *jatakas*, gods and devils, as well as well-known members of the royal court and more mundane figures from day-to-day life. Animals (lions, bears) too, feature as playful characters. This form of folk dance resembles the more serious Devil Dance in some ways – it is again performed during the night and in a similar circular, torch-lit, open-air 'stage' (originally *kolam* was performed for several nights during New Year festivities). In spite of a serious or moral undertone, a sprinkling of cartoon characters is introduced to provide comic relief. The clever play on words can only be really appreciated by a Sinhalese speaker.

mouth lined with fang-like teeth, all topped by a set of cobra hoods (see box, above). You can watch the odd craftsmen at work carving traditional masks from the light *kaduru* wood. The carvings on sale in the showroom are not of the best quality and are quite expensive. It is better to take your time to visit some of the smaller workshops around town on foot and compare prices and quality.

Traditional dancing shows take place about once a month at **Bandu Wijesooriya School of Dancing** ⓘ *417 Patabendimulla, T225 8948, www.banduwijesooriyadanceacademy.org*. A typical show will include a *kolam* dance, followed by several ritual dances, a village folk dance, and end up with some short Indian dances. Courses are also possible at the school, which is closed on Sunday, where they teach dance, drumming and mask-carving.

Excursions

At **Karandeniya**, 208 steps lead up to the **Galabuddha temple**, which has a 33-m-long lying Buddha, which a sign proudly proclaims to be the biggest in South Asia. The murals are worthy of note. The temple is 11 km inland from Ambalangoda, along the Elpitiya Road.

At **Meetiyagoda**, 16 km inland, there is a moonstone quarry. The semi-precious stone, which often has a bluish milky tinge, is polished and set in silver or gold jewellery. The road sign claims that it's the 'only natural moonstone quarry in the world'.

Hikkaduwa is Sri Lanka's beach party capital, so if you are looking for peace and a beach to yourself, then you might wish to avoid it. A victim of its own success, the island's original surfers' hangout is now its most popular resort with mass tourism bringing pollution and overcrowding, as well a reputation for unsavoury activities and beach boys. Galle Road runs the length of the town, so watch out for speeding buses and bear in mind the street noise when choosing a room. Things may change, however, when the Colombo–Matara highway opens in the future and takes the bulk of the through traffic away. Natural forces are also chipping away at Hikkaduwa's charm. The beach here is gradually disappearing with the sea noticeably encroaching inland year by year. This said, the resort still has some appeal. This coastal stretch has a vast number of high quality hotels and guesthouses of all price ranges. The food, especially seafood, is often excellent and with so much competition, reasonably priced. And the opportunities for watersports – swimming, snorkelling, scuba diving (as long as you don't expect living coral) and especially surfing – is probably unrivalled on the island.

Ins and outs

Getting there The bus station is in the centre of Hikkaduwa town. All accommodation lies to the south. The train station is about 200 m north of the bus station. Express trains and private buses are best for those travelling from or via Colombo.

Getting around There are four parts to what is known collectively as 'Hikkaduwa'. At the northern end is **Hikkaduwa** proper, the original settlement. The beach tends to be somewhat narrower here and less appealing. Further south is **Wewala**, where the beach is a wider and more attractive. Along with **Narigama** this is the main 'centre' with numerous beach bars and restaurants, and the cheapest accommodation. At the southern end is **Thirangama**, which is less frantic, but has good surfing waves and a wider beach. A major disadvantage though is the very busy main road which runs close to the beach. It is possible to walk uninterrupted along much of the beach. Three-wheelers can be stopped along the Galle Road (bus drivers are less obliging), but you will need to negotiate the price. Cycles and motorbikes can be hired.

Hikkaduwa area

To Baddegama (11km)
To Colombo, Telwatte Vihara & Ambalangoda
Gonapinuwala
HIKKADUWA
B12
WEWALA
NARIGAMA
THIRANGAMA
PUTUWATHA
Indian Ocean
A2
Polgasduwa
N
DODANDUWA
Lagoon
To Galle

1 km
1 mile

Sleeping
Eco Village **1**

Sights

Hikkaduwa's '**coral sanctuary**' is a shallow protected reef, close to the **Coral Gardens Hotel**. Once teeming with life, it was badly affected by 'bleaching' in early 1998, when sea temperatures rose causing the coral to reject the algae on which coral life fed. Recovery has been slow. The reef, and fish population, has also been degraded by tourism. Unregulated growth in the use of

Hikkaduwa & Wewala beach

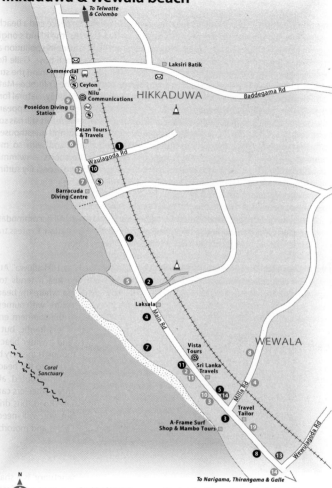

▲ To Telwatte
& Colombo

Laksiri Batik

Commercial

Ceylon

Nilu
@ Communications

HIKKADUWA

Baddegama Rd

Poseidon Diving
Station

Pasan Tours
& Travels

Waulagoda Rd

Barracuda
Diving Centre

Laksala

WEWALA

Coral
Sanctuary

Main Rd

Vista
Tours
@

Sri Lanka
Travels

Milla Rd

Travel
Tailor

A-Frame Surf
Shop & Mambo Tours

Wewulagoda Rd

To Narigama, Thirangama & Galle

N

200 metres
200 yards

Sleeping
Blue Ocean Villa 3
Chaaya Tranz 5
Citrus 2

Coral Reef Beach 6
Coral Rock 7
Coral Sands 1
El-Dorado 8
Hikkaduwa Beach 9
Lanka Super Corals 11
Mama's Coral Beach 12
Moon Beam 14
Surf Villa 4

Tandem Guest House 19
Time N Tide 10

Eating
Abba's 1
Budde's Beach 3
Cool Spot 2
Curry Bowl 4
JLH 7

Red Lobster 10
Refresh 11
Sam's Surfers Rest 5
Sea View 6
The Coffee Shop 8

Bars & clubs
Roger's Garage 14
Vibration 13

glass-bottomed boats to ferry visitors across the reef, dynamite fishing and the dumping of garbage from beachside hotels have all contributed to the denigration of the habitat, prompting the Department of Wildlife to upgrade the area to National Park status in 2002. However, it is still possible to see reef fish, which are fed by fishermen to provide an attraction for visitors. Glass-bottomed boats can be hired along the beach, though since the reef is shallow and close to shore, it is easy and less damaging to swim and snorkel to it. Despite the reduced diversity and population of coral and fish, Hikkaduwa is a good base for **scuba diving** and local operators run trips to up to 20 sites along the coast. Most rewarding close to Hikkaduwa are the rock formations, especially the deep **Kirala Gala** (21 m to 38 m), 10 minutes offshore, where there is also a wide range of pristine coral with groupers, barracuda and batfish. A number of wrecks, some in fairly shallow water, can also be visited, such as the *Earl of Shaftesbury*, though the wreck-diving is better in the bays further south at Galle or Weligama. Visibility varies from 8 m to 25 m, depending on the time of day (morning is better), and is at its best around the full moon period.

Hikkaduwa is Sri Lanka's **surf centre** from December to April, and has hosted numerous international competitions. It is particularly good for beginners as the waves are comparatively gentle, most breaking on the reefs rather than the beach. The focus is around the main break, known as the 'A-Frame' because of its distinctive apex, in Wewala, though this can be crowded in peak months. **Narigama** and **Thiragama** further south are usually quieter, though you will also need more experience.

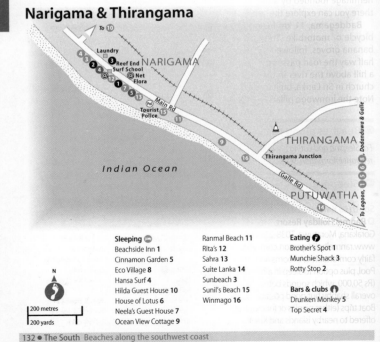

Narigama & Thirangama

Sleeping
Beachside Inn **1**
Cinnamon Garden **5**
Eco Village **8**
Hansa Surf **4**
Hilda Guest House **10**
House of Lotus **6**
Neela's Guest House **7**
Ocean View Cottage **9**
Ranmal Beach **11**
Rita's **12**
Sahra **13**
Suite Lanka **14**
Sunbeach **3**
Sunil's Beach **15**
Winmago **16**

Eating
Brother's Spot **1**
Munchie Shack **3**
Rotty Stop **2**

Bars & clubs
Drunken Monkey **5**
Top Secret **4**

Excursions

Alut Vihara (Totagama Rajamahavihara) at Telwatta, 2 km north of Hikkaduwa, dates from the early 19th century. It is the only temple to Anangaya on the island, where lovers make offerings to him. The carvings between the fine *makara* (dragon) arches leading to the sanctuary hide a cupid with his bow and flower-tipped arrows. The murals too are particularly impressive. Rarely visited by travellers, it is worth a trip and also makes a very pleasant bicycle ride.

Seenigama Temple, 6 km north, is on an island just offshore. The Devil's Temple here has enormous importance for local fishermen, who believe he will protect both their lives and wealth. You will need the services of a fisherman to get to the island. At another more easily accessible roadside temple, a few kilometres north on Galle Road, Sri Lankan travellers pay their respects, bringing most traffic to a temporary halt.

At Dodanduwa, **Kumarakanda Rajamahavihara**, 4 km south of Hikkaduwa just before Km 103 post, has some murals and statues, though it is on the tourist trail so expect a dancing monkey and 'school pen' collectors. The temple is reached by a long steep and narrow flight of stone steps. Donations are expected. The beach opposite has a very small private **Turtle Research Centre** ① *Rs 200*, which works to protect this endangered species. You can see eggs and different stages of development and a few posters under a shelter.

More relaxing as a break from the busy schedule at the beach is the picturesque **Ratgama Lake** which has abundant bird life and a large population of water monitors. There are three islands in the lagoon, one of which is **Polgasduwa**, where there is forest hermitage founded by a German monk. Touts offer trips from the beach. Once you are there you can explore the lagoon by paddleboat .

Baddegama, 11 km inland along the B153, is within easy reach of Hikkaduwa by bicycle or motorbike. The road is picturesque, cutting its way through coconut and banana groves, followed by several small plantations – rubber, tea and spices. About half way the road passes the **Nigro Dharama Mahavihara** (stupa) in Gonapinuwala. On a hill above the river in the grounds of Christ Church Girls College is the first Anglican church in Sri Lanka, built in 1818 and consecrated by Bishop Heber of Calcutta in 1825. Note the ironwood pillars.

◉ Beaches along the southwest coast listings

For Sleeping and Eating price codes and other relevant information, see pages 26-32.

◉ Sleeping

South to Kalutara *p124*

D Ranmal Holiday Resort, 346/5 Galle Rd, Gorakana, Moratuwa, T038-229 8921, www.ranmalholidayresort.com. 25 large, fairly comfortable a/c rooms and 2 bungalows. Pool, plus option to sleep in a houseboat (Rs 50,000, which sounds better than it is), overall shabby but good position on the lake. Boat trips (either picnics or for overnight stay) offered to nearby islands and Kalutara.

Kalutara *p124*

LL-L Blue Water, Thalpitiya, Wadduwa, T223 5067, www.bluewatersrilanka.com. Excellent rooms, in luxurious hotel with top facilities amidst palm groves, designed by Geoffrey Bawa, with spacious public areas, understated decor, ethnic feel (copied but not excelled by other hotels along the coast), spa and large imaginative pool with resident monitor lizard.

AL Privilege, 260 Samanthura Rd, Molligoda, Wadduwa, T038-229 5367, privilege@ sltnet.lk. 24 luxurious, well-furnished suites, with TV, some with jacuzzi, jewellery shop with imaginative designs. Half board only

(7-course dinner). Self-consciously 'boutiquey', though rather cramped.

AL Royal Palms Beach, De Abrew Rd, Kalutara North, T222 8113, www.tangerinehotels.com. 124 superb fully equipped rooms plus suites, private balcony or patio with sea or garden views, disco and pub, sports facilities shared with **Tangerine Beach Hotel**, huge pool (you can almost swim around the hotel).

A Tangerine Beach, De Abrews Rd, Waskaduwa, T222 6640, www.tangerine hotels.com. 166 a/c rooms and suites, full facilities though reception can be slow, beautifully laid out with huge lawns and ponds stretching beneath coconut palms to the sea, popular with package groups.

A-B Hibiscus Beach, Mahawaskaduwa, T508 2222, www.hibiscusbeachhotel.com. 50 large rooms, and villas with jacuzzis, lounge bar overlooks colourful hibiscus garden, pool, sports, good beach.

A-B Mermaid Hotel & Club, Mahawaskaduwa, T222 2613, www.mermaidhotelnclub.com. 72 a/c rooms, split-level restaurant, bars, sports, excursions, mainly tour groups, beautiful location in coconut plantation, attractive lawn runs down to beach.

B Kani Lanka Resort & Spa, St Sebastian's Rd, Katukurunda, T428 0801, www.kanilanka.com. 105 comfortable a/c rooms and suites, some with private balcony and tub, in a good location sandwiched between sea and lagoon, floating restaurant, pool, mini-golf, watersports on lagoon, Ayurvedic health centre, traditional-style spa, cultural shows.

Ayurvedic resort
Siddhalepa Ayurveda Health Resort, 861 Samanthara Rd, Wadduwa, T229 6967, www.ayurvedaresort.com. Siddhalepa is one of the most famous names in Sri Lankan Ayurvedic therapy, with a 200-year history. The resort is less 'authentic' than other new creations as it accepts non-Ayurveda guests and possesses a bar. There are 50 rooms, including 6 suites, in beautiful gardens full of Ayurveda plants. Suites are themed – 2 'caves', 2 made from clay and 2 Chandra Vasa,

traditional Sri Lankan *kabok* and stone with furniture of magobe wood (recommended). Other rooms resemble a Dutch fort with mini canal system outside (kids can paddle around on a boat). Packages range from 1-4 weeks including consultation and all treatments for non-Ayurveda guests.

Beruwela p125, map p126
LL-AL Eden Resort & Spa, Kaluwamodara, T227 6075, www.edenresortandspa.com. 158 rooms, suites and penthouses, grand entrance, large pool, spa, full entertainment and sports facilities. Friendly staff.

AL Club Palm Garden, T227 6217, www.lolcleisure.com. 140 a/c rooms with either garden view, pool view or sea view. Restaurant, bars, pool, lots of activities.

AL-A Riverina, Kaluwamodara, T227 6044, www.riverinahotel.com. 192 a/c rooms, full facilities including tennis, watersports, good indoor games room, 3 restaurants, Ayurvedic centre, well organized.

B The Palms, T227 6041, resvthepalms@ sltnet.lk. 100 large a/c, sea-facing rooms. Pool, Ayurvedic centre.

C Bavarian Guest House, 92 Barberyn Rd, T227 6129, www.bavarianguesthouse.com. 7 large modern a/c and fan rooms around attractive courtyard with pool, hot water bath, restaurant, bar. German and English spoken.

C Belfry Guest House, 13/4 Galle Rd, T558 1138, www.belfryguesthousesrilanka.com. ·5 a/c and fan rooms with terrace or balcony, some overlooking the pool and others with sea view. Restaurant, helpful and friendly staff.

C-D Ypsylon Guest House, T227 6132, ypsylon@slt.lk. 25 a/c and fan rooms, hot water, breakfast included, pool, German-run diving school (see Tour operators, page 140).

F Panorama, Maradana Rd, T227 7091, www.hotelpanoramalk.com. 10 simple, clean fan rooms in small guesthouse, restaurant, good value for the area.

Ayurvedic resorts
Barberyn Reef, Moragalla, T227 6036, www.barberynresorts.comcom. Opened in

1982, the 1st Ayurvedic centre in Sri Lanka. A range of rooms, some with a/c and some split-level with a living area. Extensive Ayurvedic health centre, safe swimming enclosed by a reef.

Muthumuni, T227 6766, www.muthumuni resort.com. German-run resort in very peaceful setting on the lagoon (own boat service to meditation temple). 1- to 2-week Ayurvedic packages. Also has an Ayurvedic beach resort.

Aluthgama *p126, map p127*

AL-A Club Bentota, 'Island Paradise', T227 5167, www.clubbentota.com. 146 bungalows, suites and rooms with ocean or river views on small spit of land accessible by shuttle boat, full facilities.

C Ganga Garden, 126/27 Galle Rd, Kaluwamodara, T428 9444, www.ganga-garden.com. 6 spotless, well-furnished, a/c and fan rooms, in attractive setting overlooking river, hot bath, restaurant, watersports and fishing.

C-D Nilwala, Galle Rd (on the river), Kaluwamodara, T227 5017, www.hotel nilwala.com. 10 clean a/c rooms, although a/c units are noisy, overlooking river, watersports.

D Hemadan, 25 Riverside Rd (on the river bank), T227 5320, www.hemadan.dk. 10 good clean a/c and fan rooms, some with balcony, though bigger without. Danish-owned, quiet, hot bath, restaurant, watersports, free boat shuttle to beach.

D-E Terrena, Riverside Rd, closest guesthouse to the bridge, T428 9015. 6 clean small but attractive a/c and fan rooms with hot water, Austrian-owned, pleasant terrace and garden. Good restaurant.

E Sun and Moon, 104/8 Galle Rd, T494 3453, www.sunandmoonsrilanka.com. 10 decent-sized a/c rooms. Good location on the river.

Ayurvedic resorts

Lanka Princess, Kaluwamodara, T227 6711, www.lankaprincess.com. German-managed hotel offering 110 sea-facing rooms and suites. A/c, wide range of Ayurvedic treatments, yoga, tai chi and pool.

Bentota *p126, map p127*

LL Saman Villas, Aturuwella, on a rocky headland 5 km south, T227 5435, www.samanvilla.com. 27 magnificent suites with sea views set on a spectacular rocky headland. All have attractive furnishings, and 'astonishing' open-air baths with rain shower. Superb pool high above sea which seems to merge with the ocean, panoramic views and access to long beaches either side. Good spa. Expensive but worth every rupee.

LL-L Club Villa, 138/15 Galle Rd, T227 5312, www.club-villa.com. 17 beautiful, though simple rooms (1 suite) in a Dutch-style villa, restaurant, wonderfully peaceful palm-shaded garden, small pool, beach a short walk across coastal railway line, friendly staff, superb ambience.

LL-L The Villa (Paradise Rd), 138/18-22 Galle Rd (1.5 km south of Bentota), T227 5311, www.paradiseroadhotels.com. A former residence of Geoffrey Bawa, exquisite rooms in a large villa dated 1880, each individually designed, decorated and furnished with antique furniture. Superb bathrooms (open-air bath), beautiful shaded garden, understated pool. Sublime.

L-AL Vivanta by Taj, T555 5555, www.vivantabytaj.com. 162 large a/c rooms (higher floors best) in magnificent top-class hotel in a superb location on a headland, all with sea-facing balcony or terrace, good food, fantastic pool.

AL Bentota Beach (Keels), south of Bentota Bridge, T227 5176, www.johnkeellshotels.com. 133 comfortable a/c rooms and suites, design reminiscent (and built on the site of) a Dutch fort, luxurious layout in extensive gardens, good beach, full facilities including pool and Ayurvedic spa, location of **Club Inter Sport** (see page 140).

B-C Wunderbar Beach Club, Robolgoda, T227 5908, www.hotel-wunderbar.com. 14 a/c rooms some with sea views, and 1 private bungalow (**A**). Restaurant, watersports and a turtle project.

B-E Ayubowan, 171 Galle Rd, Bentota South, T227 5913, www.ayubowan.ch.

Bright, spacious and spotless bungalows with attractive furniture, in pleasant gardens, as well as a suite and a cheap backpacker room. Restaurant has wide selection of food, including pizza. Swiss-owned.

D-E Susantha, Resort Rd, Pitaramba, next to Bentota railway station (5 mins from beach, across from the rail track), T227 5324, www.hotelsusanthas.com. 18 spotless good-sized rooms with bath in pleasant chalets, prices vary according to facilities. Bar, good restaurant and Ayurvedic centre. Suites also available (**C**).

Ayurvedic resorts

Aida Ayurveda Resort, 12a Managala Mawatha, Bentota, T227 1137, www.aidaayurveda.com. Spacious courtyards with good local furniture in great setting on Bentota River. 40 comfortable rooms with TV, small balcony. 1-day Ayurveda packages available for non-residents, including consultation, massage or herbal bath/sauna.

Ayurveda Walauwa, Galle Rd, Warahena, T275 3378, www.ayurvedawalauwabentota. com. 20 a/c rooms in treatment centre, 2-week stays are advised for best effect.

Dalmanuta Gardens, Meegama Rd, Warapitiya, T077-343 4434, www.dalma nuta.com. 9 bungalows in pleasant gardens near the river. Good food, the full-board Ayurveda rate includes all meals, doctor's consultation, daily massages, yoga, etc. Half-day Ayurveda packages also available. Very welcoming to non-Ayurvedic guests as well.

Niroga Ayurveda Health Centre, next to **Saman Villas**, T227 0312, www.niroga ayurvedaresort.com. 8 simple fan rooms, minimum stay 1 week. Also 1-day courses possible (phone in advance). Restaurant serving meals based on Ayurvedic diagnosis.

Induruwa to Ambalangoda *p127*
LL-L Heritance Ahungalla (Aitken Spence), Ahungalla, 6 km south of Kosgoda, T555 5000 www.heritancehotels.com/ahungalla. 152 a/c rooms, including 9 suites, excellent

food, full sports and entertainment facilities, imaginative landscaping merging ponds into swimming pool into sea; you can virtually swim up to reception (pool open to non-residents who stay for a meal). Excellent beach, well-run hotel.

L-AL La Maison Nil Manel, 162/4 Wathuregama, Ahungalla, T226 4331, www.nilmanel.info. Small French/Sri Lankan-owned hotel offering 6 a/c rooms (1 suite), tastefully decorated. Pool, excellent food, relaxing atmosphere.

A Kosgoda Beach Resort, between the sea and lagoon, T226 4017, www.kosgoda beachresort.lk. 42 comfortable and attractive a/c rooms, including 12 suites, open-air tubs, large garden, lovely pool, boating, restaurant.

B Royal Beach Resort, Galle Rd, Galaboda, Induruwa, T227 4351, www.royalbeach.asia. British-owned, light and spacious if slightly tacky (map of Sri Lanka in the pond), gleaming hotel in colonial style. Attractive a/c rooms with TV, tubs and veranda with great views of the ocean, clean stretch of beach.

B-C Induruwa Beach Resort, Galle Rd, T227 5445, www.induruwabeachresort.com. 84 a/c rooms and 6 suites, private balconies with sea view, pool with jacuzzi, full facilities, on good section of beach but large 4-storey block with uninspired architecture, mainly package groups, good value.

F Long Beach Cottage, Galle Rd, (next to **Royal Beach Resort**), T227 5773, hanjayas@yahoo.de. 5 clean, sea-facing rooms with fan, local dishes and seafood to order, pleasant mangrove shaded garden with direct access to a fine beach, free pick-up from Aluthgama station, friendly Sri Lankan/German owners.

Ayurvedic resorts

Lotus Villa, 162/19 Wathuregama, south of Ahungalla, T226 4082, www.lotus-villa.com. 14 rooms in exclusive Ayurvedic herbal curative treatment centre, most with sea views. Prices include transfers, all meals, consultations and treatment.

Ambalangoda p128

C Dream Beach Resort, 509 Galle Rd,
T225 8873, www.dream-beach-hotel.de.
21 large comfortable a/c rooms, some with
sea view, balcony, TV, restaurant, pool, small
rocky beach, mainly German clientele.
Minimum 1-week stays preferred.

D-E Shangrela Beach Resort, 38 Sea Beach
Rd, T225 8342, www.shangrela.de. 25 clean,
comfortable fan and a/c rooms, hot water.
Large garden, organizes boat trips. Flats are
also available for rent on a weekly basis.

F-G Sumudu Tourist Guest House,
418 Main St, Patabendimulla, T225 8832.
6 fan and a/c rooms, good home-cooking,
pleasant atmosphere, good value.

Hikkaduwa p130, maps p131 and p132
There are innumerable hotels lining
the beach here, often with very little to
distinguish between them. Places away
from the beach, understandably, tend to be
cheaper than beachfront properties with
similar facilities. Many prices drop by up to
50% out of season (May-Oct). Whatever
season you visit, it is worth bargaining.

Hikkaduwa

A Chaaya Tranz, formerly **Coral Gardens**
(Keells), T227 7023, www.johnkeells
hotels.com. Currently being refurbished
and due to open end of 2011/beginning
2012. It will offer 150 a/c rooms with sea
views, restaurants, pool, spa and all the
usual facilities. At the time of writing rates
were not finalised, so prices may exceed
the code listed above.

A-B Coral Sands, 326 Galle Rd, T227 7513,
www.coralsandshotel.com. 75 clean and airy
a/c rooms with balcony, not all sea facing and
some newer than others, restaurant, bar, pools,
diving school, friendly, reasonable value.

B Citrus, formerly **Amaya Reef**, 400 Galle Rd,
T438 3244, www.citrusleisure.com. Hard to
miss from the outside, 50 a/c rooms with
balcony or terrace facing the sea. Pool,
restaurant and diving available.

B Hikkaduwa Beach, 298 Galle Rd, T227
7327, www.hbeachhotel.com. 50 clean a/c
rooms (top floor best), most with balcony
and sea view, modern block, small pool,
Ayurvedic centre.

C-E Mama's Coral Beach, 338 Galle Rd,
T567 7724, www.mamascoralbeach.com.
A/c and fan rooms with balcony, though
a narrow property so most without views,
highly rated seafood restaurant, the first in
Hikkaduwa (see Eating, page 139).

D-E Coral Reef Beach Hotel, 336 Galle Rd
(Km 99 post), T227 7197, www.coralreef
beachhotel.com. 27 a/c and fan rooms with
sea view, although a bit spartan, bar, pool
table, restaurant, **Blue Deep Diving Center**.

E-F Coral Rock, 340 Galle Rd, T227 7021,
www.coralrock.net. 40 a/c and fan rooms,
bigger and better ones are sea-facing, some
with TV, restaurant (good fish), small pool,
nightclub. Land-side rooms close to noisy road.

Wewala

C-E Time N Tide Beach Resort, 412/E Galle
Rd, T227 7781, www.time-n-tide.com.
17 rooms with a/c and hot water, Wi-Fi
available. Restaurant serving wood-fired
pizza, good sea views (although you're so
near the surf can be almost too noisy).

C-D Lanka Super Corals, 390 Galle Rd, 1 km
from Bus Stand, T227 7387, www.hotellanka
supercorals.com. 100 rooms ranging from
road-facing rooms with fan, to deluxe a/c
with hot tub, TV, minibar and sea view. Good
pool, Ayurveda centre, 24-hr coffee shop, a
bit shabby in places, new wing nicer.

D Blue Ocean Villa, 420 Galle Rd, T227
7566, www.blueoceanvilla.com. 8 large
clean rooms, upstairs better, restaurant,
hot water, good choice.

D Hotel Moon Beam, 1/548 Galle Rd,
T545 0657, hotelmoonbeam@hotmail.com.
20 clean rooms, better on upper floors with
sea views, good restaurant.

D-E Surf Villa, Milla Rd, T077-760 4620.
Down a side road but not far from the beach,
this gem is hidden amongst a lush tropical
garden. Rooms have fan or a/c and the

bathrooms are enormous with bathtub and showers. Very clean and friendly, popular with surfers.

E El-Dorado, Milla Rd, 200 m inland from Galle Rd, T227 7091, www.eldoradohikkaduwa.com. 6 a/c and fan rooms in small family-run guesthouse, use of kitchen, very clean, very peaceful setting away from busy road (but still only 10 mins from the beach), good value, good choice.

E Tandem Guest House, 465 Galle Rd, T493 3942, wewala@sltnet.lk. Not on the beach but offering 9 clean and light rooms with seating area outside. Good value.

Narigama and Thirangama

L-B Suite Lanka, T227 7136, www.suite-lanka.com. 6 beautifully furnished standard rooms, deluxe rooms and suites. Private verandas, pool, 2 bars (one on beach), very quiet and intimate, good fresh seafood.

C Sunil's Beach, T227 7186, sunilsd@sltnet,lk. 62 simple a/c rooms (more expensive with sea-view) with no TVs or phones. Decent pool and restaurant.

C-D Cinnamon Garden Hotel, T227 7081, www.cinnamon-hikkaduwa.co.uk. 10 a/c and fan rooms in bungalows. Beachfront garden, restaurant.

C-E Hotel Rita's, T227 7496, www.ritas hotel.com. Clean rooms, 5 with sea view and balcony, beach restaurant, popular with surfers. Fan rooms with cold water are cheapest.

C-F Ranmal Beach Hotel, T227 5474, www.ranmal-rest.com. Rooms ranging from cheap fan to a/c (upper rooms are newer and better), plus 2 cabanas. Sea-facing 1st-floor restaurant with lovely sunset views.

D Ocean View Cottage, T227 7237, www.oceanviewcottage.net. 14 attractive, clean a/c and fan rooms (upstairs better), 10 with sea views. Good terrace restaurant, quiet, pleasant garden.

D-E Sunbeach, T438 3163, www.sunbeach surf.com. 15 clean and cosy rooms, some with a/c, plus a treehouse with great views. Wi-Fi.

D-F Neela's Guest House, 634 Galle Rd, Narigama, T438 3166, neelas_sl@hotmail.com. Friendly and popular guesthouse offering fan rooms, or a/c rooms with sea views.

E Winmago, 794/1 Galle Rd, T227 7655, daniel.palmer@bluewin.ch. 4 fan and cold water rooms, good views but bathrooms are basic.

F Hilda Guest House, Uswatta, Wawala, 300 m from Galle Rd, T493 3383, www.hilda guesthouse.ch. 4 rooms in an attractive Swiss-owned house 10-min walk from the beach with a quiet garden. A pleasant escape from the main drag.

F Sahra, T227 6093. 6 spotless if slightly dark rooms in 2-storey building with large communal terrace.

G Hansa Surf, T222 3854, www.hansa surf.com. 26 rooms ranging from dark and basic to brighter and breezy. Shady veranda, big screen movies, friendly and helpful and popular with surfers.

Dodanduwa

B House of Lotus, 175 Galle Rd, T226 7246, www.house-of-lotus.com. A yoga retreat also offering Ayurvedic packages, but accepts non-yoga devotees as well. 7 a/c and fan rooms, pool. A week's yoga holiday is €350 per person (based on 2 people sharing). Food is mainly veggie.

D-F Beachside Inn, Galle Rd, T309 0073, www.beach-side.com. Guesthouse with 6 clean fan rooms (upstairs better). Hot water, pleasant garden, excellent food,

E Eco Village, Sri Saranajothi Mawatha (from Hikkaduwa take the next road after the turn-off to the vihara, before the bridge, see map, page 130), T077-742 4088, www.ecovillagelanka.com. On the lagoon, a former family holiday home, now converted to an Environmental Study Centre, with a plank walkway through mangrove swamp, and attractive water garden. Sleep in a houseboat or stilt house, there's also a family unit.

✪ Eating

Kalutara p124

Besides the hotel restaurants (see Sleeping, page 133), there are numerous, and cheaper, places to eat (and buy souvenirs) along the roads leading from Galle Rd to the hotels.

Beruwela p125, map p126

There are places to eat along the roads leading from Galle Rd. For further options see Sleeping, page 134.

Aluthgama p126, map p127

There are numerous restaurants around Bentota Bridge and on the narrow lanes leading down to the hotels.

♥♥ Anushka River Inn, 97 Riverside Rd, T227 5377, www.anushka-river-inn.com. Open 1100-1500 and 1900-2300. Restaurant has fine views and serves good seafood and rice and curry, as well as a variety of other Western and Asian dishes. Also has 8 guest rooms (**C**).

♥ Singharaja Bakery and Restaurant, 120 Galle Rd, Kaluwamodara. A good, clean establishment providing excellent Sri Lankan food including short eats, hoppers and curries. Popular as a roadside halt but worth visiting for a cheap and authentic alternative to hotel food.

Bentota p126, map p127

♥♥♥ Diya Sisila, T077-740 2138. Not by the sea, but a popular place for excellent seafood with tables in a pleasant garden. The owner will pick guests up if requested. BYO, and be sure to book in advance.

♥♥ Susantha's, see Sleeping, page 136. Serves simple Sri Lankan and continental dishes.

Induruwa to Ambalangoda p127

For options see Sleeping, page 136.

Hikkaduwa p130, map p131 and p132

Wewala has the best choice, particularly for seafood. A number of *rotti* shops have sprung up, these open around 1630 and are a filling

option for those on a tight budget. Crowded places may not necessarily be better; it could just be a mention in a guidebook.

Hikkaduwa

♥♥ Abba's, 7 Waulagoda Rd, T227 7110. German (not Swedish) style food, snacks and meals, good value, quiet setting. Lovely upstairs seating area, very bright. Some dishes should be ordered in advance.

♥♥ Mama's Coral Beach, see Sleeping, page 137. A rated seafood option with friendly staff.

♥♥ Red Lobster, Waulagoda Rd. Excellent food, good value, friendly owners.

♥♥-♥ Cool Spot, 327 Galle Rd, opposite Chaaya Tranz. Tasty curry and seafood, platters can be good value. Upstairs seating area is nicer, it feels further from the Galle Rd traffic.

Wewala

♥♥♥-♥♥ Refresh, 384 Galle Rd, T227 7810, www.refreshrestaurant.com. Open 0730- 2230. Classiest place in town, vast and varied menu, pizzas, jumbo prawns, enormous mixed grill, good choice of international vegetarian options, and impressive range of wines and cocktails. Overpriced.

♥♥ Budde's Beach, Galle Rd, T077-438 3004. Popular beachside place, good food (fish, pasta, noodles). Happy hour 1700-1900, Sat night barbecues.

♥♥ Curry Bowl, 368 Galle Rd. Good food and service, 'delicious garlic toasts', upmarket setting.

♥♥ Moon Beam, see Sleeping, page 137. Seafood particularly good, pleasant ambience. Some dishes overpriced.

♥♥ Sam's Surfers Rest, 403 Galle Rd, near Blue Ocean Villa. Tastefully decorated with dark wood, stripy cushions and long window benches. Reasonably priced food; seafood, burgers, noodles. Nice bar, leads through to Roger's Garage for pool tables.

♥♥ Sea View, 297 Galle Rd, T227 7014. Not beachfront but a busy place serving good pizza, pasta and seafood, outdoor seating.

♥♥ Time n Tide Beach Resort, see Sleeping page 137. Only serves wood-fired pizza and pasta, but if that's what you're after you can't do better than this.

⊓-⊓ JLH, 382 Galle Rd, T227 7139. Fresh seafood, right by the water. Good cocktails too.
⊺ The Coffee Shop, Galle Rd. Simple but effective, homemade cake and tea or coffee. Good book exchange.

Narigama and Thirangama
⊓-⊺ Munchie Shack, Galle Rd. The usual choice of tourist dishes but also offers Australian meat and a wide range of Japanese fare.
⊺ Brother's Spot, Galle Rd. 5 little tables just off the road, serving Chinese, Italian and seafood dishes for lunch and dinner. A popular breakfast spot, the pancakes are superb and the bananas fresh from the owner's garden over the road.
⊺ Rotty Stop, Narigama. Tasty rice and curries, excellent rotties, local clientele.

⊙ Bars and clubs

Hikkaduwa *p130, map p131 and p132*
The most popular bars are **Top Secret**, **Harbour**, **Mambo's** and **Vibration**. Visit **Vibration** on a Fri for live drumming. If, however, you just want a beachfront drink there are numerous other options, just pick one that grabs your fancy.
Sam's Surfers Rest, see Eating, page 139. Attractive spot for a few drinks, although with no view of the sea. Draft lager. Next door is **Roger's Garage**, which is a dingy pool hall.

⊙ Shopping

Beruwela *p125, map p126*
There are branches of the excellent **Mlesna Tea Centre** and **Laksala** government handicrafts emporium along Galle Rd with prices more reasonable than the hotel shops.

Bentota *p126, map p127*
There is also a branch of **Laksala**, in the shopping arcade by **Bentota Beach Hotel**.

Ambalangoda *p128*
Traditional masks worn for dancing, using vegetable colours instead of the brighter chemical paints, are available on the northern edge of the town. Prices vary considerably, with traditional masks being more expensive. Antique shops often sell newly crafted items which have been 'aged'. It is illegal to export any article which is more than 50 years old without a government permit.

Hikkaduwa *p130, map p131 and p132*
There are numerous batik, handicraft, leather work, jewellery and clothing stores along the length of Galle Rd. Bargaining is expected.
Ceylon Gold Tea, 355 Galle Rd, T077-620 2615. One of a number of tea shops on Galle Rd, this one offers a wide range and the prices are reasonable.
Raja's Jewellery, 403 Galle Rd, T227 7006. Not the place for gem shopping, but stocks some interesting and modern rings and pendants; silver set with semi-precious stones.

▲ Activities and tours

Beruwela *p125, map p126*
Diving is best Dec-Mar.
Ypsylon, **Ypsylon Guest House**, Moragall, T227 6132, www.ypsylon-sri-lanka.de. German-run dive centre, SSI- and PADI-registered. 2 dives for €55, Open Water Course €300, Advanced €250. Also offers wreck dives.

Bentota *p126, map p127*
A range of activities is possible on the lagoon or the open sea.
Club Inter Sport (Keells), within the grounds of **Bentota Beach** hotel, see Sleeping, page 135. Watersports include windsurfing, water skiing (lessons possible) and banana boat. Also tennis, squash, archery, badminton. Sport passes available for discounted activities on 2-day (weekend) or weekly basis. Discounts for residents of any of the Keells hotels in the area.

Confifi Marina, T224 2766 or T227 6039 at **Club Palm Garden**, www.lsr-srilanka.com. Diving, sailing, canoeing, windsurfing, snorkelling, and deep-sea fishing.
Surf Bentota, T227 5126, www.ceylonhotels.lk. Diving centre and other watersports offered.

Hikkaduwa *p130, map p131 and p132*
Ayurveda
Many places have 'Ayurveda clinics', though the treatments usually lack authenticity.

Diving
The diving season along the southwest coast is Nov-Apr, and Hikkaduwa has the most dive schools on the island, though the not the best local sites. There are several other dive schools in addition to those listed here. Check that they are SSI or PADI qualified before agreeing to a dive or course. Snorkelling equipment can be hired from shops along the main street. Glass-bottomed boats can be hired from a number of places just north of the Chaaya Tranz. Some travellers find there are too many boats chasing too few viewing spots, turtles are disturbed unnecessarily and that the glass is not as clear as you might hope.
Barracuda Diving Center, 356 Galle Rd, T077-985 3772, www.hikkaduwabarracuda.com. PADI school, US$30 for 1 dive, US$50 for 2. Also offers 'discovery dive'. Very enthusiastic and informative. French and English spoken.
Dive Sites Lanka, 279B Galle Rd, T4308 3302, www.srilanka-diving.com. PADI school, US$30 for 1 dive, US$50 for 2. Open Water €260. Also offers dive packages.
Poseidon Diving Station, just north of **Coral Sands Hotel**, T227 7294, www.divingsrilanka.com. In operation since 1973, the headquarters has an interesting selection of booty recovered by the school's Swedish founder. Single dive including equipment, €25; PADI Open Water €265; Advanced €185. Discovery dive is €55. Rooms are available (US$18 B&B) for divers or non-divers.

Surfing
A-Frame Surf Shop, **Mambo**, 434/3 Galle Rd, T545 8131, www.mambo.nu. Surf information, and surfing equipment and clothing available.
Mambo Surf Tours organizes tours, boards are for rent on the beach.
Reef End Surf School, 593 Galle Rd, Narigama, T077-704 3559, www.reefend surfschool.com. Surf lessons from US$20 per day, or 5-days (3 hrs per day) for US$150. Board rental, surf information, and surf and accommodation packages arranged. Friendly and popular.

Tour operators
Pasan Tours & Travels, 237/1 Galle Rd, T227 7898, T077-346 6706, www.pasantours.com. Offers tours and vehicle hire, excellent English spoken.
Rainforest Rescue International, Organic Garden, Galle Rd, Akurala (10 mins north of Hikkaduwa), T223 2585, www.rainforestrescue international.org. An initiative set up by environmentalists in 2002, which runs eco-tours in the Galle area. These include rainforest tours and mangrove boat trips. Early morning or evening are best for viewing wildlife.
Sri Lanka Travels, near **Sam's Surfers Rest**, T077-301 6893. Offers 1- to 5-day tours as well as longer island tours on request. Minimum 3-4 people.

⊖ Transport

Kalutara *p124*
Bus Buses run regularly between **Colombo** and **Galle** (1-1½ hrs).
Train Trains stop here on the **Colombo–Matara** line, with 5-6 intercity trains per day.

Beruwela *p125, map p126*
Bus Buses regularly ply the route between **Colombo** and **Galle**.
Train On the main **Colombo–Matara** line, though only the slower ones (1¾ hrs) stop here. Best option is to take one of the express trains from **Aluthgama** (see below).

Aluthgama p126, map p127

Aluthgama is the main transport hub for Beruwela to the north and Bentota to the south.

Bus Those running between **Colombo** and **Galle** stop here.

Train A stop on the main **Colombo–Matara** line, Aluthgama can be reached by express trains from **Colombo** (5-6 a day) in around 1½ hrs.

Bentota p126, map p127

Air Sri Lankan Airlines, T19733 5500, www.srilankan.aero, has started operating flights to/from **Bentota** and **Colombo**.

Bus Those passing through Bentota are often full; it's better to go to Aluthgama and take a bus that originates there.

Train Bentota's tiny station is on the main **Colombo–Matara** line but only the 'slow' trains stop here so it is better to travel on an express train from Aluthgama (see above).

Ambalangoda p128

Bus Regular buses run to **Colombo** and between **Ambalangoda** and **Hikkaduwa**, 13 km south.

Train 5 to 6 express trains a day run along the coast from **Colombo Fort** to Ambalangoda (2 hrs), and on to **Hikkaduwa** (15 mins).

Hikkaduwa p130, map p131 and p132

Bus The old, slow CTB variety that travel between **Galle** and **Colombo** via Hikkaduwa can take hours. A better option is to take a private minibus to Colombo's Bastian Mawatha bus station which take under 2 hrs. Frequent buses run from Hikkaduwa's bus station (at the north end of town) to **Ambalangoda** and **Galle**. However, it is almost impossible to hail a bus on the Galle Rd (even from official bus shelters) so it is worth going to the bus station or taking a taxi or 3-wheeler for short journeys.

Taxi and three-wheeler There are now designated spots along Galle Rd where licensed taxis and 3-wheelers wait for custom. Look for the signs, both on the vehicles and by the side of the road.

Train To **Colombo Fort**, express trains (2-2½ hrs) most stopping at **Ambalangoda**, **Aluthgama** (for Bentota and Beruwela), **Panadura** and **Moratuwa**. Slow trains north run as far as **Aluthgama**. Frequent trains to **Galle** (45 mins) every 1-2 hrs, some continuing to **Matara** (1½ hrs), via **Talpe**, **Ahangama** and **Weligama**. **Kandy** train (via Colombo) leaves at 1452 (5¾ hrs). Vavuniya train, via **Anuradhapura** (8 hrs) leaves at 1117.

ⓘ Directory

Kalutara p124

Medical services General Hospital T222 2261.

Beruwela p125, map p126

Useful address Tourist police, Galle Rd, Moragalla, opposite Neptune Hotel, T227 6049.

Aluthgama p126, map p127

Banks Commercial Bank has an ATM and will change TCs. **Useful address** Tourist police, Galle Rd, in Aluthgama town.

Bentota p126, map p127

Useful address Tourist police, in tourist complex by **Bentota Beach Hotel**, T227 5022.

Hikkaduwa p130, map p131 and p132

Banks People's Bank, Commercial Bank and Bank of Ceylon all offer foreign exchange (cash and TCs), whilst the latter also has a Cirrus ATM. **Internet** There are a lot of places on Galle Rd offering internet, Rs 2-3 per min. Rates are cheaper in town. Many hotels and some guesthouses offer internet or Wi-Fi and the **Drunken Monkey Bar** has free Wi-Fi upon purchase. **Post office** Mon-Sat 0800-1900, Sun 0800-1000. At the north end of town, a few mins walk inland from the bus station. **Dimasha Agency Post Office**, opposite the bus station to the north, sells stamps and arranges international calls, usually 0800-2100. **Useful address** Tourist police, Police Station, Galle Rd, T227 7222.

The south coast

Less package oriented than the west coast, the spectacularly scenic bays and beaches of the south coast are a magnet for independently travelling sun and sea worshippers, with fewer crowds and some good-value accommodation. Unawatuna, Tangalla and, increasingly, Mirissa are the main beaches here, each with long sweeps of fine sand; while city life focuses on Matara and particularly Galle, whose colonial origins provide some historical interest. While you could pass along the south coast in under four hours, those with the time might easily spend a week here, hopping from village to village and enjoying the laid-back lifestyle. ▶▶ *For listings, see pages 158-173.*

Galle → *Phone code: 091. Colour map 3, C2. Population 97,000. 115 km from Colombo.*

Galle (pronounced in Sinhala as 'Gaal-le') is the most important town in the south and its fort area, with its mighty ramparts, encloses some wonderful examples of colonial architecture. A laid-back and enchanting place to wander, it was declared a UNESCO World Heritage Site in 1988. Rather removed from the busy modern town, the fort retains a villagey atmosphere, full of local gossip, and some find themselves staying far longer than they expected. Most, however, find that they have exhausted Galle's sites in a day or so.

Ins and outs → *Beware of touts who earn commission on accommodation and shopping (gems).*
Getting there Express trains are preferable to a crowded bus journey to Galle, provided you avoid the rush hour. Both run frequently from Colombo. ▶▶ *See Transport, page 172.*

Getting around The train and bus stations are both in the new town, 10-15 minutes' walk north of the fort walls and cricket stadium. Galle Fort is so small and compact that most of the guesthouses are very easy to find. To get to the upmarket hotels outside Galle, you will need to hire a taxi or three-wheeler.

Tourist information There is a branch of the **Ceylon Tourist Board** ① *Victoria Park, daily 0900-1600,* opposite the railway station.

Background

Galle's origins as a port go back well before the arrival of the Portuguese. Ibn Batuta, the great Moroccan traveller, visited it in 1344. The historian of Ceylon Sir Emerson Tennant claimed that Galle was the ancient city of Tarshish, which had traded not only with Persians and Egyptians but with King Solomon. The origin of the name is disputed, some associating it with the Latin *gallus* (cock), so-called because the Portugese heard the crowing of cocks here at dusk, others with the Sinhala *gala* (cattle shed) or *gal* (rock).

Lorenzo de Almeida drifted into Galle by accident in 1505. It was a further 82 years before the Portuguese captured it from the Sinhala kings, and they controlled the port until the Dutch laid siege in 1640. The old Portuguese Fort, on a promontory, was strengthened by the Dutch who remained there until the British captured Galle in 1796. Dutch East India Company, VOC (*Vereenigde Oost Indische Campagnie*) ruled the waves during the 17th and 18th centuries with over 150 ships trading from around 30 settlements in Asia.

A P&O liner called at Galle in 1842 marking the start of a regular service to Europe. In 1859, Captain Bailey, an agent for the shipping company, took a fancy to the spot where a small disused Dutch fort had stood in a commanding position, 3 km across the harbour. The villa he built, set in a tropical garden (now the **Closenberg Hotel**, see page 159), was named 'Marina' after his wife. P&O's Rising Sun emblem can still be spotted on some of the old furniture.

Galle's gradual decline in importance dates back to 1875, when reconstruction of breakwaters and the enlarged harbour made Colombo the island's major port.

Old town and fort

The **fort**, enclosing about 200 houses, completely dominates the old town. You can easily spend a whole day in this area. Part of its charm is being able to wander around the streets; nothing is very far away. The Dutch left their mark here, building brick-lined sewers which the tides automatically flushed twice a day. The fort's main streets run over these old sewers and you can still see the manhole covers every 20 m or so.

There are two entry points. The more impressive **gate** is under the clocktower. The ramparts just here are massive, partly because they are the oldest and have been reinforced over the years on many occasions. There are three quite distinct bastions (Star in the west, Moon and Sun in the east). The clocktower (1883) itself is quite modern and sometimes has a huge national flag flying from it. In Queen Street is the second and much older gate.

The **ramparts**, surrounded on three sides by the sea, are marked by a series of bastions covering the promontory. The two nearest to the harbour are Sun and Zwart, followed by Aurora and Point Utrecht bastions before the **lighthouse**, then Triton, Neptune, Clippenburg, Aeolus, Star and Moon. Those on the west side are more accessible and stand much as they were built, although there is evidence of a signals post built in the Second World War on top of Neptune. The Sri Lankan army still has a base in the fort and so have a use for the Aeolus bastion. Under the ramparts between Aeolus and Star bastions is the tomb of a Muslim saint neatly painted in green and white, said to cover an old fresh water spring. The open space between Rampart Street and the ramparts is used as a recreational area and there is often an unofficial game of cricket in progress in the evenings and at weekends. Also on the Green is a small shrine; the main one, Sri Sudharmalaya temple, is across the street.

A **walking tour** around the ramparts is a must. You can try to do it on a clear evening and aim to reach the clocktower at sunset, starting at about 1630 and wandering slowly from Amangalla clockwise. An interesting route is to walk south from the hotels, all along Church Street, then east to the 20-m-high lighthouse which was built by the British in 1939, nearly on top of the old magazine with its inscription 'AJ Galle den 1st Zeber 1782'. You can get good views from the top, though you will need to get permission from the lighthouse keeper (ask in the gem store next door). You then return up Hospital Street past the Police Barracks (built in 1927 but failing to blend in with the older parts of the fort). The government offices on Hospital Street were once the Dutch 'factory' (warehouse). You then arrive at the square with the district court near the Zwart Bastion. Turn west along Queen Street which joins Church Street at the post office. The quiet fort streets are lined with substantial buildings, most with large rooms on the ground floor and an arched veranda to provide shade. The arched windows of the upper floors are covered by huge old louvered wooden shutters; the lower ones have glass nowadays. Unfortunately, quite a few of these fine houses are in need of restoration. The **Dutch Reformed Church** (1754), next to the **Amangalla** hotel (see box, page 147), is certainly worth visiting. It was built as a result of a vow taken by the Dutch governor of Galle, Casparaus de Jong, and has a number of interesting memorials. Inside, the floor is covered by about 20 gravestones (some heavily embossed, others engraved), which originated in older graveyards which were closed in 1710 and 1804. The British moved them into this church in 1853. The organ loft has a lovely semicircular balustrade surrounding the organ while the pulpit, repaired in 1996, has an enormous canopy. Opposite the church is the old bell tower erected in 1701, while the bell, open to the

Galle

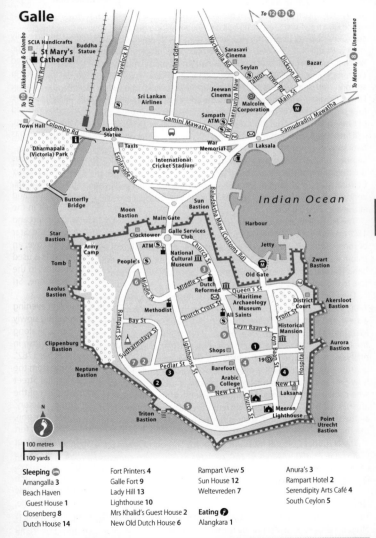

Sleeping
Amangalla **3**
Beach Haven
  Guest House **1**
Closenberg **8**
Dutch House **14**

Fort Printers **4**
Galle Fort **9**
Lady Hill **13**
Lighthouse **10**
Mrs Khalid's Guest House **2**
New Old Dutch House **6**

Rampart View **5**
Sun House **12**
Weltevreden **7**

Eating
Alangkara **1**

Anura's **3**
Rampart Hotel **2**
Serendipity Arts Café **4**
South Ceylon **5**

elements, is hung in a belfry with a large dome on top of it. Next door is the Maritime Archaeology Museum (see below). The old **post office**, restored by the Galle Heritage Trust in 1992, is a long low building with a shallow red tiled roof supported by 13 columns. It is still functioning although it is very run down inside. Further down Church Street is the All Saints Church though it is not always open. This was built in 1868 (consecrated in 1871) after much pressure from the English population who had previously worshipped at the Dutch Reform Church. Its bell has an interesting history as it came from the Liberty ship *Ocean Liberty*. When the vicar asked the Clan Shipping Company whether they could help with the cost of a bell, the chief officer who had acquired the bell from the *Liberty* when it was scrapped (and named his daughter Liberty), presented it to the church in its centenary year, 1968. There is a particularly good view of the church with its red tin roof surmounted by a cockerel and four strange little turrets, from Cross Church Street. The old **Dutch Government House**, opposite the church, is now a hotel. Note the massive door in four sections at the Queen's Street entrance, was built for entry on horseback. At the end of Church Street lies the old **Arab Quarter** with a distinct Moorish atmosphere. Here you will find the Meeran Jumma Masjid in a tall white building which resembles a church with two square towers topped by shallow domes, but with the crescent clearly visible. Slender, tubular minarets are also topped by crescent moons. The mosque was rebuilt at the beginning of the 20th century where the original stood from the 1750s. The Muslim Cultural Association and Arabic College which was established in 1892, are here. It is still very active and you will see many Muslims in the distinctive skullcaps hurrying to prayer at the appointed hours.

The **Historical Mansion Museum** ⓘ *31-39 Leyn Bann St (well signed), T223 4114, 0900-1800 (closed on Fri 1230-1400 for prayers), free*, is a restored old house. There are a number of rooms around a small courtyard containing this potentially worthwhile collection of colonial artefacts. There are several interesting and rare items which are simply 'stored' here. The real aim of the museum becomes apparent when visitors are led to the gems for sale in the adjoining shop.

The **Maritime Archaeology Museum** ⓘ *Church St, opposite the post office, daily 0900-1700, Rs 550, children Rs 250; included in Cultural Triangle Round Ticket (see box, page 52)*, is a new and enormous museum in an old Dutch warehouse, replacing the National Maritime Museum. Visitors enter on one level, follow the exhibits and leave by the exit on the lower floor. An interesting film is shown first that explains the various wrecks lying offshore, some artefacts of which are displayed in the museum. Look out for the beardman jug found at the *Avondster* wreck site in Galle harbour. Exhibits also explore how Sri Lankan dress and language (amongst other things) was influenced by visitors who came by sea to trade, and there are some interesting objects that were washed up after the tsunami. The museum currently feels a bit empty and it is disappointing that not all the objects were found, some are merely example of what would have been aboard the ships. However, there is much of interest to see.

The **National Cultural Museum** ⓘ *Church St (next to Amangalla), T223 2051, Tue-Sat 0900-1700, Rs 300, children Rs 150, cameras Rs 250, video cameras Rs 2000*, is in an old colonial stone warehouse. Exhibits include a model of Galle and the fort's Dutch and Portuguese inheritance.

New town

This area was much worse hit by the 2004 tsunami, as everything inside the fort was offered a degree of protection by the walls. Cricket fans will want to visit the rebuilt **Galle**

New conquest of Galle

After many years languishing in apparently terminal decay, Galle Fort has had a facelift. The declaration of the fort as a UNESCO World Heritage site in 1988 started the ball rolling, with the World Bank funding renovations to the town's courts. In the mid 1990's gentrification of the fort commenced, and in 2002 the Indonesian luxury chain Amanresorts bought the desperately neglected 17th-century New Oriental Hotel, former Dutch barracks and the oldest registered hotel in Sri Lanka. After substantial restoration it is now a luxury hotel (the **Amangalla**, see Sleeping, page 158).

Funding for conservation was scarce until the 2004 tsunami hit, damaging areas of the ramparts and inside the fort, after which significant donations were provided by the Dutch government. Their help enabled Sri Lanka's Central Cultural Fund to transform the warehouses opposite the Dutch Reformed Church (also restored) into a modern maritime museum (see page 146). There are plans to further renovate the fort over the coming years, with estimates that 85% of restoration work has already been completed. Investment from foreigners and the Dutch government has resulted in over 120 buildings being restored, and the repair of the fortification walls.

A recent survey showed that just under a quarter of houses in the fort were owned by foreigners, and of these only 10% lived in them permanently. The majority bought properties in 2003 when the 100% foreign land tax was abolished to encourage overseas investment. Many of the historic houses were snapped up for renovation, mainly by British bankers in the Far East, and some have become hotels, guesthouses, art galleries, restaurants and cafés. The sleepy fortified town is an attractive place to wander around, and these boutiques and galleries attract a number of visitors. The international influence is noticeable, particularly with regards hotels, and on the positive side has contributed to making Galle the South's cultural focus. The **Galle Literary Festival** takes place every year in January/February and attracts a number of well-known writers, and a successful independent British-owned publishing house now operates out of the fort.

Tourism has had a positive impact on Galle Fort in that new business opportunities have emerged. There is demand for locally produced goods, and local incomes have increased for shop keepers, guesthouse owners, cafés and other small businesses within the fort.

But amongst the buzz that investment has brought, there are critics of the new order. Some fear that as locals are priced out of the market, Galle Fort could become a 'little Europe', culturally detached from the surrounding area and devoid of local colour. As more and more foreigners buy land and houses in the fort, prices have increased significantly, making it hard for locals, some who have been here for centuries, to resist the large sums they are offered to move. Those who wish to stay are finding it almost impossible to afford to buy property.

International Cricket Stadium, where there is often a match going on. You can clamber up on the ramparts of the fort to find the spot from which Jonathan Agnew, the BBC's cricket correspondent, was forced to broadcast after the famous incident in February 2001 when he wasn't allowed into the ground.

The **new town** is quite pleasant to wander through and its bustle contrasts with the more measured pace of the fort. It is an easy walk out of the old gate and along by the sea with its rows of fishing boats neatly drawn up on the beach. On the Colombo Road to the west of Victoria Park, are several gem shops. If you take the road opposite them you can walk up to **St Mary's Cathedral** which was built in 1874 and has a very good view over the town. There is little of interest inside, though.

Unawatuna → *Phone code: 091. Colour map 3, C3. 5 km south east of Galle.*

Unawatuna's picturesque beach along a sheltered bay was once considered one of the best in the world. Although rather narrow, it is more suitable for year-round swimming than say, Hikkaduwa, as the bay is enclosed by a double reef, which lessens the impact of the waves. For divers, it is a good base to explore some of the wrecks in Galle Bay, and there is some safe snorkelling a short distance from shore (though you may be disappointed by the lack of live coral). Many find Unawatuna more appealing than its popular neighbour. However, this popularity has taken its toll. Beach restaurants have encroached to the point where the actual usable beach is very narrow, and the increasing number of visitors means that the beach is sometimes crowded, the western end of the bay particularly being popular with local day-trippers at weekends and public holidays. The erosion continues apace and some restaurants are now on wooden platforms in the sea. Petty theft has become a problem in recent years, as have drugs. Some parts of the beach can also be very noisy, with music blaring until the early hours.

During the week, however, if you are seeking somewhere with a beach safe for swimming, a wide range of clean accommodation and a variety of good beachside restaurants, then Unawatuna is a good choice.

Sights
Unawatuna's main attraction is unquestionably its beach but it isn't the only place worth visiting. There are some lovely walks in the area.

Rumassala kanda (hillock), the rocky outcrop along the coast, has a large collection of unusual medicinal herbs. In the *Ramayana* epic, Hanuman, the monkey god was sent on an errand to collect a special herb to save Rama's wounded brother Lakshmana. Having failed to identify the plant, he returned with a herb-covered section of the great mountain range, dropping a part of what he was carrying here. Another part is said to have fallen in Ritigala (see page 281). This area of forest is now protected by the state to save the rare plants from being removed indiscriminately. It offers excellent views across Galle Harbour towards the fort. On a clear day look inland to catch sight of Adam's Peak. The sea bordering Rumassala has the **Bona Vista reef** which has some of the best preserved coral in Sri Lanka. Recovery from the 1998 bleaching has been faster than elsewhere on the coast.

Jungle Beach, on the other side of the promontory, is pleasantly uncrowded and has some good snorkelling. Boat trips from some of the guesthouses run here and many three-wheelers will offer to take you. Alternatively, you can walk (around 45 minutes) from Unawatuna Beach. You might get lost but guides tend to appear as if by magic.

Unawatuna to Weligama → *Colour map 3, C3/4.*

The road running east from Unawatuna runs close to the sea offering wonderful views and linking a series of small attractive beaches. The area, with its white sandy beaches, attractive coves and first-class well-priced accommodation, is no longer known to just a few, though there still aren't the crowds that are found at Unawatuna. The coast between Talpe and Weligama was best known for its remarkable fishermen who perched for hours on poles out in the bay. Nowadays, this is a dying tradition.

Sleeping
Amma's Guest House **1**
Banana Garden **39**
Black Beauty **38**
Blue Swan Inn **4**
Brinkhaus **33**
Dream House **7**
Flower Garden **5**
French Guest House **2**
Happy Banana **10**

Heaven on Earth **11**
Milton's **13**
No Name Rest **3**
Nooit Gedacht **42**
Ocean Hill **40**
Primrose Guest House **6**
Rock House **16**
Sea View **18**
Secret Garden Villa **29**
Strand **20**

Sunil Garden Guesthouse **8**
Sun Set Point **34**
Sun-n-Sea **21**
Thambapanni Retreat **41**
Thaproban **9**
Unawatuna Beach Resort
& Diving Centre **24**
Upul Guesthouse **32**
Village Inn **26**
Weliwatta Guest House **27**

Eating
Blowhole **11**
Jina's Vegetarian & Vegan **2**
Kingfisher **10**
Lucky Tuna **1**
One Love **4**
Pink Elephant **3**
South Ceylon **5**

Dalawella and Talpe → *Phone code: 091.*

The most likely place to spot 'stilt' fishermen working is from Dalawella to Ahangama early in the morning or sometimes, if they're hungry, in the evening. At other times they tend to arrive only when visitors with cameras appear, and they expect a small tip for a photograph. Dalawella is just east of Unawatuna. Though on the main road, it has a lovely section of beach and a 'natural swimming pool' towards the eastern end. The fine beaches continue to picturesque **Talpe**, a short distance east, where an increasing number of upmarket hotels are beginning to open. Many of the new hotels and guesthouses here are better value than in Unawatuna itself.

Koggala → *Phone code: 091.*

The coast road passes the old wartime airstrip, which has been developed as a domestic airport; flights from Colombo land here.

Koggala has an attractive, tranquil lake with rocky islets to the north, and a Free Trade Zone with some light industry. The lake, actually a lagoon, is lined with mangrove and rich with birdlife. Boat trips run to the **Ananda Spice Garden** ① *T228 3805, for more details*, a temple and cinnamon island.

Just by the fortress gate, a road leads left over the railway line to the **Martin Wickramasinghe Folk Museum** ① *daily 0900-1700, Rs 200 (with explanatory leaflet), children Rs 100*. The museum houses the respected Sri Lankan writer's personal collection. His family home displays photographs and memorabilia, and some history about the area. Even if you are not a fan of Wickramasinghe, the museum is still worth visit as it contains some fascinating exhibits from traditional Sri Lankan life. Religious items and agricultural and fishing tools are well displayed behind glass cabinets, with some traditional games (from before cricket obsessed the nation). There's a colourful selection of *kolam* masks and puppets from the Ambalangoda area, and 101 different utensils for treating coconuts. The house and museum are set in an attractive garden with labelled trees, so you can swot up on your Sri Lankan flora.

Kataluva → *Phone code: 091.*

Purvarama Mahaviharaya, originally 18th century with late 19th-century additions, is 3 km along a minor road turning off at Kataluva (Km 132 mark); ask directions locally. The ambulatory has excellent examples of temple paintings illustrating different styles of Kandyan art. Young monks will happily point out interesting sections of the *Jataka* stories depicted on the wall friezes. Note the musicians and dancers on the south side and the European figures illustrating an interesting piece of social history. The priest is very welcoming and keen to speak with foreigners.

Midigama → *Phone code: 041.*

The coast from Ahangama to Midigama is regarded as the best surfing area on the south coast, and consequently it is popular with long-term surfers. However, unless you are into surfing it is probably best avoided. It is full of very cheap guesthouses, catering for surfers on long stays.

Weligama is a busy centre for the surrounding fishing villages. Though the town itself is fairly unappealing, it has a picturesque location, with a magnificent sheltered and sandy bay safe for diving and snorkelling beyond the usual season on the southwest coast and some good surf to the eastern end of the beach, and is backed by the attractive Polwatte Ganga. The western end is the home of the many fishermen operating out of Weligama and there are catamarans everywhere. At the approach to the town there is a 4-m-high **statue of Kushta Raja**, sometimes known as the 'Leper King'. Various legends surround the statue believed by some to be of Bodhisattva Samantabhadra. Look out for the *mal lali* fret-work decorated houses along the road from the centre towards the statue. The area is also known for its handmade lace, see page 169. Devil Dances are held in nearby villages.

Weligama is most famous however for its tiny **Taprobane Island**, walkable (at low tide) in the lovely bay. Once owned by the Frenchman, Count de Mauny, who built a magnificent house there, it was bought by American author Paul Bowles after his death. After a period of neglect, it was returned in the late 1990s to its former glory, and is now a luxury tourist retreat.

Weligama

Sleeping 🛏	Jaga Bay Resort **8**	Weligama Bay Inn **4**
Angel **1**	Mandara Resort **3**	Weligama Bay Resort **9**
Barbareyn Beach	Samaru Beach	Weligama Bay View **17**
Ayurveda Resort **6**	House **13**	
Green Rooms **2**	Taprobane Island **15**	Eating 🍴
Greenpeace Inn **7**	Villa Samsara **5**	Keerthi **3**

Mirissa → *Phone code: 041. Colour map 3, C3. 34 km from Galle, 149 km from Colombo.*

Of all the south coast beach resorts to have developed in recent years, Mirissa, with its beautiful wide stretch of golden sand backed by luxuriant vegetation, has received the greatest attention. For the moment the plaudits seems justified, as so far this relaxed little village, 5 km east across Weligama Bay, has been more sensitively developed than Hikkaduwa or Unawatuna, with the intrusion of guesthouses and restaurants on to the beach less obvious. Mirissa is no longer a secret hideaway though; its popularity increases each year, prompting concerns about over-development. For the moment it remains one of the most idyllic places to relax along this stretch of coast.

The west end of the beach, is popular with surfers, whilst further east, in the two beaches beyond the **Giragala Village**, is a reef where there is some good swimming and snorkelling. Giragala (or 'Parrot') Rock is a popular place to watch the sunset. Near here is a defile, known as **Bandaramulla**, where there is a Buddhist *vihara*.

Inland, you can explore the river, and there are some pleasant walks (or cycle trips) up into the jungle. In recent years Mirissa has become a centre for whale-watching, and between December and April blue whales can be viewed offshore. Nearly every guesthouse and hotel now offers tours, as do three-wheeler drivers; quality varies.
▶▶ *See Tour operators, page 170.*

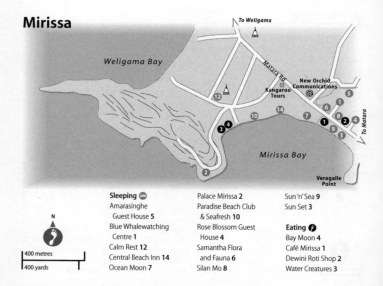

Mirissa

Sleeping 😴
Amarasinghe
  Guest House **5**
Blue Whalewatching
  Centre **1**
Calm Rest **12**
Central Beach Inn **14**
Ocean Moon **7**

Palace Mirissa **2**
Paradise Beach Club
  & Seafresh **10**
Rose Blossom Guest
  House **4**
Samantha Flora
  and Fauna **6**
Silan Mo **8**

Sun 'n' Sea **9**
Sun Set **3**

Eating 🍴
Bay Moon **4**
Café Mirissa **1**
Dewini Roti Shop **2**
Water Creatures **3**

Matara → *Phone code: 041. Colour map 3, C4. Population 44,000. 42 km from Galle, 157 km from Colombo.*

Matara (pronounced locally as Maa-tre) is the South's second biggest town, after Galle. It is also an important transport hub, with the terminus of the railway line and an enormous bus station. Locals will tell you that the city is better than Galle as it has two Dutch forts to Galle's one. Though busy and full of traffic, it does have a rich history, and the old town with its narrow streets and colonial buildings is a pleasant place to explore. In the old marketplace you might still see the local wooden hackeries (oxcarts) that are sometimes used for races. Today, Ruhuna University, 3 km east, attracts students to the town. Matara is also famous for its musical instruments, especially drums, and you can pick up some good batik. Though the beach is attractive the waters are too rough for comfortable bathing much of the year. At **Polhena**, south of the town, is a good coral beach protected by a reef which offers year-round swimming and some excellent snorkelling opportunities. There are also some good-value guesthouses, a pleasant alternative to staying in Matara town.

Sights

An important Dutch possession on the south coast, controlling the trade in cinnamon and elephants, Matara was well fortified. **Star Fort**, which is faced with coral, was built in 1763. It has a moated double-wall and six points, and was designed to house ammunition, provisions and a small garrison. The gateway that shows the VOC arms and date is particularly picturesque. As in Galle, the Dutch government has recently invested money in restoring the fort, formerly a library. Across the **Nilwala Ganga** from the fort, on the left-hand side is a gleaming and impressive **mosque**, a replica of the Meeran Jumma Masjid in Galle.

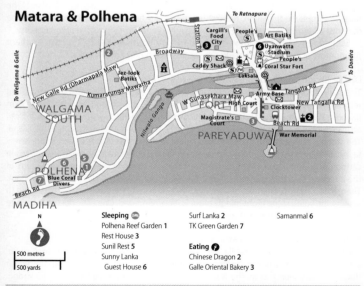

Matara & Polhena

Sleeping
Polhena Reef Garden 1
Rest House 3
Sunil Rest 5
Sunny Lanka
 Guest House 6

Surf Lanka 2
TK Green Garden 7

Eating
Chinese Dragon 2
Galle Oriental Bakery 3

Samanmal 6

The **Main Fort**, south of the *ganga*, consists of a single rampart from which guns were fired. Its inadequacy as a defence was revealed during the 'Matara rebellion' of 1762, when a Kandyan army managed to take the town by bombarding it with cannonballs that simply went over the wall. The Dutch retook the town the following year, and built the more successful **Star Fort** ⓘ *generally closed, but the caretaker will show you around*, to defend the town against siege from the river. Near the main bastion is the British clocktower (1883).

North of here, on Beach Road, is **St Mary's Church**. The date on the doorway (1769) refers to the repair work after the 'Matara rebellion'. Close by is St Servatius College, one of Matara's two exclusive public schools, whose most famous son is Sri Lankan batting hero and former cricket captain Sanath Jayasuriya.

Matara to Tangalla

Weherahena → *Phone code: 041.*

About 5 km beyond Matara, a left turn leads to this modern **Buddhist sanctuary** ⓘ *donation and tip for the guide*, which has a 40-m six-storey-high painted Buddha statue. Much older is the *vihara*, whose 600 m of tunnels are lined with some 20,000 friezes, some dating back to Portuguese times. **Perahera** takes place in November/December full moon. Catch bus No 349 from Matara.

Dondra → *Phone code: 041. Colour map 3, C4. 6 km from Matara.*

Dondra or Devinuwara (the British renamed the town as they couldn't pronounce it), which means 'City of Gods', is a fishing village famous for its Vishnu temple. The original temple, one of the most revered on the island, was destroyed by the Portuguese in a brutal attack in 1588. **Devi Nuwara Devale** retains, however, an ancient shrine possibly dating to the seventh century AD, which maybe the oldest stone built structure on the island. The modern temple, to the south, has old columns and a finely carved gate. Even today the Buddhist pilgrims continuing the ancient tradition venerate Vishnu as part of the Hindu trinity.

Some 2 km south of the town, the 50-m-high **lighthouse** (1889) on the southern promontory at Dondra Head marks the southernmost point of Sri Lanka.

Dikwella and Wewurukannala → *Phone code: 041.*

The marvellous bays and beaches continue across to Tangalla. There are some established resort hotels at the village of Dikwella offering diving and watersports in the bay, while 2 km inland at Wewuurukannala is **Buduraja Mahawehera** ⓘ *Rs 100, a guide will approach*. Until an even bigger one was built in Dambulla in 2002, this was the tallest statue on the island. The statues, tableaux and Buddhist temple are in a complex which has an impressively tacky 50-m-high seated Buddha statue with a 'library' at the back. Some 635 paintings in cartoon strip form depict events from the Buddha's life covering every square centimetre of the interior. The artists are from all over the world but retain the same style throughout. There is also a garish 'Chamber of Horrors' with depictions of the punishments meted out to sinners, including some frighteningly graphic life-size models. One critic describes the site as looking 'more like an airport terminal than a temple'.

Kudawella → *Colour map 3, C4. 6 km east of Dikwella.*

The natural blowhole at Kudawella, also known as **Hummanaya** ⓘ *Rs 200*, due to the 'hoo' sound that you hear, is one of the more bizarre attractions in Sri Lanka and worth the detour during the monsoon season. The water spray can rise to 25 m when the waves are strong.

Endangered turtles

Five of the world's seven species of turtle, the green, leatherback, olive ridley, loggerhead and the hawksbill all come ashore to nest on the beaches of Sri Lanka. All are listed by the World Conservation Union (IUCN) as either threatened or endangered. Despite the measures taken by the government, marine turtles are extensively exploited in Sri Lanka for their eggs and meat. In addition, turtle nesting beaches (rookeries) are being disturbed by tourism-related development, and feeding habitats, such as coral reefs, are being destroyed by pollution, especially polythene bags, and unsustainable harvesting. Around 13,000 turtles each year are caught, not always accidentally, in fishing gear while the illegal 'tortoise shell trade' continues to encourage

hunting of the highly endangered hawksbill turtle's carapace.

Tourism has proved a double-edged sword in the fight to save the turtles. Since the early 1980s, the government has encouraged the setting up of tourist-friendly turtle hatcheries along the coast, from Induruwa on the west coast to Yala in the southeast, though the Wildlife Department acknowledges that these sometimes do more harm than good. In 1993, the **Turtle Conservation Project**, www.tcpsrilanka.org, was set up dedicated to pursuing sustainable marine turtle conservation strategies through education, research and community participation. It currently runs tourism projects at Rekawa, Kalpitiya and Kosgoda, and education schemes for school children.

Take care when clambering on the rocks as they are wet and slippery in places. It is best to avoid weekends and go during school hours. The blowhole doesn't always 'perform' and is disappointing out of season, so check locally before making the trip. The blowhole is 1.5 km off the main road. If travelling by bus, ask the driver to drop you off at the turn-off. The route to the blowhole is well signposted by the Elephant House.

Mawella → *Colour map 3, C4. Phone code: 047.*

Mawella, 6 km west of Tangalla, has remained one of this stretch of coastline's best-kept secrets. It has a 3-km-long, very wide beach, avoids the busy main road, and offers safe swimming. It's easy to miss – turn right at the **Beach Cottage** sign.

Tangalla → *Phone code: 047. Colour map 3, C5. 40 km from Matara, 198 km from Colombo.*

Tangalla (pronounced Tunn-gaa-le), famous for its turtles, is an attractive fishing port with a palm-fringed bay. The town suffered damage during the tsunami but there are still a few distinctive colonial buildings and a picturesque *ganga*. The surrounding bays have some of the best beaches in the southern coastal belt. Even though there are a growing number of hotels and guesthouses, the beach remains quiet despite good sand and safe swimming (when the sea is not rough). There isn't an enormous amount to see or do here except lie on the beach, but it does make a useful base for visiting the **turtles** at Rekawa, and the magnificent **Mulgirigala Rock Temple**.

Sights

There is a **Dutch fort** standing on the slope above the bay. Built of coral with two bastions in opposite corners, it was turned into a jail after a report in 1837 declared it was in sound condition and able to safely hold up to 100 men. The exterior has now been covered over by cement.

There are some lovely **beaches** with visitors having a choice of three main areas to stay. The settlements of **Goyambokka** and **Pallikaduwa** are on a series of bays to the south of town, and have clean and secluded beaches.

In **Tangalla town**, there are a couple of hotels near the harbour including the Rest House. The cove in front of is fairly sheltered so is consequently quite busy. The quietest location is probably **Marakolliya** to the north. Medilla Beach is lined with budget guesthouses, hotels and restaurants. Some luxury accommodation has been built at **Rekawa**, 4 km east.

Excursions

Mulgirigala ① *Rs 100*, is a monastic site situated on an isolated 210-m-high rock. It was occupied from the second century BC and was again used as a place of Buddhist learning in the 18th century. In 1826, George Turnour discovered the *Tika*, commentaries on the *Mahavansa*, here. This allowed the ancient texts, which chronicle the island's history from the third century BC, to be translated from the original Pali to English and Sinhala.

Although not a citadel, it is in some ways similar to Sigiriya. At the base of the rock there are monks' living quarters. The fairly steep paved path goes up in stages to the main temple and image house at the top. Along the way there are three platforms. The first platform has the twin temple, Padum Rahat Vihara, with two 14-m reclining Buddhas, images of Kataragama and Vishnu among others and a Bodhi tree. The wall paintings inside illustrate the *Jatakas* while the ceiling has floral decorations. The small second platform has a *vihara* with another Buddha (reclining) with two disciples. The murals show Hindu gods including Vishnu and Kataragama and the nine planets, and elsewhere, scenes from the Buddha's life. The third has four cave temples and a pond with a 12th-century inscription. The Raja Mahavihara with a fine door frame, has several statues and good wall paintings (though they are not as fine as at Dambulla), some partially hidden behind a cabinet which hold old *ola* manuscripts. The little cave temple, **Naga Vihara**, to the far left has a small door with a painted cobra – a cobra shielded the Buddha from rain when meditating, so is considered sacred and worthy of protection. The cave is believed to be a snake pit, so take care. The final climb is steeper. You pass a Bodhi tree believed to be one of 32 saplings of the second Bodhi tree at Anuradhapura, before reaching the summit with a renovated stupa, image house and temple. The site lies some 16 km north of Tangalla: take a bus to Beliatta, then change to a Wiraketiya-bound bus or alternatively jump in a three-wheeler.

It is estimated that up to 75% of Sri Lanka's female green turtles nest at the 2.5-km **Rekawa Beach** ① *www.tcpsrilanka.org, Rs 1000, from 1900, if no turtles show up it's possible to negotiate a refund*. A 'turtle night watch' takes place each night, run by a local community tourism project which employs ex-poachers as tourist guides (see box, page 155). Visitors are encouraged to observe the females laying their eggs and returning to sea. The turtles could arrive at any time (often after midnight) so be prepared for a long wait. You will first visit a small 'museum' hut, where you can read about the turtles, and then be led on to the beach by a watcher. No flash photography or torches are permitted on the beach, but you might need one to navigate the dirt track. Rekawa's beach is 4 km east of Tangalla, then 3 km along Rekawa Road from Netolpitiya Junction. Three-wheelers from Tangalla charge around Rs 1500 including waiting. There are no facilities.

Tangalla

200 metres
200 yards

Sleeping
Amanwella 1
Beach House 2
Buckingham Place 3
Frangipani Beach Villas 4

French Residence 6
Ganesh Garden 29
Gayana Guest House 5
Green Garden Cabanas 7
Goyambokka Guest
  House 23
Ibis Guesthouse 28
Lucky Star 12
Mangrove Beach
  Cabanas 13
Mangrove Garden 14
Namal Garden Beach 8

Nature Resort 30
Nugasewana Eden 21
Palm Paradise Cabanas 9
Panorama Rock Café 31
Patini Bungalows 22
Rest House 10
Rocky Point Beach
  Bungalows 11
Sandy's 25
Shanika Beach Inn 26
Tangalla Bay 15
Touristen Gasthaus 17

Turtle's Landing 24
Wavy Ocean 16

Eating 🍴
Bay View 1
Cactus Lounge 2
Chanika's 3
Eva Lanka 5
Sea Beach 4
Starfish Beach Café 6

The south coast listings

For Sleeping and Eating price codes and other relevant information, see pages 26-32.

Sleeping

Galle p143, map p145

Beware of touts who may tell you that your guesthouse has hiked its prices or closed or that the fort itself is closed – it never shuts. If you accept a tout's recommendation, you'll be paying over the odds for their commission.

A growing number of villas in the Galle area have been bought and renovated and can be let both short and long term. **Eden Villas**, 65A Lighthouse St, T223 2568, www.villasinsrilanka.com, is a British-run agency with many beautiful properties to let in the Galle area.

Old Town and fort

LL-L Amangalla (formerly **New Oriental Hotel**), 10 Church St, T223 3388, www.amanresorts.com. 17 rooms and 8 suites, which retain the feel and elegance of Galle's most famous colonial hotel. Very attractive swimming pool, spa and good restaurant. Those who aren't staying can take a drink on the veranda or high tea in the lobby, and soak up some of the old-world atmosphere.

LL-AL Galle Fort Hotel, 28 Church St, T223 2870, www.galleforthotel.com. Restored colonial mansion with large rooms and suites, all beautifully and thoughtfully decked out. Excellent food, bar and small pool. Attentive and helpful staff.

AL-A The Fort Printers, 39 Pedlar St, T224 7977, www.thefortprinters.com. Colonial mansion converted to a small hotel with 5 tastefully decorated suites. Small courtyard with pool, where meals and drinks are served.

C New Old Dutch House, 21 Middle St, T223 2987, www.newolddutchhouse.lk. 6 rooms in gleaming house with Moorish-style decor, many arches and a great spiral staircase. Internet available in the lobby.

D-F Rampart View, 37 Rampart St, T222 6767, www.gallefortrampartview.com. 6 sizeable, clean a/c and fan rooms with attached bath in renovated colonial house. Wonderful views from the roof. Friendly, kind management. Free Wi-Fi. No alcohol.

E-F Mrs Shakira Khalid's Guest House, 102 Pedlar St, T077-317 7676, sabrik@sltnet.lk. 5 rooms in a family home, good atmosphere, excellent home-cooked food. The rooms with sea view are best. Renovation work is currently underway and by the time this goes to press there should be new bathrooms and furniture in the rooms. Free Wi-Fi.

F Weltevreden, 104 Pedlar St, T222 2650, piyasena@hotmail.com. 8 clean rooms, quiet lush garden, friendly family, very good food.

F-G Beach Haven Guest House, 65 Lighthouse St, T223 4663, www.beachhaven-galle.com. 10 spotless rooms, some with a/c, those upstairs are better as there's a communal balcony. Very friendly family-run guesthouse, great atmosphere. Popular so book in advance. Free Wi-Fi.

New Town and around

LL-L Lighthouse Hotel (Jetwing), Dadella, 4 km north of Galle, T222 3744, www.jetwinghotels.com. Member of the Small Hotels of the World Association. 60 superbly furnished a/c rooms and 3 suites, panoramic views from sea-facing terrace, 2 restaurants including excellent **Cinnamon Room** for fine dining (see Eating, page 166), and 2 pools, one of which is saltwater.

L Dutch House, 23 Upper Dickson Rd, opposite **The Sun House** (see below), T438 0275, www.thedutchhouse.com. Under the same management as **The Sun House**, this former residence of a Dutch East India admiral was built in 1712 and offers 4 magnificent suites exquisitely decorated in colonial style and a magnificent treetop infinity pool.

L-AL The Sun House, 18 Upper Dickson Rd, T438 0275, www.thesunhouse.com. 5 superbly furnished rooms, with 2 excellent suites, all with different themes in 1860s spice merchant's house. Described as a '5-star boutique hotel' it is highly exclusive with discreet service, fine dining, pool, library, very atmospheric.

B Closenberg Hotel, 11 Closenberg Rd, Magalle, T222 4313, www.closenburg hotel.com. 20 comfortable rooms in an attractive colonial house built in 1858 on promontory overlooking Galle Bay (see page 143). The modern wing is in colonial style and has a/c rooms, minibar and balcony with good sea views; the original rooms have high ceilings, beautiful antique furniture (beds have P&O Rising Sun crest) and are full of history. Attractive restaurant, bougainvillea garden, plenty of character and quiet ambience.

B-C Lady Hill, 29 Upper Dickson Rd (a little further up from **The Sun House**), T224 4322, www.ladyhillsl.com. A 19th-century mansion at the highest point of the city, with large veranda and teak ceiling. Modern extension has 15 well-furnished, if smallish, a/c rooms, with TV and balconies, **Rooftop Harbour Bar** which affords spectacular views of the fort and the harbour, and some mornings as far inland as Adam's Peak. Also very good pool.

Unawatuna p148, map p149

Book ahead at weekends as Unawatuna is a popular getaway from the city. There are a large number of hotels and guesthouses here, catering to a range of budgets. Below are just some of the places on offer.

AL-B Unawatuna Beach Resort (UBR), T438 4545, www.unawatunabeachresort.com. French-managed hotel with light and spacious rooms with balcony, best in new annexe, large private garden, pool, various sports including PADI-qualified diving (see Activities and tours, page 170), boat trips, good restaurant, spa and gym. Resort-style hotel fenced off from the crowded beach.

A-D Banana Garden, T438 1089, www.unawatunabananagarden.com. Fabulous spot very close to the beach with excellent views, and spotless rooms. Good Sri Lankan food (half-board), great atmosphere. The fan rooms are significantly cheaper.

B Dream House, T438 1541, www.dream house-srilanka.com. 4 beautifully furnished rooms in Italian-run old colonial-style house. Wonderful bougainvillea filled garden, very Italian ambience and authentic Italian food. Very peaceful.

B Thaproban, T438 1722, www.thamba pannileisure.com. Sister establishment to **Thambapanni Retreat**, this beachfront hotel offers a range of options from standard a/c to penthouse with amazing sea views. Popular restaurant.

B-C Nooit Gedacht, T222 3449, www.sriayurveda.com. Beautiful colonial mansion (built 1735), steeped in history. Simple rooms with period furniture in the main house, or brighter and more modern ones in the new bungalows. Also full, authentic Ayurveda centre (€500 per week). Very peaceful and atmospheric.

B-C Secret Garden Villa, T224 1857, www.secretgardenunawatuna.com. Tastefully decorated rooms and suites (plenty of wood) in lovely gardens, as well as more modern bungalows. Domed room in the middle for yoga lessons, see Activities and tours, page 170.

B-C Thambapanni Retreat, Yakdehimulla Rd, past **Dream House**, T223 4588, www.thambapannileisure.com. In a peaceful setting on the side of Rumassala hill, rooms on the highest level have magnificent jungle views. The best room is the one built into the side of the hill, the cheapest, standard rooms are not worth bothering with. Ayurvedic centre, inviting pool, yoga classes and reiki.

C Black Beauty, Ganahena, signposted off the main rd, T438 4978, www.black-beauty-sri-lanka.com. Look for the Ying Yang wooden door, which opens onto this very friendly, secluded guesthouse. Laid-back atmosphere, and good value (price includes breakfast), with sparkling clean rooms with a/c and hot water. Pool, play area. Can be booked up weeks and sometimes months in advance so call ahead. A good family choice.

C Flower Garden, Welladewala Rd, T222 5286, www.hotelflowergardensrilanka.com.

Rooms and a range of cabanas all with hot water. The suite cabanas are always booked up, so you'll have to plan in advance. There's a good pool, a restaurant, and it's in laid-back quiet spot in pretty gardens. Staff are friendly and helpful. Showers are amazing.

C Milton's, 368 Ganahena, T493 1201, T071-634 5567, www.miltonsbeachresort.com. Large white-walled hotel towards Matara, popular with tourists and locals, At the quieter end of the beach. Clean, if sometimes slightly small, rooms, all a/c and some with satellite TV. Large grounds, with bar and good terrace restaurant.

C No Name Rest, Dewala Rd, T225 0097. Spacious, well-appointed rooms with fan or a/c. Large restaurant area.

C Sun-n-Sea, Ganahena, east end of bay, T228 3200, ameendeane@yahoo.co.uk. Clean a/c and hot water rooms with covered verandas, on the sea edge. Good terrace restaurant overlooking the bay with excellent view. Very friendly. As you walk in notice the piece of door on the left, Mrs Perera (the previous, charming owner) clung to this as the tsunami swept through the guesthouse in 2004.

C-D The French Guest House, 90/1 Yaddehimeulla Rd, T077-912 0221, jean.muraour@cegetel.net. Fan and a/c rooms set around a peaceful garden. Wi-Fi available, as is French food. Not far from the beach but it feels like a million miles.

C-D Happy Banana, Yakdehimulla Rd, T223 2776, T077-742 4514, happybananareservation@hotmail.com. 6 high-ceilinged, decent sized but variable rooms (upstairs better) with spotless bathrooms in attractive 2-storey building, though no sea view. Popular bar and seafood restaurant.

C-D Sea View, Devala Rd, T222 4376, www.seaviewunawatuna.com. 23 spacious, clean fan and a/c rooms with large balcony in pleasant garden setting. Also a bungalow with 2 bedrooms and kitchen. One new room has an outdoor bathroom and despite being non-a/c is worth the money to shower under the stars. Plans to add kitchenettes to some rooms.

C-E Sunil Garden Guesthouse, Beach Rd, T222 6654, www.sunilgardenguesthouse.lk. A/c and fan rooms, some opening onto the garden and others looking out over the ocean, Spacious and stylishly furnished. The opportunity to have croissants and real coffee for breakfast may be the biggest draw (see Eating, page 167).

C-E Upul Guesthouse, T222 7904, www.upul-rest.com. 7 rooms, 3 with a/c and hot water. Bit cramped but the views from the rooms at the top of the building are fantastic, so try for these. The restaurant specializes in pizza.

C-F Ocean Hill, Peellagoda, T222 4827, www.hoteloceanhill.com. Good value, clean and spacious rooms with shared veranda in a friendly operation. Pleasant open areas, and a great view of Unawatuna beach from 1st floor terrace restaurant. Good food too. Prices vary depending on the amenities (cold or hot water, a/c or fan).

C-F Weliwatta Guest House, T222 6642, www.weliwatta.com. 5 fairly plain rooms, quiet, good home-cooked food. Tours arranged.

D Blue Swan Inn, Yakdehimulla Rd, T222 4691. Spotless comfortable a/c and fan rooms in English/Sri Lankan-run family guesthouse, well furnished. Rooftop restaurant.

D-E Rock House, 213A Yakdehimulla Rd, T222 4948, rockhouse2002@hotmail.com. 25 rooms in 2 blocks, all clean, some new, airy and spacious, lots of wildlife ('troop of mongooses'). Good range, good value.

D-F Primrose Guest House, Yaddehimulla, T222 4679, primroseguest@hotmail.com. 7 fan and a/c rooms in a modern building with Wi-Fi and hot water. Good value.

D-F Strand, Yakdehimulla Rd (set back from beach), T222 4358, www.homestay-strand.net. 5 spacious rooms, 1 small, and 1 apartment, in a 1920s colonial-style house in large grounds. The ground floor rooms have been renovated since the tsunami but are a bit dark. The 'nest room' is recommended, it's bright and has a private balcony looking out onto the garden. Friendly family, knowledgeable host, a little frayed around the edges. Encroaching disco music.

E Amma's Guest House, T222 5332. 13 clean, spacious rooms (upstairs better), opening onto a lovely balcony, nets, clean. Arthur C Clarke was one of the first ever guests here.

E-F Brinkhaus, Welledevala Rd, T224 2245, www.brinkhouseunawatuna.site11.com. Quiet and peaceful, decent rooms, in shaded gardens with monkeys in the trees. Lovely family who have been here for decades and are very friendly and helpful.

E-F Heaven on Earth, T224 7775. 6 quite small rooms, simple but well furnished with private seating areas. Those upstairs have breakfast and internet included in the price.

F Sun Set Point, Yakdehimulla, T393 5196, lalwhitehouse@aol.com. Spacious but slightly tired rooms with veranda in impressive house on headland, with great views. Hidden away from the rest of Unawatuna.

F-G Village Inn, T222 5375, T077-913 1802, unavillageinn@gmail.com. 13 rooms in chalets and 1 bungalow, rooms with bath and balcony, meals to order, quiet, friendly. Helpful owner has a 3-wheeler and will take you on trips.

Unawatuna to Weligama *p149*

LL-L The Fortress, Matara Rd, Koggala, T438 9400, www.thefortress.lk. Large luxury beachfront hotel hidden behind high, imposing walls. Rooms, suites and apartments have huge beds and are tastefully decorated. All the facilities you'd expect, including diving trips organized and Ayurvedic treatments. Large swimming pool.

B-C Kabalana Beach Hotel, Galle Rd, Kataluva, T228 3294, www.kabalana.com. Beachfront cabanas and a range of room options on a good stretch of sand. Decor is colonial in style, with dark wood and white furnishings. Ayurvedic treatments and surf lessons available. Restaurant. Popular with surfers. Can arrange airport transfers.

B-C Koggala Beach Hotel, Habaraduwa, Koggala, T228 3243, www.koggalabeach hotel.com. 102 sea-facing rooms, the superiors are better and newer. Popular with tour groups. Restaurants, bars, pool and lots of activities. On a good stretch of beach.

B-C Sri Gemunu, Dalawella, T228 3202, www.sri-gemunu.com. 20 comfortable sea-facing fan and a/c rooms with veranda. Pleasant gardens and good restaurant overlooking attractive beach.

C Easy Beach, Ahangama (4 km east of Koggala), T228 2028, www.easybeach.info. Set in pleasant gardens and open, breezy feel with rooms or cabanas (breakfast included). Surf boards for rent and trips organized.

D Point de Galle, 654 Matara Rd, Talpe, T077-730 4390, www.pointdegallehotel.com. 8 airy rooms with beautiful beds and balconies set in attractive gardens right on the beach.

D Star Light, Talpe, T228 2216, starlight@ sltnet.lk. Attractive a/c rooms with beautiful furniture and good attention to detail, TV, minibar and bath tubs. Lovely open areas, great pool and very smart restaurant.

D Wijaya Beach, Dalawella, T228 3610. Spotless, modern rooms with verandas. Good restaurant with great laid-back atmosphere.

E The Frangipani Tree, 812 Matara Rd, Thalpe, T228 3711, www.thefrangipanitree.com. Owned by the same people as **The Fort Printers** in Galle (see page 158), this boutique hotels offers 10 suites in 4 separate villas named after turtles. 35-m pool is at the centre of the action, there's also excellent food, yoga and tennis.

E-F Shanthi Guest House, Dalawella, T438 0081, www.shanthi-guesthouse.de. A/c and fan rooms or cabanas. Rooms are moderate size, shared balcony, facing beach. Cabanas closer to beach set amongst a series of ponds in attractive gardens. Stilt fishermen on beach, and saltwater 'pool' nearby. Excellent restaurant and pleasant, friendly atmosphere.

G Ram's Surfing Beach, Midigama, T041-225 2639. Communal surfer's hangout with range of rooms from dirt cheap to moderate. Good food and friendly.

Weligama *p151, map p151*

The better value accommodation is in Pelana, a short bus or 3-wheeler ride from Weligama town.

L Taprobane Island, T091-438 0275, www.taprobaneisland.com. Probably the most exclusive place to stay in Sri Lanka. Rent the whole house, which has 5 bedrooms and resident staff, including a private chef.

AL Barberyn Beach Ayurveda Resort, T225 2994, www.barberynresorts.com. Ayurvedic centre run by respected Beruwela-based company. 60 attractive a/c rooms, sea views and balconies, some split-level with bath-tub. Large Ayurveda clinic with full list of treatments. Yoga and meditation. Full-board only.

AL Mandara Resort, 416/A Pelena, on the border of Weligama and Mirissa, T225 3706, www.mandararesort.com. Tasteful, modern property with 20 stylish rooms and suites, some have private plunge pool and all with enormous bathrooms. Nice swimming pool, complete with fibre optic lights in 5 colours. Ayurvedic lodge, attractive beach area, gym, tours arranged.

B The Green Rooms, T077-111 9896, www.thegreenroomssrilanka.com. A surf lodge at the eastern end of the beach with very attractive wooden cabanas. The whole place can be rented, or alternatively individual rooms are available. Many visitors stay for weeks and there's a family atmosphere about the place. If you want to learn to surf there are special packages available combining tuition and accommodation. Also cookery lessons. Recommended.

B Villa Samsara, 2 km west at Kumalgama (Km 140 post), T225 1144. Beautiful colonial villa in lovely garden amongst coconut groves. 4 large, simply furnished rooms with 4 poster beds.

C Weligama Bay Resort, Matara Rd, Pelana, T225 3920, www.weligamabayresort.com. 22 a/c villas, bungalows and suites, all with sea views and contemporary furnishings. Beachfront pool, spa, and all the facilities you'd expect but a disappointing restaurant.

C Weligama Bay View, New Bypass Rd, Pelana, T225 1199, www.bayviewlk.com. Along good stretch of beach, 11 large a/c and fan rooms. Reasonably clean, good restaurant. Popular with surfers, and friendly management. Surfing equipment and surfing lessons offered.

C-D Jaga Bay Resort, New Bypass Rd, Pelana, T225 0033, www.jagabay.com. 28 large rooms with fan and a/c, plus 3 cabanas with hot bath. Good views from 1st and 2nd floors. Peaceful location, very good restaurant with palms growing out of the roof.

C-D Samaru Beach House, 544 New Bypass Rd, Pelana, T225 1417, www.guesthouse_ weligamasamaru.com. Spotless rooms, 4 a/c and 4 fan, each with own seating area. Good location on the beach, restaurant, friendly management, good value. Rents surfboards, bikes and scooters. Wi-Fi and surf lessons.

C-D Weligama Bay Inn, New Bypass Rd, almost opposite Taprobane Island, T041-225 0291, www.baynetcceylonhotels.net. 8 clean a/c and fan rooms in large gardens with sea views. Restaurant.

D-F Greenpeace Inn, New Bypass Rd, Pelana, T225 2957, greenpeaceinn@yahoo.com. 10 rooms close to the beach, the 2 on the top floor have the best views and the most light, but those downstairs are cheap (fan and cold water). 4 more rooms planned for the coming months. Restaurant. Enthusiastic owner.

Mirissa *p152, map p152*

Between Nov and Apr, book ahead. Note that most of the higher-end hotels impose a minimum of half-board on their guests.

B Hotel Silan Mo, Bandaramulla, T225 4974, hotel.silanmo@gmail.com. Newly opened hotel with 6 rooms and another 9 to come. Across the road from the beach. All a/c and with views of the ocean. The rooftop swimming pool should be completed by the time you read this. Huge balconies. Internet pending. Modern, tasteful. Half board.

B Palace Mirissa, Copparamulla, T225 1303, www.palacemirissa.com. At the top of the hill, on the headland, the 13 cabanas have good views (1 has spectacular views). Attractive landscaped gardens with peacocks wandering around and good pool. The food is not that exciting and half board is imposed on guests. Sister hotel is the **Paradise Beach Club**.

B-C Paradise Beach Club, 140 Gunasiri Mahime Mawatha, T225 1206, www.paradise mirissa.com. Rebuilt after the tsunami, offers 42 single- and 2-storey cabanas, both a/c and fan. Pool, smart restaurant (evening buffet), tours, located on beach, not bad value but enforced half board tends to be restrictive.

C Ocean Moon, Udupila Junction, T225 2326, oceanmoon46@gmail.com. 6 good cabanas on the beach, peaceful, good food, massage.

C-D The Sun Set, T225 1577, www.mirissa sunset.com. 13 rooms in 3 categories, slightly overpriced but good swimming nearby.

C-E Amarasinghe Guest House, T225 1204, chana7@sltnet.lk. 5 mins inland (follow signs). Large rooms and bungalows in a pleasant quiet garden away from the beach. Internet, cold water. Offers cookery classes. Overpriced. Has another property comprising 3 small, dark and basic rooms (1500) with verandas called **Blue Whalewatching Centre**, nearer to the beach. They're nothing special but a good price for Mirissa.

D Rose Blossom Guest House, look for the sign opposite **Giragala Village**, Bandaramulla, T077-713 3096, roseblossom.mirissa@ gmail.com. 3 rooms with hot water, set in a large garden with a restaurant serving good food. The couple who run it are friendly and helpful.

D-E Calm Rest, Sunanda Rd, T225 2546, calm.rest@yahoo.com. 4 well-furnished wooden cabanas and 3 rooms. Restaurant and gem shop.

D-E Central Beach Inn, on beach, T225 1699. 6 simple a/c and fan rooms, plus cabanas, restaurant.

F Samantha Flora and Fauna, T077-635 5068. 5 simple rooms in forest setting by log bridge and lagoon, fan and cold water.

F-G Sun 'n' Sea, T077-833 9958. This place is all about the family running it. The rooms are basic, and there's only cold water but it's near the beach and the food is fantastic.

Matara p153 map p153

Most budget travellers choose to stay in Polhena. The Broadway is also known as Dharmapala Mawatha, Colombo Rd or New Galle Rd.

C-D Rest House, main fort area south of bus station, Matara, T222 2299, resthousemh@ sltnet.lk. Badly damaged by the tsunami this rest house has recently reopened and now offers 8 modern, clean rooms (cheaper have fans) with thick mattresses, all finished to a high standard. Internet, TVs and hot water should all be installed in the next couple of months. Restaurant with good Sri Lankan breakfasts, and views of the sea.

C-E Surf Lanka Hotel, Medawatta, T222 8190, www.surf-lanka.com. 11 a/c and fan rooms with balconies and sea views (those upstairs are better), in modern white building. Restaurant.

D-F Polhena Reef Garden, 30 Beach Rd, Polhena, T222 2478, www.prghotel.com. 18 a/c rooms in a hotel that caters mainly to Sri Lankan tourists. Pool and restaurant, friendly staff.

E-F TK Green Garden, 116/1 Polhena Beach Rd, Polhena, T222 2603. 11 good, clean a/c and fan rooms, some with shared veranda, though expensive restaurant, well-run, quiet, pleasant garden.

F Sunil Rest, off Beach Rd, Polhena, T222 1983, sunilrestpolhena@yahoo.com. Very friendly and helpful guesthouse with cheap rooms. Tours organized and bike hire available.

G Sunny Lanka Guest House, Polhena Rd, Polhena, T222 3504. Clean rooms in friendly guesthouse, trips organized.

Matara to Tangalla p154

AL Claughton, Kemagoda (3 km east of Dikwella), T071-272 5470, www.claughton house.com. Sumptuous Italianate villa in magnificent setting overlooking a vast sweep of bay. 3 rooms; or hire the whole house.

AL-A Dikwella Resort, Batheegama, 1 km west of Dikwella, T225 5271, www.dick wella.net. 38 rooms, some 2-storey, and 8 suites in Italian-owned resort. All have sea views and some suites have jacuzzis over-looking the ocean. Saltwater pool, spa, tennis, watersports, excellent restaurants, very attractive location on rocky promontory. In-house PADI dive school.

D-E Kingdom Resort, Kottegoda, (5 km west of Dikwella) just before (from west) Km 175 post, T225 9364, www.kingdomsrilanka.com. 8 spotless a/c and fan rooms, some with balcony, in attractive neo-colonial house with own stretch of beach. Italian-owned, with all furnishings Italian-made. Very pleasant.

Tangalla *p155, map p157*

Tangalla is yet another place where 3-wheeler touts are very active. They meet travellers at the bus station and sing the praises of their friend's guesthouse. If you go with them you may find you're being charged an inflated price for your room, they will be pocketing the difference. In low season when there's less chance of swimming prices drop, so don't forget to bargain.

Marakolliya

The access road to some of the cheaper guesthouses is currently in a bad state of repair, however there is talk or some owners clubbing together to pay for improvements.

B-C Nature Resort, T071-177 7637. Recently reopened, spotless a/c and fan rooms with veranda or balcony. Nice bar and pool, restaurant. Body boards for hire and starting a diving operation in the near future.

C Mangrove Garden, T077-906018, www,beachcabana.lk. 6 chalets, reached by rope ferry but a bridge is being built across the lagoon. Beach bar and restaurant, rock-sheltered natural pool for swimming, and a desert island feel about the place. A 3-wheeler from town should cost Rs 250.

C-D Ganesh Garden, T224 2529, www.ganeshgarden.com. Cabanas and rooms in a quiet location, with a laid-back

atmosphere, hammocks in garden, snorkelling equipment for hire, and a reasonable restaurant. Those further from the beach have hot water and some have new bathrooms. Canoeing on lagoon also possible.

D-E Mangrove Beach Cabanas, see **Mangrove Garden**, above. Cabanas and mud houses in a beautiful spot on a secluded beach, just down from **Mangrove Garden**, check out the bathrooms. Restaurant offers a good selection of food, and staff are friendly and helpful. Internet at the chalet office.

E-F Sandy's, T077-622 5009, www.sandy cabanas.com. Family-run guesthouse with 7 cabanas, some beachfront and 1 with hot water. Home-cooked food, sheltered pool.

Medilla and Medaketiya

As the largest concentration of guesthouses is here, it's worth trying to bargain your room price down if it's quiet.

D Ibis Guesthouse, T567 4439, www.guesthouse-ibis.de. Spotless, attractive cabanas and rooms (hot water) in peaceful location where beach meets lagoon. Yoga, and windsurfing equipment and bikes for hire. Restaurant, friendly. Related to **Patini Bungalows** (see below).

D Patini Bungalows, T077-540 2679, www.patinibungalows.com. French-owned, 2 clean and attractive fan bungalows (cold water), 2 more planned, double can be made into a family room. 2 nights minimum.

D-E Gayana Guest House, T224 0659. Rooms of varying size, some fronting directly onto beach with private balconies (land-side ones are cheaper and have cold water), a/c and fan. Good restaurant, friendly staff, popular with backpackers.

D-F Panorama Rock Café, T224 0458, T077-762 0092, www.panoramarockcafe.com. Fan rooms and bungalows, some with good sea views, on lagoon. Good food (see Eating, page 168).

D-G Namal Garden Beach, T491 5533, T077-262 2798, www.namalbeach-tangalle.com. 18 rooms, upstairs better with private balcony and sea views where you can watch the fishermen hauling up the nets, terrace restaurant, beach barbecues possible, rather block-like but breezy.

E Frangipani Beach Villas, T071-533 7052, nalinemail1@gmail.com. Newly opened, 5 large, clean fan rooms with balconies overlooking the sea. Restaurant and tours. The beach it fronts is mainly frequented by fishermen rather than sunbathers. Good value.

F Wavy Ocean, T077-601 4411. Cheap, simple rooms, ignore the downstairs ones. Seafood restaurant.

F-G Shanika Beach Inn, T224 2079, T077-646 8587. 6 simple, decent-sized rooms with fan and hot water, good cheap food in upstairs restaurant. Good value and rates can be lower when things are quiet.

Tangalla town and Pallikaduwa

L Tangalla Bay Hotel, Pallikudawa, T224 0346, www.jetwinghotels.com. Recently refurbished and now one of the Jetwing hotels, it is built to look like a ship and is in a good position on the headland. The 34 rooms a/c rooms are on 4 levels, those with sea views are larger and more expensive. Restaurant, bar and nice infinity pool.

B French Residence, 260 Matara Rd, www.frenchresidence.free.fr. 10 comfortable a/c rooms, 4 with sea views, all with balcony. Nice pool rooftop terrace, good atmosphere. French management and predominantly French clientele.

C-F Nugasewana Eden, opposite **Tangalla Bay Hotel**, T224 0389, www.nugasewana.com. 9 clean and tasteful rooms, 6 a/c and 3 fan, all with hot water. Free Wi-Fi, wide balconies with sea views, good showers and a restaurant. Set back from the road in a pleasant garden, justifiably popular so book in advance. Apartment with 3 bedrooms and open kitchen/diner to be completed shortly (US$60).

D-F Rest House, on promontory overlooking harbour, Tangalla town, T224 0299. Clean fan and a/c rooms in rambling 18th-century Dutch building, balcony/verandas, restaurant with lovely views.

E Turtles' Landing, next door to **Cactus Lounge**, T071-684 0283. 1 decent-sized room above the restaurant, with small balcony and right on the beach. Nothing special but good swimming just out the front. Long-stay discounts available.

E-F Touristen Gasthaus, 13 Pallikaduwa Rd, T224 0370, sevenvilla@live.com. Popular with long-term guests, 2 bungalows with fan and cold water separate from the main house, range of rooms (a/c, fan, hot water, kitchenette), plus an apartment with kitchenette (**E**), friendly family. No restaurant, but breakfast can be arranged on request.

Goyambokka and around

LL Amanwella, Godellawela, T224 1333, www.amaresorts.com. Luxury resort nestling in a crescent-shaped bay. 30 suites, most hidden among the trees, all with private plunge pools and terrace. Beachfront infinity pool, restaurant, contemporary design and furnishings. The public beach is good for snorkelling.

LL The Beach House, contact **The Sun House** in Galle for reservations (see page 158), T091-222 2624, www.thesunhouse.com. An exquisitely furnished 4-bedroom house (sleeping 7) on a fine stretch of beach, extensive library, stunning pool, open-air bathrooms, and an extraordinary collage about the poet Keats.

B Lucky Star, 31 Tuduwewatta, at the end of the road on the headland, T077-617 4496, www.luckystar-srilanka.de. 7 clean fan rooms overlooking the ocean, shared balconies. German owners who speak limited English but the friendly staff can translate. Nice pool, restaurant.

B Palm Paradise Cabanas, T224 0338, www.palmparadisecabanas.net. 20 comfortable wooden cabanas (non-a/c) set in a spacious and shady garden close to the beach, very peaceful. Mandatory half-board during high season.

C-D Rocky Point Beach Bungalows, T224 0834, T077-497 7033, www.srilankarocky point.com. Bungalows and rooms, all large, clean with private veranda, pleasant gardens in quiet location overlooking rocky promontory, good food.

C-E Green Garden Cabanas, T077-624 7628, lankatangalla@yahoo.com. 3 wooden cabanas and 1 of stone that would look at home in the Alps, as well as a new family cabana. A couple more are planned for next year and all are dotted around the large garden. Excellent food and a welcoming and friendly family. Recommended.

D Goyambokka Guest House, opposite **Palm Paradise Cabanas**, T224 0838, T077-790 3091. 4 comfortable, clean rooms (all will have hot water and new bathrooms by the time you read this) in colonial house, with quiet, pleasant shaded garden. One room has its own private seating area, the others are quite close together so there isn't much privacy. Deals with touts, so call directly for prices.

Rekawa

L-AL Buckingham Place, T348 9447, www.buckinghamplace.lk. British-owned luxury hotel right next to the Turtle Conservation Project (see box, page 155). 11 spacious rooms and suites with colourful splashes and modern decor, all overlooking the lagoon and most with tubs and rain showers. Excellent food, beautiful gardens, pool, and almost deserted stretch of sand. Boat trips on the lagoon and bikes available for guests. Quiet and relaxing.

🍴 Eating

Galle *p143, map p145*

Some of the more upmarket hotels in the fort offer excellent dining options, guesthouses are a cheaper alternative and there are numerous cheap 'rice and curry' places around the train/bus stations,

Galle Fort Hotel, see Sleeping, page 158. Excellent European and Asian dishes served in relaxing surroundings overlooking the pool. Light lunches are available and there's a set menu in the evenings with a good choice of desserts. Not a choice if you're in a rush.

Lighthouse Hotel, see Sleeping, page 158. Highly recommended for a treat, especially in the **Cinnamon Room** (separate vegetarian menu), fine dining, superb attention to detail, order an Irish coffee just to see it being prepared. The **Cardamom Café** has lighter meals.

South Ceylon, Gamini Mawatha. For good Chinese, Sri Lankan (try pineapple curry or cashew nut curry), Continental plus bakery. Also bar.

Alangkara, 46 Pedlar St, T077-790 7878, www.alangkaralanka.com. A tour operator and a shop, but best of all a café. Enthusiastic owners with a wide menu of Sri Lankan and Western dishes. Small and welcoming. Rotti in the evenings.

Anura's, Pedlar St, T222 4354. Mediocre pizzas and curries.

Closenberg Hotel, see Sleeping, page 159. Tour groups mean service can be slow, but from under the pergola there are lovely views over the harbour, pleasant and quiet in the evenings.

Rampart View Hotel, see Sleeping, page 158. The veranda is 'a must for a sunset beer' though the food is average.

Serendipity Arts Café, Leyn Baan St. Open 0730-2130. Laid-back spot with friendly staff, serving sandwiches, burgers, Sri Lankan dishes, and cake. There are books and magazines to flip through (some published over the road) and excellent walking tours of the fort leave from here (see Activities and tours, page 169).

Unawatuna *p148, map p149*

There are numerous restaurants along the beach, with very little to choose between them. Nearly all will serve good seafood, Chinese, Sri Lankan (full meal often only to order) and Western dishes. Almost all serve alcohol (though those at the western end of the bay don't advertise it since the area close to the temple is officially 'dry'). The Rotty shop opposite **Sonja's Health Food Restaurant** is good for a light meal.

Dream House, see Sleeping, page 159. Delicious Italian food in lovely surroundings.

Book in advance as the restaurant is very popular and some meals are best ordered in advance.

¶¶-¶ Lucky Tuna. Attractive wooden bar and restaurant on the beach. Curry and the usual rice and noodle dishes, as well as some excellent fish. Reasonable beer prices.

¶ Blowhole, tucked away, past **Submarine Diving School**, turn right by the temple. In a great setting by the river (watch the wildlife), good place to stop on the way up to Jungle Beach or for a quiet breakfast. Simple but delicious food.

¶ Happy Banana, see Sleeping, page 160. With lovely beach setting, good for seafood, Fri night disco.

¶ Jina's Vegetarian and Vegan Restaurant, just down the road from **South Ceylon** (see below), serving a similar selection of veggie and vegan food. Set in pleasant gardens.

¶ Kingfisher, next to **Upul Guesthouse**. Popular place serving fresh seafood and Thai dishes, arrive early if you want a seat.

¶ Pink Elephant. Nightly set menus, 3 courses of interesting and inventive Western-inspired cuisine. It may not be beachside but it's worth tearing yourself away from the sand.

¶ South Ceylon, T077-952 6824, www.southceylonrestaurant.com. Wide vegetarian menu, and good cake.

¶ Sunil's Garden Coffee Bar, Sunil Garden Guesthouse, see Sleeping, page 160. Tables are hidden amongst the undergrowth and there's a Wi-Fi at the back on a raised platform. The menu is limited but what there is, is excellent. Food is very fresh, especially the pizzas. Homemade cake, Italian coffee, as wells as tzatziki with brown toast and others snacks.

¶ Thaproban, see Sleeping, page 159. Good selection of fish and Western dishes in pleasant surroundings. Alcohol-packed cocktails.

¶ Hot Rock. Almost dropping into the sea (literally), this is a popular hangout serving seafood and Western dishes. Bright and colourful walls, friendly staff.

¶ One Love Restaurant, next to **Upul Guesthouse**. Small, popular place with laid-back atmosphere. The curries are

fantastic, especially the pumpkin one they're renowned for, and the seafood is good. Note that food can sometimes take over an hour to reach the table.

Weligama p151, map p151
Home cooking in the privately run guesthouses is difficult to beat, see page 162.
¶¶-¶ Keerthi. After a hiatus of several years, this family-run restaurant is now back. Close to the sea and peaceful, with large whale jaw in the garden to add interest, the husband and wife team cook up a wide selection of good seafood, including mullet, snapper and sailfish, as well as usual seerfish and cuttlefish.

Mirissa p152, map p152
A number of the places listed here also rent out rooms. Those on the beach display their fresh seafood nightly so diners can choose their meals. Most guesthouses have restaurants.
¶ Bay Moon. The first in Mirissa and still one of the best, "nice beach bar ambience and they set a beach fire for effect".

¶ Café Mirissa. Has a limited selection of food – seafood, curry, Chinese – but a perfect position to survey the beach.

¶ Seafresh, part of **Paradise Beach Club**. The smartest place in Mirissa, offers a set menu.

¶ Water Creatures, at the far end of the beach. Popular with surfers, serves a good range of dishes.

¶ Dewini Roti Shop. Open 0700-2030. Roadside shack serving excellent *kottu rotti*, the tourist favourites such as banana and honey rotti, and fried rice dishes. Tables set up behind with umbrellas for shade. Friendly family running it. It may have to move soon to make way for development, if so you may find the same food being served at their house near **Amarasinghe** (see Sleeping, page 163). There are also plans for cookery lessons in the future. Popular breakfast spot.

Matara p153, map p153
¶ Chinese Dragon, 62 Tangalla Rd. Good, cheap meals.

Ψ Rest House, see Sleeping, page 163. Restaurant serving good Sri Lankan rice and curry lunches, good views of the ocean.
Ψ Samanmal, next to the **Hatton National Bank** opposite the stadium. Good for Chinese.
Ψ Galle Oriental Bakery, Dharmapala Mawatha. Good Sri Lankan meals, as well as snacks.

Tangalla *p155, map p157*
Along the beach towards the town, several restaurants and guesthouses prepare very good dishes, especially seafood. For options see page 164. There are also some shacks on the beach offering fresh seafood and BBQs.
ΨΨΨ Eva Lanka, 3 km west of Goyambokka, T077-790 5011, www.eva.lk. If you're desperate for wood-fired pizza or authentic cappuccino.
ΨΨ Bay View, next to **Touristen Gasthaus**. In a lovely spot overlooking the bay.
ΨΨ Cactus Lounge, Pallikaduwa. Has a good setting on sheltered beach, fresh seafood, plus soups and snacks.
ΨΨ Chanika's, Mahawela Rd. Small, an 'exceptional find', does excellent food, delicious and fresh, if tired of tamed down 'European' dishes, ask for Sri Lankan style. Friendly and obliging.
ΨΨ Panorama Rock Café, see Sleeping, page 164. Fresh seafood and fine BBQs in a beachfront location.
ΨΨ Sea Beach, Pallikaduwa. Good range of fish including seer, shark and mullet.
ΨΨ Starfish Beach Café, just down from **Ibis Guesthouse**, T224 1005, T077-617 8785, starfishtangallle@gmail.com. Not quite beachfront but makes up for it with the food and the free Wi-Fi. Snacks, deserts and on Sat offers BBQ and live music (3 types of fish, salad and chips).
ΨΨ Turtles' Landing, see Sleeping, page 165. Offers similar fare to **Cactus Lounge**, see above.

Ω Bars and clubs

Galle *p143, map p145*
The **Galle Fort Hotel** has a pleasant veranda bar, and the **Rampart Hotel** looks out over the ramparts. The **Rooftop Harbour Bar** at the Lady Hill Hotel is another good option for spectacular views.

Unawatuna *p148, map p149*
The places listed in the Eating section generally sell beer, see page 166. A couple of places have discos at weekends, starting at 2130. Sat is the big night.

✸ Festivals and events

Galle *p143, map p145*
Galle Literary Festival, www.galleliterary festival.com. Started in 2007, and usually takes place at the beginning of the year. Attracts a good range of well-known international authors.

O Shopping

Galle *p143, map p145*
Galle is known for its lace-making, gem polishing and ebony carving. The fort is home to a number of upmarket boutiques, as well as innumerable gem shops.
Barefoot, 41 Pedlar St, T222 6299, barefootceylon.com. A branch of the popular Colombo shop (see page 83), selling beautiful sarongs, tops and scarfs, as well as coffee table books, toys and homewares.
KK – The Collection, Pedlar St. Classy imported homewares.
Laksana, 30 Hospital St. One of a number of shops in Galle Fort selling gems and jewellery.
Natural Silk Factory, 691/1 Colombo Rd, Gintota (north of Galle), T223 4379. 0900-1830. Where you can watch silk worms (the silk being spun and weaved), showroom

and shop with reasonable prices and little
pressure to buy.

SCIA Handicraft Centre, Kandewatte Rd,
T223 4304. 5 workshops producing polished
gems, carvings (ebony), batik, lace and
leather bags, etc, employing about 50 people
(approved by the State Gem Corporation
and Tourist Board).

Shoba Display Gallery, 67A Pedlar St,
T222 4351, www.shobafashion.org.
A women's cooperative, this shops sells
colourful handicrafts and lace work.

Vijitha Yapa, 170 Main St. Branch of the
national bookshop chain, with a wide
selection of English books.

Unawatuna *p148, map p149*
There are various shops selling provisions
and tourist goods. Clothes are cheaper on
Yakdehimulla Rd, but bargain.

Weligama *p151, map p151*
Weligama lace is available at several outlets
and workshops along the road opposite
Taprobane Island.

Matara *p153, map p153*
You'll find good batiks and citronella oil.
Art Batiks, 58/6 Udyana Rd, T222 4488,
www.sites.google.com/site/artbatiks. Shirley
Dissanayake is a holder of the President's
Honorary Gold Medal 'Kala Booshana' in
arts. He produces top quality batiks, only
available on site here in his workshop.
Beware of imitations.
Jez-look Batiks, 12 St Yehiya Mawatha,
T222 2142, www.jezlookbatiks.com. Award-
winning batik workshop, wide range of
clothes and hanging batiks.
Laksala, 55 Darmapala Mawatha, by the
temple, T222 2734. For handicrafts.
Sri Madura, 21 Dharmapala Mawatha.
Specializes in locally made Pahatarata Biraya
drums, which you can buy, or simply watch
craftsmen producing.

▲ Activities and tours

Galle *p143, map p145*
Diving
There are a number of shipwrecks in Galle Bay
but better diving is at Hikkaduwa, page 130,
and Unawatuna, below.

Walking tours
Sri Serendipity, 60 Leyn Baan St, T077-683
8659, www.sriserendipity.com. Juliet Coombe
and Daisy Perry run this publishing house
in the fort, and offer guided walking tours
of the area. Tours leave from here or the
Serendipity Arts Café, just over the road
(see Eating, page 166), Rs 1500 per person.
They're usually at 1000, and 1600 if there's
enough demand. If interested in a particular
subject, such as food or architecture let them
know as walks follow certain themes.

Unawatuna *p148, map p149*
Cookery classes
There are a few places in Unawatuna offering
cookery classes, prices range from Rs 2000 for
2 hrs to Rs 3000 for a whole day.
Sonja's Health Food Restaurant, next to
South Ceylon, Unawatuna Beach Rd, T224
5815, T077-961 5310. Karuna runs very popular
cookery classes here that start at 1100 and end
about 1530. Includes a trip to Galle to visit the
market for ingredients and then pupils are
taught how to make curries, sambol, etc. In the
evening you eat what you've cooked and can
bring a guest for free. Good value.

Diving and snorkelling
Most of the beach-side restaurants hire out
snorkelling equipment, and some run their
own snorkelling trips. The diving season runs
from Nov to Apr here. There are 5 or 6 wrecks
nearby, some at a depth below 15 m, which
you can visit. The best accessible wreck is
the Rangoon in Galle Bay, though this is at
a depth of 32 m. There are also some reefs
and a rock dive on offer.
Sea Horse, off Matara Rd, T077-627 7622,
www.seahorsedivinglanka.com. Run by

Rohana (an experienced Dive Master), this is the smallest operation in Unawatuna. 1 dive €25, 10 dives €190. Open Water courses €275, Advanced €250. Also runs trips to Jungle Beach (Rs 4500) and snorkelling (Rs 3500).

Submarine Diving School, T077-719 6753, www.divinginsrilanka.com. €25 (including equipment) for 1 dive, €45-50 for 2. Hires out snorkelling gear for Rs 250 per hr and runs snorkelling trips. Dive courses. Check that a PADI-qualified instructor is on hand.

Unawatuna Diving Centre, T077-704 4886, www.unawatunadiving.com. The largest and newest dive centre, with the best equipment. Runs trips to about 15 dive sites. Open Water courses €320, Advanced €275, single dives €25. Also shallow depth refresher courses and discover dives (2 dives for €65).

Tour operators
Southlink Travels, 2nd floor, Selaka Building, 34 Gamini Mawatha, next to the Bus Station.

Yoga and meditation
A few hotels and guesthouses offer meditation and yoga classes, the best are at **Secret Garden Villa**. Yoga at 0700, 0900, 1700, Rs 1000.

Unawatuna to Weligama *p149*
For experienced surfers, the coast from Ahangama to Midigama has some excellent surf, at its best between Jan and Mar. There are various breaks at Midigama. The main (or 'left' break) is in front of **Hilten's Beach Resort**, and is good for beginners and longboarders. Further east, the 'right' breaks over a shallow reef close to **Ram's Surfing Beach**. 400 m east of here is a further break which is more suitable for beginners.

Weligama *p151, map p151*
Diving and snorkelling
There are plenty of fish in Weligama Bay (especially **Yala Rock** and **Prinz Heinrich Patch**) plus numerous wrecks here and further afield (*SS Rangoon* good but deep).

Prinz Heinrich Patch offers the chance to see huge eels and rays, whilst Yala Rock has rocks, pinnacles and caves with a swim through and lots of fish.

Bavarian Divers, Bay Beach, T077-785 8330, www.bavarian-divers.de. Highly recommended, Captain Edgar K Rupprecht has 15 years experience in the Maldives. PADI Open Water course (€375, Advanced €270), plus courses up to Dive Master. 1 dive and check dive €30, or €25 per person for 2+ people. Can arrange budget accommodation for divers (Rs 500).

Fishing
Deep-sea angling is available here mainly for marlin, yellowfin and sharks. Guesthouses can also arrange trips out on catamaran's with the local fishermen.

Mirissa *p152, map p152*
Fishing
Mirissa Water Sports, T077-359 7731, www.mirissawatersports.com. Sport fishing costs about Rs 8000 for a minimum of 4 people. Can also organize other watersports, such as sea kayaking.

Surfing
Surfboards can be rented from various places along the beach.

Tour operators
Kangaroo Tours, Galle Rd, T225 2402. Day tours, motorbike rental, whale-watching.

Whale- and dolphin-watching
Whale-watching (blue and sperm whales) has taken off in a big way in recent years and every guesthouse, 3-wheeler driver and restaurant will offer to organize a tour for you. They vary in quality and price, and probably one of the best sources of information on the ground is other travellers. Between Dec and Apr is the best time. Trips leave around 0700 and run for about 4-5 hrs, breakfast is included. **Mirissa Water Sports**, T077-359 7731, www.mirissawatersports.com. The original operator, so they know what they're doing.

The whale tale

There had been efforts for over 30 years to develop whale-watching in Sri Lanka but to little or no avail. Attempts were thwarted by the cost of setting up such a venture, the lack of suitable boats, and more than anything by the mistaken belief that whale-watching had to take place from Trincomalee, which was periodically off-limits during the war years.

Things began to change, however, in the late nineties. In 1999 marine biologist Dr Charles Anderson suggested that whale migration between the Bay of Bengal and the Arabian Sea took blue and sperm whales close to the shores of Sri Lanka between December and April. His theory was further refined in 2005 after thousands of sightings, and he identified Dondra Head as the best viewing spot because the continental shelf is at its narrowest here.

More evidence to support the migration theory was provided by **Mirissa Water Sports**, a commercial venture set up after the 2004 tsunami. Simon Scarff, Sue Evans and their crew started logging sightings and by 2008 were offering trips to see the whales (see Activities and tours, page 170).

Kalpitiya (see page 103) has also recently been identified as a whale-watching hot spot, and tours are gradually starting to gain popularity there as well. It is too early to confirm Sri Lanka's position as one of the leading whale-watching destinations in the world, but it has the potential. It is hoped by many that whale-watching will become as synonymous with Sri Lanka as leopard-spotting in Yala, but with that will come added problems. Already there are concerns about the number of boats operating out of Mirissa and their impact on the whales. Legislation and guidelines need to be adhered to for the safety of the whales and the watchers, but if this can be managed effectively then tourists should be able to experience seeing blue and sperm whales as well as dolphins, potentially all in one trip.

For more information on whale-watching in Sri Lanka, including the history and a log of sightings, see www.jetwingeco.com/index.cfm?section=page&id=1055.

Whale-watching trips can be combined with any of their other activities, 2 people minimum. Rs 8960, children half-price and under 10s free.
Raja and the Whales, T077-695 3452, www.rajaandthewhales.com. Local family-run operator, charges Rs 8000 per person and gets consistently good reports. Boat is in good shape and crew are careful not to get too close to the whales.

Matara *p153, map p153*
Diving and snorkelling
Nishantha, Blue Corals Restaurant, 36 Beach Rd, T077-760 0803. Organizes local diving excursions. Check qualifications.

Also arranges snorkelling trips (Rs 6000) and runs river safari trips for croc-spotting.

Ask at **TK Green Garden** for Titus, an excellent snorkelling guide who knows the reef like the back of his hand having had over 30 years of experience. The reef is also good for first time snorkellers ("after 10 mins I felt like Jacques Cousteau!"), and there are night trips to see moray eels.

Tangalla *p155, map p157*
Diving
Tangalla Bay Hotel (see Sleeping, page 165) used to offer diving and may well do so again under its new owners. There are also plans at **Nature Resort** (see Sleeping, page 164) to set up a diving operation in the next few months.

⊖ Transport

Galle *p143, map p145*
Bus There are regular services along the coast in both directions. Both CTB and private buses operate from the main bus stand. Frequent buses to **Colombo**, a/c express recommended (3 hrs), for normal CTB avoid Sun as it can be very busy with queues of over an hour before you actually get onto a bus. Buses east to **Unawatuna** (15 mins), **Matara** (1-1½ hrs), **Tangalla** (2-3 hrs), **Tissamaharama** (4 hrs), **Kataragama** (4½ hrs) and **Wellawaya**.

Three-wheeler Costs around Rs 300 to **Unawatuna**.

Train The station is a short walk from the bus station and the fort and town. Express trains to **Colombo** (3½ hrs, 2nd class Rs 180, 3rd class Rs 100), most via **Hikkaduwa**, **Ambalangoda**, **Aluthgama**, **Kalutara** and **Panadura** at 0540, 1355, 1705, 1430 (**Kandy** train, 7 hrs, Rs 320/175). Slow trains stop at other coastal destinations. To **Matara** trains (1½ hrs, Rs 80/40) leave every 1½-2 hrs, 0500 to 2050, stopping at **Talpe**, **Koggala**, **Ahangama** and **Weligama**. Slow trains stop at **Unawatuna** (10 mins) and **Mirissa** (1¼ hrs).

Unawatuna *p148, map p149*
It is very easy to miss Unawatuna when travelling by road. Look out for the Km 122 marker on the (sea) side of the road if coming from the east.

Bus Services between **Galle** and **Matara** will drop you at the main road on request.

Three-wheeler To **Hikkaduwa**, Rs 600, after bargaining. **Galle** Rs 300, takes 15 mins.

Train Trains pass through Unawatuna on the **Galle–Matara** line, though only the slow trains (7 a day) stop here. 10 mins to **Galle**, 1-1¼ hrs to **Matara**. If coming from **Colombo**, take the express to Galle then change on to a Matara

train. The station is to the east of the main Galle–Matara Rd, some 500 m north of the Km 122 marker (about 15-min walk to the beach). Touts and 3-wheeler drivers outside the station can be very persistent. Be sure of your destination to avoid caving in and arriving at a guesthouse of their choosing.

Unawatuna to Weligama *p148*
Many visitors to these beaches arrive by car but it is equally feasible to reach one of the resorts by public transport.

Air Sri Lankan Airlines, T19733 5500, www.srilankan.aero, has started operating flights to/from **Koggala** and **Colombo**.

Bus Between Galle and Matara, local buses can be flagged down and stopped at any of these settlements.

Train Most trains between Galle and Matara stop at **Talpe**, **Ahangama** and **Weligama**, where there are 3-wheelers, and there are also local stations at **Habaraduwa**, **Kataluva**, **Midigama** and **Mirissa**.

Weligama *p151, map p151*
Bus Services between **Galle** and **Matara** will let you off on the New Sea (Matara) Rd, though some local buses will drop you at the bus yard on the Old Matara Rd. Buses from **Colombo** about 4 hrs; from **Galle**, 45 mins. Local buses run from **Weligama** to **Pelana**.

Train Weligama is on the Colombo–Galle–Matara railway line, though check to make sure the train stops here if it's an express.

Mirissa *p152, map p152*
Bus Services between **Matara** and **Galle** pass through Mirissa. From **Weligama**, a bus or 3-wheeler costs around Rs 150.

Train Slow trains from **Galle** or **Matara** stop at Mirissa, otherwise catch an express to Weligama and then take a 3-wheeler.

Matara *p153, map p153*

Bus The station is in the Main Fort area with buses running on a 'depart when full' basis. There are regular buses to **Colombo**, **Galle**, **Hambantota**, **Kataragama**, **Tangalla**, **Tissamaharama**, and all points along the coast, as well as inland to **Ratnapura** and **Wellawaya** for the eastern highlands. There is also at least 1 early morning departure to **Nuwara Eliya** (8 hrs). Buses to **Mirissa** go regularly. Very irregular local buses run to the beach at **Polhena**. Alternatively, take a 3-wheeler.

Train Matara station, the terminus of this railway line, is 1 km away from town. 3-wheelers and taxis transfer passengers. To **Colombo** (4 hrs), plus slow trains as far as **Galle** (1½ hrs). **Kandy** train (8 hrs), Vavuniya train via **Anuradhapura** (9 hrs).

Matara to Tangalla *p154*

Air Sri Lankan Airlines, T1973 35500, www.srilankan.aero, has started operating flights to/from **Dickwella** and **Colombo**.

Bus Buses running between **Matara** and **Tangalla** link the main villages strung along Matara Rd. To visit the sights inland it is best to have your own transport.

Tangalla *p155, map p157*

Bus The station is in the town centre close to the bridge. There are regular services along the coast to **Matara** (1 hr) and **Hambantota** (1 hr), with other services continuing on to **Tissamaharama** (2 hrs) and **Kataragama** (2 hrs 45 mins). There are several morning departures for **Colombo** (5 hrs), plus some to **Wellawaya** and the hill country.

Directory

Galle *p143, map p145*

Banks Bank of Ceylon, Lighthouse St, has Visa ATM and will change TCs. **Commercial Bank** has a Cirrus ATM. **Hatton National**

Bank, HW Amarasuriya Mawatha, exchanges currency, TCs and gives cash advances on Visa and MasterCard. **People's Bank**, Middle St. **Internet** Many hotels and guesthouses offer internet access or Wi-Fi. Alternatively in the fort, try **19 Internet Café**, Pedlar St. In the new town, there are places along Main St, Rs 100 per hr. **Medical services** General Hospital, T222 2261. **Post office** The huge GPO is on Main St. It also has Poste Restante and is the only place south of Colombo that offers EMS Speedpost (though you must call before 0900). There is a branch post office on Church St, within the fort.

Unawatuna *p148, map p149*

Banks None here – head into Galle. **Internet** There are many guesthouses and hotels offering internet access and Wi-Fi. Sunil's (see Eating, page 167) has Wi-Fi access upon purchase. There are also tour operators with terminals, such as **GG Happy Tours**, whose prices are competitive. **Useful addresses** Tourist police by Unatawatuna Beach Resort.

Weligama *p151, map p151*

Banks Bank of Ceylon and People's Bank. **Post office** Main St, opposite the railway station.

Matara *p153, map p153*

Banks Amongst those around Sri Karothota Mawatha, east of the sports stadium, are Sampath Bank, with a Cirrus ATM, and Hatton Bank, changes TCs. **Internet** There are a number of places on Main St. **Post office** There is a sub post office in the Fort area, plus agency post offices on Station Rd and Dharmapala Mawatha.

Tangalla *p155, map p157*

Internet There are a few places in the town centre offering internet, as well as a number of guesthouses. The speed and age of terminals varies. **Post office** Just off the Main Rd opposite the mosque, is open Mon-Fri 0800-1700.

The dry southeast

The dry southeast offers a striking contrast with the lushness of the southwestern Wet Zone. In an astonishingly short space, east of Tangalla, everything changes. Open savanna and shallow wetlands take over from the dank forest and rich undergrowth and the increasingly frequent patches of bare earth have a burnt and arid look. From Nonagama, 25 km east of Tangalla, there are two choices of route through the Dry Zone. Both offer magnificent wildlife-spotting opportunities. The road inland takes you close to Uda Walawe, famous for its elephants, from which you can travel to Ratnapura or the Sinharaja rainforest, or into the highlands. Alternatively, you can continue east on the coastal road, visiting salt pans for some superb birdwatching, the remarkably varied wildlife of Yala, and on to the strange and wonderful pilgrimage site of Kataragama

▸▸ *For listings, see pages 184-188.*

Inland to Uda Walawe

Kalametiya Bird Sanctuary → *Colour map 3, C5.*

A short distance off the coastal road, this is ideal for watching shorebirds in the brackish lagoons and mangrove swamps. It has a beautiful beach and lagoon, excellent for birdwatching undisturbed except for a few fishermen who might pester you for money. There are no facilities, nor entry fees, though there is accommodation nearby. To get there, turn right off the A2 after Hungama at the Km 214 post and walk 2 km to the lagoon, or get off at the Km 218 post and walk 300 m to the sanctuary. Tours can be arranged in the village of Hungama nearby.

Ridiyagama and around → *Colour map 3, C5. 24 km inland north from Ambalantota.*

Close to the Walawe Ganga, the **Madungala hermitage** is claimed to have remarkable paintings. In fact, all that remains of the old monument is a square white base and some writing engraved on the rock. There is a concrete *dagoba* with murals on a hilltop. There are fine views of Ridiyagama tank and Adam's Peak from there. A walk through the forest takes you to another *dagoba*. Nearby, in an open space north of the tank, are the **Mahapalessa hot springs**. Believed to have healing powers, the bubbling water is collected in pools for bathers.

To the south, **Ridiyagama** Village is well known for its fine curd and honey. Nearby are the 100 or so ancient rocky **Karambagala Caves**, once occupied by Buddhist hermits, which were discovered in the scrub land. From the A18, take the road to the right (east) at **Siyambalagoda**, cross the Walawe Ganga, and follow the track along the stream for about 5 km.

Uda Walawe National Park → *Phone code: 047. Colour map 3, B5.*

Easily accessible from the south coast, Uda Walawe is one of the island's most popular national parks. Mainly open parkland traversed by streams, it is best known for its elephants – large herds can be seen during the dry season. However, birdwatching is more rewarding than searching for any other wildlife. The 308-sq-km park was set up in 1972 to protect the catchment of the Uda Walawe Reservoir which is at the south end of the Walawe Ganga.

Ins and outs

Getting there The park is accessible from the A18 Nonagama–Ratnapura road. Embilipitiya is the nearest major town; there is also accommodation at Timbolketiya, close to the park office. To enter the park, you follow the road along a 4-km bund across the reservoir, and take a turn after Km 11 post.

Getting around 4WD vehicles only (from Rs 4000, depending on where you start) are allowed to use the dry-weather roads and jeep tracks. These can be picked up at guesthouses or at the park gate.

Park information 0600-1800, US$15, plus the usual moveable feast of extras – vehicle fee, service charges for tracker, plus a couple more administration and tax charges. Tickets can be bought at the park entrance east of the reservoir, though the main park office is in front of the Elephant Transit Centre in Timbolketiya.

Best time to visit November to April when the resident population of water birds is joined by migrants from the north.

The park

Along the river there is thick woodland of old teak trees, but the rest of the area is mainly open parkland traversed by streams, which makes elephant viewing easy. They number 400 to 450, and can be seen in herds of up to 100 or even more. They are best seen along the river and near the numerous streams and tanks. There are also healthy populations of macaque, langur, jackal and around 15 leopard, while increasing numbers of sambar, spotted deer, barking deer, wild boar and water buffalo are beginning to re-establish themselves. Recent reports suggest that there are no sloth bear. Some 189 species of avifauna have been recorded with bee-eaters, hornbills, peafowl, hawk eagles, ibis and Indian rollers frequently seen. Birds gather in large numbers around the tanks – the best ones are around Magam, Habarlu and Kiri Ibban. You may also be able to stop at the **Palugaswewa tank**, approached from the A18, about 8 km along a dry weather track from Galpaya to the west of the reservoir. **Timbirimankada**, 3 km from Sinnukgala, at the north end of the reservoir, is particularly good for birdwatching. These are not far from **Handagiriya village** which has a prehistoric site nearby (see page 120). **Ranagala**, which can be reached in dry weather, about 7 km from Sinnukgala, is good for birdwatching. Elephants sometimes come to the river here.

Elephant Transit Centre → *Feeding time is every 3 hrs from 0600-1800.*

Set up by the Department of Wildlife in 1995, the Elephant Transit Centre cares for abandoned calves, most of which have been injured, before returning them to the wild when they reach five years of age. Its successful reintroduction scheme, supported by the Born Free Foundation, contrasts directly with the orphanage at Pinnawela, where the animals have proved to become too domesticated to fend for themselves. Twenty of the centre's 32 animals are 'foster parented', which costs Rs 10,000 per elephant per month (half the required sum for food and medical treatment). Although visitors are not allowed to get as close to the animals as at Pinnawela, it is worth visiting at mealtimes. The site's facilities are limited and entry at the time of writing was free. The centre is behind the main park office, 4 km east of the A18.

Hambantota → *Phone code: 047. Colour map 3, C6. Population: 11,500. 41 km from Tangalla, 238 km from Colombo.*

Back on the coast, Hambantota is a small fishing port with a large Muslim population, predominantly of Malay descent. The town itself, with sand dunes immediately around it, has little to recommend it – the square has its usual clocktower and a curious statue of a 'coolie'. There is an interesting if neglected Catholic cemetery to explore. It was badly hit by the 2004 tsunami and damage is still visible if you walk along the beach. The new viewing platform opposite the bus station looks a little out of place but offers good views, especially of the port and fish market down below. For most visitors, however, Hambantota is a base to visit the nearby *lewayas* (shallow lagoons) at **Bundala National Park**, excellent for birdwatching. The Karagan Lewaya and Maha Lewaya are easy to get to, where shore birds – flamingoes, gulls, plovers, terns, etc – are attracted to the salt pans.

The town is at the centre of Sri Lanka's renewed interest in shipping and an international harbour, one of the deepest in the world, is open for business. It is also the

Hambantota

To Tissamaharama & Tangalla

Maha Lewaya

Salt Corporation

Old Tissa Rd

New Tissa Rd

GALWALA

Karagan Lewaya

To Malala, Bundala, Wirawila & Tissamaharama

Cargill's Food City

Internet Box

Main St

Bridge St

People's

Catholic Cemetery

Indian Ocean

New St

Singha Communications

Terrace Rd

To & Port

Matara Rd

Jail St

Water Tower

Wilmot St

Well Rd

Local Harbour

Ceylon

N.

100 metres

100 yards

Sleeping
Joy Guest House **2**
Oasis Ayurveda Beach Hotel **1**

Peacock Beach Resort **4**
Rest House **5**

Eating
Fine Curd Food Cabin **2**
Jade Green **3**

centre for producing salt from evaporated sea water. The *lewayas* are visible from the road and you can see the salt flats of Lanka Salt Ltd stretching away inland. To protect the salt pans and access to cinnamon plantations inland, the Dutch built a stockade or 'fort'. Today's circular 'Dutch' fort, on a hill overlooking the bay, is a run-down British **Martello Tower** (circa 1796), one of a twin – the other stands in Simonstown in South Africa.

The small bay offers some swimming, but the beaches, where you will see outriggers, are not attractive – the deserted eastern side, though, is great for jogging.

Hambantota has not only seen the construction of the new harbour, the district is also home to a large convention centre, a cricket ground that was used for two of the 2011 World Cup matches and the Mattala International Airport is due to open at the end of 2012. Despite the bypass taking traffic away from the town, these changes could see Hambantota developing rapidly in the next few years.

Bundala National Park → *Colour map 3, C6.*

① *0600-1800, US$10, children under 12 US$5, plus vehicle fee and taxes (works out about US$20 per person). There is a visitor centre at the park entrance. From Weligatta, turn right for 2 km to the park entrance. To explore, you need to hire a jeep with a driver from Hambantota or Tissamaharama – the former is closer but Tissa is a popular base from which to visit both Bundala and Yala. A jeep will cost about Rs 4500 for a half-day. Guides, which are mandatory, are given on rotation, and their English may not be good.*

The area of open scrub around the coastal *lewayas* offers great opportunities for birdwatching with the added bonus of being able to spot the odd elephant and basking crocodile. The salt pans attract vast numbers of migratory shore birds, accommodating tens of thousands at any one time, making it the most important wetlands in Sri Lanka outside the Northern Province.

Much of the park boundary is contiguous with the A2, so you do not necessarily need to go in to appreciate the wildlife. Before the park, the **Malala lagoon**, reached by following the Malala River from the main road, is a birdwatchers' paradise, where you might also see crocodiles. The **Karagan**, **Maha** and particularly **Bundala** *lewayas* are also excellent for shore-bird enthusiasts.

The **reserve** itself consists of a series of shallow lagoons which are surrounded by low scrub which is really quite dense. Tracks go through the bush and connect each lagoon. The sanctuary skirts the sea and it is possible to see the lighthouse on the Great Basses some 40 km away to the east. Bundala is particularly rewarding for its winter migrants, who arrive chiefly from Eastern Europe. From September to March, you can see abundant stints, sand pipers, plovers, terns, gulls and ducks. The park's highlight is its large flocks of flamingos, which travel from the Rann of Kutch in India. In recent years, about 350 flamingos have made Bundala their year-round home. The migrants join the resident water birds – pelicans, herons, egrets, cormorants, stilts and storks – contributing to an extraordinarily variety. In the scrub jungle, you may also come across elephants (though often difficult to see), jackals, monkeys, hares (rare and carry a Rs 1000 fine for killing!) and, perhaps, snakes. The beaches attract olive ridley and leatherback turtles which come to nest here.

Inland to Tanamalwila

At **Wirawila**, east of Bundala, there is an airbase which is being prepared for domestic commercial flights. You have two choices of route, both of which eventually lead north to the hills. The A32, widened and upgraded in 2003, heads east towards Tissamaharama to Yala National Park, before turning north through Kataragama to Buttala (see page 183). The A2 continues north crossing the **Wirawila Wewa Bird Sanctuary** and running close to **Lunuganwehera National Park**, set up in 1995 to protect the elephant corridor between Yala and Uda Walawe. There are good views along here of the sacred Kataragama Peak.

Lunuganwehera Reservoir is fed by the Kirindi Oya, which runs close to the road leading up into the highlands. You can stay in a secluded forested setting along its banks, north of **Tanamalwila**, the largest settlement along this stretch, see page 185. This can also be used as a base to visit Uda Walawe to the west. From here, the road continues up to Wellawaya, passing the Handapangala tank and Buduruvagala shrine (see page 183).

Tissamaharama → *Phone code: 047. Colour map 3, C6. 32 km from Hambantota.*

Tissamaharama, or 'Tissa', is one of the oldest of the abandoned royal cities. King Dutthagamenu made it his capital before recapturing Anuradhapura. The ruins had been hidden in jungle for centuries and today there is little of interest visible. It does not, in any way, compare with the better preserved Polonnaruwa or Anuradhapura. The town

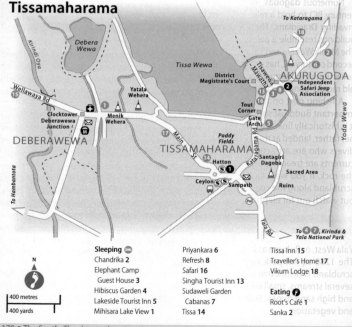

Tissamaharama

To Kataragama

Kirindi Oya
Debera Wewa
Tissa Wewa
Wellawaya Rd
Yatala Wehera
District Magistrate's Court
Theerawewa Mawatha
AKURUGODA
Independent Safari Jeep Association
Clocktower
Deberawewa Junction
Menik Wehera
Tout Corner
Gate (Arch)
DEBERAWEWA
Paddy Fields
TISSAMAHARAMA
Main St
Yoda Wewa
Santagiri Dagoba
To Hambantota
Hatton
Ceylon
Sampath
Sacred Area
Ruins
Kataragama Rd
Yala Rd
To 4 7 *, Kirinda & Yala National Park*

N

400 metres
400 yards

Sleeping 🛏
Chandrika **2**
Elephant Camp
 Guest House **3**
Hibiscus Garden **4**
Lakeside Tourist Inn **5**
Mihisara Lake View **1**

Priyankara **6**
Refresh **8**
Safari **16**
Singha Tourist Inn **13**
Sudaweli Garden
 Cabanas **7**
Tissa **14**

Tissa Inn **15**
Traveller's Home **17**
Vikum Lodge **18**

Eating 🍴
Root's Café **1**
Sanka **2**

Going on safari

It seems as if every other vehicle in Tissamaharama is a jeep and you will be constantly offered a jeep safari to the national parks. Some words of advice:

1 Remember that a tracker is included in your entrance fee. Thus don't pay extra for a driver and separate guide.

2 Make sure that the driver will stop on request, and that they will turn the engine off for photography.

3 Ask to see the vehicle first – many are ancient and noisy, which will scare away any wildlife. It has even been known for a jeep to split into two during a safari.

4 Bring binoculars.

5 Invest in a bird spotting guide, as bird life is guaranteed to be rich.

6 Speak to other travellers who have already been on safari. They are often the best source of information.

often used as a base for Yala National Park, though its plentiful accommodation is also popular with Kataragama pilgrims. If you arrive by bus, touts will probably pounce on you straight away to take you on 'safari' (see box, above).

Sights

The **Tissa Wewa tank**, thought to have been created at the end of the third century BC, was restored with two others and attracts a lot of water birds. At dawn, the view of birds roosting on large trees and then moving over the tank is very beautiful.

Numerous **dagobas**, including one that is 50 m high built by King Kavantissa (second century BC) to hold a relic, had been lost under the sand, having been destroyed by the invading Dravidians. These have now been restored entirely by local Buddhists. Other buildings resemble a palace and a multi-storeyed monastery on the edge of Tissa Wewa. The Menik Wehera and Yatala Wehera are east of the clocktower. The latter, dating from the second century BC, has a moonstone and an 'elephant wall'. It also houses a **museum** with a collection of low-impact but charming Buddha and Bodhisattva statues and a 2200-year-old monks' urinal. Excavations have been assisted by German archaeological groups.

A fishing port on the coast, 7 km south of Tissa, **Kirinda** has a good beach and an important Buddhist shrine on the rocks. Buses run regularly between Tissa and Kirinda. It is historically linked to the King Dutthagamenu. His mother, having been banished by her father, landed at the village and married the local king. Kirinda is popular with scuba divers who are attracted by the reefs at Great and Little Basses off the coast, but the currents are treacherous. You can see the Great Basses lighthouse from the temple on the rock. If you walk east along the coast towards Yala there is an area of Dry Zone scrubland along the coast, contiguous to Yala itself. It is a good place for birdwatching but watch out for elephants.

Yala West (Ruhuna) National Park → *Colour map 5, C5.*

Yala West, or Ruhuna as it alternatively known, is Sri Lanka's most popular national park. The 1260-sq-km park varies from open parkland to dense jungle on the plains. The scrubland is distinctive with its enormous rocky outcrops, or *inselbergs*. There are also several streams, small lakes and lagoons, while the ocean to the east has wide beaches and high sand dunes. Such a varied terrain supports an extraordinary range of wildlife and vegetation.

Ins and outs

Getting there The entrance is at Palatupana, 20 km from Tissamaharama, where there's an interesting visitor centre. Take the road from Tissa to Kirinda, 1 km before which a turn-off (12 km) is signposted.

Getting around A 4WD vehicle is required, a obligatory tracker is assigned to you, and marked tracks must be adhered to. Walking is not permitted within the park, visitors must remain in their vehicles and avoid excessive noise (eg radios or blaring music).

Park information Daily 0600-1800. US$15, children under 12, US$7, plus compulsory tracker fee, vehicle charge and tax (it works out about US$25 per person). If you leave the park, you will have to pay again. Entry permits, maps and leaflets are available from the visitor centre at Palatupana.

Best time to visit October to December and early morning and late afternoon.

Background

Yala comprises five 'blocks', of which tourists only visit Block One, the original 14,101-ha former shooting reserve, which became a protected area in 1938. This area is said to have the highest concentration of animals. Succeeding blocks, including a Strict Nature Reserve, were added, primarily in the late 1960s and early 1970s, giving the park its total area of 97,881 ha. In addition, there is a buffer zone which may in future form part of an expansion of the park. For the newly reopened Kumana National Park, reached from Pottuvil and Arugam Bay, see the East Coast chapter (page 315).

There are a number of remains of ancient sites in the park, suggesting that many centuries ago the area was a part of the Ruhuna Kingdom. Thousands of Buddhist monks resided at the monastery at **Situlpahuwa**, now an important pilgrimage centre, while the restored **Magul Mahavihara** and **Akasa Chetiya** date to the first and second centuries BC.

The park

For many, the search for the one of the park's 30 or so elusive leopards is a major attraction. Though sightings remain relatively rare, Yala's male leopards are quite bold and may be seen walking along tracks in dry sandy or rocky areas during the day. **Vepandeniya** is considered a favourite spot. Elephants are another attraction and are easily seen especially near water sources from January to May, though not on the scale of Uda Walawe. Other animals seen throughout the park include macaque and langur monkeys, sambar, spotted deer, jackal, wild boar, buffaloes and crocodiles. Sloth bears are occasionally spotted, particularly in June, when they feed on local fruit. There are no limits at present on the number of vehicles allowed into the park on any given day, so if a leopard or elephant is spotted it can become a little chaotic with jeeps rushing to get their tourists in the best spot.

The park is worth visiting for its birdlife alone, and a birdwatching focused day trip including the riverine forests of the **Menik Ganga** may yield over 100 species, during the migrating season. There are about 130 species overall, including barbets, hoopoes, malabar pied hornbills, orioles, Ceylon shamas, and paradise flycatchers, though pea and jungle fowl are the most frequently seen. The expanses of water attract eastern grey heron, painted stork, serpent-eagle and white-bellied sea-eagle, amongst many others. In addition a large number of migrant water-fowl arrive each winter to augment the resident population. You may be lucky enough to spot the rare black-necked stork near

Buttawa on the coast. The **Palatupana salt pans** on the Tissa Road, 6 km before the park entrance, are one of the best sites in the world for watching waders.

Kataragama → *Colour map 5, C4. 16 km north of Tissamaharama.*

Kataragama in Uva Province is, along with Sri Pada (Adam's Peak), the most important pilgrimage site in Sri Lanka. Like Adam's Peak, it holds significance for Buddhists, Hindus and Muslims. It is most famous for its two-week **Perehera** in July and August, but is popular throughout the year. A small town with clean, tree-lined roads with rows of stalls selling garlands and platters of fruit – such as coconut, mango, watermelon – it attracts thousands from across the island. The Hindu and Buddhist sanctuaries are quite separate. Buddhists visit the ancient Kirivehera dagoba, 500 m north of the plain white Hindu temple, but also consider the Kataragama Deviyo here sacred. Sri Lankan Muslims associate the town with the prophet Moses, who was said to have taught here and come to pray at the Khizr Takya mosque nearby.

Approach

From the bus stand or car park, a short walk takes you to the Menik Ganga. Steps lead down to the water which is quite shallow in places allowing pilgrims to take their ritual bath almost in the middle of the river. It is a very attractive area with large trees on the

Kataragama

Sleeping 🛏
Ceybank Rest **1**
Ceylon Tourist Board Rest House **2**

Mandara Rosen **4**
Robinson **5**
Sunil's Rest **3**

Mind over matter

Fire-walking takes place on the eve of the great procession, the culmination of the **Esala** festival. A long trench is prepared and filled with hardwood logs which are burnt to cinders. The worshippers, who will have refrained from meat or fish for a week, then walk barefoot across the burning embers shouting 'Haro hara' in front of the crowds who cry in homage to the miracle. That most firewalkers emerge unhurt is a source of mystery, though many believe that the walkers are in the deepest state of self-hypnosis, in which the body can block out pain.

The origins of the tradition may hark back to the story of Sita in the epic *Ramayana*. Ravana, the King of Lanka,

abducted Rama's wife Sita, an Indian princess, from the forest and carried her away to his island. After she is finally rescued by her husband, Sita proves her purity (chastity) by walking barefoot over fire and emerging unhurt. In southern Sri Lanka, devotees of Kataragama and Pattini follow her example and seek their blessing as they undergo the purification ritual.

To Western eyes, an even more shocking act of self-mutilation are the carts carrying men suspended by steel hooks attached to their skin. These grotesque parades, accompanied by great crowd noise and excitement, are designed to purge the devotee of his sins.

banks providing plenty of shade. Cross the bridge to enter the main temple complex. The wide street lined with tulip trees leads to the Hindu temple (300 m).

Maha Devale

Maha Devale (Hindu Temple), dedicated to Skanda (Kataragama Deviyo), is itself not particularly impressive. A small gate with a large wrought-iron peacock on the reverse, leads onto the rectangle where there is a small area where the pilgrims throw coconuts onto a stone slab to split them before making the offering. The breaking of the coconut signifies the purging of evil, so it is inauspicious if it fails to break. Trees in the rectangle are surrounded by brass railings and there are a number of places where pilgrims can light leaf-shaped candles. Here, you can see men in 'ritualistic trances': some are professionals, though, since you might see the same man, a little later, making his way to the Buddhist *dagoba*, carrying a briefcase and an umbrella.

There is often a long queue to enter the shrine (particularly on *poya* days) where platters are offered to the priests. The idea seems to be to 'hide' some money in the platter. Some say anything less than Rs 200 may be unacceptable and the gift might be refused by the deity. There is certainly evidence that the platters are 'recycled': men on bicycles can be seen returning them to the market, covered in garlands – nobody seems to mind though. There is no image of the god Skanda in the shrine – simply his vel or lance. There are separate small shrines to others in the Hindu pantheon, including Vishnu, Ganesh and Pattini, the last also linked to the fire-walking ceremony. Nearby are the two Bodhi trees.

The largest draw is the **Esala** (July/August) full moon festival which ends with fire-walking and 'water cutting' ceremonies. Thousands of pilgrims flock to the Hindu temple for the **Kataragama Festival**. They come to perform penance for sins they have committed and some of the scenes of self-mutilation, performed in a trance, are horrific. The water-cutting ceremony, in which the waters of the Manik Ganga are 'cut' with a sword at the moment of the full moon, symbolizes the separation of pure from impure.

You may see groups of pilgrims performing the Kavadi (peacock) dance when men, women and children hold semicircular blue arches above their heads as they slowly progress towards the temple.

There is a **museum** ① *Wed-Mon, US$5, children US$2.50*, next to the Maha Devale, which houses religious objects pertaining to different faiths, including statues, moonstones and ancient inscriptions.

Kirivehera

Beyond the Hindu shrine and a meeting hall on the north side of the square, starting from the east gate, there is another tulip tree avenue which leads to the milk-white Buddhist *dagoba*, about 500 m away. Stalls selling lotus buds, garlands and platters of fruit line the route but here there is competition with girls shouting out the bargains and pressing people to buy. You can often see the temple elephant shackled to the trees here, being fed a copious diet of palm leaves. The *dagoba* itself is a very peaceful place and, as usual, beautifully maintained. It is not especially large and its spire is quite squat compared with those farther north.

North of Kataragama

The remote area north of Kataragama, fringing Yala National Park, is rarely visited by tourists, though the 35 km road to Buttala is one of the main pilgrimage routes. **Buttala** ('rice mound') was known as the rice bowl of the country, and is the main centre. This is a wilderness area, with plenty of opportunities for trekking, wildlife spotting, rock-climbing and even rafting.

At **Maligawila**, southeast of Buttala, is the largest monolithic Buddha statue in Sri Lanka and is regarded by some as the finest piece of all Sinhalese sculpture. Housed inside a brick *gedige*, the *Mahavansa* suggests the 10.5-m-high, 3-m-wide crystalline limestone Buddha was crafted by Prince Aggabodhi in the seventh century. The statue was originally part of a monastic complex which had a gateway, pillared hall and terraces. It had fallen and was 'lost' in the jungle until 1934, before being restored fully in 1991. One kilometre away, at **Dambegoda**, is a mound where the island's largest image of Avalokitesvara Bodhisvata, who is said to give succour to the helpless, has been found and restored. There are direct buses to the site from Wellawaya and Buttala via Okkampitiya. It is also accessible from Moneragala.

Wellawaya → *Phone code: 055. Colour map 3, B6.*

Wellawaya is a major transport junction with many buses leading up to the hill country from here. The A4 is the main road, leading west skirting the southern highlands through Ratnapura and ultimately to Colombo, and east through Buttala and Moneragala to Pottuvil for Arugam Bay, while the A23 north climbs through picturesque country to Ella. The area is known for its sugar cane fields, and it is worth a brief stop to visit a factory and have a taste of the raw sugar cane and the resulting 'honey', which is also made into jaggery. The workers are usually very happy to show the production processes to tourists, though a tip is appreciated.

A beautiful road leads south of town past a dammed lake to the ancient Mahayana Buddhist rock carvings of **Buduruvagala** ① *Rs 200*. It is a short walk away past the monastery to the massive rock. Of the seven rock-cut figures in high relief, the 16-m-high

Buddha (Buduruvagala) in the centre – the tallest of its type in Sri Lanka – is flanked by possibly Avalokitesvara, to his right, who in turn has his consort Tara by his side, and an attendant. Traces of the original red and yellow paint remain on the Buddha itself. Close to the right foot of the Buddha is a hole in the shape of an oil lamp flame; a mustard-smelling oil is said miraculously to flow through periodically. To the Buddha's left, the figure is believed to be Maitreya who too is accompanied. The figure of Vajrayapani (or Sakra) holds a quartz implement similar to those found in Mahayana Buddhist countries such as Tibet. The quality of the carvings is more impressive close to, so it is worth removing your shoes and climbing up to the rock to view. The site itself is very peaceful and often deserted although unfortunately a pair of ugly concrete posts carrying lights have been erected in front of the carvings making photography of all seven images difficult. There is a small museum inside the meditation centre nearby. Take a Kataragama bus from Wellawaya and get off at Buduruvagala Junction (about 10 minutes). It's best to go in the morning as afternoon buses are scarce. The track to the site is an easy walk accompanied by a monk.

Some 6 km south of Buduruvagala along the A2 is a left turn for the **Handapangala tank**, where elephants migrate from Yala for water during the summer months, a danger for villagers en route. There have been clashes in recent years between environmental groups and a local sugar factory, which has periodically attempted to drive the elephants away. These came to a head in October 2002 when two baby elephants were killed, prompting calls for the government to reopen a protected elephant corridor. There is a popular local bathing spot here, about 2 km off the main road, at which you can scramble up and see the elephants at a distance on the other side of the water. Alternatively, and more rewardingly, you can take a tour to see the elephants at close hand, for which you will need a boat and guide, not least since the area is dangerous if you don't know what you're doing. **Diyaluma Falls** are also within easy reach of Wellawaya (see page 242).

◉ The dry southeast listings

For Sleeping and Eating price codes and other relevant information, see pages 26-32.

● Sleeping

Uda Walawe National Park *p174*
The best accommodation is at Embilipitiya, though there is reasonable accommodation close to the park office at Timbolketiya. Circuit bungalows can be hired but this needs to be arranged well in advance. There is also camping in the park. Telephone the Department of Wildlife, T011-288 8585, at least a month before visiting.
B Centauria, New Town, Embilipitiya, T223 0514, www.centauriahotel.com. Popular lunch spot and the most comfortable place near the park, good location next to Chandrika tank,

pool, 51 fresh, clean and quiet rooms, mostly a/c, some with TV and balcony.
B Villa, also in the grounds. Called 'the bungalow' even though it has 2 storeys, with 4 bedrooms, 3 bathrooms and 'day' kitchen. Tours to Uda Walawe, also boat trips on the tank.
B Kalu's Hideaway, Walawegama, close to the park, T492 2396, www.kalushideaway.com. 6 modern a/c or fan rooms, 1 top-floor suite and 2 chalets. Pool restaurant, camping also available. Cricket memorabilia scattered around the hotel, as Romesh Kaluwitharana owns it. Arranges trips to Uda Walawe.
C Elephant Lane, Dakunu Ela, T432 7601, www.elephant-lane.com. A/c rooms with hot water, double-storey chalet with dorms (US$8) and shared bathrooms. The restaurant serves Sri Lankan food. A budget option.

C Walawa Safari Village, Dakuna Ela Rd, Timbolketiya, T223 3201. Best option in Timbolketiya, though a little overpriced. 15 musty rooms with hot water and fan or a/c, half-board.

D-E Kottawatta Village, Colornbage Ara, 8 km from park, T223 3215. 12 average rooms and well-furnished cabanas amidst pleasant gardens leading to an oya. Friendly management, jeep tours to Uda Walawe.

E Sarathchandra Tourist Guest House, Pallegama, T223 0044. 14 clean a/c rooms and cottages, some with TV, restaurant.

Hambantota *p176, map p176*

A Oasis Ayurveda Beach Hotel, Sisilasagama, 6 km west, T222 0651, www.oasis-ayurveda. de. 40 a/c rooms, plus 10 bright, spacious chalets with TV and small tubs, set in large gardens between the sea and a lagoon, full facilities including a huge pool, good restaurant. Ayurveda centred hotel, mostly German clientele.

A-B Peacock Beach Resort, New Tissa Rd, 1 km from bus stand at Galwala, T222 0159, www.peacockbeachonline.com. 70 a/c rooms with sea views, some with bath tubs, 2 suites. Very pleasant gardens, pool, popular with groups.

C-D Rest House, T222 0299. 15 large rooms, situated in superb position on a promontory overlooking the harbour, terrific views. Old wing rooms, clean and carpeted, are better than new wing.

F Joy Guest House, Matara Rd, T222 0328. 6 small, basic rooms in guesthouse with restaurant.

Bundala National Park *p177*

Many visitors base themselves at Hambantota (above).

F Lagoon Inn, Bundala Junction, T248 9531, www.lagooninn.com. 5 fan rooms with private verandas, restaurant. In good position for visiting both Yala and Bundala.

Inland to Tanamalwila *p178*

B Tasks Safari Camp, Kithulkotte, Kudaoya, Tanamalwila, T011-486 2225,

www.taskssafari.com. 27 spacious en suite jungle tents with 'hollow log' showers, real frontier feel, hurricane lantern for light, picnics by riverside, elephants come close to drink.

Tissamaharama *p178, map p178*

There are plenty of options, so bargain hard. Tissa is plagued by touts who get a commission for the hotel room they 'fix' and also any 'safari' you may arrange through the hotel. Some places listed here are actually in **Deberawewa**, about 3 km west of Tissa, where touts sometimes jump on the bus and try to persuade you that it is Tissa. There is also accommodation at Kirinda and at Amaduwa, close to the park gate into Yala (see below).

A The Safari (CHC), Kataragama Rd, T223 7201, www.ceylonhotels.lk. Newly refurbished with 53 a/c rooms, some with lake views. Excellent location next to Tissa Wewa, with nice pool overlooking the tank. Restaurant and open-air bar.

B Priyankara, Kataragama Rd, T223 7206, www.priyankarahotel.com. 26 clean a/c standard and deluxe rooms, all with private balcony overlooking paddy fields. Inviting pool, bar, good restaurant with wide wine selection, pleasant atmosphere, friendly staff.

C Hibiscus Garden Hotel, Mahasenpura, if driving phone for directions, T492 5617, www.hibiscus-garden.com. 16 large, clean a/c rooms, restaurant and pool. Good value, birdwatchers will enjoy the gardens.

D Chandrika, Kataragama Rd, T223 7143, www.chandrikahotel.com. 20 clean rooms a/c rooms around a courtyard, good beds, fairly modern, bar, pricey restaurant, pleasant garden and pool, good value.

D Refresh, Kataragama Rd, Akurugoda, T223 7357. 5 attractive, clean a/c rooms, excellent but expensive restaurant (see Eating, page 187), friendly and welcoming, accepts Visa/MasterCard.

D-E Lakeside Tourist Inn, Kataragama Rd, Akurugoda, opposite lake, T493 1186, www.tissalakesidehotel.com. 20 clean and comfortable a/c and fan rooms, most in new block, others mustier but with views in old wing, pleasant sitting areas overlooking the lake, lots of birdlife, good restaurant.

D-E Tissa Inn, Wellawaya Rd, 1.3 km west of clocktower, Polgahawelana, T077-748 5858, T223 7233, www.tissainn.lk. 12 clean a/c and fan rooms, balcony upstairs, pleasant garden, restaurant, internet, rather pushy at selling tours but still one of the most popular.

D-E Traveller's Home, 195/4 Kachcheriyagama, T223 7958. Clean fan rooms and a/c bungalows, friendly, good food, pleasant patio, good safaris, popular with backpackers.

D-F Mihisara Lake View, Deberawewa, T223 7322. 6 clean, fresh a/c and fan rooms. Very friendly family home. Excellent food, order in advance.

D-F Singha Tourist Inn, Tissawewa Mawatha, off Kataragama Rd, Akurugoda, T223 7090. 15 dark and musty a/c and fan rooms in excellent location on the lake but hasn't realised its potential.

E Elephant Camp Guest House, Kataragama Rd, opposite The Safari, T072-493 4992, jayathunga.herath@yahoo.com. Family-run guesthouse offering 5 clean a/c and fan rooms with individual outdoor seating areas. Excellent food, small garden, friendly hosts. Recommended.

E Suduweli Garden Cabanas, down track 2 km before Kirinda from Tissa, T072-263 1059. German/Sri Lankan-run, simple but clean rooms, plus cosy bungalows with idiosyncratic Dutch-style eaved roofs, own music system in room, friendly, good menu, jeep and cycle tours.

E Vikum Lodge, off Kataragama Rd down a pot-holed rd, T223 7585. 10 cleanish rooms around attractive courtyard in quiet location. Food is pretty terrible.

F Hotel Tissa, Main St, near bus stand, T223 7104. 8 clean a/c and fan rooms, popular bar/restaurant so can be noisy.

Yala West (Ruhana) National Park *p179*
Close to the entrance, **Amaduwa**, on the coast, is an easier and more comfortable

option than sleeping inside the park itself (see below). It has a beautiful beach and lagoon. There are a number of pleasant bungalows that can be rented near the entrance to the park, www.reddottours.com has a good selection. There are also the recently reopened park bungalows (the originals were destroyed in the tsunami in 2004); contact the Department of Wildlife, T011-288 8585, but note that these need to be booked well in advance.

AL-A Yala Village, (Keels), Kirinda, T223 9450, www.johnkeellshotels.com. 60 luxurious chalets with a/c and satellite TV, most situated inland and 6 with views of the ocean. Fantastic position overlooking lagoon, observation deck, large pool, fishing, cycling.

A Hotel Elephant Reach, Kirinda, T567 7544, www.elephantreach.com. 14 a/c standard rooms and 21 spacious chalets. Restaurant and pool set in attractive gardens. Popular with tour groups.

Kataragama *p181, map p181*
There are many other pilgrims' guest-houses and hotels for all budgets on Sella Kataragama Rd.

A-B Mandara Rosen, 57 Detagamuwa, 2 km from Kataragama, T223 6030, www.rosenhotelsrilanka.com. 50 modern, comfortable a/c rooms, some with bath tubs, and 2 luxurious suites. Full facilities including pool with underwater music system.

D-E Robinson Hotel, Tissa Rd, Detagamuwa, T223 5175, robinsonhotel@infotravelsrilanka. com. 20 a/c and fan rooms with balcony in an attractive building with pleasant garden.

E-F Ceylon Tourist Board Rest House, T223 5227. Simple clean fan only rooms, or poor value a/c rooms, very cheap vegetarian restaurant, rather prison-like but friendly.

F Ceybank Rest, T011-254 4315. Attractive guesthouse with a/c and fan rooms. Good vegetarian meals.

F Sunil's Rest, Tissa Rd, T567 7172. 2 very clean rooms with attached bath, attractive garden.

North of Kataragama *p183*
L-AL Kumbuk River, Okkampitiya,
T11-452 7781, www.kumbukriver.com.
Award-winning eco-lodge in large grounds
next to a river. Accommodation is in the
form of 3 chalets, one a 12-m-high elephant.
Rented out exclusively, if privacy is what
you're after the rates aren't bad and include
full-board. As you'd expect but might forget,
there's no electricity. Minimum booking
2 nights.
C Tree Tops Jungle Lodge, Illukpitiya,
Weliara Rd (9 km from Buttala, T077-703 6554
www.treetopsjunglelodge.com. At the time
of writing it was closed for refurbishment
but previously offered traditional wood
and clay huts and camping in a genuine
wild setting, frequently visited by elephants
(don't arrive later than 1530). Excellent local
walks. Activities include 'awesome' local
treks in Yala buffer zone, rock climbing,
birdwatching. No electricity, communal
meals and well-water for washing.

Wellawaya *p183*
D-E Rest House, Ella Rd, T563 7685.
5 reasonably clean but musty and overpriced rooms, restaurant, knowledgeable
manager used to work for the
Archaeological Department.
E-F Saranga Holiday Inn, Ambawatta, 1 km
north of town, T227 4891. 15 rooms including
2 a/c, quiet, good restaurant, grubby and
overpriced but all right for a night.
G Little Rose Inn, Tissa Rd (1 km south of
town), T567 8360/227 4410, www.littlerose
wellawaya.com. 9 simple clean fan rooms.
Good home cooking.

🍴 Eating

Hambantota *p176, map p176*
For further options see Sleeping, page 185.
⑪ Jade Green, Galawala, opposite **Peacock
Beach Resort**. Smart, modern and Western
style with prices to match.

⑪ Fine Curd Food Cabin, Tissa Rd, opposite
the Bus Station (beach side). Does delicious
curd and treacle and inexpensive meals (fried
rice for Rs150).

Tissamaharama *p178, map p178*
There are a number of eating places
springing up on Kataragama Rd, and
hotels and guesthouses also do food,
see Sleeping, page 185.
⑪ Refresh, see Sleeping page 185. A branch
of the excellent Hikkaduwa-based restaurant,
offering a wide variety of good food. Portions
are large. Very popular with tourists,
overpriced and a little self-satisfied.
⑪ Sanka, Kataragama Rd, T223 7441. Serves
OK Chinese food, safari guides and drivers
hang out here.
⑪ Root's Café, look for the sign off Main St.
Very cheap rice and curry and popular
for a beer.

Kataragama *p181, map p181*
For further options see Sleeping, page 186.
Note that most places, except the more
upmarket hotels (these also serve alcohol),
will offer vegetarian-only dishes.
⑪ Nandana Hotel, 40b New Town, near
the clocktower. Offers good authentic rice
and curry.

⊛ Festivals and events

Tissamaharama *p178, map p178*
Jun The **Poson** full moon commemorates
the introduction of Buddhism with
week-long festivities ending with colourful
elephant processions accompanied by
drummers and dancers.

▲ Activities and tours

Uda Walawe National Park *p174*
Leopard Safaris, based near Colombo,
offers excellent tented safaris (for contact
details, see page 85).

Hambantota *p176, map p176*
Touts offer tours to Bundala, Yala and Uda Walawe, but it only makes sense to make Hambantota a base for the first of these. Locals currently offer to take tourists to see the new port, the new airport being built, the convention centre and tsunami sites such as the memorial. Agree a price before setting off, those who go in a taxi may be able to enter the port depending on their guide's connections.

Tissamaharama *p178, map p178*
Most hotels and guesthouses can arrange safaris to Yala and Bundala, although it may be cheaper to organize one independently through a driver at tout corner, opposite the **Independent Jeep Safari Association** office. There are also agencies in town, such as **Ajith Safari Jeep Tours**, 418/A Debarawewa, T223 7557, ajithpriyantha@yahoo.com. It's worth talking to fellow travellers as well to get an idea of their experiences. Prices can vary depending on the length or safari and also the type of jeep, those with forward-facing seating are more expensive. Half-day safaris cost around Rs 4500, full-day Rs 9000, those in the morning start around 0500, so order breakfast from your accommodation. It is possible to organize a half and half safari between Yala and Bundala, the jeep will cost the same but entry will have to be paid twice, which can be quite expensive.

Leopard Safaris, based near Colombo, offers excellent tented safaris in Yala (for contact details, see page 85).

◉ Transport

Uda Walawe National Park *p174*
Bus Local buses run between Timbolketiya and Embilipitiya. From there direct services leave for **Colombo**, **Ratnapura**, **Tangalla** and **Matara**.

Hambantota *p176, map p176*
Bus Services leave at regular intervals to **Tissamaharama** (1 hr) and **Tangalla**

(1 hr 20 mins). Buses go to **Weligata** every 15 mins. Morning departures to **Colombo** (6 hrs).

Tissamaharama *p178, map p178*
Bus To **Colombo**, (6 hrs), via Galle, or to **Ratnapura**, via Embilipitiya. There are plenty of buses to **Kataragama**.

Kataragama *p181, map p181*
Bus Services in all directions including direct bus to **Nuwara Eliya**, **Galle** and **Colombo**.

North of Kataragama *p183*
Bus To **Buttala** twice daily from **Kataragama** (1 hr), and frequently from **Wellawaya** (30 mins).

Wellawaya *p183*
Bus An important bus terminus, direct buses go to **Colombo** via **Ratnapura**, **Tissamaharama** and **Kataragama** and a few to **Matara** via **Tangalla**. For buses east to **Pottuvil** (for Arugam Bay), change at **Monaragala**. For the hills, there are plenty of buses to **Badulla**, via **Ella**, and **Haputale**.

◉ Directory

Hambantota *p176, map p176*
Banks Bank of Ceylon and Hatton National Bank deal in foreign exchange. **Internet** Internet Zone, just past the bus station.

Kataragama *p181, map p181*
Banks Bank of Ceylon has a Visa ATM and changes TCs.

Tissamaharama *p178, map p178*
Banks Plenty of banks in town.

Wellawaya *p183*
Banks There is a Hatton National Bank. **Internet** CTM Express, opposite the bus station, has internet and IDD facilities.

Contents

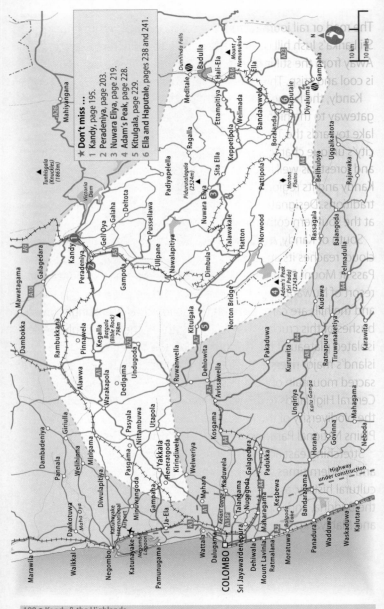

★ Don't miss ...

1 Kandy, page 195.
2 Peradeniya, page 203.
3 Nuwara Eliya, page 219.
4 Adam's Peak, page 228.
5 Kitulgala, page 229.
6 Ella and Haputale, pages 238 and 241.

10 km

10 miles

Highway under construction

The road or rail journey from the coast or dry plains up into Sri Lanka's lush hill country takes you into a different world. Away from the stifling heat of the low country, the air here is cool and crisp. This is great walking country.

Kandy, the home of the Buddha's tooth, is both capital and gateway to the highlands. The stunning view over its 18th-century lake towards the Temple of the Tooth hints at the reason for the city's unique character. Protected for centuries by its mountains and forests as well as by a fierce desire to retain its independence, Kandy and its region offer rich insights into Sri Lanka's cultural traditions. Designated a World Heritage Site in 1988, the city is at the southern corner of the Cultural Triangle.

South of Kandy, the Central Highland ridge, often shrouded in cloud, reaches its apex across the steep and spectacular Ramboda Pass at Mount Pidurutalagala near the eccentric former British hill resort of Nuwara Eliya. This is Sri Lanka's chief tea-growing region, and the hills are carpeted with the uniformly clipped bright green bushes of this crucial crop. To the south lies the hauntingly bleak isolated plateau of the Horton Plains – the source of most the island's major rivers – while to the west pilgrims flock to the sacred mountain of Adam's Peak. In 2010 UNESCO added the Central Highlands to its World Heritage list, officially recognizing the biodiversity of the Peak Wilderness Protected Area, Horton Plains National Park and the Knuckles Conservation Forest.

Stretching east across dry zone lands, irrigated in both ancient and modern times, Uva Province, like Kandy, has a rich and defiant cultural history, associated in popular legend with two visits by the Buddha, and widely celebrated in the festivals at Badulla and Mahiyangana.

Kandy and around

Kandy, Sri Lanka's second largest city and cultural capital, stands both as one of the most important symbols of Sinhalese national identity, and as the gateway to the higher hills and tea plantations. Although it has a reputation as something of a tourist trap, and has a problem with touts, the clarity of the air and its verdant, hilly outlook around the sacred lake make it a pleasant escape from the heat of the coast. It is a laid-back place and many visitors base themselves here for a few days to explore the surrounding countryside, before heading into the highlands or setting off for the ancient cities. The route northeast from Colombo across the coastal plain passes through lush scenery: paddy fields interspersed with coconut and areca nut palms, endless bananas and pineapples, which are available, graded by size and price, from roadside stalls.

Dotted around the lush Kandyan landscape are a number of important temples which make for a good day trip from the city. Thrill-seekers could head for the misty mountains of Knuckles, while for the green-fingered the magnificent botanical gardens at Peradeniya, arguably the finest of their kind in Asia, are an undoubted highlight. South of Kandy is the world's first tea museum.
▸▸ *For listings, see pages 207-216.*

Colombo to Kandy

Taking 11 years to complete, the trunk road from Colombo to Kandy was the first modern road to be opened in Sri Lanka in 1932, when the first mail service ran between the two cities. Tour groups invariably stop to visit the baby elephants at Pinnawela, but there are some lesser known sights along this busy route which are well worth a digression. Barely free of Colombo's suburbs, the road passes near the impressive temple at Kelaniya, the island's most popular, just 13 km from Colombo (see page 72). Although the road route is quicker, the train often gives better views, the last hour rattling through stunning scenery.

Sapugaskanda → *12 km north of Colombo.*
Situated on a low hill, there are beautiful views from the terrace of the small stupa here, but the temple is famous for its murals, which show the arrival of the Burmese saint Jagara Hamuduruvo in Sri Lanka. It's 3 km along a side road, a right turn off the main A1.

Heneratgoda Botanical Gardens → *Colour map 3, A2.*
ⓘ *0730-1700. Rs 600, students Rs 400.*
These beautiful gardens are particularly famous as the nursery of Asia's first rubber trees introduced from the Amazon Basin more than a century ago. Several of the early imports are now magnificent specimens. No 6, the first tree planted, is over 100 years old, but the most famous is No 2 because of its remarkable yield. The trees include *Hevea brasiliensis, Uncaria gambier*, rubber producing lianas (*Landolphia*), and the drug *ipecacuanha*. A female of the Coco de Mer was imported from the Seychelles and bore fruit in 1915. Turn off just before Yakkala. The gardens are well signposted, 1 km beyond the sizeable town of Gampaha.

Bandaranaike family home and memorial
The road passes through Yakkala, and then by the former estate of Sir Solomon Dias Bandaranaike, aide de camp to the British governor at the time of the First World War. His son, Solomon Western Ridgway Dias Bandaranaike, became prime minister of independent Ceylon in 1956 but was assassinated in 1959. His widow, Sirimavo

Bandaranaike, succeeded him becoming the world's first female prime minister. They are buried together at the memorial here. Their daughter, Chandrika Kumaratunga, was elected president in 1994. The family home, where visitors such as King George V and Jawaharlal Nehru stayed, is nearby, though it is private. The Bandaranaike memorial is by the side of the road at Nittambuwa, 39 km from Colombo. A broad walkway, about 10 m wide and 100 m long and flanked by frangipanis, leads to a raised plinth with five stone pillars behind it, the whole surrounded by a coconut grove. On the other side of the road, on a small hill, is a monument to Bandaranaike Senior.

Pasyala and around → *Colour map 3, A2.*
The area around Pasyala, 7 km further on, is noted for its *plumbago* (graphite) mines, betel nuts and above all, cashew. This is western edge of the Central Highlands massif. Passing through **Cadjugama** ('village of cashew nuts'), you will see women in brightly coloured traditional dress selling cashew nuts from stalls lining the road. Sadly, the cashews offered here are not always of the highest quality – they are often 'seconds'. Inspect and taste before you buy.

Warakapola and Ambepussa → *Phone code: 035. Colour map 2, C2. 60 km from Colombo.*
This is a convenient and popular stop en route to Kandy or Kurunegala and beyond. The busy little village of **Warakapola** provides an outlet for locally made cane baskets and mats in its bazaar. It is also a popular halt for those with a sweet tooth searching for sesame seed *thalagulis* which are freshly made at **Jinadisa's** shop, among others.

Ambepussa, 2 km north, is just off the road to the west, with a train station. Its rest house is claimed to be Sri Lanka's oldest, built in 1822, and is a popular lunch stop. About 1.5 km behind the rest house, near the Devagiri Vihara, is a series of caves which at one time formed a hermitage.

Dedigama → *Colour map 2, C3. 3 km south of the A1, from Kegalla take the B21.*
Near Ambepussa, a turn off to the south before Kegalla takes you to the two 12th-century *dagobas* at Dedigama, built by King Parakramabahu I, who was born here. One has 10 relic chambers, including one a lower level. A gem-studded golden reliquary has also been found here. The nearby **museum** ① *Wed-Mon*, is worth visiting.

Kegalla to Kandy → *See also page 203 for other sights around this area.*
Kegalla is a long straggling town in a picturesque setting. Most visitors take a detour here towards Rambukkana for the Pinnawela Elephant Orphanage (see below). After Kegalla, the hill scenery becomes increasingly beautiful, and the vegetation stunningly rich. About 1 km before Mawanella, a town surrounded by spice plantations, a sign points to the place where **Saradial** ('the local Robin Hood') lived, where there is a small monument. You then pass through **Molagoda**, a village devoted to pottery with both sides of the road lined with shops displaying a wide range of attractive pots. At the top of the Balana Pass is a precipice called **Sensation Point**.

At the Km 107 mark is an outdoor museum displaying the original equipment used to lay the Colombo–Kandy road, such as steamrollers and bitumen boilers. Next to the museum is a replica of the 300-year-old Bogoda Bridge (see page 238).

The railway goes through two tunnels to Peradeniya, where the road crosses the Mahaweli Ganga, Sri Lanka's longest river, and into the city.

Pinnawela → *Phone code: 035. Colour map 2, C3. 49 km from Kandy.*

Pinnawela, 6 km off the main Colombo–Kandy road, is the home of one of the most popular stops on the tourist circuit, the famous elephant orphanage. A number of spice gardens line the road. While most visitors are en route between Colombo and Kandy, travellers who choose to spend a night are delighted by the peace and beauty of this place with its river and jungle orphanage. The village becomes an oasis of natural quietness as calm descends when the tourist groups leave.

Pinnawela Elephant Orphanage

ⓘ *T226 6116, www.elephantorphanage.lk. 0830-1800. Rs 2000, children Rs 1000. Video camera Rs 500 (professional Rs 1500). There is a new ticketing area just down from the car park and old booths. Retain your ticket as may be checked again on the way to the elephant bath.*
The government-run elephant orphanage is a must for most visitors. It was set up in 1975 to rescue four orphaned baby elephants when they could no longer be looked after at Dehiwala Zoo. Now there are almost 90, the largest group of captive elephants in the world. The animals, some only a few weeks old, very hairy and barely 1 m high, are kept in parkland where they are nursed by adult elephants. There has been a successful captive breeding project, which at the time of visiting had produced 22 second generation births.

The elephants, which roam freely in parkland, are 'herded' just before being taken to the feeding sheds, when they are very photogenic. They may occasionally 'charge', so to avoid getting hurt stand well back. The feeding, usually around 0915, 1315 and 1700, is done in a couple of large sheds. Each baby elephant is shackled and then bottle-fed with copious amounts of milk (if visitors pay an additional Rs 250 they can hold the bottle). Adults, which need around 250 kg of food each day, are fed mainly on palm leaves. Two special farms run by the National Zoological Gardens meet part of their needs. After feeding they are driven across the road, down to the river. You can usually watch them bathing there for an hour or so at 1000 and 1400, and sometimes being trained to work. For a good view of the bathing, go down early, buy a drink and secure a table at the **Elephant Park Hotel** terrace.

Although the park has capacity for 100 elephants, the authorities are realizing that the programme cannot last forever in its current format. Since the elephants become so used to humans, it is impossible for them to be released back into the wild. Previous efforts have resulted in them returning to villages to find food. Following the success of the Elephant Transit Home scheme at Uda Walawe, see page 175, a new 19-ha safari park, which will also feature other Sri Lankan animals, is planned in the area. Another problem has been the lack of facilities and the proximity of humans to elephants to tourists, some of whom fail to realise that the elephants are still, at least in part, wild. This has led to a couple of incidents.

There is scope for up to 10 **foreign volunteers** to work at the orphanage, on programmes lasting from two weeks to three months. If you're handy with a shovel, contact **i-to-i** ⓘ *www.i-to-i.com*, or the **National Zoological Gardens** ⓘ *T011-276 1554, zoosl@slt.lk*, for further information.

Millennium Elephant Foundation → *3 km before the elephant orphanage.*

ⓘ *Hiriwadunna, Randeniya, T226 5377, www.millenniumelephantfoundation.com, 0800-1700, Rs 600.*
This registered charity, formerly Maximus Elephant Foundation, a member of WSPA, cares for elderly and disabled elephants. Although it has less of the 'aah' factor than Pinnawela, it is still worthwhile visiting. There are currently eight elephants living here, aged 21-65, but

numbers fluctuate. Pooja is the youngest elephant and was born here in 1984, the others are retired working animals. The scheme also runs a mobile veterinary unit, established in 2000, which provides healthcare across the country for domesticated and wild elephants. You can help bathe and feed the elephants and also go on rides around the grounds. As at the elephant orphanage, foreign volunteers can help with the project, and there is also an 'adopt an elephant' scheme: for US$35 (under 16s US$25) you can adopt an elephant for a year. Apply direct for voluntary work placements for up to three months.

Kandy → *Phone code: 081. Colour map 2, C4. Population 111, 700.*

The last bastion of Buddhist political power against colonial forces, the home of the Temple of the Buddha's Tooth Relic, and the site of the island's most impressive annual festival, Kandy is also the capital of the highlands. Its architectural monuments date mainly from a final surge of grandiose building by King Vikrama Rajasinha in the early 19th century. So extravagant were the edifices, and achieved only at enormous cost for the people of Kandy, that his nobles betrayed him to the British rather than continue enduring his excesses. The result is some extraordinary buildings, none of great architectural merit, but sustaining a Kandyan style dating back to the 16th century, and rich in symbolic significance of the nature of the king's view of his world.

The area with the Temple of the Tooth and associated buildings, a World Heritage Site, is the chief focus of interest. Sadly, it was the target of a bomb attack on 26 January 1998, which left over 20 dead. Security was upgraded and some roadblocks remain. Repairs to the extensive damage of the temple were completed in 1999.

Ins and outs → *Beware of accommodation touts, see page 207.*

Getting there Kandy is fairly easily accessible from all parts of the country. Some travellers head here immediately on arrival at the international airport. Intercity buses leave every half an hour, taking 3½ hours. There are also direct buses from Negombo. From Colombo, there are government buses from the Central Bus Stand in the Pettah, or private buses from Bastian Mawatha.

Getting around The bus (Goods Shed) terminus and railway station are close to each other about 1 km southwest of the centre. A three-wheeler into town will cost around Rs 100; to the guesthouses in the Saranankara Road area south of the lake will cost up to Rs 150. Air-conditioned radio cabs are very convenient, safe and reliable; telephone T223 3322, tell them your location and allow 10 minutes.

Gopallawa Mawatha, the main road into town, is horribly choked with traffic, especially at rush hour. To avoid the fumes, it's a good idea to do as the locals do and walk north along the railway line into town. Local buses ply the routes to Peradeniya, Pinnawela, etc.

Best time to visit Kandy has a pleasant climate throughout the year, lacking the humidity of the coast. In July, **Esala Perahera** is a truly magnificent spectacle.

Tourist information Hotel and guesthouse owners are usually the best source of information. There is a **Tourist Information Centre** ① *Headman's Lodge, 3 Deva Veediya (Temple St), opposite entrance to Temple of the Tooth, T222 2661, Mon-Fri 0900-1645.* There's also a very helpful tourist information in the city centre that can provide a free map of Kandy and information on buses, trains, sights, etc. See also www.kandycity.org.

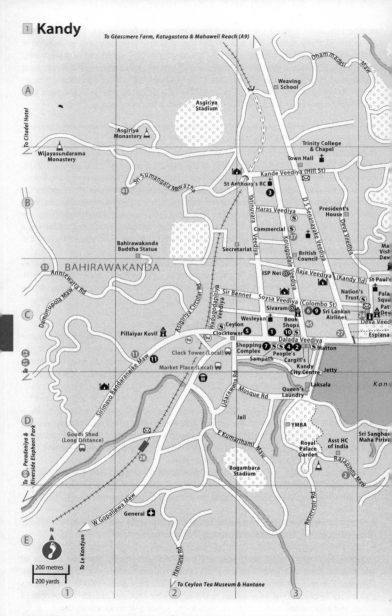

1 Kandy

To Grassmere Farm, Katugastota & Mahaweli Reach (A9)

Dhammazasi Maw

To Citadel Hotel

Weaving School

Asgiriya Stadium

Asgiriya Monastery

Wijayasundarama Monastery

Trinity College & Chapel

Town Hall

Sri Sumangala Mawatte

St Anthony's RC

Kande Veediya (Hill St)

Haras Veediya

Yatinuwara Veediya

President's House

D S Senanayake Veediya

Bahirawakanda Buddha Statue

Secretariat

Commercial

Kosugodale Veediya

British Council

Anniewatta Maw Rd

BAHIRAWAKANDA

Raja Veediya (Kandy Rd)

St Paul's

Damunupola Maw

Astigiriya Circular Rd

Sir Bennet

Soysa Veediya

ISP Net

Ma Vish Dev

Nation's Trust

Pala Squa Pat Dev

Wadugodapitiya Veediya

Sivaram

Sri Lankan Airlines

Deva Veed

Pillaiyar Kovil

Ceylon Clocktower

Wesleyan

Book Shops

Esplana

To 50 52

Clock Tower (Local)

Shopping Complex

People's

Cargill's

Hatton

Kandy City Centre

Kan

Market Place (Local)

Sampath

Udarawa Rd

Mosque Rd

Queen's Laundry

Jetty

Laksala

To Peradeniya & Riverside Elephant Park

Goods Shed (Long Distance)

Jail

E Kumarihami Maw

YMBA

Royal Palace Garden

Asst HC of India

Sri Sangha Maha Pirivu

Srimavo Bandaranaike Maw

Bogambara Stadium

Rajasinha Maw

Reservoir Rd

N

W Gopallawa Maw

General

200 metres
200 yards

To Le Kandyan

Hantane Rd

To Ceylon Tea Museum & Hantane

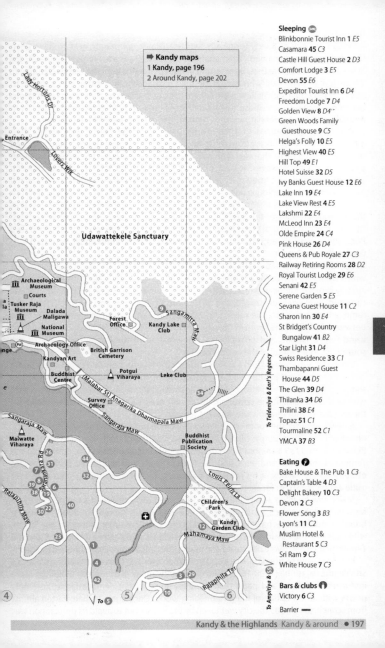

➡ **Kandy maps**
1 Kandy, page 196
2 Around Kandy, page 202

Udawattekele Sanctuary

Lady Horton's Dr
Entrance
Lovers Walk

Archaeological Museum
Courts
Tusker Raja Museum
Dalada Maligawa
National Museum
Archaeology Office
Kandyan Art
Buddhist Centre
Maiwatte Viharaya
Sangaraja Maw
Rajapihilla Rd

Forest Office
Sangamitta Maw
Kandy Lake Club
British Garrison Cemetery
Potgul Viharaya
Lake Club
(Malabar St) Anagarika Dharmapala Maw
Survey Office
Sangaraja Maw
Buddhist Publication Society

Louis Pieris La
Children's Park
Kandy Garden Club
Mahamaya Maw
Rajapihilla Ter

To Teldeniya & Earl's Regency
To Amptiya & 55

To 5
To Amptiya & 55

Kandyan Art

Sleeping
Blinkbonnie Tourist Inn **1** *E5*
Casamara **45** *C3*
Castle Hill Guest House **2** *D3*
Comfort Lodge **3** *E5*
Devon **55** *E6*
Expeditor Tourist Inn **6** *D4*
Freedom Lodge **7** *D4*
Golden View **8** *D4*
Green Woods Family
 Guesthouse **9** *C5*
Helga's Folly **10** *E5*
Highest View **40** *E5*
Hill Top **49** *E1*
Hotel Suisse **32** *D5*
Ivy Banks Guest House **12** *E6*
Lake Inn **19** *E4*
Lake View Rest **4** *E5*
Lakshmi **22** *E4*
McLeod Inn **23** *E4*
Olde Empire **24** *C4*
Pink House **26** *D4*
Queens & Pub Royale **27** *C3*
Railway Retiring Rooms **28** *D2*
Royal Tourist Lodge **29** *E6*
Senani **42** *E5*
Serene Garden **5** *E5*
Sevana Guest House **11** *C2*
Sharon Inn **30** *E4*
St Bridget's Country
 Bungalow **41** *B2*
Star Light **31** *D4*
Swiss Residence **33** *C1*
Thambapanni Guest
 House **44** *D5*
The Glen **39** *D4*
Thilaka **34** *D6*
Thilini **38** *E4*
Topaz **51** *C1*
Tourmaline **52** *C1*
YMCA **37** *B3*

Eating
Bake House & The Pub **1** *C3*
Captain's Table **4** *D3*
Delight Bakery **10** *C3*
Devon **2** *C3*
Flower Song **3** *B3*
Lyon's **11** *C2*
Muslim Hotel &
 Restaurant **5** *C3*
Sri Ram **9** *C3*
White House **7** *C3*

Bars & clubs
Victory **6** *C3*

Barrier ▬

Background

Although the city of Kandy (originally Senkadagala) is commonly held to have been founded by a general named Vikramabahu in 1472, there was a settlement on the site for at least 150 years before that. On asserting his independence from the reigning monarch, Vikramabahu made Kandy his capital. He built a palace for his mother and a shrine on pillars. In 1542 the Tooth Relic was brought to the city, stimulating a flurry of new religious building – a two-storey house for the relic itself, and 86 houses for the monks. As in Anuradhapura and Polonnaruwa, the Tooth temple was built next to the palace.

Defensive fortifications probably came only when the Portuguese began their attacks. Forced to withdraw from the town in 1594, King Vimala Dharma Suriya set half the city on fire, a tactic that was repeated by several successors in the face of expulsion by foreign armies. However, he won it back, and promptly set about building a massive wall, interspersed with huge towers. Inside, a new palace replaced the one destroyed by fire, and the city rapidly gained a reputation as a cosmopolitan centre of splendour and wealth. As early as 1597 some Portuguese showed scepticism about the claims that the enshrined tooth was the Buddha's. In 1597 De Quezroy described the seven golden caskets in which the tooth was kept, but added that it was the tooth of a buffalo. The Portuguese were already claiming that they had captured the original, exported it to Goa and incinerated it.

By 1602 the city had probably taken the form (though not the actual buildings) which would survive to the beginning of the 19th century. The major temples were also already in place. Kandy was repeatedly attacked by the Portuguese. In 1611 the city was captured and largely destroyed, and again in 1629 and 1638, and the Tooth Relic was removed for a time by the retreating King Senarat. A new earth rampart was built between the hills in the south of the city. In 1681 there is evidence of a moat being built using forced labour, and possibly the first creation of the Bogambara Lake to the southwest, as a symbol of the cosmic ocean.

Vimala Dharma Suriya I had a practical use for the lake for he is said to have kept some of his treasure sunk in the middle, guarded by crocodiles in the water. It has been suggested that there was also a symbolic link with Kubera, the mythical god of wealth, who kept his wealth at the bottom of the cosmic ocean. Crocodiles are often shown on the *makara toranas* (dragon gateways) of temples.

A new Temple of the Tooth was built by Vimala Dharma Suriya II between 1687-1707, on the old site. Three storeys high, it contained a reliquary of gold encrusted with jewels. Between 1707-1739 Narendra Sinha undertook new building in the city, renovating the Temple of the Tooth and enclosing the Natha Devala and the sacred Bodhi tree. He established the validity of his royal line by importing princesses from Madurai, and set aside a separate street for them in the town.

Major new building awaited King Kirti Sri (1747-1782). He added a temple to Vishnu northwest of the palace, but at the same time asserted his support for Buddhism, twice bringing monks from Thailand to re-validate the Sinhalese order of monks. The Dutch, who captured the city in 1765, plundered the temples and palaces. The palace and the Temple of the Tooth were destroyed and many other buildings were seriously damaged.

Kirti Sri started re-building, more opulently than ever, but it was the last king of Kandy, Sri Vikrama Rajasinha (1798-1815), who gave Kandy many of its present buildings. More interested in palaces and parks than temples, he set about demonstrating his kingly power with an exhibition of massive building works. Once again he had started almost from scratch, for in 1803 the city was taken by the British, but to avoid its desecration was once again burned to the ground. The British were thrown out, and between 1809-1812 there was massive re-building. The palace was fully renovated and a new octagonal structure added to the palace, the Patthiruppuwa. Two years later the royal complex was surrounded by a moat and a single massive stone gateway replaced the earlier entrances.

In the west, Sri Vikrama Rajasinha built new shops and houses, at the same time building more houses in the east for his Tamil relatives. But by far the greatest work was the construction of the lake. Previously the low-lying marshy land in front of the palace had been drained for paddy fields. Between 1810-1812 up to 3000 men were forced to work on building the dam at the west end of the low ground, creating an artificial lake given the cosmically symbolic name of the Ocean of Milk. A pleasure house was built in the middle of the lake, connected by drawbridge to the palace. By now the city had taken virtually its present form.

Rajasinha's rule had been so tyrannical however, violating religious laws and committing brutal murders, that the terrorized Kandyan aristocracy allied themselves with the British invaders, who garnered support for a war against the king promising to protect the people and their property. The final fall of Kandy to the British in 1815 signalled the end of independence for the whole island.

Temple of the Tooth

ⓘ *Rs 1100. Cameras Rs 150 (video cameras Rs 300). Wear a long skirt or trousers and ensure shoulders are covered. Otherwise lungis (sarongs) must be worn over shorts. Remove shoes and hats before entering (small fee for looking after your shoes). The Cultural Triangle Permit does not cover the temple here. Museum, T223 4226, Rs 500, 0900-1700. The entrance to the complex is in Palace Square opposite the Natha Devala. It is best to visit early in the morning before it gets too busy with tourist buses and pilgrims. Whilst visiting, be sure to remember that the Temple of the Tooth (Dalada Maligawa) is a genuine place of worship and not simply a site of tourist interest.*

The original temple dated from the 16th century, though most of the present building and the Patthiruppuwa or Octagon (which was badly damaged in the 1998 attack) were built in the early 19th century. The gilded roof over the Relic chamber is a recent addition. The oldest part is the inner shrine built by Kirti Sri after 1765. The drawbridge, moat and gateway were the work of Sri Vickrama Rajasinha. There is a moonstone step at the entrance to the archway, and a stone depicting Lakshmi against the wall facing the entrance. The main door to the temple is in the wall of the upper veranda, covered in restored frescoes depicting Buddhist conceptions of hell. The doorway is a typical *makara torana* showing mythical beasts. A second Kandyan-style door leads into the courtyard, across which is the building housing the Tooth Relic. The door has ivory inlay work, with copper and gold handles.

The **Udmale** (upper storey) houses the Relic. Caged behind gilded iron bars is the large outer *karandua* (casket), made of silver. Inside are seven smaller caskets, each made of gold studded with jewels. Today the temple is controlled by a layman (the *Diyawadne*) elected by the high priests of the monasteries in Kandy and Asgiriya. The administrator holds the key to the iron cage, but there are three different keys to the caskets themselves, one held by the administrator and one each by the high priests of Malwatte and Asgiriya, so that the caskets can only be opened when all four are present.

The **sanctuary** is opened at dawn. Ceremonies start at 0530, 0930 and 1830. These are moments when the temple comes to life with pilgrims making offerings of flowers amidst clouds of incense and the beating of drums. The casket is displayed for only a part of the day. The Relic itself for many years has only been displayed to the most important of

Worship of the Tooth Relic

The eyewitness account of Bella Sidney Woolf in 1914 captures something of the atmosphere when the Tooth Relic could be viewed by pilgrims.

"The relic is only shown for royal visits or, on certain occasions, to Burmese and other pilgrims. If the passenger happens to be in Kandy at such a time he should try to see the Tooth, even though it may mean many hours of waiting. It is an amazing sight. The courtyard is crammed with worshippers of all ages, bearing offerings in their hands, leaves of young coconut, scent, flowers, fruit. As the door opens, they surge up the dark and narrow stairway to the silver and ivory doors behind which lies the Tooth.

The doors are opened and a flood of hot heavy scented air pours out. The golden 'Karandua' or outer casket of the Tooth stands revealed dimly behind gilded bars. In the weird uncertain light of candles in golden candelabra the yellow-robed priests move to and fro. The Tooth is enclosed in five Karanduas and slowly and solemnly each is removed in turn; some of them are encrusted with rubies, emeralds and diamonds.

At last the great moment approaches. The last Karandua is removed – in folds of red silk lies the wondrous Relic – the centre point of the faith of millions. It is a shock to see a tooth of discoloured ivory at least three inches long – unlike any human tooth ever known. The priest sets it in a golden lotus – the Temple Korala gives a sharp cry – the tom-toms and conches and pipes blare out – the kneeling worshippers, some with tears streaming down their faces, stretch out their hands in adoration."

visitors. You can join pilgrims to see the casket but may well have to overcome pushing and jostling by those desperate to see the holy object. There is a separate enclosure in front of the Relic, which wealthy Sri Lankans pay to go into. The hall behind the Tooth Relic sanctuary has a number of golden Buddha statues from Thailand and modern paintings depicting the Buddha's life and the arrival of Buddhism on the island.

The **Temple Museum** above is accessed from the rear. It contains bronze busts of the Kandyan kings, and displays some of their garments, as well as photocopies of documents detailing some of the history of the temple. There is also a gallery of photographs showing the extent of the damage to the temple in the 1998 bomb.

The **Audience Hall** was rebuilt in the Kandyan style as a wooden pillared hall (1784). The historic document ending the Kandyan kingdom was signed here, when the territory was handed over to the British. There is excellent carving on the pillars.

Around the temple

Across from the complex is a working **monastery** and beyond its walls is **St Paul's Church** which was built in 1843 although the earliest minister, George Bisset, was here in 1816. The church was also damaged in the 1998 blast. There are various interesting memorials from 1822 to the 1870s in the British Garrison Cemetery, which is up a hill behind the Kandy National Museum. Behind the temple, in the area of the Law Courts, you can watch lawyers in black gowns and white wigs going about their business in open-sided halls.

The lake

On the lakeside, **Ulpenge**, opposite the Temple of the Tooth, was the bathing place of former queens and is now a police station. Further along to the east, is the **Buddhist Publications Society**, which has information on courses about Buddhism and meditation (see page 216). The **Royal Palace Park** (Wace Park) ⓘ *0830-1630, Rs 200*, is approached from the lake's southwest corner. There is a scenic 4-km path around the lake. Boat tours run from the jetty on the western side.

Malwatte and Asigiriya viharas

The 18th-century **Malwatte Vihara**, on the south side of the lake, where the important annual ordination of monks takes place in June, is decorated with ornate wood and metal work. Occasionally, a friendly monk shows visitors around the monastery and the small museum. This and the **Asigiriya Vihara** (northwest of town) are particularly important monasteries because of the senior position of their incumbents. The latter, which stands on a hill, has good wood carving and an impressive collection of old palm leaf manuscripts. There is a large recumbent Buddha statue and the mound of the old Royal Burial Ground nearby.

Kandy National Museum

ⓘ *Within the Queen's Palace, behind the Temple of the Tooth, T222 3867. Sun-Thu 0800-1700. Rs 500, children Rs 300, camera Rs 250.*

The collection traces a vivid history of the development and culture of the Kandyan Kingdom. It features jewels, armaments, ritual objects, sculptures, metalwork, ivory, costumes, games, medical instruments, old maps – an enormous range of everyday and exceptional objects. There is much memorabilia, and the attendants will attempt to explain it all, sometimes pointing out the obvious in expectation of a tip.

Tusker Raja Museum

The much venerated elephant which carried the Tooth Relic casket in the Esala Perahera for many years, was offered to the temple by a pious Buddhist family when he was very young. Raja was 85 when he died in 1988. He was stuffed and placed in this separate museum north (left) of the Temple of the Tooth which is more easily visited before entering the temple.

Archaeological Museum

ⓘ *Palace Sq. Wed-Mon 0800-1700. Free.*

Some good sculptures in wood and stone are housed in what remains of the old king's palace. The museum includes some architectural pieces, notably columns and capitals from the Kandyan kingdom, but the three dusty rooms are somewhat disappointing.

British Garrison Cemetery

ⓘ *Donation expected.*

To the right of the Kandy National Museum is a sign pointing the way to the British Garrison Cemetery. It is a short walk up the hill and here lie a number of colonial Brits. It was opened in 1822 until burials were all but banned in the 1870s. The cemetery was restored in the 1990s and is now a tranquil place to escape the bustle of Kandy town. The caretaker is very helpful and will show you around and point out the most interesting graves, such as the last recorded death of a European in Sri Lankan from a wild elephant.

Udawattekele Sanctuary

ⓘ *Rs 687. Kande Veediya, past the post office, leads to the entrance gate to the sanctuary.*
Once the 'forbidden forest' of the kings of Kandy, this is now the city's lung. Previously reserved for the use of the court, the British cleared vast areas soon after arrival, though declared it a 'reserved' area in 1856. The sanctuary now covers 104 ha, and contains several endemic species of flora and fauna, with over 150 species of birds (including Layard's parakeet, Sri Lankan hanging parrot, barbets, bulbuls, bee-eaters and kingfishers), monkeys, squirrels and porcupines. There are also a number of meditation centres here. Some interesting legends are attached to the forest. Look out for the trail with stone steps leading down to a cove, the Chittu Vishudi. This is where King Vickramabahu was said to have hidden here when his palace was under siege. The pond is the original bathing place of the court. Gold coins are rumoured to be concealed by its murky waters. Myth has it that a serpent with glowing red eyes guards the treasure, which surfaces once a year. Lady Horton's Drive takes you into the tropical rainforest, and further east offers good views of the Mahaweli River.

② **Around Kandy**

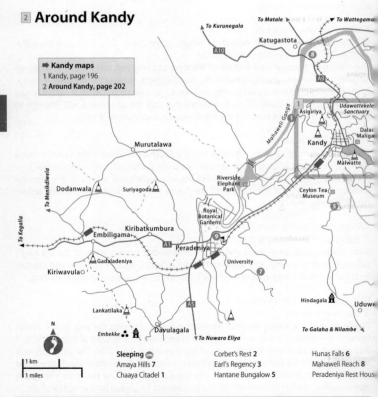

→ **Kandy maps**
1 Kandy, page 196
2 Around Kandy, page 202

Sleeping 🛏
Amaya Hills **7**
Chaaya Citadel **1**
Corbet's Rest **2**
Earl's Regency **3**
Hantane Bungalow **5**
Hunas Falls **6**
Mahaweli Reach **8**
Peradeniya Rest Hous

Trinity College

Trinity College, which is approached from DS Senanayake Veediya, has a chapel with some beautiful paintings which makes a quiet diversion from the busy part of town. It is also worth exploring the school's archives.

West of Kandy → Sights further west are covered on page 192.

Beyond the wonderful botanic gardens at Peradeniya, is a group of 14th-century temples which display ancient artistic skills of the islanders. The traditions continue to be practised in the crafts villages nearby. If you have your own transport, you can combine a visit to the gardens and some temples with a visit to the Pinnawela Elephant Orphanage (see page 194). For a temple loop on foot, you could take the bus to Embekke, walk to Lankatilaka, finishing at Galadeniya, which is close to the main road.

Peradeniya → Phone code: 035.

Colour map 2, C4. 6 km southwest of Kandy.

ⓘ Entry to the gardens is Rs 1100, students and children (under 12) Rs 550. A useful map is handed out with the tickets.

Peradeniya is famous for its magnificent **botanic gardens** justly earning the town a place on most itineraries. Conceived originally in 1371 as the queen's pleasure garden, Peradeniya became the residence of a Kandyan prince between 1747 and 1782 where royal visitors were entertained. The park was converted into a 60-ha botanical garden in 1821, six years after the fall of the last Kandyan king. There are extensive well-kept lawns, pavilions, an Orchid House with an outstanding collection, an Octagon Conservatory, fernery, banks of bamboo and numerous flower borders with cannas, hibiscus, chrysanthemums, croton and colourful bougainvillaea. The tank has water plants including the giant water lily and papyrus reeds. You will see unusual exotic species, especially palms (palmyra, talipot, royal, cabbage), and *Ficus elastica* (latex-bearing fig or 'Indian rubber tree' with buttress roots), an amazing avenue of drunken looking pines, and some magnificent old specimen trees. In all, there are about 4000 labelled species. A signboard at the entrance, with a map, features a numbered circuit from 1-30. The suggested route below closely follows this in reverse. It is best to keep to the paths to avoid the invisible large holes in the rough grass.

A **suggested walk** is to start at the **Spice Garden** (to the right of the entrance) which has many exotic spices (eg cardamom, cloves, pepper, vanilla). Follow the road to the right (east) to take in the **Orchid House**. Just off Palmyra Avenue there are Javanese Almond trees with amazing roots. The palmyra leaf was used for ancient manuscripts. The **Cabbage Palm Avenue** from South America was planted in 1905. You can then walk along the **Royal Palm Avenue** (1885) – you will notice the fruit bats in quite large colonies hanging in many of the trees. This meets the **River Drive** which follows the course of the Mahaweli Ganga. Follow the drive to the **Suspension Bridge** which is about halfway around the River Drive and you can if you wish go back via the Royal Palm Avenue. This goes through the **Great Circle**, a large grassy central area around which a remarkably diverse list of dignitaries have planted further specimens. Alongside generations of English royalty, there are trees planted by Indira Gandhi, Yuri Gagarin, Marshal Tito, U Thant and Harold Macmillan. Between the Great Circle and the Great Lawn is the **Herbarium**. Try not to miss one of the rarest plants in the gardens – the Coco de Mer. You will find it on the path leading to George Gardner's monument. This is on your right as you return to exit (left as you enter the park). This plant has the largest and heaviest fruit (or nut) in the plant kingdom, weighing on average some 10-20 kg. They take between five and eight years to mature and are surprisingly productive. It is not unusual to have over 20 nuts on a tree. They are all carefully numbered. Native Coco de Mer are only found on Praslin, an island in the Seychelles. Carry on along this path to get to the **Memorial**, a dome shaped structure. George Gardner was Superintendent of the gardens from 1844-1849. From here you overlook the lily tank which is surrounded by giant bamboo, some 40 m tall (it grows at 2-3 cm a day).

Outside the gardens a bridge across the Mahaweli River takes you to the **School of Tropical Agriculture** at Gannoruwa, where research is carried out into various important spices and medicinal herbs as well as into tea, coffee, cocoa, rubber, coconuts and varieties of rice and other cash crops. The **Economic Museum** has botanical and agricultural exhibits.

Peradeniya is also the home of the **Sri Lanka University** (1942), built in the old Kandyan style in an impressive setting of a large park with the Mahaweli Ganga running though it and the surrounding hillocks. It is worth visiting the small teaching collection **museum** ① *in the Department of Archaeology, call ahead, T238 8345 ext 518.*

Gadaladeniya Temple
① *Rs 200.*
The Buddhist temple is in a beautiful hilltop setting, built on a rock, 1 km from the main road. Built of stone, showing influence of Indian temple architecture, it has lacquered doors, carvings and frescoes and a moonstone at the entrance of the shrine. The brick superstructure, shaped like a stupa, has an octagonal base. The inscriptions on the rock by Dharmakirti date it to 1344. The principal gilded image of the Buddha (18th century, which replaced the original destroyed by the Portuguese) is framed by elaborate *makara* decoration. Unusually, there is also a shrine to Vishnu here. Outside, there is a covered stupa and a Bodhi tree. At **Kiriwavula village** nearby, craftsmen cast brass ornaments by the ancient lost-wax (*cire-perdu*) process. Some are for sale. Take a left turn off the A1 just after Pilimatalana.

Lankatilaka Mahaviharaya

The second monument of the group, 4 km away in Hiripitiya, sits on top of the rock Panhalgala. King Bhuvanekabahu IV (ruled 1341-1351) moved the Sinhalese capital from Kurunegala to Gampola nearby. When a monk reported the extraordinary vision of an elusive golden pot on the water of the tank here, the King saw this as a sign and had the temple built. He appears among the wall paintings.

The present two-storeyed blue-washed brick structure ① *donation requested*, was originally four storeys high. It was renovated and the tiled roof was added in 1845 after the two top storeys had fallen. You climb up a rock-cut stairway to the moonstone at the entrance, and the finely carved wooden doorway flanked by guardian *gajasinghas* (elephant-lions). The inner image house containing fine gold plated images of the Buddha is surrounded by a devale. The walls and ceiling have well preserved frescoes, some of the oldest and best examples of the Kandyan temple style. The west door has carved figures of Hindu gods (Saman, Skanda, Ganapathi and Vibhisena among others). There is a large rock inscription dating the temple to the thirteenth century. Craftsmen can be seen carving wood at the base of the rock.

Embekke Devale

① *Rs 200*.

The Hindu devale, dedicated to God Kataragama (Skanda), is 1.5 km away along a track through pleasant cultivated fields. The temple with its sanctuary, Dancing Hall and the Drummers' Hall, is famous for its carved wooden pillars (which may have once adorned the Audience Hall in Kandy) with vibrant figures of soldiers, wrestlers, dancers, musicians, mythical animals and birds. You can see similar stone pillars at the remains of the old Pilgrim's Rest nearby. The patterned roof tiles are attractive too. The village has craftsmen working in silver, brass and copper.

Suriyagoda Vihare

If you have your own transport and wish to visit the Suriyagoda Vihare, turn off north from the A1 at Kiribatkumbura, signed to Murutalawa. The present 18th-century *vihara*, on a 15th-century site, has striking Kandyan wall paintings.

North of Embiligama (Km 105 post), the 17th-century **Dodanwala Temple** was built by Rajasinha II. It is where the king is believed to have offered the deity his crown and sword after defeating the Portuguese. From Embiligama, to reach the textile weaving village of **Menikdiwela**, after a short distance along the Murutalawa road take the left fork for 6 km.

Riverside Elephant Park

① *0730-1630, Rs 1100*.

Opposite the War Cemetery on Deveni Rajasinghe Mawatha, tame elephants are brought here at around 1200 after a morning of work. Their *mahouts* (elephant keeper/owner) brush, sponge and splash the elephants with water – essential for the animals' health.

East of Kandy

Medawela Temple → *10 km northeast of Kandy.*

This temple marked a Buddhist revival. It was built in the 18th century, where an older 14th-century temple stood. Interesting features include the small image house built in wood and wattle-and-daub, raised above the ground on stone pillars, similar to the old Kandyan grain stores. The railed balcony forms the Pradakshina Path. Inside, the marble Buddha image sits in front of a decoratively carved and painted wooden panel with representations of a Bodhi tree, protective gods, disciples and dragons. The fine Kandyan paintings on the side walls show a line of saints and disciples along the lower level and tales from the *jatakas* along the middle (unfolding from the back of the room, to the front). Above this, the murals on the left show the weeks after the Buddha's Enlightenment, and on the right, the 16 holiest places for Buddhists. Medawela, at the junction of B36 and B37, is a metalworkers village. The **Kandyan Dance Academy** near Amunugama is 3 km south.

Nattarampota and around → *7 km east of Kandy.*

At Nattarampota, in the beautiful Dumbara Valley, you can watch traditional crafts-people at work. At **Kalapuraya Craft Village** artisans work in village homes with brass, copper, silver, wood, leather, etc. Prices are better than elsewhere but not fixed. Take a left turn down a lane off the Digana road.

Degaldoruwa Cave Temple, at Gunnepana, 3 km north of Nattarampota, has vivid wall paintings of *Jataka* stories dating from the 18th century. There is a dance academy here.

About 1.5 km along the Kalapura road from Nattarampota Junction on the Kandy–Kundasala road, the unusual incomplete 14th-century **Galmaduwa Temple** was an attempt to combine the features of Sinhalese, Indian, Islamic and Christian architectural styles.

Dumbara Hills (Knuckles Range) → *Colour map 2, C5. For tours, page 214.*

ⓘ *www.knucklesrange.orgm. Visiting hours 0600-1800. Rs 575, plus guide fees. Best time to visit Jan-Apr; be prepared for leeches.*

With peaks towering over above 1500 m and an annual rainfall range of 2500-5000 mm it follows that a wide variety of forest types would exist here from lowland dry patana to montane wet evergreen with their associated trees, shrubs, plants and epiphytes. These forests, in turn, harbour wildlife including leopard, sambar, barking deer, mouse deer, wild boar, giant squirrel, purple-faced langur, toque macaque and loris, as well as the otherwise rarely seen otter. More than 120 bird species recorded here include many endemic ones including the yellow-fronted barbet, dusky-blue flycatcher, Ceylon lorikeet, Ceylon grackle, yellow-eared bulbul and Layard's parakeet. In addition endemic amphibians and reptiles include the Kirtisinghe's rock frog and leaf-nosed lizard, which are only found here.

The importance of the range as a watershed for the Mahaweli River and the Victoria reservoir has led the government to designate the area over 1500 m as a conservation area. Soil and water conservation have become critical issues because of the way the area has been exploited so far. Cardamom cultivation, the removal of timber and fuelwood, the use of cane in basket making and the production of treacle from kitul have all been sources of concern.

South of Kandy

Ceylon Tea Museum

ⓘ *3 km south of town along Hantane Rd (past the hospital), T380 3284, www.ceylon teamuseum.com. Tue-Sun 0830-1630 (last tickets 1530). Rs 250, students Rs 100.*

Opened in December 2001, the government-backed Ceylon Tea Museum proudly claims to be the first of its kind in the world. Located in an old tea factory abandoned in 1986, it contains some impressive old machinery, polished up and laid out in manufacturing sequence, collected from various disused plantations around the highlands. The first floor holds the archive of James Taylor who set up the first tea plantation at Loolecondera in 1867, with some interesting curios such as the oldest extant packet of Ceylon Tea (still in its original packaging) and a photograph of the largest tea bush in the world, as well as a history of Thomas Lipton. The top floor has been converted into a restaurant and has a telescope for viewing the surrounding hills.

To the south, the **Hindagala Temple**, along the Galaha Road, has sixth-century rock inscriptions. The wall paintings date from different periods.

⊙ Kandy and around listings

For Sleeping and Eating price codes and other relevant information, see pages 26-32.

⊃ Sleeping

Ambepussa *p193*

C Rest House (CHC), Ambepussa, T226 7299, www.ceylonhotels.lk. Beautiful Dutch-style building with large teak veranda, close to a stream. 6 rooms with beautiful furniture, a/c, hot water and TV.

Pinnawela *p194*

Most places are along the Rambukkana Rd on the way to the elephant orphanage.
D Ralidiya, on the edge of town, T226 4069, www.ralidiyahotel.com. Catering mainly to the local wedding market, it also has 5 clean rooms with balcony and good views over the river. Restaurant.

E Elephant View, opposite the orphanage, T226 5299, eleview@sltnet.lk. 16 recently refurbished a/c rooms with hot water. Most rooms are in the main building and you can see the elephants on their way to bathe; others are in the former **Pinnawela Village Hotel** on the main road.

F Green Land Guest House, Elephant Bath Rd, T226 5668. 5 clean rooms with nets and attached bath, upstairs better as rooms have access to the balcony, excellent rice and curry dinner.

Kandy *p195, map p196*

Accommodation prices rise by about Rs 500 during peak season and the festival. In low season, try bargaining for a good price. It is best to reserve your accommodation before arriving here. Kandy is full of touts. Some board trains approaching the town. Others besiege newcomers at the bus and rail stations. They can be very persistent, will try to put you off going to certain hotels/guesthouses and then direct you to one where they can get a large commission from your host, often demanding up to 20% of everything you spend (not just the room, but food and tours as well). Insist that you want to choose your own and have a confirmed reservation. Don't tell them which hotel you will be staying at and ignore stories that your hotel/guesthouse has closed or is no good. Some touts will follow you, if you are on foot, and pretend they have taken you to your hotel – make it clear to your host that you chose the hotel of your own accord. Many guesthouse owners refuse to pay touts. These are the ones that the touts will tell you are closed or no good. Some touts will accost you in town pretending to work for your hotel (eg chef), claiming you have met them earlier. Ask them which hotel and this should get rid of them. They will often be very friendly and want to take you to a bar, if you do go drinking with them you will find yourself saddled with an inflated tab or which they get a percentage.

Saranankara Rd and Rajapihilla Mawatha, a 10- to 20-min walk southeast of the lake, are popular and have a good range of reasonably priced accommodation. This area offers a good balance. It far enough out of the centre to be peaceful though not too far out so that taxi fares bump up the costs during your stay. Some of the guesthouses here have fine views over the lake.

L-AL Helga's Folly, 70 Frederick E de Silva Mawatha, T447 4314, www.helgasfolly.com. 40 individually decorated rooms in this eccentrically designed 'anti-hotel' full of character and quirkiness, unique interior and exterior design ('the Salvador Dali of hotels') has to be seen to be believed, set in quiet wooded hills, stylish restaurant, small pool (not well maintained). Far from town but recommended for imagination and romance.

A Serene Garden Hotel, 189 Rajapihilla Mawatha, T222 7915, www.serenegarden hotel.com. Just past the **Senani**, this hotel is deceptively small from the outside. Rooms are clean and tastefully furnished, and all have balconies with a view or partial view. There is a pool, a well-stocked bar, a restaurant and internet is available.

A-B Topaz, Anniewatte (1.6 km west of town), T223 2326, www.mclarenshotels.lk. 75 a/c rooms in excellent location on high hill overlooking mountains but rather remote, balconies, good pool shared with sister hotel, **Tourmaline**. Popular with package tours.

A-B Tourmaline, Anniewatte, sister hotel of **Topaz**, T223 2326, www.mclarenshotels.lk. 29 a/c rooms with similar facilities.

A-C Thilanka, 3 Sangamitta Mawatha, T447 5200, www.thilankahotel.com. 87 well-furnished rooms and suites, private balconies

with lake views, good restaurant, nice pool, and very clean. Retains parts of original house which began as a small guesthouse, where the standard fan rooms are located. Helpful and friendly staff.

B Hotel Suisse (CHC), 30 Sangaraja Mawatha, T223 3024, www.hotelsuisse.lk. 100 a/c rooms, best with balcony on lakeside. Limited views of lake but friendly and helpful staff, restaurant, good pool (non-residents, Rs 250), tennis, snooker, herbal clinic, shopping arcade, good position, colonial-style hotel (1920s), was Lord Mountbatten's wartime HQ.

B Senani, 167/1 Rajapihilla Mawatha, T223 5118, www.senanihotel.com. Clean, spacious a/c rooms, helpful staff and good food.

B Swiss Residence, 23 Bahirawakanda, near Buddha statue, T220 4646, www.swiss residence.lk. 40 comfortable rooms, variable views, best towards Buddha statue, all with balcony, 1 stylish suite with jacuzzi (US$140). Pool, Wi-Fi, popular nightclub.

B-C Devon, 51 Ampitiya Rd, T223 5164, www.devonsrilanka.com. 27 rooms, TV, minibar, a/c, some with tubs, 24-hr coffee shop and well-renowned Devon chain food.

B-C Queens (CHC), 45 Dalada Veediya, T223 3026, www.queenshotel.lk. Full of colonial character (established 1844). 54 smallish but comfortable rooms, half a/c, but fan rooms have balcony and are better value, avoid noisy front rooms, restaurant, good bar, super pool, "hard to beat for slightly decaying colonial charm".

C Casamara, 12 Kotugodella Veediya, T222 4688, www.casamarahotel.com. Unexceptional exterior but rooms have a/c, good furniture and staff are friendly and helpful.

C Castle Hill Guest House, 22 Rajapihilla Mawatha, T222 4376, ayoni@sltnet.lk. 4 large rooms, better on garden-side, antique art-deco furniture, good food, lovely garden, magnificent views over town.

C Hill Top (Aitken Spence), 200/21 Bahirawakanda Peradeniya Rd, 2 km from centre, T222 4162, www.aitkenspence hotels.com. 73 a/c rooms in attractively designed hotel, comfortable and striking rooms, beautiful restaurant, poolside rooms better. Attention to detail could be improved.

D Comfort Lodge, 197 Rajapihilla Mawatha, T447 3707, www.hotel-comfort-kandy.com. Clean, modern and rather characterless rooms with TV, nice balconies, friendly and helpful staff.

D Sharon Inn, 59 Saranankara Rd, T220 1400, www.hotelsharoninn.com. 11 spotless rooms with balcony, restaurant, Wi-Fi, friendly, very popular.

D-E Royal Tourist Lodge, 93 Rajapihilla Mawatha, T222 2534, www.royaltouristlodge.hotels.officelive.com. 2 very large well-furnished rooms with own patio into garden, and 1 room without patio, in spacious family guesthouse. Clean and friendly, quiet.

D-E St Bridget's Country Bungalow, 125 Sri Sumangala Mawatha, Asgiriya (west of town), T221 5806, www.stbridgets-kandy.com. Pleasant rooms, peaceful surroundings, spacious garden, good food.

D-G Golden View Family Guesthouse, 46 Saranankara Rd, T223 9418. 11 clean, airy a/c and fan rooms, some with balcony, hot water. Good views of lake from rooftop, Chinese restaurant, good atmosphere. Massage treatments offered to residents.

E Lake Inn, 43 Saranankara Rd, T222 2208. 10 rooms, some with balcony. Original guesthouse on this road but no longer the best. Restaurant.

E Lakshmi, 56 Saranankara Rd, T222 2154. 10 simple, bright, clean rooms in one of the road's originals. Good food.

E Sevana Guest House, 84 Peradeniya Rd, T567 4443, www.sevanakandy.com. 15 clean rooms in family-run guesthouse, good food, friendly, excellent value.

E-F Blinkbonnie Tourist Inn, 69 Rajapihilla Mawatha, T222 2007, blinkbonnie@yahoo.com. Clean a/c and fan rooms some with private balcony, good views. Terrace restaurant with Wi-Fi, free pick-up from station.

E-F Expeditor Tourist Inn, 41 Saranankara Rd, T223 8316, www.expeditorkandy.com. Comfortable rooms some with private

balcony, 1st floor with good views, friendly. Wildlife tours, see page 214. Consistently good reports. Top floor, self-contained flat (Rs 3000) should be finished shortly.

E-F Freedom Lodge, 30 Saranankara Rd T2223506. Spotless rooms in family-run guesthouse, super friendly and helpful owners, good food.

E-F Highest View, 129/3 Saranankara Rd, T223 3778, www.highestview.com. 10 sparklingly clean rooms, price varies depending on view – the best are fantastic – and most have balconies. Restaurant with panoramic view over Kandy. Expensive but fast internet available for residents and non-residents. English and German spoken.

E-F Ivy Banks Guest House, 52 Sangaraja Mawatha (opposite **Kandy Gardens Club**), T223 4667. 7 large a/c and fan rooms in the original Ivy Banks.

E-F McLeod Inn, 65a Rajapihilla Mawatha, T222 2832, mcleod@sltnet.lk. 10 clean and pleasant rooms with hot water in the mornings and evenings, the 2 rooms with views are more expensive. The restaurant has the best view of any in this area (can be patronised by non-residents with advance warning). Very friendly and helpful. Popular so book in advance.

E-F Star Light, 15a Saranankara Rd, T223 3573. 5 clean rooms with attached bath and hot water, one larger bungalow in peaceful gardens, good value, tasty food, can be pushy though. Haggling possible if it's quiet.

E-F Thambapanni Guest House, 28 Sangaraja Mawatha (next to **Hotel Suisse**), T222 3234. 8 simple, large, moderately clean rooms, bar-cum-restaurant.

F The Glen, 58 Saranankara Rd, T223 5342. Clean rooms with attached bath, nets, good food, fruit and spice garden, peaceful, friendly family home, good value.

F Green Woods, 34a Sangamitta Mawatha, T223 2970. Quiet and rural location on edge of Udawattekele Sanctuary, doubles plus 1 family room, attached bath, friendly family, good food.

F Lake View Rest, 71 Rajapihilla Mawatha, T223 9421, www.lakeviewrest.com. 15 characterless a/c and fan rooms, with fantastic views. The restaurant looks down over the city and the lake. Family-run, friendly.

F-G Olde Empire Hotel, 21 Deva Veediya, T222 4284. 15 rooms (those with shared bathroom are cheaper) in rambling 150-year-old colonial building. Lovely veranda overlooking temple and lake, excellent location close to Dalada Maligawa. Recommended for atmosphere. Cold water only.

G Pink House, 15 Saranankara Mawatha. Basic but clean rooms, most with shared bath. Pleasant garden, home cooking, popular with backpackers.

G Railway Retiring Rooms, Kandy station, T223 4222. Basic. Book ahead.

G YMCA, 160a Kotugodale Veediya, T222 3529. 11 rooms, common bath. Dormitory accommodation for Rs 250. YMCA sports hall will allow visitors to sleep there during the **Perahera** – together with hundreds of mosquitoes.

West of Kandy *p203, map p202*

A-B Chaaya Citadel, 124 Srimanth Kuda, Ratwatte Mawatha, 5 km west on Mahaweli River, T223 4365, www.chaayahotels.com. 121 large, comfortable a/c rooms (24 deluxe) with attractive door paintings, river views, 2 restaurants, large pool, terrace gardens, popular with groups. Recommended if you can cope with monkeys jumping on the roofs.

B Amaya Hills, Heerassagala, 7 km southwest (near Peradeniya), T447 4022, www.amaya resorts.com. 100 very comfortable rooms including 4 excellent **L** split-level suites in the most stylish hotel in Kandy based on a traditional Kandyan palace, good pool, popular **Le Garage** nightclub (Fri and Sat), Ayurvedic centre, excellent views, well run.

D Peradeniya Rest House, 50 m east of the gardens entrance, T238 8299. Former residence of Captain Dawson, 10 fairly basic fan and a/c rooms, next to the noisy main road, overpriced. Better as a lunch stop.

North of Kandy *map p202*

AL-A Hunas Falls (Jetwing), Elkaduwa, 27 km north of Kandy (1-hr drive on rough road), T247 0041, www.jetwinghotels.com. 31 comfortable a/c rooms (2 suites, Scottish or Japanese styles), hot tubs, pool, boating, fishing, tennis, golf, games room for youngsters, many activities on offer, beautifully located in a tea garden by a waterfall with excellent walks, visits to tea estate, factory, farm (you can milk the cows) and spice gardens. Excellent base for birdwatching.

AL-A Mahaweli Reach, 35 PBA Weerakoon Mawatha, on river by Katugastota Bridge, 5 km north, T447 2727, www.mahaweli. com. 112 large, well-furnished a/c rooms and 4 suites (**LL-L**) in striking building overlooking river, tubs, TV, balconies with excellent river views, superb food (including good buffet choice), very attentive service, Kandy's biggest and best pool, Ayurvedic health centre, extensive sports facilities. Recommended.

East of Kandy *p206, map p202*

Very pleasant accommodation is also available at the **Victoria Golf Club**, see page 214.

AL Earl's Regency (Aitken Spence), 4 km along A26, on Mahaweli River at Thennekumbara, T242 2122, www.aitken spencehotels.com. 84 rooms, plus several suites (US$295-450), some with views overlooking Mahaweli River (and the road) although the best views are to the rear, all facilities, good free-form pool although overall the site is rather characterless.

A Rangala House, 92b Bobebila, Makuldeniya, 1 hr from Kandy on a rough road, T240 0294, T077-600 4687, www.rangalahouse.com. A converted tea-planter's bungalow with beautiful views from the veranda, Close to Knuckles and Corbett's Gap. Excellent walking and birdwatching, solar-heated swimming pool. British and Sri Lankan management. Transport from Kandy available and pick-ups from the airport. Villa basis (US$290) or the

3 rooms can be booked individually, good discount when take the whole place. Excellent food. Recommend 2-night minimum stay.

E Corbet's Rest, in the Knuckles Range, Karambaketiya. 5 cottages built on the hillside that blend well with their surroundings. There are dorms rooms and camping is available, restaurant. Popular with trekkers and birdwatchers, and there is a trekking guide on site.

South of Kandy p207, map p202

F Hantane Bungalow, Hantane Tea Estate, 6 km south, T077-755 5397, www.hantanebungalow.com. 4 rooms in cottage with lovely gardens, beautiful peaceful spot high above Kandy with panoramic views over Knuckles and Hatton Hills, horse riding possible, whole cottage available for rent (**B**).

● Eating

Colombo to Kandy p192

For options see Sleeping, page 207. There are a couple of restaurants inside the orphanage serving the usual fare of vegetable fried rice, etc. There are also restaurants strung out along the main road.

Kandy p195, map p196

The top hotels in the town are good but can be expensive. Sri Lankan rice and curry is cheap but usually only available at lunchtime There are lots of excellent bakeries in town, many of which serve lunch packets too. Beware of touts trying to take you to restaurants where they get a kick-back.

♥♥ Captain's Table, upstairs from **Devon**. Open 1100-1500, 1800-2200. Part of the Devon group, serves Indian and Chinese food. No alcohol. Large screen TV, live music at weekends.

♥♥ Flower Song, 137 Kotugodalle Veediya (1st floor), T448 1650, www.flowerdrum.net. Open 1100-2230. Excellent Chinese, good portions. A/c.

♥♥ Lyon's, 27 Peradeniya Rd, near the clocktower, T222 3073. Open 0800-2000. Specializes in Chinese (big selection), but also does Western food.

♥♥-♥ Devon, 11 Dalada Veediya, T222 4537. Open 0730-2000. The main restaurant has Sri Lankan rice and curry, Western dishes and Chinese. There is an excellent self-service area (open 1100- 1900) for very cheap Sri Lankan/Chinese/ seafood lunch and a fabulous bakery shop. Very popular with locals and tourists, waiters are miserable but the food is worth the scowls. There are other branches around town.

♥♥-♥ Sri Ram, 87 Colombo St, T567 7287. Open 1030-2100. Excellent South Indian, 1st-class service, attractive decor, immaculate. No alcohol. Offers thali and biriyani dishes at lunchtime from 1100-1500, and also sells lunch packets outside (Rs 150).

♥♥-♥ White House, 21 Dalada Veediya, T223 2765. With its white interior and glass display cases this place has a modern, Western feel to it. There are fresh juices and good cakes, and filling Chinese food. Rice and curry is served 1100-1400. The a/c draws in a number of tourists but this place is popular with the locals too.

♥ Bake House and **Delight Bakery**, both on Dalada Veediya are recommended for snacks and cakes.

♥ Muslim Hotel and Restaurant, near the clocktower. Friendly and busy place populated predominantly by locals. Cheap and excellent rice and curry at lunchtimes. Cakes and snacks are sold out the front.

● Bars and clubs

Kandy p195, map p196

There are traditional bars at **Pub Royale**, at **Queens Hotel**, usual beers available plus Three Coins' excellent Sando stout. Also **The Olde Empire**, both with good atmosphere. **Victory**, Colombo St, is a popular locals bar (it also has cheap rooms upstairs) but it's more suited to male travellers.

The Pub, 36 Dalada Veediya (above the Bake House), T223 4868. A popular tourist pub serving uninspired Western food. Draught Lion and Carlsberg are on offer (Rs 450 for 400ml or Rs 1220 for a pitcher), plus a good selection of spirits. There is a pleasant veranda overlooking street, note that the traffic noise can be a bit much during busy periods, and a/c inside. Good atmosphere.

As far as clubs go there are 2 hotel nightclubs. One at **Swiss Residence** and the other at **Amaya Hills** (see Sleeping).

🎭 Entertainment

Kandy *p195, map p196*
There are performances of Kandyan dancing in several parts of the town, most starting at 1730 and lasting 1 hr. Tickets Rs 500 (touts sell tickets around the lake but pay only the printed price). Many are disappointed by the shows, which are heavily geared towards the tourist market. The dances include snippets of several dances and the occasional fire-walking, and thus lack authenticity. They include:
Kandyan Art Association, 72 Sangaraja Mawatha, interesting to see but some have complained that it is 'stale and routine'.
Kandy Lake Club Dance Ensemble,
7 Sangamitta Mawatha (off Malabar St),
T222 3505. Performs dances of Sri Lanka.
YMBA Hall, Kandyan and low country dancing, good value.

🎪 Festivals and events

Kandy *p195, map p196*
Jul/Aug At the end of Jul/Aug is **Esala Perahera** for 10 days (see box, opposite).

🛍 Shopping

Colombo to Kandy *p192*
The roads around Pinnawela Elephant Orphanage are lined with souvenir stalls

selling a wide range of trinkets, not all elephant related. Bargaining is essential. Water is very expensive.

Kandy *p195, map p196*
There is a **Fashion Bug** on Dalada Veediya, as well as a **Cargill's** supermarket (good for water, snacks and toiletries) and the a/c **Kandy City Centre shopping mall** (with a couple of bookshops, a juice bar and a tourist information desk). The **market** near the clocktower can yield good bargains but they rely heavily on your negotiating skills.

Arts and crafts
Try the craft shops on Dalada Veediya near the Temple of the Tooth. Also several antique shops, many along the lake and on Peradeniya Rd.
   Laksala, near Lake Jetty and **Kandyan Art Association**, 72 Sangaraja Mawatha, are government sales outlets where you can watch weavers and craftsmen working on wood, silver, copper and brass, and buy lacquer-ware and batik.
Crafts village set up with government help is at Kalapuraya, Nattarampota, 7 km away (see page 206) .
Kandyan Handicrafts Centre, 10/4 Kotugodale Veediya. Good metalwork.

Batiks and silks
Check out the curio shops on south Bandaranaike Mawatha, towards the botanical gardens, just past the railway station.
Fresco, 901 Peradeniya Rd. For good batiks.
Senani Silk House, next to **Senani Restaurant**. Has a good range of quality silks.

Books
Buddhist Publications Centre, see Directory, below, for Buddhist literature.
Mark Bookshop, 151/1 Dalanda Veediya. Has a good selection of books on local history.
Vijitha Yapa Bookshop, Kotugodella Veediya. Mon-Fri 0800-1730, Sat 0800-1630. Wide range of books and magazines.

Going off with a bang

Esala Perahera (procession), Sri Lanka's greatest festival, is of special significance. It is held in the lunar month of Esala (named after the *Cassia fistula* which blossoms at this time) in which the Buddha was conceived and in which he left his father's home. It has also long been associated with rituals to ensure renewed fertility for the year ahead. The last Kandyan kings turned the Perahera into a mechanism for reinforcing their own power, trying to identify themselves with the gods who needed to be appeased. By focusing on the Tooth Relic, the Tamil kings hoped to establish their own authority and their divine legitimacy within the Buddhist community. The Sri Lankan historian Seneviratne has suggested that fear both of the king and of divine retribution encouraged nobles and peasants alike to come to the Perahera, and witnessing the scale of the spectacle reinforced their loyalty. In 1922, DH Lawrence described his experience as "wonderful – midnight – huge elephants, great flares of coconut torches, princes... tom-toms and savage music and devil dances... black eyes... of the dancers".

Today the festival is a magnificent 10-day spectacle of elephants, drummers, dancers, chieftains, acrobats, whip-crackers, torch bearers and tens of thousands of pilgrims in procession. Buddhists are drawn to the temple by the power of the Tooth Relic rather than by that of the King's authority. The power of the Relic certainly long preceded that of the Kandyan dynasty. Fa Hien described the annual festival in Anuradhapura in AD 399, which even then was a lavish procession in which roads were vividly decorated, elephants covered in jewels and flowers, and models of figures such as Bodhisattvas were paraded. When the tooth was moved to Kandy, the Perahera moved with it.

Following the Tree Planting Ceremony (Kap), the first five days, **Kumbal Perahera**, are celebrated within the grounds of the four *devalas* (temples) – Natha, Vishnu, Skanda and Pattini. The next five days are Randoli Perahera. Torch light processions set off from the temples when the Tooth Relic Casket is carried by the Maligawa Tusker accompanied by magnificently robed temple custodians. Every night the procession grows, moving from the Temple of the Tooth, along Dalada Veediya and DS Senanayake Mawatha to the Adahanamaluwa, where the relic casket is left in the keeping of the temple trustees. The separate temple processions return to their temples, coming out in the early morning for the water cutting ceremony. Originally, the temple guardians went to the lake with golden water pots to empty water collected the previous year. They would then be refilled and taken back to the temple for the following year, symbolizing the fertility protected by the gods. On the 11th day, a daylight procession accompanied the return of the Relic to the Temple. The Day Perahera continues, but today the Tooth Relic itself is no longer taken out.

You don't necessarily need to buy tickets to watch the processions since you can get good views by standing along the street. A good vantage point is that opposite or near to the Queens Hotel as much of that area is slightly better lit (the Presidential vantage point is somewhere nearby) and can provide for slightly better photography.

Markets
Municipal market, west of the lake, is well worthwhile even if you are not planning to bargain for superb Sri Lankan fruit and spices.

Tea
There are various tea outlets at **Ceylon Tea Museum** in Hantane.
Mlesna, 15 Dalada Veediya, T222 8626. Has a fine selection of teas and chinaware and is a very pleasant place to shop (they have another branch in the Kandy City Centre shopping mall).

Textiles
Shops along Colombo St sell material.
Junaid Stores, 19 Yatinuwara Veediya. Outstanding made-to-measure Western-style clothes in quality fabrics, beautifully cut and sewn, and at reasonable prices.

▲ Activities and tours

Kandy *p195, map p196*
Ayurvedic massage
Wedagedara, 76b Deveni Rajasingha Mawatha, T222 6790, www.ayurvedawedagedara.com. Authentic treatments, 1-hr head, body massage and steam bath, resident Ayurveda doctor.

Cricket
Asgiriya Stadium, northwest of town. Hosts Test matches and 1-day internationals.
Pallekelle International Cricket Stadium, east of town. Newer and hosted a match during the 2011 Cricket World Cup.

Golf
Victoria Golf Club, Rajawella, 21 km east, off A26, T237 6376, www.golfsrilanka.com. Excellently maintained 6879-yd, par 73 course surrounded on 3 sides by Victoria Reservoir with the Knuckles Range providing a further attraction. A round, including green fees, caddy, club and shoe hire will cost around Rs 5000 during the week, extra Rs 1000 at weekends. Some larger hotels

will provide free transfer for residents. There are also very pleasant a/c and fan chalets and bungalows available for visitors (you don't have to be golf fans), T077-784 0894.

Riding
Victoria Saddle Club, Rajawella, just before golf course, T237 6376. Offers lessons (Rs 2500), pony rides for young children (Rs 1550) and accompanied trail rides for experienced riders (Rs 2000-3000). Phone in advance for information and booking.

Swimming
See Sleeping, page 207, for details.
Hotel Suisse, has a large pool but during the peak season (Dec-Feb) it gets crowded.
Queens Hotel, has a pool (no chlorine), which is very clean and usually very quiet.
Mahaweli Reach, has the best pool but it is out of town.
Thilanka, has good views over town. Non-residents pay Rs 250 (includes use of towel) at these hotels.
Tourmaline/Topaz's shared uncrowded pool is worth visiting for an afternoon for the spectacular hill-top views.

Tennis
Kandy Garden Club, Sangaraja Mawatha, T2222675. Floodlit for evening use.

Tour operators
Sri Lanka Trekking, c/o **Expeditor Tourist Inn** (see Sleeping, page 209), T071-720 4722, www.srilankatrekking.com. Run by Mr Şumane Bandara Illangantilake who has 40 years' experience in leading small groups on tours of the island. Specializes in trekking, nature (he can recognize over 200 bird calls) and wildlife tours as well as rafting. Trips arranged according to experience ranging from 'smooth' to 'adventure' lasting 4-14 days. Mr Şumane's pupil, **Ravi Desappriya**, specializes in trips to the Knuckles Range, T071-499 7666, www.knucklesrange.com. These can range from 1 day to 3 days/2 nights.

Whitewater rafting
There are opportunities for rafting on the Mahaweli River, starting from near the **Chaaya Citadel**, and in the Dumbara Hills.

⊖ Transport

Colombo to Kandy p192
Bus
To Heneratgoda from **Colombo** and **Negombo** buses take 1½ hrs respectively. **Pinnawela** is 6 km northeast of Kegalla along the B32. Turn off at Udamalla if in car. Regular buses depart from **Kandy** (Goods Shed) to **Kegalla** (1 hr). Change at Kegalla clocktower for a (regular) **Rambukkana** bus, which stops at **Pinnawela** (10 mins). Some buses will drop you at the junction for Pinnawela on the A1.

Train
For **Heneratgoda Botanical Gardens** most Colombo-Kandy trains stop at **Gampaha** and from here take a 3-wheeler. Trains from Kandy to **Rambukkana (Pinnawela)** (short bus or 3-wheeler ride from the orphanage) at 0630, 1040, 1530, 1625 and 1810 (1½ hrs). Enquire at station for return times. Trains continue to **Colombo Fort** (except the 1810), taking 2½-3 hrs.

Kandy p195, map p196
Bus
The **Clocktower Bus Stand** and **Market Place Bus Stand** are for buses to 'local' destinations (including places near Kandy such as Peradeniya, Katugastota and Hantane (see below). **Goods Shed Bus Stand** near the railway station is for long-distance buses. The tourist information desk in the Kandy shopping mall (see page 212) is an excellent source of up-to-date information on bus times, where to catch them from and where to get off.

Local Buses from the Clocktower Bus Stand drop visitors nearby the **Gadaladeniya Temple**. There are hourly buses between Kandy and **Embekke village**, a short walk

away from the *devale*. For **Nattarampota** bus No 655 from the Market Bus Stand drops you at the suspension bridge across the river from the **Degaldoruwa Cave Temple**. For **Medawela**, bus No 603 departs from the Clocktower Bus Stand near the Central Market in Kandy. For the **Ceylon Tea Museum** take bus No 655 (Uduwela bus), from the Clocktower Bus Stand. Get off at the 4th mile post about 30 mins later, alternatively take a 3-wheeler. This bus runs on to **Hindagala Temple**. Regular buses to **Peradeniya** from the Market Place Bus Station, which stop outside the entrance.

Long distance Frequent buses to **Colombo**, Rs 100, 3½ hrs, last bus 2200; a/c buses (intercity express) leave from Station Rd and take 2½ hrs, Rs 250, but are often congested, nerve-wracking and far less pleasant than the train. To **Anuradhapura**, every 30 mins, 4 hrs. Both CTB and private buses run approximately every 30 mins to **Nuwara Eliya**, **Dambulla** and **Badulla**. For **Polonnaruwa** and **Trincomalee** (5 hrs), a/c buses leave every 2 hrs. There is 1 direct bus a day to **Sigiriya** at 0800.

Car hire
If time is very limited for sightseeing, it is possible to hire a car for the day to visit **Dambulla**, **Sigiriya** and **Polonnaruwa** (ask your hotel or guesthouse). While this is a very full day it can be very rewarding, although it is preferable to spend more time visiting this circuit.

Train
Tickets on the Observation Car between Kandy and **Colombo** or **Badulla** should be reserved up to 10 days in advance (window open 0530-1730). Return tickets are valid for 10 days. Intercity express to **Colombo** at 0610 and 1500 (1st class Rs 360 including observation car fare, 2nd class Rs 190, 3rd class Rs 105, 2½ hrs), plus slower trains stopping at **Rambukanna** (for **Pinnawela**, see above) at 0140, 0630, 1040, 1530 and 1625 (2nd class Rs 190, 3rd class Rs 105,

3¼ hrs). For coastal destinations south of Colombo, such as **Hikkaduwa** and **Galle**, take the 0525, which travels on to **Matara** (2nd class Rs 360, 3rd class Rs 195, 7¼ hrs). For **Kurunegala**, **Anuradhapura** and other destinations north change at Polgahawela. Train to **Badulla** (Rs 750/Rs 270/Rs 145, 7¾ hrs) leave at 0820 and 2200, via **Nanu Oya** (for **Nuwara Eliya**, Rs 300/Rs 160/Rs 90, 4 hrs), **Haputale** (5½ hrs, Rs 380, Rs 210, Rs 115), **Bandarawela** (6 hrs, Rs 420, Rs 230, Rs 125) and **Ella** (6½ hrs, Rs 440, Rs 240, Rs 130). Observation car fee Rs 50 extra. Trains to **Matale** (Rs 100, Rs 50, Rs 25, 1¼ hrs) at 0500, 0710, 1020, 1400, 1710 and 1840.

ⓘ Directory

Colombo to Kandy *p192*
Banks There is a branch of the **Hatton National Bank** opposite the orphanage.
Internet There are a couple of internet places on the Elephant Bath Rd, Pinnawela.

Kandy *p195, map p196*
Banks Plenty of banks are in town, most of which have ATMs and foreign exchange desks. ATMs at **Bank of Ceylon**, **Commercial Bank**, **Hatton National Bank**, **HSBC**, **Nations Trust**, **People's Bank** and **Sampath Bank**.
Buddhist institutes Buddhist Publication Centre, 54 Sangharaja Mawatha, T222 3679, open 0900-1630, good library, a bookshop and information on courses on Buddhism and meditation where serious visitors are welcome. **Theruwan Meditation**

Centre, Uduwela (take bus No 655, then walk 2 km). **Cultural centres** Alliance Française, 412 Peradeniya Rd, T222 4432. Has a library and also shows films (Mon-Sat, 1100-1700). **British Council**, 88/3 Kotugodella Veediya, T222 2410, www.britishcouncil.org/srilanka. Has a library plus old British papers and magazines (Tue-Sat, 0900-1700). **Embassies and consulates** Assistant High Commissioner of India, 31 Rajapihilla Mawatha, T223 4545, Mon-Fri 0830-1030, will issue Indian visas in a day. **Internet** Many hotels and guesthouses have internet access but are not the cheapest. There are a number of places offering internet in Kandy town and the going rate is Rs 60-70 per hr, including **SIT**, 77 Kotugodale Veediya, T220 1610, open 0800-2000, and **Sivaram**, 65 Kotugodale Veediya, T222 2417, open 0800-2200, machines in separate booths. If the walk down the hill is too much, **Highest View Guesthouse** (see page 209) has new computers with fast connection but is expensive (Rs 160 per hr). **Medical services** General Hospital, T222 2261. New Kandy Dispensary, Brownearigg St. **Post office** Opposite the railway station, 0700-2100, speedpost, EMS (before 1000), internet Rs 40 per hr (minimum 20), Poste Restante, Philatelic Bureau. Branch on Senanayake Veediya (crossing with Kande Veediya). **Telephone** Calling outside hotels is cheaper and there are a number of places advertising international calls (IDD), as well as Skype capability. For those with Sri Lankan phone cards, it isn't hard to find a call box.

Central Highlands

Steep mountain passes snake up through the brooding highland landscape south of Kandy, reaching their pinnacle in the Peak Wilderness Sanctuary, where the plateau of the Horton Plains represents the island's last stretch of high montane forest. It was not until the 19th century, and the coming of the British, that wild and impenetrable rainforest gave way to the familiar, intensively cultivated tea plantations of today. The British legacy has lingered longer here, most notably in the anachronistic hill station of Nuwara Eliya, nicknamed 'Little England'. Equally distinctive is the Indian Tamil culture, which dates back to the same era when migrant plantation workers were brought in from southern India. But the area's greatest appeal lies in the natural beauty of its scenery, carved by mountain streams and powerful waterfalls, and its cool, crisp air. ▸▸ *For listings, see pages 230-235.*

Kandy to the Central Highlands

By either rail or road, the journey up into the Central Highlands offers some spectacular views, climbing through tea estates and passing nearby some magnificent waterfalls. From Kandy you can either follow the direct route to Nuwara Eliya along the A5, or take the much longer but very scenic road over the Ginigathena pass to Hatton, from which a couple of hours drive takes you to Dalhousie, the most practical base for climbing Adam's Peak, Sri Lanka's holiest mountain. Both the main routes into the highlands start by crossing the Mahaweli Ganga, passing through Peradeniya and then following the river valley to the pleasant town of Gampola, a mediaeval Sinhalese capital. The Niyamgampaya *vihara* which has some interesting stone carvings, is built on the original 14th-century temple which was mostly built of brick and wood and largely disappeared.

To Nuwara Eliya
From Gampola a road leads off towards the Ginigathena Pass for the alternative Adam's Peak route through the tea estates of the Hatton-Dickoya region (see page 226), but most people continue on the more direct A5. Shortly after Gampola the road crosses the river and starts the long climb of almost 1000 m up through some of the highest tea gardens in the world to Nuwara Eliya.

Pussellawa is a busy shopping centre and has a rest house where you can stop for a meal or a drink. The tea gardens begin just below Pussellawa. The craggy hill **Monaragala** appears to the south. Legends tell that this is where King Dutthagamenu hid in a rock while escaping from his father, who had imprisoned him.

Some 5 km later the road passes the Helbodda Oya river. By **Ramboda**, you have climbed to 1000 m. There is a fine 100-m waterfall with a twin stream on the Puna Ela, a tributary of the Mahaweli River, just off the road which can be seen from the bazaar. It may be possible to visit the **Rang Buddha Tea Estate**.

After 54 km from Kandy the road climbs through a series of hairpins to the **Weddamulla Estate**, with great views to the west over Kothmale Reservoir. The area is covered with pine trees and ferns.

The 415-ha **Labookellie Estate** ⓘ *T052-223 5146, free*, one of the island's largest, follows the twisty road for miles along the hillside. Teams of women pluck the tea on fairly steep slopes, picking in all weathers – they use plastic sacks as raincoats. The women labourers are all Tamils, descendants of the labourers who migrated from Tamil Nadu before independence. They are keen to pose for photographs, and as they earn very little, tipping is customary. The tea factory, an enormous corrugated iron building, welcomes visitors to drop in to the delightful tea centre and sample a free cup of tea, indulge in a piece of chocolate cake (Rs 40), and perhaps to buy a packet or two of tea though there is no pressure to do so. The tour is quite informative – all stages of the process from picking, drying, oxidation and grading are shown if you go in the morning. There are free guided tours of the factory, available in English, German, French and Italian, which run every 20 minutes.

From the Labookellie Estate it is a short climb through more tea gardens to the narrow pass above Nuwara Eliya, and the road then drops down into the sheltered hollow in the hills now occupied by the town.

The Highlands

Kandy to Hatton and Adam's Peak

The alternative, much longer, route to Nuwara Eliya takes you close to the holy mountain of **Adam's Peak**, running close to the railway line for much of the way. It is a full day's journey, for which the train, despite its snail-like pace, offers a relaxing alternative.

From Gampola, the B43 branches to the right towards Nawalapitiya and then joins the A7, the main Colombo–Nuwara Eliya road, at the Ginigathena Pass (38 km). There are magnificent views at the top, although they are often obscured by cloud, for the pass is in one of the wettest areas of Sri Lanka. **Ginigathena** itself is a small bazaar for the tea estates and their workers. A right turn here takes you west on the A7 down to the attractively set village of Kitulgala (see page 229), or into the highlands where the road winds up through a beautiful valley, surrounded by green, evenly picked tea bushes to

Watawala (10 km) and past the **Carolina Falls** nearby, which are spectacular in the wet season. It then follows the left bank of the Mahawelia Ganga to Hatton. The air becomes noticeably cooler, and occasionally there are views right across the plains to Colombo and the Kelaniya Valley. ▶▶ *For details of the route from Hatton to Nuwara Eliya (in reverse), see page 226.*

Nuwara Eliya → *Phone code: 052. Colour map 3, A5. Population: 26,000. Altitude: 1990 m.*

Nuwara Eliya (pronounced Noo-ray-lee-ya) is one of those curiosities of history – a former British hill station. Vestiges of colonial rule are found everywhere, from the fine golf course threading through town to the creaking grand hotels, complete with overboiled vegetables and leaky roofs. Today, Sri Lanka's highest (and coolest) town remains a popular escape from the plains at long weekends and especially during the April 'season'. Visitors respond to Nuwara Eliya's fading appeal in different ways, some delighted by the tongue-in-cheek revelry in its colonial past; others are turned off by the town's lack of civic pride, depressed by its English climate (nights can get very cold), or simply confused by its archaism. For most though Nuwara Eliya represents nostalgic fun. This is also excellent walking country and a useful base for visiting Horton Plains.

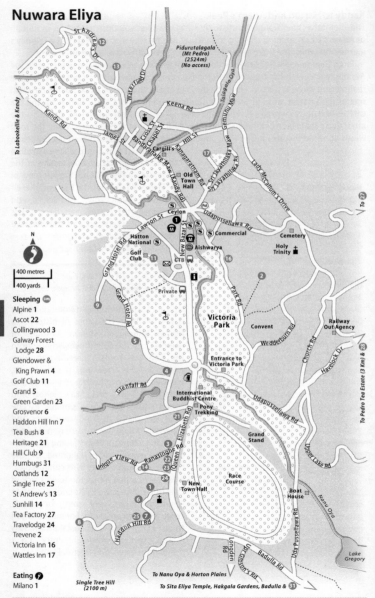

Nuwara Eliya

Sleeping
Alpine 1
Ascot 22
Collingwood 3
Galway Forest
  Lodge 28
Glendower &
  King Prawn 4
Golf Club 11
Grand 5
Green Garden 23
Grosvenor 6
Haddon Hill Inn 7
Tea Bush 8
Heritage 21
Hill Club 9
Humbugs 31
Oatlands 12
Single Tree 25
St Andrew's 13
Sunhill 14
Tea Factory 27
Travelodge 24
Trevene 2
Victoria Inn 16
Wattles Inn 17

Eating
Milano 1

Ins and outs → *Never go out without an umbrella.*

Getting there The train is a scenic though time-consuming alternative to the bus. Booking is essential for the Observation Car, especially during busy periods. During the pilgrimage season it is often full as far as Hatton. The train station is 6 km away at Nanu Oya, a short bus or taxi ride away (Rs 500, avoid the touts who will offer free transport provided you go to a hotel of their choice – buses are always available and most hotels will arrange for taxis to collect you if contacted in advance). Ask to be dropped near the Town Hall if you are planning to stay in the southern part of town where most of the hotels are clustered up the hillside opposite the racecourse. Buses arrive in the centre of town.

Getting around The town is fairly compact, so it is easy to get around on foot but carry a torch at night to avoid holes in the pavement leading to the sewers.

Best time to visit The town really comes alive during the April 'season' (see box, page 233) though accommodation is very expensive and hard to find at this time. It is often cold at night, especially during January and March, when there may be frosts, though these are also the driest months.

Tourist information Tourist information is available at www.nuwaraeliya.org.

Background

In 1846, when Samuel Baker first visited the semi-enclosed valley surrounded by hills on the west and overlooked by Pidurutalagala, the island's highest peak, he singled it out as an ideal spot for a hill country retreat. Today, with its television aerials, the highest on the island, and modern hotels, golf course and country walks, his rural idyll has been brought into the modern world.

'The City of Light' was a favourite hill station of the British and it still retains some distinctive features. The main street is the usual concrete jungle of small shops with the pink post office being an obvious exception. One of the distinctive features of Baker's plans was the introduction of European vegetables and fruit. Flowers are extensively cultivated for export to Colombo and abroad. The road out of Nuwara Eliya towards Hakgala passes through intensively cultivated fields of vegetables and a short walk up any of the surrounding hillsides shows how far intensive cultivation methods have transformed Nuwara Eliya into one of Sri Lanka's most productive agricultural areas.

The key to Nuwara Eliya's prosperity lay in the railway connection from Colombo to the hills. The line was extended from Talawakele to Nanu Oya in 1885, and a very steep narrow gauge line right into Nuwara Eliya was opened in 1910, but subsequently closed to passenger traffic in 1940 as buses began to provide effective competition.

Without the pretensions or political significance of the Raj hill stations in India, Nuwara Eliya nonetheless was an active centre of an English-style social life, with country sports including hunting, polo, cricket and tennis. It has retained all the paraphernalia of a British hill station, with its colonial houses, parks, an 18-hole golf course and trout streams (there are brown trout in the lake for anglers). The real clue to its past perhaps lies in its extensive private gardens where dahlias, snap-dragons, petunias and roses grow amongst well-kept lawns.

A superior cup

Many concur that Sri Lankan tea, with its fine, rich flavour and bright, golden colour, is the best in the world. After textiles, tea remains Sri Lanka's second biggest export, and you will notice the distinctive cropped bushes all across the hill country. Although introduced by the British, the tea industry is a source of immense national pride, and recent years have seen some ingenious methods of capitalising on the country's heritage. Near Nuwara Eliya, an old factory has been converted into a magnificent hotel, retaining its original features, while the world's first tea museum is open up near Kandy. A visit to a working tea factory is also recommended.

Tea famously originated in China (though one legend suggests it was introduced by an Indian missionary) but it was not until 1833 that the Chinese monopoly on exporting tea was abolished, and the East India Company began to grow tea in Assam in India. In Sri Lanka, the first tea bushes were planted in 1849 by James Taylor on a cleared hill slope just southeast of Kandy. It was an attempt at experimenting with a crop to replace the unfortunate diseased coffee. The experiment paid off and Sri Lanka today is the world's third biggest producer of tea, and the largest exporter, with a 20% share of global demand. The bushes now grow from sea level to the highest slopes, though the lush 'low-grown' variety lacks the flavour, colour and aroma which characterise bushes grown above 1000 m. The slow-growing bushes at greater heights produce the best flavour and aroma when picked carefully by hand – just two leaves and bud.

The old 'orthodox' method of tea processing produces the aromatic lighter coloured liquor of the Golden Flowery Orange Pekoe in its most superior grade. The fresh leaves are dried by fans on 'withering troughs' to reduce the moisture content and then rolled and pressed to express the juices which coat the leaves. These are then left to ferment in a controlled humid environment in order to produce the desired aroma. Finally the leaves are dried by passing them through a heated drying chamber and then graded – the unbroken being the best quality, down to the 'fannings' and 'dust'.

The more common 'crushing, tearing, curling' (CTC) method produces tea which gives a much darker liquor. It uses machinery which was invented in Assam in 1930. The process allows the withered leaves to be given a short, light roll before engraved metal rollers distort the leaves in a fraction of a second. The whole process can take as little as 18 hours.

Despite its name and heritage, the Ceylon tea industry (as it is still called) has lost some of its dominance in the world market, cheaper producers having wrestled away traditional export markets. Britain, for example, which once absorbed 65% of total production, now only represents 3%, importing much of its lower grade tea from East Africa. Today Russia and the Middle East are the industry's biggest customers. In recent years however, privatisation and advances in production techniques have improved yields, and producers have responded to trends in the market, beginning to embrace the vogue for green, organic and flavoured teas.

Sights

There are attractive walks round the small town, which has lawns, parks, an Anglican church and the nostalgic **Hill Club**. To the south of town are the racecourse and Lake Gregory (about 1 km from the town centre), for which boats which can be hired. Lawns and lakeside paths are currently under construction here to make the area more appealing to visitors.

Nuwara Eliya is popular birdwatching country, and there are two excellent areas close to town. **Galway's Land Bird Sanctuary** ① *0600-1730, Rs 100*, covers 60 ha to the north of Lake Gregory, while in **Victoria Park** ① *centre of town, 0700-1830, Rs 60, children Rs 30*, 38 species have been identified. The park is pleasant, well kept and provides a welcome escape from the congested New Bazaar. Take care when walking along the outside of the park where the metal fence is in poor repair and has some sharp, rusty spikes.

Pidurutalagala (Mount Pedro), the island's highest peak at 2524 m, is off limits to climbers for security of the island's first TV transmitter. **Single Tree Hill**, at 2100 m, is an alternative. The path to it winds up from Haddon Hill Road, beyond **Haddon Hill Lodge** (southwest of town), towards the transmission tower, through cultivated terraces and woods. The path then follows the ridge towards the north, through Shantipura, a small village and the island's highest settlement, eventually returning close to the golf course. This walk gives excellent views across Nuwara Eliya and beyond and takes three to four hours.

Pedro Tea Estate ① *Boralanda, T222 2016*, 3 km away, still uses some original machinery and is less commercialized than other estates. There are some very pleasant walks through the plantations here, especially down to the tank and to Warmura Ella (ask at the Tea Centre). The estate can be visited on a Boralanda bus or it is a taxi ride away. Alternatively, for those feeling active it is a very attractive walk. The **Tea Factory**, at Kandapola, which, as well as having been innovatively converted into an award-winning hotel (see page 230), still retains a small working unit, is well worth a visit. The original oil driven engine, now powered by electricity, is still in place and switched on occasionally. It is a 30-minute taxi ride away and is a good place for lunch. **Labookellie Tea Estate** is only 15 km away (see page 217).

Excursions

On the route to Hakgala Gardens you pass **Sita Eliya Temple**, a temple to Rama's wife which is thought to mark the spot where she was kept a prisoner by King Ravana. There are magnificent views.

Hakgala Botanical Gardens ① *www.botanicgardens.gov.lk/hakgala, 0800-1700, Rs 800, students/children Rs 400*, is 10 km from Nuwara Eliya. Established in 1861, it is located within a Strict Natural Reserve, and was once a Cinchona plantation. This delightful garden is now famous for its roses. The name Hakgala or 'Jaw Rock' comes from the story in the epic *Ramayana* in which the Monkey god takes back a part of the mountainside in his jaw when asked by Rama to seek out a special herb. There are monkeys here which are quite used to visitors. The different sections covering the hillside include a plant house, Japanese garden, wild orchid collection, old tea trails, arboretum, fruit garden, rock garden and oaks. Buses bound for Welimada or Bandarawela pass the entrance.

Horton Plains can be visited on a day trip if you have a car, but involve an early start (breakfast at 0600) as the plains have a reputation for bad weather after midday.

Randenigala Reservoir is good for birdwatching and in the early morning, elephants. It can easily be visited as a day trip, but is also a good camping spot (see page 295).

Horton Plains National Park → *Colour map 3, B5. Altitude: 2130 m. 32 km from Nuwara Eliya, 38 km from Haputale.*

The island's highest and most isolated plateau is contiguous with the Peak Wilderness Sanctuary. Bleak and windswept, the landscape is distinctive and unlike any other on the island. It has been compared to both the Scottish highlands and the savannah of Africa. Most people come on a day trip to see the spectacular views from the sheer 700-m drop at World's End though there is more to see within the sanctuary. In recent years, park fees have spiralled and budget travellers are increasingly choosing to forego a visit.

Ins and outs → *Carry food and water.*

Getting there Horton Plains is accessible by car from Nuwara Eliya and Haputale. Both journeys take around 1½ to two hours. Ohiya, 11 km away, is the nearest train station from which you can take a taxi or walk to the park entrance. By train, Haputale is the closest base for a day trip though World's End will probably have clouded over by the time you arrive. If you are prepared to hire transport, Nuwara Eliya may be the most convenient option for day trips. Many guesthouses and hotels organize tours. Trekkers can come from Talawakale on the Agrapatana–Diyagama track or from Belihuloya via Nagarak, though this requires serious preparation.

Getting around Horton Plains is unique amongst Sri Lanka's national parks in that walking is permitted. Keep to the footpaths, especially if misty. A number of people go missing each year.

Best time to visit The best months to visit are April and August. The winter months tend to be the driest, with the best visibility, though can be very cold. The weather can be foul at any time and it gets cold at night so come prepared. For World's End it is essential to arrive by 0930-1000, after which the area usually clouds over for the day. Avoid visiting at weekends and public holidays when it can be very noisy and busy.

Tourist information Charges for foreigners add up to around US$20 (children under 12 US$10), and fees are collected at the ticket offices situated at either end of the road bisecting the park. Locals and tourists have to pay just to use the road. There is a **visitor information centre** ① *at Farr Inn, 0600-1830*, where information on the park's flora and fauna is displayed.

Background

Horton Plains' conservation importance lies in its role as the catchment area of most of the island's major rivers. Covering 3160 ha, the area was declared a national park in 1988, though had received some protection since 1873 when logging above 1500 m was prohibited. The plains are named after former British governor Sir Robert Horton.

There is a mixture of temperate montane forest and wet patana grassland. The prominent canopy tree is the keena, its white flowers contrasting with the striking red rhododendrons lower down, which makes them in some ways reminiscent of a Scottish moor. In other ways, the gently undulating grassland has an almost savannah-like feel with stunted forest on the hill tops. There is widespread concern about the condition of the forest which appears to be slowly dying. Blame seems to be attached to the acidification of rain.

The bleak and windswept area harbours many wild animals, including a few leopards though no longer any elephants. You may see sambar (sambhur), especially at dawn and dusk close to the entrance, and possibly toque macaques, purple-faced leaf monkeys and horned lizards. Wildlife has suffered at the hands of tourism though, with visitors' discarded plastic bags responsible for the death of large numbers of sambar. There is a rich variety of hill birds, and a number of endemics, including the dull blue flycatcher, Sri Lanka white-eye, and yellow-eared bulbul as well as a good range of butterflies. Some are disappointed by how difficult it is to see the wildlife; it is not impossible to visit and spot little more than the invasive crow. However by being attentive and patient an interesting variety of flora and fauna can be observed.

Sights
Most people will take the well-trodden 4.5-km bridle path to **World's End**, returning in a loop via the scenic **Baker Falls**. The walk takes three to four hours and it is essential to visit early in the morning before the mists close in, after which only a wall of cloud is visible.

Horton Plains

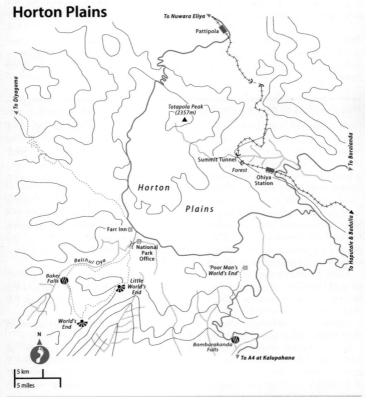

World's End The 4.5-km walk takes from 40 minutes to 1½ hours depending on how many times you stop to admire the view. You cross a small stream with lots of croaking frogs before passing across the grassland and then descending a few hundred metres through the forest. You first come to Little (or Small) World's End (2.5 km), a mere 260-m cliff overlooking a ravine (more a wide valley) with a tiny village 700 m below. You can look along the sheer cliff face to the big green rock which marks (Big) World's End about 1 km away. The path continues another 2 km up the escarpment to the astonishing (Big) World's End, a spectacular precipice with a 1050-m drop. On a clear day, you can apparently see the coast, but more realistically, it is the blue-green lake of the Samanala Wewa reservoir project. Once at Big World's End, take the small path up the hill. After only a few yards, there is a split in the rock which gives an excellent view of the valley below.

Baker's Falls Return to the main path, and a track drops down to a valley along which a 2-km walk leads to a small forested escarpment. A climb and then a scrambling descent (very slippery for the last few metres so take care) take you to the picturesque Baker's Falls. The water here is deliciously cool and refreshing, though it is said to be unsafe to swim. From Baker's Falls it is an easy 3-km walk back along the river, passing the attractive **Governor's Pool** (again prohibited to swim) on the way.

Poor Man's World's End Nicknamed Poor Man's World's End, this used to be the free alternative to paying national park fees. At the time of writing is was still accessible by several routes via the local tea plantations, but this may have changed. Ask locally for directions, or at guesthouses in Haputale.

Nuwara Eliya to Adam's Peak → *For details of the route from Kandy, see page 217.*

From Nuwara Eliya many travellers continue east to Badulla or Ella via Welimada, see page 236, or southeast from the Horton Plains to Haputale and Bandarawela, see page 240. Alternatively you can head west to Adam's Peak, and then return to Kandy, or back to Colombo, via Kitulgala. The road to Adam's Peak takes you past some spectacular waterfalls and winds through the heart of some of the finest tea-growing country in the world. For much of the way it is above 2000 m.

From Nuwara Eliya, the A7 runs through dryer country in the rain shadow of hills to the southwest and northeast. It climbs to Nanu Oya and Lindula, where a right turn leads up a beautiful mountain road to Agrapatana. In Talawakele, **Sri Lanka's Tea Research Institute** has played a major role in improving Sri Lanka's tea production (visits are possible if you get a permit from the Institute's office). The road drops as it crosses the railway line and winds through the tea estates of Dimbula.

Along this stretch, there are some magnificent views from the road. You first spy the 80-m **St Clair Falls**, dropping in three cascades down to the valley below. Opposite the viewpoint for the 98-m **Devon Falls**, an enormous bronze tea boiler introduces you to the St Clair Tea Centre, a good place to stop for a brew.

Hatton is one of the major centres of Sri Lanka's tea industry, and the base from which most pilgrims trek to the top of Adam's Peak, but the town itself is dirty and uninspiring.

It is a tortuously winding route from Hatton through Norwood up to Maskeliya at 1280 m, skirting the attractive Castlereagh Reservoir, an enormous HEP programme. If open it is worth stopping by the immaculately kept small stone **Anglican Church** (1878) at Warleigh in a picturesque setting overlooking the tank (give a donation). As you cross

Frond farewell

In 1911 Hermann Hesse wrote an evocative description of his climb to the top of Pidurutalagala at the end of a journey round India and Ceylon. He wrote, "To bid India a proper and dignified farewell in peace and quiet, on one of the last days before I left I climbed alone in the coolness of a rainy morning to the highest summit in Ceylon, Pidurutalagala.

The cool green mountain valley of Nuwara Eliya was silvery in the light morning rain, typically Anglo-Indian with its corrugated roofs and its extravagantly extensive tennis courts and golf links. The Singhalese were delousing themselves in front of their huts or sitting shivering, wrapped in woollen shawls, the landscape, resembling the Black Forest, lay lifeless and shrouded.

The path began to climb upward through a little ravine, the straggling roofs disappeared, a swift brook roared below me. Narrow and steep, the way led steadily upward for a good hour. The rain gradually stopped, the cool wind subsided, and now and again the sun came out for minutes at a time.

I had climbed the shoulder of the mountain, the path now led across flat country, springy moor, and several pretty mountain rills. Here the rhododendrons grow more luxuriantly than at home, three time a man's height.

I was approaching the last ascent of the mountain, the path suddenly began to climb again, soon I found myself surrounded once more by forest, a strange, dead, enchanted forest where trunks and branches, intertwined like serpents, stared blindly at me through long thick, whitish beards of moss; a damp, bitter smell of foliage and fog hung between.

Then the forest came to an end; I stepped, warm and somewhat breathless, out onto a gray heath, like some landscape in Ossian, and saw the bare summit capped by a small pyramid close before me. A high, cold wind was blowing against me, I pulled my coat tight and slowly climbed the last hundred paces.

What I saw there was the grandest and purest impression I took away from all Ceylon. The wind had just swept clean the whole long valley of Nuwara Eliya, I saw, deep and immense, the entire high mountain system of Ceylon piled up in mighty walls, and in its midst the beautiful, ancient and holy pyramid of Adam's Peak. Beside it at an infinite depth and distance lay the flat blue sea, in between a thousand mountains, broad valleys, narrow ravines, rivers and waterfalls, in countless folds, the whole mountainous island on which ancient legend places paradise."

the dam, which is protected by the military, and pass through the new town of Maskeliya (the old one was flooded to make way for the tank), the pyramid shape of Adam's Peak begins to loom into view, looking for all the world like the Paramount Pictures logo. The air is already strikingly fresh, and the higher road is lined with tropical ferns. Stalls selling food and souvenirs for the pilgrims line the road as you descend into the makeshift settlement of Dalhousie.

Adam's Peak (Sri Pada) → *Phone code: 051. Colour map 3, B4. Altitude: 2260 m.*

Sacred to devotees of three of Sri Lanka's major religions, Adam's Peak is one of the island's most important pilgrimage sites. The giant 'footprint' on the summit is believed to be an imprint left by either the Buddha (hence 'Sri Pada', or 'Sacred Footprint') or Siva (Sivan Adipadham) by Hindus, or Adam by Muslims. Regardless of belief, the perfectly conical shaped mountain is worth the climb, both for the buzz and for the magnificent views, especially in the first rays of dawn.

Ins and outs

Getting there The shorter (7 km) and more frequently used route is from the north, starting at Dalhousie (pronounced Dell-house). Much steeper, more difficult and more meritorious (for pilgrims) is the southern route from the Ratnapura side (11 km), starting from Palabadelle (see page 117). The really intrepid and fit could climb from Dalhousie and then walk down towards Ratnapura, a long but rewarding day.

Best time to visit The pilgrimage season runs from **Unduwap Poya** (December) to **Wesak Poya** (May), reaching its peak mid-season at **Medin Poya**. At this time, there is a constant stream of pilgrims and the top can get very crowded. The climb is still quite possible at other times of year though you will need a torch at night as the path is not lit. It often rains in the afternoon here, especially in the off-season. If it is wet, there will be leeches on the steps (see box, page 41). If climbing out of season, take a guide or climb with other people, the mountain can be dark and lonely.

Tourist information Further reading, Markus Akland, *The Sacred Footprint: A Cultural History of Adam's Peak* (Bangkok: Orchid Press, 2001).

Background

Each religion has its own myths describing the creation of the mountain's famous footprint. By far the most powerful is the Buddhist tradition, which states that the Buddha visited the mountain on his third visit to Sri Lanka on Wesak eight years to the day after Enlightenment, and was invited by the god Saman to leave an imprint. For Hindus, this is Siva's footprint, or Vishnu's in the form of the Buddha, while some Muslims believe that this was where Adam first landed on Earth after the Fall.

The mountain has been climbed for at least 1000 years. King Vijayabahu (1055-1110) built shelters along its route, work continued by Parakaramabahu II (1225-1269) who cleared jungle and built a road and bridges to the mountain. Marco Polo commented on the chains provided for pilgrims in the 13th century, while Muslim traveller Ibn Battuta visited in the 14th century and described the two approach routes still used, labelling them the Adam and Eve tracks. He warned that "anyone who goes by [the Adam – ie northern – route] is not considered... to have made the pilgrimage at all". He also mentioned the leeches which can still be a problem to this day.

The climb → *For the climb itself, it is best to base yourself in Dalhousie.*

Most people do the walk by moonlight, setting off from Dalhousie around 0300, and arriving in time to see the dawn when the sun rises behind the conical peak, casting an extraordinary shadow across the misty plains to the west. Note that it is very cold up here until well after sunrise so it is essential to take warm clothing.

It takes about three hours to reach the top (though allow an hour either way depending on your fitness). The path is clearly marked throughout, beginning fairly gently but rapidly becoming steeper, with constant steps from about halfway. The climb is completely safe, even the steepest parts being protected, and lined with teashops and stalls if you need a break. In the company of pilgrims the trek is particularly rewarding but it can be very crowded. You may notice the first-timers with white cloth on their heads.

At the top, there are some breathtaking views across the surrounding hills, though the peak itself, only 50 m sq, is not particularly impressive. Steps lead up to the sacred footprint, on top of a 4-m rock, which is covered by a huge stone slab in which has been carved another print. Pilgrims cluster round, throwing offerings in to the 1-m hollow, before moving to the Saman shrine up another flight of stairs where thanks are given. Pilgrims then ring one of the two bells at the summit, each chime representing a successful ascent. There are three official processions a day – at dawn, midday and dusk – with music, offerings and prayers, though many people perform their own ceremonies at other times.

Kitulgala → *Phone code: 036. Colour map 2, A3. 95 km from Colombo. For the route from Hatton to Kitulgala (in reverse) see page 217; for the road to Colombo (in reverse), see page 114.*

Kitulgala is a small, peaceful village lining the main road descending gently from the highlands to Colombo. It lies on the banks of the Kelaniya River and is known as a centre for *kitul* honey production. Aside from its beautiful setting, it has two other claims to fame which makes it well worth lingering. The first is that it provided the main location for the filming of David Lean's Oscar-winning film, *Bridge on the River Kwai*. You can wander down to the banks of the river to the original site of the bridge, signposted about 1 km before the Plantation Hotel (where you can pick up an interesting history of the filming), and guides will appear to show you the way. The area is surprisingly small, compared to the real bridge in Kanchanaburi, Thailand, and there is not much to see now, except for the concrete foundations of the bridge hewn into two rocks either side of the *ganga*, but for those familiar with the film the area will be recognizable. The sandbar from which the bridge was blown up has now been reclaimed by the jungle.

The other major reason to visit Kitulgala is that it is the base for the country's best **whitewater rafting**, which can be arranged at the local hotels or in Colombo. The rapids are grade III (grade IV during floods) and tend to start 5-6 km upriver, passing through six rapids to the 'bridge' area, where you can stop for a swim. There are some excellent places to stay in Kitulgala, so it is well worth a stop on the way from Colombo.

Some 5 km inland, near **Royal River Resort** (see page 232), at **Beli Lena**, are some part-excavated caves. Lying beneath a waterfall, under which you can bathe in the dry season, the caves are a wonderful place to watch butterflies and birds. Several skeletons and prehistoric tools have been found dating back 30,000 years. An old man looks after the site and will show you around (translation needed) but is so full of the dangers of the cave (vipers, cobras, even flying pigs – three once fell down the waterfall to their doom) that it's a wonder anyone survives a visit! The site is signposted off the main road. After 5 km, a track leads right at the sign for Kitulgala Tea Estate. The cave is a 1-km walk along the path from here.

For Sleeping and Eating price codes and other relevant information, see pages 26-32.

◉ Sleeping

Kandy to Nuwara Eliya *p217*
A-C Ramboda Falls, Rock Fall Estate, 76 Nuwara Eliya, Rd, Ramboda, T052-225 9582, www.rambodafall.com. 20 rooms and chalets with hot bath and excellent views, good restaurant, bar and natural pool.
B-C Taprospa Labookellie Villa, Labookellie Tea Estate, T11-267 8389, www.taprospa.com. 3 planters' bungalows furnished with antiques and great views.
C Heritage Rest House (CHC), Pussellawa, T081-247 8397, www.ceylonhotels.lk. Colonial bungalow in an attractive location, 3 rather dated rooms with bath. Pleasant (though steep) terrace garden at back with good views across the valley compensates. Seating under large permanent sun umbrellas covered with the exotic 'ladies slipper' vine.

Nuwara Eliya *p219, map p220*
Only a selection is listed here – there are more, especially on St Andrew's Dr. Some hotels are in the Raj style, well kept, with working fireplaces, good restaurants and plenty of atmosphere, and there are also a few good value 'budget' places, mainly in the southern end of town. However, prices can rise by as much as 3 times during the Apr New Year rush while long weekends can see prices double even if demand is low. It always pays to bargain. Usually bathrooms have hot water, though it may not always be on, and rooms have blankets provided. Avoid hotels introduced to you by touts, especially on the edge of town. Solo female travellers are advised to avoid **Glenfall Inn**.
L-AL Tea Factory (Aitken Spence), Kandapola, T222 9600, www.heritance hotels.com. Winner of numerous awards, including UNESCO Heritage Award, superbly

inventive conversion of old British factory retaining original features, 57 comfortable rooms (best on top floor) including 4 suites, amidst 10-ha tea plantation with magnificent views, 2 restaurants (eat at the 'TCK6685' restaurant – in a railway carriage), 9-hole putting green, riding, games, gym. Highly recommended for setting and originality.
AL-A St Andrew's (Jetwing), 10 St Andrews Dr, T222 3031, www.jetwinghotels.com. 52 good rooms in beautiful century-old building retaining a more homely colonial atmosphere than its rivals, good restaurant with show kitchen, attractive and pleasant garden, tubs, English-style country bar, good snooker room.
A-B The Grand, Grand Hotel Rd, T222 2881, www.tangerinehotels.com. 156 rooms in 2 wings: the Golf Wing is larger, carpeted and more comfortable than Governor Wing. Also 2 presidential suites, 2 restaurants (1 ballroom sized, catering for package tour buffets), considerable colonial character in Victorian former governor's residence, efficient but can lack personal touch. Popular with tour groups. Shops, exchange and gym.
A-B Hill Club, up the path from **The Grand**, T222 2653. Oozing colonial atmosphere, 39 well-furnished, comfortable rooms with fireplaces (hot water bottles in bed), including 2 **A** suites in 'modernized' 1930s Coffee Planter's Club, formal restaurant (jacket and tie for dinner, which can be borrowed), 2 bars (1 a 'casual bar'). Good public rooms (leaf through the magazines in the faded leather armchairs of the library), excellent snooker room, tennis courts. Recommended, though some feel the 'tongue-in-cheek fogeyism' has now gone a bit too far.
B Galway Forest Lodge, 89 Upper Lake Dr (1.5 km from town), T567 9556, www.galway.lk. 52 well-furnished, carpeted, comfortable rooms with TV, heater, some with king-size beds, public areas rather utilitarian, large restaurant, **Fox and Hounds**

pub, billiard room, quiet location close to Galway Forest Reserve, lovely walks through tea plantations, popular with tour groups.

C Glendower, 5 Grand Hotel Rd, overlooking the 2nd Tee of the golf course, T222 2501, hotelglendower@hotmail.com. Airy, comfortable rooms with teak floors, plus suites, stylishly decorated, attractive modern half-timbered bungalow-style hotel, pleasant lounge with good satellite TV, superb snooker table, 19th Hole Pub, Chinese restaurant (big portions), friendly and efficient service, convenient for town.

C Heritage, 96 Badulla Rd, opposite racecourse, T223 5750. Fine colonial house with 18 large, ebony furnished rooms in 2 wings (old wing better), including beautiful suite with art deco fireplace, fine sweeping staircase, restaurant, bar, open-air café outside for lunch packets. Ask for extra blankets at night.

C-D Alpine, 4 Haddon Hill Rd, T222 3500, www.alpineecotravels.com. 25 clean, warm, comfortable rooms, all with TVs.

C-D Collingwood, 112 Badulla Rd, T222 3550, www.queenshotelsrilanka.com. 12 variable rooms in old planter's house with some old-world British character, some rooms with fireplace, a few are damp so inspect first, one reader complained of "tap dancing rats", needs a coat of paint, poor restaurant.

C-D Single Tree, 1/8 Haddon Hill Rd, T222 3009. 18 clean wood-panelled rooms, some with balcony, large beds, nice views, friendly, good tours (see Tour operators, page 234).

C-E Golf Club, T222 2835, negolf@stlnet.lk. Nuwara's best-kept accommodation secret (but only if you play a round). 11 cosy, comfortable rooms, new wing better, well-furnished, good beds, plenty of atmosphere.

D Grosvenor, 6 Haddon Hill Rd, T222 2307. 10 comfortable rooms in old colonial house, fireplaces or heaters, hot water, well furnished, good value.

D Sunhill, 18 Unique View Rd, T222 2878, sunhill@itmin.com. 20 good, carpeted rooms,

though some a little damp, with attached hot bath. Deluxe rooms upstairs have balcony and TV.

D Tea Bush Hotel, 29 Haddon Hill Rd, T222 2345, T072-235 2655. 7 rooms in colonial bungalow (view before committing), restaurant with excellent views and a small roof terrace. Bikes for hire. Overpriced.

D The Trevene, 17 Park Rd, T222 2767, thetrevene@yahoo.com. Colonial bungalow, family-run, 10 clean rooms, those at the front are larger and have fireplaces and period furniture. Internet, bike hire, good food, can arrange tours but enquire elsewhere regarding public transport.

D-F Humbugs, 100 m beyond entrance to Hakgala gardens, T222 2709. 10 simple rooms, carpeted, hot water, balconies, quiet. Restaurant serves good snacks including strawberries and cream in season. Extensive views across the Uva basin, particularly attractive in the early morning mist. Good value.

D-F Oatlands, 124 St Andrew's Dr, T222 2572. Charming old bungalow, and equally charming host. 8 rooms, some with shared bath, Dining room, lounge, peaceful location in pleasant garden, homely atmosphere.

E Green Garden, 16 Unique View Rd, T223 4166, www.hotelgreengardennuwaraeliya. com. Family-run guesthouse with 8 carpeted rooms all with hot bath, deluxe with balcony and TV. Small restaurant serving home-cooked food.

E Travelodge, Badulla Rd, T222 2733. 9 large rooms in characterful old bungalow with period furniture, meals arranged on request. Management has rather given up the ghost.

E-F Haddon Hill Inn, 10 Haddon Hill Rd, T222 3304. 11 basic but clean and comfortable rooms, hot water, reasonable value.

E-F Wattles Inn, 17 Srimath Jayatilleke Mawatha, T222 2804, T077-347 4205, www.wattlesinnnuwaraeliya.com. 9 dark but reasonable, wood-panelled rooms, in half-timbered house, restaurant, bar, pleasant garden, seen better days.

F Victoria Inn, 15/2 Park Rd, T222 2321.
Attractive ivy-clad building, 9 clean rooms,
upstairs lighter, hot showers, restaurant,
friendly, though caution about tours.
F-G Ascot, 120 Badulla Rd, T222 2708.
11 large but shabby and rather damp
rooms, restaurant, friendly and the
cheapest option.

Horton Plains National Park *p224, map p225*

For all park accommodation, call the
Wildlife Conservation Dept, T011-288 8585.
Note though that park bungalows need
to be booked well in advance and that
visitors will have to pay 2 days' admission to
the park, as well as various add-ons to the
accommodation costs. Caretakers cook the
meals but visitors must bring all provisions.
It is also possible to camp in the park.

Nuwara Eliya to Adam's Peak *p226*

Hatton is the main centre (see below),
however there is basic accommodation
available in Maskeliya. Dickoya, 6 km south
of Hatton on the Maskeliya Rd, has 2 estate
bungalows managed by the Bank of Ceylon:
D Lower Glencairn, T051-222 2348. 5 large
rooms with bath tub and hot water, no food
and looking its age but good views.
D Upper Glencairn, T051-222 2348. Beautiful
100-year-old bungalow in lovely gardens
high on hill, good views, 5 well-furnished
rooms, food available, very characterful.
D-F Hatton Rest House, 1 km away from
Hatton on Colombo Rd, T051-222 2751.
7 spartan rooms, locals' bar, rundown but
good location overlooking valley.

Adam's Peak (Sri Pada) *p228*

For accommodation at Ratnapura,
see page 121.
C Slightly Chilled Guest House, formerly
the **Yellow House**, near **Wathsala Inn**,
T351 9430, www.slightlychilled.tv. Popular
guesthouse with large, bright rooms. Prices
vary, some rooms are newer and some
have balconies with views of Adam's Peak.

Mountain bikes and motor bikes for hire,
internet, restaurant serving good food,
information on local treks. Popular
so book ahead.
D-E River View Wathsala Inn, 1 km before
the bus stand in Dalhousie, T077-786 1456,
www.adamspeakhotels.com. 14 rooms
(most with hot bath), upstairs large and
clean with balcony and good views of lake,
downstairs more basic, restaurant and bar.
Will organize pick-ups from Hatton and
various trips, including whitewater rafting
at Kitulgala.
E White House, near **Wathsala Inn**,
T077-791 2009, www.whitehouse.lankabiz.lk.
Clean, basic rooms some with hot water, in
the main guesthouse. There are also basic
wooden cottages in pleasant gardens.
Guides and tours can be arranged.
Friendly and cheap.
F-G Green House, just beyond the first step,
T051-222 3956. Clean rooms with shared
bath and some newer en suites Excellent
food (massive breakfast!), snacks before
climb and herbal bath afterwards, very
friendly, welcoming and homely.

Kitulgala *p229*

Most accommodation can arrange
rafting trips.
B Royel River Resort, 6 km inland, turning
for Beli Lena (small sign) between Km 38 and
Km 39 post, T228 7575, www.plantation
grouphotels.com/royelriver. Sister hotel is
the **Plantation**, see below. Environmentally
harmonious small hotel, built around
mini-HEP system from waterfall. 4 beautiful
rooms, homely (antiques, opera posters,
working fireplaces), wonderfully refreshing
natural swimming pool built into rock.
Wonderful secluded setting with local
walks through tea and rubber plantations,
good for birders.
B-C Kitulgala Rest House (CHC), on
riverbank before Km 37 post, T228 7783,
www.ceylonhotels.lk. 19 pleasant,
comfortable rooms (4 with a/c), with porches
overlooking river. Restaurant and bar.

Blooms, bets and beauty pageants

Throughout April, and particularly over Sinhalese and Tamil New Year, Nuwara Eliya is invaded by the Colombo set. A banner across the road proudly announces "Nuwara at 6128 ft: Welcome to the salubrious climate of Nuwara Eliya: cultured drivers are welcomed with affection"!

For several weeks, the normally sedate town throngs with visitors. Many come for a day at the one of the five races, beloved by all betting mad Sri Lankans, which culminate in the nine-furlong Governor's Cup. Motor racing also draws the crowds. Over 100 Formula Three cars hare around the hills at the Mahagastota

Hill Climb, while the Fox Hill supercross at the nearby Diyatalawa circuit can be very exciting. Back in town, there are dances and beauty pageants, all culminating in the judging of the all-important flower show at the end of the month.

The town of course gets packed. Prices become inflated (tripled) and it is virtually impossible to find accommodation. Stallholders, mostly selling food and drink, pay vast amounts of money to rent a pitch alongside the main road by Victoria Park. Most hotels run all night discos (the best is said to be at the Grand Hotel) and the crowds roam the streets for much of the night.

B-C **Plantation Hotel**, at Km 39 post, T228 7575, www.plantationgrouphotels.com/plantation. A fine refurbished colonial bungalow with comfortable though expensive a/c rooms with antique furniture, TV and hot water. Excellent riverside restaurants a popular lunchtime stop for tour groups.

B-C **Rafters Retreat**, T228 7598, www.raftersretreat.com. 11 simple wooden cabins in riverside forest setting, basic and no hot water. Restaurant overlooking the river serves good food. Runs adventure tours, trips to the caves, and is a good spot for rafting.

❶ Eating

Nuwara Eliya *p219, map p220*
There are numerous cheap restaurants along Old and New Bazar Rds.

♦♦♦ **The Grand**, see Sleeping, page 230. Has 2 restaurants, one serving buffet meals all day, the other, the 'Supper Club', is only open for dinner (1930-2200).

♦♦♦ **Hill Club**, see Sleeping, page 230. Receives mixed reviews for its food, but it's a unique dining experience: dress code after 1900

(jacket and tie though fewer constraints for women), 4-course meal served promptly at 2000 (US$17), courteous service.

♦♦♦ **King Prawn**, Glendower, see Sleeping, page 231. Good but expensive Chinese food.

♦♦ **Grand Indian**, The Grand, see Sleeping page 230. Excellent Indian restaurant open for lunch and dinner, serving curries, thalis and a wide selection of breads. Recommended.

♦♦ **Milano**, 24 New Bazaar St, T222 2763. Halal restaurant, tasty seafood, Chinese and Sri Lankan, good portions, tempting wattapalam dessert, sales counter, no alcohol. Several similar restaurants nearby.

Adam's Peak (Sri Pada) *p228*
Teashops and foodstalls selling food line the approach to the mountain and the steps themselves. Good food at the **Green House** and **Slightly Chilled**, see Sleeping page 232.

❶ Bars and clubs

Nuwara Eliya *p219, map p220*
Try the **Glendower**, **The Grand**, **St Andrew's**, and most atmospherically, **Hill Club**, for old-fashioned ambience. See Sleeping, page 230.

O Shopping

Nuwara Eliya *p219, map p220*
Cargill's, Kandy Rd and **Super K**, 14 New Bazaar, are both good supermarkets and sell a wide selection of tea.

The **market**, west of New Bazaar St, sells warm jackets and fleeces, including some well-known brands, can be picked up here but bargain hard.

▲ Activities and tours

Nuwara Eliya *p219, map p220*
Boating and fishing
Boats and fishing equipment can be hired from the Lake Gregory boat house next to the lake.

Golf
Nuwara Eliya is home to a beautiful and superbly maintained 5550-yard par 70 golf course, T222 2835. Rs 15000 for 18 holes, Rs 3000 for 1-hr practice session.

Pony-trekking
Available from large hotels (eg **St Andrew's**), and at the northwestern edge of the golf course.

Snooker
Available at the **Hill Club**, though those who play like Alex Higgins may like to note the "1 million rupees first tear" sign (presumably the second one is free). 3 excellent tables at **The Grand**, plus at **St Andrew's** and an antique table at **Glendower**.

Tennis
Good clay tennis courts at the **Hill Club**.

Tour operators
Most hotels and guesthouses can arrange tours to Horton Plains, the tea plantations and the waterfalls. Some also offer an Adam's

Peak drop-off and return trip (Rs 6500), leaving at 2230. Prices do vary however, so it's worth asking around. **Single Tree**, has a range of tours on offer and at the time of writing prices were reasonable, Can also organize treks to Single Tree Hill and the highest villages. Both **Single Tree** and **Alpine Hotel** (See Sleeping page 231) should be able to arrange rafting trips to Kitulgala.

Kitulgala *p229*
Whitewater rafting trips can be arranged through the **Plantation Hotel** or **Rafters Retreat**, see Sleeping, page 233, and cost around US$30 including lunch. Alternatively, trips can be organized in advance through various tour operators (see Essentials, page 50).

⊖ Transport

Nuwara Eliya *p219, map p220*
Bus
To **Nanu Oya** every 30 mins. Frequent long-distance buses from both bus stands to **Badulla** (via Hakgala, 2½ hrs). For **Haputale** and **Bandarawela**, change at Welimada. Plenty of buses to **Hatton** (intercity 1½ hrs, normal 2½ hrs) and to **Kandy** (3-4 hrs). Several a day to **Colombo** (6 hrs) including faster a/c intercity buses (5 hrs).

Train
New arrivals are besieged by touts actually on the train and at the station and will offer free transport to the hotel of their choice. You will end up paying heavily for this service in commissions. Better to take the bus which waits for the arrival of trains or take a taxi (if none at the station walk a few hundred metres to the main road). To **Colombo**, 0927 (6¼ hrs), 1227 (7 hrs), 2333 (7 hrs). To **Kandy** 1658 (4½ hrs). To **Badulla** (3½-4 hrs), via **Haputale** (1½-2 hrs), **Bandarawela**, **Ella** (2½-3 hrs), 0505, 0933, 1227, 1525.

Nuwara Eliya to Adam's Peak p226

Bus
Intercity buses run from **Hatton** to **Colombo** (4½ hrs) and normal buses to **Kandy** and **Nuwara Eliya** (each 3 hrs), with more during the pilgrimage season.

Train
They run from **Hatton** (on the Colombo-Badulla line), with several trains a day to **Colombo** (6½ hrs), most (not all) via **Kandy** (2½ hrs), and to **Nanu Oya** (1½ hrs) and destinations further east.

Adam's Peak (Sri Pada) p228

Bus
Run regularly to Dalhousie direct during the pilgrimage season from **Colombo**, **Kandy** and **Nuwara Eliya**. You may have to change in Hatton or Maskeliya during the off-season.

Taxi
From **Hatton** should cost around Rs 2000.

Train
To **Hatton** (see above), then bus.

Kitulgala p229

Bus
Buses between **Colombo** and **Hatton** or **Nuwara Eliya** pass through Kitulgala. For Ratnapura you must change in Avissawella.

⊙ Directory

Nuwara Eliya *p219, map p220*
Banks Bank of Ceylon, on the corner of Kandy Rd and Lawson St, has a Visa ATM and foreign exchange counter. **Hatton National Bank**, just up from post office, accepts MasterCard. Other banks congregate on Park Rd, including **Commercial Bank**, **People's Bank** and **Seylan Bank**.
Buddhist centre International Buddhist Centre, Badulla Rd, T2235244.
Internet Expensive, some hotels and guesthouse offer it but facilities and speed vary. **Prine Nett**, 17/1A New Bazar St. **Chamara Computer Centre**, Park Rd.
Post office Opposite the CTB bus station, Mon-Sat 0700-2100, Sun 0800-2100.

Nuwara Eliya to Adam's Peak *p226*
Banks Hatton has several banks, including **Hatton National Bank**.

Uva Province

East of the Central Highland ridge are the picturesque hills of Uva Province. In contrast to the comparatively recently populated highland region, Uva, which stretches across the plains as far south as Kataragama, is sometimes held to be the original home of the Kandyan civilization, whose people would have used the river valleys draining into the Mahaweli Ganga as a natural migration route into the hills. Protected from the Wet Zone rains by the highland massif, it has a sunny, dry climate and a relatively bare landscape. In the hills there are impressive waterfalls and some of the best views on the island.

South of the provincial capital Badulla, whose festival draws Buddhist pilgrims from across the island, the climate of the triangle formed by Ella, Haputale and Welimada is regarded by many Sri Lankans as the most favourable on the island. This is marvellous walking country, where views, particularly at Ella and Haputale, formed by spectacular 'gaps' in its precipitous ridges come without the price tag of Horton Plains. There is a wonderful circular route from Nuwara Eliya which makes for a rewarding day tour, or there are plenty of attractive places to stay if you don't want to rush. ▸▸ *For listings, see pages 243-248.*

Nuwara Eliya to Badulla

From Nuwara Eliya, the A5 goes southeast across Wilson's Plains then east to Badulla. This is the market garden area where carrots, bean, brassicas and many other fresh vegetables are grown, much of it for export to the Middle East. Some 10 km past the Hakgala Botanical Gardens (see page 223) is a superb view southeast across the hills of Bandarawela and over the baked plains of the east coastlands. The road passes through **Keppetipola**, where you can pick up information about local attractions, as it drops rapidly through to Welimada on the Uma Oya River.

Istripura Caves, north of Welimada, are a pot-holer's delight. They are reached by a path from Parangama, which is 10 km along the road north from Welimada. The maze of damp caves holds a large lake.

From Welimada, a right turn on to the B51 leads to Bandarawela (see page 240) past terraced fields of paddy and across occasional streams. At Hali-Ela, the A5 goes to Badulla. This area is already in the rain shadow of the hills to the west, sheltered from the southwest monsoon and much drier than Nuwara Eliya. Rubber plantations cover some of the slopes before Badulla.

Badulla → *Phone code: 055. Colour map 3, A6. Population: 42,000. Altitude: 675 m.*

The capital of Uva Province is surrounded by paddy fields along the banks of the river Gallanda Oya and has an old fort against a backdrop of mountains and a small lake. It is one of the oldest towns in Sri Lanka though there are no traces of the earlier settlement. The Portuguese once occupied it but set the town on fire before leaving. At one time it was an extremely active social centre for planters, with a racecourse, golf, tennis and cricket clubs, long since fallen into disuse.

Sights → *Dunhinda Rd is also known as Mahiyangana Rd.*
Veall's Park was once a small botanical garden – some impressive specimens remain, such as the huge Australian pine. Notice the little stone grey Methodist church where

Major Rogers, an elephant hunter who died after being struck by lightning, is commemorated on a plaque.

Muthiyangana Vihara, attributed to Devanampiya Tissa, the first Buddhist convert on the island, is thought to have a 2000-year old ancient core. There is a small provincial museum behind. The Hindu **Kataragama Devale** was built in the 18th-century highland style in thanksgiving for King Vimaladharma's victory over the Portuguese. Note the plaster-on-wood statues and wooden pillars of the 'throne room'. There is also a revered Bo tree.

Next to the stadium, in a pleasant four-acre park are the **botanical gardens** ⓘ *Rs 100, free for under 12s*, welcome relief from the bustle of Badulla town.

Excursions → *Good mangoes are on sale in season at the falls.*

The island's highest perennial waterfalls, **Dunhinda Falls** ⓘ *Rs 100*, can be spectacular. Some 6 km from town, there is a small car park on a bend in the road about 2 km from the falls, which takes about 25 minutes on foot. Buses from Badulla leave every half an hour and stop about a 10-minute walk away. The path to the falls is across the road from the car park. It is quite rough and steep in places, so take care and wear suitable shoes. The valley

Badulla

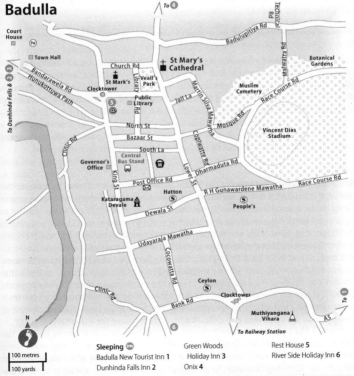

Sleeping
Badulla New Tourist Inn **1**
Dunhinda Falls Inn **2**

Green Woods
Holiday Inn **3**
Onix **4**

Rest House **5**
River Side Holiday Inn **6**

at this point is also quite narrow which can make it very hot. Numerous stalls sell cold drinks, herbs, etc, at the start of the walk and along it. As the falls are very popular with Sri Lankans, foreign travellers are not hassled too much.

Shortly after the beginning of the path you can see the lower falls (more of a cascade really), quite a long way down in the valley below. These are only about 15 m in height and much broader than the main falls. A ledge about 10 m from the top makes for a spectacular 'spurt' when the river is running high. At the main falls, the river plunges in two stages about 63 m through a 'V' in the rock which causes a misty haze (*dunhind*) which gives the falls its name. There are granite cliffs on either side and a large pool at the bottom. It is quite spectacular and well worth the effort. Here there is also a large, kidney-shaped observation platform where concrete tables and benches have been built to give a pleasant picnic spot. It can, however, be very busy at times.

Bogoda is a very peaceful place with a small monastery and rock temple. It is well off the beaten track, off the road to the north of Hali Ela, 13 km from Badulla. The attractive 16th-century wooden bridge across the Gallanda Oya is built without nails (the original claimed to date from the first century). The only surviving one of its kind, it has an unusual tiled roof in the Kandyan style supported on carved pillars. The railings are painted with natural lacquer. **Raja Maha Vihara** rock temple nearby has old murals and pre-Christian inscriptions.

Ella → *Phone code: 057. Colour map 3, A6. Altitude: 1043 m.*

Ella is little more than a handful of shops and guesthouses strung out along the main road, but it has an almost perfect climate and occupies a very scenic vantage point, with views on a fine day stretching right across to the south coast. A traveller writes, "The view through the Ella Gap was probably the best in the entire island. It was quite early and the isolated hills on the plain popped up like islands in the mist." The town is also a useful base from which to visit some local tea plantations, waterfalls and rock temples. This is excellent walking country. Persistent hotel touts besiege those arriving by train. Ignore them and go to the hotel of your choice, preferably with an advance reservation.

Sights

Rawana Ella Cave, in the massive Ella Rock, can be seen from the **Grand Ella Motel** to the right of the Ella Gap. It is associated with the *Ramayana* story, in which the demon king of Lanka, Ravana, imprisoned Rama's wife Sita. The cave, which is of particular interest to palaeontologists, has a small entrance which scarcely lets light in, and then a long drop to the floor. It is filled with water from an underground stream which has hindered exploration but excavations here have unearthed prehistoric remains of human skeletons and tools dating from 8000 to 2500 BC. The skeletons are believed to belong to *Homo sapiens balangodensis*. They are said to show evidence of a culture superior to that of the present-day Veddas (Wanniya-laeto). To reach the caves you walk downhill beyond the **Ella Rest House** for 10 minutes until you reach the road bridge, then branch up the track to the right which climbs to a rock monastery. There are often local children offering to guide you on the very steep and difficult path up to the cave, for a small fee.

Rawana Ella Falls can be quite dramatic and the 1½-hour walk from the Rawana Ella Cave to reach them can be enjoyable: the road isn't usually too busy and there are some fine views. From the cave, return to the main road, near the bridge, and walk downhill to the falls. The 90-m-high Rawana Ella (or Bambaragama) Falls are to the right (west) of the road just beyond a bridge. You can climb over the rocks up the falls for quite a way, along with the monkeys who can often been seen scampering up and down the rocks. There is also a path to the right hand side of the bathing area, and you can climb up quite far. Local 'guides' are always keen to show you the route though the way (up) is fairly obvious. At the falls themselves there is an intriguing small business in coloured stones gathered from the foot of the falls. A few enterprising vendors sell them to passing tourists. A handful of small stones should not cost much more than Rs 50 but a common method of

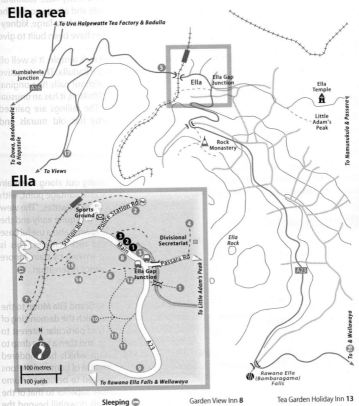

Ella area

Ella

Sleeping
Ambiente **17**
Beauty Mount Tourist
  Inn **1**
Country Comfort Inn **2**
Ella Adventure Park **16**
Ella Holiday Inn **3**
Forest Paradise
  Guest Home **4**

Garden View Inn **8**
Grand Ella Motel **11**
Highest Inn **15**
Hill Top Guest House **6**
Ravana Heights **9**
Rawana Holiday Resort **10**
Rock View Guest House **12**
Sunnyside Holiday
  Bungalow **5**

Tea Garden Holiday Inn **13**
Waterfalls Homestay **7**
Zion View **14**

Eating
Dream Café **1**
Nescoffee Shop **2**
Rotti Cart **3**

transaction is to swap the stones for a foreign coin or coins. The stone seller then waits for the next tourist, hoping to exchange the foreign coins with a native of the relevant country at the prevailing exchange rate. The falls are 6 km south of Ella on the A23 so you can get there by bus (towards Wellawaya).

There are several other walks which command magnificent views. A short walk east on the Passara Road takes you to a track, after the Km 1 post, which you follow to climb **Little Adam's Peak**. Some 10 km further east, and more strenuous, is the climb through tea plantations to **Namunukula**, which, at 2036 m, is one of Sri Lanka's highest mountains. You will need a guide for this walk.

Several **tea factories** are nearby, including the Uva Halpewatte factory off the Badulla Road. Catch a bus travelling towards Bandarawela, change at Kumbalawela Junction, on to a Badulla bound bus. At Km 27 post, take the track on the left leading uphill, and then turn left where it forks about 2 km from main road.

Dowa Rock Temple can also be visited from Ella, see below.

Bandarawela → *Phone code: 057. Colour map 3, A5. Altitude: 1230 m.*

At the centre of the Uva 'health triangle', many Sri Lankans regard Bandarawela's climate as the most favourable on the island. Averaging around 21ºC, it is invariably dry and sunny but the number of vehicles passing through means the air is no longer as clean and fresh as it once was. A centre for tea and fruit-growing, the town has a bustling market-town feel, and is good for picking up supplies or visiting the ATM. Market days are Wednesday and Sunday. Though there is little in the way of sights, the town is used mainly as a good base for walks and for exploring the Uva basin.

Bandarawela

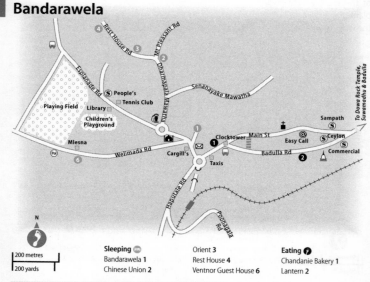

200 metres 200 yards	**Sleeping** 😴 Bandarawela 1 Chinese Union 2	Orient 3 Rest House 4 Ventnor Guest House 6	**Eating** 🍴 Chandanie Bakery 1 Lantern 2

Sights → *For details of Bandarawela's Ayurveda and herbal therapy centres, see page 247.*

Dowa Rock Temple, 6 km from Bandarawela, is squeezed between the road and the stream in the bottom of the valley. It is a pleasant walk if you follow the attractive valley down. The cliff face has an incomplete carving of a large standing Buddha with an exquisitely carved face, while inside the cave there are murals and first century BC inscriptions. The inner cave has a 'House of the Cobra' which is usually locked (ask a monk to let you in) and said to be still inhabited by serpents. Take a Badulla bus and ask the bus driver to let you off at the temple.

Haputale → *Phone code: 057. Colour map 3, B5. Altitude: 1400 m.*

Haputale, from its ridge-top position, has superb views at dawn over the low country to the east. On a clear day you can see the saltpans at Hambantota to the south, and the horizon is the sea. To the north, in magnificent contrast, are the hills. A small town with a busy shopping street, it is surrounded by great walks and the town itself, with plenty of cheap guesthouses, provides a good base in which to explore the area. The lively Sunday morning market is worth a stroll and to see a curious sight, walk down the main street from the Station Road crossing, and watch the apparent disappearance of the road over the cliff. Away from town, several tea plantations are happy to receive visitors – just stop and ask, or guesthouses can arrange transport for you. Some estates have accommodation. For more information on Haputale, see www.haputale.de.

Sights

The **Dambetenne Road**, from the town towards the Kelburne Tea Estate, must rate as one of the most spectacular walks in the whole island with breathtaking views across five provinces, several tea plantations and down to the plains. It is possible to walk the length of the road, which is not busy, or alternatively take the regular bus which ferries plantation workers the 10 km from town to the **Dambetenne (Lipton) Tea Factory**. Along the way you will pass a number of tea factories (see below).

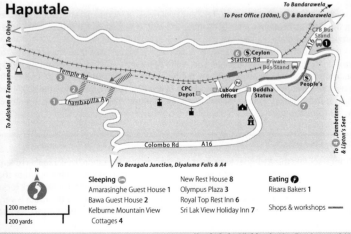

Haputale

To Ohiya
To Adisham & Tangamalai
To Bandarawela
To Post Office (300m), & Bandarawela
CTB Bus Stand
A16
6 (S)Ceylon Station Rd
Private Bus Stand
Temple Rd
Thambapilla Av
CPC Depot
Labour Office
Buddha Statue
People's
To Dambetenne & Lipton's Seat
Colombo Rd   A16
To Beragala Junction, Diyaluma Falls & A4

N
200 metres
200 yards

Sleeping
Amarasinghe Guest House 1
Bawa Guest House 2
Kelburne Mountain View Cottages 4

New Rest House 8
Olympus Plaza 3
Royal Top Rest Inn 6
Sri Lak View Holiday Inn 7

Eating
Risara Bakers 1

Shops & workshops ━━━

Some 7 km beyond the tea factory it is a short uphill walk following a clear trail up to **Lipton's Seat** from where, on a clear day, it is possible to see up to 60% of the island. This walk is highly recommended, but it's best to visit in the morning as mist tends to descend by about 1030.

Greenfields Bio Plantations ⓘ *3 km on Dambatenne Rd, T226 8102, for a tour call first*, is one of the few organic tea producers in the country, where you can ask for a tour demonstrating the various processes involved. It's a very pleasant walk or hourly buses run.

The more traditional **Dambetenne Tea Factory** ⓘ *visit 0700-1200 to see the factory in full production, Rs 200 for a 30-min tour*, has the air of a philanthropic Victorian works, which indeed is what it is. Note the quote from Ruskin at the entrance, "Quality is no accident. It is the result of intelligent effort." Built in 1890 by Sir Thomas Lipton, the 20,000 sq ft factory employs 1600 workers, 90% of which are resident, and accommodates over 4000 people. Most of the tea is now exported to Europe, Japan and South Africa. There are hourly buses to Dambatenne.

Adisham monastery ⓘ *3 km up a hill to the west, Sat-Sun, poya days and public holidays 0930-1230, 1330-1700, Rs 60*, borders the **Tangamalai Bird Sanctuary** which is good for spotting jungle and highland species. It is worth walking up to at the weekend. A quirky stone-built anachronism dating from the 1930s, it houses a Benedictine novitiate which has interesting period features. Modelled on Leeds Castle (Kent, England), it has attractive rose gardens and orchards. A few spartan rooms with cold water in an annexe are open to visitors. Reserve ahead by post or call, T226 8030. It takes about an hour to walk or is a bus ride away, No 327 or a three-wheeler will charge from Rs 400-600 return.

Excursions

The 170-m **Diyaluma Falls** drop in two stages over a huge convex outcrop. They are perhaps not as spectacular as the Dunhinda Falls, mainly because the stream is much smaller, but it is quite peaceful here and although there are no official picnic areas, there are several large rocks to sit on. Beware of the monkeys though. You can climb up to some cool bathing pools about half way up the falls: walk about 500 m (back towards Haputale) to a minor road which winds up through rubber plantations – best to ask the way. The steady climb takes about an hour. Take any Wellawaya or Moneragala bus from Haputale, getting off at Diyaluma after a 1¼-hour journey. It is best to go in the morning as afternoon buses are scarce.

If using public transport, Haputale is probably a better base than Nuwara Eliya for visiting Horton Plains National Park and World's End since you can make a round trip by train/on foot in one day. However, by the time you arrive the plains will be covered in cloud, which normally sweeps up the valleys by midday. There is a train leaving at 0747 to the nearest station, Ohiya, taking about 40 minutes. You can return on the 1636. ▸▸ *See Transport, page 247.*

From Haputale

From Haputale the A16 goes west, past the Stassen Bio Plantation, to Beragala (10 km) where it joins the A4, the main road to Colombo which hugs the southern rim of the highlands. West of Beragala is some of the most rugged scenery in Sri Lanka. Black rocks tower above the road towards Belihuloya (see page 120) and much of the route is very windy, not steep but with many blind bends. The A4 continues west to Ratnapura (see page 119).

Travelling east from Beragala, the fine views through the Haputale Gap continue, and the road leads through a marvellous area of flora – teak, rubber, pepper, cacao and coffee trees – to Koslande and past the Diyaluma waterfall to Wellawaya (see page 183).

If you wish to return to Nuwara Eliya from Haputale, the B48 goes directly through Boralanda and Nawela, and Welimada, where it rejoins the A5 to Nuwara Eliya. Alternatively you can take the slower route via Horton Plains.

⊙ Uva Province listings

For Sleeping and Eating price codes and other relevant information, see pages 26-32.

⊙ Sleeping

Badulla *p236, map p237*

D-E Hotel Onix, 69 Bandaranayaka Mawatha, north of town, T222 2426. 6 a/c and fan rooms, most with satellite TV. Quiet, restaurant, good value.

E Rest House, 800 m from railway station, T222 2299. 17 rooms around central courtyard, saggy beds, simple meals, central location.

E-G Dunhinda Falls Inn, 35/10 Bandaranaike Mawatha, 1.5 km from town centre, T222 3028. Respectable (local Rotary club meets here) despite disconcerting one-eyed leopard in entrance. 15 large a/c and fan rooms of very varying standards, restaurant, bar, car/cycle hire, visits to tea gardens.

F Badulla New Tourist Inn, 22 Mahiyangana Rd (towards Dunhinda Falls), T222 3423. 11 a/c and fan rooms (variable so check first), restaurant, courteous service, no hot water, delicious rice and curry. May see birds nesting in light fittings.

F River Side Holiday Inn, 27 Lower King's St, T222 2090. 11 decent fan rooms, rooftop restaurant, bar.

F-G Green Woods Holiday Inn, 301 Bandarawela Rd, 2.5 km before town, T223 1358. 12 reasonable a/c and fan rooms with hot bath in quiet location (although can get busy with local people), good restaurant, views would be good if you could open the windows. Also has large bungalows available.

Ella *p238, map p239*

All hotels are on the Main St, unless listed, and most have hot water though check beforehand for the cheapest rooms. It's worth booking accommodation in advance between Jan-Apr as it can be very busy.

A-B Ella Adventure Park, 12 km south of Ella on Wellawaya Rd, T011-258 8258, www.ellaadventurepark.com. Impressively environmentally sensitive lodge in forest setting spanning both banks of Kirindi Oya (river). 10 comfortable 'rooms', comprising eco-lodges, treehouse (with own ropeway), deluxe cabanas and camping tents, plus tree-top bar/restaurant. Full array of adventure sports offered, including rock-climbing, paragliding, canoeing and abseiling, some are included in the price.

B-C Grand Ella Motel (CHC), overlooking Ella Gap, 1 km south from railway station, T222 8655, www.ceylonhotels.lk. 14 large rooms, cheaper in the old wing. Wonderful garden, with its own *Ficus religiosa*, the best views in Ella.

C Ravana Heights, opposite Km 27 post, Wellawaya Rd, T222 8888, www.ravanaheights.com. 4 classy rooms, 3 with excellent views and outdoor seating areas. Intimate guesthouse just outside town, personal attention, good food. Recommended.

C Zion View, 300 m from train station, T222 8799, www.ella-guesthouse-srilanka.com. 7 spotless rooms with French windows so you can lie in bed and look at the view of Zion waterfall. Laundry service available, excellent food and an Ayurveda centre should be open by the time you read this. There are also plans for a bungalow in the future. The family are friendly and helpful and can arrange tours and onward travel. Recommended.

C-D Ella Holiday Inn, T222 8615, T072-465 6292, www.ellaholidayinn.com. Large, modern guesthouse in very central location. Range of clean rooms (some with balconies), prices vary according to facilities. Internet, free Wi-Fi available in the café, restaurant, cookery lessons, excursions and tourist information provided. Popular.

C-E Country Comfort Inn, 32 Police Station Rd, T222 8500. 12 spotless rooms in new wing with TV, 8 clean and comfortable rooms in the old wing, still good value if a little dark. Reasonable restaurant. Worth trying to bargain down the price.

D-E Waterfalls Homestay, T567 6933, www.waterfalls-guesthouse-ella.com. Hidden away in the jungle with 3 bright, clean rooms (2 have panoramic views). Friendly, good food, lovely spot. Tricky to find so take them up on their free pick-up. Recommended.

D-F Beauty Mount Tourist Inn, off Main St, T222 8760. Simple rooms and bungalows, on a forested hill just off Main St. Lovely gardens and great food. Stairs are steep so bear in mind if you have heavy bags.

D-G Tea Garden Holiday Inn, on top of the hill above the **Grand Ella Motel**, T222 2915. 12 clean basic rooms in 3-storey guesthouse, good views of the gap, food available. The rooms at the top are the most expensive, cheapest on the ground floor.

E-F Ambiente, 2 km up Kitalella Rd, high above the Ella town near Kinellan Tea Plantation, T222 8867, www.ambiente.lk. In a spectacular setting, high above the village, 8 very clean rooms, 5 in new block (can be noisy), most are spacious. Magnificent views, friendly.

E-F Hill Top Guest House, off Main St, T222 8780. Good, clean rooms, better and more expensive upstairs with excellent views, popular, good food, good choice.

E-F Rawana Holiday Resort, on hill above the village, T222 8794, nalankumara@yahoo.com. A variety of clean rooms, nice home from home touches and good food. Terrace with great views across forest, friendly. More rooms being added at the time of writing, so view before committing.

F Forest Paradise Guest Home, Passara Rd, T222 8797, www.forestparadiseella.com. Real frontier feel on edge of pine forest. 5 clean, small rooms, with private seating area. Friendly and can arrange activities. Free pick-up from station. Recommended for its setting.

F Sunnyside Holiday Bungalow, Bandarawela Rd, T561 5011, www.sunnyside. go2lk.com. Family-run guesthouse offering 3 clean rooms with attached hot bath in a bungalow surrounded by pleasant gardens. Excellent for birdwatchers. No TV, and no smoking or alcohol allowed on site. The whole bungalow can be hired (**C**). Excellent food.

F-G Rock View Guest House, T222 8561. Large rooms, newer ones are separate from the main house, and popular restaurant. Free cookery classes if you're a guest. Friendly.

G Garden View Inn, T222 8792. 3 very cheap if slightly grim rooms in a family home (bathrooms are clean). Decent food, order in advance, not very friendly.

G Highest Inn, turn left before railway bridge, or take short cut through tea plantation, T567 6933. Family-run guesthouse with good views all around. 3 rooms with shared balcony, only breakfast available. Friendly and helpful.

Bandarawela *p240, map p240*

Budget options are along Welimada Rd, as well as **Tea Estate Bungalows** which are worth looking at if you have your own wheels.

B Orient, 12 Dharmapala Mawatha, T222 2377, www.orienthotelsl.com. 50 large rooms and 4 suites, good views from top floor, billiard room, fitness centre, English-style bar and beer garden. Popular with tours. Currently undergoing some refurbishment work.

B-C Bandarawela Hotel (Aitken Spence), 14 Welimada Rd, near **Cargill's** supermarket, T222 2501, www.aitkenspencehotels.com. Old tea planters' club (1893) full of colonial charm, 35 rather cramped rooms, including 1 suite. Period furniture, including metal bedsteads, rooms built around central courtyard (look for tortoises), good gardens, passable restaurant, residents' bar with fireplace, good tours to Horton Plains, popular with groups but still recommended, though the noisy mosque will ensure you won't waste the day.

E Ventnor Guest House, 23 Welimada Rd, T222 2511. Large, carpeted rooms, well furnished, hot water, restaurant.

G Chinese Union Hotel, 8 Mount Pleasant Rd, on the corner, T222 2502. Small single storey house with clean rooms. Quiet, food available.

Haputale p241, map p241

There is a good choice of cheap guesthouses with hot water being provided by most. The owners can usually advise on good walks in the area.

There is a short cut from the railway station to Temple Rd and nearby guesthouses. Walk west along the tracks, climb the steps to Temple Rd, then follow signposts down steps on the other side.

A Kelburne Mountain View Cottages, 2 km down Dambetenne Rd, T011-257 3382 (reservations), www.kelburnemountainview.com. 3 wonderfully furnished cottages, sleeping 4 or 6, 2 with fireplaces, at least 2 bathrooms in each, meals on order or there's a restaurant, spectacular views, unique hand-painted open-air visitors book. Superb place to unwind.

C Olympus Plaza Hotel, 75 Welimada Rd, T226 8544, www.olympusplazahotel.com. The only 'real' hotel in Haputale, this place is a little soulless but the rooms are comfortable and clean and the views are excellent. Satellite TV, internet (expensive at Rs 100 per hr), a restaurant a bar with pool table, table tennis and a gym. Tours can be arranged.

E New Rest House, 100 Bandarawela Rd (1 km), T492 8888. 6 simple but comfortable rooms with hot bath, although a bit musty and could do with a spruce. Restaurant, in quiet location with garden, nice views.

E-F Sri Lak View Holiday Inn, 48 A Sirisena Mawatha, 200 m from bus stand, T226 8125, srilakv@sltnet.lk. Clean rooms, some with views. Those in the main house are better, the new building can get quite hot. Restaurant and breakfast room with excellent views, good food, internet, friendly. Rooms overpriced.

G Amarasinghe Guest House, Thambapillai Av, T226 8175, agh777@sltnet.lk. Cosy family house with homely atmosphere and clean, comfortable rooms. Very good value, including some on first floor with excellent views. Good food, friendly and knowledgeable owner. Internet available. Recommended.

G Bawa Guest House, 32 Thambapillai Av, above **Amarasinghe Guest House**, T226 8260. 3 clean, bright rooms in long-running family guesthouse. Friendly owners, Mr Bawa is a gem expert and has a small showroom. Good home-cooked vegetarian food.

G Royal Top Rest Inn, 22 Station Rd, T226 8178. Simple rooms, good restaurant, close to buses and trains, pleasant garden, inspect first.

🍽 Eating

Ella p238, map p239

Many of the guesthouses listed under Sleeping offer home-cooked rice and curry, however you will need to book by mid-afternoon. The set meal at **Zion View** is expensive but excellent, **Rawana** remains popular. Alternatively, a number of places on the main street serve food. Curd and honey is a local specialty.

🍴 **Grand Ella Motel**, see Sleeping, page 243. You come for the unrivalled setting but the food's good too.

ŤŤ-Ť **Nescoffee Shop**, Main St. A modern coffee shop serving delicious food, such as rice and curry (10 course for Rs700), pizza and burgers. Australian wine, juices, smoothies, DIY sandwich, and cocktails. Not to mention Wi-Fi, Skype and a book exchange.

ŤŤ-Ť **Dream Café**, Main St. A perennial favourite, serving curries and a wide range of excellent Western dishes in a garden tucked down away from the road. Service is good, internet is available and the pizzas are a must-have.

Ť **Rotti Cart**, next door to **Nescoffee**. Open from 1630 and serving delicious rotti, whether it be garlic or banana and honey.

Bandarawela p240, map p240

For further options see Sleeping, page 244.

Ť **Chandanie Bakery**, Main St. An appealing array of cakes and patisseries.

Ť **Lantern**, Badulla Rd, T223 2520. One of several cheap Chinese and rice and curry places on Badulla Rd, the set menus are good value.

Haputale p241, map p241

For further options see Sleeping, page 245. The home cooking at most of the guest houses is hard to beat. Several provide cheap lunch packets. No real restaurant here but you can buy rotties and snacks in food stalls, and good groceries along the road between the rail and bus stations.

Ť **Risara Bakers**, near the bus station. Serves short eats and the best samosas in Sri Lanka (spicy though). If you time it right you'll get them fresh out the fryer at the front.

⊛ Festivals and events

Badulla p236, map p237

May-Jun Wesak and Poson full moon festivals take place with drummers, dancers and elephants.

Sep Esala Perehera at Muthi-yangana Vihara when Veddas participate.

⬭ Shopping

Ella p238, map p239

Shops on Main St near the rest houses are overpriced. Walk up the street and pay half the price for water and provisions.

Bandarawela p240, map p240

Cargill's, opposite **Bandarawela Hotel**. Branch of the supermarket chain.
Mlesna, 184a Welimada Rd, T2231663. Upmarket tea shop, with a wide variety to choose from.

▲ Activities and tours

Ella p238, map p239

Ayurveda and herbal therapies
Suwamedura, 25 Grand View, Passara Rd, T567 3215. Professional establishment offering a range of treatments, including massage, steam baths and herbal saunas.

Cookery classes
A few of the guesthouses offer cookery classes (see Sleeping, page 243). **Ella Holiday Inn** organizes lessons for Rs 1700, which includes the ingredients and eating the meal at the end.

Tour operators
A number of the guesthouses can arrange tours, and onward travel if required.
Ella Holiday Inn, see Sleeping, page 244. The owner Suresh Rodrigo can provide tourist information and also organizes tours such as night-caving, jungle-trekking, rubber plantations and tea factories "not in any guidebook".
Trekking Sri Lanka, T223 1903, T077-764 6243, www.treekingsrilanka.com. Based near Bandarawela, offer excellent treks such as day trips to Lover's Leap or up Adam's Peak to 2-week excursions starting from Colombo. Also arranges tours of the Cultural Triangle and Ayurvedic getaways.

Bandarawela *p240, map p240*

Ayurveda and herbal therapies

Suwamadhu, Bindunuwewa, 3 km east,
T222 2504. Open 0800-2000. Popular herbal
treatment centre, and produces its own
creams and oils. Steam bath with 18
herbal medicines, full body massage,
longer courses available.

⊖ Transport

Badulla *p236, map p237*

Bus

Bus stand, with private and CTB
buses, is about 200 m south of the **Rest
House** along King St. Regular buses to
Bandarawela; and hourly to **Colombo**.
To **Kandy** until 1400 (every 40 mins); every
30 mins to **Nuwara Eliya** until 1650; hourly
to **Wellawaya**, via **Ella**; 1 bus a day in
the early morning to **Pottuvil**, and early
morning departure to **Galle**, via **Matara**.

Train

To **Colombo** via **Demodera** (look out for
the Loop!), **Ella**, **Bandarawela**, **Haputale**,
Ohiya (for Horton Plains) on *Udarata Menike*
0545 (9¾ hrs), *Podi Menike* 0850 (11¼ hrs),
or mail train 1805 (12 hrs). To **Kandy**, 0850
(8 hrs). Local trains run as far as **Ohiya** at
0715, and to **Bandarawela** at 1415.

Ella *p238, map p239*

Bus

Direct buses to **Nuwara Eliya** (2½ hrs)
and **Kandy**, though more frequently if
you change in Badulla. For **Colombo**, go to
Kumbalawela Junction, 3 km north on the
Haputale–Badulla road, where buses go
every half an hour. For the south coast,
direct buses go to **Matara**. Frequent buses to
Wellawaya for connections to Okkampitiya
(for Maligawila, see page 183), and to
Bandarawela (change for Haputale, 45 mins).
Buses are infrequent for **Badulla** – you may
have to go to Kumbalawela Junction.

Train

Udarate Menike departs 0643, *Podi Menike* at
0947, mail train 1907, calling at **Bandarawela**
(30 mins), **Haputale** (1 hr), **Ohiya** (for Horton
Plains), 1¾ hrs, **Nanu Oya** (for Nuwara Eliya,
2¾ hrs), **Hatton** (for Adam's Peak, 4 hrs) and
Colombo (8½-11 hrs). For **Kandy** (6 hrs), take
the 0947 or 1907, the 1309 is a slow train.
Several trains a day north to **Badulla** (1 hr).

Bandarawela *p240, map p240*

Bus

The main stand is to the west of town,
close to the playing field. Frequent buses
to **Badulla**, **Wellawaya** (via **Haputale**)
and **Colombo** (from Haputale Rd). Buses to
Matara and the south coast, or change at
Wellawaya. Direct buses to **Nuwara Eliya**,
or change at Welimada.

Train

To **Colombo** at 0713, 1017 and 1937 (1017
and 1937 via **Kandy**, there's also a slow train
at 1339). **Badulla** trains via **Ella** at 0542, 1237,
1437 and 1802.

Haputale *p241, map p241*

Bus

There are separate CTB and private bus
stands with several early morning buses for
Colombo (6 hrs), and some to **Nuwara Eliya**,
but you may have to change at Welimada.
Buses leave for **Bandarawela** every half an
hour, while express buses run to **Badulla**.
There is an early morning express bus to
Matara (via **Hambantota** and **Tangalla**),
though to get to the south coast you usually
have to change at Wellawaya (every 2 hrs).

Train

For **Colombo** (7½-10 hrs), *Udarate Menike*
departs 0747, *Podi Menike* at 1048, mail
train at 2015, calling at **Ohiya** (for Horton
Plains), **Nanu Oya** (for Nuwara Eliya), **Hatton**
(for Adam's Peak). For **Kandy** (5½-6 hrs), the
1048 or 2015 are best, although there is also
a slow train at 1437. Faster trains north to

Badulla (1¾ hrs), via **Bandarawela** (30 mins) and **Ella** (1 hr) at 0507, 1125, 1409 and 1734.

ⓘ Directory

Badulla *p236, map p237*
Banks Bank of Ceylon, Bank Rd, **Hatton National Bank**, Ward St. **Internet** Available next to the **Rest House**. **Post office** Faces the south side of the bus stand.

Ella *p238, map p239*
Banks Bank of Ceylon, Main St, has no ATM but can change money. For an ATM it's easiest to go to Bandarawela either by 3-wheeler or on the bus. **Internet** Many of the guesthouses offer Wi-Fi or computer terminals. Free Wi-Fi is available at a number of the restaurants/cafes on Main St if you buy a drink or a meal, and some have Skype as well.

Bandarawela *p240, map p240*
Banks People's Bank, Esplanade Rd. Most banks congregate at the bottom of Main St and Badulla Rd, **Sampath Bank, Bank of Ceylon, Seylan Bank**. **Internet** There are a number of places on Main St offering internet.

Haputale *p241, map p241*
Banks Bank of Ceylon, Station Rd, and **People's Bank**.

Contents

Footprint features

Ancient Cities

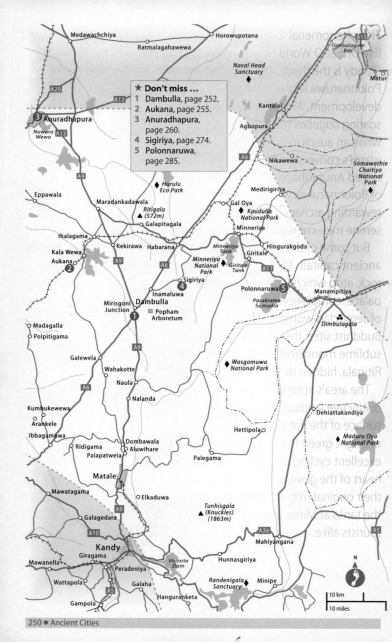

★ **Don't miss ...**
1 Dambulla, page 252.
2 Aukana, page 255.
3 Anuradhapura, page 260.
4 Sigiriya, page 274.
5 Polonnaruwa, page 285.

This phenomenal 'Cultural Triangle' encompasses no fewer than five UNESCO World Heritage Sites. At two points of the triangle (Kandy is the third), the ancient cities of Anuradhapura and Polonnaruwa represent the early phases of the nation's cultural development. Anuradhapura was the capital for 1500 years, its soaring *dagobas* testament to the lofty ambitions of its kings, while an auspicious meeting at nearby Mihintale sealed the island's conversion to Buddhism. Repeated invasions from India forced Anuradhapura's abandonment for the less exposed site of Polonnaruwa, whose city walls today encircle the island's most rewarding archaeological complex, its unmissable highlight the serene rock-cut recumbent Buddha at the Gal Vihara.

But some of the region's most inspiring treasures lie outside the ancient capitals. Most spectacular of all is the astonishing Sigiriya rock, atop which lie the remains of a sort of fifth-century playboy's palace, complete with pin-ups in the form of its famous frescoes of semi-clad women. No less remarkable are some nearby Buddhist sites: the cave paintings at Dambulla; Aukana's sublime monolithic Buddha; and the ancient monastery at Ritigala, hidden deep within the jungle.

The area's appeal extends beyond archaeology though. In this distinctive landscape, occasional boulders of granite break the surface of the flat plains, with rice fields appearing as pockets of bright green in the widespread forest. Quiet roads make it excellent cycling country – just watch out for elephants. At the heart of the government's conservation scheme to re-establish their original migration corridors, two national parks around the tanks at Minneriya and Kaudulla welcome jumbos and tourists alike.

Dambulla and around

→ *Phone code: 066. Colour map 2, B4.*

The richly painted cave temples at Dambulla, which lie atop a vast rocky outcrop, date to the first century BC and form one of Sri Lanka's World Heritage Sites (designated in 1991). Though the site is now privately run by wealthy monks, it is still considered to be part of the Cultural Triangle. Nearby, you can visit the massive rock-cut Aukana Buddha and the monastery at Sasseruwa, while Sigiriya rock is only 19 km away. Those coming from Kandy can visit the rock monastery at Aluwihare, near Matale, and the Nalanda gedige (part of the Cultural Triangle Round Ticket) en route.
▶▶ *For listings, see pages 257-259.*

Ins and outs

Getting there Dambulla lies almost in the dead centre of the country on an important junction of the Kandy–Anuradhapura and Colombo–Trincomalee roads. Consequently the town, and the sights south and northwest described in the section, can be reached by public transport with the exception of Sasseruwa where private transport is required. Buses from Kandy sometimes stop by the post office, a useful place to disembark if staying at the southern end of town.

Getting around Dambulla itself is tiny. The cave temples lie 2 km south of the junction (a short bus ride or Rs 50-100 in a three-wheeler). Most cheaper accommodation is strung out along the main road. Sights around Dambulla are best reached by bus.

Background

Dambulla is sited on a gigantic granite outcrop which towers more than 160 m above the surrounding land. The rock is more than 1.5 km around its base and the summit is at 550 m. The caves were the refuge of **King Valagambahu** (Vattagamani Abhaya) when he was in exile for 14 years. When he returned to the throne at Anuradhapura in the first century BC, he had a magnificent rock temple built at Dambulla. The site has been repaired and repainted several times in the 11th, 12th and 18th centuries. In 2001, the temple authorities completed work on an enormous gold Buddha, said to be the largest in the world, which greets you from the car park.

The caves have a mixture of religious and secular painting and sculpture. There are several reclining Buddhas, including the 15-m-long sculpture of the dying Buddha in Cave 1. The frescoes on the walls and ceilings date from the 15th to 18th centuries. The ceiling frescoes show scenes from the Buddha's life and Sinhalese history. Cave 2 is the largest and most impressive, containing more than 150 statues, illustrating the Mahayana influences on Buddhism at the time through introducing Hindu deities such as Vishnu and Ganesh.

There is little evidence of monks who are housed in monasteries in the valley below where there is a monks' school. Some monasteries and sacred sites receive large donations from Buddhists overseas (particularly Japan) and so are not dependent on government sponsorship. Gifts and your entrance fee have provided the monks here with a 4WD and many other comforts not available to others of similar calling.

Sights

Buddhist Museum

ⓘ www.goldentemple.lk. 0730-2100. Rs 100 or free with a ticket to the caves.

Beneath the big gold Buddha, you reach the bizarre Buddhist Museum inside the Golden Temple (as distinct from the Rock Temple), through a fantastically gaudy dragon's mouth.

Inside are exhibited statues gifted from around the Buddhist world, *ola* leaf manuscripts, copies of some of the cave paintings and other Buddhist objects. Its air-conditioning and piped music give it the atmosphere of a shopping mall.

Beside the museum, a flight of steps lead up into the Golden Temple, and you can climb the new Buddha, in a *dhamma chakka* pose.

The caves

ⓘ 0730-1230 and 1300-1800 (last ticket 1730). Rs 1200 from the ticket booth at the entrance to the complex. Large bags and shoes are not allowed into the complex but they can all be left with the 'shoe keepers' (Rs 25). Hats must be removed and normal temple attire should be worn (cover knees, shoulders, etc). Carry a torch if you wish to view the cave paintings in detail. It is difficult to dodge the touts and beggars who line the steps leading to the caves, and the guides as they stand in the temple doorway (Rs 500). A good alternative to a guide is to buy the Rock Temple brochure from the Buddhist book-shop before starting the ascent (Rs 200).

The climb From the car park, it can be a hot and tiring climb. It is quite steep at first, almost 100 m across at times bare granite, after which there are about 200 steps in a series of 18 terraces, some longer and steeper than others. It is not too difficult to get to the top but try to avoid the heat in the middle of the day. In any case it is best visited in the early morning. There are panoramic views from the terrace of the surrounding jungle and tanks, and of Sigiriya. The caves are about half way up the hill and form part of a temple complex.

Dambulla

N

500 metres
500 yards

Sleeping 🛏
Chamara Guest House 1
Amaya Lake 6
Gimhanala Transit 4

Little Dream 10
Kandalama 5
Oasis Tourist Welfare
Centre 2
Sun Ray Inn 8
Pelwehera Village 9
Thilanka Resort & Spa 3

Eating 🍴
Rest House 1

There are five overhung cliff caves. Monastic buildings have been built in front, complete with cloisters, and these in turn overlook a courtyard which is used for ceremonial purposes and has a wonderful view over the valley floor below. Some of the other subsidiary caves which were occupied by monks contain ancient inscriptions in Brahmi.

Cave I (Devaraja-Viharaya) Contains the huge lying *Parinirvana* Buddha which is 14 m long and carved out of solid rock. The frescoes behind the Arahat Ananda (a disciple) are said to be the oldest in the site, though unrestored they lack the lustre of those in other caves. 'Devaraja' refers to the Hindu god Vishnu. The deity may have been installed here in the Kandyan period though some believe it is older than the Buddha images. There is a Vishnu temple attached.

Cave II (Rajamaha-Viharaya) This much bigger cave is about 24 sq m and 7 m high and was named after the two kings whose images are here. The principal Buddha statue facing the entrance is in the *Abhaya mudra*, under a *makara torana* (or dragon arch). The cave has about 1500 paintings of the Buddha – almost as though the monks had tried to wallpaper the cave. The paintings of his life near the corner to the right are also interesting – you can see his parents holding him as a baby, various pictures of him meditating (counted in weeks, eg cobra hood indicates the sixth week); some have him surrounded by demons, others with cobras and another shows him being offered food by merchants. The other historical scenes are also interesting with the battle between Dutthagamenu and Elara particularly graphic, illustrating the decisive moment when the defeated falls to the ground, head first from an elephant. Here, in the right hand corner, you can see the holy pot which is never empty. Drips are collected into a bucket which sits in a wooden fenced rectangle and is used for sacred rituals by the monks.

Cave III (Maha Alut Viharaya) This cave is about 30 sq m and 18 m high. It was rebuilt in the 18th century and has about 60 images, some under *makara toranas*, and more paintings of thousands of the seated Buddha on the ceiling. This cave was a former storeroom and the frescoes are in the Kandyan style.

Cave IV (Pascima Viharaya or 'western' cave) The smallest cave and once the westernmost: it had the fifth cave constructed later to its west. It contains about 10 images though unfortunately the stupa here was damaged by thieves who came in search of Queen Somawathie's jewels. One image in particular, at the back of the cave, needed restoration. Unfortunately it is now painted in a very strong Marge Simpson yellow which jars with the rest of the cave.

Cave V (Devana Alut Viharaya) The newest, it was once used as a storeroom. The images here are built of brick and plaster and in addition to the Buddha figures, also includes the Hindu deities, Vishnu, Kataragama and Bandara (a local god).

Further reading A Seneviratna, *Golden rock temple of Dambulla*, (Colombo: Sri Lanka Central Cultural Fund, 1983). A good booklet in English and German is on sale, Rs 200.

Dambulla Museum

ⓘ *Just south of the caves and Golden Temple. Open 0800-1600. Rs 400 or included in the Cultural Triangle Round Ticket.*

Don't be discouraged by the first small room, which has exhibits demonstrating how the Dambulla murals and frescoes were created. It may at first look like any local museum with bits cobbled together but climb the stairs for a well laid-out and informative exhibition on the history of Sri Lankan painting and the development of rock and wall art. The seven rooms lead visitors from the Primitive period right through to the 20th century, via the Classical period frescoes at Sigiriya, and murals from the Kandyan period. Exhibits are excellent reproductions on canvas of paintings from all over the island, bringing inaccessible frescoes and murals to people who would otherwise have little opportunity of seeing them.

Around Dambulla → *Aukana and Sasseruwa can be visited en route to Anuradhapura, whilst Matale, Aluwihare and Nalanda can be visited on the way from (or to) Kandy.*

Popham Arboretum

ⓘ *2 km east of the caves, along Kandalama Rd towards the Kandalama Hotel. Rs 500.*

The only arboretum in the Dry Zone, it was set up by Sam Popham, a former tea planter, on his retirement in 1963. Originally planning on replanting, he discovered that clearing the scrub jungle enabled the native trees to seed and saplings to grow, and experimented on re-foresting with minimal human interference. The "Popham method" was a success and how over 70 tropical trees are preserved here, including ebony and satinwood. The woodland has been divided into blocks which are cleared at different times, and visitors have access via a set of well-maintained paths and can walk independently or organize a guided walk through the Bawa-designed visitor centre, which was Popham's house.

Aukana

ⓘ *0700-1900. Rs 500 (includes photography).*

One of the island's most elegant and perfect statues, the Aukana Buddha, to the west of the large Kala Wewa tank, has gained even greater significance to Buddhists since the destruction of the similar (but much larger) statues at Bamiyan in Afghanistan (toponymical research suggests that in ancient times Bamiyan, in the region where Mahayana Buddhism originated, was known as Vokkana or Avakana). Here is a magnificent, undamaged 12-m-high free-standing statue of the Abhayamudra Buddha, showing superhuman qualities, carved out of a single rock. The right hand is raised toward the right shoulder with the palm spread, signifying a lack of fear, while the position of the left draws the worshipper to Buddha for release from earthly bonds. It has been ascribed to King Dhatusena (AD 459-477) who was responsible for the building of several tanks, including the one here. When you walk down to the base, note the small lotus flower in between the Buddha's feet. The carving is so perfectly symmetrical that when it rains the water drops from his nose down to the centre of the 10-cm flower.

For those without their own transport, it is possible to get a bus to Aukana. There are occasional direct buses from Dambulla but more practical may be to take a bus to Kekirawa (45 minutes), and change to a Galnewa bus, getting off at Aukana Junction. From here it is a 500-m walk to the site. From Anuradhapura, buses to Kekirawa take 1½ hours. Aukana also lies on the Colombo–Batticaloa train line but trains stop more frequently at Kala Wewa (8 km from the site), where you can pick up a three-wheeler who will 'go and come back'.

Sasseruwa → Colour map 2, B3.

ⓘ *13 km west of Aukana. Rs 500. Allow 45 mins to explore – best visited early in the morning. Not accessible by public transport. The minor road from Aukana continues to the Sasseruwa via Negampaha, and the surface is poor.*

This extensive complex has an ancient monastery site with more than 100 cave cells, remains of stupas, moonstones and inscriptions, and dates back to the second century BC. Here, too, there is a similar standing Buddha framed by the dark rock, though it is either unfinished or lacks the quality of workmanship. It was possibly carved at the same time as Aukana, although some believe it to be a later copy. One legend is that the two images were carved in a competition between master and student. The master's Buddha at Aukana was completed first, so the Sasseruwa statue was abandoned. Its location, halfway up a rocky hillside, requires climbing nearly 300 steps.

Nalanda → Colour map 2, B4.

ⓘ *49 km north of Kandy, 19 km south of Dambulla. US$5 (children under 12, US$2.50); entrance to the gedige is included in the Cultural Triangle ticket. There are frequent buses to Nalanda that run between Dambulla and Kandy, stopping near the turn off opposite the rest house.*

This small reconstructed *gedige* (Buddha image house) shares some features in common with Hindu temples of southern India. Standing on the raised bund of a reservoir, it was built with stone slabs and originally dates from the seventh to the 10th centuries. Some tantric carvings have been found in the structure which combines Hindu and Buddhist (both Mahayana and Theravada) features. Note the *Karmasutra* bas-relief. It is the only extant Sri Lankan *gedige* built in the architectural style of the seventh-century Pallava shore temples at Mamallapuram near Chennai in India. The place is very atmospheric and has comparatively few visitors, which adds to its appeal. From the rest house where the bus drops visitors off there is a 1 km road, now tarred, leading east to the site.

Aluwihare → Colour map 2, C4.

ⓘ *32 km north of Kandy, 36 km south of Dambulla. Lying on a main tourist route, you will continually be asked for donations, which can get tiresome. Buses run between Matale and Dambulla and stop on the main road – the caves are on the west side. You can also take a 3-wheeler.*

Aluwihare has the renovated ruins of ancient shrines carved out of huge boulders. In the first and second century BC, the site was associated with King Vattagamani Abhaya (103-77 BC). The *Mahavansa* (Buddhist chronicle of the island) was inscribed here in Pali. The original manuscript, inscribed on palm leaves prepared by 500 monks, was destroyed in the mid-19th century, and replacements are still being inscribed today. With the expectation of a Rs 200 'contribution' to the temple (for which you are given a receipt) you are guided first into the small museum, where you will be shown the technique of writing on palmyra palm.

The palmyra palm strips were prepared for manuscripts by drying, boiling and drying again, and then flattened and coated with shell. A stylus was used for inscribing, held stationary while the leaf was moved to produce the lettering or illustration (the rounded shape of some South Asian scripts was a result of this technology). The inscribed grooves would then be rubbed with soot or powdered charcoal while colour was added with a brush. The leaves would then be stacked and sometimes strung together and sometimes 'bound' between decorative wooden 'covers'.

The path up the boulders themselves is quite steep and can be slippery when wet (a newspaper cutting in the museum commemorates how the Duke of Edinburgh "nearly had a nasty fall" during the royal visit in 1956). Four of the 10 caves have ancient inscriptions. The curious 'Chamber of Horrors' has unusual frescoes vividly illustrating punishments doled out to sinners by eager demons, including spearing of the body and pouring of boiling oil into the mouth. The sculptures in another cave show torture on a 'rack' for the wrongdoer and the distress of having one's brains exposed by the skull being cut open. The impressive painted reclining Buddhas include one about 10 m long. The stupa on top of the rock just beyond the cave temples gives fine views of the Dry Zone plains and pine covered mountains.

Matale → *Phone code: 066. Colour map 2, C4. Population: 37,000.*

ⓘ *24 km north of Kandy, 44 km south of Dambulla. To get to Matale from Kandy, the bus runs every 15 mins or so), there are also regular buses from Dambulla. Matale's railway station, in the centre of town 100 m east of the A9, is the terminus of a branch line from Kandy and several slow trains run daily (1½ hrs).*

The small but bustling town surrounded by hills has some interesting short walks as well as some longer treks into the Knuckles Range (see page 206). The British built a fort here at the beginning of the 19th century (of which only a gate remains) while the branch railway line opened in 1880. Tour groups often stop at the Sri Muthumariamman Thevasthanam temple here.

A large number of **spice gardens** line the road out of Matale towards Dambulla, as well as plantations of coffee, cocoa and rubber. While most are genuine, some so-called spice gardens which are open to visitors have very few plants and are primarily there to sell commercially grown spices and Ayurvedic herbal products.

◉ Dambulla and around listings

For Sleeping and Eating price codes and other relevant information, see pages 26-32.

● Sleeping

Dambulla *p252, map p253*

LL-AL Kandalama (Aitken Spence), head along Kandalama Rd for 4.5 km, take right fork, T555 5000, www.heritancehotels.com/kandalama. Winner of many awards including Asia's 1st Green Globe. 152 plush a/c rooms in 2 wings, and luxury suites. Unique design by Geoffrey Bawa, built between massive rock and peaceful tank and indistinguishable from its jungle surrounds. Resort-style complex with excellent cuisine and full facilities, 3 pools including one of the most spectacularly sited swimming pools in the world with crystal-clear water (filtration system based on ancient Sri Lankan technology). Magnificent views across undisturbed forest, magical details, exceptional service.

L-B Amaya Lake, follow Kandalama Rd for 4.5 km, take left fork, then follow lake around for 4.6 km, T446 1500, www.amayaresorts.com. Variety of rooms including suites, chalets and clay eco-lodges (with TVs, DVD players and minibar) with a village theme. Good pool in large gardens, restaurant, Ayurvedic health centre, very attractive setting on edge of lake.

A-B Thilanka Resort and Spa, 3 km south of Dambulla, follow Kandy Rd, T446 8001, www.thilankaresortandspa.lk. Well-proportioned and bright rooms in villas set in pleasant grounds. Huge pool, restaurant serves average food.

B Pelwehera Village, Bullagala Junction, 3 km northeast of Dambulla, T228 4281, T077-388 9052, www.pelweheraresort.com. Large, rather bare but spotless rooms, restaurant, popular with tour groups.

B-C Gimanhala Transit, 754 Anuradhapura Rd, 1 km north of Colombo Junction,

T228 4864, gimanhala@sltnet.lk. Comfortable, clean a/c rooms, good restaurant overlooking lovely large and very clean pool. Bike hire, shop. Best of the town hotels, good value.

E-F Sun Ray Inn, 156 Kandy Rd, T228 4769, urdayanandasiri@yahoo.com. 7 clean rooms, 5 with veranda, 1 with a/c, restaurant. Friendly management, tours can be arranged.

F Chamara Guest House, 121 Matale/Kandy Rd, T228 4488. Simple, moderately clean rooms, with nets, fan, restaurant and pleasant communal terrace. Prices can be negotiated in low season. Relaxed, and owner is helpful and can give advice for onward travel.

G Little Dream, close to tank along road to **Amaya Lake**, T072-289 3736. 3 simple rooms in peaceful, laid-back spot (hammocks) close to Kandalama tank with swimming hole nearby. No electricity or hot water but friendly. It's very isolated so might not be one for lone female travellers.

G Oasis Tourist Welfare Centre, down a side road opposite the caves, T228 4388. Friendly and homely though very basic. 6 dark rooms with shared bathroom you won't want to spend much time in.

Around Dambulla *p255*

A Kassapa Lions Rock, Digampathaha, 15 km towards Habarana, T567 7440, www.kassapalionsrock.com. Nestled in a rural village, 31 well-appointed chalets. Certified as a bird-friendly resort.

F Rest House, Park Rd, at crossroads south of town centre, Matale, T222 2299. 14 clean, spacious a/c and fan rooms with balcony, friendly and efficient.

F Rest House, 1.5 km from the *gedige*, Nalanda, T224 6199. Old rest house in good position, 7 basic rooms with clean attached bath.

● Eating

Dambulla *p252, map p253*
There are cheap places to eat clustered near the bus station, and most hotels also do food.
Gimanhala Transit Hotel has a good

restaurant and a snack bar at the front (open at lunchtime). The **Dambulla Rest House**, does a lunchtime rice and curry for Rs 600 as well as lunch packets, but it's nothing to write home about and the staff are disinterested.

Around Dambulla *p255*
The roadside places on the Kandy–Dambulla Rd in Aluwihare usually serve a limited selection of bland Westernized food for the tour groups on the way up from Kandy.
ᵀᵀ Aluwihare Kitchens, The Walauwe, 33 Aluwihare, T222 2404. This is the exception to the above. For parties of 6 or more is the promise of 'the biggest rice and curry in Sri Lanka' (25 curries), if booked in advance. Superb location next to the home of Ena de Silva (see Shopping, below) with stunning views of the surrounding countryside.

● Shopping

Dambulla *p252, map p253*
Branch of the **Buddhist Bookshop** in the Buddhist museum complex. Sells publications on Buddhism, meditation and the Rock Temple. Also has an informative booklet for sale on the caves.

Around Dambulla *p255*
Matale Heritage Centre, The Walauwe, 33 Aluwihare, 2 km north of Matale, T222 2404. This community-based enterprise, the brainchild of renowned designer Ena de Silva, is a rewarding stop for those with a serious interest in tapestries, batiks, furniture and brassware. Phone in advance.

● Transport

Dambulla *p252, map p253*
Bus The 'New Bus Stand' bus station is at the southern end of town and long-distance buses and those from Sigiriya can be caught from here. Local buses run to the site entrance, as do Kandy buses but catching a bus from the

bus station is easier than trying to flag one down on the road (although some guesthouse owners will help with this). Regular services to **Colombo** (4 hrs), **Anuradhapura**, **Kandy** and **Polonnaruwa** (about 2½ hrs each) and frequently to **Sigiriya** (30 mins).

than usual. There are plenty of banks with ATMs in town, including **Commercial Bank**, **Hatton National Bank**, **Seylan Bank** and **Bank of Ceylon**. **Internet** There are a number of internet places in Dambulla, including one at the junction near the post office (Rs 100 per hr). **Medical centre** Opposite Commercial Bank, T2284735. **Useful addresses** Tourist Police, New Bus Stand.

ⓘ Directory

Dambulla *p252, map p253*
Banks Trading at the 24-hr dedicated economic centre, north of the temple complex, means that banks have longer hours

Around Dambulla *p255*
Banks There are branches of all the main banks in Matale town.

Anuradhapura and Mihintale

→ *Phone code: 025. Colour map 2, A3/4. Population: 58,000.*
Anuradhapura is Sri Lanka's most sacred city. Along with Mihintale, it represents the first real home of Buddhism in Sri Lanka, and thus contains some of the island's most sacred Buddhist sites. It is here that the Sri Maha Bodhi tree was planted from a cutting from the original Bo under which the Buddha received Enlightenment, to this day drawing thousands of pilgrims from around the world. Today, Anuradhapura's ruins and monuments are widely scattered which makes a thorough tour exhausting and time-consuming, but for those with more than a passing interest in the island's past it more than repays the effort. Nearby Mihintale, where King Tissa received the Emperor Asoka's son Mahinda and converted to Buddhism, makes an excellent day-trip away from the bustle and noise, and can even be used as an alternative base. ►► *For listings, see pages 271-273.*

Ins and outs

Getting there

Many visitors arrive from Dambulla to the southeast, along the A9/A13. Others come from Colombo via Kurunegala and Yapahuwa (see page 107), though the quickest route from the capital is along the A12 from Puttalam (see page 102). From Trincomalee, the route is via Horowupatana giving you the opportunity to visit Mihintale first. Anuradhapura and Mihintale are also now accessible from the north, from Jaffna via Vavuniya (see page 328). Buses are available in all directions. By train, Anuradhapura lies on the Northern line, and all trains between Colombo and Vavuniya stop here. From Kandy, change at Polgahawela. Mihintale, 11 km east of Anuradhapura, is a short bus or cycle ride east from the city.

Getting around → *A high police presence remains in Anuradhapura, following damage in the 1998 LTTE attack.*

A three-wheeler from the train or bus station to your accommodation, assuming you are staying in the New Town, should cost around Rs 150-200. The New Town is about 2 km southeast of the central sites. If you want a full day tour, consider hiring a car or three-wheeler since the ruins, especially to the north, are very spread out and without cover can be exhausting under a hot sun. Many people use a bicycle (available from guesthouses) to get around but you should be prepared to park it and walk when told to. Bear in mind also that unless you follow a prescribed route (and even if you do) it is easy to get lost, as there are many confusing tracks and signposting can be poor. Unlike Polonnaruwa, the monuments are not clustered into convenient groups so planning an itinerary can be difficult. The order of sites below follows a 'figure-of-eight' pattern, starting in the central area, then heading 3 km north and then east to Kuttan-Pokuna, before returning south to the Jetavanarama *dagoba*, and looping across to explore the museums and lakeside monuments south of the central area.

Best time to visit

There are several festivals during the year. In April **Snana Puja** is celebrated at Sri Maha Bodhi. In June, at the full moon in **Poson**, the introduction of Buddhism to Sri Lanka is celebrated with huge processions when many pilgrims visit the area. In July/August, during **Daramiti Perahera**, locals bring firewood in a procession to the Bodhi tree, commemorating a time when bonfires were lit to keep away wild animals.

Tourist information

① *T222 4546, Mon-Fri 0900-1700, Sat 0900-1300.*

Anuradhapura tourist information office is on Sri Maha Bodhi Mawatha, the best approach road to the ancient city. Here you can pick up a local map and planning advice. There are four ticket offices: one at the Tourist Information Counter, another at the Archaeological Museum, a third at the Jetavanarama Museum, and finally one towards the Dalada Maligawa. The site is included in the Cultural Triangle Round Ticket (US$50, see page 52) though it does not cover all sights in the city. A single ticket for the main site costs US$25 (half-price for children). It is worth getting a guide, Rs 500-800 for three to four hours. There are lots of drink stalls around; the ones near the *dagobas* tend to be expensive. The souvenir sellers can be very persistent and unpleasant, so be firm. Mihintale is not covered by the Cultural Triangle Round Ticket; there is a Rs 500 charge for visiting the sacred centre.

Anuradhapura → *Allow a full day to explore the area.*

Background

From origins as a settlement in the sixth century BC, Anuradhapura was made Sri Lanka's first capital in 377 BC by King Pandukhabhaya (437-367 BC) who started the great irrigation works on which it depended, and named it after the constellation Anuradha. The first era of religious building followed the conversion of King Devanampiya Tissa (ruled 250-10 BC). In his 40-year reign these included the Thuparama Dagoba, Issurumuniyagala, and the Maha Vihara with the Sri Maha Bodhi and the Brazen Palace. A branch of the Bodhi tree (see below) under which the Buddha was believed to have gained his Enlightenment was brought from Bodhgaya in India and successfully transplanted. It is one of the holiest Buddhist sites in the world.

Anuradhapura remained a capital city until the ninth century AD, when it reached its peak of power and vigour. At this time it may have stretched 25 km. Successive waves of invasion from South India however finally took their toll. After the 13th century it almost entirely disappeared, the irrigation works on which it had depended falling into total disuse, and its political functions were taken over first by Polonnaruwa, and then by capitals to the south. 'Rediscovered' by Ralph Backhaus, archaeological research, excavation and restoration was started in 1872, and has continued ever since. In 1988, it was designated a World Heritage Site. The New Town was started in the 1950s, and is now the most important Sinhalese city of the north. It houses the headquarters of the Sri Lanka Archaeological Survey.

Approach

Anuradhapura rivals Milton Keynes for its roundabouts. If you are staying in the New Town, the best approach to the ancient city is to cycle northwest across Main Street and the railway line, to Jayanthi Mawatha where you turn right, past the two rest houses, up to **Lion Pillar**. Here you turn left on to Sri Maha Bodhi Mawatha, continue past the Tourist Information Office (where you can pick up a ticket if necessary) up to the barrier, beyond which the road leads to the **Sri Maha Bodhi**. You are not allowed to cycle past this point, and you will be asked to park your bike in the car park. Don't do this, as you will leave yourself with a long walk back from the central area to pick up your bike, though there are sometimes buses. Instead, continue past the car park for almost 1 km, heading up Nandana Mawatha (or path) towards the huge white **Ruvanwelisiya Dagoba**. Here you can park your bike (for free) close to the central area. There is a wide pedestrian walkway which leads from the *dagoba* to the Sri Maha Bodhi.

Ruvanwelisiya Dagoba

Begun by King Dutthagamenu (Dutugemunu) to house relics, this is one of the most impressive of all Sri Lanka's *dagobas*. Built with remarkable opulence, the king, who was said to have great luck, found a rich vein of silver from Ridigama to cover the expenses. Monks from as far away as Alexandria were recorded as being present at the enshrinement of the relics in 140 BC. The king however fell ill before the *dagoba*'s completion, so he asked his brother Saddhatissa to complete the work for him. Saddhatissa covered the dome with bamboo reeds and painted them with lacquer and imitation gold so that the king could witness the 'completion' of his *magnum opus* on his deathbed. Today, the dome is 80 m in diameter at its base and 53 m high. Apart from its sheer size, you will notice first the frieze on the outer wall of hundreds of life-size (and life-like) elephants, most of which are modern replacements. The *dagoba* is surrounded by the remains of sculptural pieces. You can see the columns often no more than 500 cm in height dotted around in the grass underneath huge rain trees where monkeys play. A small passage leads to the relic chamber. At the cardinal points are four 'chapels' which were reconstructed in 1873, when renovation started. The restoration has flattened the shape of the dome, and some of the painting is of questionable style, but it remains a remarkably striking monument. Today, you may find watching the *dagoba* being 'whitewashed' an interesting spectacle.

Brazen Palace

ⓘ *The site is open only on poya days.*

Follow the pedestrian walkway south towards to the Sri Maha Bodhi. Just before reaching the tree, you will see the many pillars of the Brazen Palace on your left. The name refers to the first monastery here and its now-disappeared roof, reputedly made of bronze. Built originally by Dutthagamenu, it was the heart of the monastic life of the city, the Maha Vihara. Described in the *Mahavansa* as having nine storeys, there were 1600 pillars, each just under 4 m high, laid out over an area 70 sq m. Above, each storey was supposed to have 100 windows, with 1000 rooms overall, the building adorned with coral and

White lines

The ubiquitous *dagoba* is one of the most striking features of the island, ranging in size from tiny village structures to the enormous monuments at Ruvanwelisiya in Anuradhapura and Mahaseya at Mihintale. Even in nature the stone of the canonball tree fruit is a perfectly formed white *dagoba*.

There are of course many reasons why they stand out in a landscape: partly for their position, partly their size but mostly for their colour – a dazzling white. Most are beautifully maintained and are often repainted before important Buddhist festivals.

It is no easy job to paint a large *dagoba*. A lime whitewash is used. Elaborate bamboo scaffolding cocoons the spire linked to the base by rickety bamboo ladders. Bamboo is ideal as it can be bent to conform to the shape

of the dome and the lightness makes the ladders easily moveable. A team of about five painters assembles on the ladder which is about 20 m in height. Four men are deployed with ropes attached at the top and midpoints to give it some form of stability. At each stage, a painter is responsible for about 3 m of the surface in height, and an arm's width. The topmost 1.5 m of the painter's patch is covered first. Then he takes three steps down the ladder to cover the bottom 1.5 m. Once completed, the bamboo structure is moved an arm's width round and the whole process starts again.

You'll notice that not all the *dagobas* have yet been restored – their red brick or plain plastered surface are dull in comparison with those that have been returned to their original condition.

precious stones. This requires imagination these days, though now a wooden first floor has been erected, aiming to recreate the monastery's top storey. Originally destroyed by Indian invasion, the monastery was rebuilt several times, much of what is visible today being the reconstruction of King Parakramabahu I in the last quarter of the 11th century, making use of the remnants of former buildings.

Sri Maha Bodhi tree → *This is one of Sri Lanka's most sacred sites.*
ⓘ *Rs 100. Shoes must be removed on entering the terrace – there is a booth at the eastern entrance.*

The 'Bo' ('Bodhi') tree or Pipal (*Ficus religiosa*) was planted as a cutting brought from the tree in Bodhgaya in India under which Buddha found Enlightenment, brought by Emperor Asoka's daughter, the Princess Sanghamitta, at some point after 236 BC. Guardians have kept uninterrupted watch over the tree ever since, making it, all tourist literature will proudly tell you, the oldest historically authenticated tree in the world. Today, in keeping with tradition, it is the army who guard the tree, while the Director of the Peradeniya Botanical Gardens tends to its health. Nowadays, you can only see the top of the Bo tree, on the highest terrace, which is supported by an elaborate metal structure and is surrounded by brass railings. There are other Bo trees around the Sri Maha Bodhi which are bedecked with colourful prayer flags and smaller strips of cloth which pilgrims tie in expectation of prayers being answered. In April a large number of pilgrims arrive to make offerings during the **Snana puja**, and to bathe the tree with milk. Every 12th year the ceremony is particularly auspicious.

Anuradhapura

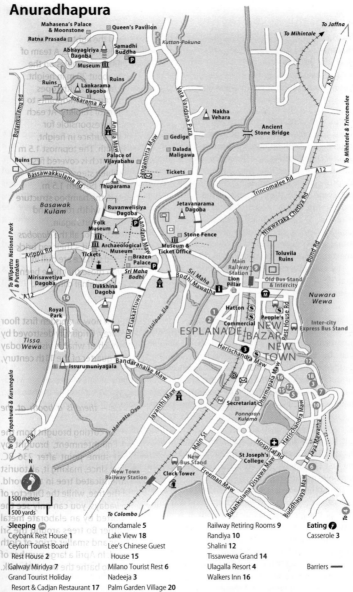

Mahasena's Palace & Moonstone
Queen's Pavilion
Ratna Prasada
Abhayagiriya Dagoba
Samadhi Buddha
Museum
Kuttan-Pokuna
To Mihintale
To Jaffna
Ruins
Lankarama Dagoba
Lankarama Rd
Ruins
Bulankulama Rd
Nakha Vehara
Gedige
Jaya Vandana Para
Ancient Stone Bridge
To Mihintale & Trincomalee
Ruins
Palace of Vijayabahu
Dalada Maligawa
Sanghamitta Para
Tickets
A20
A12
To Trincomalee & Trincomalee
Bassawakkulama Rd
Thuparama
Trincomalee Rd
Basawak Kulam
Ruvanwelisiya Dagoba
Jetavanarama Dagoba
Niwwataka Chetiya Rd
Bund Rd
Folk Museum
Vandana Para
Stone Fence
To Wilpattu National Park & Puttalam
Archaeological Museum
Tickets
Museum & Ticket Office
Arippu Rd
Brazen Palace
Sri Maha Bodhi
Main Railway Station
Toluvila Ruins
Mirisawetiya Dagoba
A12
Dakkhina Dagoba
Sri Maha Bodhi Mawatha
Lion Pillar
Old Bus Stand & Intercity
To Tissawewa
Royal Park
Halpanu Ela
Old Elakattuwa
Hatton
Commercial
People's
Nuwara Wewa
To Yapahuwa & Kurunegala
A28
Tissa Wewa
Issurumuniyagala
Bandaranaike Maw
NEW BAZAR NEW TOWN
Inter-city Express Bus Stand
ESPLANADE
Harischandra Maw
Jayanthi Maw
Malwatu Oya
Secretariat
Ponnaran Kulama
Dharmapala Maw
Rest House Rd
To Colombo
New Bus Stand
Main St
Freeman Maw
Harischandra Maw
R Jaya Mawatha
New Town Railway Station
St Joseph's College
Hospital Rd
Bulankulama Dissawa Maw
Buddhagaya Maw
Clock Tower
N
500 metres
500 yards

Sleeping
Ceybank Rest House 1
Ceylon Tourist Board Rest House 2
Galway Miridya 7
Grand Tourist Holiday Resort & Cadjan Restaurant 17

Kondamale 5
Lake View 18
Lee's Chinese Guest House 15
Milano Tourist Rest 6
Nadeeja 3
Palm Garden Village 20

Railway Retiring Rooms 9
Randiya 10
Shalini 12
Tissawewa Grand 14
Ulagalla Resort 4
Walkers Inn 16

Eating
Casserole 3

Barriers ———

Five of the best sites not to miss in Anuradhapura

Sri Maha Bodhi – one of the holiest trees in the world.
Ruvanwelisiya dagoba – impressive *dagoba* with elephant wall.
Samadhi Buddha – serene statue beloved by Jawarhalal Nehru.
Jetavananarama dagoba – simply enormous!
Issurumuniyagala – bats, reclining Buddha and 'the lovers'.

Archaeological and Folk museums

This is convenient place to visit these two museums which are both worth taking a look around. The **Archaeological Museum** ⓘ *0800-1700, closed public holidays, entry with a Cultural Triangle ticket*, is in the old colonial headquarters. It is an excellent small museum, with a large collection from all over the island, including some beautiful pieces of sculpture and finds from Mihintale. It is well laid out, with occasional informative labels and some fascinating exhibits. There are statues from several sites, moonstones, implements, and a model of Thuparama *vatadage*. Outside in the garden, there are beautifully sculpted guard stones and an array of meticulously designed latrines. Separate latrine plinths were used for urinals, solid waste and bidets. Under each immaculately carved platform was a succession of pots containing sand, charcoal and limestone to purify the waste.

The **Folk Museum** ⓘ *Tue-Sat 0900-1700, Rs 500*, nearby, is a collection that reflects rural life in the North Central Province with a large display of vessels used by villagers in Rajarata, and handicrafts.

Thuparama

Return to the Ruvanswelisiya *dagoba* to pick up your bike. Continuing north, turn left at the crossroads to the site's oldest *dagoba*, said to house the right collar-bone of the Buddha. Built by Devanampiya, the 19-m-high *dagoba* was originally in the shape of a 'paddy-heap' – its beautiful bell shape dates to renovation work completed in 1862. It is surrounded by concentric circles of graceful granite monolithic pillars of a *vatadage* which was added in the seventh century, possibly originally designed to support an over-arching thatched cover. It is a centre of active pilgrimage, decorated with flags and lights.

Abhayagiriya Dagoba

Left from the first crossroads, 2 km north along Anulla Mawatha to the Abhagiriya Dagoba. First, a detour to the west takes you to the restored **Lankarama Dagoba**. Built in the first century BC it bears some similarities to the earlier Thuparama. Some columns remain of its *vatadage*.

The Abhayagiriya Dagoba was the centre of one of Anuradhapura's largest and oldest monastic complexes. It is 400 m round and was supposedly 135 m high in its original form (part of the pinnacle has disappeared). It is now about 110 m high. Built in 88 BC by Vattagamani (and later restored by Parakramabahu I in the 12th century), it has two splendid sculpted *dwarapalas* (guardians) at the threshold. The *dagoba* and its associated monastery were built in an attempt to weaken the political hold of the Hinayana Buddhists and to give shelter to monks of the Mahayana school. It was considered an important seat of Buddhist learning and the Chinese traveller/monk Fa Hien, visiting it in the fifth century, noted that there were 5000 monks in residence. He also points out a 7-m jade Buddha, sparkling with gems, while the *dagoba* itself was said to have been built over a Buddha footprint. It is currently covered in scaffolding as restoration work is undertaken.

Abhayagiriya (Fa Hien) Museum

Abhayagiriya (Fa Hien) Museum, just south of the Abhayagiriya Dagoba, was built by the Chinese. The collection includes further examples of latrine plinths as displayed in the Archaeological Museum. There is also an extensive display detailing the excavation of the Abhayagiriya site.

Ratna Prasada

To the west of the Abhayagiriya Dagoba are the ruins of the monastery. The area had once been the 'undesirable' outskirts of Anuradhapura where the cremation grounds were sited. In protest against the king's rule, an ascetic community of monks set up a *Tapovana* community (see box, page 266) of which this is an architectural example. This type of monastery typically had two pavilions connected by a stone bridge within a high-walled enclosure which contained a pond. The main entrance was from the east, with a porch above the entrance. Here the Ratna Prasada, or 'gem palace', did not remain a peaceful haven but was the scene of bloody massacres when a rebellious group took refuge with the monks and were subsequently beheaded by the king's men. Their turn to have their heads roll in the dust followed another bloody revolt.

Mahasena Palace

The nearby Mahasena Palace has a particularly fine carved stone tablet and one of the most beautifully carved **moonstones** (see page 372), though the necessary protective railing surrounding it makes photography a little tricky. Note also the flight of steps held up by miniature stone dwarfs. You can return to the Archaeological Museum by taking the Lankarama Road to the south.

Samadhi Buddha

Continue east from the Abhayagiriya Dagoba to this superb statue of the serene Buddha, probably dating from the fourth century AD. With an expression depicting 'extinction of feeling and compassion', some used to think the expression changes as the sun's light moves across it. Sadly though it has now been roofed to protect it from the weather.

Kuttan-Pokuna

A new road through the forest leads to these two ponds – recently restored eighth- and ninth-century ritual baths with steps from each side descending to the water. They were probably for the use of the monastery or for the university nearby. Though called **'twin' ponds**, one is more than 10 m longer than the other. You can see the underground water supply channel at one end of the second bath.

South to Jetavaranama Dagoba

There are two routes south from here. Sangamitta Mawatha leads back to the central area through the site of the 11th-century palace of **Vijayabahu I**, and close to the original **Dalada Maligawa** where the Tooth Relic was first enshrined when it was brought to Ceylon in AD 313. Only the stone columns remain. Alternatively, a 2-km cycle down Vata Vandana Para takes you straight to the vast Jetavanarama Dagoba.

Forest finery

The *Pansukulika* or *Tapovana* sect of ascetic Buddhist hermits who lived a simple life of deep meditation in forests and caves around the seventh to the 11th centuries are associated with Arankale, Mihintale and Ritigala. The monks were expected to wear ragged clothing and to immerse themselves in seeking the Truth, devoid of ritualistic forms of worship associated with Buddha images, relics and relic chambers. Such communities often won the admiration and support of kings, such as Sena I (AD 831-851).

The sites had certain features in common. There was a porched entrance, ambulatories, a water pool for cleansing and the *padhanaghara*. Another similarity was an open terrace, possibly intended as a 'chapter house' connected to a smaller section which was usually roofed. These 'double platforms' were aligned east to west; the two raised stone-faced platforms were connected by a narrow walkway or bridge. An interesting contradiction of the austere life was the beautifully carved latrines or urinal stones the monks used, examples of which can be seen in the Anuradhapura Archaeological Museum (see page 264).

Jetavanarama Dagoba

This *dagoba*, looming impressively from the plain, is said to be the highest brick-bu dagoba of its kind in the world. Started by King Mahasena (AD 275-292), its massiv scale was designed in a competitive spirit to rival the orthodox Maha Vihara. The pave platform on which it stands covers more than 3 ha and it has a diameter of over 100 r In 1860 Emerson Tennent, in his book *Ceylon*, calculated that it had enough bricks build a 3-m-high brick wall 25 cm thick from London to Edinburgh, equal to th distance from the southern tip of Sri Lanka to Jaffna and back down the coast Trincomalee. The *dagoba* is being renovated with help from UNESCO, though wo periodically stops as there is a dearth of bricks.

The size of the image house here shows that Mahasena had an enormous Budd image, similar to (though larger than) the one at Aukana, installed here facing th dagoba. There is a huge lotus pedestal, with large mortices for the feet of the statue. Th image would have been destroyed by fire.

Jetavanarama Museum

ⓘ *0800-1700, closed public holidays, entry with a Cultural Triangle Round Ticket.*

This museum, well worth a visit, houses some interesting objects from the surroundir 120-ha site, including some fine guardstones and an amazingly intricate 8 mm gold cha with 14 distinguishable flowers.

To the lakeside monuments

Continuing west across the main site towards Tissawewa, you might visit th Archaeological and Folk museums at this point (see above). West of here is the **Basawa Kulam tank**, the oldest artificial lake in the city, built by King Pandukabhaya in the four century BC. The dried-up southern side is good for walks and birdwatching, and there a excellent sunset views from the eastern shore.

Alternatively, head south to stop off for lunch or a drink at the **Nuwarawewa Re House**. The Miraswetiya Dagoba is close by.

Mirisawetiya Dagoba

This was the first monument to be built by Dutthagemunu after his consecration, enshrining a miraculous sceptre which contained a Buddha relic. The sceptre which had been left here by the king when he visited the tank, could not on his return be removed by any means. After a Chola invasion, the *dagoba* was completely rebuilt during the reign of King Kasyapa V in AD 930. Surrounded by the ruins of monasteries on three sides, there are some superb sculptures of *Dhyani* Buddhas in the shrines of its chapels. It is currently being renovated.

Tissawewa and Royal Park

This tank was built by King Devanampiya Tissa, and was associated with the bathing rituals of newly crowned kings. You can walk/jog on the east and south sides along the raised tank bund and continue all round using local tracks on the west and a tarmac road on the north. The park just below the lake is very pleasant as it has few visitors. You can wander undisturbed across large rocks among ruined buildings and remains of bathing pools.

Isurumuniyagala Monastery

0800-1930. Rs 200. Ask for permission to take photos.

This small group of striking black rocks is one of the most attractive and peaceful places in town. It also has some outstanding sculptures. The temple, carved out of solid rock, houses a large statue of the reclining Buddha. There is a cleft in the rock which is full of bats which are fascinating to watch. On the terraces outside is a small square pool. Don't miss the beautifully carved elephants, showing great individual character, just above the water level as if descending to it. The small **museum** is to the left of the entrance. Some of the best sculptures in Anuradhapura are now housed here, including perhaps the most famous of all – 'the lovers', which may represent Dutthagemunu's son Saliya and his girlfriend Asokamala, for whom he forsook the throne.

Behind the temple, you can climb up steps to the top of the rock above the temple to get a good view of the countryside and tank. Here there is a footprint carved into the rock, in to which money is thrown.

Nuwara Wewa

Nuwara Wewa, which lies to the east of the New Town, is the largest of Anuradhapura's artificial lakes (1000 ha). It was probably built by Gajabahu I in the second century AD.

Mihintale → *Colour map 2, A3. 11 km east of Anuradhapura.*

Mihintale (pronounced Mihin-taalay), named as Mahinda's Hill, is revered as the place where Mahinda converted King Devanampiya Tissa to Buddhism in 243 BC, thereby enabling Buddhism to spread to the whole island. The legend tells how King Tissa was chasing a stag during a hunting expedition. The stag reached Mihintale and fled up the hillside followed by the king until he reached a place surrounded by hills, where the animal disappeared and the frustrated king was astonished to find a gentle person who spoke to him the Buddha's teachings. It was Mahinda, Asoka's son, who had come to preach Buddhism and was able to convert the king along with 40,000 followers. As well as being important historically, it is an important religious site and is well worth visiting as it a pleasant place to just stroll around away from the crowds at the more famous ancient sites. Mihintale town is little more than a junction and a few shops. It is however an important centre for pilgrims during the June festival.

Approach → *If visiting in the heat of the day bring socks to protect your feet against the hot floor.*
Mihintale is close to the Anuradhapura–Trincomalee road. The huge *dagoba* can be see
from miles around, and is especially striking at night. At the junction with the village roa
where you turn off for the main site, there are statues of six of the principal characters
the site. Follow the minor road leading to the site. On the right are the ruins of a nint
century **hospital**, which appears to have had an outer court where medicines we
ground and stored, and stone tanks for oil and herbal baths. The inner court appears t
have had small treatment rooms. A 10th-century stone inscription mentions the use
leeches in treatment. There is a small archaeological museum nearby (see below).

On the left at the foot of the steps, there is evidence of the **quincunx vihara** of
monastery (*arama*). You can avoid about half of the steps by driving round to the upp
car park, which takes you straight to the second (refectory) level.

The climb

There are 1840 granite **steps**, some carved into the rock, to the top but they are very shallo
and it is much less of a climb than it first looks. The width of the steps indicate the larg
number of pilgrims who visited the sacred site on special occasions in the past. The clim
starts gently, rising in a broad stairway of 350 steps shaded by frangipani trees which lead t
the first platform. Further steps to the right take you up to an open area with Kantaka Chetiya

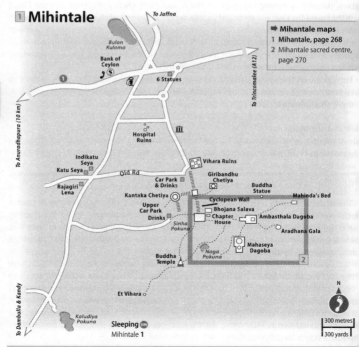

1 Mihintale

➡ **Mihintale maps**
1 Mihantale, page 268
2 Mihantale sacred centre,
   page 270

The first terrace

Kantaka Chetiya is the earliest *stupa* here. Excavated in 1932-1935, it had been severely damaged. Over 130 m in circumference, today it is only about 12 m high compared with its original height of perhaps 30 m. There is some unique stonework in the four projecting frontispieces at the cardinal points, especially to the eastern and southern points. Note the marvellously detailed friezes of geese, dwarves and a variety of other animals, flanked by *stelae* with floral designs. Around the Kantaka Chetiya are 68 caves, where the first monks here resided.

Returning to the first platform, steeper steps lead to a large refectory terrace. As you climb up (it takes under 10 minutes from the car park, at a gentle pace) you can see the impressive outer cyclopean wall of the complex. As an alternative to the steps to get to the refectory level, take a faint footpath to the left between the second and third flights. This crosses an open grassy area. Walk to the end and you will see the lake, green with algae. A path to the left takes you towards the **Giribandhu Chetiya Kiri Vehara**, though it is largely ruined and grassed over on the north side. You can look down on the lower car park and the quincunx. To the right, the path approaches the refectory from the rear and you pass a massive stone trough.

The second terrace

The Refectory Immediately on the left is the **Relic House** and the rectangular **Bhojana Salava** (Monks' refectory). There is a stone aqueduct and two granite troughs, one probably used for rice, the other for gruel. The square **Chapter House** or 'Conversation Hall' with signs of 48 pillars and a 'throne' platform, immediately to the north, is where the monks and lay members met. This has the bases of a series of evenly spaced small brick *dagobas*. At the entrance, stone slabs covered in 10th-century inscriptions on granite give detailed rules governing the sacred site.

The flat grassy terrace which can also be approached by car from the south up the old paved road or steps down from the Kantaka Chetiya, is dotted with trees and the outlines of three small shrines.

Sinha Pokuna (Lion Bath) To the west of the terrace, a short distance down the old road, this is about 2 m sq and 1.8 m deep and has excellent carvings in the form of a frieze around the bottom of the tank of elephants, lions and warriors. The finest, however, is the 2-m-high rampant lion whose mouth forms the spout. Water was gathered in the tank by channelling and feeding it through the small mystic gargoyle similar to the one that can be seen at Sigiriya.

The main path up to the Ambasthala Dagoba up the long flight of steps starts by the 'Conversation Hall' in the square. After a five-minute climb a path leads off to the right, round the hillside, to the Naga Pokuna, which you can visit on the way back down (see below). Continuing to climb, you pass a beautifully inscribed rock on the right hand side listing in second-century AD script lands owned by the king.

The sacred centre → *Rs 500, plus tip for shoes.*

Ambasthala Dagoba At the top of the steps, you reach the ticket office, where you must leave your shoes (and hat). Straight ahead at the heart of the complex is the 'mango tree' *dagoba*, the holiest part of the site, built at the traditional meeting place of King Tissa and Asoka's son Mahinda. The monk in his office makes frequent loud-speaker announcements for donations from pilgrims – these donations have funded the erection of a large white Buddha statue on a rock overlooking the central area in 1991, up to whic you can climb. The bronze Buddhas are gifts from Thailand.

Sela Cetiya A rock stupa at the site of the original mango tree has a replica of the Buddha footprint. It is quite small and is surrounded a gilt railing covered in prayer flags, with scattering of pilgrims' coins.

Mahinda's cave A path leads out of the northeast corner of the compound between small cluster of monks' houses down a rough boulder track to the cave, less than 10-minute walk away. A stall selling local herbal and forest product remedies sometimes set up halfway. The cave is formed out of an extraordinary boulder, hollowe out underneath to create a narrow platform at the very end of a ridge above the pla below. From the stone 'couch', known as **Mahinda's bed**, there are superb views to th north across the tanks and forested plains of the Dry Zone. You have to retrace your ste to the Ambasthala compound.

Aradhana Gala From the southeast corner of the compound a path with rudimenta steps cut in the bare granite rock leads to the summit of the Aradhana Gala (Meditatio Rock). It is a very steep climb, and if you have no socks, very hot on the feet. A stron railing makes access quite secure. There is nothing much to see on the rock but there a superb views from the top, especially across the compound to the Mahaseya Dagob which is at the same height.

Mahaseya dagoba A short flight of steep steps from the southwest corner of th compound, just beyond a small temple with a modern portrayal of Mahinda meeting Kin Tissa at the mango tree, leads up to the summit (310 m) with the Mahaseya Dagob According to legend this was built on the orders of King Tissa as a reliquary for a lock of th Buddha's hair or for relics of Mahinda. The renovated *dagoba*, which dominates the skylin commands superb views back towards Anuradhapura to the southwest. Another mon may ask for donations here (anything above Rs 100 is recorded in a book).

On the south side of the main *dagoba* is a smaller brick *dagoba* while abutting it on i south side is a small Buddhist temple. To the west side is a Hindu temple with mode painted images of four Hindu deities: Ganesh, Saman, Vishnu and Kataragama.

2 Mihintale sacred centre

➡ **Mihintale maps**
1 Mihintale, page 268
2 Mihintale sacred centre, page 270

aga Pokuna After collecting your shoes, and immediately below the rock inscription ee above) is a small path which leads through cool forest to the Naga Pokuna. This nake Pond', which has a five-headed cobra carving which you can still make out, is a 0-m pool carved out of solid rock which stored water for the monastery and, some elieve, is where King Tissa would have bathed. At one end is a very small tank, now ithout water. Apparently this was where the Queen would bathe. It is a peaceful and eautiful place.

: Vihara If you still have energy, a flight of 600 steps from the Naga Pokuna leads up to is inner temple, at the highest elevation in Mihintale. Though the small stupa is not very npressive, there are some magnificent views from here.

fter descending and exiting the main complex, head west to the Kandy Road (accessible om either car park). Close to the junction are the remains of a monastery complex with vo *dagobas*, of which the **Indikatu Seya** on a raised stone square platform to the north, is e larger. It shows evidence that the monks were devotees of Mahayan Buddhism in the nth century. South of here, inscriptions in the **Rajagiri Lena** (Royal Rock Caves) suggest at they may represent the first living quarters of Sri Lanka's earliest Buddhist monks.

rchaeological Museum
his small, free museum is close to the lower car park. Displays include some terracotta warves, a couple of fine Ganadevi statues and a model of the middle chamber of the ahaseya *dagoba*. There are some labels in English.

Anuradhapura and Mihintale listings

or Sleeping and Eating price codes and other elevant information, see pages 26-32.

Sleeping

nuradhapura *p260, map p263*
nuradhapura has a good selection of asonably priced hotels and guesthouses, ut is rather lacking at the top end. Except or **Ulagalla Resort** and the wonderfully :mospheric **Tissawewa Grand**, all are in the ew Town, 2-3 km from the ancient site. ne main cluster is around the junction of arischandra Mawatha and JR Jaya Mawatha. ne guesthouses on Freeman Mawatha are auch closer to the 'New' bus station and the lew Town' railway station, though even arther away from the ruins. Nearly all rent ut bicycles and can arrange guided tours.
Ulagalla Resort, Thirapanne, 23 km from nuradhapura, T11-567 1000 (reservations),

www.ulagallaresorts.com. A distance away from Anuradhapura but the most luxurious hotel around. 25 tasteful a/c chalets with private plunge pools, dotted throughout the 20 ha grounds which border Ulagalla tank, Freshwater swimming pool, spa, restaurants and activities such as kayaking, horse riding and birdwatching. Electric buggies will collect guests and ferry them to the main house.
A-B Palm Garden Village, Km 42 post, Puttalam Rd, Pandulagama, 2.5 km from the sites, T222 3961, www.palmgardenvillage.com. 40 stylish a/c rooms and 10 suites in upmarket villas dotted around gardens with deer. Full facilities including large pool, Ayurvedic centre, open-sided restaurants.
B Galway Miridya, Wasaladantha Mawatha, T222 2112, www.galway.lk. 39 comfortable a/c rooms, some with TV, attractive bathrooms, some with view over Nuwara Wewa. Restaurant, bar, pool (non-residents

pay Rs 350), pleasant atmosphere and attractive landscaped gardens with ponds overlooking tank ideal for a sunset stroll.

C Randiya, off JR Jaya Mawatha, T222 2868, www.hotelrandiya.com. Comfortable a/c rooms, standard or deluxe, all with balcony in modern house. Pleasant restaurant serving good food, excellent service. Can arrange tours to Wilpattu National Park.

C Tissawewa Grand, near the tank, T11-258 3133, www.quickshaws.com. Former Dutch governor's house with bags of colonial character, wooden floorboards and ceilings, some period furniture and fittings, beautifully situated in secluded parkland with lots of monkeys. 15 a/c and fan rooms, those downstairs are newer but darker, can be grubby so inspect first. Restaurant, bike hire, guests can use pool at **Nuwarawewa Rest House**, reasonable value, closest to archaeological sites.

D-E Milano Tourist Rest, 596/40, Stage One, JR Jaya Mawatha, T222 2364, www.milanotouristrest.com. Modern house with comfortable well-furnished rooms, fan or a/c. Bathrooms are a bit of a let-down. Good restaurant, bar, tours offered to Wilpattu National Park (2-hr drive), Rs 8000 for vehicle for half-day (find 6 people and it's a bargain). Expensive bike hire. Wi-Fi and terminals available.

D-E Shalini, 41/388 Harischandra Mawatha (opposite Water Tower Stage 1), T222 2425, www.hotelshalini.com. 14 large, clean, comfortable fan or a/c rooms, in modern house, hot water, good food in attractive roof-top restaurant, well kept, cycle hire, free transfer from/to station, internet café.

D-F Ceylon Tourist Board Rest House, Jayanthi Mawatha, T222 2188, www.national holidayresorts.lk. Reservations T011-243 7059. Set in extensive grounds, large rooms in attractive neo-colonial building, fan or a/c, attached bath, slightly grubby, reasonable value though service rather slow, popular in

the pilgrimage season, restaurant with very cheap food.

E Grand Tourist Holiday Resort, Lake Rd (off Harischandra Mawatha), T223 5173. 15 a/c and fan rooms, those in the pleasant main house are better, good views very close to tank. Friendly staff.

E-F Ceybank Rest House, Jayanthi Mawath T223 5520, ceybankhh@gmail.com. Large rooms with small balconies and some family rooms, clean, mainly for local pilgrims.

F Kondamale, 42/388 Harischandra Mawatha, T222 2029. Clean rooms with tired bathrooms but nice touches such as bottles of water for guests. Friendly owners, bike hir

F Lee's Chinese Guest House, 388/28 Harischandra Mawatha, T223 5476. Basic but clean rooms with cold water only. Good value, nice outdoor area. Can be noisy

F Nadeeja, just past Lake View, 4C6 Mihind Mawatha, T222 1904, saliya.smpth@ gmail.com. A/c and fan rooms, large open communal areas on the upper floors. Good food, welcoming.

F-G Lake View, 4C4 Harischandra Mawatha T221 1593. 10 rooms, some comfortable and clean with hot water, others a.bit dingy so inspect first, a/c or fan. Pleasant owner, Mihintale *dagoba* visible from here. Tours can be arranged, bikes for hire.

F-G Walkers Inn, 387 Harischandra Mawatha, T222 2100. Small guesthouse with 3 basic rooms, quiet, close to town. Pastry shop next door.

G Railway Retiring Rooms, T222 2571. 10 basic rooms, not too clean but cheap (single Rs 300). Rooms available for non-passengers. Rates on board as enter the railway station, enquire at the counter.

Mihintale *p267, map p268*
C Hotel Mihintale (CHC), Anuradhapura Rd 600 m west of the crossroads, T226 6599. 10 a/c rooms, those upstairs far lighter, restaurant, outdoor seating.

Eating

Anuradhapura *p260, map p263*
The north end of town lacks restaurants
but has some friendly food stalls. All the
guesthouses and hotels have restaurants,
recommended are **Milano Tourist Rest**,
Nalini (which has a terrace restaurant in the
tree-tops serving good value food, especially
the rice and curry set menus) and **Randiya.**
Casserole, above Family Bakers, 279 Main St,
222 4443. A/c offers welcome respite from
the heat, with good value Chinese (set menus
from Rs 300 upwards), but has the atmosphere
of a school gym and staff are glum.

Festivals and events

Mihintale *p267, map p268*
In **Poson** at full-moon is of particularly
importance to Buddhists who commemorate
the arrival of Buddhism on the island. Tens of
thousands flock to climb to the sacred spot,
chanting as they go: *Buddham saranam
gachchaami. Dhammam saranam gachchaami.
Sangam saranam gachchaami*, meaning
'In the Buddha I seek refuge, In Dhamma
I seek refuge, In the Sangha I seek refuge'.

Transport

Anuradhapura *p260, map p263*
Bicycle hire
From most guesthouses and hotels in the
New Town (Rs 200-300 per day). **Mihintale**
is an easy 11-km ride along a flat road.

Bus
There is a frequent bus service between
Old and New Bus stands. For long distance
services there are 2 bus stations. **New Bus
Station**, Main St, south end of town, serves
most destinations except Colombo and Kandy.
Departures for **Polonnaruwa** are frequent
(3 hrs); **Trincomalee** (3½ hrs); **Vavuniya** (1 hr);
Mannar (3 hrs). Buses to **Mihintale** can be

picked up on the main road (frequent,
30 mins). The **Old Bus Station**, Rest House Rd,
has CTB buses to **Colombo** (hourly, 5 hrs) and
Kandy via **Dambulla** (hourly, 4 hrs). Intercity
express buses leave from diagonally opposite
the Old Bus Station, to **Colombo**, **Kandy** and
to **Kurunegala** and **Negombo**.

Three-wheeler
These are everywhere and will offer 3- to 4-hr
trips around the ancient city. To **Mihintale** it
costs about Rs 1000 for a half-day trip.

Train
From the main station Intercity to **Colombo**
(4-5 hrs, Rs 520/290/160) at 0640, 0930, 1340,
1655, 2330. **Matara** (10 hrs, Rs 780/430/235),
at 0500. Change at **Polgahawela** for **Kandy**.
For **Habarana**, **Polonnaruwa**, **Trincomalee**
and other destinations east change at Maho
Junction. North to **Vavuniya** (for **Jaffna**
buses) at 0340, 0515, 0930, 1745, 1900,
2015 (1¼ hrs). Note that the branch line to
Mihintale only runs at festival time in Jul.
Be aware that the hotels around Freeman
Mawatha are closer to the New Town station
(south of the main station) though intercities
do not usually stop here.

Mihintale *p267, map p268*
Bus Regular between Mihintale and
Anuradhapura's New Bus Station (20 mins).

Train Trains only run on the branch line to
Anuradhapura during the Jun festival.

Directory

Anuradhapura *p260, map p263*
Banks Most major banks are on Main St in
New Town, all of which have foreign exchange
facilities. For ATM users, **Commercial Bank**,
Sampath Bank and **Seylan Bank** are best.
Internet Some guesthouses and hotels
offer internet access, such as the **Milano
Tourist Rest**. **Post office** Main St, south
of the Harischandra Mawatha junction.

Sigiriya

→ *Phone code: 066. Colour map 2, B5.*

The bloody history of the vast flat-topped 200-m-high Lion Rock, a tale of murder and dynast feuding, is as dramatic as its position, rearing starkly from the plain beneath. An exception natural site for a fortress, the rock dominates the surrounding countryside of the central fore and from the top offers views that stretch as far as the Dry Zone and south to the Centre Highlands. Deriving its name (Sinha-Giri) from the lions which were believed to occupy the cave for many visitors this impressive site is their favourite in the whole of Sri Lanka. The rewards c Sigiriya (pronounced See-gi-ri-ya), with its palace, famous frescoes and beautiful water garden justify the steep climb. Frequently labelled the 'Eighth Wonder of the World', it was designated World Heritage Site in 1982. ▸▸ For listings, see pages 279-280.

Ins and outs → *Allow at least two hours for a visit. Evenings bring out armies of mosquitoes, so take precautions and cover up.*

Getting there and around

The main bus stop is close to the bridge by the exit (at the south of the rock) so those without their own transport have to undertake the 10 minute walk round to the entranc (to the west) to buy their ticket (the track is signposted off the road 1 km west from th bus stand, past the rest house). Those visiting by car are dropped at the entrance – the driver will then drive round to the car park at the exit. Be careful in Sigiriya at night especially if you're a lone female.

Best time to visit

Early morning is beautiful and the site is very quiet until 0730, but the late afternoon light i better for the frescoes. Avoid the high sun around noon. There can be long queues on public holidays and the rock can be very crowded from mid-morning. If you wish to make a early start (avoiding groups which start arriving by 0800) buy your ticket the day before.

Tourist information

The ticket office is near the entrance. US$25 (half price for children). Cultural Triangl Round Tickets (US$50) can also be bought here. The Cultural Triangle ticket (see page 52 only allows for a single entry at each site. The ticket office is open 0700-1700, but those holding the Cultural Triangle ticket can enter as soon as it is light. It is advisable not to take food as the site is over-run by dogs who will follow you around. There is a road leading to the base of the rock for ease of access for disabled visitors.

The **Centre for Eco-Cultural Studies (CES)** ① *T567 5523, www.cessrilanka.org*, is east o the bus station near the tank and should be able to provide more information about the flora and fauna in the area, and arrange tours (see Activities and tours, page 280). *Sigiriya* by RH De Silva, Ceylon, Department of Archaeology, 1971, is recommended for furthe background information.

Background

ieroglyphs suggest that the site was occupied by humans from times long before the
ortress was built. The royal citadel, built between AD 477-485, was surrounded by an
npressive wall and a double moat. As well as the palace, the city had quarters for the
rdinary people who built the royal pavilions, pools and fortifications.

The engineering skills required to build the palace, gardens, cisterns and ponds
ecome even more extraordinary when you realise that the entire site was built over a
eriod of seven years and effectively abandoned after 18 years. For the famous frescoes
asyapa gathered together the best artists of his day.

Water, a scarce commodity in the Dry Zone, was conserved and diverted cleverly
hrough pipes and rock-cut channels to provide bathing pools for the palace above,
nd to enhance the gardens below with pools and fountains. The water pumps are
nought to have been powered by windmills. On the islands in the two pools in the
vater garden near the entrance stood pavilions, while the shallow marble pools
eflected the changing patterns of the clouds. Excavations have revealed surface and
nderground drainage systems.

When the citadel ceased to be a palace after Moggallana's reign, it was inhabited by
nonks till 1155, and then abandoned. It was rediscovered by archaeologists in 1828.

ights

Approach

ntering the site across the moat from the west, you will pass the fifth-century **water
ardens** (restored by the Central Cultural Fund with UNESCO sponsorship) with walks,
avilions, ponds and fountains which are gravity fed from the moats as they were 1500
ears ago. You can see the secret changing room doors. Legend states that Kaspaya used
o watch his concubines bathe here from his palace.

A straight path leads through the group of four fountain gardens with small water jets
originally fifth century), some with pretty lotuses attracting a number of water birds.
inally you reach the flower garden with colourful beds and flowering trees. To the right
s you walk up to the rock is a **miniature water garden**. The whole area (including the
noat and drive) is immaculate. It is difficult to visualize the winter palace as there are no
isible foundations.

The rock

he top of the rock has a surface area of 1.5 ha. It is easy to forget that the site was in fact
leveloped as a massive defensive fortress. Lookout points were located on ledges
linging to the rock. Steer clear of the aggressive monkeys in this area.

Base of the rock Before reaching the steps the path goes through the boulder garden
vhere clusters of rocks, including the **preaching rock** with 'seats', are marked with rows of
iotches and occasional 'gashes'. These may have been used for decorating the area with
amps during festivals. To the right at the start of the climb, under a natural overhang, is the
Cobra Hood rock which has a drip ledge inscription in Brahmi script dating from the
econd century BC. The floor and ceiling have lime plaster, the latter is decorated with
paintings and floral patterns. A headless Buddha statue is placed horizontally. It is thought
o have been a monk's cell originally. The **Cistern** and the **Audience Hall** rocks are parts of a

single massive boulder which had split, and half of which had fallen away. The exposed fl. surface had a 'throne' at one end and came to be called the Audience Hall while the upp. part of the standing half retained the rectangular cistern. A second set of steps is und. construction from the end of the new road to the Lion Terrace.

The climb This begins in earnest with steps leading through the Elephant Gate on wel. maintained brick-lined stairways. These lead up to the second checkpoint immediate. below the gallery containing the frescoes. Steps continue up to the **Fresco gallery**, painte. under an overhanging rock and reached by a spiral staircase which was built in 1938. second staircase has been added to ease congestion. Of the original 500 or so frescoes, whic. vie with those in Ajanta in Western India, only 21 remain. They are remarkably well preserve. as they are sheltered from the elements in a niche. In the style of Ajanta, the first drawing w. done on wet plaster and then painted with red, yellow, green and black. The figures ar. 'portraits' of well-endowed *apsaras* (celestial nymphs) and attendants above clouds. offering flowers, scattering petals or bathing. Here, guides are keen to point out the girl wit. three hands and another with three nipples. Note the girls of African and Mongolian origin.

Sigiriya

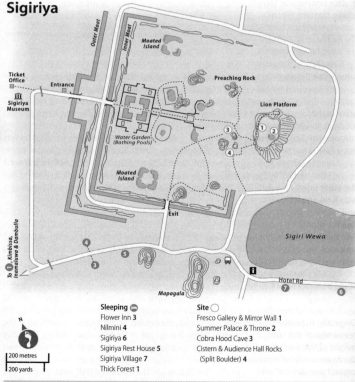

Sleeping	Site
Flower Inn 3	Fresco Gallery & Mirror Wall 1
Nilmini 4	Summer Palace & Throne 2
Sigiriya 6	Cobra Hood Cave 3
Sigiriya Rest House 5	Cistern & Audience Hall Rocks
Sigiriya Village 7	(Split Boulder) 4
Thick Forest 1	

Legends of Sigiriya

The romance of Sigiriya, the playboy's palace in the sky, has provided inspiration for many books, plays and even films, with more than one legend to explain its origins. All theories hinge around the cult of King Kasyapa.

The *Mahavansa* records that King Kasyapa (reigned AD 477-495) killed his father, King Dhatusena, by plastering him alive to a wall, in order to gain the throne, after which he lived in terror that his half brother, Moggallana, who had taken refuge in India, would return to kill him. He did come back, after 18 years, to find that Kasyapa had built a combination of pleasure palace and massive fortress. Kasyapa came down from the hill to face his half brother's army on elephant back. Mistakenly thinking he had been abandoned by his supporters, he killed himself with his dagger.

A conflicting, if equally bloody alternative theory, propounded by historian Senarat Paranavitana, is claimed to have been deciphered from inscriptions by a 15th-century monk. In this, Dhatusena is told that he can obtain imperial status by becoming a *Parvataraja*, or mountain king, ruling from a palace built on a rock summit. In the struggle for succession, Kasyapa on return from exile in India mistakenly attacks and defeats his father's army, believing it to belong to his brother, at which Dhatusena beheads himself. Remorseful as the cause of his father's death, Kasyapa, now king, attempts to put his father's dream into reality. In order to be accepted by overseas merchants, he proclaims himself as *Kubera*, the God of Wealth, and attempts to recreate his legendary palace on earth. He issues a gold coinage and establishes free ports, which accrue great wealth for the kingdom. In this theory Kasyapa dies in his palace after Moggallana persuades his wife to poison him.

proof of the kingdom's widespread trade at this time. Some paintings were destroyed by a madman in 1967 and you can see pictures of this in the small museum, and others may be cordoned off because the rusty walkway may be unsafe. You may photograph the frescoes but a flash is not permitted. Note that there is no entry to the frescoes after 1700.

Mirror wall Immediately beyond the foot of the spiral staircases the path is protected on the outer side by the 3-m-high, highly polished plaster wall believed to have been coated with lime, egg white and wild honey. After 15 centuries it still has a reflective sheen. Visitors and pilgrims (mostly between seventh and 11th century) wrote verses in Sinhalese – 'graffiti' prompted by the frescoes and by verses written by previous visitors. Some, today, find this section a little disappointing. Despite the threat of a large fine or a two-year jail sentence, there is plenty of modern graffiti to obscure the originals and it can be difficult to stop and study because of the pressure of people when the rock is busy. As you continue to climb, note the massive rock, close to the Guard House, wedged with stone supports which could be knocked out to enable it to crash on the enemy far below.

Lion Terrace Here, the giant plaster-covered brick paws of the lion become visible. Originally, the entire head and front part of the body would have awed visitors. Though the remainder of the structure has disappeared, the size of the paws gives some clue to the height of the lion's head. The terrace marks the halfway point of the climb where cool drinks are available and where many touts wait for customers. The wire cage is supposed to protect people from wild bees. You can see their nests under the metal staircase.

Final stairway The final stage of the ascent on the north ledge leads through the lion paws to the top of the rock up the steep west and north sides. It is worth studying th remaining climb to the summit. You can clearly see the outline of small steps cut into th granite. The king was apparently scared of heights so these steps would also have bee enclosed by a 3-m-high mirror wall. Here was the lion's gate after which the place named: *Si* (shortened form of *Sinha*, lion) *Giriya* (throat). The stairway of 25 flights mostly on iron steps with a small guard rail and is steep (particularly in one place where small flight resemble a ship's ladder). Small children can find this quite frightening.

Summer Palace At the top are the ruins of the palace. The foundations reveal the likel size, surprisingly small when compared with the size of the stone throne underneath i although it was only built for the king and queen. There was the granite throne, dancin terraces, a small pool fed by rain water, drinking water tanks, sleeping quarters of th concubines, a small flower garden and precariously positioned platforms for guards. you walk to the sign on the west, there is a very good birds-eye view of the winter palac and its surrounding moat.

Descent Retrace your steps to the second checkpoint. Just below this, the path splits t the left from where you can get a view of the king's audience chamber and his anteroom Once again, there is a huge throne in a semicircle where his advisors would sit – justic was swift and often brutal. Immediately below the audience chamber was anothe granite slab: this was the place of execution. Again to the left is the ante-chamber whic was cooled by a tank of water cut into the rock above the ceiling. It too would have bee covered in frescoes. Much of the construction is in brick, faced with lime plaster but ther are sections built with limestone slabs which would have been carried up. The uppe structures which have disappeared were probably wooden. Finally you exit through th cobra gate – a huge, overhanging rock.

Other sights

These include the **Mapagala Rock** with evidence of dressed stone work, a *dagoba* an other ruins on the roadside just over a kilometre away. **Pidurangala Royal Cave Templ** and Buddhist Meditation centre are 1.5 km away and signposted from the car park. Th cave on the rock Pidurangala, where there had been an ancient monastery, still has stupa with a 10th-century reclining Buddha and an inscription dating from the firs century BC. These, and other finds of early settlement in **Rama Kale** nearby, point at th ancient nature of the spot chosen by Kasyapa for his palace fortress. The **Sigiriya Museu** ① *0830-1730 (last ticket 1700), closed 1st Mon of every month, price currently included in th Sigiriya ticket or as part of the Cultural Triangle Round Ticket*, is the re-vampe archaeological museum. The empty echoing building may be off-putting but whe entering the gallery the museum comes into its own. It showcases the history of the roc from its formation, to its use as a Buddhist monastery and palace. Archaeological finds ar displayed and there is an interesting reproduction of the 'Golden Age' of Sigiriya, as we as translations of some of the graffiti from the mirror wall. The Fresco Gallery is of interes if you do not make it up the spiral stairs to see the originals. The museum also provide some tourist information on sights and accommodation and there are plans for a café.

For Sleeping and Eating price codes and other relevant information, see pages 26-32.

Sleeping

Sigiriya *p274, map p276*

Inamaluwa and Kimbissa, 4-6 km west of the rock, are good options for mid-price accommodation, which tends to be expensive or basic in Sigiriya itself. Regular buses leave from these villages to the site from early morning onwards.

L-L Elephant Corridor, Inamaluwa, T228 6950, www.elephantcorridor.com. 80-ha site overlooking tank with stunning views of the rock. 21 suites in 5 categories (from deluxe to presidential). Each room has private plunge pool, DVD player, individual garden and lots of gadgets (eg night-vision binoculars, painting easel). Sports facilities include tables and 3-hole golf course. Not all rooms have good views and are slightly overpriced.

L Vil Uyana (Jetwing), Inamaluwa, T492 3584, www.jetwinghotels.com. An artificially created wetland with 25 spacious chalets, some with private plunge pools and sunken baths, in a choice of 4 habitats (marsh, paddy, forest or lake). All have private decks for wildlife viewing. Beautiful infinity pool, and all facilities you'd expect. The walk to the main building can be hard going if you're not very mobile.

A Sigiriya Village, Sigiriya, T228 6803, sigiriyavillage@sltnet.lk. Tastefully furnished standard or deluxe rooms with small terraces, large bathrooms, a/c, good open-sided restaurants, beautifully planted site with carefully landscaped gardens and theme clusters of cottages, each with its own colour scheme and accessories. Good Ayurvedic centre, own farm, friendly and efficient management. Internet access.

B Sigiriya, Sigiriya, T223 1940, www.serendib leisure.lk. 79 well-decorated, comfortable a/c rooms, some with TV and DVD player. Started

as a small guesthouse, arranged around 2 terraces, reasonable food, large pleasant garden, birdwatching walks, attractive wooded setting, cultural shows, good freshwater pool, good value. Great rock view from pool and bar, Internet available.

B The Thick Forest, Sigiriya, T777 74240. 3 raised wooden chalets built amidst the forest, with views of the rock. Basic with fan and hot water. Quiet, excellent for birdwatching, good food and a good chance of seeing elephants.

C Eden Garden, Sigiriya Rd, Inamaluwa, T228 4635, www.edengardenlk.com. 35 large, clean a/c rooms, pool, attractive gardens, restaurant.

C Sigiriya Rest House (CHC), Sigiriya, T223 1899, www.ceylonhotels.lk. The refurbished rooms with a/c and new bathrooms are those to opt for. The rest are fan rooms and rather tired, musty and overpriced. There are plans to upgrade these to a/c and charge the same as the newer rooms, so ask to view before committing. Pleasant dining area and terrace with great view of the rock though, site tickets available here.

D Banana Rest, 164/A, TB Tennakoon Mawatha, Kimbissa, 5 km from the site, T266 5055. Family-run guesthouse with 5 a/c and fan rooms with hot water. Good food, quiet surrounds, friendly.

D Grand Tourist Holiday Resort, Kimbissa, 5 km from site, T567 0136. Not grand (or for grand tourists) but large, well-furnished a/c and fan rooms in Dutch-style bungalows in attractive gardens.

F-G Flower Inn, Sigiriya, T567 2197. Family-run guesthouse with 3 rooms in the main house and newer ones at the back (cold water). Good food, friendly owner.

F-G Nilmini, opposite **Flower Inn**, Sigiriya, T223 3313. Simple rooms (shared bath cheaper) in rather dilapidated house, good food, very friendly, free bicycle hire. Pleasant terrace and can arrange tours and taxis.

🍴 Eating

Sigiriya *p274, map p276*
There are not many eating options in Sigiriya and most people eat in their hotel or guesthouse.
🍴 Sigiriya Rest House, see Sleeping, page 279. An option for lunchtime rice and curry.

🛍 Shopping

Sigiriya *p274, map p276*
Shops in the village sell bottled water and film.
Kottegoda Batik, Inamaluwa. For batik.

⛰ Activities and tours

Sigiriya *p274, map p276*
Elephant rides
There are elephant rides available for US$30-40 per person, they leave from just after the Sigiriya Rock exit.

Night safaris
The **Centre for Eco-Cultural Studies** (see page 274) can organize night safaris in the Sigiriya Wildlife Sanctuary, Rs 5000 (4-5 people) from 2030-2330.

🚌 Transport

Sigiriya *p274, map p276*
Car
The journey by car to **Colombo** takes about 4 hrs and to **Kandy** about 2½ hrs.

Bus
The main stop is close to the exit from the site. Non-stop bus to **Colombo** from **Dambulla** (3 hrs), to reach Dambulla take an hourly local bus from Sigiriya (30 mins) or arrange a 3-wheeler or taxi. From **Sigiriya**, there is 1 direct bus a day to **Colombo**. A 3-wheeler to Inamaluwa Junction, Rs 300.

ⓘ Directory

Sigiriya *p274, map p276*
Useful addresses Tourist police, T223 1808, near the entrance to the rock, though only during office hours.

Sigiriya to Polonnaruwa

From Sigiriya, a right turn at Moragaswewa leads east through low forest clad hills, skirting the picturesque tanks at Minneriya and Giritale, to the ancient city of Polonnaruwa. Elephants migrate across this route in the late afternoon. To the north of Habarana lies the Kaudulla tank, around which Sri Lanka's newest national park has been formed, while northwest of town, the remote hermitage of Ritigala, buried deep within the jungle, is well worth the detour off the Anuradhapura road. ⏩ *For listings, see pages 283-284.*

Habarana → *Phone code: 066. Colour map 2, B5.*

Habarana is an important crossroads, with roads extending southwest to Colombo or Kandy, northwest to Anuradhapura and Jaffna, northeast to Trincomalee, and southeast to Polonnaruwa and Batticaloa. Tour groups often spend a night here, though apart from a scattering of hotels and rest houses and its accessibility, it has little to offer. It is however a good base for visiting Kaudulla or Minneriya national parks (see page 282), both close by, though shop around for jeeps. Elephant 'safaris' are also available though they are expensive. Nearby there is an attractive **Buddhist temple** with excellent paintings. Behind the tank, next to the temple, you can climb a rock for superb views over the forest to Sigiriya.

Ritigala → *Colour map 2, B4.*

ⓘ *US$10, covered by the Cultural Triangle Round Ticket. There is a visitor centre where you can arrange a guide*

The 148-ha archaeological site is located within a 1570-ha Strict Nature Reserve, where wildlife includes elephants, sloth bear and leopard and varied bird life. The area, rich in unusual plants and herbs, is associated with the *Ramayana* story in which Hanuman dropped a section of herb-covered Himalaya here (see page 148).

The forest hermitage complex here was occupied by the ascetic *Pansakulika* monks. The structures found here include the typical double platforms joined by stone bridges, stone columns, ambulatories, herbal baths filled by rain water, sluices and monks' cells. There are many natural caves on the mountain slopes, some quite large, in which priests would meditate. Brahmi inscriptions here date the site from the third and second centuries BC.

As you enter the site, you will clamber over ruined steps leading down to the now overgrown two-acre bathing tank, the **Banda Pokuna**. Over an original stone bridge, follow a part-restored pathway, laid with interlocking ashlar, to the first major clearing, the monastery hospital, where you can see the remains of a stone bed, oil bath and medicine grinder. The next set of ruins is believed to be a library, now partly restored, perched atop a rock with magnificent views across to the jungle below. Beyond here, you come to the monastery, with a remarkably well-preserved urinal which would have had three clay pots beneath, of charcoal, sand and *kabok* for filtration. Here are the distinctive raised double-platforms, characteristic of Ritigala and other forest monasteries (see box, page 266). The platforms were probably for congregational use.

Platform 17 marks the end of the excavated territory – special permission is required from the Wildlife Department to venture further, and guides are in any case fearful of wild animals (workers have been maimed or killed in this area by elephants). Though in the Dry Zone, the Ritigala summit has a strange cool, wet micro-climate, with vegetation reminiscent of Horton Plains (see page 224).

You need your own vehicle to reach Ritigala. From Habarana, follow the A11 for 22 km west towards Maradankadawala, taking a right turn at Galapitagala for 5 km into the forest, then turn left along a track (suitable for a two-wheel drive) for about 3 km where an ancient rock-cut path leads to the site.

Kaudulla National Park → Colour map 2, A5.

ⓘ *The turn-off for the park is 17 km north of Habarana at Hatarasgoduwa from where it is a 5-km ride to the visitor centre. Jeeps from Habarana will usually charge Rs 4500 for a 3-hr 'safari', leaving 1500-1600. Entry costs US$15 plus service charge, tracker, etc. Best time to visit Aug-Dec.*

Sri Lanka's newest national park was opened to the public in September 2002, partly as another step in establishing protection for the elephants' ancient migration routes. It completes a network of protected areas around the Polonnaruwa area, comprising Minneriya National Park, Minneriya-Giritale Nature Reserve and Wasgomuwa National Park to the south, and Flood Plains and Somawathie to the east and north. The 6936-ha park acts mainly as a catchment to the Kaudulla tank, which dates back to the 17th century. Its most prominent feature is its large herds of elephant (up to 250), which can be seen at the tank during the dry season when water is scarce elsewhere. The vegetation, which consists of semi-mixed evergreen, grasslands and riverine forest, supports a small population of leopard and sloth bear, while birdlife is excellent.

Outside the dry season, elephants are easier to see from the main Habarana–Trincomalee road (on the left coming from Habarana) than in the park itself. These are their preferred feeding grounds due to the lushness of the vegetation. Jeeps in Habarana are keen to take you to this area in these months but if you already have a vehicle there is little point getting a jeep since they feed very close to the road.

Minneriya National Park

ⓘ *26 km west of Polonnaruwa. US$15 plus service charge, tracker, etc. Best time to visit May-Oct. Keep a look out for wild elephants on the Minneriya–Giritale Rd, and don't drive this route at night.*

A sanctuary since 1938, Minneriya was upgraded to national park status in 1997. Here is King Mahasena's magnificent Minneriya tank (fourth century AD) covering 3000 ha, which dominates the park. It is an important wetlands, feeding around 8900 ha of paddy fields, and supporting many aquatic birds, such as painted storks, spot-billed pelicans, openbill storks and grey herons. At the end of the dry season there is little evidence of the tank which gets covered in weeds, the vegetation on its bed becoming a vital source of food for many animals. Around September and October, an influx or local migration of elephants takes place in a spectacular wildlife event. The high forest canopy also provides ideal conditions for purple-faced leaf monkey and toque monkey, while the short bushes and grasslands provide food for sambhar and chital. There are small populations of leopard and sloth bear. Mugger crocodiles and land and water monitors can also be seen. The park entrance is at Ambagaswewa, east of Habarana on the Batticaloa Road. Jeeps charge the same as to Kaudulla (see above).

Hurulu Eco Park

① *US$15 plus service charge.*

On the Habarana to Trincomalee road, Hurulu Eco Park is often suggested as an alternative when it's too wet to visit Kaudulla and Minneriya. Part of Hurulu Forest Reserve, which was designated as a biosphere reserve in January 1977, it is a good place to see elephants and for birdwatching. Taking up 10,000 ha of the 25,500-ha reserve, there are a number of waterway intersecting in the area there are plans to make a large tank from the smaller, abandoned tanks. Among the species living in the area are the turtle, Ceylon junglefowl, and small populations of leopard and the rusty-spotted cat. Facilities are limited at the moment, but there are plans to develop the park for tourists and re-open some of the walking trails.

Giritale → *Phone code: 027. Colour map 2, B5.*

Giritale also has a fine tank, which dates from the seventh century AD, and occupies a site which was once a wealthy suburb of ancient Polonnaruwa. Legend has it that King Parakramabahu met his future bride, the daughter of his uncle Girikandasiva, here, to whom he donated the tank and from whom it derives its name. There is little reason to stay here other than its position and its proximity to Minneriya and Polonnaruwa – the hotels here are more upmarket than in the ancient city itself. The road that skirts the tank south leads to Wasgomuwa National Park (see page 295), to which hotels also arrange trips (as well as to Minneriya and Kaudulla). As you drive out of town towards Polonnaruwa you will see a copy of the Aukana Buddha by the tank, erected in 2001. If you haven't made it to Aukana, you will get an idea how impressive is the real thing.

◉ Sigiriya to Polonnaruwa listings

For Sleeping and Eating price codes and other relevant information, see pages 26-32.

◓ Sleeping

Habarana *p281*

Habarana is usually used as a base for visiting the national parks, and is a good transport hub.

AL-A Cinnamon Lodge, T227 0011, www.cinnamonhotels.com. 150 tastefully decorated a/c rooms in bungalows, some deluxe with tubs and TV, and 2 suites (Rs 45,000). Excellent facilities and lush grounds with woods, good pool, good service.

A-B Chaaya Village, T227 0047, www.chaayahotels.com. 106 a/c rooms in 'rustic' cottages (deluxe have lake views), as well as 2 lodges. On the banks of the lake

with extensive gardens, an excellent pool and good food. Popular with tours.

C Rest House, Habarana Junction, T227 0003, www.ceylonhotels.lk. 4 large, basic rooms (1 with a/c) back from the road.

E-F Habarana Rest, south of Habarana Junction, T227 0010. 7 simple fan rooms on main road (can be noisy), 4 very clean and good value, others mainly designed for locals. Have proved to be dishonest in running safaris though – shop elsewhere.

Giritale *p283*

The upmarket hotels in Giritale, just off the main road overlook the tank in beautiful settings, can make a convenient base for Polonnaruwa. Other cheaper hotels are all on the Habarana–Polonnaruwa Rd.

A Deer Park, T224 6272, www.angsana.com. Luxurious 1- and 2-storey cottages set in grounds overlooking Giritale tank, most with open-air showers. Upmarket facilities with 3 restaurants, spa, pool. Popular with tour groups.

B Giritale Hotel, T224 6311. 42 reasonable a/c rooms high above the Giritale tank. Small pool, unattractive public areas, but good facilities and superb views from the restaurant and terrace. Plenty of wildlife within hotel grounds, including chital and monkeys.

B Royal Lotus, T224 6316, www.theroyallotus.com. Comfortable a/c rooms, including 2 suites (US$95). The deluxe upstairs have better views, the chalets are a little tired. Fine views over Giritale tank, pool, good food, friendly and efficient staff.

D-E Himalee, Polonnaruwa Rd, T224 6257. 16 large, basic fan rooms, helpful staff but overpriced.

F-G Woodside Tour Inn, Polonnaruwa Rd, T224 6307. 15 large and clean fan and a/c rooms.

☺ Eating

Habarana *p281*
Most groups choose to stop in Habarana, where local restaurants compete with each other to impress tourists with the number of curries they can serve at lunchtime. Prices are usually around Rs 800. Best of the bunch are:

♔♔ **Acme Transit Hotel**, 1 km east of Habarana Junction, T227 0016. 11 curries with friendly management. Rooms available, though not well maintained.

♔♔ **Rukmali Rest**, 1 km further east, T227 0059. A mighty 17 varieties of curry.

☉ Transport

Habarana *p281*
Bus
Habarana Junction is a good place to pick up buses in all directions: **Dambulla** (20 mins), **Trincomalee** (2 hrs), **Polonnaruwa** (1 hr), **Batticaloa** (3 hrs), **Colombo** (5 hrs); **Anuradhapura** (1½ hrs). Note that the buses passing through Habarana are very busy, especially the long-distance to Trincomalee. Unless travelling very light, try and catch the earliest of the day.

Train
The station is 2 km north of Habarana Junction and is on the Colombo–Batticaloa line. Trains to **Colombo**, **Trincomalee**, **Batticaloa** and **Polonnaruwa**.

☉ Directory

Habarana *p281*
Banks Branch of **People's Bank** just south of Habarana junction.

Polonnaruwa

→ *Phone code: 027. Colour map 2, B5. Population: 12,500.*

Polonnaruwa, the island's medieval capital between the 11th and 13th century, is for many visitors the most rewarding of the ancient cities. Flowering principally under three kings over a short period of less than 100 years, it is, in contrast to Anuradhapura, historically as well as geographically compact, and so it feels easier to assimilate. Today, the ruins, built alongside the vast and beautiful Parakrama Samudra, stand witness to a lavish phase of building, culminating in the sublime Gal Vihara. In its imperial intentions, and the brevity of its existence, Polonnaruwa may be compared to the great Mughal emperor Akbar's city of Fatehpur Sikri, near Agra in India.
▶▶ *For listings, see pages 291-293.*

Ins and outs → *Allow at least 3 hrs but a whole day is better to get an impression of this ancient site.*

Getting there
Trains and buses arrive at Kaduruwela, 4 km east. From here, local buses run frequently to Polonnaruwa, or take a three-wheeler.

Getting around
Under a hot sun the site is too spread out to walk around. Even if you have a car, cycling is the most practical and fun way to explore the town (Rs 150-200 per day, available from most hotels), though take it easy as brakes are a luxury and the tracks are rough in places – you'll do well if you get round without a puncture. It is best to get your bearings before starting a tour. The ruins can be split broadly into five groups, though your ticket is only needed for three. Close to the entrance and within the old walls are the **Royal Citadel Group** to the south and the **Quadrangle** to the north. The **Northern Monuments**, which include the magnificent Gal Vihara, are spread out for 3 km north of here. Across the main road from the main site, close to the museum and bund is the small **Rest House Group**, and finally, the **Southern Group** is about 3 km south of town. The museum, unless you arrive early morning, is a good place to start. The entrance to the main site is 500 m from here though you may wish to see the Rest House Group first as it is closest to the museum. Once in the main site, there is a one-way route through the sacred site that is generally quite well signed.

Best time to visit
As ever, early morning or late evening is best, out of the heat. To visit many sites you will need to remove your shoes – even in the blazing sun when the stones are scorching so taking socks is a good idea. Avoid visiting more remote ruins late in the day, as attacks on lone tourists have been known.

Tourist information
Tickets are available from the counter at the Archaeological Museum, close to the Rest House, which also acts as an information desk and sometimes sells maps of the city. Though the museum itself doesn't open till 0900, the desk is open from 0700. Tickets cost US$25, or you can also buy a Cultural Triangle Round Ticket (US$50, students and children half price). A book on Polonnaruwa is available from the bookshop for Rs 250.

Background

The Sinhalese kings of Anuradhapura in AD 369 used Polonnaruwa as their residence but it did not rank as a capital until the eighth century. The Cholas from South India destroyed the Sinhalese Kingdom at the beginning of the 11th century, and taking control of most of the island, they established their capital at Polonnaruwa. In 1056 King Vijayabahu I defeated the Cholas, setting up his own capital in the city. It remained a vibrant centre of Sinhalese culture under his successors, notably Parakramabahu I (1153-1186) who maintained very close ties with India, importing architects and engineers, and Nissankamalla (1187-1196). The rectangular shaped city was enclosed by three concentric walls, and was made attractive with parks and gardens. Polonnaruwa owes much of its glory to the artistic conception of King Parakramabahu I who planned the whole as an expression and statement of imperial power. Its great artificial lake provided cooling breezes through the city, water for irrigation and at the same time, defence along its entire west flank. The bund is over 14 km long and 1 m high, and the tank irrigates over 90 sq km of paddy fields. Fed by a 40-km-long canal and a link from the Giritale tank, it was named after its imperial designer the Parakrama Samudra (Topa Wewa).

After Parakramabahu, the kingdom went into terminal decline and the city was finally abandoned in 1288, after the tank embankment was breached. Fortunately, many of the remains are in an excellent state of repair though several of the residential buildings remain to be excavated. In 1982, it was designated a World Heritage Site. The restoration at the site is by the UNESCO-sponsored Central Cultural Fund. Today it attracts numerous water birds, including cormorants and pelicans.

Sights

Archaeological Museum
ⓘ *0900-1800. Entry is covered by the site ticket.*
This is an excellent place to start a tour of the ancient ruins, and you may wish to return afterwards. In addition to the clearly presented exhibits found on site, and many photographs, there is also a well-written commentary on Sri Lanka's ancient history. Scaled down representations give you an idea of how the buildings would have looked during the city's prime. In the final (seventh) room, there are some extraordinarily well-preserved bronze statues.

Rest House Group
Nissankamalla built his own 'New' Palace close to the water's edge in a beautiful garden setting. Today, the ruins are sadly in a poor state of repair. Just north of the rest house, beyond the sunken royal baths, are a stone 'mausoleum', the Audience Hall, and lastly the interesting Council Chamber which had the stone lion throne (now housed in the Colombo National Museum). The four rows of 12 sculpted columns have inscriptions indicating the seating order in the chamber – from the king at the head, with the princes, army chiefs and ministers, down to the record keepers on his right, while to his left were placed government administrators, and representatives of the business community. Across the water, to the northwest, the mound on the narrow strip of land which remains above flood water, has the ruins of the King Parakramabahu's 'Summer House' which was decorated with wall paintings.

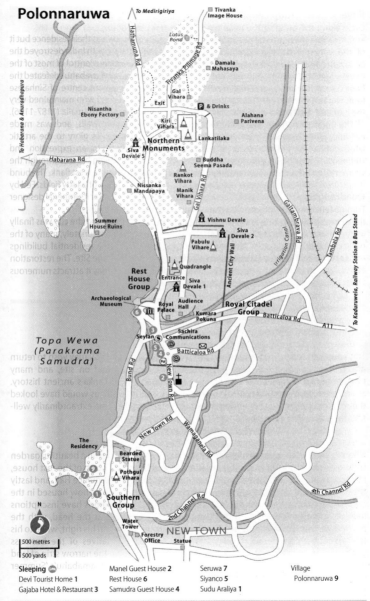

Polonnaruwa

To Medirigiriya

To Tivanka Image House

Lotus Pond

Hathamuna Rd

Tivanka Pilimage Rd

Damala Mahasaya

Gal Vihara

Exit

P & Drinks

Nisantha Ebony Factory

Kiri Vihara

Lankatilaka

Alahana Parivena

Northern Monuments

Siva Devale 5

Buddha Seema Pasada

Habarana Rd

To Habarana & Anuradhapura

Rankot Vihara

Nissanka Mandapaya

Manik Vihara

Gal Vihara Rd

Vishnu Devale

Summer House Ruins

Pabulu Vihare

Siva Devale 2

Ancient City Wall

Gattambrava Rd

Irrigation Canal

Tambala Rd

To Kaduruwela, Railway Station & Bus Stand

Quadrangle

Rest House Group

Entrance

Siva Devale 1

Archaeological Museum

Royal Palace

Audience Hall

Kumara Pokuna

Royal Citadel Group

Batticaloa Rd

A11

*Topa Wewa
(Parakrama
Samudra)*

6

III

Seylan 3

Sachira Communications

@

Batticaloa Rd

@

5

4

2

Pu Pung

New Town Rd

New Town Rd

Wannganela Rd

The Residency

Bearded Statue

Pothgul Vihara

9

7

Southern Group

1

N

500 metres
500 yards

NEW TOWN

Water Tower

Forestry Office

Statue

2nd Channel Rd

4th Channel Rd

Sleeping			
Devi Tourist Home 1	Manel Guest House 2	Seruwa 7	Village
Gajaba Hotel & Restaurant 3	Rest House 6	Siyanco 5	Polonnaruwa 9
	Samudra Guest House 4	Sudu Araliya 1	

Royal Citadel Group

Cycle along the bund to the main road, where stalls sell drinks and snacks. The main entrance, for which you will need a ticket, is opposite, across the road. About 200 m south of the entrance (to the right as you enter), stands King Parakramabahu's Palace (Vejayanta Prasada). It is described in the Chronicles as originally having had seven storeys and 1000 rooms, but much of it was of wood and so was destroyed by fire. The large central hall on the ground floor (31 m x 13 m) had 30 columns which supported the roof. You can see the holes for the beams in the 3-m-thick brick walls. It has porticoes on the east and west and a wide stairway.

The Council Chamber (sometimes called Audience Hall) is immediately to its east. It has fine, partly octagonal, granite pillars and friezes of elephants, lions and dwarves, which follow the entire exterior of the base. Nearby, outside the palace wall, is the stepped Kumara Pokuna (Prince's Bath), restored in the 1930s. You can still see the spouts where the water is channelled through the open jaws of crocodiles.

Quadrangle

Turning left from the entrance, you come first to the Siva Devale I, a Hindu Temple (one of the many Siva and Vishnu temples here), built in about AD 1200, which has lost its brick

Polonnaruwa Quadrangle

roof. An example of the Dravidian Indian architectural style, it shows exceptional stone carving, and the fine bronze statues discovered in the ruins have been transferred to the Colombo Museum.

Some 50 m further on, steps lead up to the **Quadrangle**, the highlight of the ruins within the ancient city wall. Though the structures here are comparatively modest in size, they are carved in fine detail. This is still regarded as a sanctuary and shoes and hats have to be removed.

The **Vatadage** ('hall of the relic') to the left as you enter the Quadrangle is a circular building with a *dagoba* on concentric terraces with sculptured railings, the largest with a diameter of 18 m. A superbly planned and executed 12th-century masterpiece attributed to Nissankamalla (1187-1196), the Vatadage has modest proportions but remarkably graceful lines. It was almost certainly intended to house the Tooth Relic. There are impressive guard stones at the entrances of the second terrace and wing stones with *makaras* enclosing lion figures. The moonstone to the north entrance of the top terrace is superb. The *dagoba* at the centre has four Buddhas (some damaged) with a later stone screen.

The **Hatadage**, with extraordinary moonstones at its entrance, is the sanctuary built by Nissankamalla and is also referred to as the Temple of the Tooth, since the relic may have been placed here for a time. See the Buddha statue here framed by three solid doorways, and then look back at one of the Buddha statues in the Vatadage, again beautifully framed by the doorways.

Gal Pota, to the east of the Hatadage, the 'Book of Stone' is to the side of the path and can easily be missed. According to the inscription it weighs 25 tons, and was brought over 90 km from Mihintale. It is in the form of a palm leaf measuring over 9 m by 1.2 m, over 60 cm thick in places, with Sinhalese inscriptions praising the works of the King Nissankamalla including his conquests in India. The **Chapter House** nearby dates from the seventh century. The ziggurat-like **Satmahal Prasada** (originally seven-storeyed) in the northeast corner, decorated with stucco figures, has lost its top level. The 9-m-sq base decreases at each level as in Cambodian *prasats*.

West of the Hatadage, the **Atadage** ('house of eight relics') was the first Tooth Relic temple, constructed by Vijayabahu when the capital was moved here. There are some handsome carved pillars. The ruins of the **Patimaghara**, west of here, reveal the remains of a reclining Buddha.

The **Bo Tree shrine** is to the west of the main Vatadage. The **Nissankalata** (Lotus Mandapa) nearby was built by King Nissankamalla (1187-1196) for a *dagoba*. This small pavilion has the remains of a stone seat (from which the king listened to chanting of scriptures), steps and a stone fence imitating a latticed wooden railing with posts. The ornamental stone pillars which surround the *dagoba* are in the form of thrice-bent lotus buds on stalks, a design which has become one of Sri Lanka's emblems. A statue of a *Bodhisattva* is to its east. The impressive **Thuparama**, in the south of the Quadrangle, is a *gedige* which was developed as a fusion of Indian and Sinhalese Buddhist architecture. This has the only surviving vaulted dome of its type and houses a number of Buddha statues. It has very thick plaster-covered brick walls with a staircase embedded in them. Exiting the Quadrangle by the same steps that brought you in, 500 m to the northeast are two temples which belong to different periods. If you walk past the **Pabulu Vihare**, a squat stupa up to the north wall of the ancient city, you come to one of the earliest temples with Tamil inscriptions, **Siva Devala 2**. Built of stone by the Indian Cholas in a style they were developing in Tamil Nadu (as at Thanjavur), but using brick rather than stone, it is almost perfectly preserved.

Northern monuments

Beyond the original city wall, another group of scattered monuments stretches several kilometres further north. First, the **Alahana Parivena** (Royal Crematory Monastery) Complex, which was set aside by Parakramabahu, is worth exploring. The UNESCO restoration project is concentrated in this area. At the **Manik Vihara**, the squat cloistered stupa was restored in 1991. This originally housed precious gems.

The **Rankot Vihara**, further on, is the fourth largest *dagoba* on the island with a height of 55 m. It was built by Nissankamalla in the 12th century. Note the perfection of the spire and the clarity of the statues round the drum. The tall **Buddha Seema Pasada** was the Chapter House or convocation hall where you can still make out the central throne of the chief abbot, which was surrounded by monks' cells.

The large *gedige* **Lankatilaka** ('ornament of Lanka'), the image house with a Buddha statue, had five storeys. It has walls which are 4 m thick and still stand 17 m high, although the roof has crumbled. The design illustrates the development in thinking which underlay the massive building, for it marks a turning away from the abstract form of the *dagoba* to a much more personalized faith in the Buddha in human form. The building is essentially a shrine, built to focus the attention of worshippers on the 18-m-high statue of the Buddha at the end of the nave. Though built of brick and covered in stucco, the overall design of the building shows strong Tamil influence. The exterior bas-relief sculpture, most of which is impressively well preserved, sheds light on contemporary architectural styles. To the south of the Lankatilaka is a *madipa* with carved columns

Queen Subhadra is believed to have built the 'milk white' **Kiri Vihara** stupa next to it, so named because of its unspoilt white plaster work when it was first discovered. It remains the best preserved of the island's unrestored *dagobas*. The plasterwork is intact although the whitewash is only visible in place, such as around the relic box. There are excellent views from the Chapter House which has the foundations only just visible.

The **Gal Vihara** (Cave of the Spirits of Knowledge) is rightly regarded as one of the foremost attractions of Sri Lanka and has great significance to Buddhists. It forms a part of Parakramabahu's monastery where a Buddha seated on a pedestal under a canopy was carved out of an 8-m-high rock. On either side of the rock shrine are further vast carvings of a seated Buddha and a 14-m recumbent Buddha in *Parinirvana* (rather than death), indicated, in part, by the way the higher foot is shown slightly withdrawn. The grain of the rock is beautiful as is the expression. Near the head of the reclining figure, the 7-m standing image of banded granite with folded arms was once believed to be his grieving disciple Ananda but is now thought to be of the Buddha himself. The foundation courses of the brick buildings which originally enclosed the sculptures, are visible. Sadly, the presentation of the magnificent carved Buddhas is rather disappointing. An unattractive, protective canopy now shields the seated Buddha, which is caged in with rusty metal bars and a scratched plastic 'viewing window' making clear viewing and photography impossible.

A path continues north to rejoin the road. The **Lotus Pond**, a little further along, is a small bathing pool, empty in the dry season, with five concentric circles of eight petals which form the steps down into the water. The road ends at the **Tivanka Image House** where the Buddha image is in the unusual 'thrice bent' posture (shoulder, waist and knee) associated with a female figure, possibly emphasizing his gentle aspect. This is the largest brick-built shrine here, now substantially renovated (though work continues). There are remarkable frescoes inside depicting scenes from the *Jatakas*, though not as fine as those in Sigiriya. Under the 13th-century frescoes, even earlier original paintings have been discovered. The decorations on the outside of the building are excellent with delightful carvings of dwarves on the plinth. The image house actually has a double skin, and for a small tip the guardian will unlock a door about half way inside the building. You can then walk between the outer and inner walls. The passage is lit from windows high up in the wall. It is an excellent way of seeing the corbel building technique. The guardian may also unroll the painted copies of the frescoes, which eventually will be repainted onto the walls.

Southern Group

This group is quite separate from the rest of the ruins, though it makes sense to start here if you are staying nearby. It is well worth walking or cycling down here along the bund as the view is lovely, though the main entrance is from the main road. You will first see the giant 3.5-m-high **statue** of a bearded figure, now believed to be King Parakramabahu himself, looking away from the city he restored, holding in his hand the palm leaf manuscript of the 'Book of Law' (some suggest it represents 'the burden of royalty' in the shape of a rope). Sadly, the statue is covered by an ugly canopy.

To its south is the part-restored **Pothgul Vihara**, which houses a circular *gedige* (instead of being corbelled from two sides), with four small solid *dagobas* around. The central circular room, with 5-m-thick walls, is thought to have housed a library.

Other sights

Once you've exhausted the ruins, a few peaceful hours can be spent cycling along the bund and attractive tree-lined **canals**, perhaps catching sight of a giant water monitor. The water system is so well planned it is hard to believe it is almost 1000 years old. Some 4 km south past the Southern Group along the east bank of the tank you come to a weir, a popular spot for bathing. If you have a 4WD, you can drive down to the dam at **Angamedilla**, a beautiful spot where the tank is fed by the Amban Ganga. Here is an (unofficial) entry point for Wasgomuwa National Park (see page 295), though make sure you're with someone who knows the way.

At **Medirigiriya**, 30 km north of Polonnaruwa, is **Mandalagiri Vihara** ① *US$5, covered by the Cultural Triangle Round Ticket*, a seventh- to eighth-century *vatadage* almost identical in measurement and construction to that in the ancient city's Quadrangle. The circular image house with concentric pillared terraces is located up a flight of granite steps on a hilltop site. It has lost its facing and, despite its atmospheric location, is less impressive than Polonnaruwa. The site it best reached by bus from Kaduruwela to Hingurakgoda, 15 km from the site, from which you can take another bus or three-wheeler.

◉ Polonnaruwa listings

For Sleeping and Eating price codes and other relevant information, see pages 26-32.

● Sleeping

Polonnaruwa *p285, map p287*
There are some good choices right in the centre, near the tank and entrance to the ruins. For hotels near the New Town you can get a bus from the railway station or the Old Town bus stop, and take the path signposted

beyond the Statue, for 1 km to the east. Hotels in the complex west of the Pothgul Vihara by the tank, near the Southern Group, are 3 km from the old town so transport is essential. Bikes are available. Many of the guesthouses have tiered pricing, the cheapest rooms are fan and cold water, then fan and hot water and the most expensive are a/c and hot water.
B Sudu Araliya, near the Southern Group, T222 4849, www.hotelsuduaraliya.com.

Attractive light open spaces, comfortable a/c rooms, with more being built shortly. TV, minibar, some rooms with tank view, bar, nice pool, herbal treatment, etc.

B-C Rest House (CHC), by Parakrama Samudra, T222 2299, www.ceylonhotels.lk. Magnificent setting by the tank, the a/c rooms aren't as good but some have tank views. Queen Elizabeth II stayed here when she visited in 1954 and there's the opportunity to stay in the very room, which might interest monarchists. There's also a suite **A**, which has a garden overlooking the tank.

C Seruwa (CHC), near the Southern Group, T077-237 7051, www.ceylonhotels.com. 37 clean if rather dark and tired rooms, all with lake view, a/c upstairs with private balcony, non-a/c downstairs. Cold water. Restaurant, well-located bar, popular with tour groups.

C-D The Village Polonnaruwa, near the Southern Group, T222 2405, www.villapol.com. 37 a/c rooms, pool, restaurant, bar and attractive gardens.

D Siyanco, 1 Canal Rd, behind Habarana Rd, T222 6868, www.siyancotravel.com. Tucked away behind Habarana Rd. 16 a/c rooms that are clean and modern, although some are on the small side. There are plans for more next year and at the time of writing a pool was underway. Inviting restaurant, friendly.

E-F Devi Tourist Home, Lake View Garden Rd, off New Town Rd, T222 3181, T077-908 1250. Very clean and comfortable a/c and fan rooms with attached bath. Extremely welcoming family, excellent vegetarian home cooking, bike hire, free pick-up from Old Town, peaceful location. Recommended.

E-F Gajaba Hotel & Restaurant, opposite museum, near tank, T222 2394, T077-913 1156, www.hotelgajaba.com. 25 comfortable rooms, including some with hot water and a/c (price reflects amenities). Good garden restaurant and cheap bike hire. Friendly and helpful, can arrange safaris to the national parks.

E-F Manel Guest House, New Town Rd, New Town, T222 2481. Rooms are large and

spacious and those in the new building at the back have verandas and good views of paddy fields. Fan or a/c and hot or cold water (price varies accordingly). Service can be chaotic. Bike hire available. Co-owner Mr Bandula and his tuk-tuk patrol the streets and the bus station looking for new guests, most may find him overbearing.

F-G Samudra Guest House, Habarana Rd, T222 2817. The rooms here have more character than a lot of the other guesthouses. They vary in size, price and amenities so look at what's available before committing, and there are 2 wooden cabanas in the garden. Friendly and popular with backpackers. Restaurant and bike hire available.

⓪ Eating

Polonnaruwa *p285, map p287*

There are several cheap eating places along Habarana Rd and the guesthouses and hotels offer meals. **Devi Tourist Home** offers excellent home-cooked food but you'll have to let them know in advance if you want to eat there, and the **Rest House**'s dining room is in a beautiful spot on the water (but stick to rice and curry).

††-† Gajaba Restaurant, see Sleeping. Offers good food at a reasonable price with many guests from other hotels dining here. There is a good selection of Sri Lankan food.

††-† Siyanco, see Sleeping. Large, pleasant dining room. Wide range of dishes, the Sri Lankans offerings are the best. Accommodating staff.

⊖ Transport

Polonnaruwa *p285, map p287*
Bus

When leaving Polonnaruwa, it pays to get on at Kaduruwela to get a seat. The out-of-town bus stop is near the railway station in **Kaduruwela**. There is a counter is the bus station that can provide information on times and routes. Hourly buses to **Colombo** (6 hrs), via **Dambulla** (1½ hrs), regular buses to **Anuradhapura** (3 hrs), and to **Kandy** (3 hrs), and plenty to **Habarana** (1 hr). For **Sigiriya**, travel to Sigiriya Junction in Inamaluwa, and change to a CTB/private bus. Buses leave for **Batticaloa** from outside the railway station. For **Trincomalee** (4 hrs), there are few direct buses so it may be best to travel to Habarana Junction and change.

Train
The station is in Kaduruwela, 4 km east of the Old Town on Batticaloa Rd. To **Colombo** 0958, 2030 and 2228; to **Trincomalee** 1315; to **Batticaloa** 0440, 1310, 1610.

O Directory

Polonnaruwa *p285, map p287*
Banks Seylan Bank, corner of Habarana Rd and road to Rest House, has Visa ATM and will change TCs. More choice in Kaduruwela, where there are branches of the **Commercial** (nearest to the Old Town), **Hatton** and **Sampath** banks, all with ATMs. **Internet** Sachiri Communications, open 0830-2000, Rs 60 per hr, friendly and sells drinks and snacks; **PG Focus Communication**, on the round- about opposite the police station is more expensive at Rs 100 per hr. **Useful addresses** Tourist police, junction on Habarana Rd, Batticaloa Rd, New Town Rd, T222 3099. Near the Gal Vihara at the main site.

Polonnaruwa to Kandy via Mahiyangana

Only 15 km longer than the Dambulla road, though rarely used by tourists, this route takes you through wild and isolated country, across the vast Dry Zone plains irrigated by the enormously ambitious Mahaweli Ganga Project. The road comes close to some rarely visited archaeological sites and national parks which are worth breaking the journey for. The route also provides respite from the hordes attracted by the many 'star' attractions in the area. ▸ For listings, see page 296.

South to Mahiyangana
East of Polonnaruwa, the A11 follows the railway line towards the coast, leading ultimately south to Batticaloa. Road and rail converge at the impressive Manampitiya iron bridge to cross the wide Amban Ganga, after which there is an important turn-off for Maduru Oya National Park and Mahiyangana (see below). Elephants are often sighted feeding close to the road here.

Dimbulagala → *Colour map 2, B6.*
Dimbulagala archaeological complex is a spread out series of over 100 caves carved into an imposing rock, also known as Gunner's Quoin. The caves have been in continuous use for thousands of years, first by the Veddas, while scattered ruins have been found from various periods between 300 BC and AD 1200. Parts of the complex are still used as a forest hermitage. One Brahmi inscription shows that the caves were once used by Queen Sundari, the daughter-in-law of King Vijayabahu I of Polonnaruwa. Follow the signs for 8 km and you will reach first the sign for **Namal Pokuna**, where a 1-km climb brings you to a small complex with a restored *dagoba*, a *gedige* and *bodhigaraya* (wall around a Bo tree). Nearby is a lily pond (the Namal Pokuna itself), and an ancient stone bridge. Another climb brings you to a perfectly clear drinking pool and a set of meditation caves. Some 4 km south of here, past the **Ahasmaligawa** ('sky palace'), a recent stupa built high

The island's original people

There are few remaining homes for the Veddas. Living in isolated pockets (in particular in the Nilgala and Dambane jungles), normally out of sight, these aboriginal peoples can still occasionally be seen. Once hunter-gatherers, the matrilineal Veddas worshipped ancestral spirits, but most have lost their old hunting grounds and have been forced to find alternative methods of survival by adopting local Sinhalese ways, and with that many of their tribal beliefs and customs. Those in the Eastern Province,

around Gal Oya, have become assimilated into the local Tamil community.

The government's resettlement schemes have been strongly resisted by some, who have remained on the forest edge carrying out subsistence farming by the *chena* ('slash and burn') method, having abandoned their customary bow and arrow. Under increasing pressure to allow some Vedda groups to return to their old settlements, the government has set aside 'reserved' areas for them and given them hunting rights.

on a steep rock, you come to **Pulligoda**, where there is a 12th-century cave fresco depicting five gods, four in the *anjali mudra* (palms together showing obeisance) position, seated on an embroidered scarf. They are painted using the plaster and lime method of Sigiriya, though nowhere near as impressive.

Maduru Oya National Park → *Colour map 4, C1.*
① *Main entrance is 25 km south of Manampitiya. US$15.*
The Mahiyangana road turns back towards the hills with Wasgomuwa National Park to the right (see page 295). The 58,850-ha Maduru Oya National Park is to the left. It was designated a national park in 1983 to protect the catchment of the reservoirs in its neighbourhood and also to conserve the natural habitat of the large marsh frequenting elephant which is found particularly in the Mahaweli flood plain. It is proposed to link the park with Gal Oya to the southeast via the Nilgala jungle corridor. Deer, sambar and the rare leopard and bear can be spotted and there is abundant, varied bird life.

Vedda lands
The area to the east of Mahiyangana is one of the few areas left where Veddas, or Wanniya-laeto, the original inhabitants of Sri Lanka, are found. They live on the edge of the Maduru Oya forest and, transformed from hunter-gatherers to 'poachers' overnight by the park's creation, have since successfully fought for rights to hunt in some areas of the park (though bows and arrows may have been superseded by the gun). On this route guides are often keen to take tourists to the meet the chief of the local Vedda village at **Dambane**, where you can witness some of their remarkable skills and dexterity, and buy ornaments and honey, though some visitors feel uncomfortable at this incursion of the privacy of this fragile community. If you choose to visit Dambane, note that the traditional Vedda greeting (men only) is to grasp forearms. Money is not requested but will be accepted.

This is a bustling town with a long history. In legend it is associated with the Buddha's first visit to Sri Lanka, while the late President Premadasa had a new temple built here to resemble the famous Buddhist temple at Bodhgaya in Bihar, India. Opposite the temple, north of Kandy Road, six statues of symbolically important Sri Lankan leaders have been erected: three ancient kings, Devanampiya Tissa, Dutthagamenu and Parakramabahu; Kirti Sri who reigned over an 18th-century Buddhist revival (see page 198); and two modern political figures – first Prime Minister DS Senanayake, and son Dudley, who oversaw the Mahaweli Ganga Project, the source of the town's importance and prosperity.

Rajamaha Dagoba, 1.5 km south from the main Kandy road, is of special importance since the Buddha was supposed to have visited the spot and preached to the tribal people. The large *dagoba*, which was expanded by Dutthagemunu and has been restored many times, is said to enshrine a fistful of the Buddha's hair. The area is very attractive – the park with the *dagoba* in it is well kept and is overlooked by the hills on the far bank of the Mahaweli.

Sorabora Wewa is just on the outskirts of Mahiyangana on the road to Bibile. According to legend a giant is said to have created the dam. You will probably have to ask someone to find the road for you. You can see two enormous outcrops (the Sorabora Gate) through which the run off from the lake is channelled.

Mahiyangana to Kandy

There are three possible routes. The first route goes via a little visited national park and then traverses what is often referred to as Sri Lanka's most dangerous road. West of Mahiyangana, at Hasalaka you can turn off the main road for **Wasgomuwa National Park** ① *US$15 plus taxes*, created in 1984 to conserve wildlife displaced by the Mahaweli project. From Hasalaka it is 45 km north to the park entrance at Handungamuwa. The park's isolation, hemmed in on three sides by rivers, and the lack of human disturbance, have made it a rich feeding ground with a population of around 150 elephants. There is a belt of woodland on both sides of the river but otherwise the vegetation consists of grass, scrub and low bushes.

After Hasalaka, the A26 climbs into the hills through a series of 18 hairpin bends between 62 km and 57 km from Kandy. The relatively gentle climb and forested slopes present little sense of hazard but buses often take the bends too fast for safety. There are spectacular views across the plains of the Dry Zone, now irrigated by the Mahaweli Ganga Project. Don't forget to stop near the top to look back on the glistening Mahaweli crossing the plains below. Approaching Kandy the road passes the dolomite quarries of Rajooda and the Kandy Free Trade Zone before crossing to the west bank of the Mahaweli Ganga.

These two pleasant alternatives to the A26 go through the **Randenigala Sanctuary**. The slightly shorter route crosses the Mahaweli Ganga at Mahiyangana and then goes due south to Weragantota immediately after crossing the river. The road climbs to the south side of the Randenigala Reservoir, then crosses the Victoria Dam to rejoin the A26 about 20 km from Kandy.

To take the second alternative, you have to take the B-road southeast out of Mahiyangana to **Pangarammana**, then join the road which also climbs to the southern edge of the **Randenigala Reservoir**. Here elephants can often be seen roaming along the shores of the lake. The irrigation development has created an area of intensive rice production and during the **maha** harvest (April-May) you will come across farmers winnowing and the stalks being constructed into quite large circular walls. After passing through **Minipe** the road follows the 30-km-long Minipe Right Bank Canal, then slowly starts to rise. It crosses the river at the base of the **Randenigala Reservoir Dam**, which straddles the last gorge before the Mahaweli Ganga plunges to the plains. Its crest is 485 m long and 94 m high. The road then winds spectacularly around the southern side of the upper lake. Notice too the 'contour lines' on the lakeside as the water level drops during the dry season. The road continues to climb over a small pass – you see paddy fields in the valley below. Once over the pass you can see the **Victoria Dam**. There are a couple of vantage points from which you can take photographs. Towering more than 120 m high, the dam is a massive structure, even bigger than the Randenigala Dam. There is a restaurant and look out place on the dam's north side. Not surprisingly both dams are quite heavily guarded.

◉ Polonnaruwa to Kandy via Mahiyangana listings

For Sleeping and Eating price codes and other relevant information, see pages 26-32.

● Sleeping

Mahiyangana *p295*
Most of the accommodation listed below is along Rest House Rd, 750 m west of the clocktower. Ask the bus to drop you at the **Old Rest House** stop. For eating the best option is at the **New Rest House**. There are also small food stalls and 'bakeries' in the bazaar.

E Sorabora Gedara Hotel, on the road to the lake, T225 8307. 12 comfortable, modern a/c rooms, pool, bar and restaurant serving decent food.

E-F New Rest House, 500 m south of A26, T225 7304. 10 fan and a/c rooms, restaurant serving good food, rooms are large but not of a particularly good standard, nice position overlooking the river, pleasant garden, quiet (the river is dangerous for bathing).

G (Old) Rest House, closer to the main road, T225 7299. 3 rooms at the back, meals in dining room, basic.

Mahiyangana to Kandy *p295*
Safari Village, 10 mins from Wasgomuwa National Park, T011-259 1728. Has cabanas on the lake front. There are also jeeps available for hire.

● Transport

Mahiyangana *p295*
Bus
Regular buses to **Kandy** (2½-3 hrs). Also to **Colombo** (5 hrs), normal buses frequently to **Badulla** and **Bibile**; and 2-3 a day to **Batticaloa** (3-3½ hrs) and **Polonnaruwa** (3½-4 hrs). You will need to have your own transport to visit **Dimbulagala**, the **national parks** (or organize a tour via your guesthouse or hotel) and **Dambane village**. It is also best to have your own transport to visit sites en route between Mahiyangana and Kandy.

● Directory

Mahiyangana *p295*
Banks Several close to the new temple west of Clocktower Junction, parallel with Kandy Rd.

Contents

The East

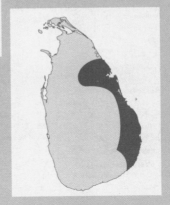

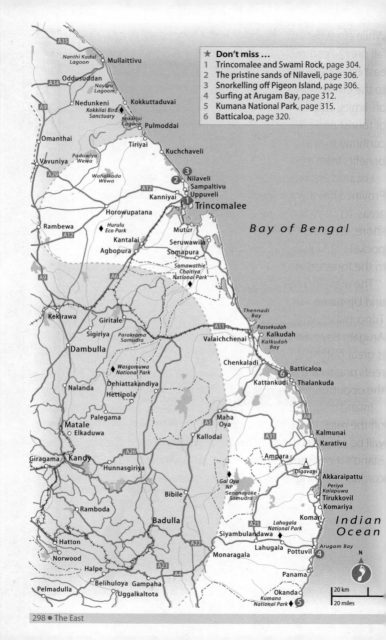

Bay of Bengal

Indian Ocean

20 km
20 miles

While elsewhere the island's magnificent beaches have begun to fall prey to commercialism, the remote and beautiful beaches of the east coast have lain almost forgotten, isolated for long periods due to the ethnic fighting. As word spreads that the area is no longer off-limits, curious visitors are beginning to be drawn by its lack of tourist paraphernalia. Though bleak reminders of the conflict continue to scar the landscape, the province may yet derive some benefits from its years without development.

Located entirely within the Dry Zone, Sri Lanka's Eastern Province has always been one of its most sparsely populated areas. Its coastline, dotted with hamlets along its lagoon-fringed shore, supports Tamil and Muslim fishing communities, while pockets of Sinhalese have traditionally eked out a hard existence in the forested interior.

The main focuses of interest are the idyllic beaches of Nilaveli and Uppuveli, just north of the magnificent natural harbour at Trincomalee, while to the south of the province, surfing centre Arugam Bay is Sri Lanka's latest hotspot. All along the coast, there is great potential, largely unexplored, for diving and snorkelling on reefs unaffected by the 'bleaching' elsewhere on the island, while the opportunities for whale watching are only now being assessed.

Inland is some of Sri Lanka's wildest country, where a short trip off the main roads, often requiring a 4WD and plenty of patience, will be rewarded with a sense of discovery. Here are some the island's most impressive national parks, which form an elephant corridor allowing the animals a free passage right across the region.

To Trincomalee

There are two routes east across the dry zone plains to Trincomalee. The coastal routes north and south of the city, which involve numerous ferry crossings where shallow lagoons flow into the sea, have had no work on them for years, but plans are underway to develop the roads and rebuild the bridges. At the time of writing, however, the route was impassable due to heavy flooding, which may have caused further damage. Enquire locally for the most up-to-date information ▸▸ For listings, see page 302.

Habarana to Trincomalee

This is the fastest and most frequently used route to Trincomalee. Nearly all barriers and checkpoints have been removed, and Trincomalee is now accessible within two hours. The effects of the war are still visible – for long stretches you will see where the forest has been cleared on each side of the road to provide a clear firing zone for military bunkers. It is now beginning to grow back. The landscape is increasingly bleak and barren, forested hills giving way to sparse areas of bush land, though there is evidence of some Western aid agency-led irrigation schemes. About 18 km north of Habarana, you reach the turn-off for the Kaudulla National Park (see page 282).

Kantalai → Phone code: 026. Colour map 2, A5.

At Agbopura, the large Kantalai tank become visible, and there are many stalls by the side of the road selling fresh curd in attractive clay pots. Kantalai is the centre of a very intensive farming area made possible from the irrigation provided by its beautiful tank, originally dating from the seventh century, which provides water to extensive rice fields to the southeast of the main road. The restored tank bund (retaining dam) was breached in 1987 with hundreds killed. Before the war, the rest house, in a scenic position by the lake, was particularly enjoyed by those with an interest in water birds, but was commandeered by the army as a headquarters. The army withdrew in March 2003, and the rest house is currently being restored. About 3 km off the main road, Kantalai town has little going for it except a turn-off for the coast which is likely to increase in importance when the fine beaches south of Trincomalee become more popular. This road is the quickest land route to **Seruwawila** (see page 307). At Somapura it passes an approach road to Somawathie Chaitiya National Park.

Anuradhapura to Trincomalee

The A12 from Anuradhapura to Trincomalee via Mihintale is open but is in bad condition, and takes at least an hour longer than the Habarana road. The route runs through one of Sri Lanka's least populated regions. Abandoned irrigation tanks and marshy ground are interspersed with forest and occasional fields of paddy land. Most of the journey is across the flat plain, broken by a few isolated granite blocks, giving way to the low range of hills just inland of the coast.

Northeast of Mihintale, in the direction of **Rambewa**, an ancient stone bridge on the Mahakanadarawa tank was discovered accidentally. It suggests a road once linked Anuradhapura with the ancient harbour at Gokanna (Trincomalee). You can break at the dusty crossroads town of **Horowupatana**, 42 km east of Mihintale, where an attractive

The east rises again

Trincomalee has long been the focus of plans to regenerate the troubled east. After the ceasefire in 2002 there was talk of redeveloping the port and industrial wasteland, and coastal areas were opened up to foreign investments. Things however did not proceed as planned. The Boxing Day tsunami in 2004 ravaged the south and east coasts of Sri Lanka, killing 31,000 people and destroying over 70,000 homes. Then, as the south concentrated on rebuilding, fighting recommenced here in 2005 until the war ended in 2009. More recently, in early 2011, the areas around Batticaloa and Kalmunai were affected by severe flooding, and yet the populace remains cautiously optimistic about the future.

Rebuilding has been slow and controversial, and the debate about misappropriation of tsunami funds continues to rumble on. In 2009, Transparency International demanded an audit of the money received by the Sri Lankan government to help victims of the Asian tsunami. It was claimed that nearly half a billion dollars in aid is unaccounted for and over 600 million dollars has been spent on projects unrelated to the disaster. This was brought to the fore again recently, when in January locals took to the streets in Batticaloa district to demand relief after the flooding drove many from their homes and decimated rice crops.

With the advent of peace Sri Lankans all over the island are looking to the future. Those on the east are picking themselves up once more, and the tourist resorts at Nilaveli and Uppuveli are drawing crowds again. Whale-watching tours have recommenced, diving trips are running to the wrecks around Trincomalee, and even Kalkudah and Passekudah are readying themselves for visitors. There are plans to develop the east coast more heavily for tourism, particularly around Arugam Bay and Trincomalee, and even Batticaloa has a new tourist information office. The east, however, still shows the scars of its past and the struggles will not be forgotten easily, but perhaps this is what makes it so different from other parts of Sri Lanka. There is something to be said for visiting before the beach settlements resemble Hikkaduwa or Unawatuna, as at the moment people are still pleased you've come and want to talk.

road leads northwest to Vavuniya (see page 328). A turn-off after Rathmale leads up to the *vatadage* at **Tiriyai** (see page 307).

About 8 km before Trincomalee is a turn-off to the hot wells at **Kanniyai**. This is a popular spot with locals who perform certain rites following the death of friends or family here. Hindu legend states that Vishnu appeared to Rawana here to tell him that his mother, after whom the wells are named, had died in order to prevent him from embarking on a foolish project. Vishnu then disappeared, touched his sword to the ground and the wells burst forth in his place. There are seven springs here, each formed into small bathing pools enclosed in tiled tubs. You can only splash the water over yourself with a bucket (the tubs are not big enough to bathe in) but the water is a perfect temperature (37-41°C) and very refreshing. The wells are located 1 km south of A12 (signposted). Independent travellers often make the trip to the wells in a three-wheeler from Uppeveli. It is possible to combine the journey with a stop at the remains of the Velgam Vihara.

For Sleeping and Eating price codes and other relevant information, see pages 26-32.

Sleeping

Habarana to Trincomalee *p300*

G Larkhchein Gest, 50 m off main road, Kantalai, T223 4748. Reasonable rooms

with grimy attached bath, Chinese restaurant, chiefly services local weddings.

Transport

For transport to Trincomalee see page 310. 3-wheelers offer trips **Kanniyai Hot Wells**.

Trincomalee and around

→ *Phone code: 026. Colour map 4, A1.*

Easily accessible from the south once again, Trincomalee, the largest city in Eastern Province, is undergoing something of a renaissance. Trinco's fame – and perhaps one day its fortune – lies in its magnificent natural harbour, described by Nelson as the finest in the world. Fiercely contested for centuries, it was a crucial naval base for the British during the Second World War. Today, after a recent past it would rather forget, this dusty port, still heavily militarized and displaying the scars of war, is for most tourists the gateway to the magnificent deserted northern beaches. The city itself, a uniquely balanced ethnic blend, is also worth exploring.

Leaving Trincomalee city behind, most visitors take the route north to the famous white-sand beaches at Uppuveli and, especially, Nilaveli. As the area slowly begins to draw back tourists, resort hotels and guesthouses have renovated been and more are being built, though some visitors find the debris of war and continued high military presence rather off-putting. Further afield, some important religious sites are once again accessible, but on terrible roads require a 4WD and infinite patience.▸▸ *For listings, see pages 308-310.*

Ins and outs

Getting there

Trincomalee is easily reached by bus from Colombo and Kandy via Habarana, and from Anuradhapura via Horowupatana. The coastal route from Batticaloa is currently not recommended, although renovation way is underway, enquire locally. There is a daily train from Colombo via Gal Oya.

Getting around

The centre of Trincomalee is quite compact, though you will need to take a bus or three-wheeler to get to the beaches north of town. Orr's Hill, 15 minutes walk from the centre, is the main expat area with NGO offices and the town's only luxury hotel. Kanniyai hot wells, the Commonwealth War Cemetery and the beaches north of Trinco can easily be visited from the city but north of Nilaveli the coastal road deteriorates. If visiting Mutur, catch a boat across the bay from the jetty on Inner Harbour Road.▸▸ *See Transport page 310.*

Best time to visit

Trincomalee and its surrounding beaches are best visited between April and October, when the area is at its driest. Between November and March, the east is sometimes battered by strong wind and rains, and the sea in unsuitable for swimming during these months. The area has recently been subjected to the worst monsoon in 50 years and there has been widespread flooding, this has damaged a number of the roads.

Background

Originally known as Gokanna, Trincomalee was one of the earliest settlements of Indian Tamils in Sri Lanka, and later was used as a port by the Kandyan kings. The scale of its advantages was however only fully realized by successive European invaders.

The town is a remarkable exception to the typical pattern of colonial ports which, once established, became the focal points for political and economic development of their entire regions. In India, Madras (Chennai), Calcutta (Kolkata) and Bombay (Mumbai) each owed their origin to colonial development and succeeded in re-orienting the geography and economy of their entire regions. However, Trincomalee was established as a colonial port purely for its wider strategic potential: the finest natural harbour in Asia, dominating the vital navigation lanes between Europe and Asia, especially significant from the late 19th century when steam power saw a massive increase in the size and draught of naval

Trincomalee

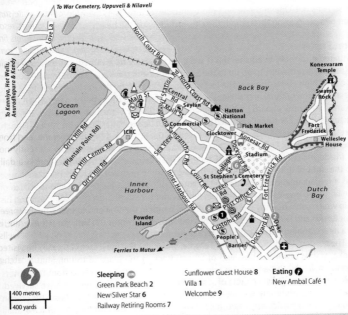

Sleeping
Green Park Beach 2
New Silver Star 6
Railway Retiring Rooms 7

Sunflower Guest House 8
Villa 1
Welcombe 9

Eating
New Ambal Café 1

ships. Trincomalee was home to the South East Asia Command of the British Navy during the Second World War, and its bombing by the Japanese in 1942 was seen as a major threat to the Allies' lifeline to Australasia and the Pacific.

Despite the port's global strategic importance it had virtually no impact on its immediate hinterland. Barren and thinly populated, the region around the city saw no development, and economically Trincomalee District remained one of Sri Lanka's most backward regions. The town itself has never been very important, but that reflects its location in Sri Lanka's dry northeastern region, where the interior has been difficult to cultivate and malaria-infested for centuries. Only today, with the completion of the Victoria Dam and the re-settlement scheme of colonizers using irrigation from the Mahaweli Ganga Project, is the area inland developing into an important agricultural region.

Torn by political strife since 1983 and damaged by the tsunami in 2004, the future for the town is at last beginning to brighten. A resurgence in tourism offers one opportunity for increasing revenue, and the end of the war should stimulate significant economic development in its hinterland (see box, page 301).

 Jane Austen's younger brother Charles is buried in St Stephen's Cemetery.

Sights

The main town is built on a fairly narrow piece of land between Back Bay and the Inner Harbour, and, while much of the harbour remains off-limits, Fort Frederick provides the main point of tourist interest. At any one point it is only possible to see sections of the magnificent bay which gives the harbour its reputation, but there are some good views from Orr's Hill. One of the town's more unusual features is its many spotted deer which can be seen grazing throughout the city, including on the beach.

Fort Frederick

Situated on a rocky headland, this is still an active army base but visitors may enter. It is especially worthwhile to go up to the **Swami Rock** and the Konesvaram Temple built on the cliffs high above the sea. The fort was originally built by the Portuguese in 1623 who destroyed the original and ancient Siva temple. Entering through the gate, which dates from 1676, a noticeboard on the left gives a short history of the fort's complex vacillating fortunes: it was continually handed back and forth between the Dutch, British and French, a result of wars in Europe, until finally taken by the British in 1796. It was christened Fort Frederick after the Duke of York, son of George III, who was stationed here.

Inside, in a cordoned-off military zone, there are two cannons, a howitzer and a mortar. To the right of the path is **Wellesley House**, now the home of the Kachcheri. The house has a remarkable role in changing the course of European history. In 1800 the Duke of Wellington convalesced here from an illness after his South India campaign, missing his ship which subsequently went down with all hands in the Gulf of Aden. Nearby there are four British and Dutch gravestones from the early 18th century. Taking the left fork leads to a new standing Buddha, from where there are good views.

The modern Hindu **Konesvaram Temple**, one of the five most sacred Saivite sites in Sri Lanka, stands at the farthest end of **Swami Rock** in the place of the original. It has a lingam, believed to be from the original shrine, which was recovered from the waters below by a diver. Only a couple of stone pillars from the original temple have survived. The new temple is highly decorated and painted; regular services are held with the one on Friday evening particularly colourful. Leave your shoes at the entrance, for which a small donation will be requested. Go behind the temple to find **'Lovers Leap'**, apparently so-called after the legend according to which the daughter of a Dutch official, Francina van Rhede, threw herself from the rock after her lover sailed away. The truth seems to be more prosaic than the fiction, however, for according to government archives she was alive and well when the Dutch memorial was placed here! A memorial stands on an old temple column on the rock summit though is now sealed off to prevent others following the same fate. There is, however, renovation work currently underway to open up the area underneath and around the rock. It should be open by the time you read this. Nearby, on a precarious ledge on the cliff side a tree has typical strips of coloured cloth tied on its branches, left there by devotees of the temple in the hope of having their prayers answered.

The market

North of the stadium and clocktower, Main Street, Central Street and North Coastal (NC) Road form a thriving shopping area where small single-storey shops and pawnbrokers, many Muslim-run, sell all sorts of goods. Just by the clocktower is a busy fish market, where you can watch tuna, rays and swordfish change hands.

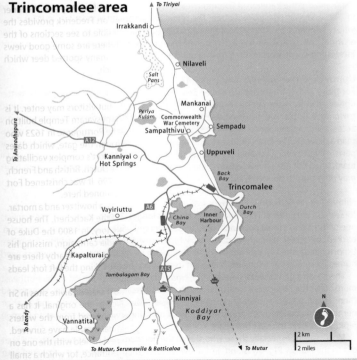

Trincomalee area

Other sights

Sadly, many of Trinco's interesting buildings, such as Admiralty House, the British Dockyard and Fort Ostenburg, built on a hill east of Inner Bay, are not open to visitors. There is little left of the British naval days apart from vivid and graphic names on the map: Marble Bay, Sweat Bay, Yard Cove, Deadman's Cove, Powder and Sober Islands. French Pass marks the passage where the French fleet escaped.

North of Trincomalee

Commonwealth War Cemetery → *Colour map 4, A1.*

At **Sampalthivu**, about 5 km north of Trinco, just before the road crosses the Uppuveli creek, is the Commonwealth War Cemetery. During the Second World War, Trinco was an important naval and air force base and the harbour was the focus of Japanese air raids in April 1942. Five Blenheim bombers were shot down, and the aircraft carrier *HMS Hermes*, along with the destroyer *Vampire* and corvette *HMS Hollyhock,* were sunk off Kalkudah and Passekudah bays to the south; many graves date from this time. As the island was a leave recuperation centre, still more died as a result of their wounds.

The cemetery was damaged by bombing during Sri Lanka's civil war in the late 1980s. The damaged headstones have now been replaced and the garden is beautifully maintained in the tradition of Commonwealth War cemeteries. HRH Princess Anne visited in 1995 and planted a *margosa* tree. The cemetery has great sentimental value for many whose families were stationed at the naval base, and a visit is a sobering experience for anyone. The custodian has a register of the graves and will show the visitor some interesting documents relating to Trincomalee.

Uppuveli → *Phone code: 026. Colour map 4, A1.*

For those without transport, Uppuveli Beach, 4 km north of Trinco, is probably a better option than its more famous northerly neighbour. It is more convenient for trips into town with buses and three-wheelers running regularly, and the main road is more accessible from the beach. While the scars from the war are still visible it is less obvious than at Nilaveli. The influx of tourists and the reopening of a major hotels has meant that parts of the beach, suitable for swimming from March to December, are now well maintained but during low season there can be a lot of debris and rubbish. Guesthouses may offer trips to the Hot Wells.

Nilaveli → *Phone code: 026. Colour map 4, A1.*

Nilaveli, 16 km north of Trincomalee, is Sri Lanka's longest beach, and before the war was one of the island's most popular. It used to be a straight wide strip of inviting white sand, backed by screw pines and palmyras which provided shade, stretching for miles. Unfortunately, the tsunami which hit this area with incredible force not only destroyed homes, businesses and families, it also left its mark on the sand.

The beach's gentle waters are safe for swimming outside the period of the northeast monsoons. The collapse of tourism through the war years has taken its toll, though and there is still a visible military presence. However, tourists are returning and as their numbers rise, building and improvement work gets underway. Expect things to change rapidly here over the next few years.

Most visitors, especially those who stay in the northern part of the beach, hire a boat out to the narrow **Pigeon Island**, just a few hundred metres offshore. It is covered with rocks but has some sandy stretches and offers snorkelling to view corals and fish. There is some good diving too. The island is named after blue rock pigeons which breed here (the island was once used by the British fleet for target practice). Their eggs are prized by Sri Lankans. There are no facilities and little shade, so go prepared. Hotels run trips to the island while local fisherman often approach tourists direct, undercutting hotel prices. The area around the **Nilaveli Beach Hotel** is the best place to leave from – trips are quickest and cheapest from here. Hotels can also arrange dolphin- and whale-watching trips (see page 308).

North of Nilaveli → *Colour map 1, C6.*

Travelling north is not encouraged at the present time, but as this part of Sri Lanka is rapidly opening up so it is worth asking locally what the current situation is. If you do manage to make the journey, be prepared to be stopped frequently by the army.

This area has a stark and desolate beauty. White sandy beaches are backed by inland lagoons though detritus from the civil war is found everywhere. Few pre-war structures remain; most are empty shells. The majority of local people have yet to return. Beyond Nilaveli, the coastal road deteriorates rapidly and you will need a 4WD beyond Kuchchaveli. Bring plenty of drinking water and expect to be stopped frequently for questions at the many checkpoints and army camps. Foreigners are usually allowed to pass through unhindered, but slow right down and make sure that they have acknowledged you before continuing.

At **Tiriyai**, 35 km north of Nilaveli, there are the part-restored remains of an eighth-century *vatadage* with a small stupa inside and fine guardstones atop a hill, reminiscent of Medirigiriya. Sri Lanka's first temple is said to have been built here during the Buddha's lifetime, enshrining a hair relic he gave to two Indian merchants as a reward, though nothing remains of this period. At the top of the hill there are fine views across to sea, 4 km away, and inland. The modern temple at the foot of the hill was destroyed by the LTTE (Liberation Tigers of Tamil Eelam), but monks returned here in May 2002 protected by a strong military presence. Elephants are often seen in this area in the evening. The site can be reached directly from Trinco or it is also accessible from a turn-off on the Anuradhapura–Trinco road near Pankulam via Gomarankadawela, though the road is again said to be poor.

South of Trincomalee

Mutur → *Colour map 4, A1. 12 km from Trincomalee.*

Sri Lanka's longest river, the Mahaweli Ganga, drains into the sea at Mutur. Here, there is also a stone memorial under a tree to Sir Robert Knox, who was captured here by King Rajasinha II in 1660, taken upriver and imprisoned for almost 20 years. Knox's *An Historical Relation of Ceylon* (see page 390) was one of the inspirations for Defoe's *Robinson Crusoe*.

Seruwawila → *Colour map 4, A1.*

Seruwawila Raja Maha Vihara, close to Allai tank, was originally built by King Kavantissa in the second century AD in an attempt to extend his authority to the ancient kingdom of Seru here. The small restored *dagoba* is said to enshrine the Buddha's frontal bone, around which several ancient structures remain. Nearby are two caves housing Buddha figures under the cobra hood of a Naga king.

For Sleeping and Eating price codes and other relevant information, see pages 26-32.

◉ Sleeping

Trincomalee *p302, map 303*

The end of the war has resulted in a mini-spate of hotel renovation, but there is still little choice of accommodation. Many travellers press on to Uppeveli and Nilaveli.

B Welcombe, 66 Lower Rd, Orr's Hill, T222 3885, www.welcombehotel.com. Trinco's 1st luxury hotel, is in an architecturally interesting boat design. Stylishly furnished and spacious rooms, all with balconies (those at 'stern' and 'bow' are best) and harbour views, naval-themed wood-panelled bar, inviting pool.

D Villa Hotel, 22 Lower Rd, Orr's, T222 2284, kandiahrajh@hotmail.com. Good position overlooking the harbour with a/c rooms, restaurant and bar.

D-F Green Park Beach Hotel, 312 Dyke St, T222 2369, lathu@sltnet.lk. Green uniforms, green paint, hence the name. Rooms are a/c in the main building, or fan and cold water in the older block next door. Good restaurant (see Eating, page 309).

E-G New Silver Star, 27 College St, T222 2348. Fairly clean a/c or fan rooms around a central courtyard. Currently undergoing some renovation work on the upper floors.

G Railway Retiring Rooms. 6 rooms with fan, shower, some with nets, all share a sitting area with balcony, eats downstairs.

G Sunflower Guest House, 154 Post Office Rd, T222 2963. This place is cheap and the bus can drop travellers right outside. Other than that, it's dirty and run down and there are no nets. There is a bakery downstairs for breakfast and 3-wheelers often hang around metres down the road if needed.

North of Trincomalee *p306*

There is currently a lot of redevelopment going on here and so new places will be opening all the time, Below are a few

suggestions of places receiving guests at the moment. Note that during high season (Apr-Oct) prices can rise significantly. In low season deals may be available, so it's worth enquiring.

L-AL Chaaya Blu, on beach 4.5 km north of Trinco, 600 m off road, (and 300 m before war cemetery), T222 2307, www.chaaya hotels.com. Previously the **Club Oceanic**, this hotel offers 79 rooms, including the more expensive beach chalets. 2 suites are also available (US$285). All rooms have sea views, a/c and Wi-Fi. There is a swimming pool, a dive centre, an exchange, bar and 2 restaurants, one serving buffet food and the other specializing in crab dishes. Popular with tour groups. Offers whale-watching trips, fishing, snorkelling and excursions to Mutur. Good location right on a curved bay.

A Pigeon Island Beach Resort, 2 km past Nilaveli Beach, 11th Mile post, Nilaveli, T492 0633, www.pigeonislandresort.com. Formerly **Maura Beach Hotel**. 34 a/c rooms and suites (some with sea views and balcony) in an attractive white- and wood-finished hotel. Organizes whale and dolphin cruises, fishing, and diving in season (Mar-Oct). There's a pool, a beach bar and shaded seating areas on the beach with view of Pigeon Island. Currently building a gym and a 2nd restaurant.

A-B Nilaveli Beach Hotel (**NBH**), 11th mile post, 4 km north of Nilaveli Village, T223 2295/6, www.tangerinehotels.com. 45 rooms, half of which are deluxe (tubs, TVs and DVD players). Some standard rooms are currently being upgraded. Restaurant, indoor a/c bar, beach bar, pool and large tree- shaded area with hammocks. Excellent location on best part of beach. PADI diving school (open Apr-Oct), trips to Pigeon Island (Rs 1600 for 2), sport fishing (Rs 2500 first hr, additional hrs Rs 1250), tennis and badminton.

B-C Lotus Park Hotel, 32 Alles Garden, Uppeveli, T222 5327, www.lotustrinco.com. Beachfront rooms with private verandas and standard rooms with balconies. A new block of large deluxe rooms has just been built and will be open by the time this you read this, there are also 6 suites available. Those on the top floor have the best sea views. All rooms are a/c. Swimming pool and good restaurant (see Eating, below).

D Nilaveli Garden Inn, near **NBH**, Nilaveli, T223 2228. Simple but clean rooms with terrace. 200 m from beach, set amongst lovely gardens, restaurant.

D Palm Beach Resort, 12 Alles Garden, Nilaveli Rd, Uppeveli, T222 1250, lpalermi@ hotmail.com. Friendly Italian-managed guesthouse offering a/c and fan rooms. Closed during the monsoon season (Nov to mid-Jan) and busy the rest of the time so book early. The breakfast offers more variety than the average guesthouse and can be enjoyed in garden restaurant. Excellent Italian food (see Eating, below right) and 'real' coffee. Recommended.

D-E Coral Bay, 389 Fisherman's Lane, 1st hotel on beach in Nilaveli village, T326 6196. Clean a/c and fan rooms with nice bathrooms. Well-kept garden in front of beach, nice pool. Restaurant. Organizes snorkelling, fishing and diving trips Mar-Oct, as well as excursions to Pigeon Island. Large army presence nearby.

D-E Jaysh Beach Resort, 7/42 Alles Garden, next door to **Lotus Park Hotel**, T077-605 5821, jaymano@hotmail.co.uk. Clean a/c or fan rooms with verandas. Quiet and although not beachfront the sea is a quick walk down a side passage. Hot water can be arranged and meals are available. The manager spent years at sea and so has a supply of stories. Friendly and accommodating.

E-F Golden Beach Cottages, next to **Chaaya Blu**, Uppuveli, T721 1243, T077-628 2658. Small, dark but fairly clean a/c or fan rooms with large attached bath. Beachfront setting, restaurant.

F French Garden Pragash, Uppuveli, T077-772 8266, edp.french@yahoo.com. Small, basic, sweaty rooms, some with sea view. Beware the low ceiling fans. Excellent beachfront location, restaurant.

F Shahira, 10th mile post (1.5 km south of **NBH**), Liyanage Rd, Nilaveli, T567 0276. Clean, large rooms with fan around shady garden, attached bath (cold water), restaurant and bar. 200 m from beach, friendly and good value.

🍴 Eating

Trincomalee *p302, map 303*
🍴 **Welcombe Restaurant**, see Sleeping. Magnificent position overlooking Inner Harbour. Your best bet in town for Western food.
🍴-🍴 **Green Park Beach Hotel**, see Sleeping. Serves a wide range of good Indian food, as well as some Sri Lankan and Western dishes. There is a rice and curry buffet at lunchtimes. No alcohol. Staff can be surly and disinterested.
🍴 **New Ambal Café**, 79 Post Office Rd. Offers good dosai and short eats. One of several good cheap eateries at the junction of Post Office and Court roads. There are others by the bus stand.

North of Trincomalee *p306*
All guesthouses and hotels listed here offer food, sometimes guests have to forewarn hosts by a few hours that they wish to stay in for dinner and this will usually be rice and curry.
🍴-🍴 **Lotus Park Hotel**, see Sleeping. Restaurant looking out over the ocean, with extensive menu and good food served all day. Staff are efficient and helpful.
🍴 **Palm Beach Resort**, see Sleeping. Home-cooked Italian food, simple but tasty. If craving real espresso this is the place to come.

🍸 Bars and clubs

Trincomalee *p302, map 303*
Welcombe Restaurant, see Eating.
A stylish place for a drink but enjoy the view from the dining room or the veranda rather than stay cloistered in the bar.

North of Trincomalee p306

Nilaveli Beach Hotel, see Sleeping, page 308. It has 2 bars, including 1 a/c with sports TV, though drinks are expensive. **Toddy Tavern**, on the main road just after Shahira turn-off. No-nonsense drinking den full of belching one-eyed old fishermen but toddy is cheap. Female travellers might want to give this one a miss.

▲ Activities and tours

North of Trincomalee p306

A number of the hotels and guesthouses listed under Sleeping, see page 308, organize diving (Nov-Mar), snorkelling, whale- and dolphin-watching trips (Dec-Apr). It is also possible to visit Pigeon Island and Mutur, and have a go at sport fishing. Ensure dive instructors are PADI or SSI certified.
Sri Lanka Diving Tours, based at **Chaaya Blu** (see Sleeping, page 308), T077-764 8459, www.srilanka-divingtours.com. Runs diving and snorkelling trips, as well as operating a glass-bottomed boat. Instructors are PADI certified.

◉ Transport

Trincomalee p302, map 303
Bus

CTB and private bus stations are adjacent to each other. To **Colombo** private buses (via **Habarana** and **Dambulla**) depart when full during the morning and early afternoon

(5-6 hrs). CTB buses leave every 30 mins-1 hr (5½-7 hrs). Fairly frequent buses to **Kandy** (5 hrs). To **Habarana** hourly. To **Polonnaruwa** (4 hrs) or change in Habarana. Fairly regular buses to **Anuradhapura** (33½ hrs). Buses to **Batticaloa** run via Habarana.

Train

The station is at the north end of town about 800 m northwest of the clocktower. To **Colombo Fort**, 1000 and 1930, (8 hrs, 2nd class Rs 270, 3rd class Rs 205). Change at Habarana for **Polonnaruwa** and destinations east. To reach **Batticaloa**, change at **Galga** (2nd class Rs 150, 3rd class Rs 150).

North of Trincomalee p306
Bus

Frequent buses run to **Uppuveli** and **Nilaveli** from Trincomalee or you can take a 3-wheeler (Rs 200-300 to Uppuveli, Rs 600-800 to Nilaveli).

South of Trincomalee p307
Ferry

Ferries leave Inner Bay for **Mutur** (1½ hrs).

◉ Directory

Trincomalee p302, map 303

Banks Plenty of banks in the centre of town, including **Commercial Bank**, Central Rd and **Hatton National Bank**, NC Rd. **Internet** There are several internet cafés near the post office, Court Rd. **Post office** Corner of Power House and Court roads, offers internet.

Arugam Bay and around

Even while civil war raged through the beach resorts along the coast to the north, a small but persistent body of travellers has always been drawn to the surfer's paradise of Arugam Bay. But if this laid-back little village invitingly set between a picturesque lagoon and a magnificent sandy bay has something of a reputation as a long-stay hippy hideaway, the opening up of the surrounding area should attract a different crowd. The growing range of good-value (and sometimes quirky) accommodation here make an excellent base for exploring some of the wildest countryside in Sri Lanka. This feels like frontier territory, largely deserted during the civil war and rebuilt after the devastation wrought by the tsunami, and ideal for those tired of the commercialism of the west coast.➤ *For listings, see pages 317-319.*

Ins and outs

Getting there
There are few direct buses to Arugam Bay – one early morning from Colombo and one from Batticaloa. Badulla and Wellawaya are the best starting points, though you may need to change in Monaragala. For details of these routes, see East to Arugam Bay (below). The main bus stand is in Pottuvil, about 3 km north of the accommodation at Arugam Bay – a few buses a day make the trip across the lagoon, or a three-wheeler costs around Rs 200.

Getting around
The roads around Arugam Bay are quiet and flat, so cycling (available from guesthouses) is a convenient way to get around the local area. For excursions further afield and to the national parks, you will need a jeep or motorbike.

Best time to visit
Most travellers come for the surfing season from April to October, when it is dry and there are constant breezes. Off-season many guesthouses close, though the area still has its attractions: from January to March windsurfing, fishing and swimming are good, and birdwatching is most rewarding when winter migrants arrive.

Tourist information
The long-established hotels, **Stardust** and **Siam View**, are valuable resources with good websites: www.arugambay.com and www.arugam.com respectively. There is also a tourist information booth opposite the **Siam View Beach Hotel** (see Sleeping, page 317).

East to Arugam Bay

Routes to Monaragala
There are two routes to Arugam Bay from the west. The quickest is the A4 from Wellawaya, via Buttala, and Okkampitiya, where there is open-pit garnet and sapphire mining. At Kumbakkana, a turn-off leads to the ancient site at Malagawila (see page 183). The alternative longer but more scenic route descends from the hills on the A22 from Badulla, passing Mount Namunukula and through tea country. It joins the A4 at Hulanduwa, which takes you to on to Monaragala.

Monaragala → *Phone code: 055. Colour map 5, B4. 71 km from Pottuvil.*

Most people pass through the small town of Monaragala ('Peacock Rock'), backed by forested hills, in the rush for the coast. But this small district headquarters, deep within the Dry Zone, is surprisingly lush and verdant owing to its own Wet Zone micro-climate. There's little to do in Monaragala itself but it has a laid-back appeal and is both a useful stop halfway to Arugam Bay and an excellent base from which to explore the surrounding countryside, rich in wildlife and unfairly ignored by tourists.

To the north are the remains of the 12th-century palace of **Galabedda**, with a fine bathing pool reminiscent of the Kumara Pokuna in Polonnaruwa, while to the south there are some attractive walks into the cool **Geelong Hills**.

Monaragala to Arugam Bay

The road surface is good until **Siyambalanduwa**, a former major checkpoint at which all vehicles travelling west would be searched. There is still a large police presence but now little fuss. The A25 here leads north to Ampara and Batticaloa. East of here, potholes begin to appear and the pace of life (never very fast) slows still further. Ox-pulled cart becomes a common mode of transport and it is a peaceful drive through the dappling, the road lined with jack, margosa and tamarind trees. The road passes through **Lahugala National Park**, and elephants are frequently seen from the road in the afternoon. For details of Lahugala and the nearby Magul Mahavihara (see page 314).

Arugam Bay → *Phone code: 063. Colour map 5, B6.*

The bay

Arugam Bay's wonderful wide sweep of sandy beach is usually deserted, except at the southwest corner, where some fishing boats and thatch huts reveal the tiny fishing village of **Ulla**, just to the south of the guesthouse area. This is also the safest area for swimming, which has led to a tussle between local hoteliers and fishermen (only ever one winner, the boats will probably relocate to the next beach). The lack of tourists, especially in the off-season, means that the beach can be dirty in some places, strewn with plastic bags and bottles.

The bay lies between two headlands and is excellent for surfing. **Arugam Point**, to the south, is the main break, regarded by many as the best in the country, with a clean wall of surf allowing a ride of up to 400 m. In season it can get crowded. In contrast, **Pottuvil Point** at the northern end of the bay, is often deserted and is popular with more experienced surfers. The journey to the beach here takes you across some attractive meadows teeming with wildlife. From Arugam Bay three-wheeler drivers charge Rs 1500 return to Pottuvil Point, including waiting time.

There are various opportunities for wreck diving in the bay with five pre-1850 ships within 5 km of each other.

Lagoons → *For boat trips, see page 319.*

Arugam's picturesque lagoon divides Ulla village from Pottuvil town. The bridge is an excellent vantage point for the sunset, and at night you can watch prawn fishermen throwing, gathering and emptying their nets. Pottuvil lagoon, north of town, supports a wide variety of wildlife including crocodiles, monkeys, water snakes and plenty of birds, though partial destruction of the lagoon's mangrove forest has had a negative effect on wildlife. There are re-planting schemes afoot.

Pottuvil

The dusty Muslim town of Pottuvil, 3 km north of Ulla, has little of interest, except for the ruins, half-submerged amongst the sand-dunes, of the **Mudu Maha Vihara**, where a Buddha statue and two Avalokiteswara figures, around ninth or 10th century, can be found in a pillared structure, along with the boundary wall of an image house.

Pottuvil & Arugam Bay

Crocodile Rock
The Crocodile Rock is 2 km south of Arugam Point along another deserted beach to **Kudakalliya**. Scrambling across the dunes and fording the lagoon where it joins the sea, you reach the rock, at the top of which there are magnificent views inland across the paddies and lagoon. Eagles swoop overhead, and you can sometimes spot elephants. There is another good surf point nearby. Do be careful getting here though. Currents sometimes render it impossible to cross the lagoon to the rock, and beware of large mugger crocodiles and the occasional elephants that attempt to climb the rock. Seek advice first.

Around Arugam Bay

Lahugala National Park → Colour map 5, B5. 14 km west of Pottuvil.
This small national park (15 sq km) is good for watching birds and large elephant herds. Lying between Gal Oya and Yala, the park is part of the 'elephant corridor' for the elephant population to move freely across the southeastern part of the island and trips can be organized from Arugam Bay.

The **Lahugala**, **Mahawewa** and **Kitulana tanks** here attract numerous species of water birds, while in the dry season (especially July to August) herds of 100 or more elephants are drawn to the *beru* grass that grows in the shallow tanks. The best time to watch them is in the late afternoon. The climbing perch fish is said to slither across from the Mahawewa to Kitulana tanks when the former runs dry.

Sleeping 🛏
Aloha Cabanas **13**
Arugam Bay **4**
Arugam Bay Surf
Resort **2**
Beach Hut **7**
Galaxy Lounge **16**
Hang Loose **15**
Hideaway **1**
Kudakkaliya Bungalow **5**
Point View **6**
Rupa's Beach **14**
Sea Shore **17**
Siam View Beach **8**
Stardust Beach **10**

Eating 🍴
Gecko's **1**
Green Room **2**

Pada Yatra

The traditional annual **Pada Yatra** from Nagadipa in the Jaffna peninsula to Kataragama is one of the world's great pilgrimages, on a par with the trip to Mount Kailasa in Tibet. Though ethnic strife nearly put an end to the trek in the 1980s, the foundation of the Kataragama Devotees Trust in 1988 has sparked a revival in recent years. Each **Wesak Poya**, an increasing band of pilgrims, predominantly but not exclusively Hindu, set out on the perilous six-week journey down the east coast along the country's ancient tracks. Dressed as beggars (*antis*) and formed into small groups (*kuttams*), they cover 8-10 km a day, bathing in rivers, sleeping in camps, and worshipping at over 70 temples en route where they are offered alms. The final section from Pottuvil, via Okanda and through Yala National Park (the only occasion on which people are allowed on foot in the park), is the most popular and dangerous. Some get lost, and even die en route, which is said to be the ultimate distinction and a sign of Kataragama's grace. The goal is the flag-hoisting ceremony at Kataragama which marks the beginning of **Esala Perahera**.

Magul Mahavihara → *8 km west of Pottuvil along the A4.*

An inscription plate here testifies that the extensive 80-ha monastery complex here (of which 20 ha have now been excavated) is a 14th-century reconstruction, though the site was originally constructed by King Dhatusena in the sixth century. There is an unrestored *dagoba*, a *vatadage* with an unusual moonstone, a *bodhigara* (for enclosing a bo tree) and several pavilions. A kilometre south, a circular structure with dressed slabs of stone may be an elephant stable.

South to Kumana

The coastal scenery south of Arugam Bay is highly distinctive. Rising from the flat landscape are giant boulders in bizarre formations, at the foot of many of which are abandoned now overgrown cave monasteries and hermitages, some dating back almost 2000 years. Cultivated paddy fields are interspersed with open parkland and scrub jungle, all supporting a remarkable variety of birdlife. This is wild country, largely abandoned during the war, where elephants roam freely.

The paved road ends 12 km to the south at **Panama**, the last inhabited village before Yala. Turtles can be seen in the attractive lagoon here, and crocodiles sometimes bask on its banks. A track leads to the sand dunes approaching Panama's seemingly endless beach, with its pink rocks shimmering in the distance.

At **Okanda**, 28 km south of Arugam Bay, there is an ancient Skanda shrine at the foot of a rocky outcrop. There are several associated legends. Ravana was supposed to have stopped here on his way to Koneswaram, while Skanda (Kataragama) landed here in a stone boat, with consort Valli, in order to fight Sooran. She is venerated by the Valli Amman *kovil* at the top of the rock. Kataragama-bound pilgrims usually stop at the shrine for the 15-day festival in July. Some 2 km inland, around Helawa lagoon, the large **Kudimbigala** rock houses a forest hermitage with a part-restored stupa and drop-ledge caves from the second century BC at its base.

Kumana National Park (formerly Yala East National Park) → *Colour map 5, B6.*
ⓘ *The park entrance is at Kumana. US$10 plus extra charges.*

Kumana National Park reopened to the public in March 2003 after 18 years of closure owing to the war, it suffered damage in the boxing day tsunami in 2004 and then was closed again in 2006 when hostilities resumed in earnest. It reopened again in early 2010. As at Wilpattu (see page 104) there has been some despoliation of the park's habitats and wildlife population in the intervening years. The focus is the wetland formed by the Kumana *villu*, fed by a channel from the Kumbukkan-oya when a sandbar forms at the mouth of the river in the dry season. In recent years, the tank has been unable to fill with sufficient water killing off part of the mangrove, though it has recently been reconstructed and is said to be filling up.

Large flocks of painted storks may be seen, while many birds can be spotted along the Kumbukkan-oya. The park still supports an elephant population, though herds are smaller, and it is evident that deer and wild boar have been poached, though some arrests have recently been made.

Arugam Bay to Batticaloa

The quiet but well-laid coastal road north of Arugam Bay passes through alternating Hindu and Muslim fishing villages on its way to Batticaloa, now accessible within three hours. Though the sea is rarely in sight, this is a beautiful drive rich in bird life. Rice paddies and lagoons dominate the landscape, though cultivation can be affected by frequent cyclones and flooding. There is evidence of numerous income-generating projects developed by Western aid agencies, and much new construction in some of the larger towns, such as **Akkaraipattu**, **Kalmunai** and **Kattankudi**, much of it an Islamic style. The Danish government is planning a harbour at Oluvil, with a new industrial zone, which will help regenerate the local area. The places of interest to visitors however lie a short distance inland.

Digavapi → *Colour map 5, A6.*
ⓘ *Donations requested (part of the complex was destroyed during the war).*

The enormous part-restored *dagoba* here, originally 98 m high, built by King Sadhatissa in the first century BC, is one of the sixteen holiest Buddhist sites in Sri Lanka. The site is said to have been visited by Buddha on his third visit. Amongst the scattered remains of this ancient complex are shrine rooms, monastic quarters, *bodhigaras* and hospitals. Three gold caskets were also found during excavations. There is a small archaeological museum nearby. From the A4, take the B607 towards Ampara and turn right at the village of Varipathanchenai.

Ampara → *Phone code: 063. Colour map 5, A5.*

The modern district headquarters of Ampara has a recent bloody history, though is well connected and, if safe, could be a used as a base for Gal Oya National Park. It has accommodation, restaurants and banks. Near the Kandavatavana tank on the road to Inginiyagala is the gleaming white *dagoba* of a peace pagoda, donated by the Japanese government in 1988.

Elephas maximus maximus

Cumbersome yet capable of remarkable grace, full of charisma yet mortally dangerous if rankled, universally revered yet critically endangered, the Asian variety of the world's largest land mammal has a complex relationship with man.

Once widespread across the country, elephants have been tamed for over 2000 years. Their massive power was harnessed by the ancient Sinhalese in wars against invaders, used to construct ancient palaces, temples and reservoirs, while some were exported as far afield as Burma and Egypt. Seemingly without paradox, they also possess a mythical and religious status: the *Jataka* tales refer to the birth of Buddha in the body of an elephant, while a caparisoned elephant carries the Buddha's Tooth in Kandy's Esala Perahera; for Hindus, they represent Lord Ganesh.

Yet, despite protection, Sri Lanka's wild elephants, now mainly confined to the Dry Zone, are in crisis, numbers falling from around 10,000 at the turn of the 18th century to between 3000 and 4000 today. The population was drastically reduced by the British, who shot them for sport and declared them an agricultural pest, and the hill country was all but cleared of herds to make way for tea plantations. Yet after a period of recovery aided by the establishment of protected areas, numbers since the 1960s have again declined rapidly: almost 1400 elephants were killed in the 1990s, 162 in 2001 alone, or the equivalent of around 5% of the total population in one year. Sri Lanka's ethnic troubles have been a contributory factor.

The problem lies of course in what is termed the 'human-elephant conflict'. Given the rarity of tuskers ivory is not a major issue, but deforestation, agricultural expansion and the explosion of the human population (set to double by 2035) have all deprived the elephants of their natural habitat. And while there is a growing network of protected reserves, buffer zones and elephant corridors, in practice these areas are usually too small to accommodate these enormous animals which require 200 kg of food and 200 litres of water per day, and are forced to push into adjacent agricultural lands.

Yet life is hard too for the farmer who may have his entire annual staple crop destroyed in one night, or who may even have to defend his own life from a marauding bull. Various solutions have been tried for this seemingly intractable problem – in periodic elephant 'drives' the animals are immobilized and transferred to a national park, while electric fences are a common management tool. Some suggest that compensation should be introduced for crop damage (to counter the heavy fines and/or imprisonment for killing an animal). But many experts agree the real key is in attempting to converge of the interests of people and elephants by encouraging compatible land use, such as grazing. One way forward is for farmers to derive economic benefits from elephant products such as manure for organic farming.

The Department of Wildlife Conservation (DWLC) is due to carry out an elephant census in 2011, hoping to ascertain the total number of wild elephants in Sri Lanka and their distribution throughout the island. A better idea of the number of elephants should aid future planning.

Gal Oya National Park → *Colour map 5, A5.*

This magnificent park was established to protect the catchment area of the Senanayake Samudra, an enormous reservoir created in 1948 by damming the Gal Oya. It remains testament to one of the most ambitious development schemes to irrigate the barren lands of the east and resettle Sinhalese from the west. Backed by sheer forested slopes, the lake is the largest in Sri Lanka, and highly impressive. The park extends over 540 sq km of rolling country most of which is covered in tall grass (*illuk* and *mana*) or dry evergreen forest which escaped being submerged. The hilly country to the west was one of the last strongholds of the Veddas, and certain areas of the park still harbour medicinal herbs and plants which are believed to have been planted centuries ago. Recent reports however suggest extensive illicit logging as well as poaching during the period of the park's closure. Gal Oya is famous for its elephants and a variety of water birds which are attracted by the lake. Crocodiles and birds such as the white-bellied sea-eagle are also often seen.

At the time of writing there were few facilities for visitors. A good road leads southwest from Ampara to Inginiyagala where you enter the park, or alternatively turn north from the A4 at Siyambalanduwa. The few tracks inside however are overgrown and in a poor state.

◉ Arugam Bay and around listings

For Sleeping and Eating price codes and other relevant information, see pages 26-32.

● Sleeping

East to Arugam Bay *p311*

F Victory Inn, 65 Wellawaya Rd, Monaragala, T227 6082. Clean, modern a/c and fan rooms, upstairs with balcony (though not much to see), restaurant, bar.

F-G Wellassa Inn Rest House, 500 m before bus stand, Monaragala, T227 6815. 6 simple a/c and fan rooms, set in attractive well-maintained gardens, restaurant with good rice and curry lunch.

G Asiri Guest Inn, 8 Pottuvil Rd (behind service station), Monaragala, T227 6618. 6 clean, simple rooms, restaurant, decent option 2 mins walk from bus stand.

Arugam Bay *p312, map p313*

Some guesthouses close in off-season. Many properties are currently being restored or built, but the 5 or 6 well-established places that have carried on through the war years and the tsunami tend to have the best local knowledge. Note that most places only have cold water bathrooms.

B Kudakkaliya Bungalow, 2 km south of Arugam Bay, 20-min walk from Elephant Rock, T071-273 3630. Attractive eco-bungalow in secluded position with own beach and surf point, choice of bedroom or sleeping *al fresco* on (protected) veranda, cook provided or self-cater. Water from the well, solar power, veranda with magnificent views. From Rs 12,000 to rent whole house.

B-D Stardust Beach Hotel, T224 8191, www.arugambay.com. Danish-run, Arugam's original hotel is in a beautiful location where the beach meets the lagoon and has been for many years a traveller's oasis. There's a choice of beach cabanas with private terrace, and 'luxury' rooms (upstairs more expensive and with sea views), pleasant beach garden, excellent if pricey restaurant, cycle hire, attentive service, good source of local information, quiet, civilized.

C Siam View Beach Hotel, T224 8195, www.arugam.com. Arugam's party centre in a Thai setting, with an excellent restaurant (see Eating, page 318). Outside is a red British phone box. Inside, the rooms are a/c with satellite TV and open onto an attractive garden. Free Wi-Fi, and surf lessons are on offer. Try the home-brewed beer.

C-D Hideaway, T077-459 6670, T077-305 7888, www.hideawayarugambay.com. Beautiful house, 5 rooms with veranda overlooking a garden, plus 9 excellent cool cabanas, tastefully decorated, pleasant restaurant, satellite TV, peaceful, relaxed atmosphere.

C-E Point View, Main St, T224 8462, www.pointviewarugambay.com. 20 a/c and fan rooms, restaurant, shaded garden area with access onto the beach.

D Sea Shore, T224 8410. Large, clean rooms with spotless bath, plus cabanas, restaurant, good position at northern end of beach.

D-E Galaxy Lounge, T224 8415, www.galaxy srilanka.com. 8 beach cabanas (2 are on stilts and 3 have sea views), simple, clean, popular, friendly, good food. Good value.

D-F Aloha Cabanas, T224 8379. Rooms, cabanas (some with roof accessed by a ladder for sitting/sleeping) and treehouse in an attractive plot with hanging baskets, all sea facing. Surf shop, board hire.

E Rupa's Beach Hotel, T224 8258, www.arugam-bay.com. Rooms with attached bath, plus 8 cabanas.

E-F Arugam Bay Surf Resort, formerly **Arugam Bay Hilton**, T224 8189. 12 spotless rooms, bungalows and basic cabanas with good beds, satellite TV, internet. Runs tours and eco-trips on the lagoon. The restaurant serves decent food, including Mexican.

E-G Arugam Bay Hotel, formerly **Tsunami Hotel**, T077-664 2991, www.thearugambay hotel.com. Founded in 1999 before the tsunami, this hotel recently decided to change its name. 11 simple, cleanish, basic rooms, nets, fan, some with terrace, plus wooden cabanas in a shaded palm garden (with hammocks) on the beach, small restaurant.

F-G Beach Hut, T224 8202. Range of good-value accommodation especially popular with long-termers in the form of coconut-thatch and *kadjan* cabanas (some in the trees). Good cheap food.

G Hang Loose, T224 8225. 7 clean, small rooms with attached bath, and 5 cabanas with shared facilities. Bike and surf board hire, set back from the road, friendly.

🍴 Eating

East to Arugam Bay *p311*
For options see Sleeping, page 317. There are also some simple roadside places serving local food near the bus stand.

Arugam Bay *p312, map p313*
There are a number of places along the main drag serving food, as well as most of the guesthouses.

🍴🍴🍴 **Siam View Beach Hotel**, see Sleeping, page 317. Authentic Thai food, as well as other international dishes including pizza. The terrace overlooking the street is a great spot for people-watching over a beer.

🍴🍴🍴 **Stardust Beach Hotel**, see Sleeping, page 317. 1st-class Western dishes (chefs and most ingredients imported from Denmark) served in a laid-back setting. Expensive but worth it.

🍴🍴 **Geckos**, Main St. For the homesick, this Sri Lankan/British-owned place serves excellent Western meals to fill up on after a day of surfing, such as burgers, fish and chips and the daily specials. Breakfast is available all day and includes the full English, pancakes, porridge and muesli. A bakery will be opening in 2011 selling fresh home-made bread and cakes. Tries to use local produce, home-grown veggies and herbs, free range chicken, fairtrade coffee and organic tea. Will fill up plastic water bottles with drinking water for a small fee. Also has rooms.

🍴 **The Green Room**, Main St, on the opposite side of the road from the sea. A characterful open-air restaurant with excellent curries and seafood dishes.

🍸 Bars and clubs

Arugam Bay *p312, map p313*
There are a number of places serving alcohol and hosting full-moon parties. Take a wander along the sand to find somewhere you like the look of. If eating in some 'dry' places you can bring booze but corkage is high.

▲ Activities and tours

Arugam Bay *p312, map p313*
The guesthouses in Arugam Bay can organize watersports, trips to nearby national parks and onward travel if required. Surfing is the main activity here, but don't despair if you don't ride waves as there are a number of other activities on offer or you can just huddle in a hammock with a good book.

Birdwatching
At its best from Nov-Dec when the winter migrants arrive in the area. The nearby lagoons are great places for twitching.

Diving
Only possible May-Jul. Ask at **Stardust**.

Dolphin-watching
2-hr boat trips are available May-Sep.

Surfing
The season runs Mar-Oct. Equipment is widely available from guesthouses.
A-Bay Surf Shop, T224 8187. Has a good selection of boards for rent, as well as other surf bits and pieces

Tour operators
The **Hidayapuram Fishermen's Cooperative Society** runs 2-hr trips in outrigger canoes on Pottuvil lagoon in season, contact **Arugam Bay Surf Resort** to arrange (see Sleeping, page 318).

Around Arugam Bay *p313*
Tour operators
Guided trips to Lahugala National Park are organized by guesthouses in Arugam Bay, usually leaving around 1530-1600.

⊖ Transport

East to Arugam Bay *p311*
Bus
From Monaragala, hourly buses to **Colombo**. Morning CTB buses for **Pottuvil** (Arugam Bay). For the highlands it is best to change at **Wellawaya**, though there are infrequent direct buses to **Badulla**. Direct buses also go to **Kataragama** and **Matara**.

Three-wheeler
They will run to Arugam Bay if you miss the bus, but this is dangerous as there may be elephants on the road, and it is expensive.

Arugam Bay *p312, map p313*
Bus
A **Colombo**-bound CTB bus originating in Panama passes through Pottuvil at 0630 each morning, or private bus leaves at around 1700. There may also be buses between Pottuvil and **Wellawaya**, though generally you have to change at Monaragala. There is a bus to **Batticaloa**, plus several buses a day to **Akkaraipattu**, where you can change.

Around Arugam Bay *p313*
Bus
Buses occasionally run to **Panama**, or you can take a 3-wheeler.

❶ Directory

East to Arugam Bay *p311*
Banks Bank of Ceylon and People's Bank at north end of Monaragala town.

Arugam Bay *p312, map p313*
Banks Bank of Ceylon in Pottuvil town. **Internet** Available at a number of places on Main St, but is expensive at Rs 100 per hr. Some guesthouses offer internet terminals and/or Wi-Fi. **Post office** In Pottuvil and a small branch at the south end of Arugam Bay's Main St. **Tourist police** Next to Point View, T224 8022.

Batticaloa and around

Until late 2009, the Tamil town of Batticaloa, along with its two famous beaches, Passekudah and Kalkudah, was well off the tourist map. Accessible once more, curious locals and foreigners are beginning to visit this remote part of the coast, and have found not a war-ravaged shell but a likeable town cautiously coming to terms with its recent troubles. Batticaloa (or 'Batti' as it is frequently called), famous for the 'singing fish' in its picturesque lagoon, has few sights but the friendliness of its people, who are genuinely pleased that you came, can make a stop on the way through to Arugam Bay or Polonnaruwa a rewarding experience. It is a relaxed place, with bicycle the chief mode of transport. ▶▶ *For listings, see pages 323-324.*

Ins and outs

Getting there

Buses run to Batticaloa from Colombo and Kandy via Habarana and Polonnaruwa, although it is also possible to travel from Badulla and the eastern hill country via Bibile (see page 322). From Pottuvil and Arugam Bay, you may need to change in Ampara or Kalmunai. From Trincomalee, you will need to take the inland route via Habarana, or if taking the train change at Gal Oya. There is a train from Colombo via Polonnaruwa, alight at Valaichchenai for Passekudah and Kalkudah.

Getting around

Batticaloa is small enough to walk or cycle around, but you will need your own transport or to take a bus or train to reach the beaches north of town.

Batticaloa → *Phone code: 065. Colour map 4, C2.*

The fort area

The coast to the south of Batticaloa was the first landing point of the Dutch in Sri Lanka in 1602, who were welcomed by the Kandyan king to help drive out the Portuguese. They subsequently captured the Portuguese fort here in 1638, which was later rebuilt. Although overgrown and neglected, the ramparts remain intact and it is possible to walk most of the way round them. The area is now home to the Kachcheri and there is a smattering of government agencies and NGOs installed within the walls.

Enter from Court House Road. Take a look at the tunnel, now sadly shut off and clogged up with rubbish, which ran parallel to the lagoon, formerly providing access to a jetty. At the eastern side of the fort is a VOC gate which has been widened to let in traffic, flanked by two cannons facing out to the lagoon. A small **museum** ① *0900-1630*, in the complex holds various artefacts from the Portuguese, Dutch and British periods. This was being renovated at the time of writing.

The lagoon → *Apr-Oct at full moon is said to be the best time to hear the fish.*

At 48 sq km, this is Sri Lanka's longest navigable lagoon, and is home of course to the **singing fish**. Numerous theories abound to the cause of this strange phenomenon, sometimes likened to a single sustained note on a guitar, one being that it is the courting call of mussels resonating against the rocks beneath. It is usually only possible to hear the fish around full moon and clearest if you go out at night with a local fisherman, who will know where to find the rocks, and for maximum effect put an oar into the lagoon with the other end to your ear.

Other sights

Batticaloa's most impressive sight lies 60 m under water, 5 km offshore, and unless you are very experienced diver, you are very unlikely to see it. It is the gargantuan wreck of *HMS Hermes*, the British aircraft carrier sunk in 1942 by the Japanese. Several dive teams from Hikkaduwa explored the wreck in 2002-2003 and reported it to be in good condition. Dive trips are available. ▶▶ *See Activities and tours, page 324.*

Though not really a sight, visitors won't be able to miss the new vast, blue bus stand that stands next to the river. The bridge is an excellent place to watch the fishermen casting their nets.

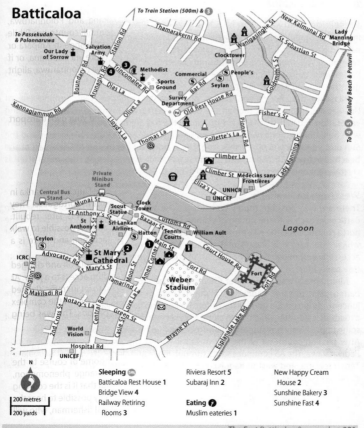

Batticaloa

Sleeping
Batticaloa Rest House 1
Bridge View 4
Railway Retiring
  Rooms 3

Riviera Resort 5
Subaraj Inn 2

Eating
Muslim eateries 1

New Happy Cream
  House 2
Sunshine Bakery 3
Sunshine Fast 4

The nearest beach to Batti is at **Kallady**, 3 km from the centre of town, though those at Passekudah and Kalkudah, see below, are better. Kallady beach has fine sand though the seas are rough, it needs a bit of a clean-up and is not suitable for swimming. There are no facilities but you'll have it to yourself. To get to Kallady Beach, cross Lady Manning Bridge and turn left. Otherwise, buses take 20 minutes.

There are some fine restored kovils and churches around town, as well as a couple of curious monuments: one an unexpected statue of a boy scout by the clocktower, commemorating the 80th anniversary of Baden-Powell's movement, the other near the fort is a bronze statue of William Ault, a pioneer of education on the east coast. Taking you out of town to the south is the British-period iron **Lady Manning Bridge**, open to traffic with a pedestrian walkway alongside. It's just too small for two sets of traffic, so crossing by vehicle can be a bruising experience.

Around Batticaloa

Passekudah and Kalkudah beaches → *Phone code: 065. 32 km north of Batticaloa*.

In peaceful times, the resorts at Passekudah and Kalkudah were one of the honey pots of east coast tourism, drawing large crowds each day to their gentle waters, safe for swimming year-round, and glorious sandy beaches. At the time of writing Kalkudah and Passekudah were beginning to recover from the years of army occupation and guesthouses had opened again.

Passekudah's fine 4-km sweep of horse-shoe shaped bay, reminiscent of Unawatuna, is still there, though the beach is narrower, hemmed in by encroaching vegetation and in need of a clean-up. Lining the bay are the bombed out husks, ridden with bullet holes, of its two abandoned package hotels, the **Imperial Oceanic** and the **Sun and Fun** which is pretty shocking. Life is however beginning to stir – part of the beach is active with fishing boats, and a tea stalls have opened. The water itself is crystal-clear and very shallow up to 500 m out to sea.

West from Batticaloa

There are two possible routes west across the scrub jungles of the Dry Zone from Batticaloa, each with the option of visiting some hot springs. The quickest route to the north continues on the A15 through the slowly recovering town of **Valaichchenai**, near which you can visit Passekudah Beach (see above). From here, Polonnaruwa is accessible within two hours, or you can stop off at **Dimbulagala** cave complex en route (see page 293).

Alternatively, a left turn off at Chenkaladi heads southwest on the A5 across a vast barren plain towards Kandy (via Mahiyangana), or via **Bibile** to Badulla. Maha Oya junction, 40 km on, is a good place to stop for lunch. Excellent rice and curry is available at a roadside café, after which, 2 km along a gravel road from Maha Oya town, you can visit some impressively **hot sulphuric springs**, rather unattractively pooled in concrete pots. After passing southeast of the 687-m Kokagala hill, the road is joined by the A26 at Padiyatalawa. The A5 continues south through Bibile and climbs steeply to Lunugala and Tennugewatta, and west to Badulla. ▶ *For the route along the A26 to Mahiyangana and Kandy see page 295.*

For Sleeping and Eating price codes and other relevant information, see pages 26-32.

◉ Sleeping

Batticaloa *p320, map p321*
There aren't many places to stay in Batticaloa. Most can be found on the north bank of the lagoon off Trinco Rd, or 2 km out of town across the bridge in Kallady.

D Batticaloa Rest House, Brayne Dr, T222 7882. Since the army moved out, this place has been renovated and now offers modern clean rooms with gardens overlooking the lagoon. There is also a restaurant serving good seafood. It's in a lovely location and is the best option in the town centre.

D-E Deep Sea Resort, New Fisheries St, Nawalady, T077-764 8459, www.deepsea resort.webs.com. Built to accommodate divers wishing to visit the *HMS Hermes* wreck with **Sri Lanka Diving Tours** (see page 324). Offers 6 spotless a/c and fan rooms, and a good restaurant. Visitors don't have to be divers to stay here, but will need their own transport to reach it independently.

D-F Riviera Resort, New Dutch Bar Rd, Kallady, T222 2165, www.riviera-online.com. 4-ha garden in beautiful position overlooking the bridge and lagoon, a range of clean rooms, including a 3-room bungalow suite and rooms with terrace near water's edge. The restaurant serves good food.

E-G Subaraj Inn, 6/1 Lloyds Av, T222 5983. At the time of writing the claustrophobic fan rooms were disturbingly mouldy, the a/c options in the main building may be a better bet but they are significantly more expensive. Things may change, however, so view before committing. Restaurant with good food.

F-G Bridge View, 63/24 New Dutch Bar Rd, Kallady (500 m from beach), T222 3723, www.hotelbridgeview.com. Near the lagoon, 25 a/c and fan rooms, clean, comfortable, restaurant.

G Railway Retiring Rooms, ask at the counter in the station. Cheap basic fan rooms with net, good if you're desperate.

Around Batticaloa *p322*
Accommodation in Passekudah/Kalkudah is some way from the beach.

E New Pearl Inn, Valaichchenai Rd, Kalkudah, T2257 9870. 6 rooms in large rambling house, attached bath, cool, clean, food available.

F-G Simla Inn, 100m from **New Pearl Inn**, Kalkudah, T077-603 1272. Family-run guesthouse continuously open since 1981 (the last comments book lasted 19 years), but in a new spot since the tsunami. 2 simple clean rooms with (Rs 400-500), very friendly, basic.

◉ Eating

Batticaloa *p320, map p321*
There are Muslim eateries on Main St which are a friendly stop for lunch or a cup of tea, though hygiene may not be high on the agenda.

🍴 **Subaraj Inn**, see Sleeping. Offers a full English breakfast for Rs 385 (although it's not always available), Chinese and Sri Lankan dishes and good desserts.

🍴 **New Happy Cream House**, 19 Central Rd, T365 5491. Good small eats, as well as fresh juices and ice cream.

🍴 **Sunshine Bakery**, 136 Trinco Rd, T222 5159. Cheap rolls and samosas, enticing cakes, seating area at back of bakery. They are also opening **Sunshine Fast** opposite, which serves up fresh dosai.

◉ Bars and clubs

Batticaloa *p320, map p321*
Riviera Resort, see Sleeping. A lovely place for a sunset drink.

○ Shopping

Batticaloa *p320, map p321*
The market on the north side of the lagoon is a noisy and fascinating place to pick up clothes, fresh produce, etc, or for range you might consider a visit to the busy modern Muslim town of Kattankudi to the south.

▲ Activities and tours

Batticaloa *p320, map p321*
Sri Lanka Diving Tours, based in Negombo (see page 100), T077-764 8459, www.srilanka-divingtours.com. Has started organizing dive trips to the *HMS Hermes* wreck, as well as a number of other wrecks in the surrounding area. Accommodation is offered in Batticaloa at the **Deep Sea Resort** (see Sleeping, page 323). Trips are available with pick-ups from Colombo airport, contact for prices and details.

○ Transport

Batticaloa *p320, map p321*
Bus
CTB and private bus station in Batticaloa are situated next to each other on Munai St, south of the lagoon. A new Central Bus Stand nearby will be opening shortly. Buses leave for **Passekudah** 4 times a day, and **Kalmunai** every half an hour. To get to **Passekudah** you can also take a Kandy bus and get off at Valaichchenai. CTB buses run to **Colombo**); **Trincomalee**; **Pottuvil**; **Badulla** and **Kandy** via **Polonnaruwa**; and **Dambulla**. Private buses also cover the major routes. Buses can be picked up in all directions on the main road near Passekudah.

Train
Trains to **Trincomalee**, via **Gal Oya**. To **Colombo Fort** 0745, 1745, 2015, via **Valaichchenai**, **Polonnaruwa**, **Mineriya**, **Gal Oya** and **Maho**. The 1015 train also passes through **Gal Oya**.

○ Directory

Batticaloa *p320, map p321*
Banks Plenty of banks in town, especially on Bar Rd. **Commercial Bank**, Cirrus, MasterCard, Visa ATM, **Seylan Bank** has 24-hr Visa ATM. **Internet** Available for Rs 30-40 per hr. **Post office** South of Weber Stadium, open 0900-1700.

Contents

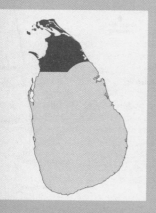

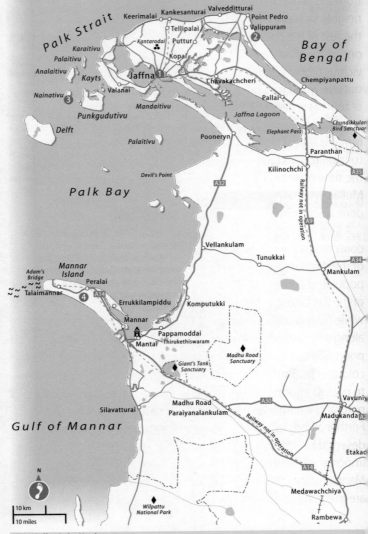

Palk Strait

Keerimalai Kankesanturai Valvedditturai

Kantarodai Tellipalai Point Pedro

Puttur Valippuram

Karaitivu Kopai

Bay of Bengal

Palaitivu

Analaitivu Kayts

Jaffna

Nainativu Valanai Chavakachcheri

Mandaitivu Chempiyanpattu

Pallai

Punkgudutivu *Jaffna Lagoon*

Delft

Pooneryn *Elephant Pass* *Chundikkular Bird Sanctuary*

Palaitivu

Paranthan

Devil's Point

Kilinochchi

Palk Bay

Vellankulam Tunukkai Mankulam

Mannar Island Peralai

Adam's Bridge Errukkilampiddu Komputukki

Talaimannar Mannar

Pappamoddai Thirukethiswaram Mantai

Giant's Tank Sanctuary *Madhu Road Sanctuary*

Silavatturai Madhu Road Vavuniy

Paraiyanalankulam Madukanda

Gulf of Mannar

Etakad

N

10 km
10 miles

Medawachchiya

Wilpattu National Park

Rambewa

Sri Lanka's Northern Province has for centuries been the cultural heartland of the island's Tamil population. With the northern and western tips of the province only a few kilometres boat ride from the coast of southwest India, affinity with Sri Lanka's larger neighbour has always been strong. Yet owing to its isolation from the rest of the country and its harsh, dry climate, the north was one of the least visited of the island's regions even before the vicious ethnic fighting that sealed off much of the province to the outside world for over 20 years. Now the war has ended a trickle of tourists is beginning to unearth the region's almost forgotten attractions. Tragically, the worst fears have been confirmed; little remains untouched by the destruction of conflict. There are few tourist facilities here, and those available are basic. Note that at the time of writing travel to the north (Jaffna, Kilinochchi, Mannar, Mullaittivu and Vavuniya) could only be undertaken with permission from the Sri Lankan Ministry of Defence in Colombo.

A visit to the north provides rewards precisely because of its contrasts to the rest of the island. The main focus of interest, north of the desolate and largely barren Wanni region, is the densely populated Jaffna peninsula. Here, amongst the war detritus, some of the flat landscape remains cultivated despite the arid climate, while fishing continues in the peninsula's shallow lagoons and along its coastline. Jaffna town's historic centre has taken a pounding but its rebuilt temples and churches are flourishing, and colourful festivals across the peninsula are once again beginning to pack in enormous crowds. Away from town are some curious natural phenomena: a desert of dunes and a bottomless well. Further afield, Jaffna's abandoned islands possess some truly deserted beaches and, at Nainativu, a pilgrimage site of national importance. Further south, recent evidence shows that off Mannar island, the narrow finger of land pointing towards India, are the remains of a causeway almost two million years old.

Anuradhapura to Jaffna

The hot, arid Wanni region was at the heart of Sri Lanka's ethnic conflict, and was ravaged by fighting, it is a desolate wasteland of war detritus – cleared forest and uncleared minefields, military bunkers and shelled homes. As you travel north, uncultivated scrub takes over the flat landscape. The Wanni swelled with refugees after the Tamil exodus from Jaffna in 1995, though many are now returning home. Except for Kilinochchi and Vavuniya, there is little settlement along the A9. ▸▸ *For listings, see pages 329-330.*

North to Vavuniya

Heading northeast from Anuradhapura, the A20 joins the A9 at Rambewa. **Medawachchiya** is the last Sinhalese town of any size, where there is a rest house. Some 2 km north, on top of **Issin Bessa Gala rock**, is a modern temple of ancient origins, with an elephant frieze and restored *dagoba*. There are excellent views south to Anuradhapura and Mihintale. The A14 leads northwest from Medawachchiya to Madhu Road and Mannar, though the A30 from Vavuniya is a better road.

Vavuniya → *Phone code: 024. Colour map 1, C4.*

About 1½ hours north of Anuradhapura, Vavuniya, now the terminus of the railway line, has the feel of a bustling frontier town. That it once marked the start of disputed territory is evident in its heavy fortification and strong military presence, and due to its strategic crossroads position its importance and prosperity have grown with the conflict. There is little to do here, though you might visit the small **museum**, where there are some ancient Buddha statues. About 4 km east at **Madukanda** is a *vihara* on the spot where the Tooth Relic was said to have rested on its way to Anuradhapura.

Kilinochchi → *Phone code: 024. Colour map 1, B3.*

Close to the large, modern Iranamadu tank, the dusty uninspiring town of Kilinochchi was the Liberation Tigers of Tamil Eelam (LTTE) headquarters, or the 'capital of Tamil Eelam', housing the Tigers' court complex, police headquarters and other government buildings. There had been some investment in the town and there are banks and accommodation. Some 5 km west of the A9 at Kanagapuram is a **Tamil Tiger war cemetery**, where almost 2000 cadres are interred.

North to Jaffna → *Colour map 1, A2/3.*

Separating the Jaffna peninsula from the mainland, **Elephant Pass** is so-called because elephants were once driven through its shallow waters on their way to export from Jaffna. Strategically important since the Dutch built a fort here, it is now notorious as the site of one of the army's most humiliating defeats: in April 2000, groups of LTTE cadres stormed into the heavily fortified camp, forcing an abrupt capitulation from the 15,000-strong military garrison. The shell of an army tank remains by the side of the road as you enter the peninsula. The area is still mined so do not get out of your vehicle.

    Chundikkulam Bird Sanctuary at the southeastern edge of the peninsula traditionally attracted a large winter flamingo population, and migrants in spring and autumn, though remains off-limits.

    After Elephant Pass, Jaffna's distinctive palmyras become the dominant feature, though around the Pallai checkpoint even these have been reduced to stumps. The

Word of warning

Between 1983 and 2009, most of Northern Province, including the Jaffna peninsula, and much of Eastern Province was off-limits to travellers due to intermittent fighting between the Sri Lanka government's military forces and the Liberation Tigers of Tamil Eelam (LTTE). Many roads were sealed off by military checkpoint. However, following end of the war most roads have reopened and flights to Jaffna have resumed.

Much of the landscape of the Jaffna peninsula and the Wanni region remains inaccessible due to landmines and unexploded ordnance not all of which is accounted for and sealed off with

warnings. You are advised not to step off roads, and in particular travel off the main A9 route into the interior of the Wanni region is not recommended. Moreover, a high military presence remains throughout the region, and the peninsula has a number of army High Security Zones which are normally inaccessible to travellers. Sri Lanka is opening up more every day, but at the time of writing permission was needed from the Ministry of Defence in Colombo to travel to the northern districts of Jaffna, Kilinochchi, Mannar, Mullaittivu and Vavuniya (see page 90). Without the proper paperwork buses and trains will not allow you to travel.

sizeable town of **Chavakachcheri** was retaken by the LTTE for several months in 2000 and reduced to rubble. After crossing numerous restored colonial bridges over the shallow lagoons, you approach the suburbs of Jaffna town.

◉ Anuradhapura to Jaffna listings

For Sleeping and Eating price codes and other relevant information, see pages 26-32.

⊜ Sleeping

Anuradhapura to Jaffna *p328*
The main place to stay on this route is Vavuniya. Lots of places to stay and eat near the bus and rail stations, though all are quite basic.

D-E 1-9 Lodge, 167 Kandy Rd, Kilinochchi, T071-234 5629. 8 rooms, 2 with attached bath, clean, nets, fan, restaurant (fried rice, noodles, devilled dishes).

E Rest House (CHC), Medawachchiya, T025-224 5699. Comfortable, clean rooms (1 with a/c), useful stopover.

E-F Kanathenu Lodge, Kilinochchi, T021-222 3954. 14 rooms, some with attached bath, spartan but fairly clean, food on request.

E-F Vanni Inn, Gnanavairavar Kovil Lane, off 2nd Cross St, Vavuniya, T024-222 1406.

Better from outside than in, but quiet and the best of the bunch, functional a/c and fan rooms, restaurant. Very little English spoken.

❼ Eating

Anuradhapura to Jaffna *p328*
For further options, see Sleeping.
❢ **Prince Hotel**, 111 Kandy Rd, Vavuniya. Serves good short eats.

⊖ Transport

Anuradhapura to Jaffna *p328*
Vavuniya is the transport hub for the region.
Bus Buses leave for **Colombo** (5 hrs) regularly. For **Anuradhapura**, take a Kandy or Colombo bus. Many buses to **Omantai** (for Jaffna), but best to leave early. Regular buses to **Mannar**; **Trincomalee**; and **Batticaloa**.

Private van For **Jaffna** can be picked up here along Kandy Rd in Vavuniya.
Train To **Colombo**, via **Anuradhapura**, then on to **Matara**.

ⓘ Directory

Anuradhapura to Jaffna *p328*
Banks Vavuniya has branches of most major banks, with ATMs. **Internet** Infonet, 28 Station Rd (close to the railway), Vavuniya.

Jaffna

→ *Phone code: 021. Colour map 1, A2.*

As the centre of Sri Lankan Tamil culture and, in peaceful times, the country's second most populous city, Jaffna has been the greatest pawn, and the greatest victim, of the 20-year ethnic conflict of the north. Devastated by shelling, much of the town today resembles a depressing post-apocalyptic wasteland. However, the ceasefire and the reopening of the land route to the south have brought a glimmer of hope: month by month, Jaffna's displaced citizens are beginning to return home, and whilst many houses remain uninhabitable, lacking roofs and basic facilities, and widespread mines will render the surrounding lands inaccessible for years to come, many of the town's schools, temples, churches and mosques have been rebuilt – a testament to the spirit of this proud community, as well as to its support from abroad. With most of its heritage and 'sights' destroyed, Jaffna is be no place for a holiday, but those who do make the trip are often unexpectedly charmed. The city can throw up some surprises from its lively festivals and glorious old cars to its distinctive cuisine and famous ice cream parlours. The most lasting memories however are of its people. Despite, or perhaps because of, the scars of battle they are amongst the warmest and most genuine on the island. ⋫ *For listings, see pages 333-334.*

Ins and outs

Getting there By far the easiest, and most expensive, way to reach Jaffna is by air from Ratmalana Airport, south of Colombo. **Expo Aviation** and **Helitours** fly regularly to **Palaly Airport** (KKS) in the north of the peninsula. The main bus stand is in Hospital Road, about 2 km west of Chundikuli, the main guesthouse and expat area. The bus route passes along Kandy Road – you can ask to be let off before the terminus. At the time of writing it is necessary to obtain permission in advance from the Ministry of Defence in Colombo before visiting Jaffna (see page 90), thus the most popular way to arrive is by night train from Colombo to Vavuniya (see page 86) and then travel by bus to Jaffna. The buses between Vavuniya and Jaffna run regularly. ⋫ *See Transport page 334.*

Getting around The city is quite spread out, and walking it can be tiring in the heat. There is a good local bus network but cycling is the best way to get around. You may be able to borrow one from your guesthouse. Note that taking a three-wheeler here will be a lot more expensive than in other parts of the country, don't forget to bargain for your fare.

Best time to visit April to May can be unbearably hot when the southwest monsoon and heatwaves from South India conspire to drive up temperatures towards 40ºC. August to September is also very hot. December and January is the coolest time. The biggest festival is at Nallur in August (see page 334).

Tourist information Further reading: Philippe Fabry, *Essential Guide for Jaffna and its region* (Negombo: Viator Publications, 2003).

Background → *See page 350 for the political history.*

There are few archaeological or literary clues to the early period of Jaffna's history, but the peninsula's proximity to India ensured that when Tamil settlers came to Sri Lanka 2000 years ago Jaffna was one of their earliest homes. Ruins at Kantarodai suggest that Buddhism was once the dominant religion of the peninsula, then known as Nagadipa, or the island of the Naga people, who may have had links to Greece and Rome. The period of the Kingdom of Jaffna, often invoked by nationalists today, began in the 13th century under the Indian King Kalinga, lasting, except for a brief period of Sinhalese occupation in the 15th century, until the execution of King Sankili by the Portuguese in 1620.

Over the centuries Jaffna's Tamils built a wholly distinctive culture. Despite the unsuitability of much of the thin red soil for agriculture, Tamil cultivators developed techniques of well irrigation which capitalized on the reserves of groundwater held in the limestone, making intensive rice cultivation the basis of a successful economy. Diversity was provided by coconut and palmyra palms, tobacco and a wide range of other crops, but the Tamil population was also international in its outlook. It maintained trading links not only with the Tamil regions across the Palk Straits but also with Southeast Asia.

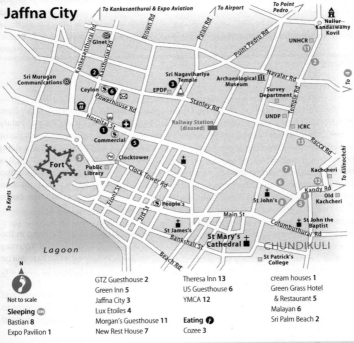

Jaffna City

Not to scale

Sleeping 🛏
Bastian 8
Expo Pavilion 1
GTZ Guesthouse 2
Green Inn 5
Jaffna City 3
Lux Etoiles 4
Morgan's Guesthouse 11
New Rest House 7
Theresa Inn 13
US Guesthouse 6
YMCA 12

Eating 🍴
Cozee 3
cream houses 1
Green Grass Hotel
  & Restaurant 5
Malayan 6
Sri Palm Beach 2

Vintage survivors

For fans of old British cars Jaffna is an unlikely Mecca. Fleets of Morris Minors, Austin Cambridges and Morris Oxfords still rattle around the town's dusty streets, preserved for posterity by Jaffna's unique situation. Their lifeline came in the late 1980s when owners of newer vehicles were forced to turn them in for the war effort, leaving the sturdy old beauties as kings of the road. The peninsula cut off since then, their owners were forced to find ever more ingenious methods of keeping them on the road, hammering out spare parts in local metal shops, and, when fuel costs spiralled out of control, by feeding these vintage survivors on a steady diet on kerosene, the carburettors fooled by just a drop of petrol. Today, Sri Lanka does a roaring trade in exporting parts to enthusiasts worldwide. Of around 70,000 Morris Minors on the road in Britain, it is estimated that more than half are sustained by the metalworkers of Sri Lanka.

The Dutch captured Jaffna from the Portuguese in 1658, losing it to the British in 1796. It was not until 1833 however that they politically unified Tamil regions with Sinhalese for administration purposes, ending the separateness of Tamil identity. From the mid-19th century Jaffna Tamils took up the educational opportunities which came with an extended period of British rule, and rapidly became numerically dominant in a range of government services and jobs both inside and outside Sri Lanka. In the early 1970s, this led to the 'quota' systems for education and employment which aimed to reduce Tamil influence, another contributory factor to today's conflict (see page 351).

Sights

Historic centre

Jaffna's historic centre has been devastated by the fighting. The 20-ha **Dutch fort**, built on the site of an earlier Portuguese building to control the trade route to India, was arguably the strongest fortification in Asia. Though the black coralline walls surrounded by a huge moat remain intact, all buildings inside, including the fine Groote Kerk, took a pummelling in 1990 when the army camp was shelled. Once taken by the LTTE, the Dutch buildings, regarded as a symbol of oppression, were demolished to prevent reoccupation. Though the approach road to the fort is open, the entrance is sealed off by barbed wire and guarded by sentries, who claim that it is mined. Nearby the town hall, rest house and post office have all been destroyed.

In contrast, across the stadium to the east is the gleaming, restored Moghul-style **public library**. The original building was torched by an anti-Tamil mob in June 1981, tragically destroying almost 100,000 books and priceless *ola* leaf manuscripts. Thousands of volumes have been donated to the new library from abroad, particularly France and India. In the library garden is a statue of its founder, Reverend Long, said to have died on hearing the news of the original library's demise. Jaffna's restored **clocktower** reopened in June 2002, with clocks donated by HRH the Prince of Wales.

Commercial centre

Life has returned to a semblance of normality in the busy **market area** between Stanley and Hospital roads. Along Kankasanthurai (KKS) Road, it is still possible to pick up some traditional palmyra craftwork, while jewellery shops cluster along Kasturiya Road.

Temples and churches

Some 3 km northeast of the fort, the ornate **Kandaswamy Temple** at Nallur hosts a spectacular 25-day **chariot festival** in July/August, which can attract up to a million devotees. The festival reaches its zenith on the 24th day, when decorated *ratham* (chariots) are paraded from dawn until midnight in honour of the god. The current temple dates from the 19th century. The original, believed to have dated back to the 10th century, was razed by the Portuguese. **Puja** takes place seven times a day. Men must remove shirts before entering and photography in the inner sanctum is not allowed.

The legacy of successive waves of proselytising Christians from Europe, most notably Roman Catholics, is visible in Jaffna's many churches, some of which, like the Goan-style **St Mary's Cathedral** and **St James's**, are enormous edifices. Post-war restoration has been speedy though not always of great architectural merit. The **Sri Nagaviharaya** with its restored *dagoba* and 'elephant wall' is Jaffna's only active Buddhist temple.

Archaeological Museum

This museum contains various artefacts excavated from Kantarodai, though anti-royalists may enjoy best the portrait of Queen Victoria with a bullet-hole through her. The museum is found on Navaly Road behind the Navalar Maddapam Hall.

◉ Jaffna listings

For Sleeping and Eating price codes and other relevant information, see pages 26-32.

◉ Sleeping

Jaffna *p330, map p331*

Most accommodation is in the expat area of Chundukuli-Old Park, 2 km east of the bus stand, but new places are opening all the time as the number of visitors increase, and there is now quite a choice along Kandy Rd. That being said, most are basic guesthouses and are overpriced for what's on offer. Note that weekends can be busy and noisy.

B Expo Pavilion, 40 Kandy Rd, T222 3790. Belonging to Expo Aviation, 7 tasteful a/c rooms with TV in a restored colonial house (some with private veranda), but they vary in size so ask to see before committing. Expensive restaurant, and Wi-Fi.
C Jaffna City Hotel, 70/6 KKS Rd, T222 5969, www.tilkojaffna.com. A modern hotel with

a/c and fan rooms, including 2 penthouse suites with good views. Restaurant serving decent food, and a bar.
C Morgan's Guesthouse, 103 Temple Rd, T222 3666. Clean and comfortable a/c rooms, bar, garden. Popular and often full.
C-E Green Inn, 60 Kandy Rd, T222 3898. 8 basic rooms, ranging from a/c with attached bath to fan only with shared bath. Restaurant, a/c van and driver, pick-up from airport can be arranged (though there is a free bus), can be pushy.
D Bastian Hotel, 37 Kandy Rd, T222 2605. 18 a/c and fan rooms, some with TV in 2 hotels (the other building is at No 11). Restaurant, helpful owners.
D-E New Rest House, 19 Somasundarum Av, T222 7839. Rooms with fan and attached bath, meals available.
E US Guesthouse, 874 Hospital Rd, opposite John the Baptist Church, T222 21018, T222 7029. A/c rooms with clean bathrooms and

hot water in the guesthouse or in their other properties nearby. Restaurant serves good and reasonably priced food.

E-F Theresa Inn, 72A Racca Rd, T222 8615, calistusjoseph89@gmail.com. Clean rooms, 1 with balcony (often on long-term rent to NGOs), a/c and fan, those without hot water cheaper. Internet, TV, very friendly and helpful.

F GTZ Guesthouse, 114A Temple Rd, T222 2203. 5 a/c rooms with large, clean shared bathrooms. Library of German books, meals arranged on request.

F Lux Etoiles, 34 Chetty St Lane, T222 3966, www.luxetoiles.com. A/c rooms with TV (some newer than others). Restaurant serves excellent seafood. English and French spoken.

G YMCA, 109 Kandy Rd, at the corner with Kachcheri Rd, T222 2499. 18 rooms, common bath, basic, meals at canteen, noisy.

🍴 Eating

Jaffna *p330, map p331*

There are plenty of cheap 'hotels' close to the market. Jaffna's cream houses are legendary. Serving delicious *wadais* and other short eats as well as ice cream. They cluster on Hospital Rd and are busy with local families during the daytime.

¶¶ Cozee, 15 Sirambiyadi Lane (off Stanley Rd), T222 5899. South Indian specialists (the cook is from Chennai), smart, clean. Kebabs recommended. Also has rooms available.

¶¶ Green Grass Hotel and Restaurant, off Hospital Rd, T222 4385, www.jaffnagreengrass.com. Seating is in a pleasant garden and menu is wide-ranging. It's a good place to try curry, Jaffna-style. Some meals may need to be ordered a day in advance. Also has (**F**) rooms.

¶¶ Sri Palm Beach, 205 Kasturiya Rd. A/c restaurant and takeaway, large menu of South Indian curries, dosai, noodles, even pizzas.

¶ Malayan, 36-38 Grand Bazaar, near the bus station. Excellent vegetarian food, including good value rice and curry, all served on a banana leaf. Cheap, cheerful and popular.

⊛ Festivals and events

Jaffna *p330, map p331*

Mar-Apr Easter is widely celebrated with passion plays performed in churches and at Jaffna's open-air theatre.

Jul-Aug Nallur kovil has the biggest Hindu festival in the north but there are many others – ask locally.

⊙ Shopping

Jaffna *p330, map p331*

Palmyra handicrafts can still be picked up in the market area, as can Jaffna wine, arrack and jaggery. The wine, along with nelli crush, is produced by the **Rosarian sisters**, 123 Main St.

⊖ Transport

Jaffna *p330, map p331*

Air Regular services between Jaffna and **Colombo**, 1 hr. **Expo Aviation**, 144 Brown Rd T222 3891, www.expoavi.com, runs flights up to 4 times a day; and **Helitours** the Sri Lankan air force), T011-314 4244, fly 3 times a week (Mon, Wed and Fri).

Bus Good bus network around town, across the peninsula, and to **Kayts**, **Karaitivu** and **Pungudutivu**. Public buses leave regularly for **Muhamalai** (1 hr). Buses to **Vavuniya** and **Colombo**.

⊙ Directory

Jaffna *p330, map p331*

Banks Most banks can be found on Hospital St in town; those with ATMs include **Commercial** and **Seylan** banks. **Internet** Gl@netcafé, 379 Kasthuriar Rd (corner with Navalar Rd), open 0930-2100, and **Sri Murugan**, 303 KKS Rd, open 0700-2200. **Post office** In a lane just north of the bus stand.

Peninsula and islands

An extensive road criss-crosses the low, flat Jaffna landscape. Areas of sandy scrubland with palmyras alternate with intensively cultivated tobacco, banana and manioc plantations, although large areas remain mined. Another obstacle is the presence of High Security Zones (HSZs), areas regarded as strategically important in which security is high and movement restricted. At least you won't need to struggle with Tamil's legendarily unpronounceable names – most major towns have a user-friendly three-letter short form. The coastal road from Thondamanaru through Valvedditturai to Point Pedro is a pleasant cycle ride. ▶▶ *For listings, see page 339.*

Northeast to Point Pedro

Getting there and around The peninsula and islands can easily be visited on a day trip from Jaffna town. All buses originate from Jaffna town: to reach Nilavarai take an Achchuveli bus; for Kantarodai take the bus from Jaffna to Alveddi, from where you can take a three-wheeler. Tellipalai buses terminate close to the temple. North of Tellipalai is inaccessible by public transport. To reach Karaitivu, there are several buses a day direct to Casuarina, or take an (hourly) bus to Karainagar and get a three-wheeler. For Nainativu take the bus which crosses Kayts island to the jetty point at Kurukkaduwan on Pungudutivu. Boats for the 20-minute crossing leave hourly. For Delft, ferries leave the KKD jetty at 0700 and 1330, returning at 1030 and 1530. There is also a boat from Nainativu at 0530, returning at 1700. A bus traverses the island, or you might hire a tractor.

Thirunelveli

Poongani Solai (Poonkanichcholai) ① *about 1 km west of Nallur temple, Ramalingam Rd, Mudamayadi, T222 2976, Rs 100,* offer some light relief. These small pleasure gardens, impeccably kept, feature some imaginative fountains, brightly painted statues and a grotto, though the enjoyment is marred by the shackled animals on show. On some days around 1500-1600, locals come dressed up to have photos or videos taken. The gardens are 3 km northeast of town. Follow Temple Road going west and the gardens are found on the right hand side.

Kopai

The **LTTE war cemetery** at Kopai, is a sobering experience. Over 1700 cadres are buried here in row upon row of neatly laid out graves. In the corner is a display of remains of LTTE monuments destroyed by the army on re-taking Jaffna in 1995. Buses bound for Point Pedro pass nearby.

Nilavarai

The square **tidal well** at Nilavarai, 10 km from Jaffna town, near Puttur, is an interesting natural phenomenon. Legend states that Rama plunged his arrow into the soil here, quenching his thirst from its 'bottomless' spring. The water, fairly fresh at the surface, increases in salinity with depth, and a fissure in the limestone probably connects it directly to the sea. You can walk down to the well, though locals warn against swimming here.

Valvedditturai

Valvedditturai (VVT) is a small fishing town with a reputation as a centre for smuggling from India and beyond. The **festival** at the large Muthumari Amman *kovil* here, featuring processions and fire-walking, was resurrected in 2003 and draws enormous crowds each April, but the town is now most famous as the birthplace of the leader of the LTTE. After the end of the war, thousands of tourists from the south were flocking to visit his childhood home 100 m west of the Amman temple, and it had become one of the 'must see' attraction in Jaffna. In 2010, however, it was destroyed, with some pointing the finger at the army.

Point Pedro

Bustling little Point Pedro (PPD), 8 km east, is the peninsula's second largest town. In peaceful times, a local challenge was to swim to India from here. As well as several large churches, there is a fishing harbour, a beach and a lighthouse, which marks the most northerly point of Sri Lanka (see also page 154), though these are located within an High Security Zone. A 20- to 25-km tunnel built in the 10th century is said to connect Point Pedro to Nallur.

Manalkadu Desert

Off the main road south of Point Pedro, is an area of **white sand dunes** known as the Manalkadu Desert. Some 15 m high in places, the dunes are formed by sand blown onshore from South India by the winds during monsoons. There are the remains of the old **St Anthony's Church** here, atmospherically half-submerged in the sand. The small village of **Valippuram**, 6 km from Point Pedro, was once the capital of Jaffna and has a

Jaffna Peninsula & Islands

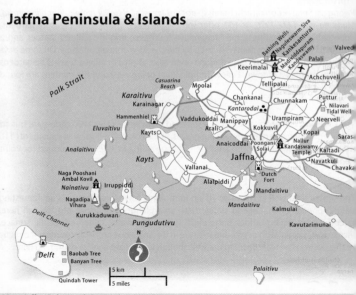

thriving temple, second in size on the peninsula only to Nallur. Vishnu was said to have appeared here as a fish. An inscription on a gold plate discovered here suggests that a *vihara* existed here during the reign of King Vasaba in the first century.

The road to Kankesanthurai → *Bring your passport to visit Keerimalai.*

Kantarodai

At Kantarodai, about halfway to Kankesanthurai (KKS), are the remains of around 30 squat Buddhist stupas, most between 2-4 m in height, crammed into a small plot. Excavations in 1918 discovered ancient Indian coins here, suggesting a 2000-year history. Some commentators have likened the stupas in form and origin to those in the upper platform at Borobudur in Indonesia. Though no theories for their existence have proved conclusive, many agree that they represent a monastic burial ground. Kantarodai is 2 km left off the KKS road at Chunnakam junction, then another left (300 m), and then right at the junction. The site is on the left, 600 m from here.

Tellipalai

Sri Durga Devasthanam here is a fine Durga temple with an enormous *gopuram*. There is a two-week festival in August with a **water-cutting ceremony**. The temple is especially active on Tuesdays.

North of Tellipalai

The area north of Tellipalai is currently inaccessible by public transport, and travelling to Kankesanthurai and Keerimalai can involve a lengthy wait for security clearance.

Kankesanthurai (KKS) was during the time of the ancient Jaffna kingdom the peninsula's most important port, though it is now in ruins and almost completely abandoned.

Naguleswaram Siva Kovil at **Keerimalai** is one of the earliest and most venerated Hindu temples in Sri Lanka. Largely destroyed in an aerial attack in 1990, and subsequently stripped of its antiquities, it was not until 1996 that worshippers were allowed to return. At the time of writing, new deities by Indian craftsmen were being carved. Close to the beach behind the kovil, spring water flows up through a rock fissure to form two popular **bathing wells** (one male, one female), associated with the visit by the Chola Princess Sangamittha in the seventh century, whose disfigured face looked like a horse's head. She was cured, legend states, by bathing in its healing waters, and in gratitude constructed the Madividdapuram Kandaswamy Kovil, 2 km south, which has a tall *gopuram* and a

Tree of Life

Jaffna's palmyras are as much the dominant feature of the northern landscape as the southern coconut, and are a cornerstone of the local economy. These tall, straight trees, which can grow up to 30 m in height, have an astonishing variety of uses. The leathery, fan-shaped leaves can be worked into mats, baskets and roof thatch, while the fruits, which grow in clusters on the stem when young, can be punctured with a finger and the water sucked out; when mature the pulp is roasted and sun-dried. The sap ferments a few hours after sunrise (just in time for the fishermen's return from their catch), and the toddy is often drunk from an attractive cup (*pila*) ingeniously shaped from a frond and tied at one end. Alternatively it is distilled into arrack. The sap also makes jaggery, a more nutritious alternative to cane sugar. The seedlings can be eaten fresh or are used in cooking, while all parts of the plant may be used in local medicines. The trees also have an important ecological role – their drought-resistant roots help retain water in the soil, paramount in this driest of regions, and the tall trunks act as natural barriers during strong winds common to the north.

Predictably, the conflict was an ecological disaster for the north's palmyras. Over 2.5 million trees were uprooted, not only for firewood and to create military bunkers, but 500 m of land either side of the region's major arteries was bulldozed in order to deter ambushes. A ban on felling palmyras was put in place to try and aid reforestation programmes, and there are calls for the Palmyra Development Board to do more to help this national industry. There are, however, supposed to be ambitious plans in the pipeline, which include expanding the foreign market for palmyra products.

festival in July/August. The water in the wells is very pleasant, though the large military presence can be disconcerting. Swimming in the sea at Keerimalai is forbidden.

The islands

The religious site of Nainativu (Nagadipa), sacred to both Buddhists and Hindus, is the only place in this area that receives a significant amount of visitors – the site is increasingly thronged with day-trippers from around the country. Kayts and Karainagar are linked to the mainland by separate causeways, while a third which cuts seemingly endlessly through dazzling blue sea, joins Kayts to Punguditivu, at the southwestern corner of which ferries can be caught to the outlying islands. The islands are rich in birdlife. Watch out for flamingos on the causeway to Kayts.

Kayts

To the north of the island, the nearest to Jaffna town, is Kayts town, once a wealthy and sought-after area – look out for the ruins of beautiful villas lining the approach road. The road ends at a jetty for boats to Karaitivu Island. Here you can see Indian fishing boats impounded for fishing in Sri Lankan waters, and to the west, the well-preserved island fort of **Hammenheil**, a long-term navy base and one-time prison. At the south of Kayts island, **Velanai** is a popular beach.

Karaitivu

The road to the Karaitivu causeway passes through Vadukoddai, where there is a large Portuguese church. Behind the church are 27 gravestones, predominantly Dutch, rescued from the Groote Kerk in Jaffna's fort. To the east at **Chankanai**, are the overgrown remains of another Portuguese church, constructed of coral in 1641. At the north end of Karaitivu, is **Casuarina Beach**, the most popular in Jaffna, where swimming is safe in the calm, shallow waters. A few stalls sell drinks and snacks. The beach is so-called after the beefwood (*casuarina*) trees found here.

Nainativu

Accessed by ferry from the deserted **Punguditivu**, the tiny island of Nainativu has great religious importance to both Buddhists and Hindus. For the former it is Nagadipa, the point at which the Buddha set foot on his second visit to the island, four years after the first, in order to settle a quarrel between two Naga kings over a throne, said to be enshrined here. A *vihara*, with a restored silver *dagoba* and image house, guarded by a large military presence (your battered sandals will line up against many neat pairs of shiny black boots at the entrance to the temple), marks the spot. There is a bo tree opposite. The *vihara* is a 10-minute walk along the road leading left from the jetty point.

In a Hindu-dominated area however, the **Naga Pooshani Ambal kovil** at the jetty point is the livelier temple, and can be the focus of a day-trip. Regular *pujas* are taken, with colourful processions, clattering drums, bells and pipes, and gasps as the inner sanctum of the temple is revealed. In its 15-day festival in June, a 30-m Ambal is paraded. In order to take advantage of Ambal's generosity, it is a good idea to arrive for the important *puja* at 1300, after which crowds of several hundred line up in the hall behind the temple for rice and curry, ladled out on to a banana leaf. Lunch is usually finished in time to catch the 1430 boat back to Pungudituvu.

Delft

The windswept and bleak landscape of Delft, the outermost inhabited island, has been less affected by the conflict and contains various reminders of the Portuguese and Dutch periods. Famous for its wild ponies, which come from a Portuguese breeding stock, there are also the remains of a coral fort, fairly tumbledown but still recognizable, behind the hospital. South of the jetty is a single baobab tree (see page 341) and, further on, a large banyan, while at the southern tip the Quindah tower is an ancient navigational landmark.

◉ Peninsula and islands listings

For Sleeping and Eating price codes and other relevant information, see pages 26-32.

◉ Sleeping

Peninsula and islands *p335*
Jaffna should be used as a base if travelling in this area as there are few accommodation options elsewhere.

◉ Eating

Peninsula and islands *p335*
Choices are limited. To be on the safe side take provisions from Jaffna.
♯ **Millennium**, 76/60 Ramanathan Rd (Campus Rd), Kaladdy, T222 2810. A bit off the beaten track, but attractive beer garden popular with locals and expats, with tasty snacks (eg devilled prawns), relaxed.

Mannar

→ *Phone code: 023. Colour map 1, B1.*

Mannar Island is one of the driest and most barren places in the country, yet is also one of the most intriguing. Linked by a 3-km dam and iron bridge to the mainland it is quite remote from the rest of Sri Lanka. Mannar's historical importance lies in its proximity to India to which it is linked by an ancient causeway. ▶▶ *For listings, see page 342.*

Ins and outs

Getting there and around The remote island of Mannar is accessible by road from Medawachchiya (86 km along the A14), though the A30 from Vavuniya (78 km) is the faster route. Both roads run through elephant country, and meet at Paraiyanalankulam, where the A30 continues northwest past the turning for Madhu Road and Giant's Tank. Palmyras and umbrella thorns are increasingly visible in this barren, open landscape interspersed with some paddy cultivation. The road between Puttalam and Mannar has now been improved, cutting journey times for those coming from Colombo, although it remains controversial as it passes through Wilpattu National Park.

For Madhu Road Church buses leave from Vavuniya and Mannar, and for Thirukethiswaram and Talaimannar, catch a bus from Mannar town. The bus to Pesalai leaves from the main bus stand.

Madhu Road → *Colour map 1, C2. 12 km northeast of the A30 from Madhu Road Junction.*

The rebuilt **church** at Madhu Road is the most important Catholic pilgrimage site in Sri Lanka. Its altar houses the sacred **Our Lady of Madhu statue**, which was brought here in 1670 by 20 Catholic families fleeing persecution by the Dutch at Mantai, near Mannar. Amongst the fugitives was Helena, the daughter of a Portuguese captain, who was sanctified and founded the first church here. The Madhu statue is venerated throughout the country for its miracles, especially the cure of snakebite, and major festivals are held here throughout the year. The largest, on 15 August, attracts up to half a million visitors.

Giant's Tank → *20 km east of Mannar Town.*

Possibly built by King Parakramabahu I, Giant's Tank, is rich in scrub and shore birds. There are a couple of vantage points along the A14, though the tank is often empty.

Thirukethiswaram kovil

A short distance inland from the Mannar causeway, the restored Saivite Thirukethiswaram kovil near Mantai is one of five ancient temples in Sri Lanka said to pre-date the arrival of Buddhism. Around the 1500-year-old inner sanctum are various statues of deities in scenes from stories. Apparently, after bathing in the adjacent Palavi tank childless women bring a pot of water to pour over Siva's lingam and drink. With most of its worshippers still refugees living in India, the temple was, at the time of visiting, usually deserted except on Fridays when there is a big *puja* at 1200. There is also a 40-day festival in July with a **water-cutting ceremony**. Remove shoes and shirts. If arriving from the east, turn right off the A14 5 km before the Mannar causeway.

Mannar Island

The island's distinctive character has been forged by its settlers, who first crossed Adam's Bridge from India almost two million years ago, while nearby Mantai was the ancient port of Mahatittha, which pre-dates Sinhalese times and brought at various times traders and invaders. Arabs brought Islam, the baobab tree and the ubiquitous donkey, rare elsewhere in the country, while Portuguese influence is also strong, the Catholic church claiming the majority of islanders. The Dutch developed their fort into one of the strongholds of the north. Historically famous for its long-abandoned pearl banks to the south, Mannar today is an impoverished and marginalised backwater, its ferry route across to India and railway inland victims of the conflict. Yet its isolation has also helped preserve the island – sealed off for seven years when its road bridge was blown up in 1990, it has avoided much of the destruction elsewhere in the region. At the time of writing, there were plans underway to resume ferry services from here.

Mannar town

The town is dominated by its mosques and churches. The Goan-style St Sebastian's has ornate latticework giving it a Moorish appearance. It is impossible to miss Mannar's **fort**, which stands proudly on the right as you cross the mudflats to enter the town. Constructed by the Portuguese in 1560, it was taken by the Dutch in 1658 and rebuilt. The fort's ramparts and four bastions, part surrounded by a moat, are intact, although most buildings inside have been blasted. There is an ornate Dutch stone tablet close to the main gate. A tunnel is said to connect Mannar's fort to the remains of another at Arippu, two hours south. The police occupy the fort, though permission for visits is usually granted.

Mannar is famous for its baobab trees and 2 km south at Pallimunai is what is claimed to be the **largest tree in Asia**. With a circumference of 19.5 m, a board states that it was probably planted in 1477. Other baobabs on the island have been radio-carbon dated to 1000 years old. Bus No 946 travels to Pallimunai .

Around the island

The A14 continues, following and at one point crossing the old railway line, through the sandy wastes and jungle scrub to Talaimannar, the westernmost point of the island. The Muslim village of **Erukkulampiddu**, 15 km from Mannar (turn right at Toddaveli) along the A14, is known locally for its mat-weaving.

Pesalai is a Catholic fishing village with one of the largest churches in Sri Lanka (rebuilt in 1999), where there is an image of Christ under a mosquito net. A Passion play is performed at Easter here using life-size dolls. Sadly, there have been some ugly clashes in recent years with Indian fishermen, whose superior trawlers have encroached on local waters.

A left-turn at **Talaimannar** takes you to South Point, close to which begins **Adam's Bridge**, a series of rocks, sandbanks and shallows which links Mannar to Rameswaram in India. In 2002, NASA space images revealed the crossing to be man-made because of its composition and curvature, proving that settlers arrived in Sri Lanka at least 1,750,000 years ago. This sheds light on the *Ramayana* legend in which Hanuman constructed a causeway in his attempt to rescue Sita from the demon-god Ravana. Closer relations with India have prompted talks of developing a modern bridge to Rameswaram from here, but this is likely to be years away. The toddy tavern here serves good toddy from traditional palmyra cups. Fishermen will offer to take you to for a 30- to 40-minute boat ride to the 'fourth island' of Adam's Bridge.

A kilometre north of Talaimannar town is the old pier from which, until 1984, ferry boats crossed to India. Sri Lanka and India are currently working on the infrastructure required to re-start the service, and it is hoped it will be up and running by the end of the year. There is an attractive but abandoned and rather forlorn lighthouse on the mined beach here – take care. Even so, the beach buzzes with fishermen (and women) in the morning. Close to Talaimannar is a Muslim shrine which, a legend states, is the burial place of Adam and Eve.

⊚ Mannar listings

For Sleeping and Eating price codes and other relevant information, see pages 26-32.

● Sleeping

Mannar *p340*
F Manjula Inn, 2nd Cross St, T223 2037. Clean and comfortable rooms with common bath, good home-cooked food.
F-G Hawaii Residency, T071-757 2942, T077-925 1531. 6 a/c and fan rooms with clean shared baths (cold water only). Food can be arranged if ordered in advance.
F-G Star Guest House, 298 Moor St, T222 2177. A/c rooms with attached baths or cheap fan rooms with grubby shared facilities. Food can be arranged if ordered in advance.

❼ Eating

Mannar *p340*
For options see Sleeping, above, or visit the **Weligama Bakery** for good short eats and snacks.

● Transport

Mannar *p340*
Bus From Mannar town buses run regularly to **Vavuniya** ; to **Colombo** (7 hrs); and there are daily buses to **Anuradhapura**, **Trincomalee** and **Kalpitiya**.

● Directory

Mannar *p340*
Banks Several banks in Mannar town including **Hatton National Bank**.

Contents

Footprint features

Background

History

Sri Lanka has a rich cultural history. In this sense it is no different to much of South Asia where religion and the migration of people are interlocked. What makes it so interesting to the traveller is its accessibility. Few will fail to imagine the great battle involving kings atop elephants as they look over the plains from the heights of the fortress at Sigiriya. Others will be moved as they watch the sun set over the Sun and Moon bastions at the colonial fortification in Galle.

Settlement and early history

Stone tools from the Middle Palaeolithic Age have been found in several places, evidence of settlement in Sri Lanka perhaps as much as 500,000 years ago. Recent genetic research however suggests that *Homo sapiens* may not have evolved until very much later, and spread from Africa in the last 100,000 years.

The early record of settlement in Sri Lanka is scanty. Archaeologists believe today that the first *Homo sapiens* arrived perhaps 75,000 years ago, bringing with them a life of hunting and gathering centred on open-air campsites. Evidence of their activity has been found in a variety of habitats. However, no Neolithic tools have been found, and no tools from the Copper Age, which is so well represented in peninsular India from the second millennium BC.

The picture changes with the arrival of the Iron Age, for the megalithic graves, associated with black and red pottery, suggest that Sri Lanka had direct contact with South India well before the Aryans immigrated from North India from around 500 BC. Sri Lanka's archaeological record remains comparatively sparse, with barely any evidence with which to date the development of Stone Age cultures or the later spread of domesticated animals and cultivation. At some point in the first millennium BC rice cultivation made its appearance, though whether as a result of migration from either North India or Southeast Asia remains controversial.

The earliest aboriginal settlers, of Australoid, Negrito and Mediterranean stock, have now been almost entirely absorbed in the settled populations. The earliest named culture is that of **Balangoda**, distributed across the whole island between 5000 and 500 BC. The **Veddas** are the only inhabitants today whose ancestors were in Sri Lanka before the Aryan migrations. Related to the Dravidian jungle peoples in South India, they dwelt in caves and rock shelters, and lived by hunting and gathering. They practised a cult of the dead, communicating with ancestors through reincarnated spirits. Today the Veddas have been largely absorbed into the Sinhalese community and have virtually ceased to have a separate existence. Their numbers have shrunk to just a few hundred. See the box on page 294 for further details.

Migration from India

The overwhelming majority of the present population of Sri Lanka owes its origins to successive waves of migration from two different regions of India. Most people are of Indo-Aryan origin and came from North India. The earliest migrations from North India may have taken place as early as the fifth century BC. Although these migrants brought with them a North Indian language which had its roots in the Sanskrit tradition, they were not yet Buddhists, for Buddhism did not arrive in Sri Lanka until the third century

BC. It is most likely that the Sinhalese came from India's northwest, possibly Punjab or Gujarat, and it seems probable that Gujarati traders were already sailing down India's west coast by this time. The origins of Tamil settlement are unclear, but are thought to go back at least to the third century BC, when there is clear evidence of trade between Sri Lanka and South India.

Today the **Sinhalese** make up 74% of the total population. Sri Lanka's **Tamil** population comprises the long settled Tamils of the north and east (12.6%) and the migrant workers on the tea plantations in the Central Highlands (5.5%) who settled in Sri Lanka from the late 19th century onwards. At the height of the conflict, up to 750,000 Tamils had repatriated abroad, though many have since returned. The so-called '**Moors**', Tamil speaking Muslims of Indian-Arab descent, were traders on the east coast and now number over 1.1 million (7.7%). A much smaller but highly distinct community is that of the **Burghers**, numbering about 50,000. The Dutch (mainly members of the Dutch Reformed Church) and the Portuguese intermarried with local people, and their descendants were urban and ultimately English speaking. There are similar numbers of Malays and smaller groups of Kaffirs. The Malays are Muslims who were brought by the Dutch from Java. The Kaffirs were brought by the Portuguese from Mozambique and other parts of East Africa as mercenaries.

A literate society

With the development of agriculture came the origins of a literate and complex society. Tradition associates the founding of Sri Lanka's first kingdom with Devanampiya Tissa (250-221 BC), who was converted to Buddhism by Mahinda, son of the great Indian Emperor Asoka. Myth and legend are bound up with many of the events of South Asian history, but the Sri Lankan historian KM de Silva has noted that the historical mythology of the Sinhalese "is the basis of their conception of themselves as the chosen guardians of Buddhism". The basic text through which this view of the island's history has been passed on by successive generations of Buddhist monks is the **Mahavansa** (*Great Dynasty* or *Lineage*), which de Silva suggests possibly goes back to the sixth century AD, but is probably much more recent. It is the epic history from Prince Vijaya, the legendary founder of Sri Lanka, to King Mahasena (died AD 303) and is a major source on early history and legend. It was continued in the 13th-century text by the *Culavansa*, which gives a very full account of the medieval history of the island. These works were compiled by **bhikkus** (Buddhist monks) and inevitably they have the marks of their sectarian origins.

Interpretation of Sri Lanka's early history does not depend entirely on the writings of the Buddhist monks who ultimately wrote the *Mahavansa*. The first known writings are inscriptions discovered near caves in several parts of the island. Written in the Brahmi script (which was also used in India on the great inscriptions of the Emperor Asoka to express his principles of government and to mark out the limits of his territorial power), in Sri Lanka the inscriptions are brief epigraphs, testifying to the donation of caves or rock shelters to Buddhist monks. Written in an early form of Sinhala, rather than in the Prakrit which was the language used by Asoka, they give vivid testimony to the existence of prosperous, literate agricultural societies. The alphabet and the language were common right across the country, and even from early times it is clear that wet rice cultivation using sophisticated irrigation technology was the basis of the economy. Settlement spread steadily right through to the 13th century. A notable feature of this early settlement and culture was its restriction to the Dry Zone and to altitudes below 300 m.

From the origins of this agricultural civilization in the third century BC there was a progressive economic and social evolution. The economy and the culture developed around the creation of extraordinarily sophisticated irrigation systems, using the rivers flowing from the Central Highlands across the much drier northern and eastern plains. Traditional agriculture had depended entirely on the rainfall brought by the retreating monsoon between October and December. The developing kingdoms of north Sri Lanka realized the need to control water to improve the reliability of agriculture, and a system of tank irrigation was already well advanced by the first century BC. This developed into possibly the most advanced contemporary system of hydraulic engineering in the world by the end of the fifth century AD. Many of these developments were quite small scale and today it is impossible to identify their creators. Others however were of a previously unparalleled size and are clearly identified with powerful kings, for example King Mahasena (AD 274-302) and the 15-m-high dam which impounded the Kantalai tank, covering 2000 ha and is served by a 40-km-long canal. King Dhatusena (AD 460-478) constructed the Kalawewa Lake in Anuradhapura, then by far the largest tank in Sri Lanka, to be surpassed in the late 12th century by King Parakramabahu's Parakrama Samudra ('Sea'), retained by an embankment 14 km long.

Political developments in pre-colonial Sri Lanka

Proximity to India has played a permanent part in Sri Lanka's developing history. Not only have the peoples of the island themselves originated from the mainland, but through more than 2000 years, contact has been an essential element in all Sri Lanka's political equations.

According to the *Mahavansa*, the Buddha commanded the king of the gods, Sakra, to protect Lanka as the home in which Buddhism would flourish. In recent years, much has been read into both the text and to more recent history to suggest that the Sinhalese have always been at war with the Tamils. The truth is far more complicated. The earliest settlement of the island took place in the northeast, the area now known as the Dry Zone. Until the 13th century AD this was the region of political and cultural development for Sinhalese and Tamil alike.

The political history of the island after the establishment of the first recorded kingdom was not as smooth as might be inferred from the steady expansion of settled agriculture and the spread of sophisticated irrigation technology. Before the 13th century AD three regions played a major role in the island's political life. **Rajarata** in the north-central part of the island's plains grew into one of the major core regions of developing Sinhalese culture. To its north was **Uttaradesa** ('northern country'), while in the southeast, **Rohana** (Ruhunu) developed as the third political centre.

Periodically these centres of Sinhalese power came into conflict with each other, and with Tamil kings from India. The *Mahavansa* records how the Rohana Sinhalese King Dutthagamenu defeated the Chola Tamil King Elara, who had ruled northern Sri Lanka from Anuradhapura, in 140 BC. Dutthagamenu's victory was claimed by the chroniclers as a historic assertion of Buddhism's inalienable hold on Sri Lanka. In fact it is clear that at the time this was not a Tamil-Sinhalese or Buddhist-Hindu conflict, for the armies and leadership of both sides contained Sinhalese and Tamils, Buddhists and Hindus. By that time Buddhism had already been a power in the island for two centuries, when the king Devanampiya Tissa (307-267 BC) converted to Buddhism.

Buddhism became the state religion, identified with the growth of Sinhalese culture and political power. The power of the central kingdom based at Anuradhapura was rarely unchallenged or complete. Power was decentralized, with a large measure of local autonomy. Furthermore, provincial centres periodically established their independence. Anuradhapura became one of Asia's pre-eminent cities, but from the 11th century AD, Polonnaruwa took over as capital.

Tamil involvement

Although Buddhist power was predominant in Sri Lanka from the first century BC, Sri Lankan kings often deliberately sought Tamil support in their own disputes. As a result Sri Lanka was affected by political developments in South India. The rise of the expansionist Tamil kingdoms of the Pandiyas, Pallavas and Cholas from the fifth century AD increased the scope for interaction with the mainland. In de Silva's words, "South Indian auxiliaries became in time a vitally important, if not the most powerful element in the armies of the Sinhalese rulers, and an unpredictable, turbulent group who were often a threat to political stability. They were also the nucleus of a powerful Tamil influence in the court."

It was not a one-way flow. Occasionally the Sinhalese were themselves drawn in to attack Tamil kings in India, as in the ninth century when to their enormous cost they joined with their beleaguered allies the Pandiyans and attacked the Cholas. The Chola emperor **Rajaraja I** defeated them in India and then carried the war into Sri Lanka, adding Jaffna and the northern plains, including Anuradhapura, to his empire.

The Cholas ruled from Polonnaruwa for 75 years, finally being driven out by the Rohana king **Vijayabahu I** in AD 1070. He established peace and a return to some prosperity in the north before civil war broke out and disrupted the civil administration again. Only the 33-year rule of **Parakramabahu I** (1153-1186) interrupted the decline. Some of Sri Lanka's most remarkable monuments date from his reign, including the Parakrama Samudra at Polonnaruwa. However, it was the collapse of this kingdom and its ultimate annihilation by the Tamils in the 13th century that left not only its physical imprint on the north Sri Lankan landscape, but also an indelible psychological mark on the Sri Lankan perception of neighbouring Tamil Hindus.

Sinhalese move south

Other factors, such as the spread of malaria, which occurred with the deterioration in maintenance of the irrigation system, may have led to the progressive desertion of the northern and eastern plains and the movement south of the centre of gravity of the Island's population. Between the 12th and 17th centuries Sinhalese moved from the Dry Zone to the Wet Zone. This required a change in agriculture from irrigated to rain-fed crops. Trade also increased, especially in cinnamon – an activity controlled by the rising population of Muslim seafarers. A **Tamil kingdom** was set up in Jaffna for the first time, briefly coming back under Sinhalese power (under the Sinhalese king **Parakramabahu VI**, 1412-1467, based in his capital at **Kotte**), but generally remaining independent, and a frequent threat to the power of the Sinhalese kingdoms to the south. Other threats came from overseas. As early as the 13th century, a Buddhist king from Malaya invaded Sri Lanka twice to try and capture the Tooth Relic and the Buddha's alms bowl. In the early 15th century the island was even invaded by a fleet of Chinese junks sent by the Ming emperors.

The Kandyan kingdom

Between the southern and northern kingdoms, Kandy became the capital of a new power base around 1480. Established in the Central Highlands, it became fully independent by the end of the 15th century. By the early 16th century the Sinhalese kingdom of Kotte in the south was hopelessly fragmented, giving impetus to Kandy's rise to independent power. Its remote and inaccessible position gave it added protection from the early colonial invasions. Using both force and diplomacy to capitalize on its geographical advantages, it survived as the last independent Sinhalese kingdom until 1815. It had played the game of seeking alliances with one colonial power against another with considerable success, first seeking the help of the Dutch against the Portuguese, then of the British against the Dutch. However, this policy ran out of potential allies when the British established their supremacy over all the territory surrounding the Central Highlands in 1796. By 1815 the last Kandyan king, a Tamil Hindu converted to Buddhism, was deposed by his Sinhalese chiefs, who sought an accord with the new British rulers in exchange for retaining a large measure of their own power.

Colonial power

The succession of three colonial powers – the Portuguese, Dutch and the British – finally ended the independent Sinhalese and Tamil rule. Expanding Islam, evidenced in the conversion of the inhabitants of islands on the Arab trading routes such as the Maldives and the Laccadives as well as significant numbers on the southwest coast of India, had also been making its presence felt. The Portuguese arrived in Sri Lanka in 1605 and established control over some of the island's narrow coastal plains around Colombo. They were responsible for large-scale conversions to Roman Catholicism which today accounts for 90% of the island's Christians, leaving both a linguistic legacy and an imprint on the population, evidenced today in many names of Portuguese origin. During this period the rest of the island was dominated by the rulers of Sitavaka, who overpowered the Kotte kingdom in 1565 and controlled the whole of the southwest apart from Colombo. For 10 years they occupied Kandy itself, nearly evicted the Portuguese and came close to reasserting Sinhalese power in the far north.

By 1619 the Portuguese had annexed Jaffna, which thereafter was treated by the Dutch, and more importantly the British, as simply part of the island state. They were less successful in subjugating Kandy, and in 1650 the Portuguese were ousted by the Dutch. The Dutch extended their own colonial control from Negombo (40 km north of Colombo) south, right round the coast to Trincomalee, as well as the entire northern peninsula, leaving the Kandyan kingdom surrounded in the Central Highlands. Because the Portuguese and Dutch were interested in little other than the spice trade, they bent most of their efforts to producing the goods necessary for their trade. The British replaced the Dutch in 1795-1796 when British power was being consolidated in South India at the expense of the French and the Mysore Muslim raja, Tipu Sultan. Their original purpose was to secure the important Indian Ocean port of Trincomalee. Initially the British imported administrators and officials from Madras, but as BH Farmer points out, by 1802 "it was apparent that Madras-trained officials were, apart from other disabilities, quite unable to understand the language and customs of the Sinhalese, and Ceylon became a Crown Colony".

When the British came to control the whole island after 1815 they established a quite distinctive imprint on the island's society and economy. This was most obvious in the introduction of plantation agriculture. During the British period coffee took over from cinnamon, but by the beginning of the 20th century, even though coffee had largely been wiped out by disease, plantation agriculture was the dominant pillar of the cash economy. Rice production stagnated and then declined, and Sri Lanka became dependent on the export of cash crops and the import of food. In 1948 it was only producing about 35% of its rice needs.

The colonial period also saw major social changes take place. Under the Portuguese and then the Dutch the development of commercial activity in the coastal lowlands encouraged many 'low country' Sinhalese to become involved in the newly emerging economic activity. In a process which continued in the early British colonial period, the low country Sinhalese became increasingly Westernized, with the widespread adoption of an English education and the rise of an urban middle class, while the Kandyan Sinhalese retained far stronger links with traditional and rural social customs. Despite British reforms in 1833 which introduced a uniform administrative system across the whole of Ceylon, wiping out the Kandyan political system, a contrast between Kandyan and low country Sinhalese persisted into the modern period.

However, an even more significant change took place in the 19th century. British commercial interests saw the opportunities presented for the cultivation of cash crops. Cinnamon and coconuts had been planted by the Dutch and become particularly important, but after 1815 coffee production was spread to the Kandyan hills. Despite ups and downs production increased dramatically until 1875, when a catastrophic attack of a fungus disease wiped out almost the entire crop. It was replaced, particularly in the higher regions, by tea.

Labour had already begun to prove a problem on the coffee plantations, and as tea plantations spread the shortage became acute. Private labour contractors were recruited to persuade labourers to come to Ceylon from the Tamil country of South India. Between 1843-1859 over 900,000 men, women and children migrated to work as indentured labour. The cost of their transport was deducted from their wages after they arrived, and they could not leave until they had repaid their debt. Immigration on that scale created a massive change in the ethnic mix of the highlands, with a particularly significant effect on the Kandyan farmers, whose land was increasingly hemmed in by the spread of estates. The Indian Tamils however remained entirely separate from the Sinhalese, returning to South India whenever possible and sending cash remittances home.

The move to independence

Dominated by Buddhists and Sinhalese in its early stages, no one in the Independence movement at the beginning of the 20th century would have believed that British rule would end within 50 years – nor would many have wanted it to. The **Ceylon National Congress**, formed in 1919, was conservative and pragmatic, but the pressures of imminent democratic self-rule made themselves felt throughout the 1930s, as minority groups pressed to protect their position. Universal suffrage came in 1931, along with the promise of self-rule from the British government. It had the positive benefit of encouraging the development of welfare policies such as health care, nutrition and public education. However, it also had the immediate impact of encouraging a resurgence of nationalism linked with Buddhist revivalism.

Independence came with scarcely a murmur on 4 February 1948, six months after that of India and Pakistan. Ceylon's first prime minister was **Don Stephen Senanayake**. His son **Dudley Senanayake**, who followed, was identified with a pragmatic nationalism. The heart of his programme was the re-colonization of the deserted Sinhalese heartlands of the Dry Zone. It was a programme deliberately calculated to recapture the glories of the past while laying the groundwork for post-independence prosperity. In the event, its results have proved far more complex than even its critics fully recognized.

Modern Sri Lanka

Sri Lanka is a parliamentary democracy with an elected president and freely contested elections. Sri Lankans enjoy a long life expectancy, a high literacy rate that belies its low per capita income, and generally an advanced health system. Over the last 50 years the island has continued to see rapid economic and social change. The plantation economy remains important though no longer as dominant as it was during the colonial period, while newer industries, including tourism, have taken on the prime role.

In the early post-independence years, Sri Lanka was regarded as a 'model colony'. The country started on a strong economic footing with a strong Sterling balance and little internal division. Within the new constitution there was also a commitment to religious neutrality. Both the island's main languages, Sinhala and Tamil, had been declared national languages and equitable access to political and administrative positions was guaranteed. However, successive governments failed to maintain commitment to either equality or economic development in the face of greater welfare spending and a rapidly growing young and literate population. The pattern of the early post-independence governments was to manipulate disaffection within the electorate in an effort to gain votes, with the effect of stirring up communal emotions between racial and religious groups. Within 10 years the seeds had been sown for the faction fighting of the last two decades which threatened to tear the country apart. Between 1983 and 2009, Sri Lanka was involved in a bitter internal ethnic conflict, predominantly in the north and east, between the government and separatist Tamil rebels, the **Liberation Tigers of Tamil Eelam (LTTE)** or 'Tamil Tigers'.

Post-independence and the Bandaranaikes

The origins of Sri Lanka's ethnic conflict are complex. Here, a brief sketch of significant post-war events is offered which aims to elucidate some of the immediate causes. Sri Lanka's first government was formed by the **United National Party (UNP)**, a broad union of conservative ideologies led by **DS Senanayake**, Minister of Agriculture during the last years of British rule. Senanayake saw Sri Lanka's pluralism as its strength, thwarting any divisive forces. He concentrated on economic progress, particularly in agricultural policy, including the setting up of the massive Gal Oya project in the east of the country, designed to increase rice production, as well as planting subsidies on rice. The party however was wrought by internal divisions with the first serious break occurring in 1951 when its left bloc broke away under the leadership of **SWRD Bandaranaike**, to form the **Sri Lanka Freedom Party (SLFP)**. After Senanayake's death in a riding accident in 1952, his son Dudley succeeded him but failed to maintain the UNP's popularity when it became clear that the country faced significant economic problems. Senanayake's massive spending on welfare (up to 35% of the budget) forced him to reduce the government rice subsidy, leading to massive protests and his resignation.

Fact file

Official name Sri Lanka Prajatantrika Samajawadi Janarajaya (Democratic Socialist Republic of Sri Lanka).

The name Sri Lanka, first recorded in the *Ramayana*, means 'Resplendent Land' in Sanskrit. It reverted to its original name from Ceylon on 22 May 1972.

Capital Sri Jayawardenepura Kotte (Legislative); Colombo (Commercial)

Population 20.6 million (UN 2010).

Annual growth rate 0.9%.

Crude birth rate 1.7%.

Crude death rate 0.6%.

Urban population 14%.

Life expectancy at birth 75.7 (female 79 and male 72).

Adult literacy 90.7% (male 92% and female 89% (in comparison to India: male 73.4% and female 48%).

Area 66,000 sq km.

Population density 329 per sq km.

GDP US$104.7 billion.

GDP per capita US$4900.

Unemployment 5.4%.

Average annual growth rate 6%.

HDI (Human Development Index) 93.

Against this background, the SLFP emerged as the main opposition party. Bandaranaike, part of a wealthy Sinhalese family, had been educated – and discriminated against – at Oxford. Returning to Sri Lanka, he rejected Western values and embraced Buddhism. His election campaign of 1956 sought to provoke the nationalist passions of the Buddhist majority in order to eradicate traces of colonial rule. While this was initially targeted at Christian influence, it coincided with a greater awareness amongst Sinhalese that they had 'lost out' at independence. During the British colonial period, a disproportionate number of government and administrative positions had been given to the traditionally hardworking Tamils, who tended to be better educated than the Sinhalese and occupied a greater number of university places, a trend that continued after independence. English had been, and continued to be, the main language of administration, and since the Tamils tended to have greater mastery, Bandaranaike chose to fight the 1956 election on a platform making Sinhala the only official language. After winning the election, Bandaranaike successfully passed the **Sinhala Only Act**, which led to widespread Tamil resentment and, within two years, the first violent clashes in which hundreds, mainly Tamils, died.

Bandaranaike pursued popular but economically unfeasible nationalization policies, expanding the public sector and draining the nation's resources. By the time he was assassinated by a Buddhist monk in 1959, the country faced grave instability. The SLFP however maintained popular support, and in July 1960 his widow, **Sirimavo Bandaranaike** swept to power, becoming the world's first female prime minister. She continued her husband's socialist-style legislation, nationalizing significant sectors of the economy, including foreign-controlled industries such as petroleum, and forced a government takeover of denominational schools. This soured relations with the country's many Catholics, while her aggressive reinforcement of Sinhala as the only official language led to Tamil disobedience in the north and east, whose political activity was subsequently curtailed in a state of emergency. In 1965, Dudley Senanayake and the UNP regained power, but despite improving relations with the US (who had suspended aid in 1963) and doubling private sector investment, the economy failed to show any significant improvement, and the government was blighted by greater civil violence and states of emergency.

Rise of the LTTE

Mrs Bandaranaike returned to power in 1970 under the banner of the **United Front**, a three-party coalition, promising land reform and further nationalization, and extending diplomatic relations to countries such as the GDR, Vietnam and North Korea. The radical left mobilized at this time, and in 1971 a Sinhalese Maoist youth movement, the **Janatha Vimukthi Peramuna (JVP)** or People's Liberation Front, attempted a blitzkrieg, with fierce fighting in the North Central and Southern Provinces leaving more than 1000 dead. Ruthlessly repressed by the military, the uprising gave the government reign to force through a new constitution in May 1972, verging on the authoritarian. The military were given greater powers, while Sinhala was enshrined as the official language and the country was given a new name, Sri Lanka, invoking the ancient Sinhalese kingdoms. The constitution lacked any hint of federalism, which dismayed Tamils. Instead, it removed many minority rights, conferring greater status on Buddhism. Even more irksome to Tamils was the 'standardization' policy on university admissions, which lowered the standard required by Sinhalese to gain university places. With many Tamils disenfranchised and disillusioned, this iniquitous change in the system, combined with heavy handed treatment by the army, was the fundamental cause of the breakdown of ethnic relations in the 1970s and the radicalization of Tamil politics. The proportion of Tamils in public service had fallen from 60% in 1956 to 10% by 1970, and from 40% to 1% in the military, while the percentage of university places held by Tamils almost halved between 1970 and 1975. In 1976, the Tamil leadership (the newly formed **Tamil United Liberation Front**, or **TULF**) for the first time advocated a separate Tamil state. The LTTE at this time emerged as the most powerful of a number of underground separatist groups. They first gained notoriety in 1975 when they assassinated the Mayor of Jaffna, and from a handful of guerrilla fighters in the early years, they grew with the help of funding and military training from abroad (notably from Tamil Nadu) into a well-disciplined military unit.

During this period support for the UNP had declined but when political divisions between left and right began to split the United Front, the UNP under a new leader, **JR Jayawardene**, actively improved their image and won a convincing victory at the polls in 1977. Promising a fairer society, he radically altered the constitution the following year, replacing the Westminster-style of governance with a French-style presidential system, the democratically elected president to appoint a prime minister, with parliamentary approval. While the new constitution also included concessions to the Tamils, including giving Tamil the status of a 'national' language and abrogating the 'standardization' policy for universities, it was a case of too little too late. The country's worst rioting in 19 years had greeted the new government's inception, and in 1979 the government passed an act, condemned by international groups, to attempt to curb the rapid proliferation of Tamil terrorist groups. The possibility of an effective solution became increasingly distant when the TULF boycotted the 1982 presidential elections (which saw a confirmation of Jayawardene's presidency whose economic advances had proved popular with the Sinhalese). When TULF members were expelled from parliament for refusing to recite allegiance to the constitution, Tamil hopes of a political solution effectively ended.

Sporadic rioting continued to increase, notably over a three-month period in 1981 during which Jaffna's historic library was destroyed, but it was during 'Black July' in 1983 that the country descended into turmoil. In retaliation for an ambush of an army patrol, organized Sinhalese mobs went on the rampage, first in Colombo, where Tamil areas were devastated and hundreds were killed, and then spreading throughout the country. More than 150,000 Tamils fled as refugees to India, many finding new homes in Europe and North America.

Civil war

Between 1983 and 1987 the LTTE waged an increasingly successful battle for control of 'Eelam' – roughly Sri Lanka's Northern and Eastern provinces. Brutal acts were perpetrated on both sides. The conflict began to assume an international dimension when the Sri Lankan government accused India of supporting the Tamil cause, and as the situation reached deadlock, Indian leader Rajiv Gandhi agreed to intervene. On 29 July 1987, Gandhi and Jayawardene signed the Indo-Lanka accord, under which the Sri Lankan government made a number of concessions to the Tamils, including some devolution of power to the provinces and a merger of the Northern and Eastern provinces. Fifty thousand troops, the **Indian Peace Keeping Force (IPKF)**, were sent in to disarm the rebels. Most groups agreed to surrender their weapons. Within weeks, however, the LTTE announced their intention to continue the fight for Eelam, entering into a bloody battle with the Indian peacekeepers. The government pressed on with reform, holding council elections, but a return to peace was complicated when Sinhalese nationalism, opposed to concessions to the Tamils and an Indian presence on Lankan soil, rose again and the JVP, which had been quiet since the early 1970s, began to reassert itself. There followed one of the ugliest periods in Sri Lankan history. The JVP embarked on a systematic attempt to bring down the government, through strikes, sabotage, closure of schools and hospitals, assassination of politicians and the murder of hundreds of government supporters. The government, relieved of its burden in the north, responded violently. By the time the JVP insurrection was finally quashed in 1990, many thousands of suspected insurgents had been killed or 'disappeared'. The systematic abuse of human rights by the government and military at this time drew widespread condemnation from the international community.

Meanwhile, presidential elections in 1988 had been won by **Ranasinghe Premadasa**. He promptly demanded that Indian troops leave and opened up discussions with the LTTE, who agreed to a ceasefire and talks in order to speed up the Indian withdrawal. Within three months of their eventual departure in March 1990, the LTTE had resumed hostilities, 'Eelam War II', at one point murdering 600 police officers in the north whom they had promised free passage. Having been pushed back to Jaffna in 1987, they now took control of large sections of the north and east. Vendettas were also pursued. In 1991, they assassinated Rajiv Gandhi in Madras and two years later at a May Day rally, Premadasa himself. With the UNP weakened after 17 years of rule, tainted by corruption, political scandal and continued failure to solve the conflict, new president Dingiri Banda Wijetunga called elections in August 1994. Chandrika Kumaratunga, daughter of Sirimavo Bandaranaike, had by now assumed the leadership of the SLFP and led a loose coalition of parties, the **People's Alliance (PA)**, to a narrow victory over the UNP. After appointing her mother as prime minister, she entered into negotiations with the LTTE. Once again these broke down when the LTTE's 'Black Sea Tigers' sank two naval gunboats off the coast of Trincomalee. But in launching 'Eelam War III' it soon became evident that the LTTE had themselves miscalculated. In a huge gamble, the army launched **Operation Riviresa** (Sunshine), a successful attempt to retake Jaffna in October 1995, preceded by a mass evacuation of its residents. Jaffna has remained narrowly under government control ever since.

Between 1996 and 2000, the LTTE achieved a series of military victories. Chased out of Jaffna, they regrouped in the east, assuming control of vast sections of Trincomalee and Batticaloa districts as well as the Wanni. In April 1996, they killed more than 1200 soldiers and police in retaking Mullaitivu, and successfully continued their campaign of attacking key civilian targets, including, in January 1996, a bomb at Colombo's Central Bank which killed more than 100 people. In May 1997 the army launched **Operation Sure Victory** which saw almost 30,000 troops attempt to reopen the vital northern highway to Jaffna. The Tigers resisted fiercely, retaking Kilinochchi in September 1998 and forcing the government forces to abandon its programme. By late 1999, the army had been forced back to Vavuniya, while in April 2000 it launched a massive and successful onslaught on the strategic Elephant Pass garrison, located on the isthmus between the Jaffna peninsula and the mainland. This was one of the bloodiest periods of the war, with thousands killed on both sides.

Kumaratunga herself was the target of a suicide bomber in December 1999 whilst on the campaign trail for re-election. She survived, though lost the sight of one eye, and won the election with 62% of the vote. Prior to 2000's parliamentary elections, in August the government presented parliament with a modified constitutional package with far greater autonomy for Tamil majority regions, but it failed to pass parliament. The PA was narrowly re-elected in October, but it was hardly a vote of confidence. Successive attempts to achieve a constitutional and political solution to the confrontation had met with repeated failure, and alienated not just the LTTE but much of the Sinhalese majority.

Ceasefire

With all other options exhausted, Kumaratunga accepted the Norwegian government's proposal to act as a facilitator with the LTTE, even though the LTTE refused to give up its claim to Eelam. The first meeting took place in November 2000 but it was not until the snap elections of December 2001, and the re-election of the UNP under Prime Minister **Ranil Wickremasinghe** that serious strides could be made towards peace. Wickremasinghe had been secretly negotiating with the LTTE for peace whilst in opposition. By now, all sides, as well as public opinion, were exhausted by war, the economy had slowed down, and the government faced bankruptcy. Two earth-shattering events precipitated discussions. The first was the LTTE's overrunning of the massively guarded international airport at Katunayake in July 2001. A crack unit of Tiger commandos destroyed almost half the national airline's fleet, as well as eight military planes and helicopters. It exacerbated economic ruin for the government and was the death-knell for the PA. The second was the events of 11 September 2001, which turned worldwide attention on terrorist groups, leading to the closing down of many of the LTTE's foreign sources of revenue, and greater US support for the government.

After the election of a new government in December 2001 a formal ceasefire agreement was signed in February 2002 between Prime Minister Ranil Wickremasinghe and LTTE leader Vellupillai Prabhakaran, to be monitored by the Norwegian government. This Memorandum of Understanding (MoU) successfully put a stop to hostilities and prompted several rounds of peace talks between September 2002 and March 2003, but the LTTE pulled out of the talks in April 2003 after accusing the government of failing to deliver on its promises. In late 2003, after months of tension, President Chandrika Bandaranaike Kumaratunga dissolved parliament whilst Wickremasinghe was in Washington meeting with George W Bush, and called for an election. Kumaratunga created a coalition government with the **Janatha Vimukthi Peramuna** (JVP) or People's Liberation Front, and **Mahinda Rajapakse** was appointed prime minister. The peace process stalled completely. In 2004 there was trouble within the LTTE and Colonel Karuna, commander in the east, broke away from the movement and took several thousand troops with him. He later renounced terrorism and joined the government as a member of parliament in 2008.

The tsunami

On 26 December 2004 the tsunami struck Sri Lanka, killing thousands, displacing millions and destroying homes and businesses. The economic loss was huge and the damage stood at over US$1 billion. It was hoped this tragedy would finally bring the country together, but instead there were arguments over aid distribution, reconstruction and land ownership. An aid-sharing agreement between the government and the LTTE was ratified in 2005 but the JVP pressured the Supreme Court into suspending it, believing it would establish the LTTE as the de facto government in the north.

Rajapakse comes to power

In August 2005 Lakshman Kadirgamar, Sri Lankan foreign minister, was assassinated by the LTTE. The LTTE boycotted the elections and no Tamils living in LTTE-controlled areas were allowed to vote. The reason remains unclear, however some suggest it was to encourage a return to hostilities, Ranil Wickramasinghe, who would traditionally have benefited from the Tamil vote, lost by a narrow margin to Mahinda Rajapakse. Rajapakse invited the Norwegians back and in early 2006 a statement was negotiated that included commitments to a ceasefire and further talks, and it was signed in February. By March, the fighting had begun again in earnest. In April an LTTE suicide bomber killed eight people in the main military compound in Colombo, and in retaliation the military launched air strikes on Tamil Tiger targets in the north, displacing thousands of civilians in the process. There followed months of intense fighting before the rebels were driven from the east; the country had well and truly returned to a state of undeclared civil war. Peace talks in Geneva in October failed. Once it became obvious the peace process was no more, a massive recruitment drive for the armed forces was launched. Personnel numbers almost doubled, and new weapons were purchased from countries including China, Pakistan and Russia. The army also changed tactics and started using a more guerrilla-style of warfare, sending small teams of commandos behind enemy lines.

Official ceasefire ends

After weeks of heavy fighting in 2007, the army took back the LTTE-held town of Vakarai. June saw thousands of non-resident Tamils forced from Colombo due to 'security reasons' before a court ordered an end to the expulsions, and in November SP Thamilselvan, leader of the LTTE's political wing and the Tiger's main point of contact for the outside world, was killed in an air raid.

The government pulled out of the official ceasefire in January 2008, which by this point was meaningless anyway, and concentrated on a military solution to the problem. It pledged to win the war within a year and launched a massive offensive. Bombings, assassinations, disappearances, and heavy fighting in the north continued. The LTTE offered a unilateral ceasefire but this was dismissed by the government. The army captured the LTTE administrative capital of Kilinochchi in January 2009, and failed to heed international calls for a ceasefire as they forced the LTTE back onto a narrow strip of land. Thousands of civilians were trapped in the ever-decreasing war zone as the LTTE abandoned the Jaffna peninsula and retreated to the jungle. Many were used as human shields by the Tigers, children were forced into soldiering, and others were bombed indiscriminately by the army whilst in supposed 'no-fire' zones. It is estimated that more than 7000 civilians died in the final months of the war, and as many as 118,000 were sheltering in a 14-sq-km no-fire zone towards the end of the fighting. The UN High Commissioner for Human Rights, Navi Pillay, stated around this time that certain actions undertaken by both sides could constitute violations of humanitarian law. The LTTE again offered a ceasefire, but the government could smell victory and the request was declared a joke.

Peace, but at what cost?

By May 2009 the LTTE were hemmed in, and they surrendered. Several senior LTTE figures were reported killed, including their leader Vellupillai Prabhakaran. Later, there were allegations that the government had ordered the execution of captured or surrendering rebels. Immediately following the end of hostilities, 250,000 Tamil refugees were interned in camps and kept there for months in less than ideal conditions while they were screened for possible links with the rebels. Rajapakse declared victory, and called for an early election in January 2010. He won a landslide victory. Former army chief, General Sarath Fonseka, who led the final campaign that crushed the LTTE, ran against Rajapakse. He lost but stated he would contest the result. Soon after, he was put on trial on charges of engaging in politics before leaving the army, and was also court martialled for breaching arms procurement guidelines. He is currently in jail and is expected to lose his parliamentary seat. Later in the year, MPs passed a constitutional amendment allowing Rajapakse to stand for unlimited terms in office. Some have described this as taking the country one step closer to a dictatorship, whilst the prime minister states it is providing Sri Lanka with the stability it needs.

Since the war ended, there have been calls for an independent investigation into what took place during the last five months of fighting. At the end of 2010 Tamil campaigners in the UK tried to serve a war crimes arrest warrant on Mahinda Rajapakse whilst he was visiting Britain, as they blame him and his senior officers for the deaths of 40,000 civilians during the war. The Sri Lankan government, irritated by continued criticism, established an internal panel of inquiry, the **Lessons Learnt and Reconciliation Commission (LLRC)** in May 2010. However, its credibility was quickly brought into question and some humanitarian groups refused to work with it. Sri Lanka's failure to improve its human rights record, led to the European Union withdrawing its preferential trade agreement with the country in July 2010. A UN-appointed panel was declined admission to the country to conduct research, and the government rejected their subsequent report, which will be made public in the near future. It is considered unacceptable that thousands of civilians died and the report was to look into issues of accountability connected with the events. That is to say, the allegations that war crimes may have been committed by the government or the Tamil Tigers (whose top leaders are all now dead).

New beginnings

Peace has brought hope and optimism to Sri Lanka, and yet there remains a lot to be done. The east and north are still struggling to recover from the damage inflicted by the war years and also by the tsunami. People are gradually returning to their homes, but many are still displaced. De-mining work also needs to continue. The east of Sri Lanka suffered the worst floods in 50 years in early 2011, which drove thousands from their homes and ruined rice crops which will lead to food shortages. There are also continuing concerns about human rights, freedom of speech, and the safety of journalists who criticize the government. Reporters Without Borders called for a boycott of the Galle Literary Festival in 2011, saying dissident voices were being victimized by the government. However, it is worth taking note of what the festival curator and Sri Lankan novelist, Shyam Selvadurai, said after hearing that South African author Damon Galgut had pulled out, "This event does a lot of good….There have been very open debates about controversial issues at past events. It's exactly the wrong thing to shut down".

Economy

Key statistics

In 2010 Sri Lanka's main agricultural products were as follows: tea 329,000 tonnes; rubber 52,000 tonnes; paddy 2695 tonnes; coconut 2317 million nuts. The major exports were: textiles and garments Rs 383,855 million; tea Rs 151,295 million; rubber Rs 18,729 million; coconut products Rs 18,156 million; petroleum products Rs 16,036 million; and gems Rs 15,716 million.

Agriculture and fishing

Approximately 25% of Sri Lanka's area is cultivated by sedentary farmers or under cultivated forests, a further 15% being under shifting cultivation. About half is under forest, grassland, swamp and waste land. In the Wet Zone virtually all the cultivable land is now taken up.

Sri Lanka has not produced enough food to meet the needs of its population since the 18th century, yet in many respects it has been the most obviously prosperous state in South Asia. In the 1970s more than half the money earned from the export of tea, rubber and coconuts was spent on importing food grains, leaving little for investment. In 1999, for the first time for over a decade, agriculture grew as fast as the rest of the economy. Agriculture has lost its relative importance to the Sri Lankan economy in recent decades. It employs 31% of the working population, but only accounts for about 11% of GDP. Domestic agriculture such as rice and other food crops improved significantly with the return of peace to the Eastern and Northern Provinces, but the floods in early 2011 destroyed many crops and livestock, including rice, in the main cultivation period. A high proportion of Sri Lanka's farmers remain poor, and 25% of the total population is below the government's poverty line.

Sri Lanka has two main **rice** growing seasons. The *Maha* crop is harvested between January and March, the *Yala* crop between August and September. Attempts to increase rice production have ranged from land reform to the introduction of High Yielding Varieties (HYV). By the early 1980s there was virtually a 100% take-up of new varieties. Yields have increased significantly, and by 2000 Sri Lanka was producing over 80% of its domestic needs despite the speed of population growth. In addition to the intensification programme the government has also carried out major colonization schemes, bringing new land under rice cultivation though these were stalled by the ethnic conflict.

The **cash crops** of tea, rubber and coconuts continue to contribute the lion's share of Sri Lanka's foreign exchange earnings with approximately 15% of foreign exchange earnings still coming from these three products alone. The **coconut** palm (*Cocos nucifer*) grows easily along the south and west coast and in the Kurunegala District. Kernel products rather than fresh nuts remain more important for export (see box, page 358). **Tea** suffered for many years from inadequate investment and fierce competition from expanding production in other countries of cheaper, lower quality tea. The area cropped under tea fell steadily, though production improved between 1948 and 1965, only to decline again. Since the mid-1980s there has been a remarkable turn-around and the last four years have seen a resurgence in global tea consumption, with tea production trailing behind. The commercially important **rubber** tree, a native of Brazil, is cultivated in plantations in areas of high rainfall. New clones have been developed which are disease resistant and high yielding (see box, page 359). Sri Lanka is, however, trying to diversify into more remunerative crops. **Spices** (cinnamon, pepper, clove, nutmeg/mace and cardamom), coffee and cocoa also contribute a significant percentage of earnings from export.

Indispensable coconut

The coconut, so much a part of the coastal scene on the island, particularly to the west, is the country's third most important crop, and sometimes called the 'money tree'.

The inland palm is often short enough to be harvested by cutting bunches of mature nuts with a sharp knife tied to the end of a long bamboo pole which the 'picker' skilfully manipulates from the ground. The coastal palm is too tall to be harvested this way so the nuts must be collected by climbing each tree.

Every bit of the palm is put to use. The green fruit produces an excellent refreshing 'milk' which is on tap when the top is cut off. The 'shell' is split open to expose the soft white kernel which is edible. The outer fibrous coir, just under the skin, is removed and soaked in tanks before being woven into mats, twisted

into rope or used as mattress filling and even exported for agricultural and garden use to improved soil texture.

The dry, older nut yields a white layer of 'flesh' or kernel, which is grated or pounded for cooking while some of the best is turned into desiccated coconut (a small industry which employs women) for use at home and abroad.

The fresh sap which is 'tapped' from a proportion of trees is prized by most Sri Lankans who drink the fermented toddy or the more alcoholic arrack. The sweet juice is also turned into jaggery or treacle. See also the box on page 125.

Palm oil and cattle feed in the shape of oil cakes are products in demand. The shell itself ends up as fuel, the leaves as thatch or for basket weaving throughout the year, and finally (when the tree dies) the strong trunk is cut up for building.

The potentially rich **fishery resources** have yet to be fully developed. Freshwater stocking programmes have increased the yield of rivers and lakes, and brackish water fishing is becoming increasingly commercialized. However, nearly 40% of households which depend on fishing have no boats or equipment, and despite the potential of the export market production does not meet domestic demand. Political uncertainty has been a major barrier to expansion in the north and east, though fishing has now resumed.

Resources and industry

Sri Lanka has few fossil fuels or metallic minerals. Gemstones, graphite (crystalline carbon) and heavy mineral sands are the most valuable resources. Gemstones include sapphires, rubies, topaz, zircon, tourmaline and many others. Gem-bearing gravels are common, especially in the southwest. The greatest concentration of heavy mineral sands – ilmenite, rutile and monazite – is north of Trincomalee, where deposits are 95% pure. High evaporation rates make shallow lagoons, suitable for salt manufacture especially around Hambantota.

Due to the lack of fossil fuel resources, 95% of the island's electricity is now generated by hydroelectric power. The first HEP project was opened in the 1930s, but firewood still accounts for more than half of all energy used. Supplies are under increasing pressure, and the **Mahaweli Project** has meant that most of the HEP is now developed.

Sri Lanka had very little industry at Independence, manufacturing accounting for less than 5% of GDP. Since then a number of new industries have developed – cement, mineral sands, ceramics and most importantly textiles. These were all planned originally in the state-controlled sector. The socialist government under Mrs Bandaranaike

Growing on trees

The country's third most important crop (after tea and coconuts), rubber trees were introduced to Sri Lanka from their native Brazil via Kew gardens in London towards the end of the 19th century. In the decade after 1904 Sri Lanka experienced a rubber boom, the Wet Zone between the sea and the Central Highlands providing particularly fruitful conditions. The apparently sparsely populated land, combined with an ideal climate, encouraged widespread planting. In fact the shifting cultivation which had dominated much of the region around Kalutara, now one of the most important centres of the rubber industry, was severely curtailed by the planting of rubber trees, which spread up the valley sides, leaving paddy the dominant crops in the valley bottoms.

The pale cream sap (latex) of the rubber plant is gathered (or 'tapped') from a fine cut in the bark, renewed two or three times a week. The latex is collected in a tin cup or coconut shell hung beneath the cut. You can ask to be shown round a rubber estate and the processing plant, where you can see the latex being mixed with water, strained and hung out to dry after having been rolled into sheets.

envisaged public ownership of all major industries, but the United National Party government elected under President Jayawardene's leadership in 1977 reversed this policy, moving towards a free trade economy.

Among the leading sectors of the new policy was **tourism**. Although tourism has been seriously affected by the political unrest, the end of the war has triggered a significant recovery. Shipping is also staging a strong recovery as a direct result of the improved political climate.

Current indicators

The period of aggressive economic reform under the UNP-led government from 2002-2004 was followed by a more statist approach under President Mahinda Rajapakse, and economic growth has averaged around 5% in the last 10 years. Due to the global recession and the escalation of violence during the final months of the war, GDP slowed to 3.5% in 2009, but business confidence soon rebounded and GDP grew by 8% in 2010. Tourism is now reaching record levels, and exports grew by 17% in 2010 despite the EU suspending its trading agreement. Exports for 2010 were estimated at US$8.3 billion and imports were estimated at US$13.5 billion. Inflation is currently running at about 8%.

The **information technology** (IT) and **business process outsourcing** (BPO) sector is small but growing. Offices in Sri Lanka are currently doing financial work for some of the world's biggest companies. With widespread use of English and a high literacy rate Sri Lanka hopes to transform itself into an outsourcing powerhouse. About 50,000 Sri Lankans now work in more common outsourcing like information technology and the figure is growing by 20% a year. The government is offering incentives, including tax breaks, subsidized telecommunications and streamlined procedures for setting up new businesses to encourage international companies to come to Sri Lanka instead of going to India, Eastern Europe or the Philippines. Unemployment dropped to 4.5% at the end of 2010.

There are 1.7 million Sri Lankan citizens working abroad at the moment, the majority are women with domestic positions in the Middle East. Remittances from migrant workers, estimated at around US$4.1 billion in 2010, are the most important source of foreign exchange for Sri Lanka, surpassing earnings from apparel exports. Sri Lanka's income inequality remains severe, with striking differences between rural and urban areas. About 15% of the country's population remains under the poverty line, partly as a result of the civil war, and also falling agricultural productivity.

Religion

The white stupas of Anuradhapura and the serene stillness of the Buddha's image captured in stone across the island testify to the interweaving of Buddhism with Sinhalese life. Yet Sri Lanka has always been a diverse society. Hinduism is the dominant religion of Tamils in the north for over 2000 years and of many of the tea plantation workers today. Islam arrived with the Arab traders across the Indian Ocean over a thousand years ago, and the three main colonial powers – the Portuguese, Dutch and British – brought Catholicism and Protestant Christianity to the island from the 17th century onwards. In Colombo these religions all have a visible presence, and Buddhists, Christians and Muslims live peacefully side by side in many parts of the island, despite present-day political conflicts. Statistically the population is split: Buddhists 69%; Hindus 15%; Christians 7.5%; Muslims 7.5%; others 1%.

Buddhism

In Sri Lanka Buddhism is the most widespread religion of the majority Sinhalese community. Although India was the original home of Buddhism, today it is practised largely on the margins of the sub-continent, and is widely followed in Ladakh, Nepal and Bhutan as well as Sri Lanka.

Buddha's life

Siddharta Gautama, who came to be given the title of the Buddha – the Enlightened One – was born about 563 BC in the Nepal/India foothills of the Himalaya. A prince in a warrior caste, he was married at the age of 16 and his wife had a son. When he reached the age of 29 he left home and wandered as a beggar and ascetic. After about six years he spent some time in Bodh Gaya in the modern Indian state of Bihar. Sitting under the Bo tree, meditating, he was tempted by the demon Mara, with all the desires of the world. Resisting these temptations, he received Enlightenment.

These scenes are common motifs of Buddhist art. The next landmark was the preaching of his first sermon on 'The Foundation of Righteousness' and set in motion the *Dharma Chakra* (Wheel of the Law) in the deer park at Sarnath near Benaras (Varanasi) to his first five disciples. This was followed by other sermons during his travels when he gathered more disciples. Ananta (his closest disciple) was a cousin. Another cousin, Devdutta, opposed the Buddha and made three attempts to have him killed but failed – a hired assassin was converted, a boulder rolled downhill split in two and finally the wild elephant sent to crush the Buddha underfoot was calmed by his sermon. By the time he died the Buddha had established a small band of monks and nuns known as the *Sangha*, and had followers across North India. The male monks were divided into *sramana* (ascetics), *bhikku* (mendicants), *upasaka* (disciples) and *sravaka* (laymen); the nuns were known as *bhikkuni*.

On the Buddha's death or *parinirvana* (Parinibbana or 'final extinction') at the age of 80, his body was cremated, and the ashes, regarded as precious relics, were divided up among the peoples to whom he had preached. Some have been discovered as far west as Peshawar, in the northwest frontier of Pakistan, and at Piprawa, close to his birthplace.

Sri Lankan Buddhism

The recent history of Sri Lanka's **Theravada** Buddhism may conceal the importance of the cultural and historical links between Sri Lanka and India in the early stages of its development. The first great stupas in Anuradhapura were built when Buddhism was still a religious force to be reckoned with in mainland India, and as some of the sculptures from Sigiriya suggest there were important contacts with Amaravati, another major centre of Buddhist art and thought, up to the 5th century AD.

The origins of Buddhism in Sri Lanka are explained in a legend which tells how King Devanampiya Tissa (died 207 BC) was converted by Mahinda, widely believed to have been Asoka's son, who was sent to Sri Lanka specifically to bring the faith to the Island's people. He established the Mahavihara monastery in Anuradhapura. Successors repeatedly struggled to preserve Sri Lankan Buddhism's distinct identity from that of neighbouring Hinduism and Tantrism. It was also constantly struggling with Mahayana Buddhism, which gained the periodic support of successive royal patrons. King Mahasena (AD 276-303) and his son Sri Meghavarna, who received the famous 'Tooth of the Buddha' when it was brought to the island from Kalinga in the fourth century AD, both advocated Mahayana forms of the faith. Even then Sri Lanka's Buddhism is not strictly orthodox, for the personal character of the Buddha is emphasized, as was the virtue of being a disciple of the Buddha. Maitreya, the 'future' Buddha, is recognized as the only Bodhisattva, and it has been a feature of Buddhism in the island for kings to identify themselves with this incarnation of the Buddha.

The Sinhalese see themselves as guardians of the original Buddhist faith. They believe that the scripture in Pali was first written down by King Vattagamani Abhaya in the first century BC. The Pali Theravada canon of scripture is referred to as *Tipitakam Tripitaka* ('three baskets'), because the palm leaf texts on which they were written were stored in baskets (*pitakas*). They are conduct (*vinaya*), consisting of 227 rules binding on monks and nuns; discourses (*sutta*), the largest and most important, divided into five groups (*niyakas*) of basic doctrine which are believed to be the actual discourses of the Buddha recording his exact words as handed down by word of mouth; and metaphysics (*abhidhamma*) which develop the ideas further both philosophically and psychologically. There are also several works that lack the full authority of the canon but are nonetheless important. Basham suggests that the main propositions of the literature are psychological rather than metaphysical. Suffering, sorrow and dissatisfaction are the nature of ordinary life, and can only be eliminated by giving up desire. In turn, desire is a result of the misplaced belief in the reality of individual existence. In its Theravada form, Hinayana Buddhism taught that there is no soul and ultimately no God. *Nirvana* was a state of rest beyond the universe, once found never lost.

The cosmology

Although the Buddha discouraged the development of cosmologies, the Hinayana Buddhists produced a cyclical view of the universe, evolving through four time periods.

Period 1 Man slowly declines until everything is destroyed except the highest heaven. The good go to this heaven, the remainder to various hells.

Period 2 A quiescent phase.

Period 3 Evolution begins again. However, 'the good *karma* of beings in the highest heaven' now begins to fail, and a lower heaven evolves, a *world of form*. During this period a great being in the higher heaven dies, and is re-born in the world of form as Brahma. Feeling lonely, he wishes that others were with him. Soon other beings from the higher heaven die and are reborn in this world. Brahma interprets these people as his own creation, and himself as The Creator.

Period 4 The first men, who initially had supernatural qualities, deteriorate and become earthbound, and the period fluctuates between advance and deterioration.

The four-period cycles continue for eternity, alternating between 'Buddha cycles' – one of which we live in today – and 'empty cycles'. It is believed that in the present cycle four Buddhas – *Krakucchanda, Kanakamuni, Kasyapa,* and *Sakyamuni* – have already taught, and one, *Maitreya*, is still to come.

In Sri Lanka the scriptures came to be attributed with almost magical powers. Close ties developed between Buddhist belief and **Sinhalese nationalism**. The Sinhalese scholar *Buddhaghosa* translated Sinhalese texts into Pali in the fifth century AD. At the beginning of the 11th century Sri Lankan missionaries were responsible for the conversion of Thailand, Burma, Cambodia and Laos to Theravada Buddhism. Subsequently, in the face of continued threats to their continued survival, Sri Lanka's Buddhist monks had to be re-ordained into the valid line of Theravada lineage by monks from Southeast Asia. Buddhist links with Thailand remain close.

Buddhist practice

By the time Buddhism was brought to Sri Lanka there was a well developed religious organization which had strong links with secular authorities. Developments in Buddhist thought and belief had made it possible for peasants and lay people to share in the religious beliefs of the faith. As it developed in Sri Lanka the main outlines of practice became clearly defined. The king and the orders of monks became interdependent; a monastic hierarchy was established; most monks were learning and teaching, rather than practising withdrawal from the world. Most important, Buddhism accepted a much wider range of goals for living than simply the release from permanent rebirth.

The most important of these were 'good rebirth', the prevention of misfortune and the increase in good fortune during the present life. These additions to original Buddhist thought led to a number of contradictions and tensions, summarized by Tambiah as: the Buddha as a unique individual, rather than a type of person (*Bodhisattva*) coming into the world periodically to help achieve release from *samsara* (rebirth), or rebirth into a better life; Buddhism as a path to salvation for all, or as a particular, nationalist religion; Buddhism as renunciation of the world and all its obligations, in contrast with playing a positive social role; and finally, whether monasteries should be run by the monks themselves, or with the support and involvement of secular authorities. These tensions are reflected in many aspects of Buddhism in Sri Lanka today, as in debates between monks who argue for political action as against withdrawal from the world.

Four Noble Truths

The Buddha preached Four Noble Truths: that life is painful; that suffering is caused by ignorance and desire; that beyond the suffering of life there is a state which cannot be described but which he termed *nirvana*; and that nirvana can be reached by following an eightfold path.

The concept of nirvana is often understood in the West in an entirely negative sense – that of 'non-being'.

The word has the rough meaning of 'blow out' or 'extinguish', meaning to blow out the fires of greed, lust and desire. In a positive sense it has been described by one Buddhist scholar as 'the state of absolute illumination, supreme bliss, infinite love and compassion, unshakeable serenity, and unrestricted spiritual freedom'. The essential elements of the eightfold path are the perfection of wisdom, morality and meditation.

Sects Until the 16th century Buddhism in Sri Lanka enjoyed the active support of the state. It remained longest in Kandy, but was withdrawn steadily after the British took control in 1815. The 18th-century revival of Buddhism in the Wet Zone was sponsored by the landowning village headmen, not by royalty, and castes such as the *Goyigama* and *Salagama* played a prominent role. Through the 19th century they became the dominant influence on Buddhist thought, while the remaining traditional Buddhist authority in Kandy, the *Siyam Nikaya*, suffered permanent loss of influence.

The *Siyam Nikaya*, one of the three sects of Sri Lankan Buddhism today, originated in the 18th mission of the Kandyan kings to Ayuthya in Thailand (Siam) to revalidate the Buddhist clergy. By a royal order admission to the sect's two branches was restricted to high caste Sinhalese. Today their monks are distinguished by carrying umbrellas and wearing their robe over one shoulder only. The exclusion of lower castes from this sect however bred resentment, and in 1803 a new sect, the *Amarapura Nikaya*, was established to be open to all castes, while in 1835 the third contemporary sect, the *Ramanya Nikaya*, was set up in protest at the supposedly excessive materialism of the other two. Both these sects wear robes which cover both shoulders, but while the *Amarapura* sect carry umbrellas the *Ramanya* carries a traditional shade. Sri Lankan monks wear orange robes and take the vows of celibacy and non-possession of worldly wealth, owning only the very basic necessities including two robes, begging bowl, a razor, needle and thread. They do not eat after midday and spend part of the day in study and meditation. The order of nuns which was introduced in Sri Lanka in the early days was short-lived.

This new, independent Buddhism, became active and militant. It entered into direct competition with Christians in proselytizing, and in setting up schools, special associations and social work. After Independence, political forces converged to encourage State support for Buddhism. The lay leadership pressed the government to protect Buddhists from competition with other religious groups. The Sinhalese political parties saw benefits in emphasizing the role of Buddhism in society.

Buddhist worship

The Buddha himself refuted all ideas of a personal God and of worshipping a deity, but subsequent trends in Buddhism have often found a place for popular worship. Even in the relatively orthodox Theravada Buddhism of Sri Lanka personal devotion and worship are common, focused on key elements of the faith. Temple complexes (*pansalas*) commonly have several features which can serve as foci for individual devotion. Stupas or *dagobas*, which enshrine personal relics of the Buddha, are the most prominent, but Bodhi or Bo trees and images of the Buddha also act as objects of veneration.

Sri Lankan Buddhists place particular emphasis on the sanctity of the relics of the Buddha which are believed to have been brought to the island. The two most important are the sacred Bo tree and the tooth of the Buddha. The Bo tree at Anuradhapura is believed to be a cutting from the Bo tree under which the Buddha himself achieved Enlightenment at Bodh Gaya in modern Bihar. The Emperor Asoka is recorded as having entrusted the cutting to Mahinda's sister Sanghamitta to be carried to Sri Lanka on their mission of taking Buddhism to the island. As the original Bo tree in Bodh Gaya was cut down, this is the only tree in the world believed to come directly from the original tree under which the Buddha sat, and is visited by Buddhists from all over the world. Many other Bo trees in Sri Lanka have been grown from cuttings of the Anuradhapura Bo tree.

The tooth of the Buddha, now enshrined at the Dalada Maligawa in Kandy, was not brought to Sri Lanka until the fourth century AD. The Portuguese reported that they had captured and destroyed the original tooth in their attempt to wipe out all evidence of other religious faiths, but the Sinhalese claimed to have hidden it and allowed a replica to have been stolen. Today pilgrims flock from all over the island, queuing for days on special occasions when special access is granted to the casket holding the tooth in the Dalada Maligawa.

In ordinary daily life many Buddhists will visit temples at least once a week on *poya* days, which correspond with the four quarters of the moon. Full moon day, a national holiday, is a particularly important festival day (see page 32). It is also an opportunity for the worship of non-Buddhist deities who have become a part of popular Buddhist religion. Some have their origins explicitly in Hinduism. The four Guardian Deities seen as future Buddhas, include Natha, Vishnu, Skanda and Saman. **Skanda**, described below, the Hindu god of war, is worshipped as Kataragama, and **Vishnu** is seen as the island's protector. It is not surprising, therefore, to see the Hindu deities in Buddhist temples. Other deities have come from the Mahayana branch of Buddhism, such as **Natha**, or *Maitreya*, the future Buddha. Thus in worship as in many other aspects of daily life, Sinhalese Buddhism shares much in common with Hindu belief and practice with which it has lived side by side for more than 2000 years.

A final feature of Buddhist worship which is held in common with Hindu worship is its individualism. Congregational worship is usually absent, and individuals will normally visit the temple, sometimes soliciting the help of a *bhikku* in making an offering or saying special prayers. One of the chief aims of the Buddhist is to earn merit (*punya karma*), for this is the path to achieving nirvana. Merit can be earned by selfless giving, often of donations in the temple, or by gifts to *bhikkus*, who make regular house calls early in the morning seeking alms. In addition merit can be gained by right living, and especially by propagating the faith both by speech and listening.

Caste system

Some elements of the caste system were probably present in pre-Buddhist Sri Lanka, with both the priestly caste of Brahmins and a range of low caste groups such as scavengers. Although Buddhism encouraged its followers to eradicate distinctions based on caste, the system clearly survived and became a universal feature of social structures among Buddhists and subsequently Christians, despite their beliefs which explicitly condemn such social stratification. However, the complexities and some of the harsh exclusiveness of the caste system as practised in India was modified in Sri Lanka.

Sinhalese Buddhism has no Brahmin or Kshatriya caste, although some groups claim a warrior lineage. The caste enjoying highest social status and the greatest numbers is the Goyigama, a caste of cultivators and landowners who are widely seen as roughly equivalent to the Vellala caste among Jaffna Tamils. The Bandaras and the Radalas comprise a sub-caste of the Goyigamas who for generations have formed a recognizable aristocracy. Among many other castes lower down the social hierarchy come fishermen (Karavas), washermen (Hena), and toddy tappers (Durava).

Some caste groups, such as the **Karava**, have achieved significant changes in their status. Ryan suggests for example that the original Karava community came from South India and converted to Buddhism and began to speak Sinhalese while retaining their fishing livelihoods. Subsequently many converted to Roman Catholicism, located as they were in the heart of the coastal region just north of modern Colombo controlled by the Portuguese. Through their conversion many Karavas received privileges reserved by the Portuguese for Christians, enabling them to climb up the social ladder. Thus today, unlike the fishing communities of Tamil Nadu who remain among the lowest castes, the Karava are now among Sri Lanka's upper caste communities.

Hinduism

Hinduism in northern Sri Lanka was brought over by successive Tamil kings and their followers. It has always been easier to define Hinduism by what it is not than by what it is. Indeed, the name Hinduism was given by foreigners to the peoples of the sub-continent who did not profess the other major faiths, such as Muslims, Christians or Buddhists. The beliefs and practices of modern Hinduism began to take shape in the centuries on either side of the birth of Christ. But while some aspects of modern Hinduism can be traced back more than 2000 years before that, other features are recent. Hinduism has undergone major changes both in belief and practice. Such changes came from outside as well as from within. As early as sixth century BC the Buddhists and Jains had tried to reform the religion of Vedism (or Brahmanism) which had been dominant in some parts of South Asia for 500 years.

Modern Hinduism

A number of ideas run like a thread through intellectual and popular Hinduism, some being shared with Buddhism. Some Hindu scholars and philosophers talk of Hinduism as one religious and cultural tradition, in which the enormous variety of belief and practice can ultimately be interpreted as interwoven in a common view of the world. Yet there is no Hindu organization, like a church, with the authority to define belief or establish official practice. Although the Vedas are still regarded as sacred by most Hindus, virtually no modern Hindu either shares the beliefs of the Vedic writers or their practices, such as sacrifice, which died out 1500 years ago. Not all Hindu groups believe in a single supreme God. In view of these characteristics, many authorities argue that it is misleading to think of Hinduism as a religion at all.

Be that as it may, the evidence of the living importance of Hinduism is visible among Hindu communities in Sri Lanka as well as in India. Hindu philosophy and practice has also touched many of those who belong to other religious traditions, particularly in terms of social institutions such as caste.

Four human goals

For many Hindus there are four major human goals: material prosperity (*artha*), the satisfaction of desires (*kama*), and performing the duties laid down according to your position in life (*dharma*). Beyond those is the goal of achieving liberation from the endless cycle of rebirths into which everyone is locked (*moksha*). It is to the search for liberation that the major schools of Indian philosophy have devoted most attention. Together with *dharma*, it is basic to Hindu thought.

Dharma

Dharma (dhamma to Buddhists) represents the order inherent in human life. It is essentially secular rather than religious, for it doesn't depend on any revelation or command of God but rather has 10 'embodiments': good name, truth, self-control, cleanness of mind and body, simplicity, endurance, resoluteness of character, giving and sharing, austerities and continence. In *dharmic* thinking these are inseparable from five patterns of behaviour: non-violence, an attitude of equality, peace and tranquillity, lack of aggression and cruelty, and absence of envy.

Karma

According to *karma*, every person, animal or god has a being or self which has existed without beginning. Every action, except those that are done without any consideration of the results, leaves an indelible mark on that self. This is carried forward into the next life, and the overall character of the imprint on each person's 'self' determines three features of the next life. It controls the nature of his next birth (animal, human or god) and the kind of family he will be born into if human. It determines the length of the next life. Finally, it controls the good or bad experiences that the self will experience. However, it does not imply a fatalistic belief that the nature of action in this life is unimportant. Rather, it suggests that the path followed by the individual in the present life is vital to the nature of its next life, and ultimately to the chance of gaining release from this world.

Rebirth

The belief in the transmigration of souls (*samsara*) in a never-ending cycle of rebirth has been Hinduism's most distinctive and important contribution to the culture of India and Sri Lanka. The earliest reference to the belief is found in one of the Upanishads, around the seventh century BC, at about the same time as the doctrine of karma made its first appearance. By the late Upanishads it was universally accepted, and in Buddhism there is never any questioning of the belief.

Ahimsa

AL Basham pointed out that belief in transmigration must have encouraged a further distinctive doctrine, that of non-violence or non-injury – *ahimsa*. Buddhism campaigned particularly vigorously against the then-existing practice of animal sacrifice. The belief in rebirth meant that all living things and creatures of the spirit – people, devils, gods, animals, even worms – possessed the same essential soul.

Hindu philosophy

It is common now to talk of six major schools of Hindu philosophy. The best known are yoga and Vedanta. Yoga is concerned with systems of meditation that can lead ultimately to release from the cycle of rebirth. It can be traced back as a system of thought to at least the third century AD. It is just one part of the wider system known as Vedanta, literally the final parts of the Vedantic literature, the *Upanishads*. The basic texts also include the *Brahmasutra of Badrayana*, written about the first century AD, and the most important of all, the *Bhagavadgita*, which is a part of the epic the *Mahabharata*.

Hindu worship

Some Hindus believe in one all-powerful God who created all the lesser gods and the universe. The Hindu gods include many whose origins lie in the Vedic deities of the early Aryans. These were often associated with the **forces of nature**, and Hindus have always revered many natural objects. Mountain tops, trees, rocks and above all rivers, are regarded as sites of special religious significance. They all have their own guardian spirits. You can see the signs of the continuing lively belief in these gods and demons wherever you travel. Thus trees for example are often painted with vertical red and white stripes and will have a small shrine at their base. Occasionally branches of trees will have numerous pieces of thread or strips of coloured cloth tied to them – placed there by devotees with the prayer for fulfilment of a favour. Hilltops will frequently have a shrine of some kind at the highest point, dedicated to a particularly powerful god. Pilgrimage to some important Hindu shrines is often undertaken by Buddhists as well as Hindus.

For most Hindus today worship (often referred to as 'performing **puja**') is an integral part of their faith. The great majority of Hindu homes will have a shrine to one of the gods of the Hindu pantheon. Individuals and families will often visit shrines or temples, and on special occasions will travel long distances to particularly holy places such as Kataragama. Acts of devotion are often aimed at the granting of favours and the meeting of urgent needs for this life – good health, finding a suitable wife or husband, the birth of a son, prosperity and good fortune. In this respect the popular devotion of simple pilgrims of all faiths in South Asia is remarkably similar when they visit shrines, whether Hindu, Buddhist or Jain temples, the tombs of Muslim saints or even churches. Performing *puja* involves making an offering to God, and darshan – having a view of the deity. Although there are devotional movements among Hindus in which singing and praying is practised in groups, Hindu worship is generally an act performed by individuals. Thus Hindu temples may be little more than a shrine in the middle of the street, housing an image of the deity which will be tended by a priest and visited at special times when a darshan of the resident God can be obtained. When it has been consecrated, the image, if exactly made, becomes the channel for the godhead to work.

The **image** of the deity may be in one of many forms. Temples may be dedicated to Vishnu or Siva, for example, or to any one of their other representations. The image of the deity becomes the object of worship and the centre of the temple's rituals. These often follow through the cycle of day and night, as well as yearly life cycles. The priests may wake the deity from sleep, bathe, clothe and feed it. Worshippers will be invited to share in this process by bringing offerings of clothes and food. Gifts of money will usually be made, and in some temples there is a charge levied for taking up positions in front of the deity in order to obtain a darshan at the appropriate times.

Hindu sects

Today three Gods are widely seen as all-powerful: **Brahma**, **Vishnu** and **Siva**. Their functions and character are not readily separated. While Brahma is regarded as the ultimate source of creation, Siva also has a creative role alongside his function as destroyer. Vishnu in contrast is seen as the preserver or protector of the universe. There are very few images and sculptures of Brahma, but Vishnu and Siva are far more widely represented and have come to be seen as the most powerful and important. Their followers are referred to as Vaishnavite and Saivites respectively, the majority in Sri Lanka today being Saivites.

Caste

One of the defining characteristics of South Asian societies, caste has helped to shape the social life of most religious communities in South Asia. Although the word caste (meaning 'unmixed' or 'pure') was given by the Portuguese in the 15th century AD, the main features of the system emerged at the end of the Vedic period. In Sri Lanka the Tamils of Jaffna have a modified form of the caste social structure typical of neighbouring Tamil Nadu. Brahmins occupy the same priestly position that they hold in India, and have also played an important role in education. Beneath them in ritual hierarchy but occupying a dominant social and political position, until recent times at least, were the cultivating and landlord caste known as the *vellalas*. Below them in rank was a range of low and outcaste groups, filling such occupations as washermen, sweepers and barbers, such as the Pallas and Nallavas. The tea plantation workers are all regarded as low caste.

Virtually all Hindu temples in Sri Lanka were destroyed by the Portuguese and the Dutch. Those that have been rebuilt never had the resources available to compare with those in India. However, they play a prominent part in Hindu life. De Silva suggests that Arumuga Navalar's failure to argue for social reform meant that caste – and untouchability – were virtually untouched. The high caste Vellalas, a small minority of the total Hindu population, maintained their power unchallenged until after Independence. Removal of caste disabilities started in the 1950s. The civil war over the demand for a separate Tamil state, Tamil Eelam, during which the Liberation Tigers of Tamil Eelam (LTTE) took complete control of social and political life in Jaffna and the north, may have changed the whole basis of caste far more thoroughly than any programme of social reform.

Islam

Islam was brought to Sri Lanka by Arab traders. Long before the followers of the Prophet Mohammad spread the new religion of Islam, Arabs had been trading across the Indian Ocean with southwest India, the Maldives, Sri Lanka and South East Asia. When the Arab world became Muslim the newly converted Arab traders brought Islam with them, and existing communities of Arab origin adopted the new faith. However, numbers were also swelled by conversion from both Buddhists and Hindus, and by immigrant Muslims from South India who fled the Portuguese along the west coast of India. The great majority of the present Muslim population of Sri Lanka is Tamil speaking, although there are also Muslims of Malay origin. Both in Kandy and the coastal districts Muslims have generally lived side by side with Buddhists, often sharing common interests against the colonial powers. However, one of the means by which Muslims maintained their identity was to refuse to be drawn into colonial education. As a result, by the end of the 19th century the Muslims were among the least educated groups. A Muslim lawyer, Siddi Lebbe, helped to change attitudes and encourage participation by Muslims.

In 1915 there were major Sinhalese-Muslim riots, and Muslims began a period of active collaboration with the British, joining other minorities led by the Tamils in the search for security and protection of their rights against the Sinhalese. The Muslims have been particularly anxious to maintain Muslim family law, and to gain concessions on education.

One of the chief of these is the teaching of Arabic in government schools to Muslim children. Until 1974 Muslims were unique among minorities in having the right to choose which of three languages – Sinhala, Tamil or English – would be their medium of instruction. Since then a new category of Muslim schools has been set up, allowing them to distance themselves from the Tamil Hindu community, whose language most of them speak.

Muslim beliefs

The beliefs of Islam (which means 'submission to God') could apparently scarcely be more different from those of Buddhism or Hinduism. Islam has a fundamental creed; 'There is no God but God; and Mohammad is the Prophet of God' (*La Illaha illa 'Ilah Mohammad Rasulu 'Ilah*). One book, the Qur'an, is the supreme authority on Islamic teaching and faith. Islam preaches the belief in bodily resurrection after death, and in the reality of heaven and hell.

The idea of heaven as paradise is pre-Islamic. Alexander the Great is believed to have introduced the word paradise into Greek from Persia, where he used it to describe the walled Persian gardens that were found even three centuries before the birth of Christ. For Muslims, paradise is believed to be filled with sensuous delights and pleasures, while hell is a place of eternal terror and torture, which is the certain fate of all who deny the unity of God.

Islam has no priesthood. The authority of Imams derives from social custom, and from their authority to interpret the scriptures, rather than from a defined status within the Islamic community. Islam also prohibits any distinction on the basis of race or colour, and there is a strong antipathy to the representation of the human figure. It is often thought, inaccurately, that this ban stems from the Qur'an itself. In fact it probably has its origins in the belief of Mohammad that images were likely to be turned into idols.

Muslim sects

During the first century of its existence Islam split in two sects which were divided on political and religious grounds, the Shi'is and Sunnis. The religious basis for the division lay in the interpretation of verses in the Qur'an and of traditional sayings of Mohammad, the *Hadis*. Both sects venerate the Qur'an but have different *Hadis*. They also have different views as to Mohammad's successor.

The **Sunnis** – always the majority in South Asia – believe that Mohammad did not appoint a successor, and that Abu Bak'r, Omar and Othman were the first three caliphs (or vice-regents) after Mohammad's death. Ali, whom the Sunni's count as the fourth Caliph, is regarded as the first legitimate Caliph by the Shi'is, who consider Abu Bak'r and Omar to be usurpers. While the Sunni's believe in the principle of election of caliphs, **Shi'is** believe that although Mohammad is the last prophet there is a continuing need for intermediaries between God and man. Such intermediaries are termed Imams, and they base both their law and religious practice on the teaching of the Imams.

From the Mughal Emperors in India, who enjoyed an unparalleled degree of political power, down to the poorest fishermen in Sri Lanka, Muslims in South Asia have found different ways of adjusting to their Hindu or Buddhist environment. Some have reacted by accepting or even incorporating features of Hindu belief and practice in their own. Akbar, the most eclectic of Mughal emperors, went as far as banning activities like cow slaughter which were offensive to Hindus and celebrating Hindu festivals in court.

Muslim year

The first day of the Muslim calendar is AD 16 July 622. This was the date of the prophet's migration from Mecca to Medina, the Hijra, from which the date's name is taken (AH = Anno Hijrae). The Muslim year is divided into 12 lunar months, alternating between 29 and 30 days. The first month of the year is *Moharram*, followed by *Safar, Rabi-ul-Awwal, Rabi-ul- Sani, Jumada-ul-Awwal, Jumada-ul-Sani, Rajab, Shaban, Ramadan, Shawwal, Ziquad* and *Zilhaj*.

Significant dates

New Year's Day – 1st of *Moharram*

Anniversary of the killing of the Prophet's grandson Hussain, commemorated by Shi'i Muslims – 9th and 10th of *Moharram*

Birthday of the Prophet (Milad-ul-Nabi) – 12th of *Rabi-ul-Awwal*

Start of the fasting month – 1st of *Ramadan*

Night of prayer (Shab-e-Qadr) – 21st of *Ramadan*

Three-day festival to mark the end of Ramadan – 1st of *Shawwal: Id-ul-Fitr*

Two-day festival commemorating the sacrifice of Ismail; the main time of pilgrimage to Mecca (the Haj). An animal (goat) is sacrificed and special meat and vermicelli dishes are prepared – 10th of *Zilhaj: Id-ul-Ajha*

Christianity

Christianity was introduced by the Portuguese. Unlike India, where Christian missionary work from the late 18th century was often carried out in spite of colonial government rather than with its active support, in Sri Lanka missionary activity enjoyed various forms of state backing. One Sinhalese king, Dharmapala, was converted, endowing the church, and even some high caste families became Christian. When the Dutch evicted the Portuguese they tried to suppress Roman Catholicism, and the Dutch Reformed Church found some converts. Other Protestant denominations followed the arrival of the British, though not always with official support or encouragement. Many of the churches remained dependent on outside support. Between the two World Wars Christian influence in government was radically reduced. Denominational schools lost their protection and special status, and since the 1960s have had to come to terms with a completely different role in Sri Lanka.

Christian beliefs

Christian theology had its roots in Judaism, with its belief in one eternal God, the Creator of the universe. Judaism saw the Jewish people as the vehicle for God's salvation, the 'chosen people of God', and pointed to a time when God would send his Saviour, or Messiah. Jesus, whom Christians believe was 'the Christ' or Messiah, was born in the village of Bethlehem, some 20 km south of Jerusalem. Very little is known of his early life except that he was brought up in a devout Jewish family. At the age of 29 or 30 he gathered a small group of followers and began to preach in the region between the Dead Sea and the Sea of Galilee. Two years later he was crucified in Jerusalem by the authorities on the charge of blasphemy – that he claimed to be the son of God.

Christians believe that all people live in a state of sin, in the sense that they are separated from God and fail to do his will. They believe that God is personal, 'like a father'. As God's son, Jesus accepted the cost of that separation and sinfulness himself through his death on the cross. Christians believe that Jesus was raised from the dead on the third day after he was crucified, and that he appeared to his closest followers. They believe that his spirit continues to live today, and that he makes it possible for people to come back to God.

The New Testament of the Bible, which, alongside the Old Testament, is the text to which Christians refer as the ultimate scriptural authority, consists of four 'Gospels' (meaning 'good news'), and a series of letters by several early Christians referring to the nature of the Christian life.

Christian worship

Although Christians are encouraged to worship individually as well as together, most forms of Christian worship centre on the gathering of the church congregation for praise, prayer the preaching of God's word, which usually takes verses from the Bible as its starting point. Different denominations place varying emphases on the main elements of worship, but in most church services today the congregation will take part in singing hymns (songs of praise), prayers will be led by the minister, priest or a member of the congregation, readings from the Bible will be given and a sermon preached. For many Christians the most important service is the act of Holy Communion (Protestant) or Mass (Catholic) which celebrates the death and resurrection of Jesus in sharing bread and wine, which are held to represent Christ's body and blood given to save people from their sin. Although Christian services may be held daily in some churches most Christian congregations in Sri Lanka meet for worship on Sunday, and services are held in Sinhala and Tamil as well as in English. They are open to all.

Denominations

Between the second and the fourth centuries AD there were numerous debates about the interpretation of Christian doctrine, sometimes resulting in the formation of specific groups focusing on particular interpretations of faith. One such group was that of the Nestorian Christians, who played a major part in the theology of the Syrian Church in Kerala. They regarded the Syrian patriarch of the east their spiritual head, and followed the Nestorian tradition that there were two distinct natures in Christ, the divine and human. However, although some believe that St Thomas and other early Christians came to Sri Lanka as well as South India the early church left no real mark on the island.

Today Roman Catholics account for 90% of the island's Christians. The Roman Catholic church believes that Christ declared that his disciple Peter should be the first spiritual head of the Church, and that his successors should lead the Church on earth. Modern Catholic churches still recognize the spiritual authority of the Pope and cardinals.

The reformation which took place in Europe from the 16th century onwards resulted in the creation of the Protestant churches, which became dominant in several European countries. They reasserted the authority of the Bible over that of the church. A number of new denominations were created. This process of division left a profound mark on the nature of the Christian church as it spread into South Asia. The Dutch brought with them their Dutch Reformed faith and left a number of churches, and subsequently during British colonial period the Anglican Church (Church of England) also became established, and several Protestant missionary denominations including Baptist and Methodist, established small churches. The reunification of the Protestant Christian churches which has taken significant steps since 1947 has progressed faster in South Asia than in most other parts of the world.

Architecture

Sri Lankan architecture has many elements in common with Buddhist and Hindu Indian traditions, but the long period of relative isolation, and the determined preservation of Buddhism long after its demise in India, have contributed to some very distinctive features.

Buddhist architecture

Buddhist and Hindu architecture probably began with wooden building, for the rock carving and cave excavated temples show clear evidence of copying styles which must have been developed first in wooden buildings. The third and second century BC caves of the Buddhists were followed in the seventh and eighth centuries AD by free standing but rock-cut temples.

Stupas

Stupas were the most striking feature of Buddhist architecture in India. Originally they were funeral mounds, built to house the remains of the Buddha and his disciples. The tradition of building stupas was developed by Sri Lanka's Sinhalese kings, notably in the golden age of the fourth and fifth centuries AD, and the revival during the 11th and 12th centuries. In Sri Lanka, a stupa is often referred to as '*dagoba*' (from Sanskrit *dhatu* – relic, *garbha* – womb chamber) and sometimes named '*saya*' (from *cetiya* - funeral mound) or '*wehera*' (from *vihara* – monastery). Some of the stupas (*dagobas*) are huge structures, and even those such as the fourth century *Jetavana* at Anuradhapura, now simply a grassed-over brick mound, is impressively large.

Few of the older Buddhist monuments are in their original form, either having become ruins or been renovated. Hemispherical mounds built of brick and filled with brick and rubble, they stand on a square terrace, surmounted by three concentric platforms. In its original or its restored form, the brick mound is covered with plaster and painted white. Surrounding it on a low platform (*vahalakadas*) is the ambulatory, or circular path, reached from the cardinal directions by stone stairways. Around some of the *dagobas* there are fine sculptures on these circular paths at the head of each stairway.

The design is filled with symbolic meaning. The hemisphere is the dome of heaven, the axis of the cosmos being represented by the central finial on top, while the umbrella-like tiers are the rising heavens of the gods. Worshippers walk round the stupa on the raised platform in a clockwise direction (*pradakshina*), following the rotational movement of the celestial bodies.

Many smaller stupas were built within circular buildings. These were covered with a metal and timber roof resting on concentric rows of stone pillars. Today the roofs have disappeared, but examples such as the Vatadage at Polonnaruwa can still be seen. King Parakramabahu I also built another feature of Sri Lankan architecture at Polonnaruwa, a large rectangular hall in which was placed an image of the Buddha. Most of Sri Lanka's early secular architecture has disappeared. Made of wood, there are remnants of magnificent royal palaces at both Anuradhapura and Sigiriya.

Moonstones

Sri Lanka's moonstones (not the gem) are among the world's finest artistic achievements. Polished semi-circular granite, they are carved in concentric semi-circular rings ('half-moons', about 1 m in radius) portraying various animals, flowers and birds, and normally placed at the foot of flights of steps or entrances to important buildings. There are particularly fine examples in Anuradhapura and Polonnaruwa.

The moonstones of pure Buddhist art at Anuradhapura comprise a series of rings and are often interpreted in the following way. You step over the flames of fire, through which one must pass to be purified. The next ring shows animals which represent the four stages of life: 1 Elephant - birth; 2 Horse - old age; 3 Lion - illness; 4 Bull – death and decay. These continue in an endless cycle symbolizing the continuous rebirths to which one is subject. The third row represents the twisting serpent of lust and desire, while the fourth is that of geese carrying lotus buds, representing purity. The lotus in the centre is a symbol of nirvana.

The steps have on either side beautifully carved **guard stones** with *makaras* designed to incorporate features from eight symbolically significant creatures: the foot of the lion, the crocodile's mouth and teeth, an elephant's tusk, the body of a fish, the peacock's feather, the serpent inside the mouth and the monkey's eyes.

Hindu architecture

Hindu temple building

The principles of religious building were laid down in the *Sastras*, sets of rules compiled by priests. Every aspect of Hindu and Buddhist religious building is identified with conceptions of the structure of the universe. This applies as much to the process of building – the timing of which must be undertaken at astrologically propitious times – as to the formal layout of the buildings. The cardinal directions of north, south, east and west are the basic fix on which buildings are planned. The east-west axis is nearly always a fundamental building axis.

Hindu temples were nearly always built to a clear and universal design, which had built into it philosophical understandings of the universe. This cosmology, of an infinite number of universes, isolated from each other in space, proceeds by imagining various possibilities as to its nature. Its centre is seen as dominated by **Mount Meru** which keeps earth and heaven apart. The concept of separation is crucial to Hindu thought and social practice. Continents, rivers and oceans occupy concentric rings around the mountain, while the stars encircle the mountain in another plane. Humans live on the continent of **Jambudvipa**, characterized by the rose apple tree (*jambu*).

The *Sastras* show plans of this continent, organized in concentric rings and entered at the cardinal points. This type of diagram was known as a **mandala**. Such a geometric scheme could then be subdivided into almost limitless small compartments, each of which could be designated as having special properties or be devoted to a particular deity. The centre of the mandala would be the seat of the major god. Mandalas provided the ground rules for the building of stupas and temples across India, and provided the key to the symbolic meaning attached to every aspect of religious buildings.

Temple design

Hindu temples developed characteristic plans and elevations. The focal point of the temple lay in its sanctuary, the home of the presiding deity, known as the womb-chamber (*garbhagriha*). A series of doorways, in large temples leading through a succession of buildings, allowed the worshipper to move towards the final encounter with the deity himself and to obtain *darshan* – a sight of the god. Both Buddhist and Hindu worship encourages the worshipper to walk clockwise around the shrine, performing *pradakshina*.

Grand designs

In May 2003, Sri Lanka mourned the death of Geoffrey Bawa, the island's best known, most prolific and most influential architect. Amongst his many projects Bawa was the creative visionary behind some of the Sri Lanka's most spectacular hotels, from the austerity of the 1-km-long camouflaged jungle palace of Kandalama near Dambulla, to the colonial-influenced Lighthouse at Galle. He also constructed Sri Lanka's first purpose-built tourist complex, the Bentota Beach in 1968.

Bawa's work blends traditional Sri Lankan architecture and use of materials with modern ideas of composition and space. Hallmarks include a careful balance, and blurring of the boundaries, between inside and outside, the creation of vistas, courtyards and walkways that offer a range of perspectives, and an acute sensitivity to setting and environment. His work builds on Sri Lanka's past, absorbing ideas from the west and east, while creating something innovative and definably Sri Lankan.

Born in 1919 to wealthy parents, Bawa went to England in 1938, where he studied English at Cambridge and took up the law. Soon tiring of this, he spent some years drifting and it was not until 1957, at the age of 38, that he qualified as an architect. On his return to Ceylon, he gathered together a group of talented young artists who shared his interest in the island's forgotten architectural heritage, including batik artist Ena de Silva (see page 258) and designer Barbara Sansoni (see page 83). The prolific practice he established set new standards in design over the next 20 years for all styles of buildings, from the residential and commercial to the religious and the educational.

Bawa's fame was sealed in 1979 when he was invited by President Jayawardene to design the new parliament building in Kotte. The result, which required the dredging of a swamp to create an artificial lake and island, itself symbolising the great irrigation of the ancient period, was a series of terraces with copper domed roofs rising from the water, with references to monastic architecture, Kandyan temples and South Indian palace architecture, all within a Modernist framework. Other high profile buildings followed including the Ruhuna University near Matara, dramatically arranged on two rocky hills overlooking the ocean.

In 1998 he suffered a massive stroke. Although it rendered him paralysed his colleagues completed his projects with a nod of assent or shake of the head from the bed-ridden master. In the same year he was honoured privately by his friend the Prince of Wales who snuck away from the official 50th anniversary celebrations to pay him tribute; official recognition followed in 2001 when he was awarded the prestigious Chairman's Award for Lifetime Achievements by the Aga Khan.

The elevations are designed to be symbolic representations of the home of the gods, the tallest towers rising above the *garbagriha* itself, symbolizing the meeting of earth and heaven in the person of the enshrined deity. In both, the basic structure is usually richly embellished with sculpture. When first built this would usually have been plastered and painted, and often covered in gems. In contrast to the extraordinary profusion of colour and life on the outside, the interior is dark and cramped. Here is the true centre of power.

Hindu architecture on the island bears close resemblances with the Dravida styles of neighbouring Tamil Nadu. Although all the important Hindu temples in Sri Lanka were destroyed by the Portuguese, the style in which they have been re-built continues to reflect those southern Indian traditions.

Tamil Nadu has been at the heart of southern Indian religious development for 2000 years. Temple building was a comparatively late development in Hindu worship. Long before the first temple was built shrines were dotted across the land, the focus of **pilgrimage**, each with its own mythology. Even the most majestic of South Indian temples have basic features in common with these original shrines, and many of them have simply grown by a process of accretion around a shrine which may have been in that spot for centuries. The **myths** that grew around the shrines were expressed first by word of mouth. Most temples today still have versions of the stories which were held to justify their existence in the eyes of pilgrims. There are several basic features in common. David Shulman has written that the story will include 'the (usually miraculous) discovery of the site and the adventures of those important exemplars (such as gods, demons, serpents, and men) who were freed from sorrow of one kind or another by worshipping there'. The shrine which is the object of the story nearly always claims to be supreme, better than all others. Many stories illustrate these claims of superiority: for example, we are often told that the **Goddess Ganga** herself is forced to worship in a South Indian shrine in order to become free of the sins deposited by evil-doers who bathe in the river at Benares. Through all its great diversity Hindu temple architecture repeatedly expresses these beliefs, shared though not necessarily expressed, by the thousands of Sri Lankan Hindus who make visiting temples such a vital and living part of their life.

Today the most striking external features of Hindu temples in Sri Lanka are their elaborately carved towering gateways (*gopurams*). These were first introduced by the **Pandiyas** in the 10th century, who succeeded the Cholas a century later. The *gopuram* took its name from the 'cow gate' of the Vedic village, which later became the city gate and finally the monumental temple entrance. This type of tower has an oblong plan at the top which is an elongated vaulted roof with gable ends. It has sloping sides, usually 65°, so that the section at the top is about half the size of the base. Although the first two storeys are usually built solidly of stone masonry, the rest is of lighter material.

By the 15th century the Vijayanagar kings established their empire across much of South India. Their temples were built on an unprecedented scale, with huge *gopurams* studding the outside walls. None of the Sri Lankan temples were built on a scale anywhere near that of the 16th- and 17th-century Vijayanagar temples of South India. Furthermore, all Hindu temples were destroyed by the Portuguese during the period in which Vijayanagar architecture was flourishing across the Palk Straits. Thus contemporary Hindu temples in Sri Lanka, while retaining some of the elements common to Hindu temples in Tamil Nadu, are always on a much smaller scale.

Art

Sculpture

Early Sri Lankan sculpture shows close links with Indian Buddhist sculpture. The first images of the Buddha, some of which are still in Anuradhapura, are similar to second and third century AD images from Amaravati in modern Andhra Pradesh. The middle period of the fifth to 11th centuries AD contains some magnificent sculptures on rocks, but there is a range of other sculpture, notably moonstones. There are decorated bands of flower motifs, geese and a variety of animals, both Anuradhapura and Polonnaruwa having outstanding examples. While the moonstones are brilliant works in miniature, Sri Lankan sculptors also produced outstanding colossal works, such as the 13-m-high Buddha at Aukana, now dated as from the ninth century, or the 13th-century reclining Buddha at Polonnaruwa.

Painting

Sri Lanka's most famous art is its rock paintings from Sigiriya, dating from the sixth century AD. The *apsaras* (heavenly nymphs), scattering flowers from the clouds, are shown with extraordinary grace and beauty (you may notice the absence of the black pigment). Polonnaruwa saw a later flowering of the painting tradition in the 12th and 13th centuries. The Thivanka murals depict tales from the *Jatakas* and the Buddha's life, some elaborating and extending the strictly religious subject by introducing scenery and architectural elements. The wall paintings of Dambulla are also noteworthy (although many of the original paintings were covered by later ones), but thereafter classical Sri Lankan art declined though the folk tradition of scroll painting carried on.

The mid-18th century saw a new revival of painting in the Kandyan kingdom, this time based on folk art which were inspired by traditional tales instead of religious themes. Many survive in temples around Kandy and elsewhere in the southwest.

Crafts

Local craft skills are still practised widely in households across the country. Pottery, coir fibre, carpentry, handloom weaving and metalwork all receive government assistance. Some of the crafts are concentrated in just a few villages. **Brasswork**, for example, is restricted to a small area around Kandy, where the 'city of arts', Kalapura, has over 70 families of craftsmen making superb brass, wood, silver and gold items. Fine **gold and silver chain work** is done in the Pettah area of Colombo. **Batiks**, from wall hangings to *lungis* (sarongs), and a wide range of cotton **handloom**, in vibrant colours and textures are widely available. **Silver jewellery** (also from Kandy), trays, ornaments and inlay work is a further specialization. **Masks** are a popular product in the southwest of the island, especially around Ambalangoda, based on traditional masks used in dance dramas, while Galle is famous for pillow **lace** and crochet. **Reed**, cane, rattan are fashioned into attractive household goods, while fine **woodcarving** and colourful **lacquer ware** can reach a high standard.

Language

Sinhala

Sinhala (or Sinhalese), the language of the Sinhalese, is an Indo-European language with North Indian affinities, unlike the Dravidian language, Tamil. Brought by the North Indian migrants, possibly in the fifth century BC, the language can be traced from inscriptions dating from the second century BC onwards which show how it had developed away from the original Sanskrit. The spoken language had changed several vowel sounds and absorbed words from the indigenous races and also from Tamil. Sinhala language had acquired a distinct identity by the beginning of the first century.

Although at first glance the **script** might suggest a link with the South Indian scripts, it developed independently. The rounded form was dictated by the use of a sharp stylus to inscribe on palm-leaf which would later be filled in with 'ink' instead of the North Indian technique of writing on bark.

The early verse and later prose **literature** were religious (Buddhist) and apart from inscriptions, date from the 10th century although there is evidence of some existing 300 years earlier. Non-religious texts only gained prominence in the last century.

Tamil

Like Sinhala, Tamil is also one of South Asia's oldest languages, but belongs to the Dravidian language family. It originated on the Indian mainland, and although Sri Lankan Tamil has retained some expressions which have a 'pure', even slightly archaic touch to them, it remains essentially an identical language both in speech and writing to that found in Tamil Nadu.

The first Tamil literature dates from approximately the second century AD. At that time a poets' academy known as the **Sangam** was established in Madurai. The poetry was devoted to religious subjects. From the beginning of the Christian era a development began to take place in Tamil religious thought and writing. Krishna became transformed from a remote and heroic figure of the epics into the focus of a new and passionate devotional worship – *bhakti*. Jordens has written that this new worship was 'emotional, ardent, ecstatic, often using erotic imagery'. From the seventh to the 10th century there was a surge of writing new hymns of praise, sometimes referred to as 'the Tamil *Veda*'. Attention focused on the 'marvels of Krishna's birth and infancy and his heroic and amorous exploits as a youth among the cowherds and cowherdesses of Gokula'. In the ninth century Vaishnavite Brahmans produced the *Bhagavata Purana*, which, through frequent translation into all India's major languages, became the vehicle for the new worship of Krishna. Its tenth book has been called 'one of the truly great books of Hinduism'. There are over 40 translations into Bengali alone. These influences were transmitted directly into Hindu Tamil culture in Sri Lanka, which retained intimate ties with the southern Tamil region.

Cinema

As in India, cinema is a favourite pastime in Sri Lanka, and while Hindi and Tamil films are predictably popular, there is a Sri Lankan tradition, which is worth searching out.

Although Sri Lanka is credited with opening, in 1903, the first film society in Asia, it was not until 1947, and the release of *Kadawunu Poronduwa* (Broken Promise) that Sinhalese dialogue was first heard in cinemas. Like most of Sri Lanka's early movies it was produced in India and though it began a spate of film-making in India using Sri Lankan actors, most followed formulaic South Indian storyline and acting styles. The post-independence creation of a **Government Film Unit** however established a breeding ground for a national style, and in 1956 British-trained director Lester James Peries became the father of a new wave in Sri Lankan cinema with his first feature, *Rekawa* (Line of Destiny). Shown at Cannes, and receiving awards at three international festivals, it was the first to portray Sri Lankan culture realistically, using amateur actors and shooting in natural light. His subsequent film *Gamperaliya* (Changing of the Village, 1963), based on a story by novelist Martin Wickremasinghe, was successful both critically and commercially abroad, and was a great influence on a new breed of Sri Lankan directors in the 1960s. More recent Peries films include *Beddegama* (1981), based on Leonard Woolf's *Village in the Jungle*, *Kaliyugaya* (1982, the second in his Wickremasinghe trilogy), and, in 2003, *Wekande Walauwa* (Mansion by the Lake), depicting an upper-class Buddhist family in the late 1980s and part-based on Chekhov's *The Cherry Orchard*. Peries received a Legion d'Honneur in 1997 and a UNESCO Fellini Gold Medal (alongside Clint Eastwood) at Cannes in 2003.

In 1970, the SLFP nationalized the film industry, with an aim of fostering an indigenous style, giving rise to a decade of experimentation from directors such as Dharmasena Pathiraja (*Ahas Gauwa* and *Bambaru Avith*), who introduced social realism, HD Premaratne (*Sikuruliya*, 1975) and Vasantha Obeysekera (*Wesgaththo*, 1970). The 1980s were a mixed decade – Tissa Abeysekara's *Viragaya* (1987) regarded as a highlight – but by the end of the decade and throughout the 1990s, the film industry was in decline, a victim of the government monopoly's restrictive policies and lack of investment.

There are however some significant films of recent years, often made with the help of foreign investment. The ethnic conflict has been a subject of a number of films, Prasanna Withanage's *Purahanda Kaluwara* (Death on a Full Moon Day, 1997), which was initially banned in Sri Lanka, is perhaps the most notable of these. Set in the quintessentially Buddhist North Central Province, the film exposes the chauvinism of the modern-day institution of Buddhism by focusing on a naive father who refuses to believe that his son, a soldier in the SLA, has been killed. *Saroja* (Somaratne Dissanayake, 1999) sets the innocent friendship between a Sinhalese and a Tamil child against a backdrop of racial hatred and violence, with fateful consequences. *Punchi Surunganavi* (Little Angel, 2001) has a similar theme. Vimukthi Jayasundara's *Sulanga Enu Pinisa* (The Foresaken Land, 2005) was considered Tamil Tiger propaganda by the Sri Lankan military but went on to win the Caméra d'Or at the 2005 Cannes Film Festival. A haunting film about people in wartime, it heralds a powerful new voice in Sri Lankan cinema.

The film industry was liberalized in 2000 with the removal of the government's monopoly, but 2010 saw the lowest attendance figures in the history of Sri Lankan cinema. The number of domestically produced films screened in Sri Lanka in 2009 was a paltry 15. If things continue in a similar vein, the future of Sri Lankan film-making looks bleak.

Land and environment

Geography

Sri Lanka is practically on the equator so there is little difference between the length of night and day, both being about 12 hours. The sun rises around 0600 and it is completely dark by 1900. Its position has meant that Sri Lanka is at the heart of the Indian Ocean trading routes. The opening of the route round the Cape of Good Hope by Vasco da Gama in 1498 brought the island into direct contact with Western Europe. The opening of the Suez Canal in 1869 further strengthened the trading links with the West.

Origins

Only 100 million years ago Sri Lanka was still attached to the great land mass of what geologists call 'Pangaea', of which South Africa, Antarctica and the Indian Peninsula were a part. Indeed, Sri Lanka is a continuation of the Indian Peninsula, from which it was separated less than 10,000 years when sea level rose to create the 10-m-deep and 35-km-wide **Palk Straits**. It is 432 km long and at its broadest 224 km wide. Its 1600 km of coastline is lined with fine sandy beaches, coral reefs and lagoons.

Many of the rocks that comprise over 90% of Sri Lanka and the Indian Peninsula were formed alongside their then neighbours in South Africa, South America, Australia and Antarctica. Generally crystalline, contorted and faulted, the Archaean rocks of Sri Lanka and the Indian Peninsula are some of the oldest in the world.

The fault line that severed India from Africa was marked by a north–south ridge of mountains. These run north from the Central Highlands of Sri Lanka through the Western Ghats, which form a spine running up the west coast of India. Both in Sri Lanka and India the hills are set back from the sea by a coastal plain which varies from 10 km to over 80 km wide while the hills are over 2500 m high.

The oldest series are the **Charnockites**, intrusive rocks named after the founder of Calcutta and enthusiastic amateur geologist, Job Charnock. These are between 2000 and 3000 million years old. In Sri Lanka they run like a broad belt across the island's heart, important partly because they contain most of Sri Lanka's minerals, including gems, though these are found largely in the gravelly river deposits rather than in their original rocks.

Unlike the central Himalaya to their north which did not begin to rise until about 35 million years ago, the highlands of Sri Lanka have been upland regions for several hundred million years. The island has never been completely covered by the sea, the only exception being in the far north where the Jaffna peninsula was submerged, allowing the distinctive Jaffna limestones to be deposited in shallow seas between seven million and 26 million years ago.

Today the ancient crystalline rocks form an ancient highland massif rising to its highest points just south and southwest of the geographical centre of the pear-shaped island. The highlands rise in three dissected steps to **Piduratalagala** (Sri Lanka's highest mountain at 2524 m) and the sacred **Adam's Peak** (2260 m). The steps are separated from each other by steep scarp slopes. Recent evidence suggests that the very early folding of the ancient rocks, followed by erosion at different speeds, formed the scarps and plateaus, often deeply cut by the rivers which radiate from the centre of the island. Even though the origin of these steps is not fully understood the steep scarps separating them have created some beautiful waterfalls and enormous hydro-electric power potential. Some of this has now been realized, notably through the huge Victoria Dam project on the Mahaweli Ganga, but in the process some of the most scenic waterfalls have been lost.

Rivers lakes and floods

By far the largest of the 103 river basins in Sri Lanka is that of the Mahaweli Ganga, which covers nearly one fifth of the island's total area. The river itself has a winding course, rising about 50 km south of Kandy and flowing north then northeast to the sea near Trincomalee, covering a distance of 320 km. It is the only perennial river to cross the Dry Zone. Its name is a reference to the Ganga of North India, and in Sri Lanka all perennial rivers are called *ganga*, while seasonal streams are called *oya* (Sinhalese) or *aru* (Tamil). A number of the rivers have been developed both for irrigation and power, the Victoria project on the Mahaweli Ganga being one of the biggest in Asia – and one of the most controversial. It has created island's largest lake, the Victoria Reservoir.

The short rivers of Sri Lanka's Wet Zone sometimes have severe floods, and the Kelani, which ultimately reaches the sea at Colombo, has had four catastrophic floods in the last century. Others can also be turbulent during the wet season, tumbling through steamy forests and cultivated fields on their short courses to the sea.

Climate

Sri Lanka's location, just north of the equator, places it on the main track of the two monsoons which dominate South Asia's weather systems. Derived from the Arabic word *mausim* (meaning season), the 'monsoon' is now synonymous with 'rains'. Strictly however it refers to the wind reversal which replaces the relatively cool, dry and stable northeasterlies, characteristic from October to May, with the very warm and wet southwesterlies from May to October. However, the northeasterlies, which originate in the arid interior of China, have crossed over 1500 km of the Bay of Bengal by the time they reach Sri Lanka, and thus even the northeast monsoon brings rain, especially to the north and east of the island.

Rainfall

Nearly three quarters of Sri Lanka lies in what is widely known as the '**Dry Zone**', comprising the northern half and the whole of the east of the country. Extensively forested and with an average annual rainfall of between 1200-1800 mm, much of the region does not seem unduly dry, but like much of southeast India, virtually all of the region's rain falls between October and January. The rain often comes in relatively short but dramatic bursts. Habarana, for example, located between Polonnaruwa and Anuradhapura received 1240 mm (nearly 50 in) of rain in the three days around Christmas in 1957. These rains caused catastrophic floods right across the Dry Zone.

The '**Wet Zone**' (the mountains and the southwestern part of the country) also receives some rain during this period, although the coastal regions of the southwest are in the rain shadow of the Central Highlands, and are much drier than the northeast between November and January. The southwest corner of Sri Lanka has its main wet season from May to October, when the southwest monsoon sweeps across the Arabian Sea like a massive wall of warm moist air, often over 10,000 m thick. The higher slopes of the Central Highlands receive as much as 4000 mm during this period, while even the coastal lowlands receive over 500 mm.

Agriculture in the north and east suffers badly during the southwest monsoon because the moisture bearing winds dry out as they descend over the Central Highlands, producing hot, drying and often very strong winds. Thus June, July and August are almost totally rainless throughout the Dry Zone. For much of the time a strong, hot wind, called *val hulunga* by the Sinhalese peasantry and *kachchan* by the Tamils, desiccates the land.

From late October to December cyclonic storms often form over the Bay of Bengal, sometimes causing havoc from the southern coast of India northwards to Bangladesh. Sri Lanka is far enough south to miss many of the worst of these, but it occasionally suffers major cyclones. These generally come later in the season, in December and January and can cause enormous damage and loss of life.

The Wet Zone rarely experiences long periods without rain. Even between the major monsoon periods widespread rain can occur. Convectional thunderstorms bring short loudbursts to the south and southwest between March and May, and depressions tracking across the Bay of Bengal can bring heavy rain in October and November.

Temperatures

Lowland Sri Lanka is always relatively hot and humid. On the plains temperature reflects the degree of cloud cover. Colombo has a minimum of 25°C in December and a maximum of 28°C in May. At Nuwara Eliya, over 2000 m up in the Central Highlands, the average daytime temperatures hover around 16°C, but you need to be prepared for the chill in the evenings. Only the northeast occasionally experiences temperatures of above 38°C.

Wildlife

For one small island Sri Lanka packs an enormous variety of wildlife. This is largely because in that small space there is a wide range in altitude. The Central Highlands rise to over 2500 m with damp evergreen forests, cool uplands and high rainfall. Within 100 km there are the dry coastal plain and sandy beaches. The climatic division of the island into the larger, dry, mainly northern and eastern region, and the smaller, wet, southwestern section is of importance to observers of wildlife. In the Dry Zone remnants of evergreen and deciduous forests are interspersed with cultivation, and in the east of this region the savanna grasslands are dominated by the metre high grass, *Imperata cylindrica*, widely regarded as a scourge. The whole vegetation complex differs sharply from both the Central Highlands and the Wet Zone of the southwest. These different areas support very different species. Many species occur only in one particular zone, but there are some, often the ones associated with man, which are found throughout. ▶ *See Books, page 391.*

Mammals

The **Asiatic elephant** (*Elephas maximus*) has a sizeable population, some wild which can be seen in several of the national parks. The animals come down to the water in the evening, either in family groups or herds of 20 or so. The 'Marsh Elephants', an interesting, significantly larger sub-species, are found in the marshy basin of the Mahaweli River. Wild elephants increasingly come into contact with humans in the growing settlements along their traditional migration routes between the northwest and southeast of the island and so the Wildlife Conservation Department is attempting to protect migration corridors from development. Visitors travelling away from the coast may get a chance to see domesticated animals being put to work or watch them at Pinnawela near Kandy.

The solid looking **Asiatic wild buffalo** (*Bubalus bubalis*), with a black coat and wide-spreading curved horns, stands about 170 cm at the shoulder. When domesticated, it is known as the water buffalo.

The **leopard or panther** (*Panthera pardus*), the only big cat in Sri Lanka, is found both in the dry lowland areas and in the forested hills. Being shy and elusive, it is rarely seen. The greyish **fishing cat** (*Felis viverrina*), with dark spots and dashes with somewhat webbed feet, search for prey in marshes and on the edge of streams.

The **sloth bear** (*Melursus ursinus*), about 75 cm at the shoulder, can be seen in areas of scrub and rock. It has an unkempt shaggy coat and is the only bear of the island.

The deer on the island are widespread. The commonest, the **chital (or spotted) deer** (*Axis axis*), only about 90 cm tall, is seen in herds of 20 or so in grassy areas. The bright rufous coat spotted with white is unmistakable. The stags carry antlers with three tines. The magnificent **sambar** (*Cervus unicolor*) (150 cm tall) with its shaggy coat varying from brownish grey to almost black in older stags, is seen in wooded hillsides. The stags carry large three-tined antlers and have a mane-like thickening of the coat around the neck. The **muntjac or barking deer** (*Muntiacus muntjak*) is small and shy (60 cm at the shoulder). It is brown with darker legs with white underparts and chest. The **stag** carries a small pair of antlers. Usually found in pairs, their staccato bark is heard more often than they are seen.

The **wild pig** (*Sus scrofa*) is easily identified by its affinity to the domestic pig. It has a mainly black body sparsely covered with hair except for a thick line along the spine; the young are striped. Only the male (boar) bears tusks. Commonly seen in grass and light bush, near water, it can do great damage to crops.

The interesting **purple-faced langur** (*Presbytis senex*) is only found in Sri Lanka. A long-tailed, long-legged monkey about 125 cm in length, nearly half of it tail, it has a dark coat contrasting with an almost white head. Hair on the head grows long to form swept back whiskers, but the face itself is almost black. Usually seen in groups of a dozen or so, it lives mainly in the dense, damp mountain forests but is also found in open woodland.

Apart from animals that still live truly in the wild, others have adapted to village and town life and are often seen near temples. The most widespread of the monkeys is the **grey langur** (*Presbytis entellus*), another long-tailed monkey with a black face, hands and feet. The **tocque macaque** (*Macaca sinica*), 60 cm, is a much more solid looking animal with shorter limbs. It varies in colour from grey to brown or even reddish brown above, with much paler limbs and underparts. The pale, sometimes reddish, face has whorls of hair on the cheeks. On top of the head the hair grows flat and cap-like, from a distinct parting!

Look out for the **flying fox** (*Pteropus giganteus*) which has a wingspan of 120 cm. These are actually fruit-eating bats, found throughout, except in the driest areas. They roost in large, sometimes huge, noisy colonies in tree tops, often in the middle of towns or villages, where they look like folded umbrellas hanging from the trees. In the evening they can be seen leaving the roost with slow measured wing beats.

The **ruddy mongoose** (*Herpestes ismithii*) is usually found in scrub and open jungle. The **brown mongoose** (*Herpestes fuscus*) can also be seen in gardens and fields. The mongoose is well known as a killer of snakes, but it will also take rats, mice, chickens and bird's eggs.

Birds

Sri Lanka is also an ornithologist's paradise with over 250 resident species, mostly found in the Wet Zone, including the Sri Lanka myna, Sri Lanka whistling thrush, yellow-eared bulbul, red-faced malkoha and brown-capped babbler. The winter migrants come from distant Siberia and western Europe, the reservoirs attracting vast numbers of water birds such as stilts, sandpipers, terns and plover, as well as herons, egrets and storks. The forests attract species of warblers, thrushes, cuckoo and many others. The endemic **jungle fowl** (*Gallus lafayetti*) is Sri Lanka's national bird. It is common to see large ornaments topped by a brass jungle fowl which has an honoured place in the home on special occasions. The recently reopened **Kumana** sanctuary in the southeast, and **Bundala** (famed for flamingoes) and **Kalametiya** sanctuaries between Tissamaharama and Hambantota in the south, both with lagoons, are the principal bird sanctuaries.

Reptiles

Two species of crocodile are found in Sri Lanka. The rather docile **mugger (or marsh) crocodile** (*Crocodilus palustrus*), 3-4 m in length, lives in freshwater rivers and tanks in many parts of the island. The **estuarine (or saltwater) crocodile** (*Crocodilus porosus*) prefers the brackish waters of the larger rivers where it can grow to 7 m. Among the lizards, the large water **monitor** (*Varanus*), up to 2 m long, greyish brown with black and yellow markings, is found in a variety of habitats. They have become quite widespread and tame and can even be seen scavenging in the rubbish dumps and market places. The land monitor lacks the yellow markings.

Seashore and marine life

Among the living coral swim a bewildering variety of colourful fish. There are shoals of silvery **sardinella** and stately, colourful **angelfish** (*Pomacanthus*) often with noticeable mouths in a different colour. Butterfly fish (*Chaetodontidae*) are similar to small angelfish but their fins are rounded at the end. The **surgeon fish** (*Acanthuridae*) get their name from the sharp blades at the base of their tails. Rounded in outline, with compressed bodies and pouting lips, they are often very brightly coloured (eg 17-cm **blue surgeon**). Striped like a zebra, the **scorpion fish** (*Pteriois*) is seen among live coral, and sometimes trapped in pools of the dead reef by the retreating tide. Although it has poisonous dorsal spines it will not attack if you leave it alone.

Corals are living organisms and consist of two basic types: the typical hard coral (eg Staghorn) and the less familiar soft corals which anchor themselves to the hard coral – one form looks like the greyish pink sea anemone. The commonest shells are the **cowries** which you can find on the beach. The **ringed cowrie** (*Cypraea annulus*) has a pretty grey and pinkish white shell with a golden ring, while the **money cowrie** which was once used as currency in Africa, varies from greenish grey to pink, according to its age. The big and beautiful **tiger cowrie** (*Cypraea tigris*) (up to 8 cm), has a very shiny shell marked like a leopard. The spectacular **spider conch** (*Lambis*) and the common **murex** (*Chicoreus*) can grow 15-20 cm. **Sea urchins** (*Echinoidea*), fairly common on sandy beaches and dead coral, are extremely painful to tread on, so be sure to wear shoes when beach combing.

Of the seven species of marine turtle in the world, five return to lay their eggs on Sri Lankan beaches but all are on the endangered list. One of the rarer species is the giant **leather-back turtle** (*Dermochelys coriacea*) which grows to 2 m in length, has a ridged leathery skin on its back instead of a shell. The smaller **olive ridley turtle** (*Lepidochelys olivacea*) has the typical rows of shields along the shell. The Turtle Conservation Project is carrying out a very worthwhile programme near Tangalla on the south coast, see page 155.

Watching wildlife: A brief introduction

Information provided by Gehan de Silva Wijeyeratne, see www.jetwingeco.com.

Classical biogeographic theory predicts that small islands do not have large animals. However, the largest terrestrial mammal, the **elephant**, roams the remaining wildernesses in Sri Lanka. You have the best chance of seeing the wild Asian elephant on this island than anywhere else on the globe. At Uda Walawe National Park, a sighting is virtually guaranteed. Other national parks such as Wasgomuwa National Park and Yala National Park are also good for seeing elephants. During August to September, probably the largest congregation of wild elephants in a single place occurs. As the waters of the Minneriya Lake recede in Minneriya National Park, grasses flourish on the exposed lake bed. At times over 300 elephants maybe gathered on the lake bed, in clusters of small family groups which coalesce into super units, at times numbering over a 100. It is one of the most impressive spectacles in the international wildlife calendar.

The coastal waters of Sri Lanka are rich in marine mammals and are particularly noted as being one of the best places in the world for observing a high diversity of marine mammals. These include the world's largest marine mammal, the **blue whale**. The **humpback whale**, another marine giant, is also found in good numbers. However, whale watching is yet in its infancy.

On land is a spotted predator. Glamorous and at times elusive, the **leopard** is the highlight of a big game safari. Largely nocturnal, with some good daytime sightings, the Sri Lanka leopard is one of potentially eight sub species and is unique to the island. Yala National Park is the best place in Asia for leopard watching. In Block 1 of the park, which is usually visited by tourists, the density is as high as one per 1.1 per sq km according to a study (see www.jetwingeco.com). This, combined with the stretches of open terrain and the leopard's position an emboldened top predator, makes it relatively easy to see. In 2003, Wilpattu National Park reopened after nearly two decades. Leopard enthusiasts are hopeful that over time the park will regain its glory as a destination for leopards and other wildlife.

Another largely nocturnal hunter is the **sloth bear**. During June and July, it gorges itself on the yellow berries of the Palu Tree found in the dry zone. The best chances of a diurnal viewing are during this time. The low country parks in the Dry Zone host a number of mammals which visitors have a good chance of seeing including **spotted deer**, **sambar**, **wild pig**, **jackal**, **black-naped hare**, **ruddy**, **grey** and **stripe-necked mongoose**, **civet cat**, etc.

On the southern coastal line is the Kalametiya Sanctuary, Bundala National Park and Palatupana Salt Pans, famous for their wintering shorebirds. Every year, tens of thousands of migrant **shorebirds** and **ducks** from Asia and Europe winter in the estuaries, lagoons and wetlands in these areas. At times, clouds of **pintail** and **garganey** (ducks) or waders such as **black-tailed godwit**, take to the air. Soon after arrival, the migrants spread out. Many of the migrant shorebirds, also called **waders**, will be familiar to foreign visitors. What makes places such as Palatupana so special is the diversity and close proximity of the birds. **Little stints, Temminck's stints, lesser and greater sand plover, redshank, broad-billed sandpiper, ruff, greenshank**, etc, crowd along the water's edge. Birdwatchers in search of birds such as **black** and **yellow bitterns** of freshwater wetlands should try the Talangama Wetland, near Colombo, or the Muthurajawela Wetland, close to the International Airport. Around Tissamaharama are a complex of inland, man-made lakes that is also popular with birdwatchers. In fact the island is dotted with hundreds of lakes that are refuges for wildlife.

Much of Sri Lanka's endemic bio-diversity is confined to what is known as the Wet Zone in the southwest of the island. The most visited and best known of these is the Sinharaja Man and Biosphere Reserve. Visitors to Galle could try the Kottawa Rainforest and Arboretum, or, less than half an hour's drive or about three hours away is the Kanneliya Forest Reserve. Kottawa has interesting endemic animals such as the **hump-nosed lizard** but is a relatively small forest patch, lacking the species diversity of larger rainforests such as Sinharaja and Morapitiya. Kanneliya rainforest is vast, but was once heavily logged and has lost the richness of animal species of Sinharaja.

Sinharaja is the jewel in the crown and one of the best places for observing 'mixed species feeding flocks'. Birds of many species forage together to enhance security and feeding efficiency, combing through the rainforest like a giant vacuum cleaner. Birdwatchers should look out or more likely listen for clues from the garrulous **orange-billed babbler** which forms a 'nucleus species'. The **crested drongo**, a courageous bird, acts as sentinel to the flock and also utters far carrying calls. When a feeding flock is encountered, it is easy to be distracted by the commotion of **babblers**, **drongos** and **barbets**. Carefully observing the mid canopy will often reveal **Malabar trogon**. The female is dull, but the male has a striking scarlet breast. In the canopy is the discrete and enigmatic **red-faced malkoha**. This relatively large bird can surprisingly go unnoticed. In the lowland streams gaudily coloured endemic **paradise combtails** swim. Shoals of **cherry barbs** may swim by. Endemic **stone suckers** cling to the stone bed, as currents swirl past them.

Even a short visit to Sinharaja will result in a number of **butterflies** and **dragonflies** being seen. The glamour set of the insect world. Endemic **tree nymphs** in black and white splotches look like Chinese art work. They float lazily on barely discernible air currents. Common **bluebottles** and **commanders** fly by more purposefully. Dragonflies, voracious predators hunt in adjoining paddy fields as well as in the gloomy forest interior. Eastern **scarlet darters** have their red set off vividly against green foliage.

The rainforests also harbour one of the most significant radiations of animal species to be discovered in the past few decades. It is believed that as many as 200 new species of **tree frogs** are awaiting scientific description. Sri Lanka could surpass countries like Costa Rica in the number of tree frog species, making it the frog capital of the world. A key to this extraordinary diversity is the evolution of 'direct development'. Most amphibians including frogs are usually dependent on water in which they lay their eggs. Sri Lanka frogs have developed an ability to lay their eggs in a moist, foam nest. The eggs develop into small frogs within the eggs and emerge as adults by passing the water dependent tadpole stage.

In Sri Lanka, designated national parks are under the purview of the Department of Wildlife Conservation. The Horton Plains National Park, about 45 minutes' drive from Nuwara Eliya, is the only national park where visitors are allowed to travel on foot, subject to designated footpaths. The Horton Plains are characterized by wind swept grasslands interspersed with patches of cloud forest. Some species of plants and animals are confined to the cloud forests. Birdwatchers visit the plains to look for montane specialties such as the Sri Lanka **whistling thrush**, Sri Lanka **wood pigeon** and **dull-blue flycatcher**.

Despite its small size, the presence of a mountainous core and two monsoons create sharply defined climatic zones in Sri Lanka. As a result, sub species have evolved in different climatic zones. A good example is the highland race of the **purple-faced leaf monkey**. This race, also called the bear monkey, on account of its thick coat, can be seen in the cloud forest.

Vegetation

From tropical thorn forest in the driest regions of the southeast and northwest, (generally with a rainfall of less than 1200 mm) the vegetation ranges through to montane temperate forest of the Central Highlands and then to mangroves of some stretches of the coast. Today mangroves are restricted almost exclusively to a stretch of the west coast, north of Puttalam and of the southeast coast, east of Hambantota and in the northern peninsula.

None of the original forest cover has been unaffected by human activity, and much has now been either converted to cultivated land, or given over to a range of tree cash crops, notably coconut and rubber at low altitudes and tea at higher levels. Indeed most of the forest cover is now restricted to the Dry Zone. Here dry evergreen forest, with trees generally less than 12 m in height, and moist deciduous forest, whose canopy level is usually up to 20-25 m, provide an excellent habitat for wildlife, and continue to cover extensive tracts of land. Even here the original forest has been much altered, most having re-colonized land which was extensively cultivated until 500 years ago. Sri Lanka also has four different types of grassland, all the result of human activity.

Common trees

In addition to the endless lines of **coconut palms** (*Cocos nucifer*) along the coastal belt and the Kurunegala district, the **sago** or **fish-tail palm** (*Caryota urens*), locally called 'kitul', is a regular feature on the island. The leaves are large and distinctive consisting of many small leaflets, each shaped like a fish tail while the flowers hang down like horses' tails. Sago comes from the pith, toddy and jaggery from the sap and the fibres are used to make bristles in brushes, as well as rope.

The **rain tree** (*Samanea saman*) is a large tree from South America, with a spreading canopy, often planted as a roadside shade tree. The dark green feathery leaves are peculiar in that they become horizontal in the daytime, thus maximizing the amount of shade thrown by the tree. At night time and in the rain they fold downwards. The flowers are pale pink, silky looking tufts.

The **eucalyptus or gum tree** (*Eucalyptus grandis*), introduced from Australia in the 19th century, is now widespread and is planted near villages to provide both shade and firewood. All the varieties have characteristic long, thin leaves and the colourful peeling bark and fresh pleasant smell. **Bamboo** (*Bambusa*) strictly speaking is a grass which is found almost everywhere. It can vary in size from small ornamental clumps to the enormous wild plant whose stems are so strong and thick that they are used for construction and as pipes for irrigation in small holdings.

The **banyan** (*Ficus benghalensis*), featured widely in eastern literature, is planted by temples, in villages and along roads. Curiously its seeds germinate in crevices in the bark of other trees. It sends down roots to the ground as it grows until the original host tree is surrounded by a cage-like structure which eventually strangles it. So a single banyan appears to have multiple 'trunks' which are in fact roots.

Related to the banyan, the **peepal** (*Ficus religiosa*) is distinguishable by the absence of aerial roots, and pointed heart shaped leaves which taper into a pronounced 'tail'. It too is commonly found near temples and shrines where it cracks open walls and strangles other trees with its roots. The purplish figs it bears in abundance are about 1 cm across.

Holy but not wholly efficacious

The sal tree is one of the most widespread and abundant trees in the tropical and subtropical Ganges plains and Himalayan foothills; it was the tree under which Gautama Buddha was born. Like the pipal (*Ficus religiosa*), under which the Buddha was enlightened, the sal is greatly revered in Sri Lanka. It is often planted near temples, for example on the lawn close to the Temple of the Tooth Relic in Kandy. However, the sal in Sri Lanka is very different to the one found in northern South Asia, and the difference has been known to have serious consequences since extracts from the tree are widely used for medicinal preparations. The sal tree proper is *Shorea robusta* (*dipterocarpaceae*), whereas the sal of Sri Lanka is the tree known all over the tropics as the cannon ball tree (*Couroupita surenamensis*). Unfortunately, the difference is not widely known and it is not unknown for Ayurvedic medicinal preparations using the Sri Lankan sal but following recipes of Indian origin, to have been taken without any effect.

Flowering trees

Visitors to Sri Lanka cannot fail to notice the many flowering trees planted along the roadside. The **golden mohur** *(Delonix regia)*, a native of Madagascar, grows throughout the island. A good shade tree, it grows only to about 8-9 m in height and has spreading branches. The leaves are an attractive feathery shape, and a bright light green in colour. The fiery coloured flowers which appear after it has shed its leaves, make a magnificent display.

The **jacaranda** *(Jacaranda mimosaefolia)*, originally from Brazil, though rather straggly in shape, has attractive feathery foliage. The purple-blue thimble-shaped flowers (up to 4 cm long) make a striking splash of colour.

The **tamarind** *(Tamarindus indica)* is an evergreen with feathery leaves and small yellow and red flowers which grow in clusters in its spreading crown. The noticeable fruit pods are long, curved and swollen at intervals.

The large and dramatic **silk cotton tree** *(Bombax ceiba)* can be up to 25 m in height. The bark is often light grey with conical spines; the bigger trees have noticeable buttress roots. The wide spreading branches keep their leaves for most of the year, the cup-shaped fleshy red flowers appearing only when the tree is leafless. The dry fruit pod produces the fine silky cotton which gives it its name.

The **Ceylon ironwood** *(Mesua ferrea)* is often planted near Buddhist temples. Its long slender leaves, reddish when young set off the white four-petalled flowers with yellow centres.

The beautiful flowering **rhododendron** *(Rhododendron Zeylanicum)* is common in the highland regions. It grows as either a sprawling shrub or a tree up to 12 m high. In the wild, the flowers are usually crimson or pale purple.

Fruit trees

The **mango** *(Mangifera indica)*, a fairly large tree ranging from 6-15 m high or more, has spreading branches forming a rounded canopy. The dense shade it casts makes it a very attractive village meeting place. The distinctively shaped fruit is quite delicious and unlike any other in taste.

The **jackfruit** (*Artocarpus heterophyllus*) is one of the most remarkable trees. A large evergreen with dark green leathery leaves, its huge fruit can be as much as 1 m long and 40 cm thick, growing from a short stem directly off the trunk and branches. The skin is thick and rough, almost prickly. The strong smelling fruit of the main eating variety is sickly sweet and an acquired taste.

The **banana plant** (*Musa*) is actually a gigantic herb arising from an underground stem. The very large leaves grow directly off the trunk which is about 5 m in height. The fruiting stem bears a large purple flower, which yields up to 100 fruit.

The **papaya** (*Carica papaya*) which often grows to 4 m has distinctive palm-shaped leaves. Only the female tree bears the shapely fruit which hang down close to the crown.

The **cashew nut** (*Anacardium occidentale*) tree, a native of tropical America, was introduced into Sri Lanka, but now grows wild as well as being cultivated. Usually less than 7 m in height, it has bright green, shiny, rounded leaves. The nut hangs from a fleshy bitter fruit called a cashew apple.

Originally from tropical America, the **avocado pear** (*Persea*) grows well in the Wet Zone. The broad-leaved tree up to 10m in height, with oval, pointed leaves, bear the familiar fruit at the ends of the branches.

Flowering plants

Many flowering plants are cultivated in parks, gardens and roadside verges. The **frangipani** (*Plumeria rubra*) is particularly attractive with a crooked trunk and regular branches which bear leaves with noticeable parallel veins which taper to a point at each end. The sweetly-scented waxy flowers are usually white, pale yellow or pink.

The **bougainvillea** grows everywhere as a dense bush or a strong climber, often completely covered in flowers of striking colours from pinks to purples, oranges to yellows, and brilliant white. If you look carefully you will see that the paper-thin colourful 'petals' are really large bracts.

The trumpet-shaped flowers of the **hibiscus** too, come in brilliant scarlet, pink and yellow or simply white. **Orchids** abound but sadly most go unnoticed because of their tiny flowers. The large flowered, deep mauve **Dendrobium macarthiae** can be seen around Ratnapura in May. From spring to summer you may find the varicoloured, sweet-scented **vanda tessellata** in bloom everywhere.

Books

Art and architecture

Archer, WG & Paranavitana, S *Ceylon, paintings from Temple Shrine and Rock* (1958) Paris: New York Graphic Soc.

Arumugam, S *Ancient Hindu temples of Sri Lanka* (1982) Colombo.

Basnayake, HT *Sri Lankan Monastic architecture* (1986) Delhi: Sri Satguru. A detailed account of Polonnaruwa.

Coomaraswamy, AK *Medieval Sinhalese Art* (1956) New York: Pantheon.

Godakumbure, CE *Architecture of Sri Lanka* (1963) Colombo: Department of Cultural Affairs Monograph.

Manjusri, LTP *Design elements from Sri Lankan Temple Paintings* (1977) Colombo: Archaeological Survey of Sri Lanka. A fine collection of line drawings from the 18th and 19th century, particularly of the Kandyan style.

Robson, D *Bawa: the Complete Works* (2002) London: Thames & Hudson.

Robson, D and Sansoni, D *Bawa: The Sri Lankan Gardens* (2008) London: Thames & Hudson.

Seneviratna, A *The Temple of the Sacred Tooth Relic* (1987) Govt of Sri Lanka (State Engineering Corp). A well-illustrated survey of the various temples in ancient Sinhalese capitals that held the sacred relic, in addition to Kandy. Also *Ancient Anuradhapura* (1994) Colombo: Archaeological Survey Department. Readable but detailed guide to the archaeological sites, including Mihintale. Others on Kandy, Dambulla and Polonnaruwa.

Cookery

Coombe, J & Perry, D *Addicted: Generation T* (2010) Sri Serendipity. All about tea in Sri Lanka, including information on travelling through tea country and even tea recipes.

Kuruvita, P *Serendip: My Sri Lankan Kitchen* (2009) Murdoch Books. A book for your coffee table rather than your kitchen, with traditional recipes and sumptuous photographs.

Stein, R *Rick Stein's Far Eastern Odyssey* (2009) BBC Books. The book to accompany the BBC series of the same name, includes the chef's favourite recipes from the region as well as anecdotes and photographs.

Current affairs and politics

De Silva, KM *Reaping the Whirlwind* (1998) New Delhi: Penguin. Tirelessly researched but readable analysis of the origins of the ethnic conflict.

Little, D *Sri Lanka: the invention of enmity* (1994) Washington: United States Institute of Peace Press. An attempt to provide a balanced interpretation of conflict in Sri Lanka.

McGowan, W *Only man is vile: The Tragedy of Sri Lanka* (1983) Picador. An account of the background to the 1983 Tamil-Sinhalese conflict.

Moore, MP *The State and Peasant Politics in Sri Lanka* (1985) London. An academic account of contemporary Sri Lankan political development.

Narayan Swamy, MR *Tigers of Lanka* (2002) Colombo: Vijitha Yapa. Updated edition of a study of Tamil militancy and the Indian role from an Indian perspective.

Narayan Swamy, MR *The Tiger Vanquished: LTTE's Story* (2010) Sage Publications. A collection of news stories and commentaries written by the author, compiled here to examine why the Tamil Tiger's lost the war.

Peiris, GH *Twilight of the Tigers: Peace Efforts and Power Struggles in Sri Lanka* (2009) OUP India. Focuses on the 2001 ceasefire and what happened afterwards, presenting a detailed account of events and trends.

Weiss, G *The Cage: The fight for Sri Lanka and the Last Days of the Tamil Tigers* (2011) Bodley Head. Written by a journalist and former UN official, looks at the last days of the war including the plight of the humanitarian aid workers and the media.

History: pre-history and early history

Deraniyagala, SU *The Prehistory of Sri Lanka* (1992) Colombo: Department of Archaeological Survey of Sri Lanka, 2 Vols. An erudite and detailed account of the current state of research into pre-historic Sri Lanka, available in Colombo and at the Anuradhapura Museum.

History: medieval and modern

de Lanerolle, Nalini *A Reign of Ten Kings* (1990) Colombo: CTB.
de Silva, KM *A History of Sri Lanka* (1981) London: OUP. Arguably the most authoritative historical account of Sri Lanka.
de Silva, RK and Beumer, WGM *Illustrations and views of Dutch Ceylon* (1988). Superbly illustrated.
Geiger, W *Culture of Ceylon in Mediaeval times* (1960) Wiesbaden: Harrassowitz.
Knox, Robert *An Historical Relation of Ceylon* (1981) Dehiwala: Tisara Prakasayo. Fascinating 17th-century account of the experiences of a British seaman imprisoned by a Kandyan king for 20 years.
Robinson, Francis (ed) *Cambridge Encyclopedia of India, Pakistan, Bangladesh, Sri Lanka* (1989). Excellent and readable introduction to many aspects of South Asian society.

Language

Dissanayake, JB *Say it in Sinhala.*
Pragnaratne, Swarna *Sinhala Phrasebook* (2008) Lonely Planet.

Literature

Clarke, Arthur C *View from Serendib (among many others)* (1977) New York: Random House. A personal view from the prolific author who has made Sri Lanka his home.
Goonetileke, HAI *Lanka, their Lanka* (1984) New Delhi: Navrang. Delightful cameos of Sri Lanka seen through the eyes of foreign travellers and writers.
Goonetileke, DCRA (ed) *The Penguin New Writing in Sri Lanka* (1992).
Gunesekhara, Romesh *Monkfish Moon* (1998) Penguin. Evocative collection of short stories of an island paradise haunted by violent undercurrents; *Reef* (1994). The story of a young boy growing up in modern Sri Lanka; and *Heaven's Edge* (2003) Bloomsbury. College graduate returns to a (thinly disguised) Sri Lanka to connect with his dead father's memory.
Muller, Carl *The Jam Fruit Tree* (the 1st of a series) about the free-and-easy Burghers; other books from this prolific author include *Colombo*, and *A Funny Thing Happened on the Way to the Cemetery.*
Obeyesekere, R & Fernando, C, Eds *An anthology of modern writing from Sri Lanka.* (1981) Tucson.
Ondaatje, Michael Writing by modern novelist, including the amusing auto-biographical, *Running in the family* (1983) Penguin, and *Anil's Ghost* (2000) Picador. Winner of the Irish Book Prize, a young forensic anthropologist returns to Sri Lanka to investigate the 'disappearances' of the late 80s, rich and evocative.
Reynolds, CHB, Ed *An anthology of Sinhalese Literature of the 20th century* (1987) London.
Selvadurai, Shyam *Funny Boy* (1995) Vintage. A Tamil boy comes to terms with his homosexuality and racism in 1980s Colombo. *Cinnamon Gardens* (2000) Anchor Books. A young school teacher is caught between her own and her parents' desires for her future.
Sivanandan, A *When Memory Dies* (1998) Arcadia. Explores racial tensions across 3 generations of one family.

Tearne, R *Mosquito* (new edition 2010) HarperPress. A love story between an English writer and a Sri Lankan woman. Sri Lanka is vividly and beautifully captured in the text. She also written *Brixton Beach* (2010) set in London and Sri Lanka.

Woolf, L *The Village in the Jungle* (new edition 2005) Eland. First published in 1913 and translated into both Tamil and Sinhalese, this is a classic novel of colonial Ceylon.

People and places

Coombe, J; Perry, D & Tennekoon, D *Around the Fort in 80 Lives* (2008) Sri Serendipity. Galle Fort's history told by the people who live there.

Cordiner, James *A description of Ceylon*. An account of the country, inhabitants and natural productions (1807), now reprinted by Colombo: Tisara Prakasakayo (1983).

Beny, Rolf *Island Ceylon* (1971) London: Thames & Hudson. Large coffee-table book with some excellent photos and illustrative quotes.

Brohier, RL *Changing face of Colombo 1505-1972* (1984) Colombo: Lake House. Excellent history of Colombo.

Maloney, Clarence *Peoples of South Asia* (1974) New York: Holt, Rheinhart & Winston. A wide ranging and authoritative review, perhaps over-emphasising the Dravidian connection with Sri Lanka.

Religion

Malangoda, K *Buddhism in Sinhalese Society, 1750-1900* (1976) Berkeley.

Perera, HR *Buddhism in Ceylon, Past and Present* (1966) Kandy: Buddhist Publication Society.

Qureshi, IH *The Muslim Community of the Indo-Pakistan Sub-Continent 610-1947* (1977) Karachi: OUP.

Travel

Handbook for the Ceylon Traveller, 2nd ed, (1983) Colombo: Studio Times. A good collection of essays from many writers (who live in and plainly love the island) about people, places and everything Sri Lankan. Now dated, but many interesting insights.

Boyle, Emma *Sri Lanka – the essential guide to customs & culture* (2009). One in a series from Culture Smart!, providing travellers with a good background on the country and culture. Written by a British journalist living in Sri Lanka.

Hatt, John *The tropical traveller: the essential guide to travel in hot countries*, 3rd ed (1992). Excellent, wide ranging and clearly written common sense, based on extensive experience and research.

Leestemaker, J, and others *Trekkers' guide to Sri Lanka* (1994) Colombo: Trekking Unlimited. A well-described selection of popular (and some off-the-beaten-track) treks and walks, pointing out wildlife and interesting features, and with maps to help.

Woolf, Bella Sidney *How to See Ceylon* (reprinted 2002) Boralesgamuwa: Visidunu Prakashakayo. Entertaining colonial-era guidebook from the sister of Leonard Woolf.

Natural history

Department of Wildlife Conservation's Guide to the National Parks of Sri Lanka (2001) Colombo: DWLC. Useful practical guide to all the parks, including maps.

The Pica traveller Sri Lanka, Pica Press, UK. Covers wildlife in general and also cultural sites.

Bond, Thomas *Wild Flowers to the Ceylon Hills* (1953) OUP.

Harrison, John & Worfolk, Tim *A Field Guide to the Birds of Sri Lanka* (2011) OUP. Excellent user-friendly pocket guide.

Henry, GM *Guide to the birds of Ceylon* (1978) 3rd ed. India: OUP.

Kazmierczak, K & van Perlo, B *A Field Guide to the Birds of the Indian Subcontinent*, (2008) A&C Black.

Munro, Ian *Marine and Fresh water fishes of Ceylon* (1955) Canberra: Australian Department of External Affairs.

Oriental Bird Club's *A bird-watcher's guide to Sri Lanka* (1997) Basingstoke: Ruby Publications. A good, illustrated leaflet giving all you need to know about the numerous reserves on the island.

Wijesinghe, DP *Checklist of birds of Sri Lanka* (1994) Colombo: Ceylon Bird Club.

Wijeyeratne, Gehan de Silva *Sri Lankan Wildlife* (2007) Bradt. Clear, concise and well-illustrated.

Wijeyeratne, Gehan de Silva *A Photographic Guide to Birds of Sri Lanka* (2008) London: New Holland. Excellent user-friendly pocket guide.

Woodcock, Martin *Handguide to Birds of the Indian Sub-Continent*, London: Collins.

Contents

Footnotes

Language

Sinhalese useful words and phrases

Pronunciation

ah is shown **ā** as in car
ee is shown **ī** as in see
oh is shown **ō** as in old
These marks, to help with pronunciation, do not appear in the main text

General greetings	*Ayubowan*
Thank you / No thank you	*Es-thu-thee / mata epa*
Excuse me, sorry	*Samavenna*
Pardon?	*Ah?*
Yes/no	*Ou/na*
Nevermind/that's all right	*Kamak na*
Please	*Karunakara*
What is your name?	*Nama mokakda?*
My name is ...	*Mage nama ...*
How are you?	*Kohamada?*
I am well thanks	*Mama hondin innava*
Not very well	*Wadiya honda ne*
Do you speak English?	*Ingirisi kathakaranawatha?*

Shopping

How much is this?	*Mīka kīyada?*
That will be 20 rupees	*Rupial wissai*
Please make it a bit cheaper	*Karunakara gana adukaranna*

The hotel

What is the room charge?	*Kamarayakata gana kiyada?*
May I see the room please?	*Kamaraya karnakara penvanna?*
Is there an a/c room?	*A/c kamarayak thiyenawada?*
Is there hot water?	*unuwathura thiyenawada?*
... a fan/mosquito net	*... fan/maduru delak*
Please clean the room	*Karnaka kamaraya suddakaranna*
This is OK	*Meka hondai*
Bill please	*Karunakara bila gaynna*

Travel

Where is the railway station?	*Dumriyapola koheda?*
When does the Colombo bus leave?	*Colombata bus eka yanne kīyatada?*
How much is it to Colombo?	*Colombota kīyada?*
Will you go for 10 rupees?	*Rupiyal dahayakata yanawada?*
Left/right	*Wama/dakuna*
Staight on	*Kelin yanna*
Nearby	*Langa*
Please wait here	*Karunakara mehe enna*
Please come here at 8	*Karunakara mehata atata enna*
Stop	*Nawathinna*

Time and days

right now	*dang*	week	*sathiya*
morning	*ude*	month	*masey*
afternoon	*dawal*	Sunday	*irrida*
evening	*sawasa*	Monday	*sanduda*
night	*raya*	Tuesday	*angaharuwada*
today	*atha*	Wednesday	*badhada*
tomorrow	*heta*	Thursday	*brahaspathinda*
yesterday	*īye*	Friday	*sikurada*
day	*dawasa*	Saturday	*senasurada*

Numbers

1	*eka*	9	*namaya*
2	*deka*	10	*dahaya*
3	*thuna*	20	*wissai*
4	*hathara*	30	*thihai*
5	*paha*	40	*hathalihai*
6	*haya*	50	*panahai*
7	*hatha*	100/200	*sīayaī/desiyai*
8	*ata*	1000/2000	*dāhai/dedāhai*

Basic vocabulary

Some English words are widely used such as airport, bathroom, bus, embassy, ferry, hospital, stamp, taxi, ticket, train (though often pronounced a little differently).

bank	*bankuwa*
café/food stall	*kamata kadyak*
chemist	*beheth sappuwa*
clean	*sudda*
closed	*wahala*
cold	*sī thai*
dirty	*apirisidui*
doctor	*dosthara*
excellent	*hari honthai*
ferry	*bottuwa*
food/to eat	*kanda/kāma*
hospital	*rohala*
hot (temperature)	*rasnai*
hotel	*hōtalaya*
open	*arala*
police station	*policiya*
restaurant	*kāmata*
road	*pāra*
room	*kamaraya*
shop	*kade*
sick (ill)	*asaneepai*
station	*istashama*
this	*meka*
that	*araka*
water	*wathura*
when?	*kawathatha?*
where?	*koheda?*

Useful words and phrases: Sri Lankan Tamil

general greeting	*vanakkam*
Thank you/no thank you	*nandri*
Excuse me, sorry, pardon	*mannikkavum*
Yes/no	*ām/illai*
never mind/that's all right	*paruvai illai*
please	*thayavu seithu*
What is your name?	*ungaludaya peyr enna*
My name is...	*ennudaya peyr*
How are you?	*ningal eppadi irukkirirgal?*
I am well, thanks	*nan nantraga irrukkirain*
Not very well	*paruvayillai*
Do you speak English?	*ningal angilam kathappirgala*

Shopping

How much is this?	*ithan vilai enna?*
That will be 20 rupees	*athan vilai irupatha rupa*
Please make it a bit cheaper!	*thayavu seithu konjam kuraikavuam!*

The hotel

What is the room charge?	*arayin vilai enna?*
May I see the room please?	*thayavu seithu arayai parka mudiyama?*
Is there an a/c room?	*kulir sathana arai irrukkatha?*
Is there hot water?	*sudu thanir irukkuma?*
...a bathroom?	*oru kuliyal arai...?*
...a fan/mosquito net?	*katotra sathanam/kosu valai...?*
Please clean the room	*thayavu seithu arayai suththap paduthava*
This is OK	*ithuru seri*
Bill please	*bill tharavum*

Travel

Where's the railway station?	*station enge?*
When does the Galle bus leave?	*eppa Galle bus pogum?*
How much is it to Kandy?	*Kandy poga evalavu?*
Will you go to Kandy for 10 rupees?	*paththu rupavitku Kandy poga mudiyami?*
left/right	*idathu/valathu*
straight on	*naerakapogavum*
nearby	*aruqil*
Please wait here	*thayavu seithu ingu nitkavum*
Please come here at 8	*thayavu seithu ingu ettu*
stop	*nivuthu*

Time and days

right now	*ippoh*
morning	*kalai*
afternoon	*pitpagal*
evening	*malai*
night	*iravu*
today	*indru*
tomorrow/yesterday	*nalai/naetru*
day	*thinam*
week	*vaaram*
month	*maatham*

Sunday	*gnatruk kilamai*		
Monday	*thinkat kilamai*		
Tuesday	*sevai kilamai*		
Wednesday	*puthan kilamai*		
Thursday	*viyalak kilamai*		
Friday	*velli kilamai*		
Saturday	*sanik kilamai*		

Numbers

1	*ontru*	10	*pattu*
2	*erantru*	20	*erupathu*
3	*moontru*	30	*muppathu*
4	*nangu*	40	*natpathu*
5	*ainthu*	50	*ompathu*
6	*aru*	100/200	*nooru/irunooru*
7	*aelu*	1000/2000	*aiyuram/iranda*
8	*ettu*		*iuram*
9	*onpathu*		

Basic vocabulary

Some English words are widely used, often alongside Tamil equivalents, such as, airport, bank, bathroom, bus, embassy, ferry, hospital, hotel, restaurant, station, stamp, taxi, ticket, train (though often pronounced a little differently).

airport	*agaya vimana*
	nilayam
bank	*vungi*
bathroom	*kulikkum arai*
café/food stall	*unavu kadai*
chemist	*marunthu kadai*
clean	*suththam*
closed	*moodu*
cold	*kulir*
dirty	*alukku*
embassy	*thootharalayam*
excellent	*miga nailathu*
ferry	*padagu*
hospital	*aspathri*
hot (temp)	*ushnamana*
hotel/restaurant	*sapathu*
juice	*saru/viduthi*
open	*thira*
road	*pathai*
room	*arai*
shop	*kadi*
sick (ill)	*viyathi*
stamp	*muththirai*
station	*nilayam*
this	*ithu*
that	*athu*
ticket	*anumati situ*
train	*rayil*
water	*thannir*
when?	*eppa?*
where?	*enge?*

Glossary

A

aarti (arati) Hindu worship with lamps

abhaya mudra Buddha posture signifying protection; forearm raised, palm facing outward fingers together

ahimsa non-harming, non-violence

ambulatory processional path

amla/amalaka circular ribbed pattern (based on a gourd) on top of a temple tower

Ananda the Buddha's chief disciple

anda lit 'egg', spherical part of the stupa

antechamber chamber in front of the sanctuary

apse semi-circular plan, as in apse of a church

arama monastery (as in Tissamaharama)

architrave horizontal beam across posts or gateways

Arjuna hero of the Mahabharata, to whom Krishna delivered the Bhagavad Gita

arrack spirit distilled from palm sap

aru river (Tamil)

Aryans literally 'noble' (Sanskrit); prehistoric peoples who settled in Persia and N India

asana a seat or throne; symbolic posture

ashlar blocks of stone

ashram hermitage or retreat

Avalokiteshwara Lord who looks down; Bodhisattva, the Compassionate

avatara 'descent'; incarnation of a divinity, usually Vishnu's incarnations

B

banamaduwa monastic pulpit

Bandaras sub-caste of the Goyigama caste, part of the Sinhalese aristocracy

bas-relief carving of low projection

basement lower part of walls, usually adorned with decorated mouldings

bazar market

beru elephant grass

Bhagavad-Gita Song of the Lord from the Mahabharata in which Krishna preaches a sermon to Arjuna

bhikku Buddhist monk

bhumi 'earth'; refers to a horizontal moulding of a *shikhara* (tower)

bhumisparasa mudra earth-witnessing Buddha posture

Bo-tree Ficus religiosa, large spreading tree associated with the Buddha; also Bodhi

Bodhisattva Enlightened One, destined to become Buddha

Brahma universal self-existing power; Creator in the Hindu Triad. Often represented in art, with four heads

Brahman (Brahmin) highest Hindu (and Jain) caste of priests

Brahmanism ancient Indian religion, precursor of modern Hinduism and Buddhism

Buddha The Enlightened One; founder of Buddhism who is worshipped as god by certain sects

bund an embankment; a causeway by a reservoir (tank)

Burghers Sri Lankans of mixed Dutch-Sinhalese descent

C

cantonment large planned military or civil area in town

capital upper part of a column or pilaster

catamaran log raft, logs (*maram*) tied (*kattu*) together (Tamil)

cave temple rock-cut shrine or monastery

chakra sacred Buddhist Wheel of Law; also Vishnu's discus

chapati unleavened Indian bread cooked on a griddle

chena shifting cultivation

chhatra, chatta honorific umbrella; a pavilion (Buddhist)

Chola early and medieval Tamil kingdom (India)

circumambulation clockwise movement around a stupa or shrine while worshipping

cloister passage usually around an open square

coir coconut fibre used for making rope and mats

copra dried sections of coconut flesh, used for oil

corbel horizontal block supporting a vertical structure or covering an opening

cornice horizontal band at the top of a wall

crore 10 million

Culavansa Historical sequel to Mahavansa, the first part dating from 13th century, later extended to 16th century

dagoba stupa (Sinhalese)

darshan (darshana) viewing of a deity

Dasara (dassara/dussehra/dassehra) 10-day Hindu festival (September-October)

devala temple or shrine (Buddhist or Hindu)

Devi Goddess; later, the Supreme Goddess; Siva's consort, Parvati

dhal (daal) lentil 'soup'

dharma (dhamma) Hindu and Buddhist concepts of moral and religious duty

dharmachakra wheel of 'moral' law (Buddhist)

dhyana meditation

dhyani mudra meditation posture of the Buddha, cupped hands rest in the lap

distributary river that flows away from main channel, usually in deltas

Diwali festival of lights (September-October) usually marks the end of the rainy season

Dravidian languages – Tamil, Telugu, Kannada and Malayalam; and peoples mainly from S India

Durga principal goddess of the Shakti cult; rides on a tiger, armed with weapons

dvarpala doorkeeper

E

eave overhang that shelters a porch or verandah

eri tank (Tamil)

F

finial emblem at the summit of a stupa, tower or dome; often a tier of umbrella-like motifs or a pot

frieze horizontal band of figures or decorative designs

G

gable end of an angled roof

ganga perennial river

garbhagriha literally 'womb-chamber'; a temple sanctuary

gedige arched Buddhist image house built of stone slabs and brick

gopura towered gateway in S Indian temples

Goyigama landowning and cultivating caste among Sinhalese Buddhists

H

Haj (Hajj) annual Muslim pilgrimage to Mecca (Haji, one who has performed the Haj)

hakim judge; a physician (usually Muslim)

Hanuman Monkey hero of the Ramayana; devotee of Rama; bringer of success to armies

Hari Vishnu

harmika the finial of a stupa; a pedestal where the honorific umbrella was set

Hasan the murdered eldest son of Ali, commemorated at Muharram

howdah seat on elephant's back

Hussain the second murdered son of Ali, commemorated at Muharram

I

illam lens of gem-bearing coarse river gravel

imam Muslim religious leader in a mosque

Indra King of the gods; God of rain; guardian of the East

Isvar Lord Sanskrit

J

jaggery brown sugar made from palm sap

jataka stories accounts of the previous lives of the Buddha

JVP Janatha Vimukhti Peramuna (People's Liberation Army) – violent revolutionary political movement in 1970s and 1980s

K

kadu forest (Tamil)

kalapuwa salty or brackish lagoon

Kali lit 'black'; terrifying form of the goddess Durga, wearing a necklace of skulls/heads

kalyanmandapa (Tamil) hall with columns, used for the symbolic marriage ceremony of the temple deity

kapok the silk cotton tree

kapurala officiating priest in a shrine (devala)

karandua replica of the Tooth Relic casket, dagoba-shaped

Karavas fishing caste, many converted to Roman Catholicism

karma present consequences of past lives

Kataragama the Hindu god of war; Skanda

Kartikkeya/Kartik Son of Siva, also known as Skanda or Subrahmanyam

katcheri (cutchery, Kachcheri) public office or court

khondalite crudely grained basalt

kolam masked dance drama (Sinhalese)

kovil temple (Tamil)

kitul fish-tailed sago palm, whose sap is used for jaggery

Krishna Eighth incarnation of Vishnu; the cowherd (Gopala, Govinda)

Kubera Chief yaksha; keeper of the earth's treasures, Guardian of the North

kulam tank or pond (Tamil)

L

laddu round sweet snack

lakh 100,000

Lakshmana younger brother of Rama in the Ramayana

Lakshmi Goddess of wealth and good fortune, consort of Vishnu

lattice screen of cross laths: perforated

lena cave, usually a rock-cut sanctuary

lingam (linga) Siva as the phallic emblem

Lokeshwar 'Lord of the World', Avalokiteshwara to Buddhists and of Siva to Hindus

LTTE Liberation Tigers of Tamil Eelam, or "The Tigers", force rebelling against Sri Lankan Government

lungi wrap-around loin cloth

M

maha great; in Sri Lanka, the main rice crop

Mahabodhi Great Enlightenment of Buddha

Mahadeva literally 'Great Lord'; Siva

Mahavansa literally "Great Dynasty or Chronicle", a major source on early history and legend

Mahayana The Greater Vehicle; form of Buddhism practised in East Asia, Tibet and Nepal

Mahesha (Maheshvara) Great Lord; Siva

mahout elephant driver/keeper

Maitreya the future Buddha

makara crocodile-shaped mythical creature

malai hill (Tamil)

mandapa columned hall preceding the sanctuary in a Jain or Hindu temple

mandir temple

mantra sacred chant for meditation by Hindus and Buddhists

Mara Tempter, who sent his daughters (and soldiers) to disturb the Buddha's meditation

mawatha roadway

maya illusion

Minakshi literally 'fish-eyed'; Parvati, Siva's consort

Mohammad 'the praised'; The Prophet; founder of Islam

moksha salvation, enlightenment; lit `release'

moonstone the semi-circular stone step before a shrine; also a gem

mudra symbolic hand gesture and posture associated with the Buddha

Muharram period of mourning in remembrance of Hasan and Hussain, two murdered sons of Ali

N

Naga (nagi/nagini) Snake deity; associated with fertility and protection

Nandi a bull, Siva's vehicle and a symbol of fertility

Narayana Vishnu as the creator of life

Nataraja Siva, Lord of the cosmic dance

Natha worshipped by Mahayana Buddhists as the bodhisattva Maitreya

navagraha nine planets, represented usually on the lintel of a temple door

navaratri literally '9 nights'; name of the Dasara festival

niche wall recess containing a sculpted image or emblem,

nirvana enlightenment; (literally 'extinguished')

O

ola palm manuscripts
oriel projecting window
oya seasonal river

P

pada foot or base
paddy rice in the husk
padma lotus flower. Padmasana, lotus seat; posture of meditating figures
pagoda tall structure in several stories
Pali language of Buddhist scriptures
pankah (punkha) fan, formerly pulled by a cord
pansukulika Buddhist sect dwelling in forest hermitages
parapet wall extending above the roof
Parinirvana (parinibbana) the Buddha's state prior to nirvana, shown usually as a reclining figure
Parvati daughter of the Mountain; Siva's consort
pilimage Buddhist image house
potgul library
pradakshina patha processional passage or ambulatory
puja ritual offerings to the gods; worship (Hindu)
pujari worshipper; one who performs puja
punya karma merit earned through actions and religious devotion (Buddhist)

R

raj rule or government
raja king, ruler; prefix 'maha' means great
Rama seventh incarnation of Vishnu; hero of the Ramayana epic
Ramayana ancient Sanskrit epic
Ravana Demon king of Lanka; kidnapper of Sita
rickshaw 3-wheeled bicycle-powered (or 2-wheeled hand-powered) vehicle
Rig Veda (Rg) oldest and most sacred of the Vedas
rupee unit of currency in Sri Lanka, India, Pakistan and Nepal

S

sagar lake; reservoir
Saiva (Shaiva) the cult of Siva
sal hardwood tree of the lower mountains

sala hall
salaam greeting (Muslim); literally 'peace'
samadhi funerary memorial, like a temple but enshrining an image of the deceased; meditation state
samsara eternal transmigration of the soul
samudra sea, or large artificial lake
sangarama monastery
sangha ascetic order founded by Buddha
Saraswati wife of Brahma and goddess of knowledge; usually seated on a swan, holding a veena
Shakti Energy; female divinity often associated with Siva; also a name of the cult
shaman doctor/priest, using magic
Shankara Siva
sharia corpus of Muslim theological law
shikhara temple tower
singh (sinha) lion
Sita Rama's wife, heroine of the Ramayana epic.
Siva The Destroyer among Hindu gods; often worshipped as a lingam (phallic symbol)
Sivaratri literally 'Siva's night'; festival (February-March) dedicated to Siva
Skanda the Hindu god of war
sri (shri) honorific title, often used for 'Mr'
stucco plasterwork
stupa hemispheric funerary mound; principal votive monument in a Buddhist religious complex
Subrahmanya Skanda, one of Siva's sons; Kartikkeya in South India
sudra lowest of the Hindu castes
svami (swami) holy man
svastika (swastika) auspicious Hindu/Buddhist emblem

T

tale tank (Sinhalese)
tank lake created for irrigation
Tara historically a Nepalese princess, now worshipped by Buddhists and Hindus
thali South and West Indian vegetarian meal
torana gateway with two posts linked by architraves
tottam garden (Tamil)

Trimurti Triad of Hindu divinities, Brahma, Vishnu and Siva

U

Upanishads ancient Sanskrit philosophical texts, part of the Vedas

ur village (Tamil)

V

Valmiki sage, author of the Ramayana epic

varam village (Tamil)

varna 'colour'; social division of Hindus into Brahmin, Kshatriya, Vaishya and Sudra

Varuna Guardian of the West, accompanied by Makara (see above)

vatadage literally circular relic house, protective pillard and roofed outer cover for dagoba

Veda (Vedic) oldest known religious texts; include hymns to Agni, Indra and Varuna, adopted as Hindu deities

vel Skanda's trident

Vellala Tamil Hindu farming caste

verandah enlarged porch in front of a hall

vihara Buddhist or Jain monastery with cells opening off a central court

villu small lake (Sri Lanka)

Vishnu a principal Hindu deity; creator and preserver of universal order; appears in 10 incarnations (Dashavatara)

vitarka mudra Buddhist posture of discourse, the fingers raised

W

Wesak Commemoration day of the Buddha's birth, enlightenment and death

wewa tank or lake (Sinhalese)

Y

yala summer rice crop

yoga school of philosophy concentrating on different mental and physical disciplines (yogi, a practitioner)

yoni female genital symbol, associated with the worship of the Siva Linga (phallus)

Food Glossary

Basic vocabulary	Sinhalese	Tamil
bread	*pān*	*rotti/pān*
butter		*butter/vennai*
(too much) chilli	*miris wadi*	*kāram*
drink	*bīma*	*kudi*
egg	*biththara*	*muttai*
fish	*malu*	*min*
fruit	*palathuru*	*palam*
food	*kama*	*unavu*
jaggery	*hakuru*	*sini/vellam*
juice	*isma*	*sāru*
meat	*mus*	*iraichchi*
oil	*thel*	*ennai*
pepper	*gammiris*	*milagu*
pulses (beans, lentils)	*parippu*	*thāniyam*
rice	*buth*	*arisi*
salt	*lunu*	*uppu*
savoury		*suvai*
spices	*kulubadu*	*milagu*
sweetmeats	*rasakevili*	*inippu pondangal*
treacle	*pani*	*pāni*
vegetables	*elawalu*	*kai kari vagaigal*
water	*wathura*	*thanneer*

Fruit		
avocado	*alkigetapera*	
banana	*keselkan*	*valaippalam*
cashew	*cadju*	*muruthivi*
coconut	*pol*	*thengali*
green coconut	*kurumba*	*pachcha niramulla thengai*
jackfruit	*(jak) kos ambul*	
mango	*amba*	*mangai*
orange	*dodam*	
papaya	*papol*	*pappa palam*
pineapple	*annasi*	*annasi*

Vegetables		
aubergine	*vambatu*	*kathirikai*
beans (green)	*bonchi*	*avarai*
cabbage	*gowa*	*muttaikosu*
gourd (green)	*pathola*	*pudalankai*
mushrooms		*kalān*
okra	*bandakka*	*vendikkai*
onion	*luunu*	*venkayam*
pea		*pattani*
pepper	*miris*	*kāram*
prawns	*isso*	*irāl*
potato	*ala*	*uruka kilangu*
spinach	*niwithi*	*pasali*
tomato	*thakkali*	*thakkali*

Meat, fish and seafood

chicken	kukulmas	koli
crab	kakuluvo	nandu
pork	ōroomas	pantri
potato	ala	uruka kilangu
spinach	niwithi	pasali
tomato	thakkali	thakkali

Ordering a meal in a restaurant: Sinhalese

Please show the menu	menu eka penwanna
sugar/milk/ice	sini/kiri/ice
A bottle of mineral water please	drink botalayak genna
do not open it	arinna epa

Order a meal in a restaurant: Tamil

Please show the menu	thayavu seithu thinpandangal patti tharavum
sugar/milk/ice	sini/pāl/ice
A bottle of mineral water please	oru pothal soda panam tharavum

Sri Lankan specialities

amblulthial sour fish curry

kaha buth kaha rice (yellow, cooked in coconut milk with spices and saffron/turmeric colouring) kiri rice is similar but white and unspiced, served with treacle, chilli or pickle

biththara rotti rotti mixed with eggs

buriyani rice cooked in meat stock and pieces of spiced meat sometimes garnished with boiled egg slices

hoppers (āppa) cupped pancakes made of fermented rice flour, coconut milk, yeast, eaten with savoury (or sweet) curry

lamprais rice cooked in stock parcelled in a banana leaf with dry meat and vegetable curries, fried meat and fish balls and baked gently

mallung boiled, shredded vegetables cooked with spice and coconut

pittu rice-flour and grated coconut steamed in bamboo moulds, eaten with coconut milk and curry

polos pahi pieces of young jackfruit (tree lamb) replaces meat in this dry curry

rotty or rotti flat, circular, unleavened bread cooked on a griddle

sambol hot and spicy accompaniment usually made with onions, grated coconut, pepper (and sometimes dried fish)

sathai spicy meat pieces baked on skewers (sometimes sweet and sour)

'short eats' a selection of meat and vegetable snacks (in pastry or crumbled and fried) charged as eaten.

string hoppers (indiappa) flat circles of steamed rice flour noodles eaten usually at breakfast with thin curry

thosai or **dosai** large crisp pancake made with rice and lentil-flour batter

vadai deep-fried savoury lentil dough-nut rings

Sweets (rasakavilis)

curd rich, creamy, buffalo-milk yoghurt served with treacle or jaggery

gulab jamun dark, fried spongy balls of milk curd and flour soaked in syrup

halwal aluva fudge-like, made with milk, nuts and fruit

kadju kordial fudge squares made with cashew nuts and jaggery

kaludodol dark, mil-based, semi solid sweet mixed with jaggery, cashew and spices (a moorish delicacy)

rasgulla syrup-filled white spongy balls of milk-curd and flour

thalaguli balls formed after pounding roasted sesame seeds with jaggery

wattalappam set 'custard' of coconut, milk, eggs and cashew, flavoured with spices and jaggery

Index → Entries in bold refer to maps.

Advertisers' index

Acknowledgements

Thanks must go first and foremost to Bob and Roma Bradnock for writing the first three editions of this guide, and Edward Aves for writing the fourth. Thank you also to Gehan de Silva Wijeyeratne of Jetwing Eco Tours for his contribution to the Background chapter.

This edition could not have come about without three-wheeler drivers, and the help and kindness of the Sri Lankan people. I'm particularly grateful to those bus drivers with the best Bollywood soundtracks.

Ravi Desappriya of *Sri Lanka Trekking* deserves a mention not only for introducing me to the beauty of the Knuckles Range but also teaching me that I can walk much further than I ever thought possible. Thanks to Sanjika Perera at the *Sri Lanka Tourism Development Authority* for guidance before I set off, Nic Abley for her tips and advice, Alan Murphy for trusting me in the first place and Nicola Gibbs for her excellent editing.

Finally, I would like to thank Tom for his patience and support, and for his unfailing cheerfulness when faced with fruit and fried eggs for the umpteenth time.

Most importantly, thanks to those readers and travellers who wrote in with their comments, advice, corrections and updates, in particular Simon Gasser, Louise Gray, Peter Phillips, PH Wallace, Clive Walker and Adam Williams. Thanks must also go to fellow travellers we met along the way, especially the retired French couple in Aurgam Bay with their document wallet full of business cards, receipts and leaflets.

Credits

Footprint credits

Project editor: Nicola Gibbs
Layout and production: Emma Bryers
Cover and colour section: Pepi Bluck
Maps: Kevin Feeney

Managing Director: Andy Riddle
Commercial Director: Patrick Dawson
Publisher: Alan Murphy
Publishing Managers: Felicity Laughton,
Nicola Gibbs
Digital Editors: Jo Williams, Tom Mellors
Marketing and PR: Liz Harper
Sales: Diane McEntee
Advertising: Renu Sibal
Finance and administration:
Elizabeth Taylor

Photography credits

Front cover: GR. RICHARDSON /
photolibrary.com
Back cover: Gavin Hellier / Robert Harding

Colour section photography credits

P1: Kimberley Coole / Robert Harding
P2-3: David Beaty / Robert Harding
P6-7: James Strachan / Robert Harding
P8: Mickael David / Authors Image /
Robert Harding

Every effort has been made to ensure that
the facts in this guidebook are accurate.
However, travellers should still obtain advice
from consulates, airlines, etc, about travel
and visa requirements before travelling.
The authors and publishers cannot
accept responsibility for any loss, injury
or inconvenience however caused.

Publishing information

Footprint Sri Lanka
5th edition
© Footprint Handbooks Ltd
October 2011

ISBN: 978 1 907263 521
CIP DATA: A catalogue record for this book
is available from the British Library

® Footprint Handbooks and the Footprint
mark are a registered trademark of Footprint
Handbooks Ltd

Published by Footprint
6 Riverside Court
Lower Bristol Road
Bath BA2 3DZ, UK
T +44 (0)1225 469141
F +44 (0)1225 469461
footprinttravelguides.com

Distributed in the USA by Globe Pequot Pre
Guilford, Connecticut

Footprint Mini Atlas
Sri Lanka

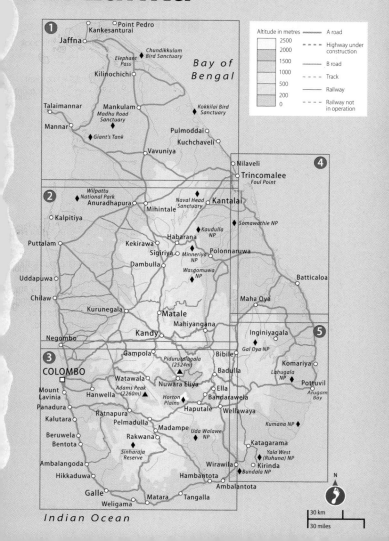

Altitude in metres

2500	A road
2000	Highway under construction
1500	B road
1000	
500	Track
200	Railway
0	Railway not in operation

Point Pedro
Kankesanturai
Jaffna
Chundikkulum Bird Sanctuary
Elephant Pass
Kilinochichi
Bay of Bengal
Talaimannar
Mankulam
Madhu Road Sanctuary
Kokkilai Bird Sanctuary
Mannar
Giant's Tank
Pulmoddai
Kuchchaveli
Vavuniya
Nilaveli
Trincomalee
Foul Point
Wilpattu National Park
Anuradhapura
Mihintale
Naval Head Sanctuary
Kantalai
Kalpitiya
Somawathie NP
Habarana
Kaudulla NP
Puttalam
Kekirawa
Sigiriya
Minneriya NP
Polonnaruwa
Dambulla
Wasgomuwa NP
Uddapuwa
Batticaloa
Chilaw
Maha Oya
Kurunegala
Matale
Mahiyangana
Negombo
Kandy
Inginiyagala
Gampola
Bibile
Gal Oya NP
COLOMBO
Watawala
Pidurutalagala (2524m)
Badulla
Komariya
Nuwara Eliya
Lahugala NP
Mount Lavinia
Hanwella
Adams Peak (2260m)
Ella
Pottuvil
Panadura
Horton Plains
Bandarawela
Arugam Bay
Kalutara
Ratnapura
Haputale
Wellawaya
Pelmadulla
Beruwela
Madampe
Uda Walawe NP
Kumana NP
Bentota
Rakwana
Katagarama
Ambalangoda
Sinharaja Reserve
Yala West (Ruhuna) NP
Hikkaduwa
Wirawila
Kirinda
Bundala NP
Galle
Hambantota
Matara
Ambalantota
Weligama
Tangalla

Indian Ocean

N

30 km
30 miles

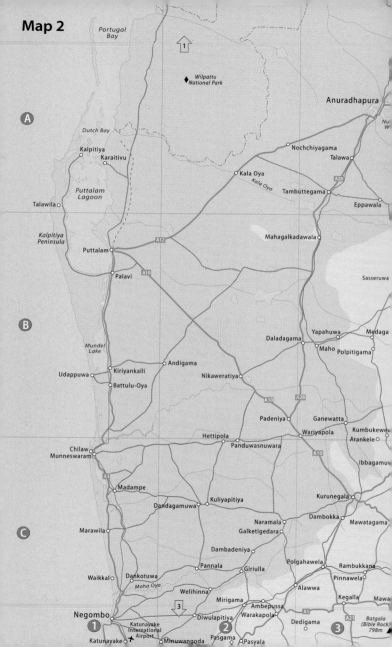

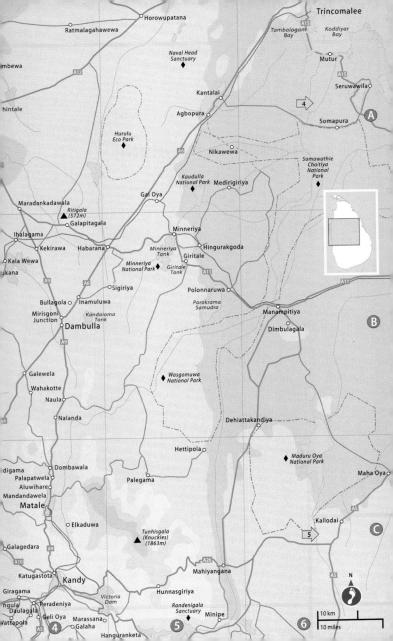

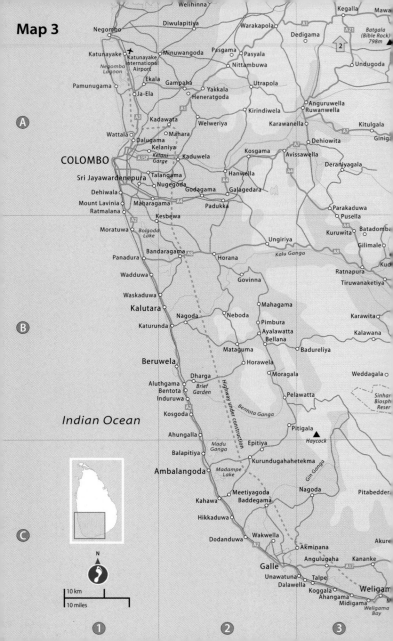

Map 4

Bay of Bengal

Nilaveli
Kanniyi   Sampaltivu
         Uppuveli
Trincomalee
Koddiyar Bay
Foul Point
alagam ay
Mutur
Seruwawila   *Ullackalie Lagoon*
         Allai Wewa
Somapura
         Sunkankuli
         Verugal
Somawathie Chaitiya National Park
Uppar Lagoon   Vakarai
         Panichchankeni
Thennadi Bay
         Vandeloos Bay
         Passekudah
         Kalkudah
Valaichchenai   *Kalkudah Bay*
ampitiya
Dimbulagala
Chenkaladi
         Batticaloa
         Kattankudi
         Thalankuda
Maduru Oya National Park
         Maha Oya
Kallodai
         Kalmunai

N

10 km
10 miles

Map 5

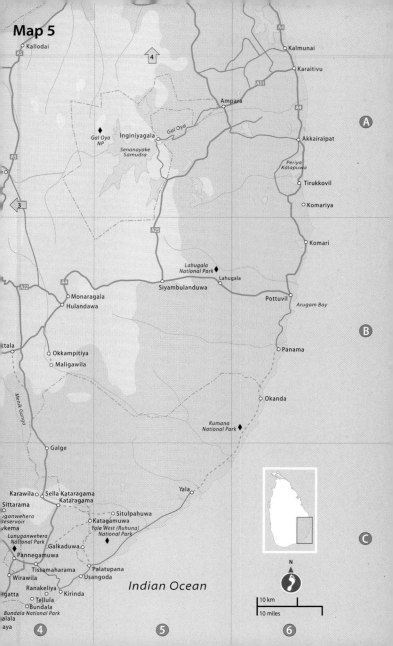

Kallodai

Kalmunai

Karaitivu

A4

A31

Ampara

A4

Gal Oya NP

Inginiyagala

Gal Oya

Senanayake Samudra

Akkairaipat

Periya Kalapuwa

Tirukkovil

Komariya

A5

3

Komari

A25

Lahugala National Park

Siyambulanduwa

Lahugala

Pottuvil

Arugam Bay

Monaragala

Hulandawa

A4

A25

Panama

Okkampitiya

Maligawila

Menik Ganga

Okanda

Kumana National Park

Galge

Yala

Karawila

Sella Kataragama

Kataragama

Sittarama

Situlpahuwa

uganwehera Reservoir

Katagamuwa

ukema

Yala West (Ruhuna) National Park

Lunugamwehera National Park

Galkaduwa

Pannegamuwa

Tissamaharama

Palatupana

Wirawila

Usangoda

igatta

Ranakeliya

Kirinda

Tellula

Bundala

Bundala National Park

aya

Indian Ocean

4

5

6

N

10 km

10 miles

Colour map index

Map symbols

□ Capital city	▦ Building
○ Other city, town	▪ Sight
International border	⬩⬩ Cathedral, church
Regional border	🏯 Chinese temple
⊖ Customs	🏛 Hindu temple
Contours (approx)	⚑ Meru
▲ Mountain, volcano	🕌 Mosque
Mountain pass	⌂ Stupa
Escarpment	✡ Synagogue
Glacier	ⓘ Tourist office
Salt flat	🏛 Museum
Rocks	✉ Post office
Seasonal marshland	Ⓟ Police
Beach, sandbank	Ⓢ Bank
◍ Waterfall	@ Internet
Reef	♪ Telephone
National highway	☎ Market
Paved road	✚ Medical services
Unpaved or *ripio* (gravel) road	Ⓟ Parking
Track	🛢 Petrol
Footpath	⚑ Golf
Railway	⚘ Archaeological site
Railway with station	♦ National park,
✈ Airport	wildlife reserve
🚌 Bus station	✿ Viewing point
Ⓜ Metro station	▲ Campsite
Cable car	⌂ Refuge, lodge
Funicular	🏰 Castle, fort
⛴ Ferry	✈ Diving
Pedestrianized street	🌲 Deciduous, coniferous,
Tunnel	palm trees
One way-street	🌴 Mangrove
Steps	⌂ Hide
Bridge	♪ Vineyard, winery
Fortified wall	⚗ Distillery
Park, garden, stadium	Shipwreck
● Sleeping	✕ Historic battlefield
❶ Eating	⇨ Related map
❶ Bars & clubs	

Join us online...

Follow us on **Twitter** and **Facebook** – ask us questions, speak to our authors, swap your stories, and be kept up to date with travel news and exclusive discounts and competitions.

Upload your travel pics to our **Flickr** site – inspire others on where to go next, and have your photos considered for inclusion in Footprint guides.

And don't forget to visit us at footprinttravelguides.com

Footprint story

It was 1921

Ireland had just been partitioned, the British miners were striking for more pay and the federation of British industry had an idea. Exports were booming in South America – how about a handbook for businessmen trading in that far away continent? The Anglo-South American Handbook was born that year, written by W Koebel, the most prolific writer on Latin America of his day.

1924

Two editions later the book was 'privatized' and in 1924, in the hands of Royal Mail, the steamship company for South America, it became The South American Handbook, subtitled 'South America in a nutshell'. This annual publication became the 'bible' for generations of travellers to South America and remains so to this day. In the early days travel was by sea and the Handbook gave all the details needed for the long voyage from Europe. What to wear for dinner; how to arrange a cricket match with the Cable & Wireless staff on the Cape Verde Islands and a full account of the journey from Liverpool up the Amazon to Manaus: 5898 miles without changing cabin!

1939

As the continent opened up, the South American Handbook reported the new Pan Am flying boat services, and the fortnightly airship service from Rio to Europe on the Graf Zeppelin. For reasons still unclear but with extraordinary determination, the annual editions continued through the Second World War.

1970s

Many more people discovered South America and the backpacking trail started to develop. All the while the Handbook was gathering fans, including literary vagabonds such as Paul Theroux and Graham Greene (who once sent some updates addressed to "The publishers of the best travel guide in the world, Bath, England").

1990s

During the 1990s the company set about developing a new travel guide series using this legendary title as the flagship. By 1997 there were over a dozen guides in the series and the Footprint imprint was launched.

2000s

The series grew quickly and there were soon Footprint travel guides covering more than 150 countries. In 2004, Footprint launched its first thematic guide: Surfing Europe, packed with colour photographs, maps and charts. This was followed by further thematic guides such as Diving the World, Snowboarding the World, Body and Soul escapes, Travel with Kids and European City Breaks.

2011

Today we continue the traditions of the last 90 years that have served legions of travellers so well. We believe that these help to make Footprint guides different. Our policy is to use authors who are genuine experts who write for independent travellers; people possessing a spirit of adventure, looking to get off the beaten track.